THE

NOVELS

AND

MISCELLANEOUS WORKS

OF

DANIEL DE FOE.

WITH PREFACES AND NOTES, INCLUDING THOSE ATTRIBUTED TO

SIR WALTER SCOTT.

————

MOLL FLANDERS,

AND

HISTORY OF THE DEVIL.

————

LONDON: GEORGE BELL AND SONS, YORK STREET,
COVENT GARDEN.
1884.

CONTENTS.

POLITICAL AND MODERN HISTORY OF . THE DEVIL.

PART I.

PART II.

CHAPTER I.

THE

FORTUNES

AND

MISFORTUNES

Of the FAMOUS

MOLL FLANDERS, &c.

Who was BORN in

NEWGATE,

And during a Life of continu'd Variety for Three-score Years, besides her Childhood, was Twelve Year a *Whore*, five times a *Wife* (whereof once to her own Brother) Twelve Year a *Thief*, Eight Year a Transported *Felon* in *Virginia*, at last grew *Rich*, liv'd *Honest*, and died a *Penitent.*

Written from her own MEMORANDUMS.

𝕮𝖍𝖊 𝕮𝖍𝖎𝖗𝖉 𝕰𝖉𝖎𝖙𝖎𝖔𝖓 𝕮𝖔𝖗𝖗𝖊𝖈𝖙𝖊𝖉.

LONDON:

Printed for, and Sold by W. CHETWOOD, at *Cato's-Head,* in *Russel-street, Covent-Garden;* and T. EDLIN, at the *Prince's-Arms,* over-against *Exeter-Change* in the *Strand;* W. MEARS, at the *Lamb* without *Temple-Bar;* J. BROTHERTON, by the *Royal-Exchange;* C. KING, and J. STAGG, in *Westminster-Hall.* MDCCXXII.

[The following history is reprinted from the third edition, which seems to have been finally corrected for the press by the author; it has however been collated with the first edition, from which it only differs in the omission of some redundant expressions.]

THE PREFACE

THE world is so taken up of late with Novels and Romances, that it will be hard for a private history to be taken for genuine, where the names and other circumstances of the person are concealed ; and on this account we must be content to leave the reader to pass his own opinion upon the ensuing sheets, and take it just as he pleases.

The author is here supposed to be writing her own history, and in the very beginning of her account she gives the reasons why she thinks fit to conceal her true name, after which there is no occasion to say any more about that.

It is true that the original of this story is put into new words, and the style of the famous lady we here speak of is a little altered, particnlarly she is made to tell her own tale in modester words than she told it at first ; the copy which came first to hand, having been written in language more like one still in Newgate, than one grown penitent and humble, as she afterward pretends to be.

The pen employed in finishing her story, and making it what you now see it to be, has had no little difficulty to put it into a dress fit to be seen, and to make it speak language fit to be read. When a woman debauched from her youth, nay, even being the offspring of debauchery and vice, comes to give an account of all her vicious practices, and even to descend to the particular occasions and circumstances by which she first became wicked, and of all the progressions of crime which she run through in threescore years, an author must be hard put to it to wrap it up so clean as not to give room, especially for vicious readers, to turn it to his disadvantage.

All possible care, however, has been taken to give no lewd ideas, no immodest turns in the new dressing up this story, no, not to the worst part of her expressions ; to this purpose some of the vicious part of her life, which could not be modestly told, is quite left out, and several other parts are very much shortened ; what is left 'tis hoped will not offend the chastest reader, or the modestest hearer ; and as the best use is to be made even of the worst story, the moral, 'tis hoped, will keep the reader serious, even where the story might incline him to be otherwise. To give the history of a wicked life repented of, necessarily requires that the wicked part should be made as wicked as the real history of it will bear, to illustrate and give a beauty to the penitent part, which is certainly the best and brightest, if related with equal spirit and life.

It is suggested there cannot be the same life, the same brightness and beauty in relating the penitent part, as is in the criminal part : if there is any truth in that suggestion, I must be allowed to say, 'tis because there is not the same taste and relish in the reading; and indeed it is too true that the difference lies not in the real worth of the subject so much as in the gust and palate of the reader.

But as this work is chiefly recommended to those who know how to read it, and how to make the good uses of it which the story all along recommends to them, so it is to be hoped that such readers will be much more pleased with the moral than the fable, with the application than with the relation, and with the end of the writer than with the life of the person written of.

There is in this story abundance of delightful incidents, and all of them usefully applied. There is an agreeable turn artfully given them in the relating, that naturally instructs the reader, either one way or another. The first part of her lewd life with the young gentleman at Colchester, has so many happy turns given it to expose the crime, and warn all whose circumstances are adapted to it, of the ruinous end of such things, and the foolish, thoughtless, and abhorred conduct of both the parties, that it abundantly atones for all the lively description she gives of her folly and wickedness.

The repentance of her lover at Bath, and how brought by the just alarm of his fit of sickness to abandon her; the just caution given there against even the lawful intimacies of the dearest friends, and how unable they are to preserve the most solemn resolutions of virtue without divine assistance; these are parts, which to a just discernment will appear to have more real beauty in them than all the amorous chain of story which introduces it.

In a word, as the whole relation is carefully garbled of all the levity and looseness that was in it, so it is applied, and with the utmost care, to virtuous and religious uses. None can, without being guilty of manifest injustice, cast any reproach upon it, or upon our design in publishing it.

The advocates for the stage, have, in all ages, made this the great argument to persuade people that their plays are useful, and that they ought to be allowed in the most civil-ized, and in the most religious government; namely, that they are applied to virtuous purposes, and that, by the most lively representations, they fail not to recommend virtue and generous principles, and to discourage and expose all sorts of vice and corruption of manners; and were it true that they did so, and that they constantly adhered to that rule, as the test of their acting on the theatre, much might be said in their favour.

Throughout the infinite variety of this book, this fundamental is most strictly adhered to; there is not a wicked action in any part of it, but is first or last rendered unhappy and unfortunate; there is not a superlative villain brought upon the stage, but either he is brought to an unhappy end, or brought to be a penitent; there is not an ill thing mentioned but it is condemned, even in the relation, nor a virtuous just thing but it carries its praise along with it. What can more exactly answer the rule laid down, to recommend even those representations of things which have so many other just objections lying against them? namely, of example of bad company, obscene language, and the like.

Upon this foundation this book is recommended to the reader, as a work from every part of which something may be learned: and some just and religious inference is drawn, by which the reader will have something of instruction if he pleases to make use of it.

All the exploits of this lady of fame, in her depredations upon mankind, stand as so many warnings to honest people to beware of 'em, intimating to 'em by what methods innocent people are drawn in, plundered, and robbed, and by consequence how to avoid them. Her robbing a little child, dressed fine by the vanity of the mother, to go to the dancing school, is a good memento to such people hereafter; as is likewise her picking the gold watch from the young lady's side in the park.

Her getting a parcel from a hairbrained wench at the coaches in St. John's-street; her booty at the fire, and also at Harwich; all give us excellent warning in such cases to be more present to ourselves in sudden surprises of every sort.

Her application to a sober life and industrious management at last, in Virginia, with her transported spouse, is a story fruitful of instruction, to all the unfortunate creatures who are obliged to seek their re-establishment abroad, whether by the misery of transportation, or other disaster; letting them know that diligence and application have their due encouragement, even in the remotest part of the world, and that no case can be so low, so despicable, or so empty of prospect, but that an unwearied industry will go a great way to deliver us from it, will in time raise the meanest creature to appear again in the world, and give him a new cast for his life.

These are a few of the serious inferences which we are led by the hand to in this book, and these are fully sufficient to justify any man in recommending it to the world, and much more to justify the publication of it.

There are two of the most beautiful parts still behind, which this story gives some idea of, and lets us into the parts of them, but they are either of them too long to be brought into the same volume; and indeed are, as I may call them, whole volumes of themselves, viz., 1. The life of her governess, as she calls her, who had run through, it seems, in a few years, all the eminent degrees of a gentlewoman, a whore, and a bawd; a midwife, and a midwife keeper, as they are called; a pawnbroker, a child taker, a receiver of thieves, and of stolen goods; and in a word, herself a thief, a breeder up of thieves, and the like, and yet at last a penitent.

The second is the life of her transported husband, a highwayman; who, it seems, lived a twelve years' life of successful villany upon the road, and even at last came off so well as to be a volunteer transport, not a convict; and in whose life there is an incredible variety.

But as I said, these are things too long to bring in here, so neither can I make a promise of their coming out by themselves.

We cannot say indeed, that this history is carried on quite to the end of the life of this famous Moll Flanders, for nobody can write their own life to the full end of it, unless they can write it after they are dead: but her husband's life being written by a third hand, gives a full account of them both, how long they lived together in that country, and how they came both to England again, after about eight years, in which time they were grown very rich, and where she lived, it seems, to be very old, but was not so extraordinary a penitent as she was at first; it seems only that indeed she always spoke with abhorrence of her former life, and of every part of it.

In her last scene, at Maryland and Virginia, many pleasant things happened, which makes that part of her life very agreeable, but they are not told with the same elegancy as those accounted for by herself; so it is still to the more advantage that we break off here.

THE

FORTUNES AND MISFORTUNES

OF THE FAMOUS

MOLL FLANDERS.

MY true name is so well known in the records or registers at Newgate, and in the Old Bailey, and there are some things of such consequence still depending there, relating to my particular conduct, that it is not to be expected I should set my name, or the account of my family to this work; perhaps after my death it may be better known; at present it would not be proper, no, not though a general pardon should be issued, even without exceptions of persons or crimes.

It is enough to tell you, that as some of my worst comrades, who are out of the way of doing me harm (having gone out of the world by the steps and the string, as I often expected to go), knew me by the name of Moll Flanders, so you may give me leave to go under that name till I dare own who I have been, as well as who I am.

I have been told, that in one of our neighbour nations, whether it be in France, or where else, I know not, they have an order from the king, that when any criminal is condemned, either to die, or to the galleys, or to be transported, if they leave any children, as such are generally unprovided for, by the forfeiture of their parents, so they are immediately taken into the care of the government, and put into an hospital called the House of Orphans, where they are bred up, clothed, fed, taught, and when fit to go out, are placed to trades, or to services, so as to be well able to provide for themselves by an honest industrious behaviour.

Had this been the custom in our country, I had not been

left a poor desolate girl without friends, without clothes, without help or helper, as was my fate; and by which, I was not only exposed to very great distresses, even before I was capable either of understanding my case, or how to amend it, but brought into a course of life, scandalous in itself, and which in its ordinary course, tended to the swift destruction both of soul and body.

But the case was otherwise here : my mother was convicted of felony for a petty theft, scarce worth naming, viz., borrowing three pieces of fine holland, of a certain draper in Cheapside : the circumstances are too long to repeat, and I have heard them related so many ways, that I can scarce tell which is the right account.

However it was, they all agree in this, that my mother pleaded her belly, and being found quick with child, she was respited for about seven months; after which she was called down, as they term it, to her former judgment, but obtained the favour afterward of being transported to the plantations, and left me about half a year old; and in bad hands you may be sure.

This is too near the first hours of my life, for me to relate anything of myself, but by hearsay; 'tis enough to mention, that as I was born in such an unhappy place, I had no parish to have recourse to for my nourishment in my infancy, nor can I give the least account how I was kept alive; other, than that, as I have been told, some relation of my mother took me away, but at whose expense, or by whose direction, I know nothing at all of it.

The first account that I can recollect, or could ever learn of myself, was that I had wandered among a crew of those people they call gipsies, or Egyptians; but I believe it was but a little while that I had been among them, for I had not had my skin discoloured, as they do to all children they carry about with them, nor can I tell how I came among them, or how I got from them.

It was at Colchester in Essex, that those people left me; and I have a notion in my head, that I left them there (that is, that I hid myself and would not go any farther with them), but I am not able to be particular in that account; only this I remember, that being taken up by some of the parish officers of Colchester, I gave an account, that I came into the town with the gipsies, but that I would not go any farther with them, and that so they had left me, but whither they were gone that I knew not; for though they sent round the country to inquire after them, it seems, they could not be found.

I was now in a way to be provided for; for though I was not a parish charge upon this or that part of the town by law, yet as my case came to be known, and that I was too young to do any work, being not above three years old, compassion moved the magistrates of the town to take care of me, and I became one of their own as much as if I had been born in the place.

In the provision they made for me, it was my good hap to be put to nurse, as they call it, to a woman who was indeed poor, but had been in better circumstances, and who got a little livelihood by taking such as I was supposed to be; and keeping them with all necessaries, till they were at a certain age, in which it might be supposed they might go to service, or get their own bread.

This woman had also a little school, which she kept to teach children to read and to work; and having, I say, lived before that in good fashion, she bred up the children with a great deal of art, as well as with a great deal of care.

But which was worth all the rest, she bred them up very religiously also, being herself a very sober, pious woman; 2ndly, very housewifely and clean, and, 3rdly, very mannerly, and with good behaviour. So that excepting a plain diet, coarse lodging, and mean clothes, we were brought up as mannerly as if we had been at the dancing school.

I was continued here till I was eight years old, when I was terrified with news that the magistrates (as I think they called them), had ordered that I should go to service; I was able to do but very little, wherever I was to go, except it was to run of errands, and be a drudge to some cookmaid, and this they told me often, which put me into a great fright; for I had a thorough aversion to going to service, as they called it, though I was so young; and I told my nurse, that I believed I could get my living without going to service, if she pleased to let me; for she had taught me to work with my needle, and spin worsted, which is the chief trade of that city, and I told her that if she would keep me, I would work for her, and I would work very hard.

I talked to her almost every day of working hard; and in

short I did nothing but work and cry all day, which grieved the good kind woman so much, that at last she began to be concerned for me, for she loved me very well.

One day after this, as she came into the room, where all the poor children were at work, she sat down just over against me, not in her usual place as mistress, but as if she had set herself on purpose to observe me, and see me work; I was doing something she had set me to, as I remember it was marking some shirts, which she had taken to make, and after a while she began to talk to me: Thou foolish child, says she, thou art always crying (for I was crying then); prithee, what do'st cry for? Because they will take me away, says I, and put me to service, and I can't work house-work. Well, child, says she, but though you can't work house-work you will learn it in time, and they won't put you to hard things, at first. Yes they will, says I, and if I can't do it they will beat me, and the maids will beat me to make me do great work, and I am but a little girl, and I can't do it; and then I cried again, till I could not speak any more.

This moved my good motherly nurse, so that she resolved I should not go to service yet; so she bid me not cry, and she would speak to Mr. Mayor, and I should not go to service till I was bigger.

Well, this did not satisfy me, for to think of going to service at all was such a frightful thing to me, that if she had assured me I should not have gone till I was twenty years' old, it would have been the same to me, I should have cried all the time, with the very apprehension of its being to be so at last.

When she saw that I was not pacified yet, she began to be angry with me: And what would you have, says she, don't I tell you that you shall not go to service till you are bigger? Ay, says I, but then I must go at last. Why, what, said she, is the girl mad? what would you be a gentlewoman? Yes, says I, and cried heartily till I roared out again.

This set the old gentlewoman a laughing at me, as you may be sure it would. Well, madam, forsooth, says she, gibing at me; you would be a gentlewoman, and how will you come to be a gentlewoman? what will you do it by your fingers' ends?

Yes, says I again, very innocently.

Why, what can you earn, says she: what can you get a-day at your work?

Three-pence, said I, when I spin, and four-pence when I work plain work.

Alas! poor gentlewoman, said she again, laughing, what will that do for thee?

It will keep me, says I, if you will let me live with you; and this I said in such a poor petitioning tone, that it made the poor woman's heart yearn to me, as she told me afterwards.

But, says she, that will not keep you and buy you clothes too; and who must buy the little gentlewoman clothes, says she, and smiled all the while at me.

I will work harder then, says I, and you shall have it all.

Poor child! it won't keep you, said she: it will hardly find you in victuals.

Then I would have no victuals, says I again, very innocently, let me but live with you.

Why, can you live without victuals? says she. Yes, again says I, very much like a child, you may be sure, and still I cried heartily.

I had no policy in all this, you may easily see it was all nature, but it was joined with so much innocence, and so much passion, that in short it set the good motherly creature a weeping too, and at last she cried as fast as I did, and then took me and led me out of the teaching-room: Come, says she, you shan't go to service, you shall live with me; and this pacified me for the present.

After this, she going to wait on the mayor, my story came up, and my good nurse told Mr. Mayor the whole tale: he was so pleased with it, that he would call his lady and his two daughters to hear it, and it made mirth enough among them you may be sure.

However, not a week had passed over, but on a sudden comes Mrs. Mayoress and her two daughters to the house to see my old nurse, and to see her school and the children. When they had looked about them a little, Well Mrs. ⸺ says the mayoress to my nurse, and pray which is the little lass that is to be a gentlewoman? I heard her, and I was terrible frighted, though I did not know why neither; but Mrs. Mayoress comes up to me, Well Miss, says she, and

what are you at work upon?   The word Miss was a language
that had hardly been heard of in our school, and I wondered
what sad name it was she called me; however, I stood
up, made a curtsy, and she took my work out of my hand,
looked on it, and said it was very well; then she looked upon
one of my hands: Nay, she may come to be a gentlewoman,
says she, for aught I know; she has a lady's hand, I assure
you.   This pleased me mightily; but Mrs. Mayoress did not
stop there, but put her hand in her pocket, gave me a shilling,
and bid me mind my work, and learn to work well, and I
might be a gentlewoman for aught she knew.

All this while my good old nurse, Mrs. Mayoress, and all
the rest of them, did not understand me at all, for they meant
one sort of thing by the word gentlewoman, and I meant
quite another: for alas, all I understood by being a gentlewoman, was to be able to work for myself, and get enough
to keep me without going to service, whereas they meant
to live great and high, and I know not what.

Well, after Mrs. Mayoress was gone, her two daughters
came in, and they called for the gentlewoman too, and they
talked a long while to me, and I answered them in my
innocent way; but always if they asked me whether I
resolved to be a gentlewoman, I answered, yes: at last they
asked me, what a gentlewoman was?   That puzzled me much:
however, I explained myself negatively, that it was one that
did not go to service, to do house-work; they were mightily
pleased, and liked my little prattle to them, which it seems
was agreeable enough to them, and they gave me money too.

As for my money, I gave it all to my mistress-nurse, as I
called her, and told her she should have all I got when I
was a gentlewoman, as well as now; by this and some other
of my talk. my old tutoress began to understand what I meant
by being a gentlewoman; and that it was no more than to
be able to get my bread by my own work; and at last she
asked me whether it was not so.

I told her, yes, and insisted on it, that to do so, was to be
a gentlewoman; for, says I, there is such a one, naming a
woman that mended lace, and washed the ladies' laced heads;
she, says I, is a gentlewoman, and they call her madam.

Poor child, says my good old nurse, you may soon be
such a gentlewoman as that, for she is a person of ill fame,
and has had two bastards.

I did not understand anything of that; but I answered, I am sure they call her madam, and she does not go to service nor do house-work; and therefore I insisted that she was a gentlewoman, and I would be such a gentlewoman as that.

The ladies were told all this again, and they made themselves merry with it, and every now and then Mr. Mayor's daughters would come and see me, and ask where the little gentlewoman was, which made me not a little proud of myself besides. I was often visited by these young ladies, and sometimes they brought others with them; so that I was known by it, almost all over the town.

I was now about ten years old, and began to look a little womanish, for I was mighty grave, very mannerly, and as I had often heard the ladies say I was pretty, and would be very handsome, you may be sure it made me not a little proud: however, that pride had no ill effect upon me yet, only as they often gave me money, and I gave it my old nurse, she, honest woman, was so just as to lay it out again for me, and gave me head-dresses, and linen, and gloves, and I went very neat, for if I had rags on, I would always be clean, or else I would dabble them in water myself; but I say, my good nurse, when I had money given me, very honestly laid it out for me, and would always tell the ladies this or that was bought with their money; and this made them give me more, till at last, I was indeed called upon by the magistrates to go out to service; but then I was become so good a workwoman myself, and the ladies were so kind to me, that I was past it; for I could earn as much for my nurse as was enough to keep me; so she told them, that if they would give her leave, she would keep the gentlewoman, as she called me, to be her assistant, and teach the children, which I was very well able to do; for I was very nimble at my work, though I was yet very young.

But the kindness of the ladies did not end here, for when they understood that I was no more maintained by the town as before, they gave me money oftener; and as I grew up, they brought me work to do for them; such as linen to make, laces to mend, and heads to dress up, and not only paid me for doing them, but even taught me how to do them; so that I was a gentlewoman indeed, as I understood that word; for before I was twelve years old, I not only found myself clothes, and paid my nurse for my keeping, but got money in my pocket too.

The ladies also gave me clothes frequently of their own or their childrens'; some stockings, some petticoats, some gowns, some one thing, some another, and these my old woman managed for me like a mother, and kept them for me, obliged me to mend them, and turn them to the best advantage; for she was a rare housewife.

At last one of the ladies took such a fancy to me, that she would have me home to her house, for a month, she said, to be among her daughters.

Now though this was exceeding kind in her, yet as my good woman said to her, unless she resolved to keep me for good and all, she would do the little gentlewoman more harm than good: Well, says the lady, that's true, I'll only take her home for a week then, that I may see how my daughters and she agree, and how I like her temper, and then I'll tell you more; and in the mean time, if nobody comes to see her as they used to do, you may only tell them you have sent her out to my house.

This was prudently managed enough, and I went to the lady's house, but I was so pleased there with the young ladies, and they so pleased with me, that I had enough to do to come away, and they were as unwilling to part with me.

However, I did come away, and lived almost a year more with my honest old woman, and began now to be very helpful to her; for I was almost fourteen years old, was tall of my age, and looked a little womanish; but I had such a taste of genteel living at the lady's house, that I was not so easy in my old quarters as I used to be, and I thought it was fine to be a gentlewoman indeed, for I had quite other notions of a gentlewoman now, than I had before; and as I thought that it was fine to be a gentlewoman, so I loved to be among gentlewomen, and therefore I longed to be there again.

When I was about fourteen years and a quarter old, my good old nurse, mother I ought to call her, fell sick and died; I was then in a sad condition indeed, for as there is no great bustle in putting an end to a poor body's family, when once they are carried to the grave; so the poor good woman being buried, the parish children were immediately removed by the churchwardens; the school was at an end, and the day children of it had no more to do but just stay at home till they were sent somewhere else; as for what she left, a daughter, a married woman, came and swept it all away, and removing the goods, they had no more to say to me than to jest with me, and tell me that the little gentlewoman might set up for herself if she pleased.

I was frighted out of my wits almost, and knew not what to do; for I was, as it were, turned out of doors to the wide world, and that which was still worse, the old honest woman had two-and-twenty shillings of mine in her hand, which was all the estate the little gentlewoman had in the world; and when I asked the daughter for it, she huft me, and told me she had nothing to do with it.

It was true the good poor woman had told her daughter of it, and that it lay in such a place, that it was the child's money, and had called once or twice for me to give it me, but I was unhappily out of the way, and when I came back she was past being in a condition to speak of it: however, the daughter was so honest afterwards, as to give it me, though at first she used me cruelly about it.

Now was I a poor gentlewoman indeed, and I was just that very night to be turned into the wide world; for the daughter removed all the goods, and I had not so much as a lodging to go to, or a bit of bread to eat: but it seems some of the neighbours took so much compassion of me, as to acquaint the lady in whose family I had been; and immediately she sent her maid to fetch me; and away I went with them bag and baggage, and with a glad heart you may be sure: the fright of my condition had made such an impression upon me, that I did not want now to be a gentlewoman, but was very willing to be a servant, and that any kind of servant they thought fit to have me be.

But my new generous mistress had better thoughts for me. I call her generous, for she exceeded the good woman I was with before in everything, as in estate; I say, in everything except honesty; and for that, though this was a lady most exactly just, yet I must not forget to say on all occcasions, that the first, though poor, was as uprightly honest as it was possible.

I was no sooner carried away as I have said by this good gentlewoman, but the first lady, that is to say, the mayoress that was, sent her daughters to take care of me; and another family which had taken notice of me when I was the little gentlewoman, sent for me after her, so that I was mightily made of; nay, and they were not a little angry, especially the mayoress, that her friend had taken me away from her; for, as she said, I was hers by right, she having been the first that took any notice of me: but they that had me, would not part with me; and as for me I could not be better than where I was.

Here I continued till I was between seventeen and eighteen years' old, and here I had all the advantages for my education, that could be imagined; the lady had masters home to teach her daughters to dance, and to speak French, and to write, and others to teach them music; and as I was always with them, I learned as fast as they; and though the masters were not appointed to teach me, yet I learned by imitation and inquiry, all that they learned by instruction and direction. So that in short, I learned to dance and speak French as well as any of them, and to sing much better, for I had a better voice than any of them; I could not so readily come at playing the harpsichord or spinet, because I had no instrument of my own to practice on, and could only come at theirs in the intervals when they left it; but yet I learned tolerably well, and the young ladies at length got two instruments, that is to say, a harpsichord and a spinet too, and then they taught me themselves; but as to dancing they could hardly help my learning country dances, because they always wanted me to make up even number; and on the other hand, they were as heartily willing to learn me everything that they had been taught themselves, as I could be to take the learning.

By this means I had, as I have said, all the advantages of education that I could have had, if I had been as much a gentlewoman as they were with whom I lived; and in some things I had the advantage of my ladies, though they were my superiors, viz., that mine were all the gifts of nature, and which all their fortunes could not furnish. First, I was apparently handsomer than any of them; secondly, I was better shaped; and thirdly, I sung better, by which I mean, I had a better voice; in all which you will, I hope, allow me to say, I do not speak my own conceit, but the opinion of all that knew the family.

I had with all these the common vanity of my sex, viz,

that being really taken for very handsome, or if you please, for a great beauty, I very well knew it, and had as good an opinion of myself, as anybody else could have of me, and particularly I loved to hear anybody speak of it, which happened often, and was a great satisfaction to me.

Thus far I have had a smooth story to tell of myself, and in all this part of my life, I not only had the reputation of living in a very good family, and a family noted and respected everywhere for virtue and sobriety, and for every valuable thing; but I had the character too of a very sober, modest, and virtuous young woman, and such I had always been; neither had I yet any occasion to think of anything else, or to know what a temptation to wickedness meant.

But that which I was too vain of, was my ruin, or rather my vanity was the cause of it. The lady in the house where I was, had two sons, young gentlemen of extraordinary parts and behaviour; and it was my misfortune to be very well with them both, but they managed themselves with me in a quite different manner.

The eldest, a gay gentleman, that knew the town as well as the country; and though he had levity enough to do an ill-natured thing, yet had too much judgment of things to pay too dear for his pleasures; he began with that unhappy snare to all women, viz., taking notice upon all occasions how pretty I was, as he called it, how agreeable, how well-carriaged, and the like; and this he contrived so subtly, as if he had known as well how to catch a woman in his net, as a partridge when he went a setting; for he would contrive to be talking this to his sisters, when, though I was not by, yet when he knew I was not so far off but that I should be sure to hear him: his sisters would return softly to him, Hush brother, she will hear you, she is but in the next room; then he would put it off, and talk softlier, as if he had not known it, and begin to acknowledge he was wrong; and then as if he had forgot himself, he would speak aloud again, and I that was so well pleased to hear it was sure to listen for it upon all occasions.

After he had thus baited his hook, and found easily enough the method how to lay it in my way, he played an open game; and one day going by his sister's chamber when I was there, he comes in with an air of gaiety, O! Mrs. Betty, said he to me, how do you do Mrs. Betty? don't your cheeks burn Mrs.

Betty? I made a curtsy, and blushed, but said nothing. What makes you talk so, brother? said the lady. Why, says he, we have been talking of her below-stairs this half hour. Well, says his sister, you can say no harm of her, that I am sure, so 'tis no matter what you have been talking about. Nay, says he, 'tis so far from talking harm of her, that we have been talking a great deal of good, and a great many fine things have been said of Mrs. Betty, I assure you; and particularly, that she is the handsomest young woman in Colchester, and, in short, they begin to toast her health in the town.

I wonder at you, brother, says the sister, Betty wants but one thing, but she had as good want everything, for the market is against our sex just now; and if a young woman has beauty, birth, breeding, wit, sense, manners, modesty, and all to an extreme; yet if she has not money, she's nobody, she had as good want them all; nothing but money now recommends a woman; the men play the game all into their own hands.

Her younger brother, who was by, cried, Hold, sister, you run too fast, I am an exception to your rule: I assure you, if I find a woman so accomplished as you talk of, I won't trouble myself about the money. O, says the sister, but you will take care not to fancy one then without the money.

You don't know that neither, says the brother.

But why, sister (says the elder brother), why do you exclaim so about the fortune? you are none of them that want a fortune, whatever else you want.

I understand you, brother (replies the lady very smartly); you suppose I have the money and want the beauty; but as times go now, the first will do, so I have the better of my neighbours.

Well, says the younger brother, but your neighbours may be even with you; for beauty will steal a husband sometimes in spite of money; and when the maid chances to be handsomer than the mistress, she oftentimes makes as good a market, and rides in a coach before her.

I thought it was time for me to withdraw, and I did so; but not so far, but that I heard all their discourse, in which I heard abundance of fine things said of myself, which prompted my vanity, but, as I soon found, was not the way to increase my interest in the family, for the sister and the younger brother fell grievously out about it; and as he said some very disobliging things to her, upon my account, so I could easily see that she resented them, by her future conduct to me, which indeed was very unjust; for I had never had the least thought of what she suspected, as to her younger brother: indeed the elder brother in his distant remote way had said a great many things as in jest, which I had the folly to believe were in earnest, or to flatter myself with the hopes of what I ought to have supposed he never intended.

It happened one day that he came running up stairs, towards the room where his sister used to sit and work, as he often used to do; and calling to them before he came in, as was his way too, I being there alone, stept to the door, and said, Sir, the ladies are not here, they are walked down the garden: as I stept forward to say this, he was just got to the door, and clasping me in his arms, as if it had been by chance, O! Mrs. Betty, says he, are you here? that's better still, I want to speak with you, more than I do with them; and then having me in his arms he kissed me three or four times.

I struggled to get away, and yet did it but faintly neither, and he held me fast, and still kissed me, till he was out of breath, and, sitting down, says he, Dear Betty, I am in love with you.

His words, I must confess, fired my blood; all my spirits flew about my heart, and put me into disorder enough. He repeated it afterwards several times, that he was in love with me, and my heart spoke as plain as a voice that I liked it; nay, whenever he said I am in love with you, my blushes plainly replied, Would you were, Sir. However, nothing else passed at that time; it was but a surprise, and I soon recovered myself. He had stayed longer with me, but he happened to look out at the window and see his sisters coming up the garden, so he took his leave, kissed me again, told me he was very serious, and I should hear more of him very quickly, and away he went infinitely pleased, and, had there not been one misfortune in it, I had been in the right, but the mistake lay here, that Mrs. Betty was in earnest, and the gentleman was not.

From this time my head run upon strange things, and I may truly say I was not myself, to have such a gentleman talk to me of being in love with me, and of my being such a charming creature, as he told me I was: these were things I knew not how to bear, my vanity was elevated to the last degree. It is true I had my head full of pride, but, knowing nothing of the wickedness of the times, I had not one thought of my virtue about me; and had my young master offered it at first sight, he might have taken any liberty he thought fit with me; but he did not see his advantage, which was my happiness for that time.

It was not long but he found an opportunity to catch me again, and almost in the same posture; indeed it had more of design in it on his part, though not on my part. It was thus: the young ladies were gone a visiting with their mother; his brother was out of town, and as for his father, he had been at London for a week before; he had so well watched me, that he knew where I was, though I did not so much as know that he was in the house, and he briskly comes up the stairs, and, seeing me at work, comes into the room to me directly, and began. just as he did before, with taking me in his arms, and kissing me for almost a quarter of an hour together.

It was his younger sister's chamber that I was in, and, as there was nobody in the house but the maid below stairs, he was it may be the ruder: in short, he began to be in earnest with me indeed; perhaps he found me a little too easy, for I made no resistance to him while he only held me in his arms and kissed me; indeed I was too well pleased with it to resist him much.

Well, tired with that kind of work, we sat down, and there he talked with me a great while; he said he was charmed with me, and that he could not rest till he had told me how he was in love with me, and, if I could love him again, and would make him happy, I should be the saving of his life, and many such fine things. I said little to him again, but easily discovered that I was a fool, and that I did not in the least perceive what he meant.

Then he walked about the room, and, taking me by the hand, I walked with him; and by and by taking his advantage, he threw me down upon the bed, and kissed me there most violently; but to give him his due, offered no manner of rudeness to me, only kissed me a great while; after this he thought he had heard somebody come up stairs, so he got off from the bed, lifted me up, professing a great deal of love for me, but told me it was all an honest affection, and that he meant no ill to me, and with that put five guineas into my hand, and went down stairs.

I was more confounded with the money than I was before with the love; and began to be so elevated, that I scarce knew the ground I stood on. I am the more particular in this, that if it comes to be read by any innocent young body, they may learn from it to guard themselves against the mischiefs which attend an early knowledge of their own beauty: if a young woman once thinks herself handsome, she never doubts the truth of any man that tells her he is in love with her; for if she believes herself charming enough to captivate him, 'tis natural to expect the effects of it.

This gentleman had now fired his inclination, as much as he had my vanity, and, as if he had found that he had an opportunity, and was sorry he did not take hold of it, he comes up again in about half an hour, and falls to work with me again just as he did before, only with a little less introduction.

And first, when he entered the room, he turned about, and shut the door. Mrs. Betty, said he, I fancied before somebody was coming up stairs, but it was not so; however, adds he, if they find me in the room with you, they shan't catch me a kissing of you. I told him I did not know who should be coming up stairs, for I believed there was nobody in the house but the cook and the other maid, and they never came up those stairs. Well, my dear, says he, 'Tis good to be sure however, and so he sits down and we began to talk; and now, though I was still on fire with his first visit, and said little, he did as it were put words in my mouth, telling me how passionately he loved me, and that though he could not till he came to his estate, yet he was resolved to make me happy then, and himself too: that is to say, to marry me, and abundance of such things, which I, poor fool, did not understand the drift of, but acted as if there was no kind of love but that which tended to matrimony; and if he had spoken of that, I had no room, as well as no power, to have said no; but we were not come to that length yet.

We had not sat long, but he got up, and, stopping my very breath with kisses, threw me upon the bed again; but then he went farther with me than decency permits me to

mention, nor had it been in my power to have denied him at
that moment, had he offered much more than he did.

However, though he took these freedoms with me, it did
not go to that which they call the last favour, which, to do
him justice, he did not attempt; and he made that self-denial
of his a plea for all his freedoms with me upon other
occasions after this. When this was over, he stayed but a
little while, but he put almost a handful of gold in my hand,
and left me a thousand protestations of his passion for me,
and of his loving me above all the women in the world.

It will not be strange if I now began to think; but alas!
it was but with very little solid reflection. I had a most
unbounded stock of vanity and pride, and but a very little
stock of virtue. I did indeed cast sometimes with myself
what my young master aimed at, but thought of nothing but
the fine words and the gold; whether he intended to marry
me, or not, seemed a matter of no great consequence to me;
nor did I so much as think of making any capitulation for
myself, till he made a kind of formal proposal to me, as you
shall hear presently.

Thus I gave up myself to ruin without the least concern,
and am a fair memento to all young women whose vanity
prevails over their virtue. Nothing was ever so stupid on
both sides: had I acted as became me, and resisted as virtue
and honour required, he had either desisted his attacks, finding
no room to expect the end of his design, or had made fair
and honourable proposals of marriage; in which case,
whoever blamed him, nobody could have blamed me. In
short, if he had known me, and how easy the trifle he aimed
at was to be had, he would have troubled his head no farther,
but have given me four or five guineas, and have lain with
me the next time he had come at me. On the other hand,
if I had known his thoughts, and how hard he supposed I
would be to be gained, I might have made my own terms,
and if I had not capitulated for an immediate marriage, I
might for a maintenance till marriage, and might have had
what I would; for he was rich to excess, besides what he
had in expectation; but I had wholly abandoned all such
thoughts, and was taken up only with the pride of my beauty,
and of being beloved by such a gentleman; as for the gold,
I spent whole hours in looking upon it; I told the guineas
over a thousand times a day. Never poor vain creature was

so wrapt up with every part of the story, as I was, not considering what was before me, and how near my ruin was at the door; and indeed I think I rather wished for that ruin, than studied to avoid it.

In the mean time, however, I was cunning enough, not to give the least room to any in the family to imagine that I had the least correspondence with him. I scarce ever looked towards him in public, or answered if he spoke to me; when, but for all that, we had every now and then a little encounter, where we had room for a word or two, and now and then a kiss, but no fair opportunity for the mischief intended; and especially considering that he made more circumlocution than he had occasion for, and the work appearing difficult to him, he really made it so.

But as the devil is an unwearied tempter, so he never fails to find an opportunity for the wickedness he invites to. It was one evening that I was in the garden, with his two younger sisters, and himself, when he found means to convey a note into my hand, by which he told me that he would to-morrow desire me publicly to go of an errand for him, and that I should see him somewhere by the way.

Accordingly, after dinner, he very gravely says to me, his sisters being all by, Mrs. Betty, I must ask a favour of you. What's that? says the second sister. Nay, sister, says he very gravely, if you can't spare Mrs. Betty to-day, any other time will do. Yes, they said, they could spare her well enough, and the sister begged pardon for asking. Well, but says the eldest sister, you must tell Mrs. Betty what it is; if it be any private business, that we must not hear, you may call her out, there she is. Why sister, says the gentleman very gravely, what do you mean? I only desire her to go into the High-street (and then he pulls out a turnover), to such a shop; and then he tells them a long story of two fine neckcloths he had bid money for, and he wanted to have me go and make an errand to buy a neck to that turnover that he showed, and if they would not take my money for the neckcloths, to bid a shilling more, and haggle with them; and then he made more errands, and so continued to have such petty business to do, that I should be sure to stay a good while.

When he had given me my errands, he told them a long story of a visit he was going to make to a family they all knew, and where was to be such and such gentlemen, and very formally asked his sisters to go with him, and they as formally excused themselves, because of company that they had notice was to come and visit them that afternoon; all which, by the way, he had contrived on purpose.

He had scarce done speaking, but his man came up to tell him that Sir W—— H——'s coach stopped at the door; so he runs down, and comes up again immediately: Alas! says he aloud, there's all my mirth spoiled at once; Sir W—— has sent his coach for me, and desires to speak with me. It seems this Sir W—— was a gentleman who lived about three miles off, to whom he had spoke on purpose to lend him his chariot for a particular occasion, and had appointed it to call for him, as it did, about three o'clock.

Immediately he calls for his best wig, hat, and sword, and ordering his man to go to the other place to make his excuse; that was to say, he made an excuse to send his man away, he prepares to go into the coach. As he was going, he stopped awhile, and speaks mightily earnestly to me about his business, and finds an opportunity to say very softly, Come away, my dear, as soon as ever you can. I said nothing, but made a curtsy, as if I had done so to what he said in public. In about a quarter of an hour I went out too; I had no dress, other than before, except that I had a hood, a mask, a fan, and a pair of gloves in my pocket; so that there was not the least suspicion in the house. He waited for me in a back lane, which he knew I must pass by, and the coachman knew whither to go, which was to a certain place, called Mile-end, where lived a confidant of his, where we went in, and where was all the convenience in the world to be as wicked as we pleased.

When we were together, he began to talk very gravely to me, and to tell me he did not bring me there to betray me; that his passion for me would not suffer him to abuse me; that he resolved to marry me as soon as he came to his estate; that in the mean time, if I would grant his request, he would maintain me very honourably; and made me a thousand protestations of his sincerity, and of his affection to me; and that he would never abandon me, and, as I may say, made a thousand more preambles than he need to have done.

However, as he pressed me to speak, I told him I had no reason to question the sincerity of his love to me, after so many protestations, but —— and there I stopped, as if I left him to guess the rest; But what, my dear, says he, I guess what you mean, what if you should be with child, is not that it? Why then, says he, I'll take care of you, and provide for you, and the child too; and that you may see I am not in jest, says he, here's an earnest for you, and with that he pulls out a silk purse with an hundred guineas in it, and gave it me; and I'll give you such another, says he, every year till I marry you.

My colour came and went at the sight of the purse, and with the fire of his proposal together, so that I could not say a word, and he easily perceived it; so putting the purse into my bosom, I made no more resistance to him, but let him do just what he pleased, and as often as he pleased; and thus I finished my own destruction at once, for from this day, being forsaken of my virtue, and my modesty, I had nothing of value left to recommend me, either to God's blessing, or man's assistance.

But things did not end here. I went back to the town, did the business he directed me to, and was at home before anybody thought me long; as for my gentleman, he stayed out till late at night, and there was not the least suspicion in the family, either on his account or on mine.

We had after this, frequent opportunities to repeat our crime, and especially at home, when his mother and the young ladies went abroad a visiting, which he watched so narrowly, as never to miss; knowing always beforehand when they went out, and then failed not to catch me all alone, and securely enough; so that we took our fill of our wicked pleasures for near half a year; and yet, which was the most to my satisfaction, I was not with child.

But before this half year was expired, his younger brother, of whom I have made some mention in the beginning of the story, falls to work with me; and he finding me alone in the garden one evening, begins a story of the same kind to me, made good honest professions of being in love with me, and in short, proposes fairly and honourably to marry me.

I was now confounded, and driven to such an extremity, as the like was never known to me; I resisted the proposal with obstinacy, and began to arm myself with arguments: I laid before him the inequality of the match, the treatment I should meet with in the family, the ingratitude it would be to his good father and mother, who had taken me into their house upon such generous principles, and when I was in such a low condition; and, in short, I said everything to dissuade him that I could imagine except telling him the truth, which would indeed have put an end to it all, but that I durst not think of mentioning.

But here happened a circumstance that I did not expect indeed, which put me to my shifts; for this young gentleman, as he was plain and honest, so he pretended to nothing but what was so too; and knowing his own innocence, he was not so careful to make his having a kindness for Mrs. Betty a secret in the house, as his brother was; and though he did not let them know that he had talked to me about it, yet he said enough to let his sisters perceive he loved me, and his mother saw it too, which though they took no notice of to me, yet they did to him, and immediately I found their carriage to me altered more than ever before.

I saw the cloud, though I did not foresee the storm; it was easy, I say, to see their carriage was altered, and that it grew worse and worse every day, till at last I got information that I should in a very little while be desired to remove.

I was not alarmed at the news, having a full satisfaction that I should be provided for; and especially considering that I had reason every day to expect I should be with child, and that then I should be obliged to remove without any pretences for it.

After some time, the younger gentleman took an opportunity to tell me, that the kindness he had for me had got vent in the family; he did not charge me with it, he said, for he knew well enough which way it came out; he told me his way of talking had been the occasion of it, for that he did not make his respect for me so much a secret as he might have done, and the reason was, that he was at a point, that if I would consent to have him, he would tell them all openly that he loved me, and that he intended to marry me: that it was true, his father and mother might resent it, and be unkind, but he was now in a way to live, being bred to the law, and he did not fear maintaining me, and that, in short, as he believed I would not be ashamed of him, so he was resolved not to be ashamed of me, and that he scorned to be afraid to own me now, whom he resolved to own after I was his wife, and therefore I had nothing to do but to give him my hand, and he would answer for all the rest.

I was now in a dreadful condition indeed, and now I repented heartily my easiness with the eldest brother; not from any reflection of conscience, for I was a stranger to those things, but I could not think of being a whore to one brother and a wife to the other; it came also into my thoughts, that the first brother had promised to make me his wife when he came to his estate; but I presently remembered, what I had often thought of, that he had never spoken a word of having me for a wife, after he had conquered me for a mistress; and indeed, till now, though I said I thought of it often, yet it gave no disturbance at all, for as he did not seem in the least to lessen his affection to me, so neither did he lessen his bounty, though he had the discretion himself to desire me not to lay out a penny in clothes, or to make the least show extraordinary, because it would necessarily give jealousy in the family, since everybody knew I could come at such things no manner of ordinary way, but by some private friendship, which they would presently have suspected.

I was now in a great strait, and knew not what to do; the main difficulty was this, the younger brother not only laid close siege to me, but suffered it to be seen; he would come into his sister's room, and his mother's room, and sit down, and talk a thousand kind things to me, even before their faces; so that the whole house talked of it, and his mother reproved him for it, and their carriage to me appeared quite altered: in short, his mother had let fall some speeches, as if she intended to put me out of the family, that is, in English, to turn me out of doors. Now I was sure this could not be a secret to his brother, only that he might think, as indeed nobody else yet did, that the youngest brother had made any proposal to me about it; but as I could easily see that it would go farther, so I saw likewise there was an absolute necessity to speak of it to him, or that he would speak of it to me, but knew not whether I should break it to him, or let it alone till he should break it to me.

Upon serious consideration, for indeed now I began to consider things very seriously, and never till now, I resolved to tell him of it first, and it was not long before I had an opportunity, for the very next day his brother went to London

upon some business, and the family being out a visiting, just
as it happened before, and as indeed was often the case, he
came according to his custom to spend an hour or two with
Mrs. Betty.

When he had sat down a while, he easily perceived there
was an alteration in my countenance, that I was not so free
and pleasant with him as I used to be, and particularly, that
I had been a crying; he was not long before he took notice
of it, and asked me in very kind terms what was the matter,
and if anything troubled me. I would have put it off if I could,
but it was not to be concealed; so after suffering many
importunities to draw that out of me, which I longed as much
as possible to disclose, I told him that it was true, something
did trouble me, and something of such a nature, that I could
hardly conceal from him, and yet that I could not tell how to
tell him of it neither; that it was a thing that not only
surprised me, but greatly perplext me, and that I knew not
what course to take, unless he would direct me: he told me
with great tenderness, that let it be what it would, I should not
let it trouble me, for he would protect me from all the world.

I then began at a distance, and told him I was afraid the
ladies had got some secret information of our correspondence;
for that it was easy to see that their conduct was very much
changed towards me, and that now it was come to pass, that
they frequently found fault with me, and sometimes fell quite
out with me, though I never gave them the least occasion:
that whereas I used always to lie with the elder sister, I was
lately put to lie by myself, or with one of the maids; and
that I had overheard them several times talking very unkindly
about me; but that which confirmed it all was, that one of
the servants had told me that she had heard I was to be
turned out, and that it was not safe for the family that I
should be any longer in the house.

He smiled when he heard of this, and I asked him how he
could make so light of it, when he must need know, that if
there was any discovery, I was undone, and that it would
hurt him, though not ruin him, as it would me: I upbraided
him, that he was like the rest of his sex, that when they had
the character of a woman at their mercy, oftentimes made it
their jest, and at least looked upon it as a trifle, and counted
the ruin of those they had had their will of, as a thing of no
value.

He saw me warm and serious, and he changed his style immediately; he told me he was sorry I should have such a thought of him : that he had never given me the least occasion for it, but had been as tender of my reputation, as he could be of his own; that he was sure our correspondence had been managed with so much address, that not one creature in the family had so much as a suspicion of it; that if he smiled when I told him my thoughts, it was at the assurance he lately received, that our understanding one another was not so much as guessed at, and that when he had told me how much reason he had to be easy, I should smile as he did, for he was very certain it would give me a full satisfaction.

This is a mystery I cannot understand, says I, or how it should be to my satisfaction, that I am to be turned out of doors; for if our correspondence is not discovered, I know not what else I have done to change the faces of the whole family to me, who formerly used me with so much tenderness, as if I had been one of their own children.

Why look you, child, says he; that they are uneasy about you, that is true, but that they have the least suspicion of the case as it is, and as it respects you and I, is so far from being true, that they suspect my brother Robin, and, in short, they are fully pursuaded he makes love to you: nay, the fool has put it into their heads too himself, for he is continually bantering them about it, and making a jest of himself; I confess I think he is wrong to do so, because he cannot but see it vexes them, and makes them unkind to you : but it is a satisfaction to me, because of the assurance it gives me, that they do not suspect me in the least, and I hope this will be to your satisfaction too.

So it is, says I, one way, but this does not reach my case at all, nor is this the chief thing that troubles me, though I have been concerned about that too. What is it then, says he? With which, I fell into tears, and could say nothing to him at all : he strove to pacify me all he could, but began at last to be very pressing upon me, to tell what it was; at last I answered, that I thought I ought to tell him too, and that he had some right to know it : besides, that I wanted his direction in the case, for I was in such perplexity, that I knew not what course to take, and then I related the whole affair to him : I told him how imprudently his brother had managed himself, in making himself so public; for that if he

had kept it a secret, I could but have denied him positively,
without giving any reason for it, and he would in time have
ceased his solicitations; but that he had the vanity, first, to
depend upon it that I would not deny him, and then had taken
the freedom to tell his design to the whole house.

I told him how far I had resisted him, and how sincere
and honourable his offers were; but, says I, my case will be
doubly hard; for as they carry it ill to me now, because he
desires to have me, they'll carry it worse when they shall find
I have denied him; and they will presently say, there's
something else in it, and that I am married already to somebody else, or that I would never refuse a match so much
above me as this was.

This discourse surprised him indeed very much: he told
me, that it was a critical point indeed for me to manage, and
he did not see which way I should get out of it; but he would
consider of it, and let me know next time we met, what
resolution he was come to about it; and in the mean time,
desired I would not give my consent to his brother, nor yet
give him a flat denial, but that I would hold him in suspense
a while.

I seemed to start at his saying, I should not give him my
consent; I told him, he knew very well, I had no consent to
give; that he had engaged himself to marry me, and that I
was thereby engaged to him; that he had all along told me
I was his wife, and I looked upon myself as effectually so, as
if the ceremony had passed; and that it was from his own
mouth that I did so, he having all along persuaded me to call
myself his wife.

Well, my dear, says he, don't be concerned at that now;
if I am not your husband, I'll be as good as a husband to you,
and do not let those things trouble you now, but let me look
a little farther into this affair, and I shall be able to say more
next time we meet.

He pacified me as well as he could with this, but I found
he was very thoughtful, and that though he was very kind to
me, and kissed me a thousand times, and more I believe, and
gave me money too, yet he offered no more all the while we
were together, which was above two hours, and which I much
wondered at, considering how it used to be, and what opportunity we had.

His brother did not come from London for five or six days,

and it was two days more before he got an opportunity to
talk with him; but then getting him by himself, he talked
very close to him about it; and the same evening found
means (for we had a long conference together) to repeat all
their discourse to me, which as near as I can remember, was
to the purpose following. He told him he heard strange
news of him since he went, viz., that he made love to Mrs.
Betty. Well, says his brother, a little angrily, and what
then?' what has anybody to do with that? Nay, says his
brother, don't be angry, Robin, I don't pretend to have anything to do with it; but I find they do concern themselves
about it, and that they have used the poor girl ill about it,
which I should take as done to myself. Who do you mean
by THEY? says Robin. I mean my mother, and the girls,
says the elder brother.

But hark ye, says his brother, are you in earnest; do you
really love the girl? Why then, says Robin, I will be free
with you; I do love her above all the women in the world,
and I will have her, let them say and do what they will; I
believe the girl will not deny me.

It stuck me to the heart when he told me this, for though
it was most rational to think I would not deny him, yet I
knew in my own conscience, I must, and I saw my ruin in
my being obliged to do so; but I knew it was my business
to talk otherwise then, so I interrupted him in his story thus:
Ay! said I, does he think I cannot deny him? but he shall
find I can deny him for all that. Well, my dear, says he,
but let me give you the whole story as it went on between
us, and then say what you will.

Then he went on and told me, that he replied thus: But
brother, you know she has nothing, and you may have several
ladies with good fortunes. 'Tis no matter for that, said
Robin, I love the girl; and I will never please my pocket in
marrying, and not please my fancy. And so my dear, adds
he, there is no opposing him.

Yes, yes, says I, I can oppose him; I have learned to say
no, now, though I had not learnt it before; if the best lord
in the land offered me marriage now, I could very cheerfully
say no to him.

Well, but my dear, says he, what can you say to him?
You know, as you said before, he will ask you many questions

about it, and all the house will wonder what .he meaning of
it should be.

Why, says I, smiling, I can stop all their mouths, at one
clap, by telling him and them too, that I am married already
to his elder brother.

He smiled a little too at the word, but I could see it
startled him, and he could not hide the disorder it put him
into : however, he returned, Why though that may be true,
in some sense, yet I suppose you are but in jest, when you
talk of giving such an answer as that; it may not be convenient on many accounts.

No, no, says I pleasantly, I am not so fond of letting that
secret come out, without your consent.

But what then can you say to them, says he, when they
find you positive against a match, which would be apparently
so much to your advantage?   Why, says I, should I be at a
loss?   First, I am not obliged to give them any reason : on
the other hand, I may tell them I am married already, and
stop there, and that will be a full stop too to him, for he can
have no reason to ask one question after it.

Ay, says he, but the whole house will teaze you about that,
and if you deny them positively, they will be disobliged at
you, and suspicious besides.

Why, says I, what can I do? What would you have me
do? I was in strait enough before, as I told you; and
acquainted you with the circumstances, that I might have
your advice.

My dear, says he, I have been considering very much upon
it, you may be sure, and though the advice has many mortifications in it to me, and may at first seem strange to you,
yet all things considered, I see no better way for you than to
let him go on ; and if you find him hearty and in earnest,
marry him.

I gave him a look full of horror at those words, and turning
pale as death, was at the very point of sinking down out of
the chair I sat in ; when giving a start, My dear, says he
aloud, what's the matter with you? where are you a-going?
and a great many such things; and with jogging and calling
to me, fetched me a little to myself, though it was a good
while before I fully recovered my senses, and was not able to
speak for several minutes.

When I was fully recovered, he began again; My dear, says he, I would have you consider seriously of it: you may see plainly how the family stand in this case, and they would be stark mad if it was my case, as it is my brother's; and for aught I see, it would be my ruin and yours too.

Ay! says I, still speaking angrily; are all your protestations and vows to be shaken by the dislike of the family? did I not always object that to you, and you made a light thing of it, as what you were above, and would not value; and is it come to this now? Is this your faith and honour, your love, and the solidity of your promises?

He continued perfectly calm, notwithstanding all my reproaches, and I was not sparing of them at all; but he replied at last, My dear, I have not broken one promise with you yet; I did tell you I would marry you when I was come to my estate; but you see my father is a hale, healthy man, and may live these thirty years still, and not be older than several are round us in the town; and you never proposed my marrying you sooner, because you know it might be my ruin; and as to the rest, I have not failed you in anything.

I could not deny a word of this: But why then, says I, can you persuade me to such a horrid step, as leaving you, since you have not left me? Will you allow no affection, no love on my side, where there has been so much on your side? Have I made you no returns? Have I given no testimony of my sincerity, and of my passion? Are the sacrifices I have made of honour and modesty to you, no proof of my being tied to you in bonds too strong to be broken?

But here, my dear, says he, you may come into a safe station, and appear with honour, and the remembrance of what we have done may be wrapt up in an eternal silence, as if it had never happened; you shall always have my sincere affection, only then it shall be honest, and perfectly just to my brother; you shall be my dear sister, as now you are my dear——and there he stopt.

Your dear whore, says I, you would have said, and you might as well have said it; but I understand you: however, I desire you to remember the long discourses you have had with me, and the many hours' pains you have taken to persuade me to believe myself an honest woman; that I was

your wife intentionally, and that it was as effectual a
marriage that had passed between us, as if we had been
publicly wedded by the parson of the parish; you know
these have been your own words to me.

I found this was a little too close upon him, but I made it
up in what follows; he stood stockstill for awhile, and said
nothing, and I went on thus: You cannot, says I, without
the highest injustice, believe that I yielded upon all these
persuasions without a love not to be questioned, not to be
shaken again by anything that could happen afterward: if
you have such dishonourable thoughts of me, I must ask you
what foundation have I given for such a suggestion.

If then I have yielded to the importunities of my affection;
and if I have been persuaded to believe that I am really your
wife, shall I now give the lie to all those arguments, and call
myself your whore, or mistress, which is the same thing?
and will you transfer me to your brother? can you transfer
my affection? can you bid me cease loving you, and bid me
love him? is it in my power, think you, to make such a
change at demand? No sir, said I, depend upon it 'tis
impossible, and whatever the change on your side may be, I
will ever be true; and I had much rather, since it is come
that unhappy length, be your whore than your brother's wife.

He appeared pleased, and touched with the impression of
this last discourse, and told me that he stood where he did
before; that he had not been unfaithful to me in any one
promise he had ever made yet, but that there were so many
terrible things presented themselves to his view in the affair
before me, that he had thought of the other as a remedy, only
that he thought this would not be an entire parting us, but
we might love as friends all our days, and perhaps with
more satisfaction than we should in the station we were now
in; that he durst say, I could not apprehend anything from
him, as to betraying a secret, which could not but be the
destruction of, us both if it came out: that he had but one
question to ask of me, that could lie in the way of it, and
if that question was answered, he could not but think still it
was the only step I could take.

I guessed at his question presently, viz., whether I was not
with child? As to that, I told him, he need not be concerned
about it, for I was not with child. Why then, my dear,
says he, we have no time to talk farther now; consider of

It, I cannot but be of the opinion still, that it will be the best course you can take. And with this he took his leave, and the more hastily too, his mother and sisters ringing at the gate just at the moment he had risen up to go.

He left me in the utmost confusion of thought; and he easily perceived it the next day, and all the rest week, but he had no opportunity to come at me all that week, till the Sunday after, when I being indisposed, did not go to church, and he, making some excuse, stayed at home.

And now he had me an hour and half again by myself, and we fell into the same arguments all over again; at last, I asked him warmly, what opinion he must have of my modesty, that he could suppose I should so much as entertain a thought of lying with two brothers? and assured him it could never be: I added, if he was to tell me that he would never see me more, than which nothing but death could be more terrible, yet I could never entertain a thought so dishonourable to myself, and so base to him; and therefore, I entreated him, if he had one grain of respect or affection left for me, that he would speak no more of it to me, or that he would pull his sword out and kill me. He appeared surprised at my obstinacy, as he called it; told me I was unkind to myself, and unkind to him in it; that it was a crisis unlooked for upon us both, but that he did not see any other way to save us both from ruin, and therefore he thought it the more unkind; but that if he must say no more of it to me, he added with an unusual coldness, that he did not know anything else we had to talk of; and so he rose up to take his leave; I rose up too, as if with the same indifference, but when he came to give me as it were a parting kiss, I burst out into such a passion of crying, that though I would have spoke, I could not, and only pressing his hand, seemed to give him the adieu, but cried vehemently.

He was sensibly moved with this; so he sat down again, and said a great many kind things to me, but still urged the necessity of what he had proposed; all the while insisting, that if I did refuse, he would notwithstanding provide for me; but letting me plainly see, that he would decline me in the main point: nay, even as a mistress; making it a point of honour not to lie with the woman, that for aught he knew, might one time or other come to be his brother's wife.

The bare loss of him as a gallant was not so much my
affliction, as the loss of his person, whom indeed I loved to
distraction; and the loss of all the expectations I had, and
which I always built my hopes upon, of having him one day
for my husband: these things oppressed my mind so much,
that in short, the agonies of my mind threw me into a high
fever, and long it was, that none in the family expected my
life.

I was reduced very low indeed, and was often delirious;
but nothing lay so near me, as the fear that when I was
light-headed, I should say something or other to his prejudice.
I was distressed in my mind also to see him, and so he was
to see me, for he really loved me most passionately; but it
could not be; there was not the least room to desire it on
one side, or other.

It was near five weeks that I kept my bed; and though
the violence of my fever abated in three weeks, yet it several
times returned; and the physicians said two or three times,
they could do no more for me, but that they must leave
nature and the distemper to fight it out: after the end of
five weeks I grew better, but was so weak, so altered, and
recovered so slowly, that the physicians apprehended I
should go into a consumption; and which vexed me most,
they gave their opinion, that my mind was oppressed, that
something troubled me, and, in short, that I was in love.
Upon this, the whole house set upon me to press me to tell,
whether I was in love or not, and with whom? but as I well
might, I denied my being in love at all.

They had on this occasion a squabble one day about me
at table, that had like to put the whole family in an uproar.
They happened to be all at table, but the father; as for me,
I was ill, and in my chamber: at the beginning of the talk,
the old gentlewoman, who had sent me somewhat to eat, bid
her maid go up and ask me if I would have any more; but
the maid brought down word, I had not eaten half what she
had sent me already. Alas, says the old lady, that poor girl!
I am afraid she will never be well. Well! says the elder
brother, How should Mrs. Betty be well, they say she is in
love? I believe nothing of it, says the old gentlewoman.
I don't know, says the elder sister, what to say to it, they
have made such a rout about her being so handsome, and so
charming, and I know not what, and that in her hearing too,

that has turned the creature's head, I believe, and who knows what possessions may follow such doings? for my part, I don't know what to make of it.

Why sister, you must acknowledge she is very handsome, says the elder brother. Ay, and a great deal handsomer than you, sister, says Robin, and that's your mortification. Well, well, that is not the question, says his sister; the girl is well enough, and she knows it; she need not be told of it to make her vain.

We don't talk of her being vain, says the elder brother, but of her being in love: may be she is in love with herself: it seems my sisters think so.

I would she was in love with me, says Robin; I'd quickly put her out of her pain. What d'ye mean by that, son? says the old lady: how can you talk so. Why madam, says Robin again, very honestly, do you think I'd let the poor girl die for love, and of me too, that is so near at hand to be had. Fie brother, says the second sister, how can you talk so? Would you take a creature that has not a groat in the world? Prithee child, says Robin, beauty's a portion, and good humour with it is a double portion; I wish thou hadst half her stock of both for thy portion: so there was her mouth stopt.

I find, says the eldest sister, if Betty is not in love, my brother is; I wonder he has not broke his mind to Betty; I warrant she won't say NO. They that yield when they are asked, says Robin, are one step before them that were never asked to yield, and two steps before them that yield before they are asked; and that's an answer to you, sister.

This fired the sister, and she flew into a passion, and said, things were come to that pass, that it was time the wench, meaning me, was out of the family; and but that she was not fit to be turned out, she hoped her father and mother would consider of it, as soon as she could be removed.

Robin replied, that was for the master and mistress of the family, who were not to be taught by one that had so little judgment as his eldest sister.

It run up a great deal farther; the sister scolded, Robin rallied and bantered, but poor Betty lost ground by it extremely in the family. I heard of it, and cried heartily, and the old lady came up to me, somebody having told her that I was so much concerned about it. I complained to her, that it was very hard the doctors should pass such a censure upon me, for which they had no ground; and that it was still harder, considering the circumstances I was under in the family; that I hoped I had done nothing to lessen her esteem for me, or given any occasion for the bickering between her sons and daughters; and had more need to think of a coffin, than of being in love, and begged she would not let me suffer in her opinion for anybody's mistakes, but my own.

She was sensible of the justice of what I said, but told me, since there had been such a clamour among them, and that her younger son talked after such a rattling way as he did, she desired I would be so faithful to her, as to answer her but one question sincerely. I told her I would, and with the utmost plainness and sincerity. Why then the question was, whether there was anything between her son Robert and me? I told her with all the protestations of sincerity that I was able to make, and as I might well do, that there was not, nor ever had been; I told her that Mr. Robert had rattled and jested, as she knew it was his way, and that I took it always as I supposed he meant it, to be a wild airy way of discourse that had no signification in it; and assured her, that there was not the least tittle of what she understood by it between us; and that those who had suggested it, had done me a great deal of wrong, and Mr. Robert no service at all.

The old lady was fully satisfied, and kissed me, spoke cheerfully to me, and bid me take care of my health, and want for nothing, and so took her leave; but when she came down, she found the brother and all his sisters together by the ears; they were angry even to passion, at his upbraiding them with their being homely, and having never had any sweethearts, never having been asked the question, their being so forward as almost to ask first, and the like; he rallied them with Mrs. Betty; how pretty, how good-humoured, how she sung better than they did, and danced better, and how much handsomer she was; and in doing this, he omitted no ill-natured thing that could vex them. The old lady came down in the height of it, and to stop it, told them the discourse she had had with me, and how I answered, that there was nothing between Mr. Robert and I.

She's wrong there, says Robin, for if there was not a great deal between us, we should be closer together than we are: I told her I loved her hugely, says he, but I could never make the jade believe I was in earnest. I do not know how you should, says his mother, nobody in their senses could believe you were in earnest, to talk so to a poor girl, whose circumstances you know so well.

But prithee son, adds she, since you tell us you could not make her believe you were in earnest, what must we believe about it? For you ramble so in your discourse, that nobody knows whether you are in earnest or in jest; but as I find the girl, by your own confession, has answered truly, I wish you would do so too, and tell me seriously, so that I may depend upon it; is there anything in it or no? Are you in earnest or no? Are you distracted indeed, or are you not? 'Tis a weighty question, I wish you would make us easy about it.

By my faith, madam, says Robin, 'tis in vain to mince the matter, or tell any more lies about it; I am in earnest, as much as a man is that's going to be hanged. If Mrs. Betty would say she loved me, and that she would marry me, I'd have her to-morrow morning fasting; and say, To have and to hold, instead of eating my breakfast.

Well, says the mother, then there's one son lost; and she said it in a very mournful tone, as one greatly concerned at it. I hope not madam, says Robin, no man is lost when a good wife has found him. Why, but child, says the old lady, she is a beggar. Why then madam, she has the more need of charity, says Robin; I'll take her off the hands of the parish, and she and I'll beg together. It's bad jesting with such things, says the mother. I don't jest, madam, says Robin: we'll come and beg your pardon, madam; and your blessing, madam, and my father's. This is all out of the way, son, says the mother; if you are in earnest you are undone. I am afraid not, says he, for I am really afraid she won't have me; after all my sister's huffing, I believe I shall never be able to persuade her to it.

That's a fine tale indeed; she is not so far gone neither; Mrs. Betty is no fool, says the youngest sister: Do you think she has learned to say NO, any more than other people? No, Mrs. Mirth-wit, says Robin, Mrs. Betty's no fool, but Mrs. Betty may be engaged some other way, and what then? Nay, says the eldest sister, we can say nothing to that; who must it be to then? she is never out of the doors, it must be between you. I have nothing to say to that, says Robin; I have been examined enough, there's my brother; if it must be between us, go to work with him.

This stung the elder brother to the quick, and he concluded that Robin had discovered something; however, he kept himself from appearing disturbed; Prithee, says he, don't go to sham your stories off upon me; I tell you I deal in no such ware, I have nothing to say to no Mrs. Betty's in the parish; and with that he rose up, and brushed off. No, says the eldest sister, I dare answer for my brother; he knows the world better.

Thus the discourse ended; but it left the eldest brother quite confounded: he concluded his brother had made a full discovery, and he began to doubt whether I had been concerned in it or not; but with all his management, he could not bring it about to get at me; at last he was so perplexed, that he was quite desperate, and resolved he would see me whatever came of it. In order to this, he contrived it so, that one day after dinner, watching his eldest sister, till he could see her go up stairs, he runs after her; Hark ye, sister, says he, where is this sick woman? may not a body see her? Yes, says the sister, I believe you may, but let me go in first a little, and I'll tell you; so she run up to the door, and gave me notice, and presently called to him again: Brother, says she, you may come in if you please; so in he came, just in the same kind of rant: Well, says he, at the door, as he came in, where's this sick body that's in love? How do ye do Mrs. Betty? I would have got up out of my chair, but was so weak I could not for a good while; and he saw it, and his sister too; and she said, Come do not strive to stand up, my brother desires no ceremony, especially now you are so weak. No, no, Mrs. Betty, pray sit still, says he, and so sits himself down in a chair over against me, and appeared as if he was mighty merry.

He talked a deal of rambling stuff to his sister, and to me; sometimes of one thing, sometimes another, on purpose to amuse her, and every now and then would turn it upon the old story. Poor Mrs. Betty, says he, it is a sad thing to be in love, why it has reduced you sadly; at last I spoke a little. I am glad to see you so merry, sir, says I, but I think the doctor might have found something better to do

than to make his game of his patients: if I had been ill of
no other distemper, I know the proverb too well to have let
him come to me. What proverb? says he: what,

> " Where love is the case,
> The doctor's an ass."

Is not that it, Mrs. Betty? I smiled, and said nothing.
Nay, says he, I think the effect has proved it to be love; for
it seems the doctor has done you little service; you mend
very slowly, they say; I doubt there's somewhat in it,
Mrs. Betty; I doubt you are sick of the incurables. I
smiled, and said, No indeed, sir, that's none of my distemper.

We had a deal of such discourse, and sometimes others
that signified as little: by and bye he asked me to sing them
a song; at which I smiled, and said, my singing days were
over. At last he asked me, if he should play upon his flute
to me; his sister said, she believed my head could not bear
it; I bowed, and said, Pray, madam, do not hinder it, I love
the flute very much; then his sister said, Well, do then,
brother; with that he pulled out the key of his closet; Dear
sister, says he, I am very lazy, do step and fetch my flute, it
·lies in such a drawer, naming a place where he was sure it
was not, that she might be a little while a looking for it.

As soon as she was gone, he related the whole story to me
of the discourse his brother had about me, and his concern
about it, which was the reason of his contriving this visit.
I assured him I had never opened my mouth, either to his
brother or to anybody else: I told him the dreadful exigence
I was in; that my love to him, and his offering to have me
forget that affection, and remove it to another, had thrown
me down; and that I had a thousand times wished I might
die, rather than recover, and to have the same circumstances
to struggle with as I had before: I added that I foresaw that
as soon as I was well I must quit the family, and that as for
marrying his brother, I abhorred the thoughts of it, after
what had been my case with him, and that he might depend
upon it I would never see his brother again upon that subject. That if he would break all his vows and oaths, and
engagements with me, be that between his conscience and
himself; but he should never be able to say, that I whom he
had persuaded to call myself his wife, and who had given

D 2

him the liberty to use me as a wife, was not as faithful to him as a wife ought to be, whatever he might be to me.

He was going to reply, and had said that he was sorry I could not be persuaded, and was a-going to say more, but he heard his sister a-coming, and so did I; and yet I forced out these few words as a reply, that I could never be persuaded to love one brother and marry the other. He shook his head, and said, Then I am ruined, meaning himself; and that moment his sister entered the room, and told him she could not find the flute. Well, says he, merrily, this laziness won't do, so he gets up, and goes himself to look for it, but comes back without it too, not but that he could have found it, but he had no mind to play; and, besides, the errand he sent his sister on was answered another way; for he only wanted to speak to me, which he had done, though not much to his satisfaction.

I had, however, a great deal of satisfaction in having spoken my mind to him in freedom, and with such an honest plainness, as I have related; and though it did not at all work the way I desired, that is to say, to oblige the person to me the more; yet it took from him all possibility of quitting me, but by a downright breach of honour, and giving up all the faith of a gentleman, which he had so often engaged by, never to abandon me, but to make me his wife as soon as he came to his estate.

It was not many weeks after this before I was about the house again, and began to grow well; but I continued melancholy and retired, which amazed the whole family, except he that knew the reason of it; yet it was a great while before he took any notice of it, and I, as backward to speak as he, carried as respectfully to him, but never offered to speak a word that was particular of any kind whatsoever; and this continued for sixteen or seventeen weeks; so that as I expected every day to be dismissed the family, on account of what distaste they had taken another way, in which I had no guilt, I expected to hear no more of this gentleman, after all his solemn vows, but to be ruined and abandoned.

At last I broke the way myself in the family, for my removing; for being talking seriously with the old lady one day, about my own circumstances, and how my distemper had left a heaviness upon my spirits: the old lady said, I am afraid, Betty, what I have said to you about my son has had some influence upon you, and that you are melancholy on his account; pray, will you let me know how the matter stands with you both? if it may not be improper? for, as for Robin, he does nothing but rally and banter when I speak of it to him. Why truly madam, said I, that matter stands as I wish it did not, and I shall be very sincere with you in it, whatever befalls me. Mr. Robert has several times proposed marriage to me, which is what I had no reason to expect, my poor circumstances considered; but I have always resisted him, and that perhaps in terms more positive than became me, considering the regard that I ought to have for every branch of your family; but, said I, madam, I could never so far forget my obligations to you, and all your house, to offer to consent to a thing which I knew must needs be disobliging to you, and have positively told him that I would never entertain a thought of that kind, unless I had your consent, and his father's also, to whom I was bound by so many invincible obligations.

And is this possible, Mrs. Betty? says the old lady. Then you have been much juster to us than we have been to you; for we have all looked upon you as a kind of a snare to my son; and I had a proposal to make you, for your removing, for fear of it; but I had not yet mentioned it to you, because I was afraid of grieving you too much, lest it should throw you down again; for we have a respect for you still, though not so much as to have it be the ruin of my son; but if it be as you say, we have all wronged you very much.

As to the truth of what I say, madam, said I, I refer to your son himself: if he will do me any justice he must tell you the story just as I have told it.

Away goes the old lady to her daughters, and tells them the whole story, just as I had told it her, and they were surprised at it, you may be sure, as I believed they would be; one said she could never have thought it, another said Robin was a fool; a third said, she would not believe a word of it, and she would warrant that Robin would tell the story another way; but the old lady, who was resolved to go to the bottom of it, before I could have the least opportunity of acquainting her son with what had passed, resolved too, that she would talk with her son immediately, and to that purpose sent for him, for he was gone but to a lawyer's house in the town, and upon her sending he returned immediately.

Upon his coming up to them, for they were all together, Sit down Robin, says the old lady, I must have some talk with you. With all my heart, madam, says Robin, looking very merry; I hope it is about a good wife, for I am at a great loss in that affair. How can that be, says his mother, did not you say you resolved to have Mrs. Betty? Ay, madam, says Robin, but there is one that has forbid the banns. Forbid the banns, who can that be? Even Mrs. Betty herself, says Robin. How so, says his mother, have you asked her the question then? Yes indeed madam, says Robin, I have attacked her in form five times since she was sick, and am beaten off: the jade is so stout, she won't capitulate, nor yield upon any terms, except such as I can't effectually grant. Explain yourself, says the mother, for I am surprised, I do not understand you; I hope you are not in earnest.

Why, madam, says he, the case is plain enough upon me, it explains itself; she won't have me, she says, is not that plain enough? I think 'tis plain, and pretty rough too. Well, but, says the mother, you talk of conditions, that you cannot grant, what does she want a settlement? her jointure ought to be according to her portion; what does she bring? Nay, as to fortune, says Robin, she is rich enough; I am satisfied in that point; but 'tis I that am not able to come up to her terms, and she is positive she will not have me without.

Here the sisters put in. Madam, says the second sister, 'tis impossible to be serious with him, he will never give a direct answer to anything; you had better let him alone, and talk no more of it; you know how to dispose of her out of his way. Robin was a little warmed with his sister's rudeness, but he was even with her presently. There are two sorts of people, madam, says he, turning to his mother, that there is no contending with; that is a wise body and a fool; 'tis a little hard I should engage with both of them together.

The younger sister then put in. We must be fools indeed, says she, in my brother's opinion, that he should make us believe he has seriously asked Mrs. Betty to marry him, and she has refused him.

Answer, and answer not, says Solomon, replied her brother: when your brother had said that he had asked her no less than five times, and that she positively denied him, methinks a younger sister need not question the truth of it, when her mother did not. My mother, you see, did not understand it, says the second sister. There's some difference, says Robin, between desiring me to explain it, and telling me she did not believe it.

Well, but son, says the old lady, if you are disposed to let us into the mystery of it, what were those hard conditions? Yes madam, says Robin, I had done it before now, if the teasers here had not worried me by way of interruption. The conditions are, that I bring my father and you to consent to it, and without that she protests she will never see me more upon that head; and the conditions, as I said, I suppose I shall never be able to grant; I hope my warm sisters will be answered now, and blush a little.

This answer was surprising to them all, though less to the mother, because of what I had said to her; as to the daughters, they stood mute a great while; but the mother said, with some passion, Well, I heard this before, but I could not believe it; but if it is so, then we have all done Betty wrong, and she has behaved better then I expected. Nay, says the eldest sister, if it is so, she has acted handsomely indeed. I confess, says the mother, it was none of her fault, if he was enough fool to take a fancy to her; but to give such an answer to him, shows more respect to us, than I can tell how to express; I shall value the girl the better for it, as long as I know her. But I shall not, says Robin, unless you will give your consent. I'll consider of that awhile, says the mother; I assure you, if there were not some other objections, this conduct of hers would go a great way to bring me to consent. I wish it would go quite through with it, says Robin: if you had as much thought about making me easy, as you have about making me rich, you would soon consent to it.

Why Robin, says the mother, again, are you really in earnest? would you fain have her?   Really, madam, says Robin, I think 'tis hard you should question me again upon that head; I won't say that I will have her; how can I resolve that point, when you see I cannot have her without your consent; but this I will say, I am earnest, that I will never have any anybody else, if I can help it; Betty or nobody is the word, and the question which of the two shall be in your breast to decide, madam, provided only, that my good-humoured sisters here, may have no vote in it.

All this was dreadful to me, for the mother began to yield, and Robin pressed her home in it. On the other hand, she advised with the eldest son, and he used all the arguments in the world to persuade her to consent; alleging his brother's passionate love for me, and my generous regard to the family, in refusing my own advantages upon such a nice point of honour, and a thousand such things. And as to the father, he was a man in a hurry of public affairs, and getting money, seldom at home, thoughtful of the main chance, but left all those things to his wife.

You may easily believe, that when the plot was thus, as they thought, broke out, it was not so difficult or so dangerous for the elder brother, whom nobody suspected of anything, to have a freer access than before: nay, the mother, which was just as he wished, proposed it to him to talk with Mrs. Betty: It may be, son, said she, you may see farther into the thing than I, and see if she has been so positive as Robin says she has been, or no. This was as well as he could wish, and he as it were yielding to talk with me at his mother's request, she brought me to him into her own chamber; told me her son had some business with me at her request, and then she left us together, and he shut the door after her.

He came back to me, and took me in his arms and kissed me very tenderly; but told me it was now come to that crisis, that I should make myself happy or miserable as long as I lived: that if I could not comply to his desire, we should both be ruined. Then he told me the whole story between Robin, as he called him, and his mother, and his sisters, and himself, as above. And now, dear child, says he, consider what it will be to marry a gentleman of a good family, in good circumstances, and with the consent of the whole house, and to enjoy all that the world can give you; and what on the other hand, to be sunk into the dark circumstances of a woman that has lost her reputation; and that though I shall be a private friend to you while I live, yet as I shall be suspected always, so you will be afraid to see me, and I shall be afraid to own you.

He gave me no time to reply, but went on with me thus: What has happened between us, child, so long as we both agree to do so, may be buried and forgotten : I shall always be your sincere friend, without any inclination to nearer intimacy when you become my sister ; and we shall have all the honest part of conversation without any reproaches between us, of having done amiss : I beg of you to consider it, and do not stand in the way of your own safety and prosperity ; and to satisfy you that I am sincere, added he, I here offer you five hundred pounds to make you some amends for the freedoms I have taken with you, which we shall look upon as some of the follies of our lives, which 'tis hoped we may repent of.

He spoke this in so much more moving terms than it is possible for me to express, that you may suppose as he held me above an hour and a half in this discourse ; so he answered all my objections, and fortified his discourse with all the arguments that human wit and art could devise.

I cannot say, however, that anything he said made impression enough upon me, so as to give me any thought of the matter, till he told me at last very plainly, that if I refused, he was sorry to add, that he could never go on with me in that station as we stood before ; that though he loved me as well as ever, and that I was as agreeable to him, yet the sense of virtue had not so forsaken him as to suffer him to lie with a woman that his brother courted to make his wife ; that if he took his leave of me, with a denial from me in this affair, whatever he might do for me in the point of support, grounded on his first engagement of maintaining me, yet he would not have me be surprised, that he was obliged to tell me, he could not allow himself to see me any more ; and that, indeed, I could not expect it of him.

I received this last part with some tokens of surprise and disorder, and had much ado to avoid sinking down, for indeed I loved him to an extravagance not easy to imagine ; but he perceived my disorder, and entreated me to consider seriously of it ; assured me that it was the only way to preserve our mutual affection ; that in this station we might love as friends, with the utmost passion, and with a love of relation untainted, free from our own just reproaches, and free from other people's suspicions : that he should ever acknowledge his happiness owing to me ; that he would be debtor to me as long as he lived, and would be paying that debt as long as he had breath. Thus he wrought me up, in short to a kind of hesitation in the matter; having the dangers on one side represented in lively figures, and indeed heightened by my imagination of being turned out to the wide world, a mere cast-off whore, for it was no less, and perhaps exposed as such; with little to provide for myself; with no friend, no acquaintance in the whole world, out of that town, and there I could not pretend to stay. All this terrified me to the last degree, and he took care upon all occasions to lay it home to me, in the worst colours. On the other hand, he failed not to set forth the easy prosperous life, which I was going to live.

He answered all that I could object from affection, and from former engagements, with telling me the necessity that was before us of taking other measures now; and as to his promises of marriage, the nature of things, he said, had put an end to that, by the probability of my being his brother's wife, before the time to which his promises all referred.

Thus, in a word, I may say, he reasoned me out of my reason; he conquered all my arguments, and I began to see a danger that I was in, which I had not considered of before, and that was, of being dropped by both of them, and left alone in the world to shift for myself.

This, and his persuasion, at length prevailed with me to consent, though with so much reluctance, that it was easy to see I should go to church like a bear to the stake; I had some little apprehensions about me too, lest my new spouse, who by the way, I had not the least affection for, should be skilful enough to challenge me on another account, upon our first coming to bed together; but whether he did it with design or not, I know not, but his elder brother took care to make him very much fuddled before he went to bed, so that I had the satisfaction of a drunken bedfellow the first night: how he did it, I know not, but I concluded that he certainly contrived it, that his brother might be able to make no judgment of the difference between a maid and a married woman, nor did he ever entertain any notions of it, or disturb his thoughts about it.

I should go back a little here, to where I left off. The elder brother having thus managed me, his next business was to manage his mother; and he never left till he had brought her to acquiesce, and be passive even without acquainting the father, other than by post letters: so that she consented to our marrying privately, leaving her to manage the father afterwards.

Then he cajoled with his brother, and persuaded him what service he had done him, and how he had brought his mother to consent, which though true, was not indeed done to serve him, but to serve himself; but thus diligently did he cheat him, and had the thanks of a faithful friend for shifting off his whore into his brother's arms for a wife. So naturally do men give up honour and justice, and even christianity, to secure themselves.

I must now come back to brother Robin, as we always called him, who having got his mother's consent, as above, came big with the news to me, and told me the whole story of it, with a sincerity so visible, that I must confess it grieved me, that I must be the instrument to abuse so honest a gentleman; but there was no remedy, he would have me, and I was not obliged to tell him that I was his brother's whore, though I had no other way to put him off; so I came gradually into it, and behold we were married.

Modesty forbids me to reveal the secrets of the marriage bed, but nothing could have happened more suitable to my circumstances than that, as above, my husband was so fuddled when he came to bed, that he could not remember in the morning, whether he had had any conversation with me or no, and I was obliged to tell him he had, though, in reality, he had not, that I might be sure he could make no inquiry about anything else.

It concerns the story in hand very little to enter into the farther particulars of the family, or of myself, for the five years that I lived with this husband, only to observe that I had two children by him, and that at the end of the five years he died: he had been really a very good husband to me, and we lived very agreeably together; but as he had not received much from them, and had in the little time he lived acquired no great matters, so my circumstances were not great, nor was I much mended by the match. Indeed I had preserved the elder brother's bonds to me, to pay me 500*l.* which he offered me for my consent to marry his brother; and this, with what I had saved of the money he formerly gave me, and about as much more by my husband, left me a widow with about 1200*l.* in my pocket.

My two children were indeed taken happily off of my

hands, by my husband's father and mother, and 'hat was all they got by Mrs. Betty.

I confess I was not suitably affected with the loss of my husband; nor can I say that I ever loved him as I ought to have done, or was suitable to the good usage I had from him, for he was a tender, kind, good-humoured man as any woman could desire; but his brother being so always in my sight, at least while we were in the country, was a continual snare to me; and I never was in bed with my husband, but I wished myself in the arms of his brother; and though his brother never offered me the least kindness that way, after our marriage, but carried it just as a brother ought to do, yet it was impossible for me to do so to him; in short, I committed adultery and incest with him every day in my desires, which, without doubt, was as effectually criminal.

Before my husband died, his elder brother was married, and we being then removed to London, were written to by the old lady to come and be at the wedding; my husband went, but I pretended indisposition, so I stayed behind; for in short, I could not bear the sight of his being given to another woman, though I knew I was never to have him myself.

I was now, as above, left loose to the world, and being still young and handsome, as everybody said of me, and I assure you I thought myself so, and with a tolerable fortune in my pocket, I put no small value upon myself; I was courted by several very considerable tradesmen, and particularly very warmly by one, a linen-draper, at whose house, after my husband's death, I took a lodging, his sister being my acquaintance; here I had all the liberty and opportunity to be gay and appear in company that I could desire, my landlord's sister being one of the maddest, gayest things alive, and not so much mistress of her virtue as I thought at first she had been: she brought me into a world of wild company, and even brought home several persons, such as she liked well enough to gratify, to see her pretty widow. Now as fame and fools make an assembly, I was here wonderfully caressed; had abundance of admirers, and such as called themselves lovers; but I found not one fair proposal among them all; as for their common design, that I understood too well to be drawn into any more snares of that kind. The case was altered with me, I had money in my pocket, and had nothing to say to them. I had been tricked once by that cheat called love, but the game was over; I was resolved now to be married or nothing, and to be well married or not at all.

I loved the company indeed of men of mirth and wit, and was often entertained with such, as I was also with others; but I found by just observation, that the brightest men came upon the dullest errand, that is to say, the dullest as to what I aimed at; on the other hand, those who came with the best proposals were the dullest and·most disagreeable part of the world. I was not averse to a tradesman, but then I would have a tradesman, forsooth, that was something of a gentleman too; that when my husband had a mind to carry me to the court, or to the play, he might become a sword, and look as like a gentleman as another man; and not like one that had the mark of his apron-strings upon his coat, or the mark of his hat upon his periwig; that should look as if he was set on to his sword, when his sword was put on to him, and that carried his trade in his countenance.

Well, at last I found this amphibious creature, this land-water-thing, called a gentleman tradesman; and as a just plague upon my folly, I was catched in the very snare which, as I might say, I laid for myself.

This was a draper too, for though my comrade would have bargained for me with her brother, yet when they came to the point, it was, it seems, for a mistress, and I kept true to this notion, that a woman should never be kept for a mistress, that had money to make herself a wife.

Thus my pride, not my principle, my money, not my virtue, kept me honest; though, as it proved, I found I had much better have been sold by my she comrade, to her brother, than have sold myself as I did to a tradesman, that was a rake, gentleman, shopkeeper, and beggar, all together.

But I was hurried on (by my fancy to a gentleman) to ruin myself in the grossest manner that ever woman did; for my new husband coming to a lump of money at once, fell into such a profusion of expense, that all I had, and all he had, would not have held it out above one year.

He was very fond of me for about a quarter of a year, and what I got by that was, that I had the pleasure of seeing a great deal of my money spent upon myself. Come, my dear, says he to me one day, Shall we go and take a turn into the country for a week? Ay my dear, says I, whither would

you go? I care not whither, says he, but I have a mind
to look like quality for a week, we'll go to Oxford, says
he. How, says I, shall we go, I am no horsewoman, and
'tis too far for a coach. Too far! says he, no place is too
far for a coach and six. If I carry you out, you shall
travel like a duchess. Hum, says I, my dear, 'tis a frolic,
but if you have a mind to it, I don't care. Well, the time
was appointed, we had a rich coach, very good horses, a coachman, postillion, and two footmen in very good liveries; a
gentleman on horseback, and a page with a feather in his
hat upon another horse; the servants all called him my lord,
and I was her honour the countess, and thus we travelled to
Oxford, and a pleasant journey we had; for give him his due,
not a beggar alive knew better how to be a lord than my
husband. We saw all the rarities at Oxford, talked with
two or three fellows of colleges, about putting a nephew, that
was left to his lordship's care, to the university, and of their
being his tutors; we diverted ourselves with bantering several
other poor scholars, with the hopes of being at least his lordship's chaplain and putting on a scarf; and thus having lived
like quality indeed, as to expense, we went away for North-
ampton, and, in a word, in about twelve days' ramble came
home again, to the tune of about 93l. expense.

Vanity is the perfection of a fop; my husband had this
excellence, that he valued nothing of expense. As his history,
you may be sure, has very little weight in it, 'tis enough to
tell you, that in about two years and a quarter he broke, got
into a spunging-house, being arrested in an action too heavy
for him to give bail to; so he sent for me to come to him.

It was no surprise to me, for I had foreseen some time
before that all was going to wreck, and had been taking care
to reserve something, if I could, for myself: but when he sent
for me, he behaved much better than I expected: he told me
plainly, he had played the fool, and suffered himself to be
surprised, which he might have prevented: that now he
foresaw he could not stand it, and therefore he would have
me go home, and in the night take away everything I had in
the house of any value, and secure it; and after that, he told
me, that if I could get away 100l. or 200l. in goods out of
the shop, I should do it; only, says he, let me know nothing
of it, neither what you take, or whither you carry it; for as
for me, says he, I am resolved to get out of this house and be

gone, and if you never hear of me more, my dear, says he, I wish you well; I am only sorry for the injury I have done you. He said some very handsome things to me indeed, at parting; for I told you he was a gentleman, and that was all the benefit I had of his being so; that he used me very handsomely, even to the last, only spent all I had, and left me to rob the creditors for something to subsist on.

However, I did as he bade me, that you may be sure; and having thus taken my leave of him, I never saw him more; for he found means to break out of the bailiff's house that night, or the next; how, I knew not, for I could come at no knowledge of anything, more than this, that he came home about three o'clock in the morning, caused the rest of his goods to be removed into the Mint, and the shop to be shut up; and having raised what money he could, he got over to France, from whence I had one or two letters from him, and no more.

I did not see him when he came home, for he having given me such instructions as above, and I having made the best of my time, I had no more business back again at the house, not knowing but I might have been stopped there by the creditors; for a commission of bankrupt, being soon after issued, they might have stopped me by orders from the commissioners. But my husband having desperately got out from the bailiff's by letting himself down from almost the top of the house, to the top of another building, and leaping from thence, which was almost two stories, and which was enough indeed to have broken his neck, he came home and got away his goods, before the creditors could come to seize; that is to say, before they could get out the commission, and be ready to send their officers to take possession.

My husband was so civil to me, for still I say he was much of a gentleman, that in the first letter he wrote me, he let me know where he had pawned twenty pieces of fine Holland for 30*l.* which were worth above 90*l.*, and enclosed me the token for the taking them up, paying the money, which I did, and made in time above 100*l.* of them, having leisure to cut them, and sell them to private families, as opportunity offered.

However, with all this, and all that I had secured before, I found, upon casting things up, my case was very much altered, and my fortune much lessened; for including the Hollands, and a parcel of fine muslins, which I carried off before, and some plate, and other things, I found I could hardly muster up 500*l.* ; and my condition was very odd, for though I had no child (I had had one by my gentleman draper, but it was buried), yet I was a widow bewitched, I had a husband and no husband, and I could not pretend to marry again, though I knew well enough my husband would never see England any more, if he lived fifty years. Thus, I say, I was limited from marriage, what offer soever might be made me; and I had not one friend to advise with, in the condition I was in, at least not one whom I could trust the secret of my circumstances to; for if the commissioners were to have been informed where I was, I should have been fetched up, and all I had saved be taken away.

Upon these apprehensions, the first thing I did, was to go quite out of my knowledge, and go by another name. This I did effectually, for I went into the Mint too, took lodgings in a very private place, dressed me up in the habit of a widow, and called myself Mrs. Flanders.

Here, however, I concealed myself, and though my new acquaintance knew nothing of me, yet I soon got a great deal of company about me; and whether it be that women are scarce among the people that generally are to be found there, or that some consolations in the miseries of that place, are more requisite than on other occasions, I soon found that an agreeable woman was exceedingly valuable among the sons of affliction there; and that those that could not pay half a crown in the pound to their creditors, and run in debt at the sign of the bull for their dinners, would yet find money for a supper, if they liked the woman.

However, I kept myself safe yet, though I began like my Lord Rochester's mistress, that loved his company, but would not admit him farther, to have the scandal of a whore, without the joy; and upon this score, tired with the place, and with the company too, I began to think of removing.

It was indeed a subject of strange reflection to me, to see men in the most perplexed circumstances, who were reduced some degrees below being ruined, whose families were objects of their own terror and other people's charity; yet while a penny lasted, nay even beyond it, endeavouring to drown their sorrow in their wickedness; heaping up more guilt upon themselves, labouring to forget former things, which now it was the proper time to remember, making more work for repentance, and sinning on, as a remedy for sin past.

But it is none of my talent to preach; these men were too wicked, even for me: there was something horrid and absurd in their way of sinning, for it was all a force even upon themselves; they did not only act against conscience, but against nature, and nothing was more easy than to see how sighs would interrupt their songs, and paleness and anguish sit upon their brows, in spite of the forced smiles they put on; nay, sometimes it would break out at their very mouths, when they had parted with their money for a lewd treat, or a wicked embrace; I have heard them, turning about, fetch a deep sigh, and cry, What a dog am I! well Betty, my dear, I'll drink thy health though, meaning the honest wife, that perhaps had not a halfcrown for herself, and three or four children. The next morning they were at their penitentials again, and perhaps the poor weeping wife comes over to him, either brings him some account of what his creditors are doing, and how she and the children are turned out of doors, or some other dreadful news; and this adds to his self-reproaches; but when he has thought and pored on it till he is almost mad, having no principles to support him, nothing within him, or above him, to comfort him; but finding it all darkness on every side, he flies to the same relief again, viz., to drink it away, debauch it away, and falling into company of men in just the same condition with himself, he repeats the crime, and thus he goes every day one step onward of his way to destruction.

I was not wicked enough for such fellows as these: yet, on the contrary, I began to consider here very seriously what I had to do; how things stood with me, and what course I ought to take: I knew I had no friends, no, not one friend or relation in the world; and that little I had left apparently wasted, which when it was gone, I saw nothing but misery and starving was before me: upon these considerations, I say, and filled with horror at the place I was in, I resolved to be gone.

I had made an acquaintance with a sober good sort of a woman, who was a widow too like me, but in better circumstances; her husband had been a captain of a ship, and having had the misfortune to be cast away coming home from the

West Indies, was so reduced by the loss, that though he had
saved his life then, it broke his heart, and killed him afterwards, and his widow being pursued by the creditors, was forced
to take shelter in the Mint. She soon made things up with
the help of friends, and was at liberty again; and finding
that I rather was there to be concealed, than by any particular
prosecutions, and finding also that I agreed with her, or rather
she with me, in a just abhorrence of the place, and of the
company, she invited me to go home with her, till I could put
myself in some posture of settling in the world to my mind;
withal telling me, that it was ten to one, but some good
captain of a ship might take a fancy to me, and court me, in
that part of the town where she lived.

I accepted of her offer, and was with her half a year, and
should have been longer, but in that interval what she proposed
to me happened to herself, and she married very much to her
advantage. But whose fortune soever was upon the increase,
mine seemed to be upon the wane, and I found nothing
present, except two or three boatswains, or such fellows, but
as for the commanders they were generally of two sorts.
1. Such as, having good business, that is to say, a good
ship, resolved not to marry, but with advantage. 2. Such
as, being out of employ, wanted a wife to help them to
a ship; I mean, 1. A wife who, having some money, could
enable them to hold a good part of a ship themselves, so to
encourage owners to come in; or 2. A wife who, if she had
not money, had friends who were concerned in shipping, and
so could help to put the young man into a good ship; and
neither of these was my case, so I looked like one that was
to lie on hand.

This knowledge I soon learnt by experience, viz., that the
state of things was altered as to matrimony, that marriages
were here the consequences of politic schemes, for forming
interests, carrying on business, and that love had no share, or
but very little, in the matter.

That as my sister-in-law at Colchester had said, beauty, wit,
manners, sense, good humour, good behaviour, education,
virtue, piety, or any other qualification, whether of body or
mind, had no power to recommend: that money only made
a woman agreeable: that men chose mistresses indeed by the
gust of their affection, and it was requisite for a whore to be
handsome, well-shaped, have a good mien, and a graceful

behaviour; but that for a wife, no deformity would shock the fancy, no ill qualities the judgment; the money was the thing; the portion was neither crooked, or monstrous, but the money was always agreeable, whatever the wife was.

On the other hand, as the market run all on the mens' side, I found the women had lost the privilege of saying no; that it was a favour now for a woman to have the question asked, and if any young lady had so much arrogance as to counterfeit a negative, she never had the opportunity of denying twice; much less of recovering that false step, and accepting what she had seemed to decline. The men had such choice everywhere, that the case of the women was very unhappy; for they seemed to ply at every door, and if the man was by great chance refused at one house, he was sure to be received at the next.

Besides this, I observed that the men made no scruple to set themselves out, and to go a fortune-hunting, as they call it, when they had really no fortune themselves to demand it, or merit or deserve it; and they carried it so high, that a woman was scarce allowed to inquire after the character or estate of the person that pretended to her; this, I had an example of, in a young lady at the next house to me, and with whom I had contracted an intimacy; she was courted by a young captain, and though she had near 2000l. to her fortune, she did but inquire of some of his neighbours about his character, his morals, or substance; and he took occasion at the next visit to let her know, truly, that he took it very ill, and that he should not give her the trouble of his visits any more. I heard of it, and I had begun my acquaintance with her; I went to see her upon it; she entered into a close conversation with me about it, and unbosomed herself very freely; I perceived presently that though she thought herself very ill used, yet she had no power to resent it; that she was exceedingly piqued she had lost him, and particularly that another of less fortune had gained him.

I fortified her mind against such a meanness, as I called it; I told her, that as low as I was in the world, I would have despised a man that should think I ought to take him upon his own recommendation only; also I told her, that as she had a good fortune, she had no need to stoop to the disaster of the times; that it was enough, that the men could insult us that had but little money, but if she suffered such an affront·

to pass upon her without resenting it, she would be rendered
low prized upon all occasions; that a woman can never want
an opportunity to be revenged of a man that has used her ill,
and that there were ways enough to humble such a fellow as
that, or else certainly women were the most unhappy creatures
in the world.

She was very well pleased with the discourse, and told me
seriously that she would be very glad to make him sensible
of her resentment, and either to bring him on again, or have
the satisfaction of her revenge being as public as possible.

I told her, that if she would take my advice, I would tell
her how she should obtain her wishes in both those things;
and that I would engage I would bring the man to her door
again, and make him beg to be let in: she smiled at that, and
soon let me see, that if he came to her door, her resentment
was not so great, to let him stand long there.

However, she listened very willingly to my offer of advice;
so I told her, that the first thing she ought to do, was a piece
of justice to herself; namely, that whereas he had reported
among the ladies, that he had left her, and pretended to give
the advantage of the negative to himself, she should take
care to have it well spread among the women, which she
could not fail of an opportunity to do, that she had inquired
into his circumstances, and found he was not the man he
pretended to be: let them be told too, madam, said I, that
he was not the man you expected, and that you thought it
was not safe to meddle with him; that you heard he was of
an ill temper, and that he boasted how he had used the
women ill upon many occasions, and that particularly he was
debauched in his morals, &c. The last of which indeed had
some truth in it; but I did not find that she seemed to like
him much the worse for that part.

She came most readily into all this, and immediately she
went to work to find instruments; she had very little difficulty
in the search, for telling her story in general to a couple of
her gossips, it was the chat of the tea-table all over that part
of the town, and I met with it wherever I visited: also, as it
was known that I was acquainted with the young lady herself,
my opinion was asked very often, and I confirmed it with all
the necessary aggravations, and set out his character in the
blackest colours; and as a piece of secret intelligence, I added
what the gossips knew nothing of, viz., That I had heard he

was in very bad circumstances; that he was under a necessity of a fortune to support his interest with the owners of the ship he commanded: that his own part was not paid for, and if it was not paid quickly, his owners would put him out of the ship, and his chief mate was likely to command it, who offered to buy that part which the captain had promised to take.

I added, for I was heartily piqued at the rogue, as I called him, that I had heard a rumour too, that he had a wife alive at Plymouth, and another in the West Indies, a thing which they all knew was not very uncommon for such kind of gentlemen.

This worked as we both desired it, for presently the young lady at the next door, who had a father and mother that governed both her and her fortune, was shut up, and her father forbid him the house: also in one place more the woman had the courage, however strange it was, to say no; and he could try nowhere but he was reproached with his pride, and that he pretended not to give the women leave to inquire into his character, and the like.

By this time he began to be sensible of his mistake; and seeing all the women on that side the water alarmed, he went over to Ratcliff, and got access to some of the ladies there; but though the young women there too, were, according to the fate of the day, pretty willing to be asked, yet such was his ill luck, that his character followed him over the water; so that though he might have had wives enough, yet it did not happen among the women that had good fortunes, which was what he wanted.

But this was not all; she very ingeniously managed another thing herself, for she got a young gentleman who was a relation, to come and visit her two or three times a week in a very fine chariot and good liveries, and her two agents, and I also, presently spread a report all over, that this gentleman came to court her; that he was a gentleman of a thousand pounds a year, and that he was fallen in love with her, and that she was going to her aunt's in the city, because it was inconvenient for the gentleman to come to her with his coach to Rotherhithe, the streets being so narrow and difficult.

This took immediately, the captain was laughed at in all companies, and was ready to hang himself; he tried all the

ways possible to come at her again, and wrote the most
passionate letters to her in the world, and in short, by great
application, obtained leave to wait on her again, as he said,
only to clear his reputation.

At this meeting she had her full revenge of him; for she
told him, she wondered what he took her to be, that she
should admit any man to a treaty of so much consequence as
that of marriage, without inquiring into his circumstances :
that if he thought she was to be huffed into wedlock, and
that she was in the same circumstances which her neighbours
might be in, viz., to take up with the first good christian that
came, he was mistaken; that, in a word, his character was
really bad, or he was very ill beholden to his neighbours;
and that unless he could clear up some points, in which she
had justly been prejudiced, she had no more to say to him,
but give him the satisfaction of knowing that she was not
afraid to say no, either to him, or any man else.

With that she told him what she had heard, or rather raised
herself by my means, of his character; his not having paid
for the part he pretended to own of the ship he commanded;
of the resolution of his owners to put him out of the command, and to put his mate in his stead; and of the scandal
raised on his morals; his having been reproached with such
and such women, and his having a wife at Plymouth, and
another in the West Indies, and the like; and she asked him
whether she had not good reason, if these things were not
cleared up, to refuse him, and to insist upon having satisfaction
in points so significant as they were.

He was so confounded at her discourse, that he could not
answer a word, and she began to believe that all was true, by
his disorder, though she knew that she had been the raiser of
these reports herself.

After some time he recovered a little, and from that time
was the most humble, modest, and importunate man alive in
his courtship.

She asked him if he thought she was so at her last shift
that she could or ought to bear such treatment, and if he did
not see that she did not want those who thought it worth
their while to come farther to her than he did; meaning
the gentleman whom she had brought to visit her by way
of sham.

She brought him by these tricks to submit to all possible

measures to satisfy her, as well of his circumstances, as of his behaviour. He brought her undeniable evidence of his having paid for his part of the ship; he brought her certificates from his owners, that the report of their intending to remove him from the command of the ship, was false and groundless; in short, he was quite the reverse of what he was before.

Thus I convinced her, that if the men made their advantage of our sex in the affair of marriage, upon the supposition of there being such a choice to be had, and of the women being so easy, it was only owing to this, that the women wanted courage to maintain their ground, and that according to my Lord Rochester

> " A woman's ne'er so ruined but she can
> Revenge herself on her undoer, man."

After these things this young lady played her part so well, that though she resolved to have him, and that indeed having him was the main bent of her design, yet she made his obtaining her to be to him the most difficult thing in the world; and this she did, not by a haughty, reserved carriage, but by a just policy, playing back upon him his own game; for as he pretended by a kind of lofty carriage, to place himself above the occasion of a character, she broke with him upon that subject, and at the same time that she made him submit to all possible inquiry after his affairs, she apparently shut the door against his looking into her own.

It was enough to him to obtain her for a wife; as to what she had, she told him plainly, that as he knew her circumstances, it was but just she should know his; and though at the same time he had only known her circumstances by common fame, yet he had made so many protestations of his passion for her, that he could ask no more but her hand to his grand request; and the like ramble according to the custom of lovers. In short, he left himself no room to ask any more questions about her estate, and she took the advantage of it; for she placed part of her fortune so in trustees, without letting him know anything of it, that it was quite out of his reach, and made him be very well contented with the rest.

It is true she was pretty well besides, that is to say, she had about 1400*l.* in money, which she gave him, and the other, after some time, she brought to light as a perquisite to herself, which he was to accept as a mighty favour, seeing,

though it was not to be his, it might ease him in the article
of her particular expenses; and I must add, that by this conduct, the gentleman himself became not only more humble in
his applications to her to obtain her, but also was much the
more an obliging husband when he had her. I cannot but
remind the ladies how much they place themselves below the
common station of a wife, which if I may be allowed not to
be partial, is low enough already; I say, they place themselves below their common station, and prepare their own
mortifications, by their submitting so to be insulted by the
men beforehand, which I confess I see no necessity of.

This relation may serve therefore to let the ladies see, that
the advantage is not so much on the other side, as the men
think it is; and that though it may be true, the men have
but too much choice among us, and that some women may
be found, who will dishonour themselves, be cheap, and too
easy to come at; yet if they will have women worth having,
they may find them as uncomeatable as ever; and that those
that are otherwise have often such deficiencies, when had, as
rather recommend the ladies that are difficult, than encourage
the men to go on with their easy courtship, and expect wives
equally valuable that will come at first call.

Nothing is more certain, than that the ladies always gain
of the men, by keeping their ground, and letting their pretended lovers see they can resent being slighted, and that
they are not afraid of saying no. They insult us mightily,
with telling us of the number of women; that the wars and
the sea, and trade, and other incidents have carried the men
so much away, that there is no proportion between the
numbers of the sexes; but I am far from granting that the
number of the women is so great, or the number of the men
so small; but if they will have me tell the truth, the disadvantage of the women is a terrible scandal upon the men,
and it lies here only; namely, that the age is so wicked, and
the sex so debauched, that, in short, the number of such men
as an honest woman ought to meddle with, is small indeed;
and it is but here and there that a man is to be found who is
fit for an honest woman to venture upon.

But the consequence even of that too, amounts to no more
than this; that women ought to be the more nice; for how
do we know the just character of the man that makes the
offer? To say that the woman should be the more easy on

this occasion, is to say we should be the forwarder to venture because of the greatness of the danger, which is very absurd.

On the contrary, the women have ten thousand times the more reason to be wary, and backward, by how much the hazard of being betrayed is the greater; and would the ladies act the wary part, they would discover every cheat that offered; for, in short, the lives of very few men now-a-days will bear a character; and if the ladies do but make a little inquiry, they would soon be able to distinguish the men, and deliver themselves. As for women that do not think their own safety worth their own thought, that, impatient of their present state, run into matrimony, as a horse rushes into the battle. I can say nothing to them but this, that they are a sort of ladies that are to be prayed for among the rest of distempered people, and they look like people that venture their estates in a lottery where there is a hundred thousand blanks to one prize.

No man of common sense will value a woman the less for not giving up herself at the first attack, or for not accepting his proposal without inquiring into his person or character; on the contrary, he must think her the weakest of all creatures, as the rate of men now goes: in short, he must have a very contemptible opinion of her capacities, that having but one cast for her life, shall cast that life away at once, and make matrimony, like death, be a leap in the dark.

I would fain have the conduct of my sex a little regulated in this particular, which is the same thing in which of all the parts of life, I think at this time we suffer most in: 'tis nothing but lack of courage, the fear of not being married at all, and of that frightful state of life, called an old maid. This, I say, is the woman's snare; but would the ladies once but get above that fear, and manage rightly, they would more certainly avoid it by standing their ground, in a case so absolutely necessary to their felicity, than by exposing themselves as they do; and if they did not marry so soon, they would make themselves amends by marrying safer. She is always married too soon, who gets a bad husband, and she is never married too late who gets a good one: in a word, there is no woman, deformity or lost reputation excepted, but if she manages well, may be married safely one time or other; but if she precipitates herself, it is ten thousand to one but she is undone.

But I come now to my own case, in which there was at this time no little nicety. The circumstances I was in, made the offer of a good husband, the most necessary thing in the world to me; but I found soon that to be made cheap and easy, was not the way; it soon began to be found that the widow had no fortune, and to say this, was to say all that was ill of me, being well-bred, handsome, witty, modest, and agreeable; all which I had allowed to my character, whether justly or no is not to the purpose; I say, all these would not do without the dross. In short, the widow, they said, had no money!

I resolved therefore that it was necessary to change my station, and make a new appearance in some other place, and even to pass by another name if I found occasion.

I communicated my thoughts to my intimate friend the captain's lady, whom I had so faithfully served in her case with the captain; and who was as ready to serve me in the same kind as I could desire; I made no scruple to lay my circumstances open to her; my stock was but low, for I had made but about 540*l*. at the close of my last affair, and I had wasted some of that; however, I had about 460*l*. left, a great many very rich clothes, a gold watch, and some jewels, though of no extraordinary value, and about 30*l*. or 40*l*. left in linen not disposed of.

My dear and faithful friend the captain's wife, was so sensible of the service I had done her in the affair above, that she was not only a steady friend to me, but knowing my circumstances, she frequently made me presents as money came into her hands; such as fully amounted to a maintenance; so that I spent none of my own; and at last she made this unhappy proposal to me, viz., that as we had observed, as above, how the men made no scruple to set themselves out as persons meriting a woman of fortune of their own, it was but just to deal with them in their own way, and if it was possible, to deceive the deceiver.

The captain's lady, in short, put this project into my head, and told me if I would be ruled by her, I should certainly get a husband of fortune, without leaving him any room to reproach me with want of my own: I told her that I would give up myself wholly to her directions, and that I would have neither tongue to speak, or feet to step in that affair, but as she should direct me; depending that she would extricate me out of every difficulty that she brought me into, which she said she would answer for.

The first step she put me upon, was to call her cousin, and go to a relation's house of hers in the country, where she directed me, and where she brought her husband to visit me; and calling me cousin, she worked matters so about, that her husband and she together invited me most passionately to come to town and live with them, for they now lived in a quite different place from where they were before. In the next place she tells her husband that I had at least 1500*l.* fortune, and that I was like to have a great deal more.

It was enough to tell her husband this, there needed nothing on my side; I was but to sit still and wait the event, for it presently went all over the neighbourhood that the young widow at Captain ——'s was a fortune, that she had at least 1500*l.*, and perhaps a great deal more, and that the captain said so; and if the captain was asked at any time about me, he made no scruple to affirm it, though he knew not one word of the matter, other than that his wife had told him so; and in this he thought no harm, for he really believed it to be so. With the reputation of this fortune, I presently found myself blessed with admirers enough (and that I had my choice of men), as they said they were, which by the way confirms what I was saying before; this being my case, I who had a subtle game to play, had nothing now to do, but to single out from them all, the properest man that might be for my purpose; that is to say, the man who was most likely to depend upon the hearsay of fortune, and not inquire too far into the particulars; and unless I did this, I did nothing, for my case would not bear much inquiry.

I picked out my man without much difficulty, by the judgment I made of his way of courting me: I had let him run on with his protestations that he loved me above all the world; that if I would make him happy, that was enough; all which I knew was upon supposition that I was very rich, though I never told him a word of it myself.

This was my man, but I was to try him to the bottom; and indeed in that consisted my safety, for if he balked, I knew I was undone, as surely as he was undone if he took me; and if I did not make some scruple about his fortune, it was the way to lead him to raise some about mine; and first, therefore, I pretended on all occasions to doubt his sincerity, and told him, perhaps he only courted me for my fortune; he stopped my mouth in that part, with the thunder of his protestations as above, but still I pretended to doubt.

One morning he pulls off his diamond ring, and writes upon the glass of the sash in my chamber this line,

> You I love, and you alone.

I read it, and asked him to lend me the ring, with which I wrote under it thus,

> And so in love says every one.

He takes his ring again, and writes another line thus,

> Virtue alone is an estate.

I borrowed it again; and I wrote under it,

> But money's virtue, gold is fate.

He coloured as red as fire to see me turn so quick upon him, and in a kind of rage told me he would conquer me, and wrote again thus,

> I scorn your gold, and yet I love.

I ventured all upon the last cast of poetry, as you'll see, for I wrote boldly under his last.

> I'm poor: let's see how kind you'll prove.

This was a sad truth to me, whether he believed me or no I could not tell; I supposed then that he did not. However, he flew to me, took me in his arms, and, kissing me very eagerly, and with the greatest passion imaginable, he held me fast till he called for a pen and ink, and told me he could not wait the tedious writing on a glass, but, pulling out a piece of paper, he began and wrote again,

> Be mine with all your poverty.

I took his pen, and followed immediately thus,

> Yet secretly you hope I lie.

He told me that was unkind, because it was not just, and that I put him upon contradicting me, which did not consist with good manners, and, therefore, since I had insensibly drawn him into this poetical scribble, he begged I would not oblige him to break it off; so he writes again,

> Let love alone be our debate.

I wrote again,

> She loves enough that does not hate.

This he took for a favour, and so laid down the cudgels, that is to say, the pen; I say, he took it for a favour, and a mighty one it was, if he had known all: however, he took it as I meant .it, that is, to let him think I was inclined to go on with him, as indeed I had reason to do, for he was the best humoured merry sort of a fellow that I ever met with; and I often reflected how doubly criminal it was to deceive such a man; but that necessity, which pressed me to a settlement suitable to my condition, was my authority for it; and certainly his affection to me, and the goodness of his temper, however they might argue against using him ill, yet they strongly argued to me, that he would better take the disappointment than some fiery-tempered wretch, who might have nothing to recommend him but those passions which would serve only to make a woman miserable.

Besides, though I had jested with him (as he supposed it) so often about my poverty, yet when he found it to be true, he had foreclosed all manner of objection, seeing, whether he was in jest or in earnest, he had declared he took me without any regard to my portion, and, whether I was in jest or in earnest, I had declared myself to be very poor, so that, in a word, I had him fast both ways; and though he might say afterwards he was cheated, yet he could never say that I had cheated him.

He pursued me close after this, and, as I saw there was no need to fear losing him, I played the indifferent part with him longer than prudence might otherwise have dictated to me; but I considered how much this caution and indifference would give me the advantage over him when I should come to own my circumstances to him; and I managed it the more warily, because I found he inferred from thence that I either had the more money, or the more judgment, and would not venture at all.

I took the freedom one day to tell him that it was true I had received the compliment of a lover from him, namely, that he would take me without inquiring into my fortune, and I would make him a suitable return in this, viz., that I would make as little inquiry into his as consisted with reason, but I hoped he would allow me to ask some questions, which he should answer or not as he thought fit; one of these questions related to our manner of living, and the place where, because I had heard he had a great plantation in Virginia, and I told him I did not care to be transported.

He began from this discourse to let me voluntarily into all his affairs, and to tell me in a frank open way all his circumstances, by which I found he was very well to pass in the world; but that great part of his estate consisted of three plantations, which he had in Virginia, which brought him in a very good income of about 300*l.* a year; but that if he was to live upon them, would bring him in four times as much. Very well, thought I, you shall carry me thither then as soon as you please, though I won't tell you so beforehand.

I jested with him about the figure he would make in Virginia; but I found he would do anything I desired, so I turned my tale; I told him I had good reason not to desire to go there to live, because if his plantations were worth so much there, I had not a fortune suitable to a gentleman of 1200*l.* a year, as he said his estate would be.

He replied, he did not ask what my fortune was; he had told me from the beginning he would not, and he would be as good as his word; but whatever it was, he assured me he would never desire me to go to Virginia with him, or go thither himself without me, unless I made it my choice.

All this, you may be sure, was as I wished, and indeed nothing could have happened more perfectly agreeable; I carried it on as far as this with a sort of indifferency that he often wondered at, and I mention it the rather to intimate again to the ladies that nothing but want of courage for such an indifferency makes our sex so cheap, and prepares them to be ill used as they are; would they venture the loss of a pretending fop now and then, who carries it high upon the point of his own merit, they would certainly be slighted less, and courted more; had I discovered really what my great fortune was, and that in all I had not full 500*l.* when he expected 1500*l.*, yet I hooked him so fast, and played him so long, that I was satisfied he would have had me in my worst circumstances; and indeed it was less a surprise to him when he learnt the truth than it would have been, because having not the least blame to lay on me, who had carried it with an air of indifference to the last, he could not say one word, except that indeed he thought it had been more, but that, if it had been less, he did not repent his bargain; only that he should not be able to maintain me so well as he intended.

In short, we were married, and very happily married on my side, I assure you, as to the man : for he was the best-humoured man that ever woman had, but his circumstances were not so good as I imagined, as on the other hand he had not bettered himself so much as he expected.

When we were married, I was shrewdly put to it to bring him that little stock I had, and to let him see it was no more; but there was a necessity for it, so I took my opportunity one day when we were alone, to enter into a short dialogue with him about it. My dear, said I, we have been married a fortnight, is it not time to let you know whether you have got a wife with something or with nothing? Your own time for that, my dear, says he; I am satisfied I have got the wife I love; I have not troubled you much, says he, with my inquiry after it.

That's true, said I, but I have a great difficulty about it, which I scarce know how to manage. What's that, my dear? says he. Why, says I, 'tis a little hard upon me, and 'tis harder upon you; I am told that Captain ———— (meaning my friend's husband), has told you I had a great deal more than ever I pretended to have, and I am sure I never employed him so to do.

Well, says he, Captain ———— may have told me so, but what then? if you have not so much, that may lie at his door, but you never told me what you had, so I have no reason to blame you if you have nothing at all.

That is so just, said I, and so generous, that it makes my having but a little a double affliction to me.

The less you have, my dear, says he, the worse for us both; but I hope your affliction is not caused for fear I should be unkind to you, for want of a portion; no, no, if you have nothing, tell me plainly; I may perhaps tell the captain he has cheated me, but I can never say you have, for did not you give it under your hand that you was poor, and so I ought to expect you to be.

Well, said I, my dear, I am glad I have not been concerned in deceiving you before marriage; if I deceive you since, 'tis ne'er the worse; that I am poor, 'tis too true. but not so poor as to have nothing neither; so I pulled out some bank bills,

and gave him about 160*l.*; there is something, my dear, says
I, and not quite all neither.

I had brought him so near to expecting nothing, by what
I had said before, that the money, though the sum was small in
itself, was doubly welcome; he owned it was more than he
looked for, and that he did not question by my discourse to
him, but that my fine clothes, gold watch, and a diamond
ring or two, had been all my fortune.

I let him please himself with that 160*l.* two or three days,
and then having been abroad that day, and as if I had been
to fetch it, I brought him 100*l.* more home in gold, and told
him there was a little more portion for him; and in short, in
about a week more, I brought him 180*l.* more, and about 60*l.*
in linen, which I made him believe I had been obliged to
take with the 100*l.* which I gave him in gold, as a composition for a debt of 600*l.*, being little more than five shillings in
the pound, and overvalued too.

And now, my dear, says I to him, I am very sorry to tell
you, that I have given you my whole fortune; I added, that
if the person who had my 600*l.* had not abused me, I had
been worth 1000*l.* to him, but that as it was, I had been
faithful, and reserved nothing to myself, but if it had been
more he should have had it.

He was so obliged by the manner, and so pleased with the
sum, for he had been in a terrible fright lest it had been
nothing at all, that he accepted it very thankfully. And thus
I got over the fraud of passing for a fortune without money,
and cheating a man into marrying me on pretence of it;
which by the way I take to be one of the most dangerous
steps a woman can take, and in which she runs the most
hazards of being ill used afterwards.

My husband, to give him his due, was a man of infinite
good nature, but he was no fool; and finding his income not
suited to the manner of living which he had intended, if I
had brought him what he expected, and being under a disappointment in his return of his plantations in Virginia, he
discovered many times his inclination of going over to
Virginia, to live upon his own; and often would be magnifying the way of living there, how cheap, how plentiful, how
pleasant, and the like.

I began presently to understand his meaning, and I took

him up very plainly one morning, and told him that I did so; that I found his estate turned to no account at this distance, compared to what it would do if he lived upon the spot, and that I found he had a mind to go and live there; that I was sensible he had been disappointed in a wife, and that finding his expectations not answered that way, I could do no less, to make him amends, than tell him that I was very willing to go to Virginia with him and live there.

He said a thousand kind things to me upon the subject of my making such a proposal to him. He told me that though he was disappointed in his expectations of a fortune, he was not disappointed in a wife, and that I was all to him that a wife could be, but that this offer was so kind, that it was more than he could express.

To bring the story short, we agreed to go. He told me that he had a very good house there, well furnished, that his mother lived in it, and one sister, which was all the relations he had; that as soon as he came there, they would remove to another house which was her own for life, and his after her decease; so that I should have all the house to myself; and I found it all exactly as he said.

We put on board the ship, which we went in, a large quantity of good furniture for our house, with stores of linen and other necessaries, and a good cargo for sale, and away we went.

To give an account of the manner of our voyage, which was long and full of dangers, is out of my way; I kept no journal, neither did my husband; all that I can say is, that after a terrible passage, frighted twice with dreadful storms, and once with what was still more terrible, I mean a pirate, who came on board, and took away almost all our provisions; and which would have been beyond all to me, they had once taken my husband, but by entreaties were prevailed with to leave him; I say, after all these terrible things, we arrived in York river in Virginia, and coming to our plantation, we were received with all the tenderness and affection, by my husband's mother, that could be expressed.

We lived here altogether; my mother-in-law, at my entreaty, continuing in the house, for she was too kind a mother to be parted with: my husband likewise continued the same at first, and I thought myself the happiest creature alive, when an odd and surprising event put an end to all that felicity in a moment, and rendered my condition the most uncomfortable in the world.

My mother was a mighty cheerful good-humoured old woman, I may call her so, for her son was above thirty; I say she was very pleasant good company, and used to entertain me in particular, with abundance of stories to divert me, as well of the country we were in, as of the people.

Among the rest, she often told me how the greatest part of the inhabitants of that colony came thither in very indifferent circumstances from England; that, generally speaking, they were of two sorts; either, 1st, such as were brought over by masters of ships to be sold as servants; or, 2nd, such as are transported after having been found guilty of crimes punishable with death.

When they come here, says she, we make no difference; the planters buy them, and they work together in the field, till their time is out; when 'tis expired, said she, they have encouragement given them to plant for themselves; for they have a certain number of acres of land allotted them by the country, and they go to work to clear and cure the land, and then to plant it with tobacco and corn for their own use; and as the merchants will trust them with tools and necessaries, upon the credit of their crop before it is grown, so they again plant every year a little more than the year before, and so buy whatever they want with the crop that is before them. Hence child, says she, many a Newgate-bird becomes a great man, and we have, continued she, several justices of the peace, officers of the trained bands, and magistrates of the towns they live in, that have been burnt in the hand.

She was going on with that part of the story, when her own part in it interrupted her, and with a great deal of good-humoured confidence she told me she was one of the second sort of inhabitants herself; that she came away openly, having ventured too far in a particular case, so that she was become a criminal; and here's the mark of it child, says she, and showed me a very fine white arm and hand, but branded in the inside of the hand, as in such cases it must be.

This story was very moving to me, but my mother, smiling, said, You need not think such a thing strange, daughter, for some of the best men in the country are burnt in the hand, and they are not ashamed to own it; there's Major ———, says she, he was an eminent pickpocket; there's Justice

Ba——r, was a shoplifter, and both of them were burnt in the hand, and I could name you several, such as they are.

We had frequent discourses of this kind, and abundance of instances she gave me of the like ; after some time, as she was telling some stories of one that was transported but a few weeks ago, I began in an intimate kind of way, to ask her to tell me something of her own story, which she did with the utmost plainness and sincerity ; how she had fallen into very ill company in London in her young days, occasioned by her mother sending her frequently to carry victuals to a kinswoman of hers who was a prisoner in Newgate, in a miserable starving condition, who was afterwards condemned to die, but having got respite by pleading her belly, perished afterwards in the prison.

Here my mother-in-law ran out in a long account of the wicked practices in that dreadful place ; and child, says my mother, perhaps you may know litttle of it, or, it may be, have heard nothing about it ; but depend upon it, says she, we all know here, that there are more thieves and rogues made by that one prison of Newgate, than by all the clubs and societies of villains in the nation ; 'tis that cursed place, says my mother, that half peoples this colony.

Here she went on with her own story so long, and in so particular a manner, that I began to be very uneasy ; but coming to one particular that required telling her name, I thought I should have sunk down in the place ; she perceived I was out of order, and asked me if I was not well, and what ailed me ?   I told her I was so affected with the melancholy story she had told, that it had overcome me, and I begged of her to talk no more of it. Why, my dear, says she very kindly, what need these things trouble you ?   These passages were long before your time, and they give me no trouble at all now ; nay, I look back on them with a particular satisfaction, as they have been a means to bring me to this place.   Then she went on to tell me how she fell into a good family, where behaving herself well, and her mistress dying, her master married her, by whom she had my husband and his sister, and that by her diligence and good management after her husband's death, she had improved the plantations to such a degree as they then were, so that most of the estate was of her getting, not of her husband's, for she had been a widow upwards of sixteen years.

I heard this part of the story with very little attention, because I wanted much to retire and give vent to my passions; and let any one judge what must be the anguish of my mind, when I came to reflect that this was certainly no more or less than my own mother, and that I had now had two children, and was big with another by my own brother, and lay with him still every night.

I was now the most unhappy of all women in the world. O! had the story never been told me, all had been well; it had been no crime to have lain with my husband, if I had known nothing of it.

I had now such a load on my mind that it kept me perpetually waking; to reveal it I could not find would be to any purpose, and yet to conceal it would be next to impossible; nay, I did not doubt but I should talk in my sleep, and tell my husband of it whether I would or no: if I discovered it, the least thing I could expect was to lose my husband, for he was too nice and too honest a man to have continued my husband after he had known I had been his sister; so that I was perplexed to the last degree.

I leave it to any man to judge what difficulties presented to my view: I was away from my native country at a distance prodigious, and the return to me unpassable: I lived very well, but in a circumstance unsufferable in itself; if I had discovered myself to my mother, it might be difficult to convince her of the particulars, and I had no way to prove them: on the other hand, if she had questioned or doubted me, I had been undone, for the bare suggestion would have immediately separated me from my husband, without gaining my mother or him; so that between the surprise on one hand, and the uncertainty on the other, I had been sure to be undone.

In the mean time, as I was but too sure of the fact, I lived therefore in open avowed incest and whoredom, and all under the appearance of an honest wife; and though I was not much touched with the crime of it, yet the action had something in it shocking to nature, and made my husband even nauseous to me. However, upon the most sedate consideration, I resolved that it was absolutely necessary to conceal it all, and not make the least discovery of it either to mother or husband; and thus I lived with the greatest pressure imaginable for three years more.

During this time my mother used to be frequently telling me old stories of her former adventures, which however were no ways pleasant to me; for by it, though she did not tell it me in plain terms, yet I could understand, joined with what I heard myself, of my first tutors, that in her younger days she had been whore and thief; but I verily believe she had lived to repent sincerely of both, and that she was then a very pious, sober, and religious woman.

Well, let her life have been what it would then, it was certain that my life was very uneasy to me; for I lived, as I have said, but in the worst sort of whoredom, and as I could expect no good of it, so really no good issue came of it, and all my seeming prosperity wore off, and ended in misery and destruction. It was some time indeed before it came to this, for everything went wrong with us afterwards, and that which was worse, my husband grew strangely altered, froward, jealous, and unkind, and I was as impatient of bearing his carriage, as the carriage was unreasonable and unjust. These things proceeded so far, and we came at last to be in such ill terms with one another, that I claimed a promise of him which he entered willingly into with me when I consented to come from England with him, viz., that if I did not like to live there, I should come away to England again when I pleased, giving him a year's warning to settle his affairs.

I say, I now claimed this promise of him, and I must confess I did it not in the most obliging terms that could be neither; but I insisted that he treated me ill, that I was remote from my friends, and could do myself no justice, and that he was jealous without cause, my conversation having been unblameable, and he having no pretence for it, and that to remove to England, would take away all occasion from him.

I insisted so peremptorily upon it, that he could not avoid coming to a point, either to keep his word with me, or to break it; and this, notwithstanding he used all the skill he was master of, and employed his mother and other agents to prevail with me to alter my resolutions; indeed the bottom of the thing lay at my heart, and that made all his endeavours fruitless, for my heart was alienated from him. I loathed the thoughts of bedding with him, and used a thousand pretences of illness and humour to prevent his touching me, fearing nothing more than to be with child again, which to be sure would have prevented, or at least delayed, my going over to England.

However, at last I put him so out of humour that he took up a rash and fatal resolution, that in short I should not go to England; that though he had promised me, yet it was an unreasonable thing, that it would be ruinous to his affairs, would unhinge his whole family, and be next to an undoing him in the world; that therefore I ought not to desire it of him, and that no wife in the world that valued her family and her husband's prosperity, would insist upon such a thing.

This plunged me again, for when I considered the thing calmly, and took my husband as he really was, a diligent, careful man in the main, and that he knew nothing of the dreadful circumstances that he was in, I could not but confess to myself that my proposal was very unreasonable, and what no wife that had the good of her family at heart would have desired.

But my discontents were of another nature; I looked upon him no longer as a husband, but as a near relation, the son of my own mother, and I resolved some how or other to be clear of him, but which way I did not know.

It is said by the ill-natured world, of our sex, that if we are set on a thing, it is impossible to turn us from our resolutions; in short, I never ceased poring upon the means to bring to pass my voyage, and came that length with my husband at last, as to propose going without him. This provoked him to the last degree, and he called me not only an unkind wife, but an unnatural mother, and asked me how I could entertain such a thought without horror, as that of leaving my two children (for one was dead) without a mother, and never to see them more. It was true, had things been right, I should not have done it, but now, it was my real desire never to see them, or him either, any more; and as to the charge of unnatural, I could easily answer it to myself, while I knew that the whole relation was unnatural in the highest degree.

However, there was no bringing my husband to anything; he would neither go with me, or let me go without him, and it was out of my power to stir without his consent, as any one that is acquainted with the constitution of that country knows very well.

We had many family quarrels about it, and they began to

grow up to a dangerous height; for as I was quite estranged from him in affection, so I took no heed to my words, but sometimes gave him language that was provoking; in short, I strove all I could to bring him to a parting with me, which was what above all things I desired most.

He took my carriage very ill, and indeed he might well do so, for at last I refused to bed with him, and carrying on the breach upon all occasions to extremity, he told me once he thought I was mad, and if I did not alter my conduct, he would put me under cure; that is to say, into a madhouse: I told him he should find I was far enough from mad, and that it was not in his power, or any other villain's, to murder me; I confess at the same time I was heartily frighted at his thoughts of putting me into a madhouse, which would at once have destroyed all the possibility of bringing the truth out; for that then, no one would have given credit to a word of it.

This therefore brought me to a resolution, whatever came of it, to lay open my whole case; but which way to do it, or to whom, was an inextricable difficulty; when another quarrel with my husband happened, which came up to such an extreme as almost pushed me on to tell it him all to his face; but though I kept it in so as not to come to the particulars, I spoke so much as put him into the utmost confusion, and in the end brought out the whole story.

He began with a calm expostulation upon my being so resolute to go to England; I defended it, and one hard word bringing on another, as is usual in all family strife, he told me I did not treat him as if he was my husband, or talk of my children as if I was a mother; and in short, that I did not deserve to be used as a wife: that he had used all the fair means possible with me; that he had argued with all the kindness and calmness that a husband or a christian ought to do, and that I made him such a vile return, that I treated him rather like a dog than a man, and rather like the most contemptible stranger than a husband; that he was very loath to use violence with me, but that, in short, he saw a necessity of it now, and that for the future he should be obliged to take such measures as should reduce me to my duty.

My blood was now fired to the utmost, and nothing could appear more provoked; I told him, for his fair means and his foul they were equally contemned by me; that for my

going to England, I was resolved on it, come what-would;
and that as to treating him not like a husband, and not
showing myself a mother to my children, there might be
something more in it than he understood at present, but I
thought fit to tell him thus much, that he neither was my
lawful husband, nor they lawful children, and that I had
reason to regard neither of them more than I did.

I confess I was moved to pity him when I spoke it, for he
turned pale as death, and stood mute as one thunderstruck,
and once or twice I thought he would have fainted : in short,
it put him in a fit something like an apoplex; he trembled,
a sweat or dew ran off his face, and yet he was cold as a clod,
so that I was forced to fetch something to keep life in him ;
when he recovered of that, he grew sick and vomited, and
in a little after was put to bed, and the next morning was
in a violent fever.

However, it went off again, and he recovered, though but
slowly, and when he came to be a little better, he told me I
had given him a mortal wound with my tongue, and he had
only one thing to ask before he desired an explanation; I
interrupted him, and told him I was sorry I had gone so far,
since I saw what disorder it put him into, but I desired him
not to talk to me of explanations, for that would but make
things worse.

This heightened his impatience, and indeed perplexed him
beyond all bearing; for now he began to suspect that there
was some mystery yet unfolded, but could not make the least
guess at it; all that run in his brain was, that I had another
husband alive, but I assured him there was not the least of
that in it; indeed as to my other husband he was effectually
dead to me, and had told me I should look on him as such,
so I had not the least uneasiness on that score.

But now I found the thing too far gone to conceal it much
longer, and my husband himself gave me an opportunity to
ease myself of the secret much to my satisfaction; he had
laboured with me three or four weeks, but to no purpose,
only to tell him whether I had spoken those words only to
put him in a passion, or whether there was anything of truth
in the bottom of them. But I continued inflexible, and would
explain nothing, unless he would first consent to my going
to England, which he would never do, he said, while he lived;
on the other hand. I said it was in my power to make him

willing when I pleased, nay, to make him entreat me to go; and this increased his curiosity, and made him importunate to the highest degree.

At length he tells all this story to his mother, and sets her upon me to get it out of me, and she used her utmost skill indeed; but I put her to a full stop at once, by telling her that the mystery of the whole matter lay in herself; that it was my respect to her had made me conceal it, and that, in short, I could go no farther, and therefore conjured her not to insist upon it.

She was struck dumb at this suggestion, and could not tell what to say or to think; but laying aside the supposition as a policy of mine, continued her importunity on account of her son, and if possible, to make up the breach between us two; as to that, I told her, that it was indeed a good design in her, but that it was impossible to be done; and that if I should reveal to her the truth of what she desired, she would grant it to be impossible, and cease to desire it. At last I seemed to be prevailed on by her importunity, and told her I dare trust her with a secret of the greatest importance, and she would soon see that this was so, and that I would consent to lodge it in her breast, if she would engage solemnly not to acquaint her son with it without my consent.

She was long in promising this part, but rather than not come at the main secret she agreed to that too, and after a great many other preliminaries, I began, and told her the whole story. First I told her how much she was concerned in all the unhappy breach which had happened between her son and me, by telling me her own story, and her London name; and that the surprise she saw I was in, was upon that occasion; then I told her my own story, and my name, and assured her, by such other tokens as she could not deny, that I was no other, nor more or less, than her own child, her daughter, born of her body in Newgate; the same that had saved her from the gallows by being in her belly, and that she left in such and such hands when she was transported.

It is impossible to express the astonishment she was in; she was not inclined to believe the story, or to remember the particulars; for she immediately foresaw the confusion that must follow in the family upon it; but everything concurred so exactly with the stories she had told me of herself, and

which, if she had not told me, she would perhaps have been
content to have denied, that she had stopped her own mouth,
and she had nothing to do but take me about the neck and
kiss me, and cry most vehemently over me, without speaking
one word for a long time together: at last she broke out,
Unhappy child! says she, what miserable chance could bring
thee hither? and in the arms of my son too! Dreadful girl!
says she, why we are all undone! married to thy own brother!
three children, and two alive, all of the same flesh and blood!
my son and my daughter lying together as husband and wife!
all confusion and distraction! miserable family! what will
become of us? what is to be said? what is to be done? And
thus she run on a great while, nor had I any power to speak,
or if I had, did I know what to say, for every word wounded
me to the soul. With this kind of amazement we parted for
the first time, though my mother was more surprised than I
was, because it was more news to her than to me: however,
she promised again, that she would say nothing of it to her
son, till we had talked of it again.

It was not long, you may be sure, before we had a second
conference upon the same subject; when, as if she had been
willing to forget the story she had told me of herself, or to
suppose that I had forgot some of the particulars, she began
to tell them with alterations and omissions; but I refreshed
her memory, in many things which I supposed she had forgot,
and then came in so opportunely with the whole history, that
it was impossible for her to go from it; and then she fell into
her rhapsodies again, and exclamations at the severity of her
misfortunes: when these things were a little over with her,
we fell into a close debate about what should be first done
before we gave an account of the matter to my husband. But
to what purpose could be all our consultations? we could
neither of us see our way through it, or how it could be safe
to open such a scene to him; it was impossible to make any
judgment, or give any guess at what temper he would receive
it in, or what measures he would take upon it; and if he should
have so little government of himself, as to make it public, we
easily foresaw that it would be the ruin of the whole family;
and if at last he should take the advantage the law would give
him, he might put me away with disdain, and leave me to
sue for the little portion that I had, and perhaps waste it all

in the suit, and then be a beggar; and thus I should see him perhaps in the arms of another wife in a few months, and be myself the most miserable creature alive.

My mother was as sensible of this as I; and upon the whole, we knew not what to do. After some time we came to more sober resolutions, but then it was with this misfortune too, that my mother's opinion and mine were quite different from one another, and indeed inconsistent with one another; for my mother's opinion was, that I should bury the whole thing entirely, and continue to live with him as my husband, till some other event should make the discovery of it more convenient; and that in the mean time she would endeavour to reconcile us together again, and restore our mutual comfort and family peace; that we might lie as we used to do together, and so let the whole matter remain a secret as close as death; for child, says she, we are both undone if it comes out.

To encourage me to this, she promised to make me easy in my circumstances, and to leave me what she could at her death, secured for me separately from my husband; so that if it should come out afterwards, I should be able to stand on my own feet, and procure justice too from him.

This proposal did not agree with my judgment, though it was very fair and kind in my mother; but my thoughts run quite another way.

As to keeping the thing in our own breasts, and letting it all remain as it was, I told her it was impossible; and I asked her how she could think I could bear the thoughts of lying with my own brother? In the next place I told her, that her being alive was the only support of the discovery, and that while she owned me for her child, and saw reason to be satisfied that I was so, nobody else would doubt it; but that if she should die before the discovery, I should be taken for an impudent creature that had forged such a thing to go away from my husband, or should be counted crazed and distracted. Then I told her how he had threatened already to put me into a madhouse, and what concern I had been in about it, and how that was the thing that drove me to the necessity of discovering it to her as I had done.

From all which I told her, that I had, on the most serious reflections I was able to make in the case, come to this resolution, which I hoped she would like, as a medium be-

tween both, viz., that she should use her endeavours with her
son to give me leave to go for England, as I had desired, and
to furnish me with a sufficient sum of money, either in goods
along with me, or in bills for my support there, all along
suggesting that he might one time or other think it proper to
come over to me.

That when I was gone she should then, in cold blood, discover the case to him gradually, and as her own discretion
should guide; so that he might not be surprised with it, and
fly out into any passions and excesses; and that she should
concern herself to prevent his slighting the children, or
marrying again, unless he had a certain account of my being
dead.

This was my scheme, and my reasons were good; I was
really alienated from him in the consequence of these things;
indeed I mortally hated him as a husband, and it was impossible to remove that riveted aversion I had to him; at the
same time, it being an unlawful, incestuous living, added to
that aversion, and everything added to make cohabiting with
him the most nauseous thing to me in the world; and I think
verily it was come to such a height, that I could almost as
willingly have embraced a dog, as have let him offer anything
of that kind to me, for which reason I could not bear the
thoughts of coming between the sheets with him; I cannot
say that I was right in carrying it such a length, while at
the same time I did not resolve to discover the thing to him;
but I am giving an account of what was, not of what ought
or ought not to be.

In this directly opposite opinion to one another my mother
and I continued a long time, and it was impossible to reconcile our judgments; many disputes we had about it, but we
could never either of us yield our own, or bring over the
other.

I insisted on my aversion to lying with my own brother;
and she insisted upon its being impossible to bring him to
consent to my going to England; and in this uncertainty we
continued, not differing so as to quarrel, or anything like it;
but so as not to be able to resolve what we should do to
make up that terrible breach.

At last I resolved on a desperate course, and told my
mother my resolution, viz., that in short, I would tell him
of it myself. My mother was frighted to the last degree at

the very thoughts of it; but I bid her be easy, told her I would do it gradually and softly, and with all the art and good humour I was mistress of, and time it also as well as I could, taking him in good humour too: I told her, I did not question but if I could be hypocrite enough to feign more affection to him than I really had, I should succeed in all my design, and we might part by consent, and with a good agreement, for I might love him well enough for a brother, though I could not for a husband.

All this while he lay at my mother to find out, if possible, what was the meaning of that dreadful expression of mine, as he called it, which I mentioned before; namely, that I was not his lawful wife, nor my children his legal children: my mother put him off, told him she could bring me to no explanations, but found there was something that disturbed me very much, and she hoped she should get it out of me in time, and in the mean time recommended to him earnestly to use me more tenderly, and win me with his usual good carriage; told him of his terrifying and affrighting me with his threats of sending me to a madhouse and the like, and advised him not to make a woman desperate on any account whatever.

He promised her to soften his behaviour, and bid her assure me that he loved me as well as ever, and that he had no such design as that of sending me to a madhouse, whatever he might say in his passion; also he desired my mother to use the same persuasions to me too, and we might live together as we used to do.

I found the effects of this treaty presently; my husband's conduct was immediately altered, and he was quite another man to me; nothing could be kinder and more obliging than he was to me upon all occasions; and I could do no less than make some return to it, which I did as well as I could, but it was but in an awkward manner at best, for nothing was more frightful to me than his caresses, and the apprehensions of being with child again by him, was ready to throw me into fits; and this made me see that there was an absolute necessity of breaking the case to him without any more delay, which however I did with all the caution and reserve imaginable.

He had continued his altered carriage to me near a month, and we began to live a new kind of life with one another, and could I have satisfied myself to have gone on with it, I believe it might have continued as long as we had continued alive together. One evening as we were sitting and talking together under a little awning, which served as an arbour at the entrance into the garden, he was in a very pleasant agreeable humour, and said abundance of kind things to me relating to the pleasure of our present good agreement, and the disorders of our past breach, and what a satisfaction it was to him, that we had room to hope we should never have any more of it.

I fetched a deep sigh, and told him there was nobody in the world could be more delighted than I was, in the good agreement we had always kept up, or more afflicted with the breach of it, but I was sorry to tell him that there was an unhappy circumstance in our case, which lay too close to my heart, and which I knew not how to break to him, that rendered my part of it very miserable, and took from me all the comfort of the rest.

He importuned me to tell him what it was; I told him I could not tell how to do it; that while it was concealed from him, I alone was unhappy, but if he knew it also, we should be both so; and that therefore to keep him in the dark about it was the kindest thing that I could do, and it was on that account alone that I kept a secret from him, the very keeping of which I thought would first or last be my destruction.

It is impossible to express his surprise at this relation, and the double importunity which he used with me to discover it to him: he told me I could not be called kind to him, nay, I could not be faithful to him, if I concealed it from him; I told him I thought so too, and yet I could not do it. He went back to what I had said before to him, and told me he hoped it did not relate to what I said in my passion; and that he had resolved to forget all that, as the effect of a rash, provoked spirit; I told him I wished I could forget it all too, but that it was not to be done, the impression was too deep, and it was impossible.

He then told me he was resolved not to differ with me in anything, and that therefore he would importune me no more about it, resolving to acquiesce in whatever I did or said; only begged I would then agree, that whatever it was, it should no more interrupt our quiet and our mutual kindness.

This was the most provoking thing he could have said to me, for I really wanted his farther importunities, that I might be prevailed with to bring out that which indeed was like death to me to conceal; so I answered him plainly, that I could not say I was glad not to be importuned, though I could not tell how to comply; But come, my dear, said I, what conditions will you make with me upon the opening this affair to you?

Any conditions in the world, said he, that you can in reason desire of me. Well, said I, come, give it me under your hand, that if you do not find I am in any fault, or that I am willingly concerned in the causes of the misfortunes that is to follow, you will not blame me, use me the worse, do me any injury, or make me be the sufferer for that which is not my fault.

That, says he, is the most reasonable demand in the world; not to blame you for that which is not your fault: give me a pen and ink, says he; so I ran in and fetched pen, ink, and paper, and he wrote the condition down in the very words I had proposed it, and signed it with his name. Well, says he, what is next, my dear? Why, says I, the next is, that you will not blame me for not discovering the secret to you before I knew it. Very just again, says he; with all my heart; so he wrote down that also, and signed it.

Well, my dear, says I, then I have but one condition more to make with you, and that is, that as there is nobody concerned in it but you and I, you shall not discover it to any person in the world, except your own mother; and that in all the measures you shall take upon the discovery, as I am equally concerned in it with you, though as innocent as yourself, you shall do nothing in a passion, nothing to my prejudice, or to your mother's prejudice, without my knowledge and consent.

This a little amazed him, and he wrote down the words distinctly, but read them over and over before he signed them, hesitating at them several times, and repeating them; my mother's prejudice! and your prejudice! What mysterious thing can this be? however, at last he signed it.

Well, says I, my dear, I'll ask you no more under your hand, but as you are to hear the most unexpected and surprising thing that perhaps ever befel any family in the world, I beg you to promise me you will receive it with composure and a presence of mind suitable to a man of sense.

I'll do my utmost, says he, upon condition you will keep

me no longer in suspense, for you terrify me with all these preliminaries.

Well then, says I, it is this: As I told you before in a heat, that I was not your lawful wife, and that our children were not legal children, so I must let you know now in calmness, and in kindness, but with affliction enough, that I am your own sister, and you my own brother, and that we are both the children of our mother now alive, and in the house, who is convinced of the truth of it, in a manner not to be denied or contradicted.

I saw him turn pale, and look wild; and I said, Now remember your promise, and receive it with presence of mind; for who could have said more to prepare you for it, than I have done? However, I called a servant, and got him a little glass of rum (which is the usual dram of the country), for he was fainting away.

When he was a little recovered, I said to him, This story you may be sure requires a long explanation, and therefore have patience and compose your mind to hear it out, and I'll make it as short as I can; and with this, I told him what I thought was needful of the fact, and particularly how my mother came to discover it to me, as above; And now, my dear, says I, you will see reason for my capitulations, and that I neither have been the cause of this matter, nor could be so, and that I could know nothing of it before now.

I am fully satisfied of that, says he, but 'tis a dreadful surprise to me; however, I know a remedy for it all, and a remedy that shall put an end to all your difficulties, without your going to England. That would be strange, said I, as all the rest. No, no, says he, I'll make it easy, there's nobody in the way of it all, but myself. He looked a little disordered when he said this, but I did not apprehend anything from it at that time, believing, as it used to be said, that they who do those things never talk of them; or that they who talk of such things never do them.

But things were not come to their height with him, and I observed he became pensive and melancholy; and in a word, as I thought a little distempered in his head: I endeavoured to talk him into temper, and into a kind of scheme for our government in the affair, and sometimes he would be well, and talk with some courage about it; but the weight of it lay too heavy upon his thoughts, and went so far that he made two attempts upon himself, and in one of them had actually strangled himself, and had not his mother come into the room in the very moment, he had died; but with the help of a negro servant, she cut him down and recovered him.

Things were now come to a lamentable height: my pity for him now began to revive that affection which at first I really had for him, and I endeavoured sincerely, by all the kind carriage I could, to make up the breach; but in short, it had gotten too great a head, it preyed upon his spirits, and it threw him into a lingering consumption, though it happened not to be mortal. In this distress I did not know what to do; as his life was apparently declining, and I might perhaps have married again there, very much to my advantage, had it been my business to have stayed in the country; but my mind was restless too, I hankered after coming to England, and nothing would satisfy me without it.

In short, by an unwearied importunity, my husband, who was apparently decaying, as I observed, was at last prevailed with, and so my fate pushing me on, the way was made clear for me, and my mother concurring, I obtained a very good cargo for my coming to England.

When I parted with my brother (for such I am now to call him), we agreed that after I arrived, he should pretend to have an account that I was dead in England, and so might marry again when he would; he promised, and engaged to me, to correspond with me as a sister, and to assist and support me as long as I lived; and that if he died before me, he would leave sufficient to his mother to take care of me still, in the name of a sister, and he was in some respects just to this; but it was so oddly managed that I felt the disappointments very sensibly afterwards, as you shall hear in its time.

I came away in the month of August, after I had been eight years in that country; and now a new scene of misfortunes attended me, which perhaps few women have gone through the like.

We had an indifferent good voyage, till we came just upon the coast of England, and where we arrived in two-and-thirty days, but were then ruffled with two or three storms, one of which drove us away to the coast of Ireland, and we put in at Kinsale. We remained there about thirteen days, got some refreshment on shore, and put to sea again, though we met with very bad weather again, in which the ship sprung her mainmast, as they called it: but we got at last into Milford Haven in Wales, where, though it was remote from our port, yet having my foot safe upon the firm ground of the isle of Britain, I resolved to venture it no more upon the waters, which had been so terrible to me; so getting my clothes and money on shore, with my bills of loading and other papers, I resolved to come for London, and leave the ship to get to her port as she could; the port whither she was bound, was to Bristol, where my brother's chief correspondent lived.

I got to London in about three weeks, where I heard a little while after, that the ship was arrived at Bristol, but at the same time had the misfortune to know that by the violent weather she had been in, and the breaking of her mainmast, she had great damage on board, and that a great part of her cargo was spoiled.

I had now a new scene of life upon my hands, and a dreadful appearance it had; I was come away with a kind of final farewell; what I brought with me, was indeed considerable, had it come safe, and by the help of it, I might have married again tolerably well; but as it was, I was reduced to between two or three hundred pounds in the whole, and this without any hope of recruit. I was entirely without friends, nay, even so much as without acquaintances, for I found it was absolutely necessary not to revive former acquaintance; and as for my subtle friend that set me up formerly for a fortune, she was dead and her husband also.

The looking after my cargo of goods soon after obliged me to take a journey to Bristol, and during my attendance upon that affair, I took the diversion of going to Bath, for as I was still far from being old, so my humour, which was always gay, continued so to an extreme; and being now, as it were, a woman of fortune, though I was a woman without a fortune, I expected something or other might happen in the way, that might mend my circumstances, as had been my case before.

Bath is a place of gallantry enough; expensive, and full of snares; I went thither indeed in the view of taking what might offer; but I must do myself that justice, as to protest I meant nothing but in an honest way, nor had any thoughts about me at first that looked the way which afterwards I suffered them to be guided.

Here I stayed the whole latter season, as it is called there, and contracted some unhappy acquaintance, which rather prompted the follies I fell afterwards into, than fortified me against them. I lived pleasantly enough, kept good company, that is to say, gay, fine company; but had the discouragement to find this way of living sunk me exceedingly, and that as I had no settled income, so spending upon the main stock was but a certain kind of bleeding to death; and this gave me many sad reflections. However, I shook them off, and still flattered myself that something or other might offer for my advantage.

But I was in the wrong place for it; I was not now at Redriff, where if I had set myself tolerably up, some honest sea captain or other might have talked with me upon the honourable terms of matrimony; but I was at Bath, where men find a mistress sometimes, but very rarely look for a wife; and consequently all the particular acquaintances a woman can expect there must have some tendency that way.

I had spent the first season well enough, for though I had contracted some acquaintance with a gentleman who came to Bath for his diversion, yet I had entered into no felonious treaty. I had resisted some casual offers of gallantry, and had managed that way well enough; I was not wicked enough to come into the crime for the mere vice of it, and I had no extraordinary offers that tempted me with the main thing which I wanted.

However, I went this length the first season, viz., I contracted an acquaintance with a woman in whose house I lodged, who, though she did not keep an ill house, yet had none of the best principles in herself. I had on all occasions behaved myself so well as not to get the least slur upon my reputation, and all the men that I had conversed with, were of so good reputation that I had not gotten the least reflection, by conversing with them; nor did any of them seem to think there was room for a wicked correspondence if they had offered it; yet there was one gentleman, as above, who always singled me out for the diversion for my company, as he called it, which, as he was pleased to say, was very agreeable to him, but at that time there was no more in it.

I had many melancholy hours at Bath after all the

company was gone; for though I went to Bristol sometimes
for the disposing my effects, and for recruits of money, yet
I chose to come back to Bath for my residence, because
being on good terms with the woman, in whose house I
lodged in the summer, I found that during the winter I lived
rather cheaper there than I could do anywhere else. Here,
I say, I passed the winter as heavily as I had passed the
autumn cheerfully; but having contracted a nearer intimacy
with the said woman, in whose house I lodged, I could not
avoid communicating something of what lay hardest upon
my mind, and particularly the narrowness of my circumstances : I told her also, that I had a mother and a brother
in Virginia in good circumstances; and as I had really
written back to my mother in particular to represent my
condition, and the great loss I had received, so I did not
fail to let my new friend know, that I expected a supply
from thence, and so indeed I did; and as the ships went
from Bristol, to York-river, in Virginia, and back again
generally in less time than from London, and that my
brother corresponded chiefly at Bristol, I thought it was
much better for me to wait here for my returns, than to go
to London.

My new friend appeared sensibly affected with my condition,
and indeed was so very kind, as to reduce the rate of my
living with her to so low a price during the winter, that she
convinced me she got nothing by me; and as for lodging,
during the winter I paid nothing at all.

When the spring season came on, she continued to be as
kind to me as she could, and I lodged with her for a time,
till it was found necessary to do otherwise ; she had some
persons of character that frequently lodged in her house, and
in particular the gentleman, who, as I said, singled me out
for his companion in the winter before; and he came down
again with another gentleman in his company and two
servants, and lodged in the same house ; I suspected that my
landlady had invited him thither, letting him know that I
was still with her, but she denied it.

In a word, this gentleman came down and continued to
single me out for his peculiar confidence; he was a complete
gentleman, that must be confessed, and his company was
agreeable to me, as mine, if I might believe him, was to him;
he made no professions to me but of an extraordinary respect,

and he had such an opinion of my virtue, ·that, as he often professed, he believed, if he should offer anything else, I should reject him with contempt; he soon understood from me that I was a widow, that I had arrived at Bristol from Virginia by the last ships; and that I waited at Bath till the next Virginia fleet should arrive, by which I expected considerable effects; I understood by him, that he had a wife, but that the lady was distempered in her head, and was under the conduct of her own relations, which he consented to, to avoid any reflection that might be cast upon him for mismanaging her cure; and in the mean time he came to Bath to divert his thoughts under such a melancholy circumstance.

My landlady, who of her own accord encouraged the correspondence on all occasions, gave me an advantageous character of him, as of a man of honour, and of virtue, as well as of a great estate; and indeed I had reason to say so of him too, for though we lodged both on a floor, and he had frequently come into my chamber, even when I was in bed, and I also into his, yet he never offered anything to me farther than a kiss, or so much as solicited me to anything till long after, as you shall hear.

I frequently took notice to my landlady of his exceeding modesty, and she again used to tell me, she believed it was so from the beginning; however she used to tell me that she thought I ought to expect some gratifications from him for my company, for indeed he did as it were engross me. I told her, I had not given him the least occasion to think I wanted it, or that I would accept of it from him; she told me, she would take that part upon her, and she managed it so dexterously, that the first time we were together alone, after she had talked with him, he began to inquire a little into my circumstances, as how I had subsisted myself since I came ·on shore, and whether I did not want money? I stood off very boldly; I told him that though my cargo of tobacco was damaged, yet that it was not quite lost: that the merchant that I had been consigned to had so honestly managed for me that I had not wanted, and that I hoped, with frugal management, I should make it hold out till more would come, which I expected by the next fleet; that in the mean time I had retrenched my expenses, and whereas I kept a maid last season, now I lived without; and whereas I had a chamber and a dining-room then on the first floor, I now had but one room two pair of stairs, and the like; but I live, said I, as well satisfied now as then; adding, that his company had made me live much more cheerfully than otherwise I should have done, for which I was much obliged to him; and so I put off all room for any offer at the present. It was not long before he attacked me again, and told me he found that I was backward to trust him with the secret of my circumstances, which he was sorry for; assuring me that he inquired into it with no design to satisfy his own curiosity, but merely to assist me if there was any occasion; but since I would not own myself to stand in need of any assistance, he had but one thing more to desire of me, and that was, that I would promise him that when I was any way straitened, I would frankly tell him of it, and that I would make use of him with the same freedom that he made the offer; adding, that I should always find I had a true friend, though perhaps I was afraid to trust him.

I omitted nothing that was fit to be said by one infinitely obliged, to let him know that I had a due sense of his kindness; and indeed from that time, I did not appear so much reserved to him as I had done before, though still within the bounds of the strictest virtue on both sides; but how free soever our conversation was, I could not arrive to that freedom which he desired, viz., to tell him I wanted money, though I was secretly very glad of his offer.

Some weeks passed after this, and still I never asked him for money; when my landlady, a cunning creature, who had often pressed me to it, but found that I could not do it, makes a story of her own inventing, and comes in bluntly to me when we were together, O! widow, says she, I have bad news to tell you this morning. What is that? said I; are the Virginia ships taken by the French? for that was my fear. No, no, says she, but the man you sent to Bristol yesterday for money is come back, and says he has brought none.

I could by no means like her project; I thought it looked too much like prompting him, which he did not want, and I saw that I should lose nothing by being backward, so took her up short; I can't imagine why he should say so, said I, for I assure you he brought me all the money I sent him for, and here it is, said I (pulling out my purse with about twelve guineas in it); and added, I intend you shall have most of it by and by.

He seemed distasted a little at her talking as she did, as well as I; taking it, as I fancied he would, as something forward of her; but when he saw me give such an answer, ne came immediately to himself.   The next morning we talked of it again, when I found he was fully satisfied; and smiling, said he hoped I would not want money, and not tell him of it, and that I had promised him otherwise; I told him I had been very much dissatisfied at my landlady's talking so publicly the day before of what she had nothing to do with; but I supposed she wanted what I owed her, which was about eight guineas, which I had resolved to give her, and had given it her the same night.

He was in a mighty good humour, when he heard me say I had paid her, and it went off into some other discourse at that time: but the next morning he having heard me up before him, he called to me, and I answered; he asked me to come into his chamber; he was in bed when I came in, and he made me come and sit down on his bed side, for he said he had something to say to me. After some very kind expressions, he asked me if I would be very honest to him, and give a sincere answer to one thing he would desire of me.   After some little cavil with him at the word sincere, and asking him if I had ever given him any answers which were not sincere, I promised him I would; why then his request was, he said, to let him see my purse: I immediately put my hand into my pocket, and laughing at him, pulled it out, and there was in it three guineas and a half; then he asked me if there was all the money I had? I told him no, laughing again, not by a great deal.

Well then, he said, he would have me promise to go and fetch him all the money I had, every farthing; I told him I would, and I went into my chamber, and fetched him a little private drawer, where I had about six guineas more, and some silver, and threw it all down upon the bed, and told him there was all my wealth, honestly to a shilling: he looked a little at it, but did not tell it, and huddled it all into the drawer again, and then reaching his pocket, pulled out a key, and bade me open a little walnut-tree box he had upon the table, and bring him such a drawer, which I did: in this drawer, there was a great deal of money in gold, I believe near two hundred guineas, but I knew not how much.   He took the drawer, and taking me by the hand, made me put it

in, and take a whole handful; I was backward at that, but
he held my hand hard in his hand, and put it into the drawer,
and made me take out as many guineas almost as I could
well take up at once.

When I had done so, he made me put them into my lap,
and took my little drawer, and poured out all my own money
among his, and bade me get me gone, and carry it all into
my own chamber.

I relate this story the more particularly, because of the
good humour of it, and to show the temper with which we
conversed. It was not long after this, but he began every
day to find fault with my clothes, with my laces, and head-
dresses; and in a word, pressed me to buy better, which by
the way I was willing enough to do, though I did not seem
to be so; I loved nothing in the world better than fine clothes,
but I told him I must housewife the money he had lent me,
or else I should not be able to pay him again. He then told
me in a few words, that as he had a sincere respect for me,
and knew my circumstances, he had not lent me that money,
but given it me, and that he thought I had merited it from
him, by giving him my company so entirely as I had done.
After this he made me take a maid, and keep house, and his
friend being gone, he obliged me to diet him, which I
did very willingly, believing, as it appeared, that I should
lose nothing by it, nor did the woman of the house fail to find
her account in it too.

We had lived thus near three months, when the company
beginning to wear away at Bath, he talked of going away,
and fain he would have me to go to London with him: I was
not very easy in that proposal, not knowing what posture I
was to live in there, or how he might use me; but while this
was in debate, he fell very sick; he had gone out to a place
in Somersetshire, called Shepton, and was there taken very
ill, and so ill that he could not travel; so he sent his man
back to Bath, to beg me that I would hire a coach and come
over to him. Before he went, he had left his money and
other things of value with me, and what to do with them I
did not know, but I secured them as well as I could, and
locked up the lodgings and went to him, where I found him
very ill indeed, so I persuaded him to be carried in a litter
to Bath, where was more help and better advice to be had.

He consented, and I brought him to Bath, which was about

fifteen miles, as I remember; here he continued very ill of a fever, and kept his bed five weeks, all which time I nursed him and tended him as carefully as if I had been his wife; indeed if I had been his wife I could not have done more; I sat up with him so much and so often, that at last, indeed, he would not let me sit up any longer, and then I got a pallet-bed into his room, and lay in it just at his bed's feet.

I was indeed sensibly affected with his condition, and with the apprehensions of losing such a friend as he was, and was like to be to me, and I used to sit and cry by him many hours together; at last he grew better, and gave hopes that he would recover, as indeed he did, though very slowly.

Were it otherwise than what I am going to say, I should not be backward to disclose it, as it is apparent I have done in other cases; but I affirm, through all this conversation, abating the coming into the chamber when I or he was in bed, and the necessary offices of attending him night and day, when he was sick, there had not passed the least immodest word or action between us. O! that it had been so to the last.

After some time he gathered strength and grew well apace, and I would have removed my pallet-bed, but he would not let me, till he was able to venture himself without anybody to sit up with him, when I removed to my own chamber.

He took many occasions to express his sense of my tenderness for him; and when he grew well he made me a present of fifty guineas for my care, and, as he called it, hazarding my life to save his.

And now he made deep protestations of a sincere inviolable affection for me, but with the utmost reserve for my virtue and his own: I told him I was fully satisfied of it; he carried it that length that he protested to me, that if he was naked in bed with me, he would as sacredly preserve my virtue, as he would defend it, if I was assaulted by a ravisher; I believed him, and told him I did so; but this did not satisfy him; he would, he said, wait for some opportunity to give me an undoubted testimony of it.

It was a great while after this that I had occasion, on my business, to go to Bristol, upon which he hired me a coach, and would go with me; and now indeed our intimacy increased. From Bristol he carried me to Gloucester, which was merely a journey of pleasure, to take the air; and here it was our hap to have no lodgings in the inn, but in one large chamber with two beds in it. The master of the house going with us to show his rooms, and coming into that room, said very frankly to him, Sir, it is none of my business to inquire whether the lady be your spouse or no, but if not, you may lie as honestly in these two beds, as if you were in two chambers; and with that he pulls a great curtain which drew quite cross the room, and effectually divided the beds; Well, says my friend, very readily, these beds will do, and as for the rest, we are too near akin to lie together, though we may lodge near one another; and this put an honest face on the thing too. When we came to go to bed, he decently went out of the room till I was in bed, and then went to bed in the other bed, but lay there talking to me a great while.

At last, repeating his usual saying, that he could lie naked in the bed with me, and not offer me the least injury, he starts out of his bed; And now, my dear, says he, you shall see how just I will be to you, and that I can keep my word, and away he comes to my bed.

I resisted a little, but I must confess I should not have resisted him much, if he had not made those promises at all; so after a little struggle, I lay still and let him come to bed; when he was there he took me in his arms, and so I lay all night with him, but he had no more to do with me, or offered anything to me, other than embracing me, as I say, in his arms, no, not the whole night, but rose up and dressed him in the morning, and left me as innocent for him as I was the day I was born.

This was a surprising thing to me, and perhaps may be so to others, who know how the laws of nature work; for he was a vigorous brisk person; nor did he act thus on a principle of religion at all, but of mere affection; insisting on it, that though I was to him the most agreeable woman in the world, yet, because he loved me, he could not injure me.

I own it was a noble principle, but as it was what I never saw before, so it was perfectly amazing. We travelled the rest of the journey as we did before, and came back to Bath, where, as he had opportunity to come to me when he would, he often repeated the same moderation, and I frequently lay with him, and although all the familiarities of man and wife were common to us, yet he never once offered to go any farther, and he valued himself much upon it; I do not say that I was so wholly pleased with it as he thought I was, for I own I was much wickeder than he.

We lived thus near two years, only with this exception, that he went three times to London in that time, and once he continued there four months; but to do him justice, he always supplied me with money to subsist on very handsomely.

Had we continued thus, I confess we had had much to boast of; but as wise men say, it is ill venturing too near the brink of a command, so we found it; and here again I must do him the justice to own that the first breach was not on his part. It was one night that we were in bed together warm and merry, and having drank, I think, a little more both of us than usual, though not in the least to disorder us, when after some other follies which I cannot name, and being clasped close in his arms, I told him (I repeat it with shame and horror of soul) that I could find in my heart to discharge him of his engagement for one night and no more.

He took me at my word immediately, and after that there was no resisting him; neither indeed had I any mind to resist him any more.

Thus the government of our virtue was broken, and I exchanged the place of friend for that unmusical, harsh-sounding title of whore. In the morning we were both at our penitentials, I cried very heartily, he expressed himself very sorry; but that was all either of us could do at that time, and the way being thus cleared, and the bars of virtue and conscience thus removed, we had the less to struggle with.

It was but a dull kind of conversation that we had together for all the rest of that week; I looked on him with blushes, and every now and then started that melancholy objection, What if I should be with child now? What will become of me then? He encouraged me by telling me, that as long as I was true to him, he would be so to me; and since it was gone such a length (which indeed he never intended), yet if I was with child, he would take care of that and me too. This hardened us both; I assured him if I was with child, I would die for want of a midwife rather than name him as the father of it; and he assured me I should never want if I should be with child. These mutual assurances hardened us in the thing, and after this we repeated the crime as often as we pleased, till at length, as I feared, so it came to pass, and I was indeed with child.

After I was sure it was so, and I had satisfied him of it too, we began to think of taking measures for the managing it, and I proposed trusting the secret to my landlady, and asking her advice, which he agreed to: my landlady, a woman (as I found) used to such things, made light of it; she said she knew it would come to that at last, and made us very merry about it: as I said above, we found her an experienced old lady at such work; she undertook every-thing, engaged to procure a midwife and a nurse, to satisfy all inquiries, and bring us off with reputation, and she did so very dexterously indeed.

When I grew near my time, she desired my gentleman to go away to London, or make as if he did so; when he was gone, she acquainted the parish officers that there was a lady ready to lie in at her house, but that she knew her husband very well, and gave them, as she pretended, an account of his name, which she called Sir Walter Cleave; telling them he was a worthy gentleman, and that she would answer for all inquiries, and the like. This satisfied the parish officers presently, and I lay in in as much credit as I could have done if I had really been my Lady Cleave; and was assisted in my travail by three or four of the best citizens' wives of Bath, which, however, made me a little the more expensive to him; I often expressed my concern to him about that part, but he bid me not be concerned at it.

As he had furnished me very sufficiently with money for the extraordinary expenses of my lying in, I had everything very handsome about me; but did not affect to be so gay or extravagant neither; besides, knowing the world, as I had done, and that such kind of things do not often last long, I took care to lay up as much money as I could for a wet day, as I called it; making him believe it was all spent upon the extraordinary appearance of things in my lying in.

By this means, with what he had given me as above, I had at the end of my lying in two hundred guineas by me, including also what was left of my own.

I was brought to bed of a fine boy indeed, and a charming child it was; and when he heard of it, he wrote me a very kind obliging letter about it, and then told me he thought it would look better for me to come away for London as soon as I was up and well, that he had provided apartments for me at Hammersmith, as if I came only from London, and that after a while I should go back to Bath, and he would go with me.

I liked his offer very well, and hired a coach on purpose, and taking my child and a wet nurse to tend and suckle it, and a maid servant with me, away I went for London.

He met me at Reading in his own chariot, and taking me into that, left the servant and the child in the hired coach, and so he brought me to my new lodgings at Hammersmith; with which I had abundance of reason to be very well pleased, for they were very handsome rooms.

And now I was indeed in the height of what I might call prosperity, and I wanted nothing but to be a wife, which however could not be in this case, and therefore on all occasions I studied to save what I could, as I said above, against the time of scarcity; knowing well enough that such things as these do not always continue, that men that keep mistresses often change them, grow weary of them, or jealous of them, or something or other; and sometimes the ladies that are thus well used, are not careful by a prudent conduct to preserve the esteem of their persons, or the nice article of their fidelity, and then they are justly cast off with contempt.

But I was secured in this point, for as I had no inclination to change, so I had no manner of acquaintance, so no temptation to look any farther; I kept no company but in the family where I lodged, and with a clergyman's lady at next door; so that when he was absent I visited nobody, nor did he ever find me out of my chamber or parlour whenever he came down; if I went anywhere to take the air it was always with him.

The living in this manner with him, and his with me, was certainly the most undesigned thing in the world; he often protested to me that when he became first acquainted with me, and even to the very night when we first broke in upon our rules, he never had the least design of lying with me; that he always had a sincere affection for me, but not the least real inclination to do what he had done; I assured him I never suspected him; that if I had I should not so easily

have yielded to the freedoms which brought it on, but that it
was all a surprise, and was owing to our having yielded too
far to our mutual inclinations that night; and indeed I have
often observed since, and leave it as a caution to the readers
of this story, that we ought to be cautious of gratifying our
inclinations in loose and lewd freedoms, lest we find our
resolutions of virtue fail us in the juncture when their
assistance should be most necessary.

It is true that from the first hour I began to converse with
him, I resolved to let him lie with me, if he offered it; but
it was because I wanted his help, and knew of no other way
of securing him: but when we were that night together,
and, as I have said, had gone such a length, I found my
weakness, the inclination was not to be resisted, but I was
obliged to yield up all even before he asked it.

However, he was so just to me that he never upbraided
me with that; nor did he ever express the least dislike of
my conduct on any other occasion, but always protested he
was as much delighted with my company as he was the first
hour we came together.

It is true that he had no wife, that is to say, she was no
wife to him, but the reflections of conscience oftentimes
snatch a man, especially a man of sense, from the arms of a
mistress, as it did him at last, though on another occasion.

On the other hand, though I was not without secret reproaches of my own conscience for the life I led, and that even
in the greatest height of the satisfaction I ever took, yet I
had the terrible prospect of poverty and starving, which lay
on me as a frightful spectre, so that there was no looking
behind me; but as poverty brought me into it, so fear of
poverty kept me in it, and I frequently resolved to leave it
quite off, if I could but come to lay up money enough to
maintain me: but these were thoughts of no weight, and
whenever he came to me they vanished; for his company
was so delightful, that there was no being melancholy when
he was there; the reflections were all the subject of those
hours when I was alone.

I lived six years in this happy but unhappy condition, in
which time I brought him three children, but only the first of
them lived; and though I removed twice in that six years, yet
I came back the sixth year to my first lodgings at Hammersmith: here it was that I was one morning surprised with a

kind but melancholy letter from my gentleman; intimating
that he was very ill, and was afraid he should have another
fit of sickness, but that his wife's relations being in the
house with him, it would not be practicable to have me with
him, which, however, he expressed his great dissatisfaction
in, and that he wished I could be allowed to tend and nurse
him as I did before.

I was very much concerned at this account, and was very
impatient to know how it was with him; I waited a fortnight
or thereabouts, and heard nothing, which surprised me, and
I began to be very uneasy indeed; I think, I may say, that
for the next fortnight I was near to distracted: it was my
particular difficulty, that I did not know directly where he
was; for I understood at first he was in the lodgings of his
wife's mother; but having removed myself to London, I
soon found, by the help of the direction I had for writing
my letters to him, how to inquire after him, and there I
found that he was at a house in Bloomsbury, whither he had
removed his whole family; and that his wife, and wife's
mother were in the same house, though the wife was not
suffered to know that she was in the same house with her
husband.

Here I also soon understood that he was at the last
extremity, which made me almost at the last extremity too,
to have a true account: one night I had the curiosity to
disguise myself like a servant maid, in a round cap and
straw hat, and went to the door, as sent by a lady of his
neighbourhood, where he lived before, and giving master and
mistresses service, I said I was sent to know how Mr. ———
did, and how he had rested that night: in delivering this
message I got the opportunity I desired, for speaking with
one of the maids, I held a long gossip's tale with her, and
had all the particulars of his illness, which I found was a
pleurisy, attended with a cough and fever; she told me also
who was in the house, and how his wife was, who, by her
relation, they were in some hopes might recover her understanding; but as to the gentleman himself, the doctors said
there was very little hopes of him, that in the morning they
thought he had been dying, and that he was but little better
then, for they did not expect that he could live over the next
night.

This was heavy news for me, and I began now to see an

end of my prosperity, and to see that it was well I had played the good housewife, and saved something while he was alive, for now I had no view of my own living before me.

It lay very heavy upon my mind too, that I had a son, a fine lovely boy, above five years old, and no provision made for it, at least that I knew of; with these considerations, and a sad heart, I went home that evening, and began to cast with myself how I should live, and in what manner to bestow myself, for the residue of my life.

You may be sure I could not rest without inquiring again very quickly what was become of him; and not venturing to go myself, I sent several sham messengers, till after a fortnight's waiting longer, I found that there was hopes of his life, though he was still very ill; then I abated my sending to the house, and in some time after I learnt in the neighbourhood that he was about house, and then that he was abroad again.

I made no doubt then but that I should soon hear of him, and began to comfort myself with my circumstances, being, as I thought, recovered; I waited a week, and two weeks, and with much surprise, near two months, and heard nothing, but that being recovered he was gone into the country for the air, after his distemper; after this it was yet two months more, and then I understood he was come to his city house again, but still I heard nothing from him.

I had written several letters for him, and directed them as usual, and found two or three of them had been called for, but not the rest. I wrote again in a more pressing manner than ever, and in one of them let him know that I must be forced to wait on him myself, representing my circumstances, the rent of lodgings to pay. and the provision for the child wanting, and my own deplorable condition, destitute of subsistence after his most solemn engagement to take care of and provide for me; I took a copy of this letter, and finding it lay at the house near a month, and was not called for, I found means to have the copy of it put into his hands at a coffee-house where I had found he had used to go.

This letter forced an answer from him, by which, though I found I was to be abandoned, yet I found he had sent a letter to me some time before, desiring me to go down to Bath again; its contents I shall come to presently.

It is true that sick beds are the times, when such correspondences as this are looked on with different countenances,
and seen with other eyes, than we saw them with before :
my lover had been at the gates of death, and at the very
brink of eternity; and, it seems, struck with a due remorse,
and with sad reflections upon his past life of gallantry and
levity; and among the rest, his criminal correspondence
with me, which was indeed neither more or less than a long
continued life of adultery, had represented itself as it really
was, not as it had been formerly thought by him to be, and
he looked upon it now with a just abhorrence.

I cannot but observe also, and leave it for the direction of
my sex in such cases of pleasure, that whenever sincere
repentance succeeds such a crime as this, there never fails to
attend a hatred of the object; and the more the affection
might seem to be before, the hatred will be more in proportion. It will always be so, indeed it cannot be otherwise;
for there cannot be a true and sincere abhorrence of the
offence, and the love to the cause of it remain; there will,
with an abhorrence of the sin, be found a detestation of the
fellow-sinner; you can expect no other.

I found it so here, though good manners, and justice in this
gentleman, kept him from carrying it on to any extreme;
but the short history of his part in this affair was thus; he
perceived by my last letter, and by the rest, which he went
for after, that I was not gone to Bath, and that his first letter
had not come to my hand, upon which he writes me this
following :

Madam,
I am surprised that my letter dated the 8th of last month,
did not come to your hand; I give you my word it was
delivered at your lodgings, and to the hands of your maid.

I need not acquaint you with what has been my condition
for some time past; and how, having been at the edge of the
grave, I am, by the unexpected and undeserved mercy of
heaven, restored again : in the condition I have been in, it
cannot be strange to you that our unhappy correspondence
has not been the least of the burthens which lay upon my
conscience : I need say no more ; those things that must be
repented of, must also be reformed.

I wish you would think of going back to Bath; I enclose

you here a bill for 50*l.* for clearing yourself at your lodgings, and carrying you down, and hope it will be no surprise to you to add, that on this account only, and not for any offence given me on your side, I can *see you no more;* I will take due care of the child, leave him where he is, or take him with you as you please; I wish you the like reflections, and that they may be to your advantage; I am, &c.

I was struck with this letter, as with a thousand wounds; the reproaches of my own conscience were such as I cannot express, for I was not blind to my own crime; and I reflected that I might with less offence have continued with my brother, since there was no crime in our marriage on that score, neither of us knowing it.

But I never once reflected that I was all this while a married woman, a wife to Mr. —— the linendraper, who though he had left me by the necessity of his circumstances, had no power to discharge me from the marriage contract which was between us, or to give me a legal liberty to marry again; so that I had been no less than a whore and an adulteress all this while. I then reproached myself with the liberties I had taken, and how I had been a snare to this gentleman, and that indeed I was principal in the crime; that now he was mercifully snatched out of the gulf by a convincing work upon his mind, but that I was left as if I was abandoned by heaven to a continuing in my wickedness.

Under these reflections I continued very pensive and sad for near a month, and did not go down to Bath, having no inclination to be with the woman whom I was with before, lest, as I thought, she should prompt me to some wicked course of life again, as she had done; and besides, I was loath she should know I was cast off as above.

And now I was greatly perplexed about my little boy; it was death to me to part with the child, and yet when I considered the danger of being one time or other left with him to keep without being able to support him, I then resolved to leave him; but then I concluded to be near him myself too, that I might have the satisfaction of seeing him, without the care of providing for him. So I sent my gentleman a short letter that I had obeyed his orders in all things but that of going back to Bath; that however parting from him was a wound to me that I could never recover, yet that I was fully satisfied his reflections were just, and would be very far from desiring to obstruct his reformation.

Then I represented my own circumstances to him in the most moving terms. I told him that those unhappy distresses which first moved him to a generous friendship for me, would, I hoped, move him to a little concern for me now, though the criminal part of our correspondence, which I believe neither of us intended to fall into at that time, was broken off; that I desired to repent as sincerely as he had done, but entreated him to put me in some condition that I might not be exposed to temptations from the frightful prospect of poverty and distress; and if he had the least apprehensions of my being troublesome to him, I begged he would put me in a posture to go back to my mother in Virginia, from whence he knew I came, and that would put an end to all his fears on that account; I concluded, that if he would send me 50*l.* more to facilitate my going away, I would send him back a general release, and would promise never to disturb him more with any importunities; unless it were to hear of the well-doing of the child, who, if I found my mother living, and my circumstances able, I would send for, and take him also off of his hands.

This was indeed all a cheat thus far, viz., that I had no intention to go to Virginia, as the account of my former affairs there may convince anybody of; but the business was to get this last 50*l.* of him, if possible, knowing well enough it would be the last penny I was ever to expect.

However, the argument I used, namely, of giving him a general release, and never troubling him any more, prevailed effectually, and he sent me a bill for the money by a person who brought with him a general release for me to sign, and which I frankly signed; and thus, though full sore against my will, a final end was put to this affair.

And here I cannot but reflect upon the unhappy consequence of too great freedoms between persons stated as we were, upon the pretence of innocent intentions, love of friendship, and the like; for the flesh has generally so great a share in those friendships, that it is great odds but inclination prevails at last over the most solemn resolutions; and that vice breaks in at the breaches of decency, which really innocent friendship ought to preserve with the greatest strictness; but I leave the readers of these things to their own just reflections, which they will be more able to make effectual than I, who so soon forgot myself, and am therefore but a very indifferent monitor.

I was now a single person again, as I may call myself; I was loosed from all the obligations either of wedlock or mistressship in the world; except my husband the linendraper, whom I having not now heard from in almost fifteen years, nobody could blame me for thinking myself entirely freed from; seeing also he had at his going away told me, that if I did not hear frequently from him, I should conclude he was dead, and I might freely marry again to whom I pleased.

I now began to cast up my accounts; I had by many letters, and much importunity, and with the intercession of my mother too, had a second return of some goods from my brother, as I now call him, in Virginia, to make up the damage of the cargo I brought away with me, and this too was upon the condition of my sealing a general release to him, which though I thought hard, yet I was obliged to promise. I managed so well in this case, that I got my goods away before the release was signed, and then I always found something or other to say to evade the thing, and to put off the signing it at all; till at length I pretended I must write to my brother, before I could do it.

Including this recruit, and before I got the last 50*l.*, I found my strength to amount, put all together, to about 400*l.*, so that with that I had above 450*l.* I had saved 100*l.* more, but I met with a disaster with that, which was this; that a goldsmith in whose hands I had trusted it, broke, so I lost 70*l.* of my money, the man's composition not making above 30*l.* out of his 100*l.* I had a little plate, but not much, and was well enough stocked with clothes and linen.

With this stock I had the world to begin again; but you are to consider that I was not now the same woman as when I lived at Rotherhithe; for first of all I was near twenty years older, and did not look the better for my age, nor for my rambles to Virginia and back again; and though I omitted nothing that might set me out to advantage, except painting, for that I never stooped to, yet there would always be some difference seen between five-and-twenty and two-and-forty.

I cast about innumerable ways for my future state of life, and began to consider very seriously what I should do, but nothing offered; I took care to make the world take me for

something more than I was, and had it given out that I was
a fortune, and that my estate was in my own hands, the last
of which was very true, the first of it was as above : I had
no acquaintance, which was one of my worst misfortunes,
and the consequence of that was, I had no adviser, and above
all, I had nobody to whom I could in confidence commit the
secret of my circumstances to ; and I found by experience,
that to be friendless is the worst condition, next to being
in want, that a woman can be reduced to: I say a woman,
because 'tis evident men can be their own advisers, and their
own directors, and know how to work themselves out of
difficulties and into business better than women ; but if a
woman has no friend to communicate her affairs to, and to
advise and assist her, 'tis ten to one but she is undone ; nay,
and the more money she has, the more danger she is in of
being wronged and deceived ; and this was my case in the
affair of the 100l. which I left in the hand of the goldsmith,
as above, whose credit, it seems, was upon the ebb before,
but I that had nobody to consult with, knew nothing of it,
and so lost my money.

When a woman is thus left desolate and void of counsel,
she is just like a bag of money or a jewel dropt on the highway, which is a prey to the next comer ; if a man of virtue
and upright principles happens to find it, he will have it
cried, and the owner may come to hear of it again ; but how
many times shall such a thing fall into hands that will make
no scruple of seizing it for their own, to once that it shall
come into good hands.

This was evidently my case, for I was now a loose unguided
creature, and had no help, no assistance, no guide for my
conduct ; I knew what I aimed at, and what I wanted, but
knew nothing how to pursue the end by direct means ; I
wanted to be placed in a settled state of living, and had I
happened to meet with a sober good husband, I should have
been as true a wife to him as virtue itself could have formed :
if I had been otherwise, the vice came in always at the door
of necessity, not at the door of inclination ; and I understood
too well, by the want of it, what the value of a settled life was,
to do anything to forfeit the felicity of it ; nay, I should have
made the better wife for all the difficulties I had passed through,
by a great deal; nor did I in any of the times that I had been a

wife, give my husbands the least uneasiness on account of my behaviour.

But all this was nothing; I found no encouraging prospect; I waited, I lived regularly, and with as much frugality as became my circumstances, but nothing offered; nothing presented, and the main stock wasted apace; what to do I knew not, the terror of approaching poverty lay hard upon my spirits : I had some money, but where to place it I knew not, nor would the interest of it maintain me, at least not in London.

At length a new scene opened : there was in the house where I lodged. a north-country gentlewoman, and nothing was more frequent in her discourse, than her account of the cheapness of provisions, and the easy way of living in her country; how plentiful and how cheap everything was, what good company they kept, and the like; till at last I told her she almost tempted me to go and live in her country; for I that was a widow, though I had sufficient to live on, yet had no way of increasing it, and that London was an extravagant place; that I found I could not live here under 100*l.* a-year, unless I kept no company, no servant, made no appearance, and buried myself in privacy, as if I was obliged to it by necessity.

I should have observed, that she was always made to believe, as everybody else was, that I was a great fortune, or at least that I had three or four thousand pounds, if not more, and all in my own hands; and she was mighty sweet upon me when she thought me inclined in the least to go into her country; she said she had a sister lived near Liverpool, that her brother was a considerable gentleman there, and had a great estate also in Ireland; that she would go down there in about two months, and if I would give her my company thither, I should be as welcome as herself for a month or more as I pleased, till I should see how I liked the country; and if I thought fit to live there, she would undertake they would take care, though they did not entertain lodgers themselves, they would recommend me to some agreeable family, where I should be placed to my content.

If this woman had known my real circumstances, she would never have laid so many snares, and taken so many weary steps to catch a poor desolate creature that was good for little when it was caught; and indeed I, whose case was almost desperate, and thought I could not be much worse, was not very anxious about what might befall me, provided they did me no personal injury; so I suffered myself, though not without a great deal of invitation, and great professions of sincere friendship and real kindness, I say, I suffered myself to be prevailed upon to go with her, and accordingly I put myself in a posture for a journey, though I did not absolutely know whither I was to go.

And now I found myself in great distress; what little I had in the world was all in money, except as before, a little plate, some linen, and my clothes; as for household stuff I had little or none, for I had lived always in lodgings; but I had not one friend in the world with whom to trust that little I had, or to direct me how to dispose of it; I thought of the bank, and of the other companies in London, but I had no friend to commit the management of it too, and to keep and carry about me bank bills, tallies, orders, and such things, I looked upon as unsafe; that if they were lost, my money was lost, and then I was undone; and on the other hand I might be robbed, and perhaps murdered in a strange place for them; and what to do I knew not.

It came into my thoughts one morning that I would go to the bank myself, where I had often been to receive the interest of some bills I had, and where I had found the clerk, to whom I applied myself, very honest to me, and particularly so fair one time, that when I had mistold my money, and taken less than my due, and was coming away, he set me to rights and gave me the rest, which he might have put into his own pocket.

I went to him, and asked if he would trouble himself to be my adviser, who was a poor friendless widow, and knew not what to do. He told me, if I desired his opinion of anything within the reach of his business, he would do his endeavour that I should not be wronged, but that he would also help me to a good sober person of his acquaintance, who was a clerk in such business too, though not in their house, whose judgment was good, and whose honesty I might depend upon; for, added he, I will answer for him, and for every step he takes; if he wrongs you, madam, of one farthing, it shall lie at my door; and he delights to assist people in such cases, he does it as an act of charity.

I was a little at a stand at this discourse, but after some

pause I told him I had rather have depended upon him, because I had found him honest, but if that could not be, I
would take his recommendation sooner than any one's else.
I dare say, madam, says he, that you will be as well satisfied
with my friend as with me, and he is thoroughly able to assist
you, which I am not. It seems he had his hands full of the
business of the bank, and had engaged to meddle with no
other business than that of his office : he added, that his
friend should take nothing of me for his advice or assistance,
and this indeed encouraged me.

He appointed the same evening, after the bank was shut,
for me to meet him and his friend : as soon as I saw his
friend, and he began but to talk of the affair, I was fully
satisfied I had a very honest man to deal with, his countenance
spoke it, and his character, as I heard afterwards, was everywhere so good, that I had no room for any more doubts upon me.

After the first meeting, in which I only said what I had
said before, he appointed me to come the next day, telling me
I might in the mean time satisfy myself of him by inquiry,
which, however, I knew not how to do, having no acquaintance myself.

Accordingly I met him the next day, when I entered more
freely with him into my case ; I told him my circumstances at
large, that I was a widow come over from America, perfectly
desolate and friendless : that I had a little money, and but a
little, and was almost distracted for fear of losing it, having
no friend in the world to trust with the management of it :
that I was going into the north of England to live cheap, that
my stock might not waste ; that I would willingly lodge my
money in the bank, but that I durst not carry the bills about
me; and how to correspond about it, or with whom, I knew not.

He told me I might lodge the money in the bank as an account, and its being entered in the books would entitle me to
the money at any time; and if I was in the north I might
draw bills on the cashier, and receive it when I would ; but
that then it would be esteemed as running cash, and the bank
would give no interest for it; that I might buy stock with
it, and so it would lie in store for me, but that then if I
wanted to dispose of it, I must come up to town to transfer
it, and even it would be with some difficulty I should receive
the half-yearly dividend, unless I was here in person, or had
some friend I could trust with having the stock in his name

to do it for me, and that would have the same difficulty in it as before; and with that he looked hard at me and smiled a little. At last, says he, Why do you not get a head steward, madam, that may take you and your money together, and then you would have the trouble taken off of your hands? Ay, sir, and the money too it may be, said I, for truly I find the hazard that way is as much as 'tis t'other way; but I remember I said secretly to myself, I wish you would ask me the question fairly, I would consider very seriously on it before I said NO.

He went on a good way with me, and I thought once or twice he was in earnest, but to my real affliction, I found at last he had a wife; but when he owned he had a wife he shook his head, and said with some concern, that indeed he had a wife, and no wife; I began to think he had been in the condition of my late lover, and that his wife had been lunatic, or some such thing. However, we had not much more discourse at that time, but he told me he was in too much hurry of business then, but that if I would come home to his house after their business was over, he would consider what might be done for me, to put my affairs in a posture of security: I told him I would come, and desired to know where he lived: he gave me a direction in writing, and, when he gave it me he read it to me, and said, There 'tis, madam, if you dare trust yourself with me. Yes, sir, said I, I believe I may venture to trust you with myself, for you have a wife you say, and I don't want a husband; besides, I dare trust you with my money, which is all I have in the world, and if that were gone, I may trust myself anywhere.

He said some things in jest that were very handsome and mannerly, and would have pleased me very well if they had been in earnest; but that passed over, I took the directions and appointed to be at his house at seven o'clock the same evening.

When I came he made several proposals for my placing my money in the bank, in order to my having interest for it; but still some difficulty or other came in the way, which he objected as not safe; and I found such a sincere disinterested honesty in him, that I began to think I had certainly found the honest man I wanted; and that I could never put myself into better hands; so I told him with a great deal of frankness that I had never met with a man or woman yet that I could trust, or in whom I could think myself safe, but that

I saw he was so disinterestedly concerned for my safety, that I would freely trust him with the management of that little I had, if he would accept to be steward for a poor widow that could give him no salary.

He smiled, and standing up, with great respect saluted me; he told me he could not but take it very kindly that I had so good an opinion of him; that he would not deceive me, that he would do anything in his power to serve me, and expect no salary; but that he could not by any means accept of a trust that might bring him to be suspected of self-interest, and that if I should die he might have disputes with my executors, which he should be very loath to encumber himself with.

I told him if those were all his objections I would soon remove them, and convince him that there was not the least room for any difficulty: for that, first, as for suspecting him, if ever, now was the time to suspect him, and not to put the trust into his hands; and whenever I did suspect him, he could but throw it up then, and refuse to go on; then, as to executors, I assured him I had no heirs, nor any relations in England, and I would have neither heirs or executors but himself, unless I should alter my condition, and then his trust and trouble should cease together, which, however, I had no prospect of yet; but I told him if I died as I was, it should be all his own, and he would deserve it by being so faithful to me, as I was satisfied he would be.

He changed his countenance at this discourse, and asked me, how I came to have so much good-will for him? and looking very much pleased, said, he might very lawfully wish he was single for my sake; I smiled, and told him, that as he was not, my offer could have no design upon him, and to wish, was not to be allowed, 'twas criminal to his wife.

He told me I was wrong; for, says he, as I said before, I have a wife and no wife, and 'twould be no sin to wish her hanged. I know nothing of your circumstances that way, sir, said I; but it cannot be innocent to wish your wife dead. I tell you, says he again, she is a wife and no wife; you don't know what I am, or what she is.

That's true, said I, sir, I don't know what you are, but I believe you to be an honest man, and that's the cause of all my confidence in you.

Well, well, says he, and so I am, but I am something else

too, madam; for, says he, to be plain with you, I am a cuckold, and she is a whore; he spoke it in a kind of jest, but it was with such an awkward smile, that I perceived it stuck very close to him, and he looked dismally when he said it.

That alters the case indeed, sir, said I, as to that part you were speaking of; but a cuckold you know may be an honest man, it does not alter that case at all; besides I think, said I, since your wife is so dishonest to you, you are too honest to her, to own her for your wife; but that, said I, is what I have nothing to do with. Nay, says he, I do think to clear my hands of her, for to be plain with you, madam, added he, I am no contented cuckold neither: on the other hand, I assure you it provokes me to the highest degree, but I can't help myself; she that will be a whore, will be a whore.

I waved the discourse, and began to talk of my business, but I found he could not have done with it, so I let him alone, and he went on to tell me all the circumstances of his case, too long to relate here; particularly, that having been out of England some time before he came to the post he was in, she had had two children in the mean time by an officer in the army; and that when he came to England, and, upon her submission, took her again, and maintained her very well, yet she run away from him with a linendraper's apprentice, robbed him of what she could come at, and continued to live from him still; so that, madam, says he, she is a whore not by necessity, which is the common bait, but by inclination, and for the sake of the vice.

Well, I pitied him, and wished him well rid of her, and still would have talked of my business, but it would not do; at last he looked steadily at me, Look you, madam, says he, you came to ask advice of me, and I will serve you as faithfully as if you were my own sister; but I must turn the tables, since you oblige me to do it, and are so friendly to me, and I think I must ask advice of you; tell me what must a poor abused fellow do with a whore? what can I do to do myself justice upon her?

Alas, sir, says I, 'tis a case too nice for me to advise in, but it seems to me she has run away from you, so you are rid of her fairly; what can you desire more? Ay, she is gone indeed, said he, but I am not clear of her for all that. That's true, says I, she may indeed run you into debt, but the law has furnished you with methods to prevent that also; you may cry her down as they call it.

No, no, says he, that is not the case, I have taken care of all that; 'tis not that part that I speak of, but I would be rid of her that I might marry again.

Well, sir, says I, then you must divorce her; if you can prove what you say, you may certainly get that done, and then you are free.

That's very tedious and expensive, says he.

Why, says I, if you can get any woman you like, to take your word, I suppose your wife would not dispute the liberty with you that she takes herself.

Ay, says he, but it would be hard to bring an honest woman to do that; and for the other sort, says he, I have had enough of her to meddle with any more whores.

It occurred to me presently, I would have taken your word with all my heart, if you had but asked me the question; but that was to myself: to him I replied, Why you shut the door against any honest woman accepting you, for you condemn all that should venture upon you, and conclude, that a woman that takes you now can't be honest.

Why, says he, I wish you would satisfy me that an honest woman would take me, I'd venture it; and then turns short upon me, Will you take me, madam?

That's not a fair question, says I, after what you have said; however, lest you should think I wait only a recantation of it, I shall answer you plainly, No not I, my business is of another kind with you, and I did not expect you would have turned my serious application to you in my distracted case, into a comedy.

Why, madam, says he, my case is as distracted as yours can be, and I stand in as much need of advice as you do, for I think if I have not relief somewhere, I shall be mad myself, and I know not what course to take, I protest to you.

Why sir, says I, 'tis easier to give advice in your case than mine. Speak then, says he, I beg of you, for now you encourage me.

Why, says I, if your case is so plain, you may be legally divorced, and then you may find honest women enough to ask the question of fairly; the sex is not so scarce that you can want a wife.

Well then, said he, I am in earnest, I'll take your advice; but shall I ask you one question seriously beforehand?

Any question, said I, but that you did before.

No, that answer will not do, said he, for in short that is the question I shall ask.

You may ask what questions you please, but you have my answer to that already, said I; besides, sir, said I, can you think so ill of me, as that I would give any answer to such a question beforehand? can any woman alive believe you in earnest, or think you design anything but to banter her?

Well, well, says he, I do not banter you, I am in earnest; consider of it.

But, sir, says I, a little gravely, I came to you about my own business; I beg of you to let me know what you will advise me to do?

I will be prepared, says he, against you come again.

Nay, says I, you have forbid my coming any more.

Why so? said he, and looked a little surprised.

Because, said I, you can't expect I should visit you on the account you talk of.

Well, says he, you shall promise to come again however, and I will not say any more of it till I have the divorce: but I desire you'll prepare to be better conditioned when that's done, for you shall be the woman, or I will not be divorced at all: I owe it to your unlooked-for kindness, if to nothing else, but I have other reasons too.

He could not have said anything in the world that pleased me better; however, I knew that the way to secure him was to stand off while the thing was so remote, as it appeared to be, and that it was time enough to accept of it when he was able to perform it; so I said very respectfully to him, it was time enough to consider of these things, when he was in a condition to talk of them; in the mean time I told him, I was going a great way from him, and he would find objects enough to please him better. We broke off here for the present, and he made me promise him to come again the next day, for my own business, which after some pressing I did; though had he seen farther into me, I wanted no pressing on that account.

I came the next evening accordingly, and brought my maid with me, to let him see that I kept a maid: he would have had me let the maid have stayed, but I would not, but ordered her aloud to come for me again about nine o'clock: but he forbid that, and told me he would see me safe home, which I was not very well pleased with, supposing he might do that to know where I lived, and inquire into my character and circumstances: however, I ventured that, for all the people there knew of me was to my advantage; and all the character he had of me was, that I was a woman of fortune, and that I was a very modest sober body; which whether true or not in the main, yet you may see how necessary it is for all women who expect anything in the world, to preserve the character of their virtue, even when perhaps they may have sacrificed the thing itself.

I found, and was not a little pleased with it, that he had provided a supper for me: I found also he lived very handsomely, and had a house very handsomely furnished, and which I was rejoiced at indeed, for I looked upon it as all my own.

We had now a second conference upon the subject-matter of the last: he laid his business very home indeed; he protested his affection to me, and indeed I had no room to doubt it; he declared that it began from the first moment I talked with him, and long before I had mentioned leaving my effects with him. 'Tis no matter when it began, thought I; if it will but hold, 'twill be well enough. He then told me how much the offer I had made of trusting him with my effects had engaged him; so I intended it should, thought I, but then I thought you had been a single man too. After we had supped, I observed he pressed me very hard to drink two or three glasses of wine, which however I declined, but drank one glass or two: he then told me he had a proposal to make to me, which I should promise him I would not take ill, if I should not grant it; I told him I hoped he would make no dishonourable proposal to me, especially in his own house, and that if it was such, I desired he would not mention it, that I might not be obliged to offer any resentment to him that did not become the respect I professed for him, and the trust I had placed in him, in coming to his house; and begged of him he would give me leave to go away, and accordingly began to put on my gloves, and prepare to be gone, though at the same time I no more intended it than he intended to let me.

Well, he importuned me not to talk of going; he assured me, he was very far from offering any such thing to me that was dishonourable, and if I thought so, he would choose to say no more of it.

That part I did not relish at all; I told him, I was ready to hear anything that he had to say, depending that he would say nothing unworthy of himself, or unfit for me to hear. Upon this, he told me his proposal was this; that I would marry him, though he had not yet obtained the divorce from the whore his wife; and to satisfy me that he meant honourably, he would promise not to desire me to live with him, or go to bed to him till the divorce was obtained. My heart said yes to this offer at first word, but it was necessary to play the hypocrite a little more with him; so I seemed to decline the motion with some warmth, as unfair, told him that such a proposal could be of no signification, but to entangle us both in great difficulties; for if he should not at last obtain the divorce, yet we could not dissolve the marriage, neither could we proceed in it; so that if he was disappointed in the divorce, I left him to consider what a condition we should both be in.

In short, I carried on the argument against this so far, that I convinced him it was not a proposal that had any sense in it; then he went from it to another, viz., that I would sign and seal a contract with him, conditioning to marry him as soon as the divorce was obtained, and to be void if he could not get it.

I told him that was more rational than the other; but as this was the first time that ever I could imagine him weak enough to be in earnest, I did not use to say yes at first asking, I would consider of it. I played with this lover, as an angler does with a trout: I found I had him fast on the hook, so I jested with his new proposal, and put him off: I told him he knew little of me, and bade him inquire about me; I let him also go home with me to my lodging, though I would not ask him to go in, for I told him it was not decent.

In short, I ventured to avoid signing a contract, and the reason why I did it, was because the lady that had invited me to go with her into Lancashire insisted so positively upon it, and promised me such great fortunes, and fine things there, that I was tempted to go and try; perhaps, said I, I may mend myself very much, and then I made no scruple of quitting my honest citizen, whom I was not so much in love with as not to leave him for a richer.

In a word, I avoided a contract; but told him I would go

into the north, that he would know where to write to me by
the business I had intrusted with him; that I would give him
a sufficient pledge of my respect for him, for I would leave
almost all I had in the world in his hands; and I would thus
far give him my word, that as soon as he had sued out the
divorce, if he would send me an account of it, I would come
up to London, and that then we would talk seriously of the
matter.

It was a base design I went with, that I must confess,
though I was invited thither with a design much worse, as
the sequel will discover; well, I went with my friend as I
called her, into Lancashire; all the way we went she caressed
me with the utmost appearance of a sincere undissembled
affection; treated me, except my coach-hire, all the way;
and her brother brought a gentleman's coach to Warrington
to receive us, and we were carried from thence to Liverpool
with as much ceremony as I could desire.

We were also entertained at a merchant's house in Liverpool three or four days very handsomely; I forbear to tell his
name, because of what followed; then she told me she would
carry me to an uncle's house of hers where we should be nobly
entertained; and her uncle, as she called him, sent a coach
and four horses for us, and we were carried near forty miles
I know not whither.

We came however to a gentleman's seat, where was a
numerous family, a large park, extraordinary company indeed,
and where she was called cousin; I told her if she had
resolved to bring me into such company as this, she should
have let me have furnished myself with better clothes; the
ladies took notice of that, and told me very genteelly, they
did not value people in their own country so much by their
clothes as they did in London; that their cousin had fully
informed them of my quality, and that I did not want clothes
to set me off; in short, they entertained me not like what I
was, but like what they thought I had been, namely, a widow
lady of a great fortune.

The first discovery I made here was, that the family were
all Roman Catholics, and the cousin too; however, nobody
in the world could behave better to me, and I had all the
civility shown that I could have had if I had been of their
opinion. The truth is, I had not so much principle of any
kind, as to be nice in point of religion; and I presently learned

to speak favourably of the Romish church; particularly I told them I saw little but the prejudice of education in all the differences that were among christians about religion, and if it had so happened that my father had been a Roman Catholic, I doubted not but I should have been as well pleased with their religion as my own.

This obliged them in the highest degree, and as I was besieged day and night with good company, and pleasant discourse, so I had two or three old ladies that lay at me upon the subject of religion too; I was so complaisant that I made no scruple to be present at their mass, and to conform to all their gestures as they showed me the pattern, but I would not come too cheap; so that I only in the main encouraged them to expect that I would turn Roman Catholic if I was instructed in the Catholic doctrine, as they called it; and so the matter rested.

I stayed here about six weeks; and then my conductor led me back to a country village, about six miles from Liverpool, where her brother, as she called him, came to visit me in his own chariot, with two footmen in a good livery; and the next thing was to make love to me. As it happened to me, one would think I could not have been cheated, and indeed I thought so myself, having a safe card at home, which I resolved not to quit unless I could mend myself very much. However, in all appearance this brother was a match worth my listening to, and the least his estate was valued at was a 1000l. a-year, but the sister said it was worth 1500l. a-year, and lay most of it in Ireland.

I that was a great fortune, and passed for such, was above being asked how much my estate was; and my false friend taking it upon a foolish hearsay, had raised it from 500l. to 5000l., and by the time she came into the country she called it 15,000l. The Irishman, for such I understood him to be, was stark mad at this bait: in short, he courted me, made me presents, and run in debt like a madman for the expenses of his courtship: he had, to give him his due, the appearance of an extraordinary fine gentleman; he was tall, well-shaped, and had an extraordinary address; talked as naturally of his park and his stables, of his horses, his game-keepers his woods, his tenants, and his servants, as if he had been i a mansion-house, and I had seen them all about me.

He never so much as asked me about my fortune or estate;

I

but assured me that when we came to Dublin he would
jointure me in 600*l.* a-year in good land; and that he would
enter into a deed of settlement, or contract here, for the performance of it.

This was such language indeed as I had not been used to,
and I was here beaten out of all my measures; I had a she-
devil in my bosom, every hour telling me how great her
brother lived : one time she would come for my orders, how
I would have my coach painted, and how lined; and another
time what clothes my page should wear : in short, my eyes
were dazzled, I had now lost my power of saying no, and to
cut the story short, I consented to be married ; but to be more
private, we were carried farther into the country, and married
by a priest, which I was assured would marry us as effectually
as a Church of England parson.

I cannot say but I had some reflections in this affair upon
the dishonourable forsaking my faithful citizen, who loved me
sincerely, and who was endeavouring to quit himself of a
scandalous whore by whom he had been barbarously used,
and promised himself infinite happiness in his new choice ;
which choice was now giving up herself to another in a
manner almost as scandalous as hers could be.

But the glittering show of a great estate and of fine things
which the deceived creature that was now my deceiver
represented every hour to my imagination, hurried me away,
and gave me no time to think of London, or of anything
there, much less of the obligation I had to a person of infinitely
more real merit than what was now before me.

But the thing was done, I was now in the arms of my new
spouse, who appeared still the same as before ; great even to
magnificence, and nothing less than a thousand pounds a-year
could support the ordinary equipage he appeared in.

After we had been married about a month, he began to
talk of my going to West-chester in order to embark for
Ireland.   However, he did not hurry me, for we stayed near
three weeks longer, and then he sent to Chester for a coach to
meet us at the Black Rock, as they call it, over against
Liverpool. Thither we went in a fine boat they call a pinnace,
with six oars ; his servants, and horses, and baggage going
in a ferry-boat.   He made his excuse to me, that he had no
acquaintance at Chester, but he would go before and get some
handsome apartments for me at a private house ; I asked him.

how long we should stay at Chester? he said, not at all, any longer than one night or two, but he would immediately hire a coach to go to Holyhead; then I told him he should by no means give himself the trouble to get private lodgings for one night or two, for that Chester being a great place, I made no doubt but there would be very good inns, and accommodation enough; so we lodged at an inn not far from the cathedral; I forgot what sign it was at.

Here my spouse, talking of my going to Ireland, asked me if I had no affairs to settle at London before we went off; I told him no, not of any great consequence, but what might be done as well by letter from Dublin: Madam, says he very respectfully, I suppose the greatest part of your estate, which my sister tells me is most of it in money in the Bank of England, lies secure enough, but in case it required transferring, or any way altering its property, it might be necessary to go up to London, and settle those things before we went over.

I seemed to look strange at it, and told him I knew not what he meant; that I had no effects in the Bank of England that I knew of; and I hope he could not say that I had ever told him I had. No, he said, I had not told him so, but his sister had said the greatest part of my estate lay there; and I only mentioned it, my dear, said he, that if there was any occasion to settle it, or order anything about it, we might not be obliged to the hazard and trouble of another voyage back again; for, he added, that he did not care to venture me too much upon the sea.

I was surprised at this talk, and began to consider what the meaning of it must be! and it presently occurred to me that my friend, who called him brother, had represented me in colours which were not my due; and I thought that I would know the bottom of it before I went out of England, and before I should put myself into I know not whose hands, in a strange country.

Upon this I called his sister into my chamber the next morning, and letting her know the discourse her brother and I had been upon, I conjured her to tell me what she had said to him, and upon what foot it was that she had made this marriage? She owned that she had told him that I was a great fortune, and said that she was told so at London: Told so, says I warmly, did I ever tell you so? No, she said, it was true I never did tell her so, but I had said several times that

I 2

what I had was in my own disposal: I did so, returned I
very quick, but I never told you I had anything called a
fortune; no, that I had a 100*l.* or the value of a 100*l.* in the
world; and how did it consist with my being a fortune, said
I, that I should come here into the north of England with
you, only upon the account of living cheap? At these words,
which I spoke warm and high, my husband came into the
room, and I desired him to come in and sit down, for I had
something of moment to say before them both, which it was
absolutely necessary he should hear.

He looked a little disturbed at the assurance with which I
seemed to speak it, and came and sat down by me, having
first shut the door; upon which I began, for I was very much
provoked, and turning myself to him, I am afraid, says I, my
dear (for I spoke with kindness on his side), that you have a
very great abuse put upon you, and an injury done you never to
be repaired in your marrying me, which, however, as I have
had no hand in it, I desire I may be fairly acquitted of it, and
that the blame may lie where it ought and nowhere else, for I
wash my hands of every part of it. What injury can be done
me, my dear, says he, in marrying you? I hope it is to my
honour and advantage every way. I will soon explain it to
you, says I, and I fear there will be no reason to think yourself well used, but I will convince you, my dear, says I again,
that I have had no hand in it.

He looked now scared and wild, and began, I believed, to
suspect what followed; however, looking towards me, and
saying only, Go on, he sat silent, as if to hear what I had
more to say; so I went on: I asked you last night, said I,
speaking to him, if ever I made any boast to you of my estate,
or ever told you I had any estate in the Bank of England, or
anywhere else, and you owned I had not, as is most true;
and I desire you will tell me here, before your sister, if ever
I gave you any reason from me to think so, or that ever we
had any discourse about it; and he owned again I had not;
but said, I had appeared always as a woman of fortune, and
he depended on it that I was so, and hoped he was not
deceived. I am not inquiring whether you have been
deceived, said I, I fear you have, and I too; but I am clearing
myself from being concerned in deceiving you.

I have been now asking your sister if ever I told her of
any fortune or estate I had, or gave her any particulars of

It; and she owns I never did : And pray madam, said I, be
so just to me, to charge me if you can, if ever I pretended to
you that I had an estate; and why if I had, should I ever
come down into this country with you on purpose to spare
that little I had, and live cheap? She could not deny one
word, but said she had been told in London that I had a
very great fortune, and that it lay in the Bank of England.

And now, dear sir, said I, turning myself to my new spouse
again, be so just to me as to tell me who has abused both
you and me so much, as to make you believe I was a fortune,
and prompt you to court me to this marriage? He could
not speak a word, but pointed to her; and after some more
pause, flew out in the most furious passion that ever I saw
a man in my life; cursing her, and calling her all the whores
and hard names he could think of; and that she had ruined
him, declaring that she had told him I had 15,000l., and that
she was to have 500l. of him for procuring this match for
him: he then added, directing his speech to me, that she was
none of his sister, but had been his whore for two years before;
that she had had 100l. of him in part of this bargain, and
that he was utterly undone if things were as I said; and in
his raving he swore he would let her heart's blood out
immediately, which frightened her and me too. She cried,
said she had been told so in the house where I lodged: but
this aggravated him more than before, that she should put so
far upon him, and run things such a length upon no other
authority than a hearsay; and then turning to me again, said
very honestly, he was afraid we were both undone; for to be
plain, my dear, I have no estate, says he; what little I had,
this devil has made me run out in putting me into this equipage.
She took the opportunity of his being earnest in talking with
me, and got out of the room, and I never saw her more.

I was confounded now as much as he, and knew not what
to say: I thought many ways that I had the worst of it, but
his saying he was undone, and that he had no estate neither,
put me into a mere distraction. Why, says I to him, this
has been a hellish juggle, for we are married here upon the
foot of a double fraud; you are undone by the disappointment it seems, and if I had had a fortune I had been cheated
too, for you say you have nothing.

You would indeed have been cheated, my dear, says he,
but you would not have been undone, for 15,000l. would have

maintained us both very handsomely in this country; and I
had resolved to have dedicated every groat of it to you; I
would not have wronged you of a shilling, and the rest I
would have made up in my affection to you, and tenderness
of you as long as I lived.

This was very honest indeed, and I really believe he spoke
as he intended, and that he was a man that was as well
qualified to make me happy, as to his temper and behaviour,
as any man ever was; but his having no estate, and being
run into debt on this ridiculous account in the country, made
all the prospect dismal and dreadful, and I knew not what
to say, or what to think.

I told him it was very unhappy, that so much love, and so
much good nature as I discovered in him, should be thus
precipitated into misery; that I saw nothing before us but ruin,
for as to me, it was my unhappiness, that what little I had
was not able to relieve us a week, and with that I pulled out a
bank-bill of 20l. and eleven guineas, which I told him I had
saved out of my little income; and that by the account that
creature had given me of the way of living in that country, I
expected it would maintain me three or four years; that if it
was taken from me, I was left destitute, and he knew what
the condition of a woman must be, if she had no money in
her pocket; however, I told him, if he would take it, there it
was.

He told me with great concern, and I thought I saw tears
in his eyes, that he would not touch it, that he abhorred the
thoughts of stripping me and making me miserable; that he
had fifty guineas left, which was all he had in the world, and
he pulled it out and threw it down on the table, bidding me
take it, though he were to starve for want of it.

I returned, with the same concern for him, that I could
not bear to hear him talk so; that on the contrary, if he could
propose any probable method of living, I would do anything
that became me, and that I would live as narrow as he could
desire.

He begged of me to talk no more at that rate, for it would
make him distracted; he said he was bred a gentleman,
though he was-reduced to a low fortune, and that there was
but one way left which he could think of, and that would not
do, unless I could answer him one question, which however
he said he would not press me to; I told him I would answer

it honestly; whether it would be to his satisfaction or no that I could not tell.

Why then my dear, tell me plainly, says he, will the little you have keep us together in any figure, or in any station or place, or will it not?

It was my happiness that I had not discovered myself, or my circumstances, at all; no, not so much as my name; and seeing there was nothing to be expected from him, however good-humoured, and however honest he seemed to be, but to live on what I knew would soon be wasted, I resolved to conceal everything but the bank-bill, and eleven guineas, and I would have been very glad to have lost that, and have been set down where he took me up. I had indeed another bank-bill about me of 30*l*., which was the whole of what I brought with me, as well to subsist on in the country, as not knowing what might offer; because this creature, the go-between that had thus betrayed us both, had made me believe strange things of marrying to my advantage, and I was not willing to be without money, whatever might happen. This bill I concealed, and that made me the freer of the rest, in consideration of his circumstances, for I really pitied him heartily.

But to return to this question, I told him I never willingly deceived him, and I never would. I was very sorry to tell him that the little I had would not subsist us: that it was not sufficient to subsist me alone in the south country, and that this was the reason that made me put myself into the hands of that woman who called him brother, she having assured me that I might board very handsomely at a town called Manchester, where I had not yet been, for about 6*l*. a-year, and my whole income not being above 15*l*. a-year, I thought I might live easy upon it, and wait for better things.

He shook his head, and remained silent, and a very melancholy evening we had; however we supped together, and lay together that night, and when we had almost supped he looked a little better, and more cheerful, and called for a bottle of wine; Come my dear, says he, though the case is bad, it is to no purpose to be dejected; Come, be as easy as you can, I will endeavour to find out some way or other to live; if you can but subsist yourself, that is better than nothing, I must try the world again; a man ought to think like a man; to be discouraged, is to yield to the misfortune.

With this he filled a glass, and drank to me, holding my hand all the while the wine went down, and protesting his main concern was for me.

It was really a true gallant spirit he was of, and it was the more grievous to me. 'Tis something of relief even to be undone by a man of honour, rather than by a scoundrel; but here the greatest disappointment was on his side, for he had really spent a great deal of money, and it was very remarkable on what poor terms she proceeded; first, the baseness of the creature herself is to be observed, who for the getting 100*l.* herself, could be content to let him spend three or four more, though perhaps it was all he had in the world, and more than all; when she had not the least ground more than a little tea-table chat, to say that I had any estate, or was a fortune, or the like. It is true the design of deluding a woman of a fortune, if I had been so, was base enough; the putting the face of great things upon poor circumstances was a fraud, and bad enough; but the case a little differed too, and that in his favour, for he was not a rake that made a trade to delude women, and as some have done, get six or seven fortunes after one another, and then rifle and run away from them; but he was already a gentleman, unfortunate and low, but had lived well; and though if I had had a fortune, I should have been enraged at the slut for betraying me, yet really for the man, a fortune would not have been ill bestowed on him, for he was a lovely person indeed, of generous principles, good sense, and of abundance of good humour.

We had a great deal of close conversation that night, for we neither of us slept much; he was as penitent, for having put all those cheats upon me, as if it had been felony, and that he was going to execution; he offered me again every shilling of the money he had about him, and said he would go into the army and seek for more.

I asked him why he would be so unkind to carry me into Ireland, when I might suppose he could not have subsisted me there? He took me in his arms; My dear, said he, I never designed to go to Ireland at all, much less to have carried you thither; but came hither to be out of the observation of the people, who had heard what I pretended to, and that nobody might ask me for money before I was furnished to supply them.

But, where then, said I, were we to have gone next?

Why, my dear, said he, I'll confess the whole scheme to you, as I had laid it; I purposed here to ask you something about your estate, as you see I did, and when you, as I expected you would, had entered into some account of the particulars, I would have made an excuse to have put off our voyage to Ireland for some time, and so have gone for London.

Then, my dear, says he, I resolved to have confessed all the circumstances of my own affairs to you, and let you know I had indeed made use of these artifices to obtain your consent to marry me, but had now nothing to do but to ask your pardon, and to tell you how abundantly I would endeavour to make you forget what was past, by the felicity of the days to come.

Truly, said I to him, I find you would soon have conquered me; and it is my affliction now, that I am not in a condition to let you see how easily I should have been reconciled to you, and have passed by all the tricks you had put upon me, in recompense of so much good humour; but my dear, said I, what can we do now? we are both undone, and what better are we for our being reconciled, seeing we have nothing to live on.

We proposed a great many things, but nothing could offer, where there was nothing to begin with. He begged me at last to talk no more of it, for, he said, I would break his heart; so we talked of other things a little, till at last he took a husband's leave of me, and so went to sleep.

He rose before me in the morning, and indeed having lain awake almost all night, I was very sleepy, and lay till near eleven o'clock, in this time he took his horses, and three servants, and all his linen and baggage, and away he went, leaving a short but moving letter for me on the table, as follows:

My dear,

I am a dog; I have abused you; but I have been drawn in to do it by a base creature, contrary to my principle, and the general practice of my life. Forgive me, my dear! I ask you pardon with the greatest sincerity; I am the most miserable of men, in having deluded you: I have been so happy to possess you, and am now so wretched as to be forced to fly from you. Forgive me, my dear, once more I say, forgive me! I am not able to see you ruined by me, and myself unable to support you. Our marriage is nothing; I

shall never be able to see you again; I here discharge you
from it; if you can marry to your advantage do not decline
it on my account; I here swear to you on my faith, and on
the word of a man of honour, I will never disturb your repose
if I should know of it, which however is not likely: on the
other hand, if you should not marry, and if good fortune
should befall me, it shall be all yours wherever you are.

I have put some of the stock of money I have left into your
pocket; take places for yourself and your maid in the stage
coach, and go for London; I hope it will bear your charges
thither, without breaking into your own. Again I sincerely
ask your pardon, and will do so as often as I shall ever
think of you.

Adieu, my dear, for ever!

I am yours most affectionately,

J. E.

Nothing that ever befell me in my life, sunk so deep into
my heart as this farewell: I reproached him a thousand times
in my thoughts for leaving me, for I would have gone with
him through the world, if I had begged my bread. I felt in
my pocket, and there I found ten guineas, his gold watch, and
two little rings, one a small diamond ring, worth only about
6l., and the other a plain gold ring.

I sat down and looked upon these things two hours together,
and scarce spoke a word, till my maid interrupted me, by
telling me my dinner was ready: I eat but little, and after
dinner I fell into a violent fit of crying, every now and then
calling him by his name, which was James; O Jemmy! said
I, come back, come back, I'll give you all I have; I'll beg,
I'll starve with you. And thus I ran raving about the room
several times, and then sat down between whiles, and then
walked about again, called upon him to come back, and then
cried again; and thus I passed the afternoon, till about seven
o'clock, when it was near dusk in the evening, being August,
when to my unspeakable surprise he comes back into the inn,
and comes directly up into my chamber.

I was in the greatest confusion imaginable, and so was he
too: I could not imagine what should be the occasion of it;
and began to be at odds with myself whether to be glad or
sorry; but my affection biassed all the rest, and it was impossible to conceal my joy, which was too great for smiles,

for it burst out into tears. He was no sooner entered the room, but he ran to me and took me in his arms, holding me fast, and almost stopping my breath with his kisses, but spoke not a word; at length I began. My dear, said I, how could you go away from me? to which he gave no answer, for it was impossible for him to speak.

When our ecstasies were a little over, he told me he was gone above fifteen miles, but it was not in his power to go any farther, without coming back to see me again, and to take his leave of me once more.

I told him how I had passed my time, and how loud I had called him to come back again; he told me he heard me very plain upon Delamere Forest, at a place about twelve miles off. I smiled. Nay, says he, do not think I am in jest, for if ever I heard your voice in my life, I heard you call me aloud, and sometimes I thought I saw you running after me. Why, said I, what did I say? for I had not named the words to him. You called aloud, says he, and said, O Jemmy! O Jemmy! come back, come back.

I laughed at him. My dear, says he, do not laugh, for depend upon it, I heard your voice as plain as you hear mine now; if you please, I'll go before a magistrate and make oath of it; I then began to be amazed and surprised, and indeed frighted, and told him what I had really done, and how I had called after him, as above. When we had amused ourselves awhile about this, I said to him, Well, you shall go away from me no more, I'll go all over the world with you rather. He told me, it would be a very difficult thing for him to leave me, but since it must be, he hoped I would make it as easy to me as I could; but as for him, it would be his destruction, that he foresaw.

However, he told me that he had considered he had left me to travel to London alone, which was a long journey; and that as he might as well go that way as any way else, he was resolved to see me hither, or near it; and if he did go away then without taking his leave, I should not take it ill of him; and this he made me promise.

He told me how he had dismissed his three servants, sold their horses, and sent the fellows away to seek their fortunes, and all in a little time, at a town on the road, I know not where; and, say he, it cost me some tears all alone by myself, to think how much happier they were than their master, for they could go to the next gentleman's house to see for a service, whereas, said he, I knew not whither to go, or what to do with myself.

I told him I was so completely miserable in parting with him, that I could not be worse; and that now he was come again, I would not go from him, if he would take me with him, let him go whither he would. And in the mean time I agreed that we would go together to London; but I could not be brought to consent he should go away at last, and not take his leave of me; but told him jesting, that if he did, I would call him back again as loud as I did before. Then I pulled out his watch, and gave it him back, and his two rings, and his ten guineas; but he would not take them, which made me very much suspect that he resolved to go off upon the road, and leave me.

The truth is, the circumstances he was in, the passionate expressions of his letter, the kind gentle manly treatment I had from him in all the affair, with the concern he showed for me in it, his manner of parting with that large share which he gave me of his little stock left, all these had joined to make such impressions on me, that I could not bear the thoughts of parting with him.

Two days after this we quitted Chester, I in the stage-coach, and he on horseback; I dismissed my maid at Chester; he was very much against my being without a maid, but she being hired in the country (keeping no servant at London), I told him it would have been barbarous to have taken the poor wench, and have turned her away as soon as I came to town; and it would also have been a needless charge on the road; so I satisfied him, and he was easy on that score.

He came with me as far as Dunstable, within thirty miles of London, and then he told me fate and his own misfortunes obliged him to leave me, and that it was not convenient for him to go to London, for reasons which it was of no value to me to know, and I saw him preparing to go. The stage-coach we were in did not usually stop at Dunstable, but I desiring it for a quarter of an hour, they were content to stand at an inn-door a while, and we went into the house.

Being in the inn, I told him I had but one favour more to ask him, and that was, that since he could not go any farther, he would give me leave to stay a week or two in the town with him, that we might in that time think of something to prevent such a ruinous thing to us both, as a final separation would be; and that I had something of moment to offer to him, which perhaps he might find practicable to our advantage.

This was too reasonable a proposal to be denied, so he called the landlady of the house, and told her his wife was taken ill, and so ill that she could not think of going any farther in a stage-coach, which had tired her almost to death, and asked if she could not get us a lodging for two or three days in a private house where I might rest me a little, for the journey had been too much for me? The landlady, a good sort of a woman, well-bred, and very obliging, came immediately to see me; told me, she had two or three very good rooms in a part of the house quite out of the noise, and if I saw them she did not doubt but I would like them, and I should have one of her maids, that should do nothing else but wait on me; this was so very kind, that I could not but accept of it; so I went to look on the rooms, and liked them very well, and indeed they were extraordinarily furnished, and very pleasant lodgings; so we paid the stage-coach, took out our baggage, and resolved to stay here awhile.

Here I told him I would live with him now till all my money was spent, but would not let him spend a shilling of his own: we had some kind squabble about that, but I told him it was the last time I was like to enjoy his company, and I desired that he would let me be master in that thing only, and he should govern in everything else; so he acquiesced.

Here one evening, taking a walk into the fields, I told him I would now make the proposal to him I had told him of; accordingly I related to him how I had lived in Virginia, that I had a mother, I believed was alive there still, though my husband was dead some years; I told him that had not my effects miscarried, which by the way I magnified pretty much, I might have been fortune good enough to him to have kept us from being parted in this manner. Then I entered into the manner of people's settling in those countries, how they had a quantity of land given them by the constitution of the place; and if not, that it might be purchased at so easy a rate that it was not worth naming.

I then gave him a full and distinct account of the nature

of planting, how with carrying over but two or three hundred pounds' value in English goods, with some servants and tools, a man of application would presently lay a foundation for a family, and in a few years would raise an estate.

I let him into the nature of the product of the earth, how the ground was cured and prepared, and what the usual increase of it was; and demonstrated to him, that in a very few years, with such a beginning, we should be as certain of being rich, as we were now certain of being poor.

He was surprised at my discourse; for we made it the whole subject of our conversation for near a week together, in which time I laid it down in black and white, as we say, that it was morally impossible, with a supposition of any reasonable good conduct, but that we must thrive there and do very well.

Then I told him what measures I would take to raise such a sum as 300*l.* or thereabouts; and I argued with him how good a method it would be to put an end to our misfortunes, and restore our circumstances in the world, to what we had both expected; and I added, that after seven years we might be in a posture to leave our plantation in good hands, and come over again and receive the income of it, and live here and enjoy it; and I gave him examples of some that had done so, and lived now in very good figure in London.

In short, I pressed him so to it, that he almost agreed to it, but still something or other broke it off; till at last he turned the tables, and began to talk almost to the same purpose of Ireland.

He told me that a man that could confine himself to a country life, and that could but find stock to enter upon any land, should have farms there for 50*l.* a-year, as good as were let here for 200*l.* a-year; that the produce was such, and so rich the land, that if much was not laid up, we were sure to live as handsomely upon it as a gentleman of 3000*l.* a-year could do in England ; and that he had laid a scheme to leave me in London, and go over and try ; and if he found he could lay a handsome foundation of living, suitable to the respect he had for me, as he doubted not he should do, he would come over and fetch me.

I was dreadfully afraid that upon such a proposal he would have taken me at my word, viz., to turn my little income into money, and let him carry it over into Ireland and try nis experiment with it; but he was too just to desire it, or to have accepted it if I had offered it; and he anticipated me in that, for he added, that he would go and try his fortune that way, and if he found he could do anything at it to live then by adding mine to it when I went over, we should live like ourselves; but that he would not hazard a shilling of mine till he had made the experiment with a little, and he assured me that if he found nothing to be done in Ireland, he would then come to me and join in my project for Virginia.

He was so earnest upon his project being to be tried first, that I could not withstand him; however he promised to let me hear from him in a very little time after his arriving there, to let me know whether his prospect answered his design, that if there was not a probability of success, I might take the occasion to prepare for our other voyage, and then, he assured me, he would go with me to America with all his heart.

I could bring him to nothing farther than this, and which entertained us near a month, during which I enjoyed his company, which was the most entertaining that ever I met with in my life before. In this time he let me into part of the story of his own life, which was indeed surprising, and full of an infinite variety, sufficient to fill up a much brighter history for its adventures and incidents, than any I ever saw in print; but I shall have occasion to say more of him hereafter.

We parted at last, though with the utmost reluctance on my side; and indeed he took his leave very unwillingly too, but necessity obliged him, for his reasons were very good, why he would not come to London, as I understood more fully afterwards.

I gave him a direction how to write to me, though still I reserved the grand secret, which was not to let him ever know my true name, who I was, or where to be found; he likewise let me know how to write a letter to him, so that he said he would be sure to receive it.

I came to London the next day after we parted, but did not go directly to my old lodgings; but for another nameless reason took a private lodging in St. John's-street, or, as it is vulgarly called, St. Jones's near Clerkenwell; and here being perfetly alone, I had leisure to sit down and reflect seriously

upon the last seven months' ramble I had made, for I had
been abroad no less; the pleasant hours I had with my
last husband I looked back on with an infinite deal of pleasure; but that pleasure was very much lessened, when I found
some time after that I was really with child.

This was a perplexing thing, because of the difficulty which
was before me where I should get leave to lie in; it being
one of the nicest things in the world at that time of day, for
a woman that was a stranger, and had no friends, to be entertained in that circumstance without security, which I had
not, neither could I procure any.

I had taken care all this while to preserve a correspondence
with my friend at the bank, or rather he took care to correspond with me, for he wrote to me once a week; and though
I had not spent my money so fast as to want any from him,
yet I often wrote also to let him know I was alive; I had
left directions in Lancashire, so that I had these letters conveyed to me; and during my recess at St. Jones's I received
a very obliging letter from him, assuring me that his process
for a divorce went on with success, though he met with some
difficulties in it that he did not expect.

I was not displeased with the news that his process was
more tedious than he expected; for though I was in no condition to have had him yet, not being so foolish to marry him
when I knew myself to be with child by another man, as
some I know have ventured to do; yet I was not willing to
lose him, and in a word, resolved to have him if he continued
in the same mind, as soon as I was up again; for I saw
apparently I should hear no more from my other husband;
and as he had all along pressed me to marry, and had assured
me he would not be at all disgusted at it, or ever offer to claim
me again, so I made no scruple to resolve to do it if I could,
and if my other friend stood to his bargain; and I had a
great deal of reason to be assured that he would, by the letters
he wrote to me, which were the kindest and most obliging
that could be.

I now grew big, and the people where I lodged perceived
it, and began to take notice of it to me, and as far as civility
would allow, intimated that I must think of removing; this
put me to extreme perplexity, and I grew very melancholy,
for indeed I knew not what course to take; I had money,
but no friends, and was like now to have a child upon my

hands to keep, which was a difficulty I had never. had upon me yet, as my story hitherto makes appear.

In the course of this affair I fell very ill, and my melancholy really increased my distemper; my illness proved at length to be only an ague, but my apprehensions were really that I should miscarry; I should not say apprehensions, for indeed I would have been glad to miscarry, but I could never entertain so much as a thought of taking anything to make me miscarry; I abhorred, I say, so much as the thought of it.

However, speaking of it, the gentlewoman who kept the house, proposed to me to send for a midwife; I scrupled it at first, but after some time consented, but told her I had no acquaintance with any midwife, and so left it to her.

It seems the mistress of the house was not so great a stranger to such cases as mine was, as I thought at first she had been, as will appear presently; and she sent for a midwife of the right sort, that is to say, the right sort for me.

The woman appeared to be an experienced woman in her business, I mean as a midwife, but she had another calling too, in which she was as expert as most women, if not more : my landlady had told her I was very melancholy, and that she believed that had done me harm ; and once, before me, said to her, Mrs. B———, I believe this lady's trouble is of a kind that is pretty much in your way, and therefore if you can do anything for her, pray do, for she is a very civil gentlewoman ; and so she went out of the room.

I really did not understand her, but my Mother Midnight began very seriously to explain what she meant, as soon as she was gone : Madam, says she, you seem not to understand what your landlady means, and when you do, you need not let her know at all that you do so.

She means that you are under some circumstances that may render your lying-in difficult to you, and that you are not willing to be exposed ; I need say no more, but to tell you, that if you think fit to communicate so much of your case to me as is necessary, for I do not desire to pry into those things, I perhaps may be in a condition to assist you, and to make you easy, and remove all your dull thoughts upon that subject.

Every word this creature said was a cordial to me, and put new life and new spirit into my very heart; my blood

began to circulate immediately, and I was quite another body;
I eat my victuals again, and grew better presently after it:
she said a great deal more to the same purpose, and then
having pressed me to be free with her, and promised in the
solemnest manner to be secret, she stopped a little, as if
waiting to see what impression it made on me, and what I
would say.

I was too sensible of the want I was in of such a woman,
not to accept her offer; I told her my case was partly as she
guessed, and partly not, for I was really married, and had a
husband, though he was so remote at that time, as that he
could not appear publicly.

She took me short, and told me that was none of her business; all the ladies that came under her care were married
women to her; every woman, says she, that is with child,
has a father for it, and whether that father was a husband or
no husband, was no business of hers; her business was to
assist me in my present circumstances, whether I had a husband or no; for, madam, says she, to have a husband that
cannot appear, is to have no husband, and therefore whether
you are a wife or a mistress is all one to me.

I found presently, that whether I was a whore or a wife, I
was to pass for a whore here, so I let that go: I told her it
was true, as she said, but that however, if I must tell her my
case, I must tell it her as it was: so I related it as short as I
could, and I concluded it to her: I trouble you with this,
madam, said I, not that, as you said before, it is much to the
purpose in your affair; but this is to the purpose, namely,
that I am not in any pain about being seen, or being concealed, for 'tis perfectly indifferent to me: but my difficulty
is, that I have no acquaintance in this part of the nation.

I understand you, madam, says she, you have no security
to bring to prevent the parish impertinences usual in such
cases; and perhaps, says she, do not know very well how to
dispose of the child when it comes. The last, says I, is not
so much my concern as the first. Well, madam, answers the
midwife, dare you put yourself into my hands? I live in
such a place; though I do not inquire after you, you may
inquire after me; my name is B———, I live in such a
street, naming the street, at the sign of the cradle; my profession is a midwife, and I have many ladies that come to my
house to lie in; I have given security to the parish in general

to secure them from any charge from what shall come into the world under my roof; I have but one question to ask in the whole affair, madam, says she, and if that be answered, you shall be entirely easy of the rest.

I presently understood what she meant, and told her, Madam, I believe I understand you; I thank God, though I want friends in this part of the world, I do not want money, so far as may be necessary, though I do not abound in that neither: this I added, because I would not make her expect great things. Well madam, says she, that is the thing indeed, without which nothing can be done in these cases; and yet, says she, you shall see that I will not impose upon you, or offer anything that is unkind to you, and you shall know everything beforehand, that you may suit yourself to the occasion, and be either costly or sparing as you see fit.

I told her she seemed to be so perfectly sensible of my condition, that I had nothing to ask of her but this, that as I had money sufficient, but not a great quantity, she would order it so that I might be at as little superfluous charge as possible.

She replied, that she should bring in an account of the expenses of it in two or three shapes; I should choose as I pleased; and I desired her to do so.

The next day she brought it, and the copy of her three bills was as follows:

	£.	s.	d.
1. For three months' lodging in her house, including my diet, at 10s. a week............	6	0	0
2. For a nurse for the month, and use of child-bed linen.......................................	1	10	0
3. For a minister to christen the child, and to the godfathers and clerk.......................	1	10	0
4. For a supper at the christening if I had five friends at it	1	0	0
For her fees as a midwife, and the taking off the trouble of the parish......................	3	3	0
To her maid-servant attending....................	0	10	0
	£13	13	0

This was the first bill, the second was in the same terms.

K 2

	£.	s.	d.
1. For three months' lodging and diet, &c., at 20s. per week............................	12	0	0
2. For a nurse for the month, and the use of linen and lace	2	10	0
3. For the minister to christen the child, &c. as above....................................	2	0	0
4. For a supper, and for sweetmeats............	3	3	0
For her fees as above.............................	5	5	0
For a servant maid..................................	1	0	0
	£26	18	0

This was the second rate bill; the third, she said, was for a degree higher, and when the father or friends appeared.

	£.	s.	d.
1. For three months' lodging and diet, having two rooms and a garret for a servant.........	30	0	0
2. For a nurse for the month, and the finest suit of child-bed linen..............................	4	4	0
3. For the minister to christen the child, &c....	2	10	0
4. For a supper, the gentleman to send in the wine...	6	0	0
For my fees, &c....................................	10	10	0
The maid, besides their own maid, only.........	0	10	0
	£53	14	0

I looked upon all the three bills, and smiled, and told her I did not see but that she was very reasonable in her demands, all things considered, and I did not doubt but her accommodations were good.

She told me I should be a judge of that when I saw them: I told her I was sorry to tell her that I feared I must be her lowest-rated customer; and perhaps, madam, said I, you will make me the less welcome upon that account. No, not at all, said she, for where I have one of the third sort, I have two of the second, and four of the first, and I get as much by them in proportion, as by any; but if you doubt my care of you, I will allow any friend you have to see if you are well waited on or no.

Then she explained the particulars of her bill. In the first place, madam, said she, I would have you observe that here is three months keeping you at but 10s. a week; I undertake to say you will not complain of my table: I suppose, says she, you do not live cheaper where you are now. No, indeed, said I, nor so cheap, for I give 6s. per week for my chamber, and find my own diet, which costs me a great deal more.

Then, madam, says she, if the child should not live, as it sometimes happens, there is the minister's article saved; and if you have no friends to come, you may save the expense of a supper; so that take those articles out, madam, says she, your lying-in will not cost you above 5l. 3s. more than your ordinary charge of living.

This was the most reasonable thing that I ever heard of; so I smiled, and told her I would come and be a customer; but I told her also, that as I had two months and more to go, I might perhaps be obliged to stay longer with her than three months, and desired to know if she would not be obliged to remove me before it was proper. No, she said, her house was large, and besides, she never put anybody to remove, that had lain in, 'till they were willing to go; and if she had more ladies offered, she was not so ill-beloved among her neighbours but she could provide accommodation for twenty, if there was occasion.

I found she was an eminent lady in her way, and in short, I agreed to put myself into her hands: she then talked of other things, looked about into my accommodations where I was, found fault with my wanting attendance and conveniences, and that I should not be used so at her house. I told her I was shy of speaking, for the woman of the house looked stranger, or at least I thought so, since I had been ill, because I was with child; and I was afraid she would put some affront or other upon me, supposing that I had been able to give but a slight account of myself.

O dear, says she, her ladyship is no stranger to these things; she has tried to entertain ladies in your condition, but could not secure the parish; and besides, such a nice lady, as you take her to be; however, since you are agoing, you shall not meddle with her, but I'll see you are a little better looked after while you are here, and it shall not cost you the more neither.

I did not understand her: however, I thanked her, so we parted. The next morning she sent me a chicken roasted and hot, and a bottle of sherry, and ordered the maid to tell me that she was to wait on me every day as long as I stayed there.

This was surprisingly good and kind, and I accepted it very willingly: at night she sent to me again, to know if I wanted anything, and to order the maid to come to her in the morning for dinner; the maid had orders to make me some chocolate in the morning before she came away, and at noon she brought me the sweetbread of a breast of veal, whole, and a dish of soup for my dinner; and after this manner she nursed me up at a distance, so that I was mightily well pleased, and quickly well, for indeed my dejections before were the principal part of my illness.

I expected, as is usually the case among such people, that the servant she sent me would have been some impudent brazen wench of Drury-lane breeding, and I was very uneasy upon that account; so I would not let her lie in the house the first night, but had my eyes about me as narrowly as if she had been a public thief.

My gentlewoman guessed presently what was the matter, and sent her back with a short note, that I might depend upon the honesty of her maid; that she would be answerable for her upon all accounts; and that she took no servants without very good security: I was then perfectly easy, and indeed the maid's behaviour spoke for itself, for a modester, quieter, soberer girl never came into anybody's family, and I found her so afterwards.

As soon as I was well enough to go abroad, I went with the maid to see the house, and to see the apartment I was to have; and everything was so handsome and so clean, that, in short, I had nothing to say, but was wonderfully pleased with what I had met with, which, considering the melancholy circumstances I was in, was beyond what I looked for.

It might be expected that I should give some account of the nature of the wicked practices of this woman, in whose hands I was now fallen; but it would be but too much encouragement to the vice, to let the world see what easy measures were here taken to rid the women's burthen of a child clandestinely gotten. This grave matron had several sorts of practice, and this was one, that if a child was born, though not in her house (for she had the occasion to be called to many private labours), she had people always ready, who for a piece of money would take the child off their hands, and off from the hands of the parish too; and those children, as she said, were honestly taken care of: what should become of them all, considering so many, as by her account she was concerned with, I cannot conceive.

I had many times discourses upon that subject with her; but she was full of this argument, that she saved the life of many an innocent lamb,' as she called them, which would perhaps have been murdered; and of many a woman, who, made desperate by the misfortune, would otherwise be tempted to destroy their children. I granted her that this was true, and a very commendable thing, provided the poor children fell into good hands afterwards, and were not abused and neglected by the nurses; she answered, that she always took care of that, and had no nurses in her business but what were very good people, and such as might be depended upon.

I could say nothing to the contrary, and so was obliged to say, Madam, I do not question but you do your part, but what those people do is the main question; and she stopped my mouth again with saying she took the utmost care about it.

The only thing I found in all her conversation on these subjects, that gave me any distaste, was, that one time in discoursing about my being so far gone with child, she said something that looked as if she could help me off with my burthen sooner, if I was willing; or, in English, that she could give me something to make me miscarry, if I had a desire to put an end to my troubles that way; but I soon let her see that I abhorred the thoughts of it; and to do her justice, she put it off so cleverly, that I could not say she really intended it, or whether she only mentioned the practice as a horrible thing; for she couched her words so well, and took my meaning so quickly, that she gave her negative before I could explain myself.

To bring this part into as narrow a compass as possible, I quitted my lodging at St. Jones's, and went to my new governess, for so they called her in the house, and there I was indeed treated with so much courtesy, so carefully looked to, and everything so well, that I was surprised at it, and could not at first see what advantage my governess made of it; but I found afterwards that she professed to make no profit of the lodger's diet, nor indeed could she get much by it, but that her profit lay in the other articles of her management, and she made enough that way I assure you; for 'tis scarce credible what practice she had, as well abroad as at home, and yet all upon the private account, or in plain English, the whoring account.

While I was in her house, which was near four months, she had no less than twelve ladies of pleasure brought to bed within doors, and I think she had two-and-thirty, or thereabouts, under her conduct without doors; whereof one, as nice as she was with me, was lodged with my old landlady at St. Jones's.

This was a strange testimony of the growing vice of the age, and as bad as I had been myself, it shocked my very sense; I began to nauseate the place I was in, and above all, the practice; and yet I must say that I never saw, or do I believe there was to be seen, the least indecency in the house the whole time I was there.

Not a man was ever seen to come up stairs, except to visit the lying-in ladies within their month, nor then without the old lady with them, who made it a piece of the honour of her management that no man should touch a woman, no, not his own wife, within the month; nor would she permit any man to lie in the house upon any pretence whatever, no, not though it was with his own wife; and her saying for it was, that she cared not how many children were born in her house, but she would have none got there if she could help it.

It might perhaps be carried farther than was needful, but it was an error of the right hand if it was an error, for by this she kept up the reputation, such as it was, of her business, and obtained this character, that though she did take care of the women when they were debauched, yet she was not instrumental to their being debauched at all; and yet it was a wicked trade she drove too.

While I was here, and before I was brought to bed, I received a letter from my trustee at the bank full of kind obliging things, and earnestly pressing me to return to London; it was near a fortnight old when it came to me, because it had first been sent into Lancashire, and then returned to me; he concludes with telling me that he had obtained a decree against his wife, and that he would be ready to make good his engagement to me, if I would accept of him, adding a great many protestations of kindness and affection, such as he would have been far from offering if he had known the circumstances I had been in, and which, as it was, I had been very far from deserving.

I returned an answer to this letter, and dated it at Liverpool, but sent it by a messenger, alleging that it came in cover to a friend in town ; I gave him joy of his deliverance, but raised some scruples at the lawfulness of his marrying again, and told him I supposed he would consider very seriously upon that point before he resolved on it, the consequence being too great for a man of his judgment to venture rashly upon ; so concluded wishing him very well in whatever he resolved, without letting him into anything of my own mind, or giving any answer to his proposal of my coming to London to him, but mentioned at a distance my intention to return the latter end of the year, this being dated in April.

I was brought to bed about the middle of May, and had another brave boy, and myself in as good condition as usual on such occasions : my governess did her part as a midwife with the greatest art and dexterity imaginable, and far beyond all that ever I had had any experience of before.

Her care of me in my travail, and after in my lying-in, was such, that if she had been my own mother it could not have been better. Let none be encouraged in their loose practices from this dexterous lady's management, for she is gone to her place, and I dare say has left nothing behind her that can or will come up to it.

I think I had been brought to bed about twenty days when I received another letter from my friend at the bank, with the surprising news that he had obtained a final sentence of divorce against his wife, and had served her with it on such a day, and that he had such an answer to give to all my scruples about his marrying again, as I could not expect, and as he had no desire of ; for that his wife, who had been under some remorse before for her usage of him, as soon as she heard that he had gained his point, had very unhappily destroyed herself that same evening.

He expressed himself very handsomely as to his being concerned at her disaster, but cleared himself of having any hand in it, and that he had only done himself justice in a case in which he was notoriously injured and abused : however, he said that he was extremely afflicted at it, and had no view of any satisfaction left in this world, but only in the hope that I would come and relieve him by my company; and then he pressed me violently indeed to give him some hopes, that I would at least come up to town and let him see me, when he would farther enter into discourse about it.

I was exceedingly surprised at the news, and began now seriously to reflect on my circumstances, and the inexpressible misfortune it was to have a child upon my hands; and what to do in it I knew not. At last I opened my case at a distance to my governess; I appeared melancholy for several days, and she lay at me continually to know what troubled me; I could not for my life tell her that I had an offer of marriage, after I had so often told her that I had a husband, so that I really knew not what to say to her; I owned I had something which very much troubled me, but at the same time told her I could not speak of it to any one alive.

She continued importuning me several days, but it was impossible, I told her, for me to commit the secret to anybody: this, instead of being an answer to her, increased her importunities; she urged her having been trusted with the greatest secrets of this nature, that it was her business to conceal everything, and that to discover things of that nature would be her ruin; she asked me if ever I had found her tattling of other people's affairs, and how could I suspect her? she told me, to unfold myself to her, was telling it to nobody; that she was silent as death, that it must be a very strange case indeed, that she could not help me out of; but to conceal it was to deprive myself of all possible help, or means of help, and to deprive her of the opportunity of serving me. In short, she had such a bewitching eloquence, and so great a power of persuasion, that there was no concealing anything from her.

So I resolved to unbosom myself to her; I told her the history of my Lancashire marriage, and how both of us had been disappointed; how we came together, and how we parted: how he discharged me, as far as lay in him, and gave me free liberty to marry again, protesting that if he knew it he would never claim me, or disturb, or expose me; that I thought I was free, but was dreadfully afraid to venture, for fear of the consequences that might follow in case of a discovery.

Then I told her what a good offer I had; showed her my friend's letters, inviting me to London, and with what affection they were written, but blotted out the name, and also the story about the disaster of his wife, only that she was dead.

She fell a laughing at my scruples about marrying, and told me the other was no marriage, but a cheat on both sides; and that as we were parted by mutual consent, the nature of the contract was destroyed, and the obligation was mutually discharged; she had arguments for this at the tip of her tongue; and in short, reasoned me out of my reason; not but that it was too by the help of my own inclination.

But then came the great and main difficulty, and that was the child; this, she told me, must be removed, and that so as that it should never be possible for any one to discover it. I knew there was no marrying without concealing that I had had a child, for he would soon have discovered by the age of it that it was born, nay, and gotten too, since my parley with him, and that would have destroyed all the affair.

But it touched my heart so forcibly to think of parting entirely with the child, and for aught I knew, of having it murdered, or starved by neglect and ill-usage, which was much the same, that I could not think of it without horror. I wish all those women who consent to the disposing their children out of the way, as it is called, for decency sake, would consider that 'tis only a contrived method for murder; that is to say, killing their children with safety.

It is manifest to all that understand anything of children, that we are born into the world helpless, and uncapable either to supply our own wants, or so much as make them known; and that without help we must perish; and this help requires not only an assisting hand, whether of the mother, or somebody else, but there are two things necessary in that assisting hand, that is, care and skill; without both which, half the children that are born would die; nay, though they were not to be denied food; and one half more of those that remained would be cripples or fools, lose their limbs, and perhaps their sense. I question not but that these are partly the reasons why affection was placed by nature in the hearts of mothers to their children; without which they would never be able to give themselves up, as 'tis necessary they should, to the care and waking pains needful to the support of children.

Since this care is needful to the life of children, to neglect them is to murder them; again, to give them up to be managed by those people who have none of that needful affection placed by nature in them, is to neglect them in the highest degree; nay, in some it goes farther, and is in order to their being lost; so that 'tis an intentional murder, whether the child lives or dies.

All those things represented themselves to my view, and that in the blackest and most frightful form; and as I was very free with my governess, whom I had now learned to call mother, I represented to her all the dark thoughts which I had about it, and told her what distress I was in: she seemed graver by much at this part than at the other; but as she was hardened in these things beyond all possibility of being touched with the religious part, and the scruples about the murder, so she was equally impenetrable in that part which related to affection: she asked me if she had not been careful and tender of me in my lying-in, as if I had been her own child? I told her I owned she had. Well, my dear, says she, and when you are gone, what are you to me? and what would it be to me if you were to be hanged? Do you think there are not women, who, as it is their trade, and they get their bread by it, value themselves upon their being as careful of children as their own mothers? Yes, yes, child, says she, fear it not; how were we nursed ourselves? Are you sure, you were nursed up by your own mother? and yet you look fat and fair, child, says the old beldam; and with that she stroked me over the face. Never be concerned, child, says she, going on in her drolling way: I have no murderers about me, I employ the best nurses that can be had; and have as few children miscarry under their hands, as there would if they were all nursed by mothers; we want neither care nor skill.

She touched me to the quick, when she asked if I was sure that I was nursed by my own mother; on the contrary, I was sure I was not; and I trembled and looked pale at the very expression. Sure, said I to myself, this creature cannot be a witch, or have any conversation with a spirit, that can inform her what I was, before I was able to know it myself; and I looked at her as if I had been frighted; but reflecting that it could not be possible for her to know anything about me, that went off, and I began to be easy, but it was not presently.

She perceived the disorder I was in, but did not know the meaning of it; so she run on in her wild talk upon the weakness of my supposing that children were murdered, because they were not all nursed by the mother; and to persuade me that the children she disposed of were as well used as if the mothers had the nursing of them themselves.

It may be true, mother, says I, for aught I know, but my doubts are very strongly grounded. Come then, says she, let's hear some of them. Why, first, says I, you give a piece of money to these people to take the child off the parent's hands, and to take care of it as long as it lives; now we know, mother, said I, that those are poor people, and their gain consists in being quit of the charge as soon as they can; how can I doubt but that, as it is best for them to have the child die, they are not over solicitous about its life?

This is all vapours and fancy, says she; I tell you their credit depends upon the child's life, and they are as careful as any mother of you all.

O mother, says I, if I was but sure my little baby would be carefully looked to, and have justice done it, I should be happy; but it is impossible I can be satisfied in that point, unless I saw it, and to see it would be ruin and destruction, as my case now stands; so what to do I know not.

A fine story! says the governess; you would see the child, and you would not see the child; you would be concealed and discovered both together; these are things impossible, my dear, and so you must e'en do as other conscientious mothers have done before you; and be contented with things as they must be, though not as you wish them to be.

I understood what she meant by conscientious mothers; she would have said conscientious whores, but she was not willing to disoblige me, for really in this case I was not a whore, because legally married, the force of my former marriage excepted.

However, let me be what I would, I was not come up to that pitch of hardness, common to the profession; I mean, to be unnatural, and regardless of the safety of my child, and I preserved this honest affection so long, that I was upon the point of giving up my friend at the bank, who lay so hard at

me to come to him, and marry him, that there was hardly
any room to deny him.

At last my old governess came to me, with her usual
assurance. Come, my dear, says she, I have found out a way
how you shall be at a certainty that your child shall be used
well, and yet the people that take care of it shall never know
you.

O mother, says I, if you can do so, you will engage me to
you for ever. Well, says she, are you willing to be at some
small annual expense, more than what we usually give to the
people we contract with? Ay, says I, with all my heart,
provided I may be concealed. As to that, says she, you shall
be secure, for the nurse shall never dare to inquire about you,
and you shall once or twice a year go with me and see your
child, and see how 'tis used, and be satisfied that it is in good
hands, nobody knowing who you are.

Why, said I, do you think, that when I come to see my
child, I shall be able to conceal my being the mother of it?
do you think that possible?

Well, says she, if you discover it, the nurse shall be never
the wiser: she shall be forbid to take any notice; if she offers
it, she shall lose the money which you are to be supposed to
give her, and the child be taken from her too.

I was very well pleased with this; so the next week a
countrywoman was brought from Hertford, or thereabouts,
who was to take the child off our hands entirely, for 10l. in
money; but if I would allow 5l. a year more to her, she
would be obliged to bring the child to my governess's house
as often as we desired, or we should come down and look at
it, and see how well she used it.

The woman was a very wholesome-looked likely woman.
a cottager's wife, but she had very good clothes and linen,
and everything well about her; and with a heavy heart and
many a tear, I let her have my child: I had been down at
Hertford and looked at her, and at her dwelling, which I
liked well enough; and I promised her great things if she
would be kind to the child, so she knew at first word that I
was the child's mother; but she seemed to be so much out of
the way, and to have no room to inquire after me, that I
thought I was safe enough; so in short, I consented to let her
have the child, and I gave her 10l., that is to say, I gave it
to my governess, who gave it the poor woman before my face,

she agreeing never to return the child to me, or to claim anything more for its keeping, or bringing up; only that I promised, if she took a great deal of care of it, I would give her something more as often as I came to see it; so that I was not bound to pay the 5*l.* only that I promised my governess I would do it; and thus my great care was over, after a manner, which though it did not at all satisfy my mind, yet was the most convenient for me, as my affairs then stood, of any that could be thought of at that time.

I then began to write to my friend at the bank in a more kindly style, and particularly about the beginning of July I sent him a letter, that I purposed to be in town some time in August; he returned me an answer in the most passionate terms imaginable, and desired me to let him have timely notice, and he would come and meet me two days' journey; this puzzled me scurvily, and I did not know what answer to make to it; once I was resolved to take the stage-coach to West-Chester, on purpose only to have the satisfaction of coming back, that he might see me really come in the same coach; for I had a jealous thought, though I had no ground for it at all, lest he should think I was not really in the country.

I endeavoured to reason myself out of it, but it was in vain; the impression lay so strong on my mind, that it was not to be resisted. At last it came as an addition to my new design of going into the country, that it would be an excellent blind to my old governess, and would cover entirely all my other affairs, for she did not know in the least, whether my new lover lived in London or in Lancashire; and when I told her my resolution, she was fully persuaded it was in Lancashire.

Having taken my measures for this journey, I let her know it, and sent the maid that tended me from the beginning, to take a place for me in the coach; she would have had me let the maid have waited on me down to the last stage, and come up again in the waggon, but I convinced her it would not be convenient. When I went away, she told me she would enter into no measures for correspondence, for she saw evidently that my affection to my child would cause me to write to her, and to visit her too, when I came to town again. I assured her it would, and so took my leave, well satisfied to have been freed from such a house, however good my accommodations there had been.

I took the place in the coach not to its full extent, but to

a place called Stone, in Cheshire, where I not only had no
manner of business, but not the least acquaintance with any
person in the town: but I knew that with money in the pocket
one is at home anywhere; so I lodged there two or three
days, till watching my opportunity, I found room in another
stage-coach, and took passage back again for London, sending
a letter to my gentleman, that I should be such a certain day
at Stony-Stratford, where the coachman told me he was to
lodge.

It happened to be a chance coach that I had taken up,
which having been hired on purpose to carry some gentlemen
to West-Chester, who were going for Ireland, was now returning, and did not tie itself up to exact times or places, as
the stages did; so that having been obliged to lie still on
Sunday, he had time to get himself ready to come out, which
otherwise he could not have done.

His warning was so short, that he could not reach Stony-
Stratford time enough to be with me at night, but he met me
at a place called Brickhill the next morning, just as we were
coming into the town.

I confess I was very glad to see him, for I thought myself
a little disappointed over night: he pleased me doubly too by
the figure he came in, for he brought a very handsome (gentleman's) coach, and four horses, with a servant to attend him.

He took me out of the stage-coach immediately, which
stopped at an inn in Brickhill; and putting into the same inn,
he set up his own coach, and bespoke his dinner: I asked him
what he meant by that, for I was for going forward with the
journey; he said, No, I had need of a little rest upon the
road, and that was a very good sort of a house, though it
was but a little town; so we would go no farther that night,
whatever came of it.

I did not press him much, for since he had come so far to
meet me, and put himself to so much expense, it was but
reasonable I should oblige him a little too: so I was easy
as to that point.

After dinner we walked to see the town, to see the church,
and to view the fields, and the country, as is usual for strangers to do; and our landlord was our guide in going to see
the church. I observed my gentleman inquired pretty much
about the parson, and I took the hint immediately, that
he certainly would propose to be married; and it followed

presently, that in short, I would not refuse him; for to be plain, with my circumstances I was in no condition now to say no : I had no reason now to run any more such hazards.

But while these thoughts run round in my head, which was the work but of a few moments, I observed my landlord took him aside and whispered to him, though not very softly nei- ther, for so much I overheard: Sir, if you shall have occasion ————the rest I could not hear, but it seems it was to this purpose: Sir, if you shall have occasion for a minister, I have a friend a little way off that will serve you, and be as private as you please. My gentleman answered loud enough for me to hear, Very well, I believe I shall.

I was no sooner come back to the inn, but he fell upon me with irresistible words, that since he had had the good fortune to meet me, and everything concurred, it would be hastening his felicity if I would put an end to the matter just there. What, do you mean ? says I, colouring a little : What, in an inn, and on the road ! Bless us all, said I, how can you talk so ! O ! I can talk so very well, says he ; I came on purpose to talk so, and I'll show you that I did ; and with that he pulls out a great bundle of papers. You fright me, said I, what are all these ? Don't be frighted, my dear, said he, and kissed me ; this was the first time that he had been so free to call me my dear ; then he repeated it, Don't be frighted, you shall see what it is all ; then he laid them all abroad. There was first the deed or sentence of divorce from his wife, and the full evidence of her playing the whore ; then there was the certificates of the minister and churchwardens of the parish where she lived, proving that she was buried, and inti- mating the manner of her death ; the copy of the coroner's warrant for a jury to sit upon her, and the verdict of the jury, who brought it in "Non compos mentis." All this was to give me satisfaction, though, by the way, I was not so scrupulous, had he known all, but that I might have taken him without it: however, I looked them all over as well as I could, and told him that this was all very clear indeed, but that he need not have brought them out with him, for it was time enough. Well, he said, it might be time enough for me, but no time but the present time was time enough for him.

There were other papers rolled up, and I asked him what they were ? Why, ay, says he, that's the question I wanted to have you ask me ; so he takes out a little shagreen case,

and gives me out of it a very fine diamond ring; I could not
refuse it, if I had a mind to do so, for he put it upon my finger; so I only made him a curtsy; then he takes out another
ring; And this, says he, is for another occasion, and puts that
into his pocket. Well, but let me see it though, says I, and
smiled: I guess what it is, I think you are mad. I should
have been mad if I had done less, says he; and still he did
not show it me, and I had a great mind to see it; so says I,
Well, but let me see it. Hold, says he, first look here; then
he took up the roll again, and read it, and behold! it was a
license for us to be married. Why, says I, are you distracted?
you were fully satisfied, sure, that I would yield at first word,
or resolved to take no denial. The last is certainly the case,
said he. But you may be mistaken, said I. No, no, says he,
I must not be denied, I can't be denied; and with that he
fell to kissing me so violently, I could not get rid of him.

There was a bed in the room, and we were walking to and
again, eager in the discourse: at last, he takes me by surprise
in his arms, and threw me on the bed, and himself with me,
and holding me still fast in his arms, but without the least offer
of any indecency, courted me to consent with such repeated
entreaties and arguments, protesting his affection, and vowing
he would not let me go till I had promised him, that at last I
said, Why, you resolve not to be denied indeed, I think.
No, no, says he, I must not be denied, I won't be denied, I
can't be denied. Well, well, said I, and giving him a slight
kiss, then you shan't be denied, let me get up.

He was so transported with my consent, and the kind
manner of it, that I began to think once, he took it for a
marriage, and would not stay for the form; but I wronged
him, for he took me by the hand, pulled me up again, and
then giving me two or three kisses, thanked me for my kind
yielding to him; and was so overcome with the satisfaction
of it, that I saw tears stand in his eyes.

I turned from him, for it filled my eyes with tears too; and
asked him leave to retire a little to my chamber. If I had a
grain of true repentance for an abominable life of twenty-
four years past, it was then. O! what a felicity is it to
mankind, said I to myself, that they cannot see into the hearts
of one another! How happy had it been, if I had been wife
to a man of so much honesty, and so much affection, from
the beginning!

Then it occurred to me, What an abominable creature am I! and how is this innocent gentleman going to be abused by me! How little does he think, that having divorced a whore, he is throwing himself into the arms of another! that he is going to marry one that has lain with two brothers, and has had three children by her own brother! one that was born in Newgate, whose mother was a whore, and is now a transported thief; one that has lain with thirteen men, and has had a child since he saw me! Poor gentleman! said I, What is he going to do! After this reproaching myself was over, it followed thus: Well, if I must be his wife, if it please God to give me grace, I'll be a true wife to him, and love him suitably to the strange excess of his passion for me; I will make him amends, by what he shall see, for the abuses I put upon him, which he does not see.

He was impatient for my coming out of my chamber, but finding me long, he went down stairs and talked with my landlord about the parson.

My landlord, an officious, though well-meaning fellow, had sent away for the clergyman; and when my gentleman began to speak to him of sending for him, Sir, says he to him, my friend is in the house; so without any more words he brought them together. When he came to the minister, he asked him if he would venture to marry a couple of strangers that were both willing? The parson said that Mr. —— had said something to him of it; that he hoped it was no clandestine business; that he seemed to be a grave gentleman, and he supposed madam was not a girl, so that the consent of friends should be wanted. To put you out of doubt of that, says my gentleman, read this paper, and out he pulls the license. I am satisfied, says the minister; where is the lady? You shall see her presently, says my gentleman.

When he had said thus, he comes up stairs, and I was by that time come out of my room; so he tells me the minister was below, and that upon showing him the license, he was free to marry us with all his heart, but he asks to see you: so he asked if I would let him come up.

'Tis time enough, said I, in the morning, is it not? Why, said he, my dear, he seemed to scruple whether it was not some young girl stolen from her parents, and I assured him we were both of age to command our own consent; and that made him ask to see you. Well, said I, do as you please;

L 2

so up they brings the parson, and a merry good sort of gentleman he was: he had been told, it seems, that we had met there by accident, that I came in a Chester coach, and my gentleman in his own coach to meet me: that we were to have met last night at Stony-Stratford, but that he could not reach so far. Well, sir, says the parson, every ill turn has some good in it; the disappointment, sir, says he to my gentleman, was yours, and the good turn is mine, for if you had met at Stony-Stratford I had not had the honour to marry you. Landlord, have you a Common Prayer Book?

I started as if I had been frighted; Sir, says I, what do you mean? what, to marry in an inn, and at night too! Madam, says the minister, if you will have it be in the church, you shall; but I assure you your marriage will be as firm here as in the church; we are not tied by the canons to marry nowhere but in the church; and as for the time of day, it does not at all weigh in this case; our princes are married in their chambers, and at eight or ten o'clock at night.

I was a great while before I could be persuaded, and pretended not to be willing at all to be married but in the church; but it was all grimace; so I seemed at last to be prevailed on, and my landlord, and his wife and daughter, were called up. My landlord was father and clerk and all together, and we were married, and very merry we were; though I confess the self-reproaches which I had upon me before, lay close to me, and extorted every now and then a deep sigh from me, which my bridegroom took notice of, and endeavoured to encourage me, thinking, poor man, that I had some little hesitations at the step I had taken so hastily.

We enjoyed ourselves that evening completely, and yet all was kept so private in the inn, that not a servant in the house knew of it, for my landlady and her daughter waited on me, and would not let any of the maids come up stairs. My landlady's daughter I called my bridemaid; and sending for a shopkeeper the next morning, I gave the young woman a good suit of knots, as good as the town would afford, and finding it was a lacemaking town, I gave her mother a piece of bone-lace for a head.

One reason that my landlord was so close, was, that he was unwilling that the minister of the parish should hear of it; but for all that somebody heard of it, so as that we had the bells set a ringing the next morning early, and the music, such

as the town would afford, under our window; but my landlord brazened it out, that we were married before we came
thither, only that being his former guests, we would have our
wedding-supper at his house.

We could not find in our hearts to stir the next day; for,
in short, having been disturbed by the bells in the morning,
and having perhaps not slept overmuch before, we were so
sleepy afterwards that we lay in bed till almost twelve o'clock.

I begged my landlady that we might have no more music
in the town, nor ringing of bells, and she managed it so well
that we were very quiet: but an odd passage interrupted all
my mirth for a good while; the great room of the house
looked into the street, and I had walked to the end of the
room, and it being a pleasant warm day, I had opened the
window, and was standing at it for some air, when I saw
three gentlemen ride by, and go into an inn just against us.

It was not to be concealed, nor did it leave me any room
to question it, but the second of the three was my Lancashire
husband. I was frighted to death; I never was in such a
consternation in my life; I thought I should have sunk into
the ground: my blood run chill in my veins, and I trembled
as if I had been in a cold fit of an ague. I say, there was no
room to question the truth of it, I knew his clothes, I knew
his horse, and I knew his face.

The first reflection I made was, that my husband was not
by to see my disorder, and that I was very glad of. The
gentlemen had not been long in the house but they came to
the window of their room, as is usual; but my window was
shut, you may be sure: however, I could not keep from
peeping at them, and there I saw him again, heard him call
to one of the servants for something he wanted, and received all the terrifying confirmations of its being the same
person, that were possible to be had.

My next concern was, to know what was his business
there; but that was impossible. Sometimes my imagination
formed an idea of one frightful thing, sometimes of another;
sometimes I thought he had discovered me, and was come to
upbraid me with ingratitude and breach of honour; then I
fancied he was coming up stairs to insult me; and innumerable thoughts came into my head, of what was never in his
head, nor ever could be, unless the devil had revealed it to
him.

I remained in the fright near two hours, and scarce ever kept my eye from the window or door of the inn where they were. At last, hearing a great clutter in the passage of their inn, I ran to the window, and, to my great satisfaction, I saw them all three go out again and travel on westward : had they gone towards London, I should have been still in a fright, lest I should meet him again, and that he should know me ; but he went the contrary way, and so I was eased of that disorder.

We resolved to be going the next day, but about six o'clock at night we were alarmed with a great uproar in the street, and people riding as if they had been out of their wits ; and what was it but a hue and cry after three highwaymen, that had robbed two coaches and some travellers near Dunstable-hill, and notice had, it seems, been given, that they had been seen at Brickhill, at such a house, meaning the house where those gentlemen had been.

The house was immediately beset and searched, but there were witnesses enough that the gentlemen had been gone above three hours. The crowd having gathered about, we had the news presently ; and I was heartily concerned now another way : I presently told the people of the house, that I durst say those were honest persons, for that I knew one of the gentlemen to be a very honest person, and of a good estate in Lancashire.

The constable who came with the hue and cry, was immediately informed of this, and came over to me to be satisfied from my own mouth ; and I assured him that I saw the three gentlemen as I was at the window, that I saw them afterwards at the windows of the room they dined in ; that I saw them take horse, and I would assure him I knew one of them to be such a man, that he was a gentleman of a very good estate, and an undoubted character in Lancashire, from whence I was just now upon my journey.

The assurance with which I delivered this, gave the mob gentry a check, and gave the constable such satisfaction, that he immediately sounded a retreat, told his people these were not the men, but that he had an account they were very honest gentlemen ; and so they went all back again. What the truth of the matter was I knew not, but certain it was that the coaches were robbed at Dunstable-hill, and 560l. in money taken ; besides, some of the lace merchants that always

travel that way had been visited too.   As to the three gentlemen, that remains to be explained hereafter.

Well, this alarm stopped us another day, though my spouse
told me it was always safest travelling after a robbery, for
that the thieves were sure to be gone far enough off when
they had alarmed the country ; but I was uneasy, and indeed
principally lest my old acquaintance should be upon the road
still, and should chance to see me.

I never lived four pleasanter days together in my life : I
was a mere bride all this while, and my new spouse strove to
make me easy in everything.   O could this state of life
have continued ! how had all my past troubles been forgot,
and my future sorrows been avoided ! but I had a past life
of a most wretched kind to account for, some of it in this
world as well as in another.

We came away the fifth day ; and my landlord, because
he saw me uneasy, mounted himself, his son, and three honest
country fellows with good fire-arms, and, without telling us
of it, followed the coach, and would see us safe into Dunstable.

We could do no less than treat them very handsomely at
Dunstable, which cost my spouse about ten or twelve shillings,
and something he gave the men for their time too, but my
landlord would take nothing for himself.

This was the most happy contrivance for me that could
have fallen out; for had I come to London unmarried, I
must either have come to him for the first night's entertainment, or have discovered to him that I had not one acquaintance in the whole city of London, that could receive a poor
bride for the first night's lodging with her spouse.   But now
I made no scruple of going directly home with him, and there
I took possession at once of a house well furnished, and a
ausband in very good circumstances, so that I had a prospect
of a very happy life, if I knew how to manage it ; and I had
leisure to consider of the real value of the life I was likely to
live : how different it was to be from the loose part I had
acted before, and how much happier a life of virtue and
sobriety is, than that which we call a life of pleasure !

O had this particular scene of life lasted, or had I learnt
from that time I enjoyed it, to have tasted the true sweetness
of it, and had I not fallen into that poverty which is the sure
bane of virtue, how happy had I been, not only here, but

perhaps for ever! for while I lived thus, I was really a penitent for all my life past; I looked back on it with abhorrence, and might truly be said to hate myself for it: I often reflected how my lover at Bath, struck by the hand of God, repented and abandoned me, and refused to see me any more, though he loved me to an extreme; but I, prompted by that worst of devils, poverty, returned to the vile practice, and made the advantage of what they call a handsome face, be the relief to my necessities, and beauty be a pimp to vice.

Now I seemed landed in a safe harbour, after the stormy voyage of life past was at an end, and I began to be thankful for my deliverance: I sat many an hour by myself, and wept over the remembrance of past follies, and the dreadful extravagances of a wicked life, and sometimes I flattered myself that I had sincerely repented.

But there are temptations which it is not in the power of human nature to resist, and few know what would be their case, if driven to the same exigences. As covetousness is the root of all evil, so poverty is the worst of all snares: but I waive that discourse till I come to the experiment.

I lived with this husband in the utmost tranquillity; he was a quiet, sensible, sober man; virtuous, modest, sincere, and in his business diligent and just: his business was in a narrow compass, and his income sufficient to a plentiful way of living in the ordinary way; I do not say to keep an equipage, and make a figure as the world calls it, nor did I expect it, or desire it; for as I abhorred the levity and extravagance of my former life, so I chose now to live retired, frugal, and within ourselves; I kept no company, made no visits; minded my family, and obliged my husband; and this kind of life became a pleasure to me.

We lived in an uninterrupted course of ease and content for five years, when a sudden blow from an almost invisible hand, blasted all my happiness, and turned me out into the world in a condition the reverse of all that had been before it.

My husband having trusted one of his fellow-clerks with a sum of money, too much for our fortunes to bear the loss of, the clerk failed, and the loss fell very heavy on my husband; yet it was not so great, but that if he had had courage to have looked his misfortunes in the face, his credit was so good, that as I told him, he would easily recover it; for to sink under trouble is to double the weight, and he that will die in it, shall die in it.

It was in vain to speak comfortably to him, the wound had sunk too deep, it was a stab that touched the vitals, he grew melancholy and disconsolate, and from thence lethargic, and died: I foresaw the blow, and was extremely oppressed in my mind, for I saw evidently that if he died I was undone.

I had had two children by him, and no more, for it began to be time for me to leave bearing children, for I was now eight-and-forty, and I suppose if he had lived I should have had no more.

I was now left in a dismal and disconsolate case indeed, and in several things worse than ever. First, it was past the flourishing time with me, when I might expect to be courted for a mistress; that agreeable part had declined some time, and the ruins only appeared of what had been; and that which was worse than all was this, that I was the most dejected, disconsolate creature alive; I that had encouraged my husband, and endeavoured to support his spirits under his trouble, could not support my own; I wanted that spirit in trouble which I told him was so necessary for bearing the barthen.

But my case was indeed deplorable, for I was left perfectly friendless and helpless, and the loss my husband had sustained had reduced his circumstances so low, that though indeed I was not in debt, yet I could easily foresee that what was left would not support me long; that it wasted daily for subsistence, so that it would be soon all spent, and then I saw nothing before me but the utmost distress, and this represented itself so lively to my thoughts, that it seemed as if it was come, before it was really very near; also my very apprehensions doubled the misery, for I fancied every sixpence that I paid for a loaf of bread, was the last I had in the world, and that to-morrow I was to fast, and be starved to death.

In this distress I had no assistant, no friend to comfort or advise me; I sat and cried and tormented myself night and day; wringing my hands, and sometimes raving like a distracted woman; and indeed I have often wondered it had not affected my reason, for I had the vapours to such a degree, that my understanding was sometimes quite lost in fancies and imaginations.

I lived two years in this dismal condition, wasting that little I had, weeping continually over my dismal circumstances, and as it were only bleeding to death, without the least hope or prospect of help; and now I had cried so long, and so often, that tears were exhausted, and I began to be desperate, for I grew poor apace.

For a little relief, I had put off my house and took lodgings; and as I was reducing my living, so I sold off most of my goods, which put a little money in my pocket, and I lived near a year upon that, spending very sparingly, and ekeing things out to the utmost; but still when I looked before me, my heart would sink within me at the inevitable approach of misery and want. O let none read this part without seriously reflecting on the circumstances of a desolate state, and how they would grapple with want of friends and want of bread; it will certainly make them think not of sparing what they have only, but of looking up to heaven for support, and of the wise man's prayer, Give me not poverty, lest I steal.

Let them remember that a time of distress is a time of dreadful temptation, and all the strength to resist is taken away; poverty presses, the soul is made desperate by distress, and what can be done? It was one evening, when being brought, as I may say, to the last gasp, I think I may truly say I was distracted and raving, when prompted by I know not what spirit, and as it were, doing I did not know what, or why, I dressed me (for I had still pretty good clothes), and went out: I am very sure I had no manner of design in my head, when I went out; I neither knew, or considered where to go, or on what business; but as the devil carried me out, and laid his bait for me, so he brought me to be sure to the place, for I knew not whither I was going, or what I did.

Wandering thus about, I knew not whither, I passed by an apothecary's shop in Leadenhall-street, where I saw lie on a stool just before the counter a little bundle wrapt in a white cloth; beyond it stood a maid-servant with her back to it, looking up towards the top of the shop, where the apothecary's apprentice, as I suppose, was standing upon the counter, with his back also to the door, and a candle in his hand, looking and reaching up to the upper shelf, for something he wanted, so that both were engaged, and nobody else in the shop.

This was the bait; and the devil who laid the snare,

prompted me, as if he had spoke, for I remember, and shall never forget it, 'twas like a voice spoken over my shoulder, Take the bundle; be quick; do it this moment. It was no sooner said but I stepped into the shop, and with my back to the wench, as if I had stood up for a cart that was going by, I put my hand behind me and took the bundle, and went off with it, the maid or fellow not perceiving me, or any one else.

It is impossible to express the horror of my soul all the while I did it. When I went away I had no heart to run, or scarce to mend my pace : I crossed the street indeed, and went down the first turning I came to, and I think it was a street that went through into Fenchurch-street; from thence I crossed and turned through so many ways and turnings, that I could never tell which way it was, nor where I went; I felt not the ground I stept on, and the farther I was out of danger, the faster I went, till tired and out of breath, I was forced to sit down on a little bench at a door, and then found I was got into Thames-street, near Billingsgate : I rested me a little and went on ; my blood was all in a fire, my heart beat as if I was in a sudden fright: in short, I was under such a surprise that I knew not whither I was agoing, or what to do.

After I had tired myself thus with walking a long way about, and so eagerly, I began to consider, and make home to my lodging, where I came about nine o'clock at night.

What the bundle was made up for, or on what occasion laid where I found it, I knew not, but when I came to open it, I found there was a suit of childbed-linen in it, very good, and almost new, the lace very fine ; there was a silver porringer of a pint, a small silver mug, and six spoons, with some other linen, a good smock, and three silk handkerchiefs. and in the mug a paper, 18s. 6d. in money.

All the while I was opening these things I was under such dreadful impressions of fear, and in such terror of mind, though I was perfectly safe, that I cannot express the manner of it ; I sat me down, and cried most vehemently ; Lord, said I, what am I now ? a thief! why, I shall be taken next time, and be carried to Newgate, and be tried for my life ! and with that I cried again a long time, and I am sure, as poor as I was, if I had durst for fear, I would certainly have carried the things back again ; but that went off after a while. Well,

I went to bed for that night, but slept little, the horror of the fact was upon my mind, and I knew not what I said or did all night, and all the next day. Then I was impatient to hear some news of the loss; and would fain know how it was, whether they were a poor body's goods, or a rich; perhaps, said I, it may be some poor widow like me, that had packed up these goods to go and sell them for a little bread for herself and a poor child, and are now starving and breaking their hearts, for want of that little they would have fetched; and this thought tormented me worse than all the rest, for three or four days.

But my own distresses silenced all these reflections, and the prospect of my own starving, which grew every day more frightful to me, hardened my heart by degrees. It was then particularly heavy upon my mind, that I had been reformed, and had, as I hoped, repented of all my past wickedness; that I had lived a sober, grave, retired life for several years, but now I should be driven by the dreadful necessity of my circumstances to the gates of destruction, soul and body; and two or three times I fell upon my knees, praying to God, as well as I could, for deliverance; but I cannot but say, my prayers had no hope in them: I knew not what to do, it was all fear without, and dark within; and I reflected on my past life as not repented of, that heaven was now beginning to punish me, and would make me as miserable as I had been wicked.

Had I gone on here I had perhaps been a true penitent; but I had an evil counsellor within, and he was continually prompting me to relieve myself by the worst means; so one evening he tempted me again by the same wicked impulse that had said, take that bundle, to go out again and seek for what might happen.

I went out now by daylight, and wandered about I knew not whither, and in search of I knew not what, when the devil put a snare in my way of a dreadful nature indeed, and such a one as I have never had before or since. Going through Aldersgate-street, there was a pretty little child had been at a dancing-school, and was agoing home all alone; and my prompter, like a true devil, set me upon this innocent creature. I talked to it, and it prattled to me again, and I took it by the hand and led it along till I came to a paved alley that goes into Bartholomew-close, and I led it in there; the child said, that was not its way home; I said, Yes, my dear, it is, I'll show you the way home; the child had a little necklace on of gold beads, and I had my eye upon that, and in the dark of the alley I stooped, pretending to mend the child's clog that was loose, and took off her necklace and the child never felt it, and so led the child on again. Here, I say, the devil put me upon killing the child in the dark alley, that it might not cry, but the very thought frighted me so that I was ready to drop down; but I turned the child about and bade it go back again, for that was not its way home; the child said, so she would, and I went through into Bartholomew-close, and then turned round to another passage that goes into Long-lane, so away into Charterhouse-yard, and out into St. John's-street; then crossing into Smithfield, went down Chick-lane, and into Field-lane, to Holborn-bridge, when mixing with the crowd of people usually passing there, it was not possible to have been found out; and thus I made my second sally into the world.

The thoughts of this booty put out all the thoughts of the first, and the reflections I had made wore quickly off; poverty hardened my heart, and my own necessities made me regardless of anything. The last affair left no great concern upon me, for as I did the poor child no harm, I only thought I had given the parents a just reproof for their negligence, in leaving the poor lamb to come home by itself, and it would teach them to take more care another time.

This string of beads was worth about 12l. or 14l. I suppose it might have been formerly the mother's, for it was too big for the child's wear, but that, perhaps, the vanity of the mother to have her child look fine at the dancing-school, had made her let the child wear it, and no doubt the child had a maid sent to take care of it, but she, like a careless jade, was taken up perhaps with some fellow that had met her, and so the poor baby wandered till it fell into my hands.

However, I did the child no harm; I did not so much as fright it, for I had a great many tender thoughts about me yet, and did nothing but what, as I may say, mere necessity drove me to.

I had a great many adventures after this, but I was young in the business, and did not know how to manage, otherwise than as the devil put things into my head; and indeed he was seldom backward to me. One adventure I had which was very lucky to me; I was going through Lombard-street, in the dusk of the evening, just by the end of Three King-court, when on a sudden comes a fellow running by me as swift as lightning, and throws a bundle that was in his hand just behind me, as I stood up against the corner of the house at the turning into the alley; just as he threw it in, he said, God bless you, mistress, let it lie there a little, and away he runs: after him comes two more, and immediately a young fellow without his hat, crying, Stop thief; they pursued the two last fellows so close, that they were forced to drop what they had got, and one of them was taken into the bargain; the other got off free.

I stood stockstill all this while, till they came back dragging the poor fellow they had taken, and lugging the things they had found, extremely well satisfied that they had recovered the booty, and taken the thief; and thus they passed by me, for I looked only like one who stood up while the crowd was gone.

Once or twice I asked what was the matter, but the people neglected answering me, and I was not very importunate; but after the crowd was wholly passed, I took my opportunity to turn about and take up what was behind me and walk away: this indeed I did with less disturbance than I had done formerly, for these things I did not steal, but they were stolen to my hand. I got safe to my lodgings with this cargo, which was a piece of fine black lustring silk, and a piece of velvet; the latter was but part of a piece of about eleven yards; the former was a whole piece of near fifty yards; it seems it was a mercer's shop that they had rifled; I say rifled, because the goods were so considerable that they had lost; for the goods that they recovered were pretty many, and I believe came to about six or seven several pieces of silk: how they came to get so many I could not tell; but as I had only robbed the thief, I made no scruple at taking these goods, and being very glad of them too.

I had pretty good luck thus far, and I made several adventures more, though with but small purchase, yet with good success, but I went in daily dread that some mischief would befall me, and that I should certainly come to be hanged at last. The impression this made on me was too strong to be slighted, and it kept me from making attempts, that for aught I knew, might have been very safely performed; but one thing I cannot omit, which was a bait to me many a day. I

walked frequently out into the villages round the town to
see if nothing would fall in my way there; and going by a
house near Stepney, I saw on the window-board two rings,
one a small diamond ring, and the other a plain gold ring, to
be sure laid there by some thoughtless lady, that had more
money than forecast, perhaps only till she washed her hands.

I walked several times by the window to observe if I could
see whether there was anybody in the room or no, and I
could see nobody, but still I was not sure; it came presently
into my thoughts to rap at the glass, as if I wanted to speak
with somebody, and if anybody was there they would be
sure to come to the window, and then I would tell them to
remove those rings, for that I had seen two suspicious fellows take notice of them. This was a ready thought; I
rapt once or twice, and nobody came, when I thrust hard
against the square of glass, and broke it with little noise,
and took out the two rings, and walked away; the diamond
ring was worth about 3*l.*, and the other about 9*s.*

I was now at a loss for a market for my goods, and
especially for my two pieces of silk. I was very loath to
dispose of them for a trifle, as the poor unhappy thieves in
general do, who after they have ventured their lives for
perhaps a thing of value, are forced to sell it for a song
when they have done; but I was resolved I would not do
thus, whatever shift I made; however, I did not well know
what course to take. At last I resolved to go to my old
governess, and acquaint myself with her again; I had
punctually supplied the 5*l.* a year to her for my little boy as
long as I was able; but at last was obliged to put a stop to
it. However, I had written a letter to her, wherein I had
told her that my circumstances were reduced; that I had
lost my husband, and that I was not able to do it any longer,
and begged the poor child might not suffer too much for its
mother's misfortunes.

I now made her a visit, and I found that she drove something of the old trade still, but that she was not in such
flourishing circumstances as before; for she had been sued
by a certain gentleman, who had had his daughter stolen
from him, and who it seems she had helped to convey away;
and it was very narrowly that she escaped the gallows. The
expense also had ravaged her, so that her house was but

meanly furnished, and she was not in such repute for her
practice as before; however, she stood upon her legs, as they
say, and as she was a bustling woman, and had some stock
left, she was turned pawnbroker, and lived pretty well.

She received me very civilly, and with her usual obliging
manner told me she would not have the less respect for me
for my being reduced; that she had taken care my boy was
very well looked after, though I could not pay for him, and
that the woman that had him was easy, so that I needed not
to trouble myself about him, till I might be better able to do
it effectually.

I told her I had not much money left, but that I had some
things that were money's worth, if she could tell me how I
might turn them into money. She asked what it was I had?
I pulled out the string of gold beads, and told her it was one
of my husband's presents to me; then I showed her the two
parcels of silk which I told her I had from Ireland, and
brought up to town with me; and the little diamond ring.
As to the small parcel of plate and spoons, I had found
means to dispose of them myself before; and as for the
childbed-linen I had, she offered me to take it herself, believing it to have been my own. She told me that she was
turned pawnbroker, and that she would sell those things for
me as pawned to her, and so she sent presently for proper
agents that bought them, being in her hands, without any
scruple, and gave good prices too.

I now began to think this necessary woman might help me
a little in my low condition to some business; for I would
gladly have turned my hand to any honest employment if I
could have got it; but honest business did not come within
her reach. If I had been younger, perhaps she might have
helped me, but my thoughts were off of that kind of livelihood, as being quite out of the way after fifty, which was my
case, and so I told her.

She invited me at last to come, and be at her house till I
could find something to do, and it should cost me very little,
and this I gladly accepted of; and now living a little easier,
I entered into some measures to have my little son by my
last husband taken off; and this she made easy too, reserving
a payment only of 5l. a year, if I could pay it. This was
such a help to me, that for a good while I left off the wicked

trade that I had so newly taken up; and gladly I would have got work, but that was very hard to do for one that had no acquaintance.

However, at last I got some quilting work for ladies' beds, petticoats, and the like; and this I liked very well, and worked very hard, and with this I began to live; but the diligent devil who resolved I should continue in his service, continually prompted me to go out and take a walk, that is to say, to see if anything would offer in the old way.

One evening I blindly obeyed his summons, and fetched a long circuit through the streets, but met with no purchase; but not content with that, I went out the next evening too, when going by an alehouse I saw the door of a little room open, next the very street, and on the table a silver tankard, things much in use in public-houses at that time; it seems some company had been drinking there, and the careless boys had forgot to take it away.

I went into the box frankly, and setting the silver tankard on the corner of the bench, I sat down before it, and knocked with my foot; a boy came presently, and I bade him fetch me a pint of warm ale, for it was cold weather; the boy ran, and I heard him go down the cellar to draw the ale; while the boy was gone, another boy came, and cried, D'ye call? I spoke with a melancholy air, and said, No, the boy is gone for a pint of ale for me.

While I sat here, I heard the woman in the bar say, Are they all gone in the five? which was the box I sat in, and the boy said, yes. Who fetched the tankard away? says the woman. I did, says another boy, that's it, pointing it seems to another tankard, which he had fetched from another box by mistake; or else it must be, that the rogue forgot that he had not brought it in, which certainly he had not.

I heard all this much to my satisfaction, for I found plainly that the tankard was not missed, and yet they concluded it was fetched away: so I drank my ale, called to pay, and as I went away, I said, Take care of your plate, child, meaning a silver pint mug which he brought me to drink in: the boy said, Yes madam, very welcome, and away I came.

I came home to my governess, and now I thought it was a time to try her, that if I might be put to the necessity of being exposed she might offer me some assistance. When I had been at home some time, and had an opportunity of talking to her, I told her I had a secret of the greatest consequence in the world to commit to her, if she had respect enough for me to keep it a secret: she told me she had kept one of my secrets faithfully; why should I doubt her keeping another? I told her the strangest thing in the world had befallen me, even without any design; and so told her the whole story of the tankard. And have you brought it away with you, my dear? says she. To be sure I have, says I, and showed it her. But what shall I do now, says I, must not I carry it again?

Carry it again! says she; Ay, if you want to go to Newgate. Why, says I, they can't be so base to stop me, when I carry it to them again? You don't know those sort of people, child, says she; they'll not only carry you to Newgate, but hang you too, without any regard to the honesty of returning it; or bring in an account of all the other tankards as they have lost, for you to pay for. What must I do then? says I. Nay, says she, as you have played the cunning part and stole it, you must e'en keep it, there's no going back now; besides child, says she, Don't you want it more than they do? I wish you could light of such a bargain once a week.

This gave me a new notion of my governess, and that since she was turned pawnbroker, she had a sort of people about her that were none of the honest ones that I had met with there before.

I had not been long there but I discovered it more plainly than before, for every now and then I saw hilts of swords, spoons, forks, tankards, and all such kind of ware brought in, not to be pawned, but to be sold downright; and she bought them all without asking any questions, but had good bargains, as I found by her discourse.

I found also that in following this trade she always melted down the plate she bought, that it might not be challenged; and she came to me and told me one morning that she was going to melt, and if I would, she would put my tankard in, that it might not be seen by anybody; I told her with all my heart; so she weighed it, and allowed me the full value in silver again; but I found she did not do so to the rest of her customers.

Some time after this, as I was at work, and very melancholy, she begins to ask me what the matter was? I told her my heart was very heavy, I had little work and nothing to live on, and knew not what course to take. She laughed, and told me I must go out again and try my fortune; it might be that I might meet with another piece of plate. O, mother! says I, that is a trade that I have no skill in, and if I should be taken I am undone at once. Says she, I could help you to a schoolmistress, that shall make you as dexterous as herself; 1 trembled at that proposal, for hitherto I had had no confederates nor any acquaintance among that tribe. But she conquered all my modesty, and all my fears; and in a little time, by the help of this confederate, I grew as impudent a thief, and as dexterous, as ever Moll Cutpurse was, though, if fame does not belie her, not half so handsome.

The comrade she helped me to, dealt in three sorts of craft; viz., shoplifting, stealing of shop-books and pocket-books, and taking off gold watches from the ladies' sides; and this last she did so dexterously that no woman ever arrived to the perfection of that art, like her. I liked the first and the last of these things very well, and I attended her some time in the practice, just as a deputy attends a midwife, without any pay.

At length she put me to practice. She had shown me her art, and I had several times unhooked a watch from her own side with great dexterity; at last she showed me a prize, and this was a young lady with child, who had a charming watch. The thing was to be done as she came out of the church; she goes on one side of the lady, and pretends, just as she came to the steps, to fall, and fell against the lady with so much violence as put her into a great fright, and both cried out terribly: in the very moment that she jostled the lady, I had hold of the watch, and holding it the right way, the start she gave drew the hook out and she never felt it; I made off immediately, and left my schoolmistress to come out of her fright gradually, and the lady too; and presently the watch was missed; Ay, says my comrade, then it was those rogues that thrust me down, I warrant ye; I wonder the gentlewoman did not miss her watch before, then we might have taken them.

She humoured the thing so well that nobody suspected her, and I was got home a full hour before her. This was my first adventure in company; the watch was indeed a very fine one, and had many trinkets about it, and my governess allowed us 20*l.* for it, of which I had half. And thus I was entered a complete thief, hardened to a pitch above all the reflections of conscience or modesty, and to a degree which I never thought possible in me.

Thus the devil, who began, by the help of an irresistible poverty, to push me into this wickedness, brought me to a height beyond the common rate, even when my necessities were not so terrifying; for I had now got into a little vein of work, and as I was not at a loss to handle my needle, it was very probable I might have got my bread honestly enough.

I must say, that if such a prospect of work had presented itself at first, when I began to feel the approach of my miserable circumstances; I say, had such a prospect of getting bread by working presented itself then, I had never fallen into this wicked trade, or into such a wicked gang as I was now embarked with; but practice had hardened me, and I grew audacious to the last degree; and the more so, because I had carried it on so long, and had never been taken; for in a word, my new partner in wickedness and I went on together so long, without being ever detected, that we not only grew bold, but we grew rich, and we had at one time one-and-twenty gold watches in our hands.

I remember that one day being a little more serious than ordinary, and finding I had so good a stock beforehand, as I had, for I had near 200*l.* in money for my share; it came strongly into my mind, no doubt from some kind spirit, if such there be, that as at first poverty excited me, and my distresses drove me to these dreadful shifts, so seeing those distresses were now relieved, and I could also get something towards a maintenance by working, and had so good a bank to support me, why should I not now leave off, while I was well; that I could not expect to go always free; and if I was once surprised, I was undone.

This was doubtless the happy minute, when, if I had hearkened to the blessed hint, from whatsoever hand it came, I had still a cast for an easy life. But my fate was otherwise determined; the busy devil that drew me in, had too fast hold of me to let me go back; but as poverty brought me in, so avarice kept me in, till there was no going back; as to the arguments which my reason dictated for persuading me to lay down, avarice stept in and said, Go on, you have had very good luck, go on till you have gotten four or five hundred pounds, and then you shall leave off, and then you may live easy without working at all.

Thus I that was once in the devil's clutches, was held fast there as with a charm, and had no power to go without the circle, till I was ingulfed in labyrinths of trouble too great to get out at all.

However, these thoughts left some impression upon me, and made me act with some more caution than before, and more than my directors used for themselves. My comrade, as I called her (she should have been called my teacher), with another of her scholars, was the first in the misfortune; for happening to be upon the hunt for purchase, they made an attempt upon a linendraper in Cheapside, but were snapped by a hawk's-eyed journeyman, and seized with two pieces of cambric, which were taken also upon them.

This was enough to lodge them both in Newgate, where they had the misfortune to have some of their former sins brought to remembrance; two other indictments being brought against them, and the facts being proved upon them, they were both condemned to die; they both pleaded their bellies, and were both voted quick with child; though my tutoress was no more with child than I was.

I went frequently to see them, and condole with them, expecting that it would be my turn next; but the place gave me so much horror, reflecting that it was the place of my unhappy birth, and of my mother's misfortunes, that I could not bear it, so I left off going to see them.

And O! could I but have taken warning by their disasters, I had been happy still, for I was yet free, and had nothing brought against me; but it could not be, my measure was not yet filled up.

My comrade, having the brand of an old offender, was executed; the young offender was spared, having obtained a reprieve; but lay starving a long while in prison, till at last she got her name into what they call a circuit pardon, and so came off.

This terrible example of my comrade frighted me heartily, and for a good while I made no excursions; but one night, in the neighbourhood of my governess's house, they cried, Fire; my governess looked out, for we were all up, and cried immediately that such a gentlewoman's house was all of a light fire a-top, and so indeed it was. Here she gives me a jog; Now, child, says she, there is a rare opportunity, the fire being so near that you may go to it before the street is blocked up with the crowd. She presently gave me my cue; Go, child, says she, to the house, and run in and tell the lady, or anybody you see, that you come to help them, and that you came from such a gentlewoman; that is, one of her acquaintance farther up the street.

Away I went, and, coming to the house, I found them all in confusion, you may be sure; I ran in, and finding one of the maids, Alas! sweetheart, said I, how came this dismal accident? where is your mistress? is she safe? and where are the children? I come from Madam —— to help you. Away runs the maid; Madam, madam, says she, screaming as loud as she could yell, here is a gentlewoman come from Madam —— to help us. The poor woman, half out of her wits, with a bundle under her arm, and two little children, comes towards me; Madam, says I, let me carry the poor children to Madam ——, she desires you to send them; she'll take care of the poor lambs; and so I takes one of them out of her hand, and she lifts the 'tother up into my arms: Ay, do, for God sake, says she, carry them; O thank her for her kindness. Have you anything else to secure, madam? says I; she will take care of it. O dear! says she, God bless her, take this bundle of plate and carry it to her too; O she is a good woman; O, we are utterly ruined, undone! And away she runs from me out of her wits, and the maids after her, and away comes I with the two children and the bundle.

I was no sooner got into the street, but I saw another woman come to me; O! says she, mistress, in a piteous tone, you will let fall the child; come, come, this is a sad time, let me help you; and immediately lays hold of my bundle to carry it for me. No, says I, if you will help me, take the child by the hand, and lead it for me but to the upper end of the street; I'll go with you and satisfy you for your pains.

She could not avoid going, after what I said, but the creature, in short, was one of the same business with me, and wanted nothing but the bundle; however, she went with me to the door, for she could not help it; when we were come there I whispered her, Go child, said I, I understand your trade, you may meet with purchase enough.

She understood me and walked off; I thundered at the door with the children, and as the people were raised before by the noise of the fire, I was soon let in, and I said, Is madam awake, pray tell her Mrs. ——— desires the favour of her to take the two children in; poor lady, she will be undone, their house is all of a flame. They took the children in very civilly, pitied the family in distress, and away came I with my bundle. One of the maids asked me if I was not to leave the bundle too; I said, No, sweetheart, 'tis to go to another place, it does not belong to them.

I was a great way out of the hurry now, and so I went on and brought the bundle of plate, which was very considerable, straight home, to my old governess; she told me she would not look into it, but bade me go again and look for more.

She gave me the like cue to the gentlewoman of the next house to that which was on fire, and I did my endeavour to go, but by this time the alarm of fire was so great, and so many engines playing, and the street so thronged with people, that I could not get near the house, whatever I could do; so I came back again to my governess's, and taking the bundle up into my chamber, I began to examine it. It is with horror that I tell what a treasure I found there; 'tis enough to say, that besides most of the family plate, which was considerable, I found a gold chain, an old-fashioned thing, the locket of which was broken, so that I suppose it had not been used some years, but the gold was not the worse for that; also a little box of burying rings, the lady's wedding-ring, and some broken bits of old lockets of gold, a gold watch, and a purse with about 24*l.* value in old pieces of gold coin, and several other things of value.

This was the greatest and the worst prize that ever I was concerned in; for indeed, though, as I have said above, I was hardened now beyond the power of all reflection in other cases, yet it really touched me to the very soul, when I looked into this treasure; to think of the poor disconsolate gentlewoman who had lost so much besides; and who would think to be sure that she had saved her plate and best things; how she would be surprised when she should find that she had been deceived, and that the person that took her children and her goods, had come, as was pretended, from the gentlewoman in next street, but that the children had been put upon her without her own knowledge.

I say, I confess the inhumanity of this action moved me very much, and made me relent exceedingly, and tears stood in my eyes upon that subject; but with all my sense of its being cruel and inhuman, I could never find in my heart to make any restitution. The reflection wore off, and I quickly forgot the circumstances that attended it.

Nor was this all; for though by this job I was become considerably richer than before, yet the resolution I had formerly taken of leaving off this horrid trade when I had gotten a little more; and the avarice had such success, that I had no more thoughts of coming to a timely alteration of life, though without it I could expect no safety, no tranquillity in the possession of what I had gained; a little more, and a little more, was the case still.

At length, yielding to the importunities of my crime, I cast off all remorse, and all the reflections on that head turned to no more than this, that I might perhaps come to have one booty more that might complete all; but though I certainly had that one booty, yet every hit looked towards another, and was so encouraging to me to go on with the trade, that I had no gust to the laying it down.

In this condition, hardened by success, and resolving to go on, I fell into the snare in which I was appointed to meet with my last reward for this kind of life. But even this was not yet, for I met with several successful adventures more in this way.

My governess was for awhile really concerned for the misfortune of my comrade that had been hanged, for she knew enough of my governess to have sent her the same way, and which made her very uneasy; indeed she was in a very great fright.

It is true that when she was gone and had not told what she knew, my governess was easy as to that point, and perhaps glad she was hanged, for it was in her power to have obtained a pardon at the expense of her friends; but the loss of her, and the sense of her kindness in not making her market of what she knew, moved my governess to mourn very sincerely for her. I comforted her as well as I could, and she in return hardened me to merit more completely the same fate.

However, as I have said, it made me the more wary, and particularly I was very shy of shoplifting, especially among the mercers and drapers, who are a set of fellows that have their eyes very much about them. I made a venture or two among the lace folks, and the milliners, and particularly at one shop where two young women were newly set up, and had not been bred to the trade: there I carried off a piece of bone-lace, worth six or seven pounds, and a paper of thread; but this was but once, it was a trick that would not serve again.

It was always reckoned a safe job when we heard of a new shop, and especially when the people were such as were not bred to shops; such may depend upon it that they will be visited once or twice at their beginning, and they must be very sharp indeed if they can prevent it.

I made another adventure or two after this, but they were but trifles. Nothing considerable offering for a good while, I began to think that I must give over trade in earnest; but my governess, who was not willing to lose me, and expected great things of me, brought me one day into company with a young woman and a fellow that went for her husband, though as it appeared afterwards she was not his wife, but they were partners in the trade they carried on; and in something else too. In short, they robbed together, lay together, were taken together, and at last were hanged together.

I came into a kind of league with these two by the help of my governess, and they carried me out into three or four adventures, where I rather saw them commit some coarse and unhandy robberies, in which nothing but a great stock of impudence on their side, and gross negligence on the people's side who were robbed, could have made them successful; so I resolved from that time forward to be very cautious how I adventured with them; and indeed when two or three unlucky projects were proposed by them, I declined the offer, and persuaded them against it. One time they particularly proposed robbing a watchmaker of three gold watches, which they had eyed in the daytime, and found the place where he laid them: one of them had so many keys of all kinds, that he made no question to open the place where

the watchmaker had laid them; and so we made a kind of
an appointment; but when I came to look narrowly into the
thing, I found they proposed breaking open the house, and
this I would not embark in, so they went without me.   They
did get into the house by main force, and broke up the locked
place where the watches were, but found but one of the gold
watches, and a silver one, which they took, and got out of
the house again very clear; but the family being alarmed,
cried out, Thieves, and the man was pursued and taken; the
young woman had got off too, but unhappily was stopped at
a distance, and the watches found upon her; and thus I had
a second escape, for they were convicted, and both hanged,
being old offenders, though but young people; and as I said
before, that they robbed together, so now they hanged
together, and there ended my new partnership.

I began now to be very wary, having so narrowly escaped
a scouring, and having such an example before me; but I
had a new tempter, who prompted me every day, I mean my
governess; and now a prize presented, which as it came by
her management, so she expected a good share of the booty;
there was a good quantity of Flanders lace lodged in a private
house, where she had heard of it; and Flanders lace, being
prohibited, it was a good booty to any custom-house officer
that could come at it; I had a full account from my governess, as well of the quantity as of the very place where it
was concealed, so I went to a custom-house officer, and told
him I had a discovery to make to him, if he would assure me
that I should have my due share of the reward; this was so
just an offer, that nothing could be fairer; so he agreed, and
taking a constable, and me with him, we beset the house; as
I told him I could go directly to the place, he left it to me,
and the hole being very dark, I squeezed myself into it, with
a candle in my hand, and so reached the pieces out to him,
taking care, as I gave him some, so to secure as much about
myself as I could conveniently dispose of.   There was near
300l. worth of lace in the whole; and I secured about 50l.
worth of it myself.   The people of the house were not
owners of the lace, but a merchant who had entrusted them
with it; so that they were not so surprised as I thought they
would be.

I left the officer overjoyed with his prize, and fully satisfied with what he had got, and appointed to meet him at a

house of his own directing, where I came after I had disposed of the cargo I had about me, of which he had not the least suspicion; when I came, he began to capitulate, believing I did not understand the right I had in the prize, and would fain have put me off with 20*l.*, but I let him know that I was not so ignorant as he supposed I was; and yet I was glad too, that he offered to bring me to a certainty; I asked 100*l.* and he rose up to 30*l.*; I fell to 80*l.* and he rose again to 40*l.*; in a word, he offered 50*l.* and I consented, only demanding a piece of lace, which I thought came to about 8*l.* or 9*l.*, as if it had been for my own wear, and he agreed to it; so I got 50*l.* in money paid me that same night, and made an end of the bargain; nor did he ever know who I was, or where to inquire for me; so that if it had been discovered that part of the goods were embezzled, he could have made no challenge upon me for it.

I very punctually divided this spoil with my governess, and I passed with her from this time for a very dexterous manager in the nicest cases; I found that this last was the best and easiest sort of work that was in my way, and I made it my business to inquire out prohibited goods; and after buying some, usually betrayed them, but none of these discoveries amounted to anything considerable, not like that I related just now; but I was cautious of running the great risks which I found others did, and in which they miscarried every day.

The next thing of moment, was an attempt at a gentlewoman's gold watch. It happened in a crowd, at a meetinghouse, where I was in very great danger of being taken; I had full hold of her watch, but giving a great jostle as if somebody had thrust me against her, and in the juncture giving the watch a fair pull, I found it would not come, so I let it go that moment, and cried as if I had been killed, that somebody had trod upon my foot, and that there was certainly pickpockets there, for somebody or other had given a pull at my watch; for you are to observe, that on these adventures we always went very well dressed, and I had very good clothes on, and a gold watch by my side, as like a lady as other folks.

I had no sooner said so, but the other gentlewoman cried out, A pickpocket, too, for somebody, she said, had tried to pull her watch away.

When I touched her watch, I was close to her, out when

I cried out, I stopped as it were short, and the crowd bearing her forward a little, she made a noise too, but it was at some distance from me, so that she did not in the least suspect me, but when she cried out, A pickpocket, somebody cried out, Ay, and here has been another, this gentlewoman has been attempted too.

At that very instant, a little farther in the crowd, and very luckily too, they cried out, A pickpocket, again, and really seized a young fellow in the very fact. This, though unhappy for the wretch, was very opportunely for my case, though I had carried it handsomely enough before; but now it was out of doubt, and all the loose part of the crowd ran that way, and the poor boy was delivered up to the rage of the street, which is a cruelty I need not describe, and which, however, they are always glad of, rather than be sent to Newgate, where they lie often a long time, and sometimes they are hanged, and the best they can look for, if they are convicted, is to be transported.

This was a narrow escape to me, and I was so frighted, that I ventured no more at gold watches a great while; there were indeed many circumstances in this adventure, which assisted to my escape; but the chief was, that the woman whose watch I had pulled at was a fool; that is to say, she was ignorant of the nature of the attempt, which one would have thought she should not have been, seeing she was wise enough to fasten her watch so that it could not be slipt up; but she was in such a fright, that she had no thought about her; for she, when she felt the pull, screamed out, and pushed herself forward, and put all the people about her into disorder, but said not a word of her watch, or of a pickpocket, for at least two minutes, which was time enough for me, and to spare; for as I had cried out behind her, as I have said, and bore myself back in the crowd as she bore forward, there were several people, at least seven or eight, the throng being still moving on, that were got between me and her in that time, and then I crying out, A pickpocket, rather sooner than she, she might as well be the person suspected as I, and the people were confused in their inquiry; whereas, had she with a presence of mind needful on such an occasion, as soon as she felt the pull, not screamed out as she did, but turned immediately round, and seized the next body that was behind her, she had infallibly taken me.

This is a direction not of the kindest sort to the fraternity, but 'tis certainly a key to the clew of a pickpocket's motions; and whoever can follow it, will as certainly catch the thief as he will be sure to miss if he does not.

I had another adventure, which puts this matter out of doubt, and which may be an instruction for posterity in the case of a pickpocket: my good old governess, to give a short touch at her history, though she had left off the trade, was, as I may say, born a pickpocket, and, as I understood afterward, had run through all the several degrees of that art, and yet had been taken but once; when she was so grossly detected that she was convicted, and ordered to be transported; but being a woman of a rare tongue, and withal having money in her pocket, she found means, the ship putting into Ireland for provisions, to get on shore there, where she practised her old trade some years; when falling into another sort of company, she turned midwife and procuress, and played a hundred pranks, which she gave me a little history of, in confidence between us as we grew more intimate; and it was to this wicked creature that I owed all the dexterity I arrived to, in which there were few that ever went beyond me, or that practised so long without any misfortune.

It was after those adventures in Ireland, and when she was pretty well known in that country, that she left Dublin, and came over to England, where the time of her transportation being not expired, she left her former trade, for fear of falling into bad hands again, for then she was sure to have gone to wreck. Here she set up the same trade she had followed in Ireland, in which she soon, by her admirable management, and a good tongue, arrived to the height which I have already described, and indeed began to be rich, though her trade fell again afterwards.

I mention thus much of the history of this woman here, the better to account for the concern she had in the wicked life I was now leading; into all the particulars of which she led me, as it were, by the hand, and gave me such directions, and I so well followed them, that I grew the greatest artist of my time, and worked myself out of every danger with such dexterity, that when several more of my comrades run themselves into Newgate, by that time they had been half a year at the trade, I had now practised upwards of five years, and the people at Newgate did not so much as know me; they had heard much of me indeed, and often expected me there; but I always got off, though many times in the extremest danger.

One of the greatest dangers I was now in, was that I was too well known among the trade, and some of them, whose hatred was owing rather to envy than any injury I had done them, began to be angry that I should always escape when they were always catched and hurried to Newgate. These were they that gave me the name of Moll Flanders: for it was no more of affinity with my real name, or with any of the names I had ever gone by, than black is of kin to white, except that once, as before, I called myself Mrs. Flanders, when I sheltered myself in the Mint; but that these rogues never knew, nor could I ever learn how they came to give me the name, or what the occasion of it was.

I was soon informed that some of these who were gotten fast into Newgate, had vowed to impeach me; and as I knew that two or three of them were but too able to do it, I was under a great concern, and kept within doors for a good while; but my governess, who was partner in my success, and who now played a sure game, for she had no share in the hazard, I say, my governess was something impatient of my leading such a useless unprofitable life, as she called it; and she laid a new contrivance for my going abroad, and this was to dress me up in men's clothes, and so put me into a new kind of practice.

I was tall and personable, but a little too smooth-faced for a man; however, as I seldom went abroad but in the night, it did well enough; but it was long before I could behave in my new clothes; it was impossible to be so nimble, so ready, so dexterous at these things, in a dress contrary to nature; and as I did everything clumsily, so I had neither the success, or easiness of escape that I had before, and I resolved to leave it off; but that resolution was confirmed soon after by the following accident.

As my governess had disguised me like a man, so she joined me with a man, a young fellow that was nimble enough at his business, and for about three weeks we did very well together. Our principal trade was watching shopkeepers' counters, and slipping off any kinds of goods we could see carelessly laid anywhere, and we made several good bargains, as we called them, at this work. And as we kept always together, so we grew very intimate, yet he never knew that I was not a man; nay, though I several times went home with him to his lodgings, according as our business directed, and four or five times lay with him all night: but our design lay another way, and it was absolutely necessary to me to conceal my sex from him, as appeared afterwards, the circumstances of our living, coming in late, and having such business to do as required that nobody should be trusted with coming into our lodgings, were such as 'made it impossible to me to refuse lying with him, unless I would have owned my sex; and as it was, I effectually concealed myself.

But his ill, and my good fortune, soon put an end to this life, which I must own I was sick of too. We had made several prizes in this new way of business, but the last would have been extraordinary: there was a shop in a certain street which had a warehouse behind it that looked into another street, the house making the corner.

Through the window of the warehouse we saw lying on the counter or showboard which was just before it, five pieces of silks, besides other stuffs; and though it was almost dark, yet the people being busy in the fore-shop had not had time to shut up those windows, or else had forgot it.

This the young fellow was so overjoyed with, that he could not restrain himself; it lay within his reach, he said, and he swore violently to me that he would have it, if he broke down the house for it; I dissuaded him a little, but saw there was no remedy; so he run rashly upon it, slipt out a square out of the sash window dexterously enough, and got four pieces of the silks, and came with them towards me, but was immediately pursued with a terrible clutter and noise; we were standing together indeed, but I had not taken any of the goods out of his hand, when I said to him hastily, You are undone! He run like lightning, and I too, but the pursuit was hotter after him, because he had the goods; he dropt two of the pieces, which stopped them a little, but the crowd increased, and pursued us both; they took him soon after with the other two pieces, and then the rest followed me; I run for it and got into my governess's house, whither some quick-eyed people followed me so warmly as to fix me there; they did not immediately knock at the door, by which I got time to throw off my disguise, and dress me in my own clothes; besides, when they came there, my governess, who had her tale ready, kept her door shut, and called out to them and told them there was no man came in there ; the people affirmed there did a man come in there, and swore 'they would break open the door.

My governess, not at all surprised, spoke calmly to them, told them they should very freely come and search her house, if they would bring a constable, and let in none but such as the constable would admit, for it was unreasonable to let in a whole crowd; this they could not refuse, though they were a crowd ; so a constable was fetched immediately, and she very freely opened the door, the constable kept the door, and the men he appointed searched the house, my governess going with them from room to room.   When she came to my room she called to me, and said aloud, Cousin, pray open the door, here's some gentlemen that must come and look into your room.

I had a little girl with me, which was my governess's grandchild, as she called her ; and I bade her open the door, and there sat I at work with a great litter of things about me, as if I had been at work all day, being undressed, with only night clothes on my head, and a loose morning gown about me : my governess made a kind of excuse for their disturbing me, telling partly the occasion of it, and that she had no remedy but to open the doors to them, and let them satisfy themselves, for all she could say would not satisfy them : I sat still, and bid them search if they pleased, for if there was anybody in the house, I was sure they were not in my room; and for the rest of the house I had nothing to say to that, I did not understand what they looked for.

Everything looked so innocent and so honest about me, that they treated me civiller than I expected ; but it was not till they had searched the room to a nicety, even under the bed, and in the bed, and everywhere else, where it was possible anything could be hid ; when they had done, and could find nothing, they asked my pardon and went down.

When they had thus searched the house from bottom to top, and then from top to bottom, and could find nothing, they appeased the mob pretty well ; but they carried my governess before the justice : two men swore that they saw the man, whom they pursued, go into her house ; my governess rattled and made a great noise that her house should be insulted, and that she should be used thus for nothing ; that if a man did come in, he might go out again presently for aught she knew, for she was ready to make oath that no man had been within her doors all that day as she knew of; which was very true; that it might be, that as she was above stairs, any fellow in a fright might find the door open, and run in for shelter when he was pursued, but that she knew nothing of it; and if it had been so, he certainly went out again, perhaps at the other door, for she had another door into an alley, and so had made his escape.

This was indeed probable enough, and the justice satisfied himself with giving her an oath that she had not received or admitted any man into her house to conceal him, or protect or hide him from justice: this oath she might justly take, and did so, and so she was dismissed.

It is easy to judge what a fright I was in upon this occasion, and it was impossible for my governess ever to bring me to dress in that disguise again; for, as I told her, I should certainly betray myself.

My poor partner in this mischief was now in a bad case, for he was carried away before my lord mayor, and by his worship committed to Newgate, and the people that took him were so willing, as well as able, to prosecute him, that they offered themselves to enter into recognisances to appear at the sessions, and pursue the charge against him.

However, he got his indictment deferred, upon promise to discover his accomplices, and particularly the man that was concerned with him in this robbery; and he failed not to do his endeavour, for he gave in my name, whom he called Gabriel Spencer, which was the name I went by to him; and here appeared the wisdom of my concealing myself from him, without which I had been undone.

He did all he could to discover this Gabriel Spencer; he described me; he discovered the place where he said I lodged; and in a word, all the particulars that he could of my dwelling; but having concealed the main circumstances of my sex from him, I had a vast advantage, and he could never hear of me; he brought two or three families into trouble, by his endeavouring to find me out, but they knew nothing of me, any more than that he had a fellow with him, that they had seen, but knew nothing of; and as to my governess, though she was the means of his coming to me yet it was done at secondhand, and he knew nothing of her neither.

This turned to his disadvantage; for having promised discoveries, but not being able to make it good, it was looked upon as trifling, and he was the more fiercely pursued by the shopkeeper.

I was, however, terribly uneasy all this while, and that I might be quite out of the way, I went away from my governess for a while, but not knowing whither to wander, I took a maid-servant with me, and took the stage-coach to Dunstable to my old landlord and landlady, where I lived so handsomely with my Lancashire husband: here I told her a formal story, that I expected my husband every day from Ireland, and that I had sent a letter to him that I would meet him at Dunstable at her house, and that he would certainly land if the wind was fair, in a few days; so that I was come to spend a few days with them till he could come, for he would either come post, or in the West-Chester coach, I knew not which, but whichsoever it was, he would be sure to come to that house to meet me.

My landlady was mighty glad to see me, and my landlord made such a stir with me, that if I had been a princess I could not have been better used, and here I might have been welcome a month or two if I had thought fit.

But my business was of another nature; I was very uneasy (though so well disguised that it was scarce possible to detect me) lest this fellow should find me out; and though he could not charge me with the robbery, having persuaded him not to venture, and having done nothing of it myself, yet he might have charged me with other things, and have bought his own life at the expense of mine.

This filled me with horrible apprehensions: I had no resource, no friend, no confidant but my old governess, and I knew no remedy but to put my life into her hands; and so I did, for I let her know where to send to me, and had several letters from her while I stayed here. Some of them almost scared me out of my wits; but at last she sent me the joyful news that he was hanged, which was the best news to me that I had heard a great while.

I had stayed here five weeks, and lived very comfortably indeed, the secret anxiety of my mind excepted; but when I received this letter I looked pleasantly again, and told my landlady that I had received a letter from my spouse in Ireland, that I had the good news of his being very well, but had the bad news that his business would not permit him to come away so soon as he expected, and so I was like to go back again without him.

My landlady complimented me upon the good news, however, that I had heard he was well; For I have observed, madam, says she, you han't been so pleasant as you used to be; you have been over head and ears in care for him, I dare say, says the good woman; 'tis easy to be seen there's an alteration in you for the better, says she. Well, I am sorry the 'squire can't come yet, says my landlord; I should have been heartily glad to have seen him: when you have certain news of his coming, you'll take a step hither again, madam, says he: you shall be very welcome whenever you please to come.

With all these fine compliments we parted, and I came merry enough to London, and found my governess as well pleased as I was. And now she told me she would never recommend any partner to me again, for she always found, she said, that I had the best luck when I ventured by myself. And so indeed I had, for I was seldom in any danger when I was by myself, or if I was, I got out of it with more dexterity than when I was entangled with the dull measures of other people, who had perhaps less forecast, and were more impatient than I; for though I had as much courage to venture as any of them, yet I used more caution before I undertook a thing, and had more presence of mind to bring myself off.

I have often wondered even at my own hardiness another way, that when all my companions were surprised, and fell so suddenly into the hand of justice, yet I could not all this while enter into one serious resolution to leave off this trade; and especially considering that I was now very far from being poor, that the temptation of necessity, which is the general introduction of all such wickedness, was now removed; that I had near 500*l.* by me in ready money, on which I might have lived very well, if I had thought fit to have retired; but, I say, I had not so much as the least inclination to leave off; no, not so much as I had before, when I had but 200*l.* beforehand, and when I had no such frightful examples before my eyes as these were. From hence 'tis evident, that when once we are hardened in crime, no fear can affect us, no example give us any warning.

I had indeed one comrade, whose fate went very near me for a good while, though I wore it off too in time. That case was indeed very unhappy; I had made a prize of a piece of very good damask in a mercer's shop, and went clear off myself; but had conveyed the piece to this companion of mine, when we went out of the shop; and she went one way, I went another. We had not been long out of the shop, but the mercer missed the piece of stuff, and sent his messengers, one one way, and one another, and they presently seized her that had the piece, with the damask upon her; as for me, I had very luckily stept into a house where there was a lace chamber, up one pair of stairs, and had the satisfaction, or the terror indeed, of looking out of the window, and seeing the poor creature dragged away to the justice, who immediately committed her to Newgate.

I was careful to attempt nothing in the lace chamber, but tumbled their goods pretty much to spend time; then bought a few yards of edging, and paid for it, and came away very sad-hearted indeed, for the poor woman who was in tribulation for what I only had stolen.

Here again my old caution stood me in good stead; though I often robbed with these people, yet I never let them know who I was, nor could they ever find out my lodging, though they often endeavoured to watch me to it. They all knew me by the name of Moll Flanders, though even some of them rather believed I was she, than knew me to be so; my name was public among them indeed; but how to find me out they knew not, nor so much as how to guess at my quarters, whether they were at the east end of the town, or the west; and this wariness was my safety upon all these occasions.

I kept close a great while upon the occasion of this woman's disaster; I knew that if I should do anything that should miscarry, and should be carried to prison, she would be there, and ready to witness against me, and perhaps save her life at my expense; I considered that I began to be very well known by name at the Old Bailey, though they did not know my face; and that if I should fall into their hands, I should be treated as an old offender; and for this reason, I was resolved to see what this poor creature's fate should be

before I stirred, though several times in her distress I conveyed money to her for her relief.

At length she came to her trial. She pleaded she did not
steal the things, but that one Mrs. Flanders, as she heard
her called (for she did not know her), gave the bundle to
her after they came out of the shop, and bade her carry it
home. They asked her where this Mrs. Flanders was? but
she could not produce her, neither could she give the least
account of me; and the mercer's men swearing positively
that she was in the shop when the goods were stolen, that
they immediately missed them, and pursued her, and found
them upon her, thereupon the jury brought her in guilty;
but the court considering that she really was not the person
that stole the goods, and that it was very possible she could
not find out this Mrs. Flanders, meaning me, though it would
save her life, which indeed was true, they allowed her to be
transported; which was the utmost favour she could obtain,
only that the court told her, if she could in the mean time
produce the said Mrs. Flanders, they would intercede for her
pardon; that is to say, if she could find me out, and hang
me, she should not be transported. This I took care to make
impossible to her, and so she was shipped off in pursuance of
her sentence a little while after.

I must repeat it again, that the fate of this poor woman
troubled me exceedingly; and I began to be very pensive,
knowing that I was really the instrument of her disaster:
but my own life, which was so evidently in danger, took off
my tenderness; and seeing she was not put to death, I was
easy at her transportation, because she was then out of the
way of doing me any mischief, whatever should happen.

The disaster of this woman was some months before that
of the last-recited story, and was indeed partly the occasion
of my governess proposing to dress me up in men's clothes,
that I might go about unobserved; but I was soon tired of
that disguise, as I have said, for it exposed me to too many
difficulties.

I was now easy, as to all fear of witnesses against me, for
all those that had either been concerned with me, or that
knew me by the name of Moll Flanders, were either hanged
or transported; and if I should have had the misfortune to
be taken, I might call myself anything else, as well as Moll
Flanders, and no old sins could be placed to my account; so

I began to run a-tick again, with the more freedom, and several successful adventures I made, though not such as I had made before.

We had at that time another fire happened not a great way off from the place where my governess lived, and I made an attempt there as before, but as I was not soon enough before the crowd of people came in, and could not get to the house I aimed at, instead of a prize, I got a mischief, which had almost put a period to my life and all my wicked doings together; for the fire being very furious, and the people in a great fright in removing their goods, and throwing them out of window, a wench from out of a window threw a feather-bed just upon me; it is true, the bed being soft it broke no bones: but as the weight was great, and made greater by the fall, it beat me down, and laid me dead for awhile: nor did the people concern themselves much to deliver me from it, or to recover me at all; but I lay like one dead and neglected a good while, till somebody going to remove the bed out of the way, helped me up; it was indeed a wonder the people in the house had not thrown other goods out after it, and which might have fallen upon it, and then I had been inevitably killed; but I was reserved for farther afflictions.

This accident, however, spoiled my market for that time, and I came home to my governess very much hurt, and frighted, and it was a good while before she could set me upon my feet again.

It was now a merry time of the year, and Bartholomew fair was begun; I had never made any walks that way, nor was the fair of much advantage to me; but I took a turn this year into the cloisters, and there I fell into one of the raffling shops. It was a thing of no great consequence to me, but there came a gentleman extremely well dressed, and very rich, and as 'tis frequent to talk to everybody in those shops, he singled me out, and was very particular with me; first he told me he would put in for me to raffle, and did so; and some small matter coming to his lot, he presented it to me, I think it was a feather muff; then he continued to keep talking to me with a more than common appearance of respect, but still very civil, and much like a gentleman.

He held me in talk so long, till at last he drew me out of the raffling place to the shop door, and then to take a walk in the cloister, still talking of a thousand things cursorily without anything to the purpose: at last he told me that he was charmed with my company, and asked me if I durst trust myself in a coach with him; he told me he was a man of honour, and would not offer anything to me unbecoming him. I seemed to decline it awhile, but suffered myself to be importuned a little, and then yielded.

I was at a loss in my thoughts to conclude at first what this gentleman designed; but I found afterward he had had some drink in his head, and that he was not very unwilling to have some more. He carried me to the Spring-garden, at Knightsbridge, where we walked in the gardens, and he treated me very handsomely; but I found he drank freely; he pressed me also to drink, but I declined it.

Hitherto he kept his word with me, and offered me nothing amiss; we came away in the coach again, and he brought me into the streets, and by this time it was near ten o'clock at night, when he stopped the coach at a house where it seems he was acquainted, and where they made no scruple to show us up stairs into a room with a bed in it; at first I seemed to be unwilling to go up, but after a few words I yielded to that too, being indeed willing to see the end of it, and in hopes to make something of it at last; as for the bed, &c., I was not much concerned about that part.

Here he began to be a little freer with me than he had promised; and I by little and little yielded to everything, so that in a word, he did what he pleased with me; I need say no more. All this while he drank freely too, and about one in the morning we went into the coach again; the air and the shaking of the coach made the drink get more up in his head and he grew uneasy, and was for acting over again what he had been doing before; but as I thought my game now secure, I resisted, and brought him to be a little still, which had not lasted five minutes but he fell fast asleep.

I took this opportunity to search him to a nicety; I took a gold watch, with a silk purse of gold, his fine full-bottom periwig, and silver-fringed gloves, his sword, and fine snuffbox, and gently opening the coach door, stood ready to jump out while the coach was going on; but the coach stopping in the narrow street beyond Temple-Bar to let another coach pass, I got softly out, fastened the door again, and gave my gentleman and the coach the slip together.

This was an adventure indeed unlooked for, and perfectly

undesigned by me; though I was not so past the merry part of life, as to forget how to behave, when a fop so blinded by his appetite should not know an old woman from a young. I did not indeed look so old as I was by ten or twelve years; yet I was not a young wench of seventeen, and it was easy enough to be distinguished. There is nothing so absurd, so surfeiting, so ridiculous, as a man heated by wine in his head, and a wicked gust in his inclination together; he is in the possession of two devils at once, and can no more govern himself by his reason, than a mill can grind without water vice tramples upon all that was in him that had any good in it; nay, his very sense is blinded by its own rage, and he acts absurdities even in his view; such is drinking more, when he is drunk already; picking up a common woman, without any regard to what she is, or who she is; whether sound or rotten, clean or unclean; whether ugly or handsome, old or young; and so blinded as not really to distinguish. Such a man is worse than lunatic; prompted by his vicious head he no more knows what he is doing, than this wretch of mine knew when I picked his pocket of his watch and his purse of gold.

These are the men of whom Solomon says, They go like an ox to the slaughter, till a dart strikes through their liver; an admirable description, by the way, of the foul disease, which is a poisonous deadly contagion mingling with the blood, whose centre or fountain is in the liver; from whence, by the swift circulation of the whole mass, that dreadful nauseous plague strikes immediately through his liver, and his spirits are infected, his vitals stabbed through as with a dart.

It is true this poor unguarded wretch was in no danger from me, though I was greatly apprehensive at first, what danger I might be in from him; but he was really to be pitied in one respect, that he seemed to be a good sort of a man in himself: a gentleman that had no harm in his design; a man of sense, and of a fine behaviour: a comely handsome person, a sober and solid countenance, a charming beautiful face, and everything that could be agreeable; only had unhappily had some drink the night before; had not been in bed, as he told me when we were together; was hot, and his blood fired with wine, and in that condition his reason, as it were asleep, had given him up.

As for me, my business was his money, and what I could make of him ; and after that, if I could have found out any way to have done it, I would have sent him safe home to his house, and to his family, for 'twas ten to one but he had an honest virtuous wife, and innocent children, that were anxious for his safety, and would have been glad to have gotten him home, and taken care of him, till he was restored to himself: and then with what shame and regret would he look back upon himself! how would he reproach himself with associating himself with a whore! picked up in the worst of all holes, the cloister, among the dirt and filth of the town! how would he be trembling for fear he had got the pox, for fear a dart had struck through his liver, and hate himself every time he looked back upon the madness and brutality of his debauch! how would he, if he had any principles of honour, abhor the thought of giving any ill distemper, if he had it, as for aught he knew he might, to his modest and virtuous wife, and thereby sowing the contagion in the life-blood of his posterity.

Would such gentlemen but consider the contemptible thoughts which the very women they are concerned with, in such cases as these, have of them, it would be a surfeit to them. As I said above, they value not the pleasure, they are raised by no inclination to the man, the passive jade thinks of no pleasure but the money; and when he is as it were drunk in the ecstacies of his wicked pleasure, her hands are in his pockets for what she can find there ; and of which he can no more be sensible in the moment of his folly, than he can fore-think of it when he goes about it.

I knew a woman that was so dexterous with a fellow, who indeed deserved no better usage, that while he was busy with her another way, conveyed his purse with twenty guineas in it out of his fob pocket, where he had put it for fear of her, and put another purse with gilded counters in it into the room of it. After he had done, he says to her, Now han't you picked my pocket? She jested with him, and told him she supposed he had not much to lose ; he put his hand to his fob, and with his fingers felt that his purse was there which fully satisfied him, and so she brought off his money. And this was a trade with her ; she kept a sham gold watch, and a purse of counters in her pocket to be ready on all such occasions ; and I doubt not practised it with success.

I came home with this last booty to my governess, and really when I told her the story, it so affected her, that she was hardly able to forbear tears, to think how such a gentleman run a daily risk of being undone, every time a glass of wine got into his head.

But as to the purchase I got, and how entirely I stripped him, she told me it pleased her wonderfully; Nay, child, says she, The usage may, for aught I know, do more to reform him, than all the sermons that ever he will hear in his life. And if the remainder of the story be true, so it did.

I found the next day, she was wonderful inquisitive about this gentleman; the description I gave her of him, his dress, his person, his face, all concurred to make her think of a gentleman whose character she knew; she mused awhile, and I going on in the particulars, says she, I lay a 100l. I know the man.

I am sorry if you do, says I, for I would not have him exposed on any account in the world; he has had injury enough already, and I would not be instrumental to do him any more. No, no, says she, I will do him no injury, but you may let me satisfy my curiosity a little, for if it is he, I warrant you I find it out. I was a little startled at that, and I told her with an apparent concern in my face, that by the same rule he might find me out, and then I was undone. She returned warmly, Why, do you think I will betray you child? No, no, says she, not for all he is worth in the world; I have kept your counsel in worse things than these, sure you may trust me in this. So I said no more.

She laid her scheme another way, and without acquainting me with it, but she was resolved to find it out; so she goes to a certain friend of hers, who was acquainted in the family that she guessed at, and told her she had some extraordinary business with such a gentleman (who by the way was no less than a baronet, and of a very good family), and that she knew not how to come at him without somebody to introduce her. Her friend promised her readily to do it, and accordingly goes to the house to see if the gentleman was in town.

The next day, she comes to my governess and tells her, that Sir ———— was at home, but that he had met with a disaster and was very ill, and there was no speaking to him. What disaster? says my governess, hastily, as if she was surprised at it. Why, says her friend, he had been at Hampstead to visit a gentleman of his acquaintance, and as he came back again, he was set upon and robbed! and having got a little drink too, as they suppose, the rogues abused him, and he is very ill. Robbed! says my governess, and what did they take from him? Why, says her friend, they took his gold watch, and his gold snuff-box, his fine periwig, and what money he had in his pocket, which was considerable to be sure, for Sir ———— never goes without a purse of guineas about him.

Pshaw! says my old governess, jeering, I warrant you he has got drunk now, and got a whore, and she has picked his pocket, and so he comes home to his wife and tells her he has been robbed; that's an old sham, a thousand such tricks are put upon the poor women every day.

Fie, says her friend, I find you don't know Sir ————; why he is as civil a gentleman, there is not a finer man, nor a soberer, modester person in the whole city; he abhors such things; there's nobody that knows him will think such a thing of him. Well, well, says my governess, that's none of my business; if it was, I warrant I should find there was something of that in it; your modest men in common opinion are sometimes no better than other people, only they keep a better character, or if you please, are the better hypocrites.

No, no, says her friend, I can assure you Sir ————is no hypocrite, he is really an honest, sober gentleman, and he has certainly been robbed. Nay, says my governess, it may be he has; it is no business of mine I tell you; I only want to speak with him, my business is of another nature. But, says her friend, let your business be of what nature it will, you cannot see him yet, for he his not fit to be seen, for he is very ill, and bruised very much. Ay, says my governess, nay then he has fallen into bad hands to be sure. And then she asked gravely, Pray where is he bruised? Why in his head, says her friend, and one of his hands, and his face, for they used him barbarously. Poor gentleman, says my governess. I must wait then till he recovers; and adds, I hope it will not be long.

Away she comes to me, and tells me this story. I have found out your fine gentleman, and a fine gentleman he was, says she; but mercy on him, he is in a said pickle now, I wonder what the d————. you. have done to him; why you

have almost killed him. I looked at her with disorder enough;
I killed him! says I, you must mistake the person, I am sure
I did nothing to him; he was very well when I left him, said
I, only drunk and fast asleep. I know nothing of that, says
she, but he is in a sad pickle now; and so she told me all
that her friend had said. Well then, says I, he fell into bad
hands after I left him, for I left him safe enough.

About ten days after, my governess goes again to her friend,
to introduce her to this gentleman; she had inquired other
ways in the mean time, and found that he was about again,
so she got leave to speak with him.

She was a woman of an admirable address, and wanted
nobody to introduce her; she told her tale much better than
I shall be able to tell it for her, for she was mistress of her
tongue, as I said already. She told him that she came, though
a stranger, with a single design of doing him a service, and
he should find she had no other end in it; that as she came
purely on so friendly an account, she begged a promise from
him, that if he did not accept what she should officiously
propose, he would not take it ill that she meddled with what
was not her business; she assured him that as what she had
to say was a secret that belonged to him only, so whether he
accepted her offer or not, it should remain a secret to all the
world, unless he exposed it himself; nor should his refusing
her service in it, make her so little show her respect, as to
do him the least injury, so that he should be entirely at liberty
to act as he thought fit.

He looked very shy at first, and said he knew nothing that
related to him that required much secrecy; that he had never
done any man any wrong, and cared not what anybody might
say of him; that it was no part of his character to be unjust
to anybody, nor could he imagine in what any man could
render him any service; but that if it was as she said, he
could not take it ill from any one that should endeavour
to serve him; and so, as it were, left her at liberty either to
tell him or not to tell him, as she thought fit.

She found him so perfectly indifferent, that she was almost
afraid to enter into the point with him; but, however, after
some other circumlocutions, she told him, that by a strange
and unaccountable accident she came to have a particular
knowledge of the late unhappy adventure he had fallen into;
and that in such a manner, that there was nobody in the

world but herself and him that were acquainted with it, no, not the very person that was with him.

He looked a little angrily at first. What adventure? said he. Why sir, said she, of your being robbed coming from Knightsbr—, Hampstead, sir, I should say, says she : be not surprised, sir, says she, that I am able to tell you every step you took that day from the cloister in Smithfield, to the Spring-garden at Knightsbridge, and thence to the —— in the Strand, and how you were left asleep in the coach afterwards ; I say let not this surprise you, for, sir, I do not come to make a booty of you, I ask nothing of you, and I assure you the woman that was with you knows nothing who you are, and never shall; and yet perhaps I may serve you farther still, for I did not come barely to let you know that I was informed of these things, as if I wanted a bribe to conceal them ; assure yourself, sir, said she, that whatever you think fit to do or say to me, it shall be all a secret as it is, as much as if I were in my grave.

He was astonished at her discourse, and said gravely to her, Madam, you are a stranger to me, but it is very unfortunate that you should be let into the secret of the worst action of my life, and a thing that I am justly ashamed of, in which the only satisfaction I had was, that I thought it was known only to God and my own conscience. Pray, sir, says she, do not reckon the discovery of it to me to be any part of your misfortune; it was a thing I believe you were surprised into, and perhaps the woman used some art to prompt you to it; however, you will never find any just cause, said she, to repent that I came to hear of it ; nor can your mouth be more silent in it than I have been, and ever shall be.

Well, says he, but let me do some justice to the woman too : whoever she is, I do assure you she prompted me to nothing, she rather declined me ; it was my own folly and madness that brought me into it all, ay, and brought her into it too ; I must give her her due so far. As to what she took from me, I could expect no less from her in the condition I was in, and to this hour I know not whether she robbed me or the coachman; if she did it, I forgive her : I think all gentlemen that do so, should be used in the same manner ; but I am more concerned for some other things, than I am for all that she took from me.

My governess now began to come into the whole matter,

and he opened himself freely to her; first, she said to him,
in answer to what he had said about me, I am glad, sir, you
are so just to the person that you were with; I assure you
she is a gentlewoman, and no woman of the town; and however you prevailed with her as you did, I am sure 'tis not
her practice; you run a great venture indeed, sir, but if that
be part of your care, you may be perfectly easy, for I do
assure you no man has touched her before you, since her
husband; and he has been dead now almost eight years.

It appeared that this was his grievance, and that he was
in a very great fright about it; however, when my governess
said this to him, he appeared very well pleased, and said,
Well, madam, to be plain with you, if I was satisfied of that,
I should not so much value what I lost; for as to that, the
temptation was great, and perhaps she was poor, and wanted
it. If she had not been poor, sir, says she, I assure you she
would never have yielded to you; and as her poverty first
prevailed with you to let you do as you did, so the same
poverty prevailed with her to pay herself at last, when she
saw you was in such a condition, that if she had not done it,
perhaps the next coachman or chairman might have done it
more to your hurt.

Well, says he, much good may it do her; I say again, All
the gentlemen that do so, ought to be used in the same
manner, and then they would be cautious of themselves; I
have no more concern about it, but on the score which you
hinted at before. Here he entered into some freedoms with
her on the subject of what passed between us, which are not
so proper for a woman to write, and the great terror that was
upon his mind with relation to his wife, for fear she should
have received any injury from me, and should communicate
it farther; and asked her at last if she could not procure him
an opportunity to speak with me. My governess gave him
farther assurances of my being a woman clear from any such
thing, and that he was as entirely safe in that respect, as he
was with his own lady; but as for seeing me, she said it
might be of dangerous consequence; but however, that she
would talk with me, and let him know; endeavouring at the
same time to persuade him not to desire it, and that it could
be of no service to him; seeing she hoped he had no desire
to renew the correspondence, and that on my account it was
a kind of putting my life in his hands.

He told her he had a great desire to see me, that he would give her any assurances that were in his power, not to take any advantages of me, and that in the first place he would give me a general release from all demands of any kind. She insisted how it might tend to farther divulging the secret, and might be injurious to him, entreating him not to press for it; so at length he desisted.

They had some discourse upon the subject of the things he had lost, and he seemed to be very desirous of his gold watch, and told her if she could procure that for him, he would willingly give as much for it as it was worth. She told him she would endeavour to procure it for him, and leave the valuing it to himself.

Accordingly the next day she carried the watch, and he gave her thirty guineas for it, which was more than I should have been able to make of it, though it seems it cost much more; he spoke something of his periwig, which it seems cost him three-score guineas, and his snuff-box, and in a few days more she carried them too, which obliged him very much, and he gave her thirty more: the next day I sent him his fine sword and cane gratis, and demanded nothing of him, but had no mind to see him, unless he might be satisfied I knew who he was, which he was not willing to.

Then he entered into a long talk with her of the manner how she came to know all this matter. She formed a long tale of that part; how she had it from one that I had told the whole story to, and that was to help me dispose of the goods; and this confidant brought things to her, she being by professsion a pawnbroker; and she hearing of his worship's disaster, guessed at the thing in general; that having gotten the things into her hands, she had resolved to come and try as she had done. She then gave him repeated assurances that it should never go out of her mouth, and though she knew the woman very well, yet she had not let her know, meaning me, anything of who the person was, which by the way was false; but however it was not to his damage, for I never opened my mouth of it to anybody.

I had a great many thoughts in my head about my seeing him again, and was often sorry that I had refused it; I was persuaded that if I had seen him, and let him know that I knew him, I should have made some advantage of him, and perhaps have had some maintenance from him; and though it was a life wicked enough, yet it was not so full of danger as this I was engaged in: however those thoughts wore off, and I declined seeing him again, for that time; but my governess saw him often, and he was very kind to her, giving her something almost every time he saw her. One time in particular she found him very merry, and as she thought he had some wine in his head then, and he pressed her again to let him see that woman, that, as he said, had bewitched him so that night, my governess, who was from the beginning for my seeing him, told him he was so desirous of it, that she could almost yield to it, if she could prevail upon me; adding that if he would please to come to her house in the evening, she would endeavour it, upon his repeated assurances of forgetting what was past.

Accordingly she came to me, and told me all the discourse; in short, she soon biassed me to consent, in a case which I had some regret in my mind for declining before; so I prepared to see him. I dressed me to all the advantage possible, I assure you, and for the first time used a little art; I say for the first time, for I had never yielded to the baseness of paint before, having always had vanity enough to believe I had no need of it.

At the hour appointed he came; and as she observed before, so it was plain still, that he had been drinking, though very far from what we call being in drink. He appeared exceeding pleased to see me, and entered into a long discourse with me upon the whole affair; I begged his pardon very often, for my share of it, protested I had not any such design when first I met him, that I had not gone out with him but that I took him for a very civil gentleman, and that he made me so many promises of offering no incivility to me.

He alleged the wine he drank, and that he scarce knew what he did, and that if it had not been so, he should never have taken the freedom with me he had done. He protested to me that he never touched any woman but me since he was married to his wife, and it was a surprise upon him: complimented me upon being so particularly agreeable to him, and the like, and talked so much of that kind, till I found he had talked himself almost into a temper to do the thing again. But I took him up short; I protested I had never suffered any man to touch me since my husband died,

which was near eight years : he said he believed it; and
added, that madam had intimated as much to him, and that
it was his opinion of that part which made him desire to see
me again; and since he had once broken in upon his virtue
with me, and found no ill consequences, he could be safe in
venturing again; and so in short he went on to what I
expected, and to what will not bear relating.

My old governess had foreseen it, as well as I, and therefore led him into a room which had not a bed in it, and yet
had a chamber within it which had a bed, whither we withdrew for the rest of the night, and, in short, after some time
being together, he went to bed, and lay there all night, I
withdrew, but came again undressed before it was day, and
lay with him the rest of the time.

Thus, you see, having committed a crime once is a sad
handle to the committing of it again: all the reflections wear
off when the temptation renews itself. Had I not yielded to
see him again, the corrupt desire in him had worn off, and
'tis very probable he had never fallen into it with anybody
else, as I really believe he had not done before.

When he went away, I told him I hoped he was satisfied
he had not been robbed again. He told me he was fully
satisfied in that point; and putting his hand in his pocket
gave me five guineas, which was the first money I had
gained that way for many years.

I had several visits of the like kind from him, but he
never came into a settled way of maintenance, which was
what I would have been best pleased with. Once, indeed,
he asked me how I did to live; I answered him pretty quick,
that I assured him I had never taken that course that I took
with him; but that indeed I worked at my needle, and could
just maintain myself, that sometimes it was as much as I
was able to do, and I shifted hard enough.

He seemed to reflect upon himself, that he should be the
first person to lead me into that which he assured me he
never intended to do himself; and it touched him a little, he
said, that he should be the cause of his own sin and mine too.
He would often make just reflections also upon the crime
itself and upon the particular circumstances of it, with respect
to himself; how wine introduced the inclinations, how the
devil led him to the place, and found out an object to tempt
him, and he made the moral always himself.

When these thoughts were upon him, he would go away, and pernaps not come again in a month's time or longer; but then as the serious part wore off, the lewd part would wear in, and then he came prepared for the wicked part. Thus we lived for some time; though he did not keep, as they call it, yet he never failed doing things that were handsome, and sufficient to maintain me without working; and, which was better, without following my old trade.

But this affair had its end too; for after about a year, I found that he did not come so often as usual, and at last he left it off altogether without any dislike, or bidding adieu; and so there was an end of that short scene of life, which added no great store to me, only to make more work for repentance.

During this interval, I confined myself pretty much at home; at least being thus provided for, I made no adventures, no, not for a quarter of a year after; but then finding the fund fail, and being loath to spend upon the main stock, I began to think of my old trade, and to look abroad into the street; and my first step was lucky enough.

I had dressed myself up in a very mean habit, for as I had several shapes to appear in, I was now in an ordinary stuff gown, a blue apron, and a straw hat; and I placed myself at the door of the Three Cups inn in St. John's-street. There were several carriers used the inn, and the stage-coaches for Barnet, for Totteridge, and other towns that way, stood always in the street, in the evening, when they prepared to set out; so that I was ready for anything that offered. The meaning was this; people come frequently with bundles and small parcels to those inns, and call for such carriers or coaches as they want, to carry them into the country; and there generally attends women, porters' wives or daughters, ready to take in such things for the people that employ them.

It happened very oddly that I was standing at the inn-gate, and a woman that stood there before, and which was the porter's wife belonging to the Barnet stage-coach, having observed me, asked if I waited for any of the coaches; I told her yes, I waited for my mistress, that was coming to go to Barnet; she asked me who was my mistress, and I told her any madam's name that came next me; but it seemed I happened upon a name a family of which name lived at Hadley, near Barnet.

I said no more to her, or she to me, a good while; but by and by, somebody calling her at a door a little way off, she desired me that if anybody called for the Barnet coach, I would step and call her at the house, which it seems was an alehouse; I said yes, very readily, and away she went.

She was no sooner gone; but comes a wench and a child, puffing and sweating, and asks for the Barnet coach; I answered presently, Here. Do you belong to the Barnet coach? says she. Yes sweetheart, said I, what do you want? I want room for two passengers, says she. Where are they, sweetheart? said I. Here's this girl, pray let her go into the coach, says she, and I'll go and fetch my mistress. Make haste then, sweetheart, says I, for we may be full else. The maid had a great bundle under her arm; so she put the child into the coach; and I said, You had best put your bundle into the coach too. No, said she, I am afraid somebody should slip it away from the child. Give it me then, said I. Take it then, says she, and be sure you take care of it. I'll answer for it, said I, if it were 20l. value. There, take it then, says she, and away she goes.

As soon as I got the bundle, and the maid was out of sight, I goes on towards the alehouse, where the porter's wife was; so that if I had met her, I had then only been going to give her the bundle and to call her to her business, as if I was going away, and could stay no longer; but as I did not meet her, I walked away, and turning into Charterhouse-lane, made off through Charterhouse-yard, into Long-lane, then into Bartholomew-close, so into Little-Britain, and through the Bluecoat-hospital, to Newgate-street.

To prevent being known, I pulled off my blue apron, and wrapt the bundle in it, which was made up in a piece of painted calico; I also wrapt up my straw hat in it, and so put the bundle upon my head; and it was very well that I did thus, for coming through the Bluecoat-hospital, who should I meet but the wench that had given me the bundle to hold; it seems she was going with her mistress, who she had been to fetch, to the the Barnet coaches.

I saw she was in haste, and I had no business to stop her; so away she went, and I brought my bundle safe to my governess. There was no money, plate, or jewels in it; but a very good suit of Indian damask, a gown and petticoat, a

o 2

laced head and ruffles of very good Flanders lace, and some other things, such as I knew very well the value of.

This was not indeed my own invention, but was given me by one that had practised it with success, and my governess liked it extremely; and indeed, I tried it again several times, though never twice near the same place; for the next time I tried in Whitechapel, just by the corner of Petticoat-lane, where the coaches stand that go out to Stratford and Bow, and that side of the country; and another time at the Flying-horse without Bishopsgate, where the Cheston coaches then lay; and I had always the good luck to come off with some booty.

Another time I placed myself at a warehouse by the water side, where the coasting vessels from the north come, such as Newcastle-upon-Tyne, Sunderland, and other places. Here, the warehouse being shut, comes a young fellow with a letter; and he wanted a box and a hamper that was come from Newcastle-upon-Tyne. I asked him if he had the marks of it; so he shows me the letter, by virtue of which he was to ask for it, and which gave an account of the contents, the box being full of linen, and the hamper full of glass ware. I read the letter, and took care to see the name, and the marks, the name of the person that sent the goods, and the name of the person they were sent to; then I bade the messenger come in the morning, for that the warehouse-keeper would not be there any more that night.

Away went I, and wrote a letter from Mr. John Richardson of Newcastle to his dear cousin Jemmy Cole, in London, with an account that he had sent by such a vessel (for I remembered all the particulars to a tittle), so many pieces of huckaback linen, and so many ells of Dutch holland, and the like, in a box, and a hamper of flint glasses from Mr. Henzill's glass house; and that the box was marked I. C. No. 1., and the hamper was directed by a label on the cording.

About an hour after, I came to the warehouse, found the warehouse-keeper, and had the goods delivered me without any scruple; the value of the linen being about 22l.

I could fill up this whole discourse with the variety of such adventures, which daily invention directed to, and which I managed with the utmost dexterity, and always with success.

At length, as when does the pitcher come safe home that

goes so often to the well, I fell into some broils, which though they could not affect me fatally, yet made me known, which was the worst thing next to being found guilty that could befall me.

I had taken up the disguise of a widow's dress; it was without any real design in view, but only waiting for anything that might offer, as I often did. It happened that while I was going along a street in Covent-garden, there was a great cry of Stop thief, stop thief; some artists had, it seems, put a trick upon a shopkeeper, and being pursued, some of them fled one way, and some another; and one of them was, they said, dressed up in widow's weeds, upon which the mob gathered about me, and some said I was the person, others said no. Immediately came the mercer's journeyman, and he swore aloud I was the person, and so seized on me; however, when I was brought back by the mob to the mercer's shop, the master of the house said freely that I was not the woman; and would have let me go immediately, but another fellow said gravely, Pray stay till Mr. ———, meaning the journeyman, comes back, for he knows her; so they kept me near half an hour. They had called a constable, and he stood in the shop as my jailer; in talking with the constable I inquired where he lived, and what trade he was; the man not apprehending in the least what happened afterwards, readily told me his name, and where he lived; and told me as a jest, that I might be sure to hear of his name when I came to the Old Bailey.

The servants likewise used me saucily, and had much ado to keep their hands off me, the master indeed was civiller to me than they; but he would not let me go, though he owned I was not in his shop before.

I began to be a little surly with him, and told him I hoped he would not take it ill, if I made myself amends upon him another time; and desired I might send for friends to see me have right done. No, he said, he could give no such liberty, I might ask it when I came before the justice of peace; and seeing I threatened him, he would take care of me in the mean time, and would lodge me safe in Newgate. I told him it was his time now, but it would be mine by and by, and governed my passion as well as I was able: however, I spoke to the constable to call me a porter, which he did, and then I called for pen, ink, and paper, but they would let me

have none; I asked the porter his name, and where he lived,
and the poor man told it me very willingly; I bade him
observe and remember how I was treated there; that he saw
I was detained there by force; I told him I should want him
in another place, and it should not be the worse for him to
speak.   The porter said he would serve me with all his
heart; but, madam, says he, let me hear them refuse to let
you go, then I may be able to speak the plainer.

With that, I spoke aloud to the master of the shop, and
said, Sir, you know in your own conscience that I am not
the person you look for, and that I was not in your shop
before, therefore I demand that you detain me here no
longer, or tell me the reason of your stopping me.   The
fellow grew surlier upon this than before, and said he would
do neither till he thought fit.   Very well, said I, to the
constable and to the porter, you will be pleased to remember
this, gentlemen, another time.   The porter said, Yes, madam;
and the constable began not to like it, and would have persuaded the mercer to dismiss him, and let me go, since, as he
said, he owned I was not the person.   Good sir, says the
mercer to him tauntingly, are you a justice of peace, or a
constable?   I charged you with her, pray do your duty.
The constable told him, a little moved, but very handsomely,
I know my duty, and what I am, sir; I doubt you hardly
know what you are doing.   They had some other hard
words, and in the mean time the journeymen, impudent and
unmanly to the last degree, used me barbarously, and one of
them, the same that first seized upon me, pretended he would
search me, and began to lay hands on me.   I spit in his
face, called out to the constable, and bade him take notice of
my usage; and pray, Mr. Constable, said I, ask that villain's
name, pointing to the man.   The constable reproved him
decently, told him that he did not know what he did, for he
knew that his master acknowledged I was not the person;
and, says the constable, I am afraid your master is bringing
himself and me too into trouble, if this gentlewoman comes to
prove who she is, and where she was, and it appears that
she is not the woman you pretend to.   Damn her, says the
fellow again, with an impudent hardened face, she is the
lady you may depend upon it, I'll swear she is the same
body that was in the shop, and that I gave the piece of satin
that is lost into her own hand: you shall hear more of it

when Mr. William and Mr. Anthony (those were other journeymen) come back, they will know her again as well as I.

Just as the insolent rogue was talking thus to the constable, comes back Mr. William and Mr. Anthony, as he called them, and a great rabble with them, bringing along with them the true widow that I was pretended to be; and they came sweating and blowing into the shop, and with a great deal of triumph dragging the poor creature in a most butcherly manner up towards their master, who was in the back shop; and they cried out aloud, Here's the widow, sir, we have catched her at last. What do you mean by that? says the master; why we have her already, there she sits, and Mr. —— says he can swear this is she. The other man, who they called Mr. Anthony, replied; Mr. —— may say what he will, and swear what he will, but this is the woman, and there's the remnant of satin she stole; I took it out of her clothes with my own hand.

I now began to take a better heart, but smiled, and said nothing; the master looked pale; the constable turned about and looked at me. Let 'em alone, Mr. Constable, said I; let 'em go on. The case was plain and could not be denied, so the constable was charged with the right thief, and the mercer told me very civilly he was sorry for the mistake, and hoped I would not take it ill; that they had so many things of this nature put upon them every day, that they could not be blamed for being very sharp in doing themselves justice. Not take it ill, sir! said I; how can I take it well? if you had dismissed me when your insolent fellow seized on me in the street, and brought me to you, and when you yourself acknowledged I was not the person, I would have put it by, and not have taken it ill, because of the many ill things I believe you have put upon you daily; but your treatment of me since has been insufferable, and especially that of your servant, I must and will have reparation for that.

Then he began to parley with me, said he would make me any reasonable satisfaction, and would fain have had me told him what it was I expected. I told him I should not be my own judge, the law should decide it for me, and as I was to be carried before a magistrate; I should let him hear there what I had to say. He told me there was no occasion to go before the justice now, I was at liberty to go where I pleased;

and calling to the constable, told him he might let me go, for I was discharged. The constable said calmly to him, Sir, you asked me just now, if I knew whether I was a constable or a justice, and bade me do my duty, and charged me with this gentlewoman as a prisoner; now, sir, I find you do not understand what is my duty, for you would make me a justice indeed; but I must tell you it is not in my power: I may keep a prisoner when I am charged with him, but 'tis the law and the magistrate alone that can discharge that prisoner; therefore, 'tis a mistake sir, I must carry her before a justice now, whether you think well of it or not. The mercer was very high with the constable at first; but the constable happening to be not a hired officer, but a good, substantial kind of man (I think he was a corn-chandler), and a man of good sense, stood to his business, would not discharge me without going to a justice of the peace, and I insisted upon it too. When the mercer saw that, Well, says he to the constable, you may carry her where you please, I have nothing to say to her. But, sir, says the constable, you will go with us, I hope, for 'tis you that charged me with her. No, not I, says the mercer, I tell you I have nothing to say to her. But pray, sir, do, says the constable; I desire it of you for your own sake, for the justice can do nothing without you. Prithee, fellow, says the mercer, go about your business; I tell you I have nothing to say to the gentlewoman, I charge you in the king's name to dismiss her. Sir, says the constable, I find you don't know what it is to be a constable; I beg of you don't oblige me to be rude to you. I think I need not, you are rude enough already, says the mercer. No, sir, says the constable, I am not rude; you have broken the peace in bringing an honest woman out of the street, when she was about her lawful occasions, confining her in your shop, and ill using her here by your servants; and now can you say I am rude to you? I think I am civil to you, in not commanding you in the king's name to go with me, and charging every man I see that passes your door, to aid and assist me in carrying you by force; this you know I have power to do, and yet I forbear it, and once more entreat you to go with me. Well, he would not for all this, and gave the constable ill language. However, the constable kept his temper, and would not be provoked; and then I put in and said, Come, Mr. Constable, let him alone; I shall find ways enough to fetch him before a magistrate, I don't fear that; but there's that fellow, says I, he was the man that seized on me as I was innocently going along the street, and you are a witness of his violence with me since; give me leave to charge you with him, and carry him before a justice. Yes, madam, says the constable; and turning to the fellow, Come young gentleman, says he to the journeyman, you must go along with us; I hope you are not above the constable's power, though your master is.

The fellow looked like a condemned thief, and hung back, then looked at his master, as if he could help him; and he, like a fool, encouraged the fellow to be rude, and he truly resisted the constable, and pushed him back with a good force when he went to lay hold on him, at which the constable knocked him down, and called out for help, immediately the shop was filled with people, and the constable seized the master and man, and all his servants.

The first ill consequence of this fray was, that the woman who was really the thief, made off, and got clear away in the crowd; and two others that they had stopped also; whether they were really guilty or not, that I can say nothing to.

By this time some of his neighbours having come in, and seeing how things went, had endeavoured to bring the mercer to his senses; and he began to be convinced that he was in the wrong; and so at length we went all very quietly before the justice, with a mob of about five hundred people at our heels; and all the way we went I could hear the people ask what was the matter? and others reply and say, a mercer had stopped a gentlewoman instead of a thief, and had afterwards taken the thief, and now the gentlewoman had taken the mercer, and was carrying him before the justice. This pleased the people strangely, and made the crowd increase, and they cried out as they went, which is the rogue? which is the mercer? and especially the women: then when they saw him they cried out, That's he, that's he; and every now and then came a good dab of dirt at him; and thus we marched a good while, till the mercer thought fit to desire the constable to call a coach to protect himself from the rabble; so we rode the rest of the way, the constable and I, and the mercer and his man.

When we came to the justice, which was an ancient gentleman in Bloomsbury, the constable giving first a summary

account of the matter, the justice bade me speak, and tell
what I had to say; and first he asked my name, which I was
very loath to give, but there was no remedy, so I told him my
name was Mary Flanders, that I was a widow, my husband
being a sea captain, died on a voyage to Virginia; and some
other circumstances I told which he could never contradict,
and that I lodged at present in town, with such a person,
naming my governess; but that I was preparing to go over
to America, where my husband's effects lay, and that I was
going that day to buy some clothes to put myself into second
mourning, but had not yet been in any shop, when that
fellow, pointing to the mercer's journeyman, came rushing
upon me with such fury, as very much frighted me, and
carried me back to his master's shop; where, though his
master acknowledged I was not the person, yet he would not
dismiss me, but charged a constable with me.

Then I proceeded to tell how the journeymen treated me;
how they would not suffer me to send for any of my friends;
how afterwards they found the real thief, and took the goods
they had lost upon her, and all the particulars as before.

Then the constable related his case; his dialogue with the
mercer about discharging me, and at last his servant's refusing
to go with him, when I had charged him with him, and his
master encouraging him to do so; and at last his striking the
constable, and the like, all as I have told it already.

The justice then heard the mercer and his man. The mercer indeed made a long harangue of the great loss they have
daily by the lifters and thieves; that it was easy for them to
mistake, and that when he found it, he would have dismissed
me, &c., as above. As to the journeyman, he had very little
to say, but that he pretended other of the servants told him
that I was really the person.

Upon the whole, the justice first of all told me very cour-
teously I was discharged; that he was very sorry that the
mercer's man should in his eager pursuit have so little discretion as to take up an innocent person for a guilty; that if
he had not been so unjust as to detain me afterwards, he believed I would have forgiven the first affront; that, however,
it was not in his power to award me any reparation, other
than by openly reproving them, which he should do; but he
supposed I would apply to such methods as the law directed;
in the mean time he would bind him over.

But as to the breach of the peace committed by the journeyman, he told me he should give me some satisfaction for that, for he should commit him to Newgate for assaulting the constable, and for assaulting of me also. .

Accordingly he sent the fellow to Newgate for that assault, and his master gave bail, and so we came away; but I had the satisfaction of seeing the mob wait upon them both, as they came out, hallooing and throwing stones and dirt at the coaches they rode in; and so I came home. ·

After this hustle, coming home, and telling my governess the story, she falls a laughing at me; Why are you so merry, say I? the story has not so much laughing room in it, as you imagine; I am sure I have had a great deal of hurry and fright too, with a pack of ugly rogues. Laugh, says my governess, I laugh, child, to see what a lucky creature you are; why this job will be the best bargain to you that ever you made in your life, if you manage it well. I warrant you, you shall make the mercer pay 500l. for damages, besides what you shall get of the journeyman.

I had other thoughts of the matter than she had; and especially, because I had given in my name to the justice of peace; and I knew that my name was so well known among the people at Hicks's-hall, the Old Bailey, and such places, that if this cause came to be tried openly, and my name came to be inquired into, no court would give much damages, for the reputation of a person of such a character. However, I was obliged to begin a prosecution in form, and accordingly my governess found me out a very creditable sort of man to manage it, being an attorney of very good business, and of good reputation, and she was certainly in the right of this; for had she employed a pettifogging hedge solicitor, or a man not known, I should have brought it to but little.

I met this attorney, and gave him all the particulars at large, as they are recited above; and he assured me it was a case, as he said, that he did not question but that a jury would give very considerable damages; so taking his full instructions, he began the prosecution, and the mercer being arrested, gave bail; a few days after his giving bail, he comes with his attorney to my attorney, to let him know that he desired to accomodate the matter; that it was all carried on in the heat of an unhappy passion; that his client, meaning me, had a sharp provoking tongue, and that I used them ill,

gibing at them, and jeering them, even while they believed
me to be the very person, and that I had provoked them, and
the like.

My attorney managed as well on my side; made them believe I was a widow of fortune, that I was able to do myself
justice, and had great friends to stand by me too, who had
all made me promise to sue to the utmost, if it cost me a
thousand pounds, for that the affronts I had received were
insufferable.

However, they brought my attorney to this, that he promised he would not blow the coals; that if I inclined to an
accommodation, he would not hinder me, and that he would
rather persuade me to peace than to war; for which they told
him he should be no loser; all which he told me very honestly,
and told me that if they offered him any bribe, I should certainly know it; but upon the whole he told me very honestly
that if I would take his opinion, he would advise me to make
it up with them, for that as they were in a great fright, and
were desirous above all things to make it up, and knew that
let it be what it would, they must bear all the costs, he believed they would give me freely more than any jury would
give upon a trial. I asked him what he thought they would
be brought to; he told me he could not tell, as to that, but
he would tell me more when I saw him again.

Some time after this, they came again, to know if he had
talked with me. He told them he had, that he found me not so,
averse to an accommodation as some of my friends were, who
resented the disgrace offered me, and set me on; that they
blowed the coals in secret, prompting me to revenge, or to do
myself justice, as they called it; so that he could not tell
what to say to it; he told them he would do his endeavour
to persuade me, but he ought to be able to tell me what proposal
they made. They pretended they could not make any proposal, because it might be made use of against them; and he
told them, that by the same rule he could not make any
offers, for that might be pleaded in abatement of what damages a jury might be inclined to give. However, after some
discourse, and mutual promises that no advantage should be
taken on either side, by what was transacted then, or at any
other of those meetings, they came to a kind of a treaty; but
so remote, and so wide from one another, that nothing could
be expected from it; for my attorney demanded 500*l.* and

charges, and they offered 50*l.* without charges; so they broke off, and the mercer proposed to have a meeting with me myself; and my attorney agreed to that very readily.

My attorney gave me notice to come to this meeting in good clothes, and with some state, that the mercer might see I was something more than I seemed to be that time they had me. Accordingly I came in a new suit of second mourning, according to what I had said at the justice's; I set myself out too, as well as a widow's dress would admit; my governess also furnished me with a good pearl necklace, that shut in behind with a locket of diamonds, which she had in pawn; and I had a very good gold watch by my side: so that I made a very good figure, and as I stayed till I was sure they were come, I came in a coach to the door, with my maid with me.

When I came into the room, the mercer was surprised; he stood up and made his bow, which I took a little notice of, and but a little, and went and sat down where my own attorney had appointed me to sit, for it was his house. After awhile, the mercer said, he did not know me again, and began to make some compliments. I told him, I believed he did not know me, at first; and that if he had, he would not have treated me as he did.

He told me he was very sorry for what had happened, and that it was to testify the willingness he had to make all possible reparation, that he had appointed this meeting; that he hoped I would not carry things to extremity, which might be not only too great a loss to him, but might be the ruin of his business and shop, in which case I might have the satisfaction of repaying an injury with an injury ten times greater; but that I would then get nothing, whereas he was willing to do me any justice that was in his power, without putting himself or me to the trouble or charge of a suit at law.

I told him I was glad to hear him talk so much more like a man of sense than he did before; that it was true, acknowledgment in most cases of affronts was counted reparation sufficient; but that this had gone too far to be made up so; that I was not revengeful, nor did I seek his ruin, or any man's else, but that all my friends were unanimous not to let me so far neglect my character, as to adjust a thing of this kind without reparation. That to be taken up for a thief, was such an indignity as could not be put up, that my character was above being treated so by any that knew me, but because in my condition of a widow I had been careless of myself, I might be taken for such a creature, but that for the particular usage I had from him afterward; and then I repeated all as before, it was so provoking, I had scarce patience to repeat it.

He acknowledged all, and was mighty humble indeed; he came up to 100*l*., and to pay all the law charges, and added, that he would make me a present of a very good suit of clothes; I came down to 300*l*., and demanded that I should publish an advertisment of the particulars in the common newspapers.

This was a clause he never could comply with; however, at last he came up, by good management of my attorney, to 150*l*. and a suit of black silk clothes, and there, as it were at my attorney's request, I complied; he paying my attorney's bill and charges, and gave us a good supper into the bargain.

When I came to receive the money, I brought my governess with me, dressed like an old duchess, and a gentleman very well dressed, who we pretended courted me, but I called him cousin, and the lawyer was only to hint privately to them, that this gentleman courted the widow.

He treated us handsomely indeed, and paid the money cheerfully enough; so that it cost him 200*l*. in all, or rather more. At our last meeting, when all was agreed, the case of the journeyman came up, and the mercer begged very hard for him, told me he was a man that had kept a shop of his own, and been in good business, had a wife and several children, and was very poor; that he had nothing to make satisfaction with, but should beg my pardon on his knees. I had no spleen at the saucy rogue, nor were his submissions anything to me, since there was nothing to be got by him; so I thought it was as good to throw that in generously as not, so I told him I did not desire the ruin of any man, and therefore at his request I would forgive the wretch, it was below me to seek any revenge.

When we were at supper he brought the poor fellow in to make his acknowledgment, which he would have done with as much mean humility as his offence was with insulting pride; in which he was an instance of complete baseness of spirit, imperious, cruel, and relentless when uppermost, abject and low-spirited when down   However, I abated his cringes, told him I forgave him and desired he might withdraw, as if I did not care for the sight of him, though 1 had forgiven him.

I was now in good circumstances indeed, if I could have known my time for leaving off, and my governess often said I was the richest of the trade in England, and so I believe I. was; for I had 700*l.* by me in money, besides clothes, rings, some plate, and two gold watches, and all of them stolen, for I had innumerable jobs, besides these I have mentioned. O! had I even now had the grace of repentance, I had still leisure to have looked back upon my follies, and have made some reparation; but the satisfaction I was to make for the public mischiefs I had done, was yet left behind; and I could not forbear going abroad again, as I called it now, any more than I could when my extremity really drove me out for bread.

It was not long after the affair with the mercer was made up, that I went out in an equipage quite different from any I had ever appeared in before; I dressed myself like a beggar-woman, in the coarsest and most despicable rags I could get, and I walked about peering and peeping into every door and window I came near; and indeed I was in such a plight now, that I knew as ill how to behave in, as ever I did in any; I naturally abhorred dirt and rags; I had been bred up tight and cleanly, and could be no other, whatever condition I was in; so that this was the most uneasy disguise to me that ever I put on. I said presently to myself, that this would not do, for this was a dress that everybody was shy and afraid of; and I thought everybody looked at me as if they were afraid I should come near them, lest I should take something from them, or afraid to come near me, lest they should get something from me. I wandered about all the evening the first time I went out, and made nothing of it, and came home again wet, draggled, and tired: however, I went out again the next night, and then I met with a little adventure, which had like to have cost me dear. As I was standing near a tavern door, there comes a gentleman on horseback, and lights at the door, and wanting to go into the tavern, he calls one of the drawers to hold his horse; he stayed pretty long in the tavern, and the drawer heard his master call, and thought he would be angry with him,

seeing me stand by him, he called to me, Here woman, says
he, hold this horse awhile, 'till I go in; if the gentleman
comes, he'll give you something. Yes, says I, and takes the
horse, and walks off with him soberly, and carried him to
my governess.

This had been a booty to those that had understood it; but
never was poor thief more at a loss to know what to do with
anything that was stolen; for when I came home, my
governess was quite confounded, and what to do with the
creature we neither of us knew; to send him to a stable
was doing nothing, for it was certain that notice would be
given in the gazette, and the horse described, so that we
durst not go to fetch it again.

All the remedy we had for this unlucky adventure was to
go and set up the horse at an inn, and send a note by a
porter to the tavern, that the gentleman's horse that was
lost at such a time, was left at such an inn, and that
he might be had there; that the poor woman that held
him, having led him about the street, not being able to
lead him back again, had left him there. We might have
waited till the owner had published, and offered a reward,
but we did not care to venture the receiving the reward.

So this was a robbery and no robbery, for little was lost
by it, and nothing was got by it, and I was quite sick of
going out in a beggar's dress; it did not answer at all, and
besides, I thought it ominous and threatening.

While I was in this disguise, I fell in with a parcel of folks
of a worse kind than any I ever sorted with, and I saw a little
into their ways too; these were coiners of money, and they
made some very good offers to me, as to profit; but the part
they would have had me embark in, was the most dangerous;
I mean that of the very working of the die, as they call it,
which had I been taken, had been certain death, and that at
a stake, I say, to be burnt to death at a stake. So that though
I was to appearance but a beggar, and they promised
mountains of gold and silver to me, to engage, yet it would
not do; 'tis true, if I had been really a beggar, or had been
desperate as when I began, I might perhaps have closed with
it, for what care they to die, that cannot tell how to live?
But at present that was not my condition, at least I was for
no such terrible risks as those; besides, the very thought of
being burnt at a stake, struck terror to my very soul, chilled

my blood, and gave me the vapours to such a degree as I could not think of it without trembling.

This put an end to my disguise too, for though I did not like the proposal, yet I did not tell them so, but seemed to relish it, and promised to meet again. But I durst see them no more; for if I had seen them, and not complied, though I had declined it with the greatest assurances of secrecy in the world, they would have gone near to have murdered me, to make sure work, and make themselves easy, as they call it; what kind of easiness that is, they may best judge that understand how easy men are that can murder people to prevent danger.

This and horse stealing were things quite out of my way, and I might easily resolve I would have no more to say to them; my business seemed to lie another way, and though it had hazard enough in it too, yet it was more suitable to me, and what had more of art in it, and more chances for a coming off if a surprise should happen.

I had several proposals made also to me about that time, to come into a gang of housebreakers; but that was a thing I had no mind to venture at neither, any more than I had at the coining trade. I offered to go along with two men and a woman, that made it their business to get into houses by stratagem, I was willing enough to venture, but there were three of them already, and they did not care to part, nor I to have too many in a gang; so I did not close with them, and they paid dear for their next attempt.

But at length I met with a woman that had often told me what adventures she had made, and with success, at the waterside, and I closed with her, and we drove on our business pretty well. One day we came among some Dutch people at St. Catharine's, where we went on pretence to buy goods that were privately got on shore. I was two or three times in a house where we saw a good quantity of prohibited goods, and my companion once brought away three pieces of Dutch black silk that turned to good account, and I had my share of it; but in all the journeys I made by myself, I could not get an opportunity to do anything, so I laid it aside, for I had been there so often that they began to suspect something.

This balked me a little, and I resolved to push at something or other, for I was not used to come back so often without purchase; so the next day I dressed myself up fine, and took a walk to the other end of the town; I passed through the Exchange in the Strand, but had no notion of finding anything to do there, when on a sudden I saw a great clutter in the place, and all the people, shopkeepers as well as others, standing up, and staring; and what should it be but some great duchess come into the Exchange, and they said the queen was coming; I set myself close up to a shop-side with my back to the counter, as if to let the crowd pass by, when keeping my eye upon a parcel of lace, which the shopkeeper was showing to some ladies that stood by me, the shopkeeper and her maid were so taken up with looking to see who was a coming, and what shop they would go to, that I found means to slip a paper of lace into my pocket, and come clear off with it; so the lady-milliner paid dear enough for her gaping after the queen.

I went off from the shop, as if driven along by the throng, and mingling myself with the crowd, went out at the other door of the Exchange, and so got away before they missed their lace; and because I would not be followed, I called a coach, and shut myself up in it. I had scarce shut the coach doors, but I saw the milliner's maid and five or six more come running out into the street, and crying out as if they were frighted; they did not cry Stop thief, because nobody ran away, but I could hear the word 'robbed,' and 'lace,' two or three times, and saw the wench wringing her hands, and run staring to and again, like one scared. The coachman that had taken me up, was getting up into the box, but was not quite up, and the horses had not began to move; so that I was terrible uneasy, and I took the packet of lace and laid it ready to have dropt it out at the flap of the coach, which opens before, just behind the coachman; but to my great satisfaction, in less than a minute the coach began to move, that is to say, as soon as the coachman had got up and spoken to his horses, so he drove away, and I brought off my purchase, which was worth near 20*l.*

The next day I dressed me up again, but in quite different clothes, and walked the same way again, but nothing offered till I came into St. James's park. I saw abundance of fine ladies in the park, walking in the Mall, and among the rest, there was a little miss, a young lady of about twelve or thirteen years old, and she had a sister, as I supposed, with her, that might be about nine. I observed the biggest had

a fine gold watch on, and a good necklace of pearl, and they
had a footman in livery with them; but as it is not usual for
the footmen to go behind the ladies in the Mall, so I observed
the footman stopped at their going into the Mall, and the
biggest of the sisters spoke to him, to bid him be just there
when they came back.

When I heard her dismiss the footman, I stept up to him,
and asked him what little lady that was? and held a little
chat with him, about what a pretty child it was with her,
and how genteel and well carriaged the eldest would be:
how womanish, and how grave; and the fool of a fellow
told me presently who she was, that she was Sir Thomas
——'s eldest daughter, of Essex, and that she was a great
fortune; that her mother was not come to town yet; but she
was with Sir William ——'s lady at her lodgings in Suffolk-
street, and a great deal more; that they had a maid and a
woman to wait on them, besides Sir Thomas's coach, the
coachman, and himself; and that young lady was governess
to the whole family, as well here as at home; and told me
abundance of things, enough for my business.

I was well dressed, and had my gold watch as well as she;
so I left the footman, and I puts myself in a rank with this lady,
having stayed till she had taken one turn in the Mall, and was
going forward again; by and by I saluted her by her name,
with the title of Lady Betty. I asked her when she heard
from her father? when my lady her mother would be in town,
and how she did?

I talked so familiarly to her of her whole family that she
could not suspect but that I knew them all intimately: I
asked her why she would come abroad without Mrs. Chime
with her (that was the name of her woman) to take care of
Mrs. Judith, that was her sister. Then I entered into a long
chat with her about her sister; what a fine little lady she
was; and asked her if she had learned French; and a thousand such little things, when on a sudden the guards came,
and the crowd run to see the king go by to the parliament-
house.

The ladies run all to the side of the Mall, and I helped my
lady to stand upon the edge of the boards on the side of the
Mall, that she might be high enough to see; and took the
little one and lifted her quite up; during which, I took care
to convey the gold watch so clean away from the Lady Betty,

that she never missed it till the crowd was gone, and she was gotten into the middle of the Mall.

I took my leave in the very crowd, and said, as if in haste, Dear Lady Betty take care of your little sister; and so the crowd did as it were thrust me away, and that I was unwilling to take my leave.

The hurry in such cases is immediately over, and the place clear as soon as the king is gone by; but as there is always a great running and clutter just as the king passes, so having dropt the two little ladies, and done my business with them, without any miscarriage, I kept hurrying on among the crowd, as if I run to see the king, and so I kept before the crowd 'till I came to the end of the Mall; when the king going on toward the Horse-guards; I went forward to the passage, which went then through against the end of the Haymarket, and there I bestowed a coach upon myself, and made off; and I confess I have not yet been so good as my word, viz., to go and visit my Lady Betty.

I was once in the mind to venture staying with Lady Betty till she missed the watch, and so have made a great outcry about it with her, and have got her into her coach, and put myself in the coach with her, and have gone home with her; for she appeared so fond of me, and so perfectly deceived by my so readily talking to her of all her relations and family, that I thought it was very easy to push the thing farther, and to have got at least the necklace of pearl; but when I considered that though the child would not perhaps have suspected me, other people might, and that if I was searched I should be discovered, I thought it was best to go off with what I had got.

I came accidentally afterwards to hear, that when the young lady missed her watch, she made a great outcry in the park, and sent her footman up and down to see if he could find me, she having described me so perfectly that he knew it was the same person that had stood and talked so long with him, and asked him so many questions about them; but I was gone far enough out of their reach, before she could come at her footman to tell him the story.

I made another adventure after this, of a nature different from all I had been concerned in yet, and this was at a gaming-house near Covent Garden.

I saw several people go in and out; and I stood in the

passage a good while with another woman with me, and seeing a gentleman go up that seemed to be of more than
ordinary fashion, I said to him, Sir, pray don't they give
women leave to go up? Yes, madam, says he, and to play,
too, if they please. I mean so, sir, said I. And with that, he said
he would introduce me if I had a mind; so I followed him to
the door, and he looking in, There, madam, says he, are the
gamesters, if you have a mind to venture. I looked in, and
said to my comrade aloud, Here's nothing but men, I won't
venture. At which one of the gentlemen cried out, You
need not be afraid, madam, here's none but fair gamesters,
you are very welcome to come and set what you please. So
I went a little nearer and looked on, and some of them
brought me a chair, and I sat down and saw the box and dice
go round apace; then I said to my comrade, The gentlemen
play too high for us, come let us go.

The people were all very civil, and one gentleman encouraged me, and said, Come, madam, if you please to venture,
if you dare trust me, I'll answer for it you shall have nothing
put upon you here. No sir, said I, smiling, I hope the gentlemen would not cheat a woman; but still I declined venturing, though I pulled out a purse with money in it, that
they might see I did not want money.

After I had sat awhile, one gentleman said to me, jeering,
Come madam, I see you are afraid to venture for yourself; I
always had good luck with the ladies, you shall set for me, if
you won't set for yourself. I told him, Sir, I should be very
loath to lose your money; though I added, I am pretty lucky
too; but the gentlemen play so high, that I dare not venture
my own.

Well, well, says he, There's ten guineas madam, set them
for me; so I took the money and set, himself looking on. I
run out the guineas by one and two at a time, and then the
box coming to the next man to me, my gentleman gave me
ten guineas more, and made me set five of them at once, and
the gentleman who had the box threw out, so there was five
guineas of his money again. He was encouraged at this, and
made me take the box, which was a bold venture: however,
I held the box so long that I gained him his whole money,
and had a handful of guineas in my lap; and which was the
better luck, when I threw out, I threw but at one or two of
those that had set me, and so went off easy.

When I was come this length, I offered the gentleman all the gold, for it was his own; and so would have had him play for himself, pretending that I did not understand the game well enough. He laughed, and said if I had but good luck, it was no matter whether I understood the game or no; but I should not leave off. However, he took out the fifteen guineas that he had put in first, and bade me play with the rest. I would have him to have seen how much I had got, but he said, No, no, don't tell them, I believe you are very honest, and 'tis bad luck to tell them; so I played on.

I understood the game well enough, though I pretended I did not, and played cautiously, which was to keep a good stock in my lap, out of which I every now and then conveyed some into my pocket; but in such a manner, as I was sure he could not see it.

I played a great while, and had very good luck for him; but the last time I held the box, they set me high, and I threw boldly at all, and held the box till I had gained near fourscore guineas, but lost above half of it back at the last throw; so I got up, for I was afraid I should lose it all back again, and said to him, Pray come, sir, now, and take it and play for yourself, I think I have done pretty well for you: he would have had me play on, but it grew late, and I desired to be excused. When I gave it up to him, I told him I hoped he would give me leave to tell it now, that I might see what he ·had gained, and how lucky I had been ·for him; when I told them, there were threescore and three guineas. Ay, says I, if it had not been for that unlucky throw, I had got you a hundred guineas. So I gave him all the money, but he would not take it till I had put my hand into it, and taken some for myself, and bid me please myself; I refused it, and was positive I would not take it myself; if he had a mine to do anything of that kind it should be all his own doings.

The rest of the gentlemen seeing us striving, cried, Give it her all; but I absolutely refused that. Then one of them said, D—n ye Jack, half it with her; don't you know you should be always upon even terms with the ladies; so in short, he divided it with me, and I brought away thirty guineas, besides about forty-three which I had stole privately, which I was sorry for, because he was so generous.

Thus I brought home seventy-three guineas, and let my old governess see what good luck I had at play. However it was her advice that I should not venture again, and I took her counsel, for I never went there any more ; for I knew as well as she, if the itch of play came in, I might soon lose that, and all the rest of what I had got.

Fortune had smiled upon me to that degree, and I had thriven so much, and my governess too, for she always had a share with me, that really the old gentlewoman began to talk of leaving off while we were well, and being satisfied with what we had got; but, I know not what fate guided me, I was as backward to it now, as she was when I proposed it to her before, and so in an ill hour we gave over the thoughts of it for the present, and in a word I grew more hardened and audacious than ever, and the success I had, made my name as famous as any thief of my sort ever had been.

I had sometimes taken the liberty to play the same game over again, which is not according to practice, which however succeeded not amiss ; but generally I took up new figures, and contrived to appear in new shapes every time I went abroad.

It was now a rumbling time of the year, and the gentlemen being most of them gone out of town, Tunbridge, and Epsom, and such places, were full of people, but the city was thin, and I thought our trade felt it a little, as well as others ; so that at the latter end of the year I joined myself with a gang, who usually go every year to Sturbridge fair, and from thence to Bury fair, in Suffolk. We promised ourselves great things here, but when I came to see how things were, I was weary of it presently ; for except mere picking of pockets, there was little worth meddling with ; neither if a booty had been made, was it so easy carrying it off, nor was there such a variety of occasion for business in our way, as in London ; all that I made of the whole journey, was a gold watch at Bury fair, and a small parcel of linen at Cambridge, which gave me occasion to take leave of the place. It was an old bite, and I thought might do with a country shopkeeper, though in London it would not.

I bought at a linendraper's shop, not in the fair, but in the town of Cambridge, as much fine holland, and other things, as came to about 7l. ; when I had done I bade them be sent to such an inn, where I had taken up my being the same morning, as if I was to lodge there that night.

I ordered the draper to send them home to me, about such an hour, to the inn where I lay, and I would pay him his money. At the time appointed the draper sends the goods, and I placed one of our gang at the chamber door, and when the innkeeper's maid brought the messenger to the door, who was a young fellow, an apprentice, almost a man, she tells him her mistress was asleep, but if he would leave the things and call in about an hour, I should be awake, and he might have the money. He left the parcel very readily, and goes his way, and in about half an hour my maid and I walked off, and that very evening I hired a horse, and a man to ride before me, and went to Newmarket, and from thence got my passage in a coach that was not quite full to St. Edmund's Bury; where, as I told you, I could make but little of my trade, only at a little country opera-house I got a gold watch from a lady's side, who was not only intolerably merry, but a little fuddled, which made my work much easier.

I made off with this little booty to Ipswich, and from thence to Harwich, where I went into an inn, as if I had newly arrived from Holland, not doubting but I should make some purchase among the foreigners that came on shore there; but I found them generally empty of things of value, except what was in their portmanteaus, and Dutch hampers, which were always guarded by footmen; however, I fairly got one of their portmanteaus one evening out of the chamber where the gentleman lay, the footman being fast asleep on the bed, and I suppose very drunk.

The room in which I lodged, lay next to the Dutchman's, and having dragged the heavy thing with much ado out of the chamber into mine, I went out into the street to see if I could find any possibility of carrying it off; I walked about a great while, but could see no probability either of getting out the thing, or of conveying away the goods that were in it, the town being so small, and I a perfect stranger in it; so I was returning with a resolution to carry it back again, and leave it where I found it. Just in that very moment I heard a man make a noise to some people to make haste, for the boat was going to put off, and the tide would be spent; I called the fellow, What boat is it friend, said I,

that you belong to ? The Ipswich wherry, madam, says he.
When do you go off ? says I. This moment, madam, says
he ; Do you want to go thither ? Yes, said I, if you can
stay till I fetch my things. Where are your things, madam ?
says he. At such an inn, said I. Well, I'll go with you
madam, says he, very civilly, and bring them for you. Come
away then, says I ; and takes him with me.

The people of the inn were in a great hurry, the packet
boat from Holland being just come in, and two coaches just
come also with passengers from London, for another packet-
boat that was going off for Holland, which coaches were to
go back next day with the passengers that were just landed.
In this hurry it was that I came to the bar, and paid my
reckoning, telling my landlady I had gotten my passage by
sea in a wherry.

These wherries are large vessels, with good accommodation
for carrying passengers from Harwich to London ; and
though they are called wherries, which is a word used in the
Thames for a small boat, rowed with one or two men, yet
these are vessels able to carry twenty passengers, and ten or
fifteen tons of goods, and fitted to bear the sea ; all this I
had found out by inquiring the night before into the several
ways of going to London.

My landlady was very courteous, took my money for the
reckoning, but was called away, all the house being in a
hurry ; so I left her, took the fellow up into my chamber,
gave him the trunk, or portmanteau, for it was like a trunk,
and wrapt it about with an old apron, and he went directly
to his boat with it, and I after him, nobody asking us the
least question about it. As for the drunken Dutch footman
he was still asleep, and his master with other foreign gentlemen at supper, and very merry below ; so I went clean off
with it to Ipswich, and going in the night, the people of the
house knew nothing but that I was gone to London by the
Harwich wherry, as I had told my landlady.

I was plagued at Ipswich with the custom-house officers,
who stopped my trunk, as I called it, and would open, and
search it. I was willing I told them that they should search
it, but my husband had the key, and that he was not yet
come from Harwich ; this I said, that if upon searching it
they should find all the things be such as properly belonged to
a man rather than a woman, it should not seem strange to

them; however, they being positive to open the trunk, I
consented to have it broken open, that is to say, to have the
lock taken off, which was not difficult.

They found nothing for their turn, for the trunk had been
searched before; but they discovered several things much to
my satisfaction, as particularly a parcel of money in French
pistoles, and some Dutch ducatoons, or rixdollars, and the
rest was chiefly two periwigs, wearing-linen, razors, wash-
balls, perfumes, and other useful things necessary for a
gentleman; which all passed for my husband's, and so I was
quit of them.

It was now very early in the morning, and not light, and
I knew not well what course to take; for I made no doubt
but I should be pursued in the morning, and perhaps be
taken with the things about me; so I resolved upon taking
new measures. I went publicly to an inn in the town with
my trunk, as I called it, and having taken the substance out,
I did not think the lumber of it worth my concern; however,
I gave it the landlady of the house with a charge to take
care of it, and lay it up safe till I should come again, and
away I walked into the street.

When I was got into the town a great way from the inn,
I met with an ancient woman who had just opened her door,
and I fell into chat with her, and asked her a great many
wild questions of things all remote to my purpose and design,
but in my discourse I found by her how the town was situated,
that I was in a street which went out towards Hadley; but
that such a street went towards the water-side, such a street
went into the heart of the town; and at last, such a street
went towards Colchester, and so the London road lay there.

I had soon my ends of this old woman, for I only wanted
to know which was the London road, and away I walked as
fast as I could; not that I intended to go on foot, either to
London or to Colchester, but I wanted to get quietly away
from Ipswich.

I walked about two or three miles, and then I met a plain
countryman, who was busy about some husbandry work, I
did not know what; and I asked him a great many questions,
first, not much to the purpose, but at last told him I was
going for London, and the coach was full, and I could not get
a passage, and asked him if he could not tell me where to
hire a horse that would carry double, and an honest man to

ride before me to Colchester, so that I might get a place there
in the coaches. The honest clown looked earnestly at me, and
said nothing for above half a minute; when scratching his
pole, A horse say you, and to Colchester to carry double?
why yes mistress, alack-a-day, you may have horses enough
for money. Well friend, says I, that I take for granted, I
don't expect it without money. Why, but mistress, says he,
how much are you willing to give? Nay, says I again, friend,
I don't know what your rates are in the country here, for I
am a stranger; but if you can get one for me, get it as cheap
as you can, and I'll give you somewhat for your pains.

Why that's honestly said too, says the countryman. Not
so honest neither, said I to myself, if thou knewest all. Why
mistress, says he, I have a horse that will carry double, and
I don't much care if I go myself with you, an' you like. Will
you, says I? well I believe you are an honest man; if you
will, I shall be glad of it, I'll pay you in reason. Why look
ye mistress, says he, I won't be out of reason with you; then
if I carry you to Colchester, it will be worth 5s. for myself
and my horse, for I shall hardly come back to-night.

In short, I hired the honest man and his horse; but when
we came to a town upon the road (I do not remember the
name of it, but it stands upon a river), I pretended myself
very ill, and I could go no farther that night, but if he would
stay there with me, because I was a stranger, I would pay
him for himself and his horse with all my heart.

This I did because I knew the Dutch gentlemen and their
servants would be upon the road that day, either in the
stage-coaches, or riding post, and I did not know but the
drunken fellow, or somebody else that might have seen me
at Harwich, might see me again, and I thought that in one
day's stop they would be all gone by.

We lay all that night there, and the next morning it was
not very early when I set out, so that it was near ten o'clock
by that time I got to Colchester. It was no little pleasure
that I saw the town where I had so many pleasant days, and
I made many inquiries after the good old friends I had once
had there, but could make little out, they were all dead or
removed. The young ladies had been all married or gone to
London; the old gentleman, and the old lady that had been
my early benefactress, all dead; and which troubled me most,
the young gentleman my first lover, and afterwards my

brother-in-law, was dead; but two sons, men grown, were left of him, but they too were transplanted to London.

I dismissed my old man here, and stayed incognito for three or four days in Colchester, and then took a passage in a waggon, because I would not venture being seen in the Harwich coaches; but I needed not have used so much caution, for there was nobody in Harwich, but the woman of the house, could have known me; nor was it rational to think that she, considering the hurry she was in, and that she never saw me but once, and that by candle-light, should have ever discovered me.

I was now returned to London, and though by the accident of the last adventure, I got something considerable, yet I was not fond of any more country rambles; nor should I have ventured abroad again if I had carried the trade on to the end of my days. I gave my governess a history of my travels; she liked the Harwich journey well enough, and in discoursing of these things between ourselves she observed, that a thief being a creature that watches the advantages of other people's mistakes, 'tis impossible but that to one that is vigilant and industrious many opportunities must happen, and therefore she thought that one so exquisitely keen in the trade as I was, would scarce fail of something wherever I went.

On the other hand, every branch of my story, if duly considered, may be useful to honest people, and afford a due caution to people of some sort or other to guard against the like surprises, and to have their eyes about them when they have to do with strangers of any kind, for 'tis very seldom that some snare or other is not in their way. The moral indeed of all my history is left to be gathered by the senses and judgment of the reader; I am not qualified to preach to them; let the experience of one creature completely wicked, and completely miserable, be a storehouse of useful warning to those that read.

I am drawing now towards a new variety of life. Upon my return, being hardened by a long race of crime, and success unparalleled, I had, as I have said, no thoughts of laying down a trade, which if I was to judge by the example of others, must however end at last in misery and sorrow.

It was on the Christmas-day following, in the evening, that to finish a long train of wickedness, I went abroad to see what might offer in my way; when going by a working silversmith's in Foster-lane, I saw a tempting bait indeed, and not to be resisted by one of my occupation; for the shop had nobody in it, and a great deal of loose plate lay in the window, and at the seat of the man, who I suppose worked at one side of the shop.

I went boldly in, and was just going to lay my hand upon a piece of plate, and might have done it, and carried it clear off, for any care that the men who belonged to the shop had taken of it; but an officious fellow in a house on the other side of the way, seeing me go in, and that there was nobody in the shop, comes running over the street, and without asking me what I was, or who, seizes upon me, and cries out for the people of the house.

I had not touched anything in the shop, and seeing a glimpse of somebody running over, I had so much presence of mind as to knock very hard with my foot on the floor of the house, and was just calling out too, when the fellow laid hands on me.

However, as I had always most courage when I was in most danger, so when he laid hands on me, I stood very high upon it, that I came in to buy half a dozen of silver spoons; and to my good fortune, it was a silversmith's that sold plate, as well as worked plate for other shops. The fellow laughed at that part, and put such a value upon the service that he had done his neighbour, that he would have it be, that I came not to buy, but to steal, and raising a great crowd, I said to the master of the shop, who by this time was fetched home from some neighbouring place, that it was in vain to make a noise, and enter into talk there of the case; the fellow had insisted that I came to steal, and he must prove it, and I desired we might go before a magistrate without any more words; for I began to see I should be too hard for the man that had seized me.

The master and mistress of the shop were really not so violent as the man from t'other side of the way; and the man said, Mistress, you might come into the shop with a good design for aught I know, but it seemed a dangerous thing for you to come into such a shop as mine is, when you see nobody there; and I cannot do so little justice to my neighbour, who was so kind, as not to acknowledge he had reason on his side; though upon the whole I do not find you attempted to take

anything, and I really know not what to do in it. I pressed
him to go before a magistrate with me, and if anything could
be proved on me, that was like a design, I should willingly
submit, but if not, I expected reparation.

Just while we were in this debate, and a crowd of people
gathered about the door, came by Sir T. B., an alderman of
the city, and justice of the peace, and the goldsmith hearing
of it, entreated his worship to come in and decide the case.

Give the goldsmith his due, he told his story with a great
deal of justice and moderation, and the fellow that had come
over, and seized upon me, told his with as much heat, and
foolish passion, which did me good still. It came then to my
turn to speak, and I told his worship that I was a stranger
in London, being newly come out of the north ; that I lodged
in such a place, that I was passing this street, and went into
a goldsmith's shop to buy half a dozen of spoons. By great
good luck I had an old silver spoon in my pocket, which I
pulled out, and told him I had carried that spoon to match it
with half a dozen of new ones, that it might match some I had
in the country.

That seeing nobody in the shop, I knocked with my foot
very hard to make the people hear, and had also called aloud
with my voice : 'tis true, there was loose plate in the shop,
but that nobody could say I had touched any of it; that a
fellow came running into the shop out of the street, and laid
hands on me in a furious manner, in the very moment while
I was calling for the people of the house ; that if he had really
had a mind to have done his neighbour any service, he should
have stood at a distance, and silently watched to see whether
I had touched anything, or no, and then have taken me in the
fact. That is very true, says Mr. Alderman, and turning to
the fellow that stopt me, he asked him if it was true that I
knocked with my foot ? He said yes, I had knocked, but that
might be because of his coming. Nay, says the alderman,
taking him short, now you contradict yourself, for just now
you said she was in the shop with her back to you, and did
not see you till you came upon her. Now it was true that my
back was partly to the street, but yet as my business was of
a kind that required me to have eyes every way, so I
really had a glance of him running over, as I said before,
though he did not perceive it.

After a full hearing, the alderman gave it as his opinion,

that his neighbour was under a mistake, and that I was innocent, and the goldsmith acquiesced in it too, and his wife, and so I was dismissed; but as I was going to depart, Mr. Alderman said, But hold, madam, if you were designing to buy spoons, I hope you will not let my friend here lose his customer by the mistake. I readily answered, No sir, I'll buy the spoons, still if he can match my odd spoon, which I brought for a pattern, and the goldsmith showed me some of the very same fashion; so he weighed the spoons, and they came to 35s., so I pulls out my purse to pay him, in which I had near twenty guineas, for I never went without such a sum about me, whatever might happen, and I found it of use at other times as well as now.

When Mr. Alderman saw my money, he said, Well, madam, now I am satisfied you were wronged, and it was for this reason that I moved you should buy the spoons, and stayed till you had bought them, for if you had not had money to pay for them, I should have suspected that you did not come into the shop to buy, for the sort of people who come upon those designs that you have been charged with, are seldom troubled with much gold in their pockets, as I see you are.

I smiled, and told his worship, that then I owed something of his favour to my money, but I hoped he saw reason also in the justice he had done me before. He said, Yes, he had, but this had confirmed his opinion, and he was fully satisfied now of my having been injured. So I came well off from an affair in which I was at the very brink of destruction.

It was but three days after this, that not at all made cautious by my former danger, as I used to be, and still pursuing the art which I had so long been employed in, I ventured into a house where I saw the doors open, and furnished myself as I thought verily without being perceived, with two pieces of flowered silks, such as they call brocaded silk, very rich. It was not a mercer's shop, nor a warehouse of a mercer, but looked like a private dwelling-house, and was, it seems, inhabited by a man that sold goods for a weaver to the mercers, like a broker or factor.

That I may make short of the black part of this story, I was attacked by two wenches that came open-mouthed at me just as I was going out at the door, and one of them pulled me back into the room, while the other shut the door upon me   I would have given them good words, but there was no room for it; two fiery dragons could not have been more furious; they tore my clothes, bullied and roared, as if they would have murdered me; the mistress of the house came next, and then the master, and all outrageous.

I gave the master very good words, told him the door was open, and things were a temptation to me, that I was poor and distressed, and poverty was what many could not resist, and begged him, with tears, to have pity on me. The mistress of the house was moved with compassion, and inclined to have let me go, and had almost persuaded her husband to it also, but the saucy wenches were run even before they were sent, and had fetched a constable, and then the master said he could not go back, I must go before a justice, and answered his wife, that he might come into trouble himself if he should let me go.

The sight of a constable indeed struck me, and I thought I should have sunk into the ground; I fell into faintings, and indeed the people themselves thought I would have died, when the woman argued again for me, and entreated her husband, seeing they had lost nothing, to let me go. I offered him to pay for the two pieces, whatever the value was, though I had not got them, and argued that as he had his goods, and had really lost nothing, it would be cruel to pursue me to death, and have my blood for the bare attempt of taking them. I put the constable in mind too that I had broke no doors, nor carried anything away; and when I came to the justice, and pleaded there that I had neither broken anything to get in, nor carried anything out, the justice was inclined to have released me; but the first saucy jade that stopped me, affirming that I was going out with the goods, but that she stopped me and pulled me back, the justice upon that point committed me, and I was carried to Newgate, that horrid place! My very blood chills at the mention of its name; the place where so many of my comrades had been locked up, and from whence they went to the fatal tree; the place where my mother suffered so deeply, where I was brought into the world, and from whence I expected no redemption, but by an infamous death: to conclude, the place that had so long expected me, and which with so much art and success I had so long avoided.

I was now fixed indeed; 'tis impossible to describe the terror of my mind, when I was first brought in, and when I

looked round upon all the horrors of that dismal place :
I looked on myself as lost, and that I had nothing to think of
but of going out of the world, and that with the utmost
infamy ; the hellish noise, the roaring, swearing and clamour,
the stench and nastiness, and all the dreadful afflicting things
that I saw there, joined to make the place seem an emblem
of hell itself, and a kind of an entrance into it.

Now I reproached myself with the many hints I had had,
as I have mentioned above, from my own reason, from the
sense of my good circumstances, and of the many dangers I
had escaped, to leave off while I was well, and how I had
withstood them all, and hardened my thoughts against all
fear ; it seemed to me that I was hurried on by an inevitable
fate to this day of misery, and that now I was to expiate all
my offences at the gallows ; that I was now to give satisfaction to justice with my blood, and that I was to come to
the last hour of my life and of my wickedness together.
These things poured themselves in upon my thoughts in a
confused manner, and left me overwhelmed with melancholy
and despair.

Then I repented heartily of all my life past, but that
repentance yielded me no satisfaction, no peace, no, not in
the least, because, as I said to myself, it was repenting after
the power of farther sinning was taken away. I seemed not
to mourn that I had committed such crimes, and for the fact,
as it was an offence against God and my neighbour ; but that
I was to be punished for it ; I was a penitent as I thought,
not that I had sinned, but that I was to suffer, and this took
away all the comfort of my repentance in my own thoughts.

I got no sleep for several nights or days after I came into
that wretched place, and glad I would have been for some
time to have died there, though I did not consider dying as it
ought to be considered neither ; indeed nothing could be filled
with more horror to my imagination than the very place,
nothing was more odious to me than the company that was
there.   O! if I had but been sent to any place in the world,
and not to Newgate, I should have thought myself happy.

In the next place, how did the hardened wretches that
were there before me triumph over me ! What! Mrs.
Flanders come to Newgate at last ? What, Mrs. Mary, Mrs.
Molly, and after that plain Moll Flanders ! They thought
the devil had helped me, they said, that I had reigned so

long; they expected me there many years ago, they said, and was I come at last? Then they flouted me with dejections, welcomed me to the place, wished me joy, bid me have a good heart, not be cast down, things might not be so bad as I feared, and the like; then called for brandy, and drank to me; but put it all up to my score, for they told me I was but just come to the college, as they called it, and sure I had money in my pocket, though they had none.

I asked one of this crew how long she had been there. She said four months. I asked her how the place looked to her when she first came into it? Just as it did now to me, says she, dreadful and frightful; that she thought she was in hell; and I believe so still, adds she, but it is natural to me now, I don't disturb myself about it. I suppose, says I, you are in no danger of what is to follow. Nay, says she, you are mistaken there I am sure, for I am under sentence, only I pleaded my belly, but am no more with child than the judge that tried me, and I expect to be called down next session. This 'calling down' is calling down to their former judgment, when a woman has been respited for her belly, but proves not to be with child, or if she has been with child, and has been brought to bed. Well, says I, and are you thus easy? Ay, says she, I can't help myself, what signifies being sad? if I am hanged there's an end of me. And away she turned dancing, and sings as she goes, the following piece of Newgate wit:

> If I swing by the string,
> I shall hear the bell ring *,
> And then there's an end of poor Jenny.

I mention this because it would be worth the observation of any prisoner, who shall hereafter fall into the same misfortune, and come to that dreadful place of Newgate, how time, necessity, and conversing with the wretches that are there, familiarizes the place to them; how at last they become reconciled to that which at first was the greatest dread upon their spirits in the world, and are as impudently cheerful and merry in their misery, as they were when out of it.

I cannot say, as some do, this devil is not so black as he is painted; for indeed no colours can represent that place to the life; nor any soul conceive aright of it, but those who

* The bell at St. Sepulchre's, which tolls upon execution-day.

have been sufferers there. But how hell should become by degrees so natural, and not only tolerable, but even agreeable, is a thing unintelligible, but by those who have experienced it, as I have.

The same night that I was sent to Newgate, I sent the news of it to my old governess, who was surprised at it you may be sure, and spent the night almost as ill out of Newgate, as I did in it.

The next morning she came to see me; she did what she could to comfort me, but she saw that was to no purpose; however, as she said, to sink under the weight was but to increase the weight; she immediately applied herself to all the proper methods to prevent the effects of it, which we feared, and first she found out the two fiery jades that had surprised me; she tampered with them, persuaded them, offered them money, and, in a word, tried all imaginable ways to prevent a prosecution; she offered one of the wenches 100*l.* to go away from her mistress, and not to appear against me; but she was so resolute, that though she was but a servant-maid at 3*l.* a year wages, or thereabouts, she refused it, and would have refused, as my governess said she believed, if she had offered her 500*l.* Then she attacked the other maid; she was not so hard-hearted as the other, and sometimes seemed inclined to be merciful; but the first wench kept her up, and would not so much as let my governess talk with her, but threatened to have her up for tampering with the evidence.

Then she applied to the master, that is to say, the man whose goods had been stolen, and particularly to his wife, who was inclined at first to have some compassion for me; she found the woman the same still, but the man alleged he was bound to prosecute, and that he should forfeit his recognisance.

My governess offered to find friends that should get his recognisance off of the file, as they call it, and that he should not suffer; but it was not possible to convince him that he could be safe any way in the world but by appearing against me; so I was to have three witnesses of fact against me, the master and his two maids; that is to say, I was as certain to be cast for my life as I was that I was alive, and I had nothing to do but to think of dying. I had but a sad foundation to build upon for that, as I said before, for all my repentance appeared to me to be only the effect

Q 2

of my fear of death, not a sincere regret for the wicked life
that I had lived, and which had brought this misery upon
me, or for the offending my Creator, who was now suddenly
to be my judge.

I lived many days here under the utmost horror; I had
death as it were in view, and thought of nothing night or
day, but of gibbets and halters, evil spirits and devils; it
is not to be expressed how I was harassed, between the
dreadful apprehensions of death, and the terror of my conscience reproaching me with my past horrible life.

The ordinary of Newgate came to me, and talked a little
in his way, but all his divinity run upon confessing my
crime, as he called it (though he knew not what I was in
for), making a full discovery, and the like, without which
he told me God would never forgive me; and he said so
little to the purpose that I had no manner of consolation from
him; and then to observe the poor creature preaching confession and repentance to me in the morning, and find him
drunk with brandy by noon, this had something in it so shocking, that I began to nauseate the man, and his work too by
degrees, for the sake of the man; so that I desired him to
trouble me no more.

I know not how it was, but by the indefatigable application of my diligent governess I had no bill preferred against
me the first session, I mean to the grand jury, at Guildhall;
so I had another month or five weeks before me, and without
doubt this ought to have been accepted by me as so much
time given me for reflection upon what was past, and preparation for what was to come; I ought to have esteemed it
as a space given me for repentance, and have employed it
as such; but it was not in me. I was sorry, as before, for
being in Newgate, but had few signs of repentance about
me.

On the contrary, like the water in the hollows of mountains, which petrifies and turns into stone whatever they are
suffered to drop upon; so the continual conversing with such
a crew of hell-hounds had the same common operation upon
me as upon other people; I degenerated into stone, I turned
first stupid and senseless, and then brutish and thoughtless,
and at last raving mad as any of them; in short, I become as naturally pleased and easy with the place, as if indeed I had been born there.

It is scarce possible to imagine that our natures should be capable of so much degeneracy, as to make that pleasant and agreeable, that in itself, is the most complete misery. Here was a circumstance, that I think it is scarce possible to mention a worse; I was as exquisitely miserable, as it was possible for any one to be, that had life and health, and money to help them as I had.

I had a weight of guilt upon me, enough to sink any crea ture who had the least power of reflection left, and had any sense upon them of the happiness of this life, or the misery of another; I had at first some remorse indeed, but no repentance; I had now neither remorse or repentance. I had a crime charged on me, the punishment of which was death; the proof so evident, that there was no room for me, so much as to plead Not guilty; I had the name of an old offender, so that I had nothing to expect but death, neither had I myself any thoughts of escaping, and yet a certain strange lethargy of soul possessed me; I had no trouble, no apprehensions, no sorrow about me; the first surprise was gone; I was, I may well say, I know not how; my senses, my reason, nay, my conscience, were all asleep; my course of life for forty years had been a horrid complication of wickedness, whoredom, adultery, incest, lying, theft, and, in a word, everything but murder and treason had been my practice, from the age of eighteen, or thereabouts, to threescore; and now I was ingulfed in the misery of punishment, and had an infamous death at the door, and yet I had no sense of my condition, no thought of heaven or hell, at least that went any farther than a bare flying touch, like the stitch or pain that gives a hint and goes off; I neither had a heart to ask God's mercy, or indeed to think of it. And in this I think I have given a brief description of the completest misery on earth.

All my terrifying thoughts were past, the horrors of the place were become familiar, and I felt no more uneasiness at the noise and clamours of the prison, than they did who made that noise; in a word, I was become a mere Newgate-bird, as wicked and as outrageous as any of them; nay, I scarce retained the habit and custom of good breeding and manners, which all along 'till now run through my conversation; so thorough a degeneracy had possessed me, that I was no more the same thing that I had been, than if I had never been otherwise than what I was now.

In the middle of this hardened part of my life, I had another sudden surprise, which called me back a little to that thing called sorrow, which indeed I began to be past the sense of before. They told me one night, that there was brought into the prison late the night before, three highwaymen, who had committed a robbery somewhere on Hounslow-heath, I think it was, and were pursued to Uxbridge by the country, and there taken after a gallant resistance, in which many of the country people were wounded, and some killed.

It is not to be wondered that we prisoners were all desirous enough to see these brave, topping, gentlemen, that were talked up to be such as their fellows had not been known, and especially because it was said they would in the morning be removed into the press-yard, having given money to the head master of the prison, to be allowed the liberty of that better place. So we that were women placed ourselves in the way, that we would be sure to see them; but nothing could express the amazement and surprise I was in, when the first man that came out, I knew to be my Lancashire husband, the same with whom I lived so well at Dunstable, and the same who I afterwards saw at Brickhill, when I was married to my last husband, as has been related.

I was struck dumb at the sight, and knew neither what to say, or what to do; he did not know me, and that was all the present relief I had : I quitted my company, and retired as much as that dreadful place suffers anybody to retire, and cried vehemently for a great while ; Dreadful creature that I am, said I, how many poor people have I made miserable! how many desperate wretches have I sent to the devil! This gentleman's misfortunes I placed all to my own account. He had told me at Chester, he was ruined by that match, and that his fortunes were made desperate on my account; for that thinking I had been a fortune, he was run into debt more than he was able to pay; that he would go into the army, and carry a musket, or buy a horse and take a tour, as he called it; and though I never told him that I was a fortune, and so did not actually deceive him myself, yet I did encourage the having it thought so, and so I was the occasion originally of his mischief.

The surprise of this thing only, struck deeper in my thoughts, and gave me stronger reflections than all that had befallen me before; I grieved day and night, and the more for that they told me he was the captain of the gang, and that he had committed so many robberies, that Hind, or Whitney, or the Golden Farmer were fools to him; that he would surely be hanged if there were no more men left in the country; and that there would be abundance of people come in against him.

I was overwhelmed with grief for him; my own case gave me no disturbance compared to this, and I loaded myself with reproaches on his account; I bewailed my misfortunes, and the ruin he was now come to, at such a rate, that I relished nothing now, as I did before, and the first reflections I made upon the horrid life I had lived, began to return upon me; and as these things returned, my abhorrence of the place, and of the way of living in it, returned also; in a word, I was perfectly changed, and become another body.

While I was under these influences of sorrow for him, came notice to me that the next sessions there would be a bill preferred to the grand jury against me, and that I should be tried for my life. My temper was touched before, the wretched boldness of spirit which I had acquired, abated, and conscious guilt began to flow in my mind. In short, I began to think, and to think indeed is one real advance from hell to heaven; all that hardened state and temper of soul, which I said so much of before, is but a deprivation of thought; he that is restored to his thinking, is restored to himself.

As soon as I began, I say, to think, the first thing that occurred to me broke out thus; Lord! what will become of me? I shall be cast, to be sure, and there is nothing beyond that, but death! I have no friends, what shall I do? I shall be certainly cast! Lord! have mercy upon me! what will become of me! This was a sad thought, you will say, to be the first, after so long time, that had started in my soul of that kind, and yet even this was nothing but fright at what was to come; there was not a word of sincere repentance in it all. However, I was dreadfully dejected, and disconsolate to the last degree; and as I had no friend to communicate my distressed thoughts to, it lay so heavy upon me, that it threw me into fits and swoonings several times a day. I sent for my old governess, and she, give her her due, acted the part of a true friend; she left no stone unturned to prevent the grand jury finding the bill; she went to several of the jury-men, talked with them, and endeavoured to possess them with favourable dispositions, on account that nothing was taken away, and no house broken, &c.; but all would not do, the two wenches swore home to the fact, and the jury found the bill for robbery and housebreaking, that is, for felony and burglary.

I sunk down when they brought the news of it, and after I came to myself I thought I should have died with the weight of it. My governess acted a true mother to me; she pitied me, she cried with me, and for me; but she could not help me; and to add to the terror of it, 'twas the discourse all over the house, that I should die for it; I could hear them talk it among themselves very often; and see them shake their heads, and say they were sorry for it, and the like, as is usual in the place; but still nobody came to tell me their thoughts, till at last one of the keepers came to me privately, and said with a sigh, Well, Mrs. Flanders, you will be tried a Friday (this was but a Wednesday), what do you intend to do? I turned as white as a clout, and said, God knows what I shall do, for my part I know not what to do. Why, says he, I won't flatter you, I would have you prepare for death, for I doubt you will be cast, and as you are an old offender, I doubt you will find but little mercy. They say, added he, your case is very plain, and that the witnesses swear so home against you, there will be no standing it.

This was a stab into the very vitals of one under such a burthen, and I could not speak a word, good or bad, for a great while; at last I burst out into tears, and said to him, O sir, what must I do? Do, says he, send for a minister, and talk with him? for indeed, Mrs. Flanders, unless you have very good friends, you are no woman for this world.

This was plain dealing indeed, but it was very harsh to me, at least I thought it so. He left me in the greatest confusion imaginable, and all that night I lay awake; and now I began to say my prayers, which I had scarce done before since my last husband's death, or from a little while after; and truly I may well call it saying my prayers; for I was in such a confusion, and had such horror upon my mind, that though I cried, and repeated several times the ordinary expression of, Lord have mercy upon me! I never brought myself to any sense of being a miserable sinner, as indeed I was, and of confessing my sins to God, and begging pardon for the sake of Jesus Christ; I was overwhelmed with the sense of· my condition, being tried for my life, and being sure to be executed, and on this account, I cried out all night, Lord! what will become of me? Lord! what shall I do? Lord have mercy upon me! and the like.

My poor afflicted governess was now as much concerned as I, and a great deal more truly penitent, though she had no prospect of being brought to a sentence ; not but that she deserved it as much as I, and so she said herself; but she had not done anything for many years, other than receiving what I and others had stolen, and encouraging us to steal it. But she cried and took on, like a distracted body, wringing her hands, and crying out that she was undone, that she believed there was a curse from heaven upon her, that she should be damned, that she had been the destruction of all her friends, that she brought such a one, and such a one, and such a one to the gallows ; and there she reckoned up ten or eleven people, some of which I have given an account of, that came to untimely ends, and that now she was the occasion of my ruin, for she had persuaded me to go on, when I would have left off. I interrupted her there ; No mother, no, said I, don't speak ot that, for you would have had me left off when I got the mercer's money again, and when I came home from Harwich, and I would not hearken to you ; therefore you have not been to blame, it is I only have ruined myself, I have brought myself to this misery; and thus we spent many hours together.

Well, there was no remedy, the prosecution went on, and on the Thursday I was carried down to the sessions-house, where I was arraigned, as they called it, and the next day I was appointed to be tried. At the arraignment I pleaded Not guilty, and well I might, for I was indicted for felony and burglary ; that is, for feloniously stealing two pieces of brocaded silk, value 46*l.*, the goods of Anthony Johnson, and for breaking open the doors ; whereas I knew very well they could not pretend I had broken up the doors, or so much as lifted up a latch.

On the Friday I was brought to my trial. I had exhausted my spirits with crying for two or three days before, that I slept better the Thursday night than I expected, and had more courage for my trial than I thought possible for me to have.

When the trial began, and the indictment was read, I would have spoke, but they told me the witnesses must be heard first, and then I should have time to be heard. The witnesses were the two wenches, a couple of hard-mouthed jades indeed, for though the thing was truth in the main, yet they aggravated it to the utmost extremity, and swore I had the goods wholly in my possession, that I hid them among my clothes, that I was going off with them, that I had one foot over the threshold when they discovered themselves, and then I put 'tother over, so that I was quite out of the house in the street with the goods before they took me, and then they seized me, and took the goods upon me. The fact in general was true, but I insisted upon it, that they stopped me before I had set my foot clear of the threshold: but that did not argue much, for I had taken the goods, and was bringing them away, if I had not been taken.

I pleaded that I had stole nothing, they had lost nothing, that the door was open, and I went in with design to buy: if, seeing nobody in the house, I had taken any of them up in my hand, it could not be concluded that I intended to steal them, for that I never carried them farther than the door, to look on them with the better light.

The court would not allow that by any means, and made a kind of a jest of my intending to buy the goods, that being no shop for the selling of anything; and as to carrying them to the door to look at them, the maids made their impudent mocks upon that, and spent their wit upon it very much; told the court I had looked at them sufficiently, and approved them very well, for I had packed them up, and was a going with them.

In short, I was found guilty of felony, but acquitted of the burglary, which was but small comfort to me, the first bringing me to a sentence of death, and the last would have done no more. The next day I was carried down to receive the dreadful sentence, and when they came to ask me what I had to say why sentence should not pass, I stood mute awhile, but somebody prompted me aloud to speak to the judges, for that they could represent things favourably for me. This encouraged me, and I told them I had nothing to say to stop the sentence; but that I had much to say to bespeak the mercy of the court; that I hoped they would allow something in such a case, for the circumstances of it, that I had broken

no doors, had carried nothing off, that nobody had lost anything; that the person whose goods they were, was pleased to
say he desired mercy might be shown (which indeed he very
honestly did), that at the worst it was the first offence, and
that I had never been before any court of justice before; and
in a word, I spoke with more courage than I thought I could
have done, and in such a moving tone, and though with tears,
yet not so many tears as to obstruct my speech, that I could
see it moved others to tears that heard me.

The judges sat grave and mute, gave me an easy hearing,
and time to say all that I would, but saying neither yes or no
to it, pronounced the sentence of death upon me; a sentence
to me like death itself, which confounded me; I had no more
spirit left in me; I had no tongue to speak, or eyes to look
up either to God or man.

My poor governess was utterly disconsolate, and she that
was my comforter before, wanted comfort now herself; and
sometimes mourning, sometimes raging, was as much out of
herself as any mad-woman in Bedlam. Nor was she only
disconsolate as to me, but she was struck with horror at the
sense of her own wicked life, and began to look back upon it
with a taste quite different from mine; for she was penitent to
the highest degree for her sins, as well as sorrowful for the
misfortune. She sent for a minister too, a serious, pious, good
man, and applied herself with such earnestness, by his assistance, to the work of a sincere repentance, that I believe, and so
did the minister too, that she was a true pentitent, and which
is still more, she was not only so for the occasion, and at
that juncture, but she continued so, as I was informed, to the
day of her death.

It is rather to be thought of, than expressed, what was
now my condition; I had nothing before me but death; and
as I had no friends to assist me, I expected nothing but to
find my name in the dead warrant, which was to come for
the execution, next Friday, of five more and myself.

In the mean time my poor distressed governess sent me a
minister, who at her request came to visit me. He exhorted
me seriously to repent of all my sins, and to dally no longer
with my soul; not flattering myself with hopes of life, which
he said, he was informed there was no room to expect, but
unfeignedly to look up to God with my whole soul, and to
cry for pardon in the name of Jesus Christ. He backed his

discourses with proper quotations of Scripture, encouraging the greatest sinner to repent, and turn from their evil way; and when he had done, he kneeled down and prayed with me.

It was now, that for the first time, I felt any real signs of repentance; I now began to look back upon my past life with abhorrence, and having a kind of view into the other side of time, the things of life, as I believe they do with everybody at such a time, began to look with a different aspect, and quite another shape, than they did before. The views of felicity, the joy, the griefs of life were quite other things; and I had nothing in my thoughts, but what was so infinitely superior to what I had known in life, that it appeared to be the greatest stupidity to lay a weight upon anything, though the most valuable in this world.

The word eternity represented itself with all its incomprehensible additions, and I had such extended notions of it, that I know not how to express them. Among the rest, how absurd did every pleasant thing look! I mean, that we had counted pleasant before; when I reflected that these sordid trifles were the things for which we forfeited eternal felicity.

With these reflections came in of mere course, severe reproaches for my wretched behaviour in my past life; that I had forfeited all hope of happiness in the eternity that I was just going to enter into; and, on the contrary, was entitled to all that was miserable; and all this with the frightful addition of its being also eternal.

I am not capable of reading lectures of instruction to anybody, but I relate this in the very manner in which things then appeared to me, as far as I am able; but infinitely short of the lively impressions which they made on my soul at that time; indeed those impressions are not to be explained by words, or, if they are, I am not mistress of words to express them. It must be the work of every sober reader to make just reflections, as their own circumstances may direct; and this is what every one at some time or other may feel something of; I mean, a clearer sight into things to come, than they had here, and a dark view of their own concern in them.

But I go back to my own case; the minister pressed me to tell him, as far as I thought convenient, in what state I found myself as to the sight I had of things beyond life; he told me he did not come as ordinary of the place, whose business it is to extort confessions from prisoners, for the farther detecting of other offenders; that his business was to move me to such freedom of discourse as might serve to disburthen my own mind, and furnish him to administer comfort to me as far as was in his power; and assured me, that whatever I said to him should remain with him, and be as much a secret as if it was known only to God and myself; and that he desired to know nothing of me, but to qualify him to give proper advice to me, and to pray to God for me.

The honest friendly way of treating me, unlocked all the sluices of my passions. He broke into my very soul by it; and I unravelled all the wickedness of my life to him. In a word, I gave him an abridgment of this whole history; I give him the picture of my conduct for fifty years in miniature.

I hid nothing from him, and he in return exhorted me to a sincere repentance, explained to me what he meant by repentance, and then drew out such a scheme of infinite mercy, proclaimed from heaven to sinners of the greatest magnitude, that he left me nothing to say, that looked like despair, or doubting of being accepted; and in this condition he left me the first night.

He visited me again the next morning, and went on with his method of explaining the terms of divine mercy, which according to him consisted of nothing more difficult than that of being sincerely desirous of it, and willing to accept it; only a sincere regret for, and hatred of, those things which rendered me so just an object of divine vengeance. I am not able to repeat the excellent discourses of this extraordinary man; all that I am able to do, is to say, that he revived my heart, and brought me into such a condition, that I never knew anything of in my life before. I was covered with shame and tears for things past, and yet had at the same time a secret surprising joy at the prospect of being a true penitent, and obtaining the comfort of a penitent, I mean the hope of being forgiven; and so swift did thoughts circulate, and so high did the impressions they had made upon me run, that I thought I could freely have gone out that minute to execution, without any uneasiness at all, casting my soul entirely into the arms of infinite mercy as a penitent.

The good gentleman was so moved with a view of the

influence which he saw these things had on me, that he blessed God he had come to visit me, and resolved not to leave me till the last moment.

It was no less than twelve days after our receiving sentence, before any were ordered for execution, and then the dead warrant, as they call it, came down, and I found my name was among them. A terrible blow this was to my new resolutions; indeed my heart sunk within me, and I swooned away twice, one after another, but spoke not a word. The good minister was sorely afflicted for me, and did what he could to comfort me, with the same arguments, and the same moving eloquence that he did before, and left me not that evening so long as the prison-keepers would suffer him to stay in the prison, unless he would be locked up with me all night, which he was not willing to be.

I wondered much that I did not see him all the next day, it being but the day before the time appointed for execution; and I was greatly discouraged and dejected, and indeed almost sunk for want of that comfort, which he had so often, and with such success, yielded me in his former visits; I waited with great impatience, and under the greatest oppression of spirits imaginable till about four o'clock, when he came to my apartment; for I had obtained the favour, by the help of money, nothing being to be done in that place without it, not to be kept in the condemned hole, among the rest of the prisoners who were to die, but to have a little dirty chamber to myself.

My heart leaped within me for joy, when I heard his voice at the door, even before I saw him; but let any one judge what kind of motion I found in my soul, when, after having made a short excuse for his not coming, he showed me that his time had been employed on my account, that he had obtained a favourable report from the recorder in my case, and in short that he had brought me a reprieve.

He used all the caution that he was able in letting me know what it would have been double cruelty to have concealed; for as grief had overset me before, so did joy overset me now, and I fell into a more dangerous swooning than at first, and it was not without difficulty that I was recovered at all.

The good man having made a very christian exhortation to me, not to let the joy of my reprieve put the remembrance

of my past sorrow out of my mind, and told me that he
must leave me, to go and enter the reprieve in the books,
and show it to the sheriffs, he stood up just before his going
away, and in a very earnest manner prayed to God for me,
that my repentance might be made unfeigned and sincere;
and that my coming back as it were into life again, might
not be a returning to the follies of life, which I had made
such solemn resolutions to forsake.   I joined heartily in that
petition, and must needs say, I had deeper impressions upon
my mind all that night, of the mercy of God in sparing my
life, and a greater detestation of my sins, from a sense of
that goodness, than I had in all my sorrow before.

This may be thought inconsistent in itself, and wide from
the business of this book; particularly, I reflect that many
of those who may be pleased and diverted with the relation
of the wicked part of my story may not relish this, which is
really the best part of my life, the most advantageous to
myself, and the most instructive to others; such however
will I hope allow me liberty to make my story complete.   It
would be a severe satire on such, to say they do not relish
the repentance as much as they do the crime; and they had
rather the history were a complete tragedy, as it was very
likely to have been.

But I go on with my relation.   The next morning there
was a sad scene indeed in the prison; the first thing I was
saluted with in the morning, was the tolling of the great
bell at St. Sepulchre's, which ushered in the day.   As soon
as it began to toll, a dismal groaning and crying was heard
from the condemned hole, where there lay six poor souls,
who were to be executed that day, some for one crime,
some for another, and two for murder.

This was followed by a confused clamour in the house,
among the several prisoners, expressing their awkward
sorrows for the poor creatures that were to die, but in a
manner extremely differing one from another; some cried
for them, some brutishly huzza'd, and wished them a good
journey; some damned and cursed those that had brought
them to it, many pitying them, and some few, but very few,
praying for them.

There was hardly room for so much composure of mind
as was required for me to bless the merciful providence that

had, as it were, snatched me out of the jaws of this destruction : I remained, as it were, dumb and silent, overcome with the sense of it, and not able to express what I had in my heart ; for the passions on such occasions as these, are certainly so agitated as not to be able presently to regulate their own motions.

All the while the poor condemned creatures were preparing for death, and the ordinary, as they call him, was busy with them, disposing them to submit to their sentence : I say all this while I was seized with a fit of trembling, as much as I could have been if I had been in the same condition as I was the day before ; I was so violently agitated by this surprising fit, that I shook as if it had been in an ague ; so that I could not speak or look, but like one distracted. As soon as they were all put into the carts and gone, which however I had not courage enough to see, I say, as soon as they were gone, I fell into a fit of crying involuntarily, as a mere distemper, and yet so violent, and it held me so long, that I knew not what course to take, nor could I stop, or put a check to it, no, not with all the strength and courage I had.

This fit of crying held me near two hours, and, as I believe, held me till they were all out of the world, and then a most humble penitent serious kind of joy succeeded ; a real transport it was, or passion of thankfulness, and in this I continued most part of the day.

In the evening the good minister visited me again, and fell to his usual good discourses ; he congratulated my having a space yet allowed me for repentance, whereas the state of those six poor creatures was determined, and they were now past the offers of salvation ; he pressed me to retain the same sentiments of the things of life, that I had when I had a view of eternity ; and at the end of all, told me that I should not conclude that all was over, that a reprieve was not a pardon, that he could not answer for the effects of it ; however, I had this mercy, that I had more time given me, and it was my business to improve that time.

This discourse left a kind of sadness on my heart, as if I might expect the affair would have a tragical issue still, which however he had no certainty of ; yet I did not at that time question him about it, he having said he would do his utmost to bring it to a good end, and that he hoped he might, but he would not have me be secure; and the consequence showed that he had reason for what he said.

It was about a fortnight after this, that I had some just apprehensions that I should be included in the dead warrant at the ensuing sessions; and it was not without great difficulty, and at last an humble petition for transportation, that I avoided it; so ill was I beholding to fame, and so prevailing was the report of being an old offender; though in that they did not do me strict justice, for I was not in the sense of the law an old offender, whatever I was in the eye of the judge, for I had never been before them in a judicial way before; so the judges could not charge me with being an old offender, but the recorder was pleased to represent my case as he thought fit.

I had now a certainty of life indeed, but with the hard conditions of being ordered for transportation, which was, I say, a hard condition in itself, but not when comparatively considered; and therefore I shall make no comments upon the sentence, nor upon the choice I was put to; we all shall choose anything rather than death, especially when 'tis attended with an uncomfortable prospect beyond it, which was my case.

The good minister, whose interest, though a stranger to me, had obtained me the reprieve, mourned sincerely for his part; he was in hopes, he said, that I should have ended my days under the influence of good instruction, that I might not have forgot my former distresses, and that I should not have been turned loose again among such a wretched crew as are thus sent abroad, where, he said, I must have more than ordinary secret assistance from the grace of God, if I did not turn as wicked again as ever.

I have not for a good while mentioned my governess, who had been dangerously sick, and being in as near a view of death, by her disease, as I was by my sentence, was a very great penitent; I say, I have not mentioned her, nor indeed did I see her in all this time, but being now recovering, and just able to come abroad, she came to see me.

I told her my condition, and what a different flux and reflux of fears and hopes I had been agitated with; I told her what I had escaped, and upon what terms; and she was present when the minister expressed his fears of my relapsing again

into wickedness upon my falling into the wretched company
that are generally transported.   Indeed I had a melancholy
reflection upon it in my own mind, for I knew what a dreadful
gang was always sent away together, and said to my governess
that the good minister's fears were not without cause.   Well,
well, says she, but I hope you will not be tempted with such
a horrid example as that, and as soon as the minister was gone,
she told me she would not have me discouraged, for perhaps
ways and means might be found to dispose of me in a particular
way, by myself, of which she would talk farther with me
afterward.

I looked earnestly at her, and thought she looked more
cheerfully than she usually had done, and I entertained
immediately a thousand notions of being delivered, but could
not for my life imagine the methods, or think of one that was
feasible ; but I was too much concerned in it to let her go
from me without explaining herself, which though she was
very loath to do, yet, as I was still pressing, she answered me
in a few words, thus : Why, you have money, have you not ?
Did you ever know one in your life that was transported and
had a 100l. in his pocket ; I'll warrant ye child, says she.

I understood her presently, but told her I saw no room to
hope for anything but a strict execution of the order, and as
it was a severity that was esteemed a mercy, there was no
doubt but it would be strictly observed.   She said no more
but this : We will try what can be done ; and so we parted.

I lay in the prison near fifteen weeks after this ; what the
reason of it was, I know not, but at the end of this time I was
put on board of a ship in the Thames, and with me a gang of
thirteen as hardened vile creatures as ever Newgate produced
in my time; and it would really well take up a history longer
than mine to describe the degrees of impudence and audacious
villany that those thirteen were arrived to, and the manner of
their behaviour in the voyage; of which I have a very diverting
account by me, which the captain of the ship, who carried
them over, gave me, and which he caused his mate to write
down at large.

It may, perhaps, be thought trifling to enter here into a
relation of all the little incidents which attended me in this
interval of my circumstances ; I mean, between the final order
for my transportation and the time of going on board the ship ;
and I am too near the end of my story to allow room for it ;

but something relating to me and my Lancashire husband I must not omit.

He had, as I have observed already, been carried from the master's side of the ordinary prison into the press-yard, with three of his comrades, for they found another to add to them after some time; here, for what reason I knew not, they were kept without being brought to a trial almost three months, it seems they found means to bribe or buy off some who were to come in against them, and they wanted evidence to convict them. After some puzzle on this account, they made shift to get proof enough against two of them to carry them off; but the other two, of which my Lancashire husband was one, lay still in suspense. They had, I think, one positive evidence against each of them; but the law obliging them to have two witnesses, they could make nothing of it; yet they were re solved not to part with the men neither, not doubting but evidence would at last come in; and in order to this, I think publication was made that such prisoners were taken, and any one might come to the prison and see them.

I took this opportunity to satisfy my curiosity, pretending I had been robbed in the Dunstable coach, and that I would go to see the two highwaymen; but when I came into the press-yard, I so disguised myself, and muffled my face up so that he could see little of me, and knew nothing of who I was, but when I came back, I said publicly that I knew them very well.

Immediately it was all over the prison, that Moll Flanders would turn evidence against one of the highwaymen, and that I was to come off by it from the sentence of transportation.

They heard of it, and immediately my husband desired to see this Mrs. Flanders that knew him so well, and was to be an evidence against him; and accordingly, I had leave to go to him. I dressed myself up as well as the best clothes that I suffered myself ever to appear in there would allow me, and went to the press-yard, but had a hood over my face; he said little to me at first, but asked me if I knew him; I told him, Yes, very well; but as I concealed my face, so I counterfeited my voice too, that he had no guess at who I was. He asked me where I had seen him; I told him between Dunstable and Brickhill; but turning to the keeper that stood by, I asked if I might not be admitted to talk with him alone; he said, Yes, yes, and so very civilly withdrew

R 2

As soon as he was gone, and I had shut the door, . threw off my hood, and bursting out into tears, My dear, said I, do you not know me? He turned pale and stood speechless, like one thunderstruck, and not able to conquer the surprise, said no more but this, Let me sit down; and sitting down by the table, leaning his head on his hand, fixed his eyes on the ground as one stupid. I cried so vehemently, on the other hand, that it was a good while e'er I could speak any more; but after I had given vent to my passion, I repeated the same words: My dear, do you not know me? At which he answered, Yes, and said no more a good while.

After some time continuing in the surprise, as above, he cast up his eyes towards me, and said, How could you be so cruel? I did not really understand what he meant; and I answered, How can you call me cruel? To come to me, says he, in such a place as this? is it not to insult me, I have not robbed you, at least not on the highway.

I perceived by this, that he knew nothing of the miserable circumstances I was in, and thought that having got intelligence of his being there, I had come to upbraid him with his leaving me. But I had too much to say to him to be affronted, and told him in a few words, that I was far from coming to insult him, but at best I came to condole mutually; that he would be easily satisfied that I had no such view, when I should tell him that my condition was worse than his, and that many ways. He looked a little concerned at the expression of my condition being worse than his; but with a kind of a smile, said, How can that be? When you see me fettered and in Newgate, and two of my companions executed already, can you say your condition is worse than mine?

Come, my dear, says I, we have a long piece of work to do, if I should be to relate, or you to hear my unfortunate history; but if you will hear it, you will soon conclude with me that my condition is worse than yours. How is that possible, says he, when I expect to be cast for my life the very next sessions? Yes, says I, 'tis very possible, when I shall tell you that I have been cast for my life three sessions ago, and am now under sentence of death, is not my case worse than yours?

Then indeed he stood silent again, like one struck dumb, and after a little while he starts up, Unhappy couple! says he, how can this be possible? I took him by the hand; Come, my dear, said I, sit down, and let us compare our sorrows :· I am a prisoner in this very house, and in a much worse circumstance than you, and you will be satisfied I do not come to insult you, when I tell you the particulars. And with this we sat down together, and I told him so much of my story as I thought convenient, bringing it at last to my being reduced to great poverty, and representing myself as fallen into some company that led me to relieve my distresses by a way that I had been already unacquainted with, and that they, making an attempt on a tradesman's house, I was seized upon, for having been but just at the door, the maidservant pulling me in ; that I neither had broke any lock, or taken anything away, and that notwithstanding, that I was brought in guilty, and sentenced to die ; but that the judges having been made sensible of the hardship of my circumstances, had obtained leave for me to be transported.

I told him I fared the worse for being taken in the prison for one Moll Flanders, who was a famous successful thief, that all of them had heard of, but none of them had ever seen ; but that, as he knew, was none of my name. But I placed all to the account of my ill fortune, and that under this name I was dealt with as an old offender, though this was the first thing they had ever known of me. I gave him a long account of what had befallen me since I saw him ; but told him I had seen him since he might think I had ; then gave him an account how I had seen him at Brickhill; how he was pursued, and how, by giving an account that I knew him, and that he was a very honest gentleman, the hue and cry was stopped, and the high constable went back again.

He listened most attentively to all my story, and smiled at the particulars, being all of them infinitely below what he had been at the head of; but when I came to the story of Little Brickhill he was surprised ; And was it you, my dear, said he, that gave the check to the mob, at Brickhill. Yes said I, it was I indeed : then I told him the particulars which I had observed of him there. Why then, said he, it was you that saved my life at that time, and I am glad I owe my life to you, for I will pay the debt to you now, and I'll deliver you from the present condition you are in, or I will die in the attempt.

I told him by no means; it was a risk too great, not worth his running the hazard of, and for a life not worth his saving. 'Twas no matter for that, he said, it was a life worth all the world to him; a life that had given him a new life; for, says he, I was never in real danger, but that time, till the last minute when I was taken. Indeed his danger then lay in his believing he had not been pursued that way; for they had gone off from Hockley quite another way, and had come over the enclosed country into Brickhill, and were sure they had not been seen by anybody.

Here he gave a long history of his life, which indeed would make a very strange history, and be infinitely diverting: he told me that he took the road about twelve years before he married me; that the woman which called him brother, was not any kin to him; but one that belonged to their gang, and who, keeping correspondence with them, lived always in town, having great acquaintance; that she gave them perfect intelligence of persons going out of town, and that they had made several good booties by her correspondence; that she thought she had fixed a fortune for him, when she brought me to him, but happened to be disappointed, which he really could not blame her for: that if I had had an estate, which she was informed I had, he had resolved to leave off the road, and live a new life, but never to appear in public till some general pardon had been passed, or till he could, for money, have got his name into some particular pardon, so that he might have been perfectly easy; but that, as it had proved otherwise, he was obliged to take up the old trade again.

He gave a long account of some of his adventures, and particularly one where he robbed the West Chester coaches, near Lichfield, when he got a very great booty; and after that, how he robbed five graziers in the West, going to Burford fair, in Wiltshire, to buy sheep: he told me he got so much money on those two occasions, that if he had known where to have found me, he would certainly have embraced my proposal of going with me to Virginia; or to have settled in a plantation, or some other of the English colonies in America.

He told me he wrote three letters to me, directed according to my order, but heard nothing from me. This indeed I knew to be true, but the letters coming to my hand in the time of my latter husband, I could do nothing in it, and therefore gave no answer, that so he might believe they had miscarried.

Being thus disappointed, he said he carried on the old trade ever since, though, when he had gotten so much money, he said, he did not run such desperate risks as he did before. Then he gave me some account of several hard and desperate encounters which he had with gentlemen on the road, who parted too hardly with their money; and showed me some wounds he had received; and he had one or two very terrible wounds indeed, particularly one by a pistol-bullet, which broke his arm, and another with a sword, which run him quite through the body, but that missing his vitals he was cured again; one of his comrades having kept with him so faithfully, and so friendly, as that he assisted him in riding near eighty miles before his arm was set, and then got a surgeon in a considerable city, remote from the place where it was done, pretending they were gentlemen travelling towards Carlisle, that they had been attacked on the road by highwaymen, and that one of them had shot him into the arm.

This, he said, his friend managed so well that they were not suspected, but lay still till he was cured. He gave me also so many distinct accounts of his adventures, that it is with great reluctance that I decline the relating them; but this is my own story, not his.

I then inquired into the circumstances of his present case, and what it was he expected when he came to be tried; he told me, that they had no evidence against him; for that of the three robberies, which they were all charged with, it was his good fortune that he was but in one of them, and that there was but one witness to be had to that fact, which was not sufficient; but that it was expected some others would come in, and that he thought when he first see me, I had been one that came of that errand; but that if nobody came in against him he hoped he should be cleared; that he had some intimation, that if he would submit to transport himself, he might be admitted to it without a trial, but that he could not think of it with any temper, and thought he could much easier submit to be hanged.

I blamed him for that; first, because if he was transported, there might be an hundred ways for him, that was a gentleman, and a bold enterprising man, to find his way back again, and perhaps some ways and means to come back before he went. He smiled at that part, and said he should like the last the best of the two, for he had a kind of horror upon his mind at his being sent to the plantations, as the Romans sent slaves to work in the mines; that he thought the passage into another state much more tolerable at the gallows, and that this was the general notion of all the gentlemen who were driven by the exigence of their fortunes to take the road; that at the place of execution there was at least an end of all the miseries of the present state; and as for what was to follow, a man was, in his opinion, as likely to repent sincerely in the last fortnight of his life, under the agonies of a jail, and the condemned hole, as he would ever be in the woods and wildernesses of America; that servitude and hard labour were things gentlemen could never stoop to; that it was but the way to force them to be their own executioners, which was much worse, and that he could not have any patience when he did but think of it.

I used the utmost of my endeavour to persuade him, and joined that known woman's rhetoric to it, I mean, that of tears. I told him the infamy of a public execution was certainly a greater pressure upon the spirits of a gentleman than any mortifications that he could meet with abroad; that he had at least in the other a chance for his life, whereas here he had none at all; that it was the easiest thing in the world for him to manage the captain of a ship, who were, generally speaking, men of good humour; and a small matter of conduct, especially if there was any money to be had, would make way for him to buy himself off when he came to Virginia.

He looked wishfully at me, and I guessed he meant that he had no money, but I was mistaken, his meaning was another way. You hinted just now, my dear, said he, that there might be a way of coming back before I went, by which I understood you that it might be possible to buy it off here; I had rather give 200l. to prevent going, than 100l. to be set at liberty when I came there. That is, my dear, said I, because you do not know the place so well as I do. That may be, said he; and yet I believe, as well as you know it, you would do the same, unless it is because, as you told me, you have a mother there.

I told him, as to my mother she must be dead many years before; and as for any other relations that I might have there, I knew them not: that since my misfortunes had reduced me to the condition I had been in for some years, I had not kept up any correspondence with them; and that he would easily believe I should find but a cold reception from them, if I should be put to make my first visit in the condition of a transported felon; that therefore if I went thither, I resolved not to see them; but that I had many views in going there, which took off all the uneasy part of it; and if he found himself obliged to go also, I should easily instruct him how to manage himself, so as never to go a servant at all, especially since I found he was not destitute of money, which was the only friend in such a condition.

He smiled, and said he did not tell me he had money. I took him up short, and told him I hoped he did not understand by my speaking that I should expect any supply from him if he had money; that on the other hand, though I had not a great deal, yet I did not want, and while I had any I would rather add to him than weaken him, seeing whatever he had I knew in the case of transportation he would have occasion of it all.

He expressed himself in a most tender manner upon that head. He told me, what money he had was not a great deal, but that he would never hide any of it from me if I wanted it; and assured me he did not speak with any such apprehensions; that he was only intent upon what I had hinted to him; that here he knew what to do, but there he should be the most helpless wretch alive.

I told him he frighted himself with that which had no terror in it; that if he had money, as I was glad to hear he had, he might not only avoid the servitude supposed to be the consequence of transportation, but begin the world upon such a new foundation as he could not fail of success in, with but the common application usual in such cases; that he could not but call to mind I had recommended it to him many years before, and proposed it for restoring our fortunes in the world? and I would tell him now, that to convince him both of the certainty of it, and of my being fully acquainted with the method, and also fully satisfied in the probability of success, he should first see me deliver myself from the necessity of going over at all, and then that I would go with him freely, and of my own choice, and perhaps carry enough with me to satisfy him; that I did not offer it for want of being able to live without assistance from him; but that I thought our mutual misfortunes had been such as were sufficient to reconcile us both to quitting this part of the world, and living where nobody could upbraid us with what was past, and without the agonies of a condemned hole to drive us to it, where we should look back on all our past disasters with infinite satisfaction, when we should consider that our enemies should entirely forget us, and that we should live as new people in a new world, nobody having anything to say to us, or we to them.

I pressed this home to him with so many arguments, and answered all his own passionate objections so effectually, that he embraced me, and told me I treated him with such a sincerity as overcame him; that he would take my advice, and would strive to submit to his fate in hope of having the comfort of so faithful a counsellor, and such a companion in his misery; but still he put me in mind of what I had mentioned before, namely, that there might be some way to get off before he went, and that it might be possible to avoid going at all, which he said would be much better. I told him he should see, and be fully satisfied that I would do my utmost in that part too, and if it did not succeed, yet that I would make good the rest.

We parted after this long conference with such testimonies of kindness and affection as I thought were equal if not superior to that at our parting at Dunstable; and now I saw more plainly the reason why he then declined coming with me toward London; and why when we parted there he told me it was not convenient to come to London with me, as he would otherwise have done. I have observed that the account of his life would have made a much more pleasing history than this of mine; and indeed nothing in it was more strange than this part, viz., that he carried on that desperate trade full five-and-twenty year, and had never been taken, the success he had met with had been so very uncommon, and such that sometimes he had lived handsomely and retired in one place for a year or two at a time, keeping himself and a man-servant to wait on him, and has often sat in the coffee-houses and heard the very people who he had robbed give

account of their being robbed, and of the places and circumstances, so that he could easily remember that it was the
same.

In this manner it seems he lived near Liverpool at the
time he unluckily married me for a fortune. Had I been the
fortune he expected, I verily believe he would have taken up
and lived honestly.

He had with the rest of his misfortunes the good luck not
to be actually upon the spot when the robbery was done
which they were committed for ; and so none of the persons
robbed could swear to him ; but it seems as he was taken
with the gang, one hard-mouthed countryman swore home
to him ; and according to the publication they had made,
they expected more evidence against him, and for that reason
he was kept in hold.

However, the offer which was made to him of transportation, was made, as I understood, upon the intercession of
some great person who pressed him hard to accept of it ; and
as he knew there were several that might come in against
him, I thought his friend was in the right, and I lay at him
night and day to delay it no longer.

At last, with much difficulty, he gave his consent, and as
he was not therefore admitted to transportation in court, and
on his petition, as I was, so he found himself under a difficulty to avoid embarking himself, as I had said he might
have done ; his friend having given security for him that he
should transport himself, and not return within the term.

This hardship broke all my measures for the steps I took
afterwards for my own deliverance, were hereby rendered
wholly ineffectual, unless I would abandon him, and leave
him to go to America by himself; than which he protested
he would much rather go directly to the gallows.

I must now return to my own case. The time of my
being transported was near at hand ; my governess, who
continued my fast friend, had tried to obtain a pardon, but
it could not be done unless with an expense too heavy for my
purse, considering that to be left empty, unless I had resolved
to return to my old trade, had been worse than transportation, because there I could live, here I could not. The
good minister stood very hard on another account to prevent
my being transported also ; but he was answered, that my

life had been given me at his first solicitations, and therefore he ought to ask no more; he was sensibly grieved at my going, because, as he said, he feared I should lose the good impressions which a prospect of death had at first made on me, and which were since increased by his instructions; and the pious gentleman was exceedingly concerned on that account.

On the other hand, I was not so solicitous about it now, but I concealed my reasons for it from the minister, and to the last he did not know but that I went with the utmost reluctance and affliction.

It was in the month of February that I was, with thirteen other convicts, delivered to a merchant that traded to Virginia, on board a ship riding in Deptford Reach. The officer of the prison delivered us on board, and the master of the vessel gave a discharge for us.

We were for that night clapt under hatches, and kept so close, that I thought I should have been suffocated for want of air, and the next morning the ship weighed, and fell down the river to a place called Bugby's Hole, which was done, as they told us, by the agreement of the merchant, that all opportunity of escape should be taken from us. However, when the ship came thither, and cast anchor, we were permitted to come upon the deck, but not upon the quarter-deck, that being kept particularly for the captain, and for passengers.

When by the noise of the men over my head, and the motion of the ship, I perceived they were under sail, I was at first greatly surprised, fearing we should go away, and that our friends would not be admitted to see us; but I was easy soon after, when I found they had come to an anchor, and that we had notice given by some of the men, that the next morning we should have the liberty to come upon deck, and to have our friends come to see us.

All that night I lay upon the hard deck, as the other prisoners did, but we had afterwards little cabins allowed for such as had any bedding to lay in them; and room to stow any box or trunk for clothes, and linen if we had it (which might well be put in), for some of them had neither shirt or shift, linen or woollen, but what was on their backs, or one farthing of money to help themselves; yet I did not find but they fared well enough in the ship, especially the women, who got money of the seamen for washing their clothes, &c., sufficient to purchase anything they wanted.

When the next morning we had the liberty to come upon deck, I asked one of the officers whether I might not be allowed to send a letter on shore to let my friends know where we lay, and to get some necessary things sent to me. This was the boatswain, a very civil courteous man, who told me I should have any liberty that I desired, that he could allow me with safety; I told him I desired no other; and he answered, the ship's boat would go up to London next tide, and he would order my letter to be carried.

Accordingly when the boat went off, the boatswain came and told me the boat was going off, that he went in it himself, and if my letter was ready, he would take care of it. I had prepared pen, ink, and paper beforehand, and had gotten a letter ready directed to my governess, and enclosed another to my fellow prisoner, which however I did not let her know was my husband, not to the last. In that to my governess, I let her know where the ship lay, and pressed her to send me what things she had got ready for me for my voyage.

When I gave the boatswain the letter, I gave him a shilling with it, which I told him was for the charge of a porter, which I had entreated him to send with the letter as soon as he came on shore, that if possible I might have an answer brought back by the same hand, that I might know what was become of my things, For, sir, says I, if the ship should go away before I have them, I am undone.

I took care, when I gave him the shilling, to let him see I had a little better furniture about me than the ordinary prisoners; that I had a purse, and in it a pretty deal of money; and I found that the very sight of it immediately furnished me with very different treatment from what I should otherwise have met with; for though he was courteous indeed before, in a kind of natural compassion to me, as a woman in distress, yet he was more than ordinarily so afterwards, and procured me to be better treated in the ship, than, I say, I might otherwise have been; as shall appear in its place.

He very honestly delivered my letter to my governess's own hands, and brought me back her answer. And when he gave it me, gave me the shilling again, There, says he, there's your shilling again too, for I delivered the letter myself. I could not tell what to say, I was surprised at the thing; but after some pause, I said, Sir, you are too kind, it had been but reasonable that you had paid yourself coach-hire then.

No, no, says he, I am overpaid: What is that gentlewoman? is she your sister?

No, sir, said I, she is no relation to me, but she is a dear friend, and all the friends I have in the world. Well, says he, there are few such friends: why she cries after you like a child. Ay, says I again, she would give a hundred pounds, I believe, to deliver me from this dreadful condition.

Would she so? says he: for half the money, I believe I could put you in a way how to deliver yourself. But this he spoke softly that nobody could hear.

Alas! sir, said I, but then that must be such a deliverance as if I should be taken again, would cost me my life. Nay, said he, if you were once out of the ship, you must look to yourself afterwards; that I can say nothing to. So we dropped the discourse for that time.

In the mean time, my governess, faithful to the last moment, conveyed my letter to the prison to my husband, and got an answer to it, and the next day came down herself, bringing me, in the first place, a sea-bed, as they call it, and all its ordinary furniture: she brought me also a sea-chest, that is, a chest, such as are made for seamen, with all the conveniences in it, and filled with everything almost that I could want; and in one of the corners of the chest, where there was a private drawer, was my bank of money, that is to say, so much of it as I had resolved to carry with me; for I ordered part of my stock to be left behind, to be sent afterwards in such goods as I should want when I came to settle; for money in that country is not of much use, where all things are bought for tobacco, much more is it a great loss to carry it from hence.

But my case was particular; it was by no means proper for me to go without money or goods, and for a poor convict that was to be sold as soon as I came on shore, to carry a cargo of goods, would be to have notice taken of it, and perhaps to have them seized; so I took part of my stock with me thus, and left the rest with my governess.

My governess brought me a great many other things, but it was not proper for me to appear too well, at least till I knew what kind of a captain we should have. When she came into the ship, I thought she would have died indeed; her heart sunk at the sight of me, and at the thoughts of parting with me in that condition; and she cried so intolerably, I could not for a long time have any talk with her.

I took that time to read my fellow-prisoner's letter, which greatly perplexed me; he told me it would be impossible for him to be discharged time enough for going in the same ship, and which was more than all, he began to question whether they would give him leave to go in what ship he pleased, though he did voluntarily transport himself; but that they would see him put on board such a ship as they should direct, and that he would be charged upon the captain as other convict prisoners were; so that he began to be in despair of seeing me till he came to Virginia, which made him almost desperate; seeing that, on the other hand, if I should not be there, if any accident of the sea, or of mortality, should take me away, he should be the most undone creature in the world.

This was very perplexing, and I knew not what course to take; I told my governess the story of the boatswain, and she was mighty eager with me to treat with him; but I had no mind to it, till I heard whether my husband, or fellow-prisoner, so she called him, could be at liberty to go with me or no; at last I was forced to let her into the whole matter, except only that of his being my husband; I told her that I had made a positive agreement with him to go, if he could get the liberty of going in the same ship, and I found he had money.

Then I told her what I proposed to do when we came there, how we could plant, settle, and in short grow rich without any more adventures; and as a great secret, I told her we were to marry as soon as he came on board.

She soon agreed cheerfully to my going, when she heard this, and she made it her business from that time to get him delivered in time, so that he might go in the same ship with me, which at last was brought to pass, though with great difficulty, and not without all the forms of a transported convict, which he really was not, for he had not been tried, and which was a great mortification to him. As our fate was now determined, and we were both on board, actually bound to Virginia, in the despicable quality of transported convicts, destined to be sold for slaves, I for five years, and he under bonds and security not to return to England any more, as long as he lived, he was very much dejected and cast down; the mortification of being brought on board as he was, like a prisoner, piqued him very much, since it was first told him he should transport himself, so that he might go as a gentleman at liberty: it is true he was not ordered to be sold when he came there, as we were, and for that reason he was obliged to pay for his passage to the captain, which we were not; as to the rest, he was as much at a loss as a child what to do with himself, but by directions.

However, I lay in an uncertain condition full three weeks, not knowing whether I should have my husband with me or no, and therefore not resolved how or in what manner to receive the honest boatswain's proposal, which indeed he thought a little strange.

At the end of this time, behold my husband came on board. . He looked with a dejected angry countenance; his great heart was swelled with rage and disdain, to be dragged along with three keepers of Newgate, and put on board like a convict, when he had not so much as been brought to a trial. He made loud complaints of it by his friends, for it seems he had some interest; but they got some check in their application, and were told he had had favour enough, and that they had received such an account of him since the last grant of his transportation, that he ought to think himself very well treated that he was not prosecuted anew. This answer quieted him, for he knew too much what might have happened, and what he had room to expect; and now he saw the goodness of that advice to him, which prevailed with him to accept of the offer of transportation; and after his chagrin at these hell-hounds, as he called them, was a little over, he looked more composed, began to be cheerful, and as I was telling him how glad I was to have him once more out of their hands, he took me in his arms, and acknowledged with great tenderness, that I had given him the best advice possible: My dear, says he, thou hast twice saved my life; from henceforward it shall be employed for you, and I'll always take your advice.

Our first business was to compare our stock: he was very honest to me, and told me his stock was pretty good when he came into the prison, but that living there as he did like a gentleman, and which was much more, the making of friends, and soliciting his case, had been very expensive; and in a word, all his stock left was a hundred and eight pounds, which he had about him in gold.

I gave him an account of my stock as faithfully, that is to say, what I had taken with me; for I was resolved, whatever should happen, to keep what I had left in reserve: that in case I should die, what I had was enough to give him, and what was left in my governess's hands would be her own, which she had well deserved of me indeed.

My stock which I had with me was 246*l.* some odd shillings; so that we had 354*l.* between us, but a worse gotten estate was never put together, to begin the world with.

Our greatest misfortune as to our stock was, that it was in money, an unprofitable cargo to be carried to the plantations; I believe his was really all he had left in the world, as he told me it was; but I, who had between 700*l.* and 800*l.* in bank, when this disaster befell me, and who had one of the faithfulest friends in the world to manage it for me, considering she was a woman of no principles, had still 300*l.* left in her hand, which I had reserved, as above; besides, I had some very valuable things with me, as particularly two gold watches, some small pieces of plate, and some rings; all stolen goods. With this fortune, and in the sixty-first year of my age, I launched out into a new world, as I may call it, in the condition only of a poor convict, ordered to be transported in respite from the gallows; my clothes were poor and mean, but not ragged or dirty, and none knew in the whole ship that I had anything of value about me.

However, as I had a great many very good clothes, and linen in abundance, which I had ordered to be packed up in two great boxes, I had them shipped on board, not as my goods, but as consigned to my real name in Virginia; and had the bills of loading in my pocket; and in these boxes was my plate and watches, and everything of value, except my money, which I kept by itself in a private drawer in my chest, and which could not be found, or opened, if found, without splitting the chest to pieces.

The ship began now to fill; several passengers came on board, who were embarked on no criminal account, and these had accommodations assigned them in the great cabin, and other parts of the ship, whereas we, as convicts, were thrust down below, I know not where. But when my husband came on board, I spoke to the boatswain, who had so early given me hints of his friendship; I told him he had befriended me in many things, and I had not made any suitable return to him, and with that I put a guinea into his hand; I told him that my husband was now come on board; that though we were under the present misfortunes, yet we had been persons of a differing character from the wretched crew that we came with, and desired to know whether the captain might not be moved to admit us to some conveniences in the ship, for which we would make him what satisfaction he pleased, and that we would gratify him for his pains in procuring this for us. He took the guinea, as I could see, with great satisfaction, and assured me of his assistance.

Then he told us he did not doubt but that the captain, who was one of the best-humoured gentlemen in the world, would be easily brought to accommodate us, as well as we could desire; and to make me easy, told me he would go up the next tide on purpose to speak to him about it. The next morning happening to sleep a little longer than ordinary, when I got up, and began to look abroad, I saw the boatswain among the men in his ordinary business; I was a little melancholy at seeing him there, and going forwards to speak to him, he saw me, and came towards me, but not giving him time to speak first, I said smiling, I doubt, sir, you have forgot us, for I see you are very busy. He returned presently, Come along with me, and you shall see: so he took me into the great cabin, and there sat a good sort of a gentlemanly man writing, and a great many papers before him.

Here, says the boatswain to him that was a writing, is the gentlewoman that the captain spoke to you of. And turning to me, he said, I have been so far from forgetting your business, that I have been up at the captain's house, and have represented faithfully what you said, of your being furnished with conveniences for yourself and your husband; and the captain has sent this gentleman, who is mate of the ship, down on purpose to show you everything, and to accommodate you to your content, and bid me assure you that you shall not be treated like what you were expected to be, but with the same respect as other passengers are treated.

The mate then spoke to me, and not giving me time to thank the boatswain for his kindness, confirmed what the boatswain had said, and added, that it was the captain's delight to show himself kind and charitable, especially to those that were under any misfortunes ; and with that he showed me several cabins built up, some in the great cabin, and some partitioned off, out of the steerage, but opening into the great cabin, on purpose for passengers, and gave me leave to choose where I would. I chose a cabin in the steerage, in which were very good conveniences to set our chest and boxes, and a table to eat on.

. The mate then told me that the boatswain had given so good a character of me and of my husband, that he had orders to tell me we should eat with him, if we thought fit, during the whole voyage, on the common terms of passengers; that we might lay in some fresh provisions if we pleased ; or if not, he should lay in his usual store, and that we should have share with him. This was very reviving news to me, after so many hardships and afflictions ; I thanked him, and told him the captain should make his own terms with us, and asked him leave to go and tell my husband of it, who was not very well, and was not yet out of his cabin. Accordingly I went, and my husband, whose spirits were still so much sunk with the indignity (as he understood it) offered him, that he was scarce yet himself, was so revived with the account I gave him of the reception we were like to have in the ship, that he was quite another man, and new vigour and courage appeared in his very countenance. So true is it, that the greatest spirits when overwhelmed by their afflictions, are subject to the greatest dejections.

After some little pause to recover himself, my husband came up with me, and gave the mate thanks for the kindness which he had expressed to us, and sent suitable acknowledgments by him to the captain, offering to pay him by advance, whatever he demanded for our passage, and for the conveniences he had helped us to. The mate told him that the captain would be on board in the afternoon, and that he would leave all that to him. Accordingly, in the afternoon, the captain came, and we found him the same courteous obliging man that the boatswain had represented him ; and he was so well pleased with my husband's conversation, that in short, he would not let us keep the cabin we had chosen, but gave us one that, as I said before, opened into the great cabin.

Nor were his conditions. exorbitant, or the man craving and eager to make a prey of us, but for fifteen guineas we had our whole passage and provisions, eat at the captain's table, and were very handsomely entertained.

The captain lay himself in the other part of the great cabin, having let his roundhouse, as they call it, to a rich planter, who went over with his wife and three children, who eat by themselves; he had some other ordinary passengers, who quartered in the steerage; and as for our old fraternity, they were kept under the hatches, and came very little on the deck.

I could not refrain acquainting my governess with what had happened; it was but just that she, who was really concerned for me, should have part in my good fortune; besides, I wanted her assistance to supply me with several necessaries, which before I was shy of letting anybody see me have; but now I had a cabin, and room to set things in, I ordered abundance of good things for our comfort in the voyage; as brandy, sugar, lemons, &c., to make punch, and treat our benefactor, the captain; and abundance of things for eating and drinking; also a larger bed, and bedding proportioned to it; so that in a word, we resolved to want for nothing.

All this while I had provided nothing for our assistance when we should come to the place, and begin to call ourselves·planters; and I was far from being ignorant of what was needful on that occasion; particularly all sorts of tools for the planter's work, and for building; and all kinds of house-furniture, which, if to be bought in the country, must necessarily cost double the price.

I discoursed that point with my governess, and she went and waited upon the captain, and told him that she hoped ways might be found out for her two unfortunate cousins, as she called us, to obtain our freedom when we came into the country, and so entered into a discourse with him about the means and terms also, of which I shall say more in its place; and after thus sounding the captain, she let him know, though we were unhappy in the circumstance that occasioned our going, yet that we were not unfurnished to set ourselves to work in the country; and were resolved to settle, and live there as planters. The captain readily offered his assistance, told her the method of entering upon such business, and how easy, nay, how certain it was for

industrious people to recover their fortunes in such a manner
Madam, says he, 'tis no reproach to any man in that country
to have been sent over in worse circumstances than I per
ceive your cousins are in, provided they do but apply with
good judgment to the business of the place when they come
there.

· She then inquired of him what things it was necessary we
should carry over with us, and he, like a knowing man, told
her thus: Madam, your cousins first must procure somebody
to buy them as servants in conformity to the conditions of
their transportation, and then, in the name of that person,
they may go about what they will; they may either purchase
some plantations already begun, or they may purchase land
of the government of the country, and begin where they
please, and both will be done reasonably. She bespoke his
favour in the first article, which he promised to her to take
upon himself, and indeed faithfully performed it; and as to
the rest, he promised to recommend us to such as should
give us the best advice, and not to impose upon us, which
was as much as could be desired.

She then asked him if it would not be necessery to furnish us with a stock of tools and materials for the business
of planting; and he said, Yes, by all means: then she
begged his assistance in that, and told him she would furnish us with everything that was convenient, whatever it
cost her; he accordingly gave her a list of things necessary
for a planter, which by his account came to about fourscore
or a 100l. And, in short, she went about as dexterously to
buy them as if she had been an old Virginia merchant;
only that she bought, by my direction, above twice as much
of everything as he had given her a list of.

These she put on board in her own name, took his bills of
loading for them, and endorsed those bills of loading to my
husband, insuring the cargo afterwards in her own name; so
that we were provided for all events, and for all disasters.

I should have told you that my husband gave her all his
own stock of 108l., which, as I have said, he had about him
in gold, to lay out thus, and I gave her a good sum besides,
so that I did not break into the stock which I had left in her
hands at all, but after all we had near 200l. in money, which
was more than enough for our purpose.

In this condition, very cheerful, and indeed joyful at being so happily accommodated, we set sail from Bugby's Hole to Gravesend, where the ship lay about ten days more, and where the captain came on board for good and all. Here, the captain offered us a civility which indeed we had no reason to expect, namely, to let us go on shore and refresh ourselves, upon giving our words that we would not go from him, and that we would return peaceably on board again. This was such an evidence of his confidence in us that it overcome my husband, who, in a mere principle of gratitude, told him, as he could not be in any capacity to make a suitable return for such a favour, so he could not think of accepting it, nor could he be easy that the captain should run such a risk. After some mutual civilities, I gave my husband a purse, in which was eighty guineas, and he put it into the captain's hand. There, captain, says he, there's part of a pledge for our fidelity; if we deal dishonestly with you on any account, 'tis your own; and on this we went on shore.

Indeed the captain had assurance enough of our resolutions to go, for that having made such provision to settle there, it did not seem rational that we would choose to remain here at the peril of life, for such it must have been. In a word, we went all on shore with the captain, and supped together in Gravesend, where we were very merry, stayed all night, lay at the house where we supped, and came all very honestly on board again with him in the morning. Here we bought ten dozen of bottles of good beer, some wine, some fowls, and such things as we thought might be acceptable on board.

My governess was with us all this while, and went round with us into the Downs, as did also the captain's wife, with whom she went back. I was never so sorrowful at parting with my own mother as I was at parting with her, and I never saw her more. We had a fair easterly wind the third day after we came to the Downs, and we sailed from thence the 10th of April; nor did we touch any more at any place, till being driven on the coast of Ireland by a very hard gale of wind, the ship came to an anchor in a little bay, near a river, whose name I remember not, but they said the river came down from Limerick, and that it was the largest river in Ireland.

Here, being detained by bad weather for some time, the

captain, who continued the same kind good-humoured man as at first, took us two on shore with him again. He did it now in kindness to my husband indeed, who bore the sea very ill, especially when it blew so hard. Here we bought again store of fresh provisions, beef, pork, mutton, and fowls, and the captain stayed to pickle up five or six barrels of beef to lengthen out the ship's store. We were here not above five days, when the weather turning mild, and a fair wind, we set sail again, and in two-and-forty days came safe to the coast of Virginia.

When we drew near to the shore the captain called me to him, and told me that he found by my discourse I had some relations in the place, and that I had been there before, and so he supposed I understood the custom in their disposing the convict prisoners when they arrived. I told him I did not; and that as to what relations I had in the place, he might be sure I would make myself known to none of them while in the circumstances of a prisoner, and that as to the rest we left ourselves entirely to him to assist us, as he was pleased to promise us he would do. He told me I must get somebody in the place to come and buy me as a servant, and who must answer for me to the governor of the country if he demanded me. I told him we should do as he should direct; so he brought a planter to treat with him, as it were, for the purchase of me for a servant, my husband not being ordered to be sold, and there I was formally sold to him, and went ashore with him. The captain went with us, and carried us to a certain house, whether it was to be called a tavern or not I know not, but we had a bowl of punch there made of rum, &c., and were very merry. After some time, the planter gave us a certificate of discharge, and an acknowledgment of having served him faithfully, and I was free from him the next morning to go whither I would.

For this piece of service the captain demanded of me six thousand weight of tobacco, which he said he was accountable for to his freighter, and which we immediately bought for him, and made him a present of twenty guineas besides, with which he was abundantly satisfied.

It is not proper to enter here into the particulars of what part of the colony of Virginia we settled in, for divers reasons; it may suffice to mention that we went into the great river of Potomac, the ship being bound thither; and there we intended to have settled at first, though afterwards we altered our minds.

The first thing I did of moment after having gotten all our goods on shore, and placed them in a storehouse, which, with a lodging, we hired at the small place or village where we landed: I say the first thing was to inquire after my mother, and after my brother (that fatal person who I married as a husband, as I have related at large). A little inquiry furnished me with information that Mrs. ———, that is, my mother, was dead; that my brother, or husband, was alive, and which was worse, I found he was removed from the plantation where I lived, and lived with one of his sons in a plantation just by the place where we landed, and had hired a warehouse.

I was a little surprised at first, but as I ventured to satisfy myself that he could not know me, I was not only perfectly easy, but had a great mind to see him if it was possible, without his seeing me. In order to that, I found out by inquiry the plantation where he lived, and with a woman of the place who I got to help me, like what we call a chairwoman, I rambled about towards the place as if I had only a mind to see the country, and look about me. At last I came so near that I saw the dwelling-house. I asked the woman whose plantation that was; she said it belonged to such a man, and looking out a little to our right hands, There, says she, is the gentleman that owns the plantation, and his father with him. What are their christian names? said I. I know not, said she, what the old gentleman's name is, but his son's name is Humphry; and I believe, says she, the father's is so too. You may guess, if you can, what a confused mixture of joy and fright possessed my thoughts upon this occasion, for I immediately knew that this was nobody else but my own son, by that father she showed me, who was my own brother. I had no mask, but I ruffled my hoods so about my face that I depended upon it that after above twenty years' absence, and withal not expecting any thing of me in that part of the world, he would not be able to know me. But I need not have used all that caution, for he was grown dim-sighted by some distemper which had fallen upon his eyes, and could but just see well enough to walk about, and not run against a tree or into a ditch. As they drew near to us, I said, Does he know you, Mrs. Owen? so they called the woman. Yes,

she said, if he hears me speak, he will know me; but he can't
see well enough to know me or anybody else; and so she
told me the story of his sight, as I have related. This made
me secure, and so I threw open my hoods again, and let them
pass by me. It was a wretched thing for a mother thus to
see her own son, a handsome comely young gentleman in
flourishing circumstances, and durst not make herself known
to him, and durst not take any notice of him. Let any
mother of children that reads this consider it, and but think
with what anguish of mind I restrained myself; what yearn-
ings of soul I had in me to embrace him, and weep over him;
and how I thought all my entrails turned within me, that my
very bowels moved, and I knew not what to do, as I now
know not how to express those agonies. When he went
from me I stood gazing and trembling, and looking after him
as long as I could see him; then sitting down on the grass,
just at a place I had marked, I made as if I lay down to rest
me, but turned from her, and lying on my face, wept, and
kissed the ground that he had set his foot on.

I could not conceal my disorder so much from the woman,
but that she perceived it, and thought I was not well, which
I was obliged to pretend was true; upon which she pressed
me to rise, the ground being damp and dangerous, which I
did, and walked away.

As I was going back again, and still talking of this gentleman and his son, a new occasion of melancholy offered itself,
thus: the woman began, as if she would tell me a story to
divert me; There goes, says she, a very odd tale among the
neighbours where this gentleman formerly lived. What was
that? said I. Why, says she, that old gentleman going to
England, when he was a young man, fell in love with a young
lady there, one of the finest women that ever was seen here,
and married her, and brought her over hither to his mother,
who was then living. He lived here several years with her,
continued she, and had several children by her, of which the
young gentleman that was with him now, was one; but after
some time, the old gentlewoman, his mother, talking to her
of something relating to herself, and of her circumstances in
England, which were bad enough, the daughter-in-law began
to be very much surprised and uneasy; and in short, in
examining farther into things, it appeared past all contradiction, that she, the old gentlewoman, was her own mother,

and that consequently that son was her own brother, which struck the family with horror, and put them into such confusion, that it had almost ruined them all; the young woman would not live with him, he for a time went distracted, and at last the young woman went away for England, and has never been heard of since.

It is easy to believe that I was strangely affected with this story, but 'tis impossible to describe the nature of my disturbance; I seemed astonished at the story, and asked her a thousand questions about the particulars, which I found she was thoroughly acquainted with. At last I began to inquire into the circumstances of the family, how the old gentlewoman, I mean my mother, died, and how she left what she had; for my mother had promised me, very solemnly, that when she died she would do something for me, and leave it so, as that, if I was living, I should, one way or other, come at it, without its being in the power of her son, my brother and husband, to prevent it. She told me she did not know exactly how it was ordered, but she had been told, that my mother had left a sum of money, and had tied her plantation for the payment of it, to be made good to the daughter, if ever she could be heard of, either in England or elsewhere; and that the trust was left with this son, who we saw with his father.

This was news too good for me to make light of, and you may be sure filled my heart with a thousand thoughts, what course I should take, and in what manner I should make myself known, or whether I should ever make myself known or no.

Here was a perplexity that I had not indeed skill to manage myself in, neither knew I what course to take. It lay heavy upon my mind night and day; I could neither sleep or converse, so that my husband perceived it, wondered what ailed me, and strove to divert me, but it was all to no purpose; he pressed me to tell him what it was troubled me, but I put it off, till at last importuning me continually, I was forced to form a story, which yet had a plain truth to lay it upon too; I told him I was troubled because I found we must shift our quarters, and alter our scheme of settling, for that I found I should be known if I stayed in that part of the country; for that my mother being dead, several of my relations were come into that part where we then was, and that I must either discover myself to them, which in our present circumstances was not proper on many accounts, or remove, and which to do I knew not, and that this it was that made me melancholy.

He joined with me in this, that it was by no means proper for me to make myself known to anybody in the circumstances in which we then were; and therefore he told me he would be willing to remove to any part of the country, or even to any other country if I thought fit. But now I had another difficulty, which was, that if I removed to another colony, I put myself out of the way of ever making a due search after those things which my mother had left; again, I could never so much as think of breaking the secret of my former marriage to my new husband; it was not a story would bear telling, nor could I tell what might be the consequences of it: it was impossible too, without making it public all over the country, as well who I was, as what I now was also.

This perplexity continued a great while, and made my spouse very uneasy; for he thought I was not open with him, and did not let him into every part of my grievance; and he would often say he wondered what he had done, that I would not trust him, whatever it was, especially if it was grievous and afflicting; the truth is, he ought to have been trusted with everything, for no man could deserve better of a wife; but this was a thing I knew not how to open to him, and yet having nobody to disclose any part of it to, the burthen was too heavy for my mind; for let them say what they please of our sex not being able to keep a secret, my life is a plain conviction to me of the contrary; but be it our sex, or the men's sex, a secret of moment should always have a confidant, a bosom friend to whom we may communicate the joy of it, or the grief of it, be it which it will, or it will be a double weight upon the spirits, and perhaps become even insupportable in itself; and this I appeal to human testimony for the truth of.

And this is the cause why many times men as well as women, and men of the greatest and best qualities other ways, yet have found themselves weak in this part, and have not been able to bear the weight of a secret joy, or of a secret sorrow; but have been obliged to disclose it, even for the mere giving vent to themselves, and to unbend the mind.

oppressed with the weights which attended it; nor was this any token of folly at all, but a natural consequence of the thing; and such people, had they struggled longer with the oppression, would certainly have told it in their sleep, and disclosed the secret, let it have been of what fatal nature soever, without regard to the person to whom it might be exposed. This necessity of nature is a thing which works sometimes with such vehemency in the minds of those who are guilty of any atrocious villany, such as a secret murder in particular, that they have been obliged to discover it, though the consequence has been their own destruction. Now, though it may be true that the divine justice ought to have the glory of all those discoveries and confessions, yet 'tis as certain that providence, which ordinarily works by the hands of nature, makes use here of the same natural causes to produce those extraordinary effects.

I could give several remarkable instances of this in my long conversation with crime, and with criminals; I knew one fellow, that while I was a prisoner in Newgate, was one of those they called then night-fliers, I know not what word they may have understood it by since; but he was one who by connivance was admitted to go abroad every evening, when he played his pranks, and furnished those honest people they call thief-catchers with business to find out the next day, and restore for a reward what they had stolen the evening before. This fellow was as sure to tell in his sleep all that he had done, and every step he had taken, what he had stolen, and where, as sure as if he had engaged to tell it waking, and therefore he was obliged, after he had been out, to lock himself up, or be locked up by some of the keepers that had him in fee, that nobody should hear him; but on the other hand, if he had told all the particulars, and given a full account of his rambles and success to any comrade, any brother thief, or to his employers, as I may justly call them, then all was well, and he slept as quietly as other people.

As the publishing this account of my life is for the sake of the just moral of every part of it, and for instruction, caution, warning, and improvement to every reader, so this will not pass I hope for an unnecessary digression, concerning some people being obliged to disclose the greatest secrets either of their own, or other people's affairs.

Under the oppression of this weight, I laboured in the case

I have been naming; and the only relief I found for it, was to let my husband into so much of it as I thought would convince him of the necessity there was for us to think of settling in some other part of the world; and the next consideration before us was, which part of the English settlements we should go to? My husband was a perfect stranger to the country, and had not yet so much as a geographical knowledge of the situation of the several places; and I, that till I wrote this, did not know what the word geographical signified, had only a general knowledge from long conversation with people that came from or went to several places; but this I knew, that Maryland, Pennsylvania, East and West Jersey, New York, and New England, lay all north of Virginia, and that they were consequently all colder climates, to which, for that very reason, I had an aversion : for that as I naturally loved warm weather, so now I grew into years, I had a stronger inclination to shun a cold climate; I therefore considered of going to Carolina, which is the most southern colony of the English on the Continent; and hither I proposed to go, the rather, because I might with ease come from thence at any time, when it might be proper to inquire after my mother's effects, and to demand them.

With this resolution, I proposed to my husband our going away from where we was, and carrying our effects with us to Carolina, where we resolved to settle ; for my husband readily agreed to the first part, viz., that it was not at all proper to stay where we was, since I had assured him we should be known there ; and the rest I concealed from him.

But now I found a new difficulty upon me. The main affair grew heavy upon my mind still, and I could not think of going out of the country without somehow or other making inquiry into the grand affair of what my mother had done for me; nor could I with any patience bear the thought of going away, and not make myself known to my old husband (brother), or to my child, his son ; only I would fain have had it done without my new husband having any knowledge of it, or they having any knowledge of him.

I cast about innumerable ways in my thoughts how this might be done. I would gladly have sent my husband away to Carolina, and have come after myself; but this was impracticable, he would not stir without me, being himself unacquainted with the country, and with the methods of settling anywhere. Then I thought we would both go first, and that when we were settled I should come back to Virginia; but even then I knew he would never part with me, and be left there alone; the case was plain, he was bred a gentleman, and was not only unacquainted, but indolent, and when we did settle, would much rather go into the woods with his gun, which they call there hunting, and which is the ordinary work of the Indians; I say he would much rather do that than attend the natural business of the plantation.

These were therefore difficulties unsurmountable, and such as I knew not what to do in. I had such strong impressions on my mind about discovering myself to my old husband, that I could not withstand them; and the rather, because it run in my thoughts, that if I did not while he lived, I might in vain endeavour to convince my son afterward, that I was really the same person, and that I was his mother, and so might both lose the assistance and comfort of the relation, and lose whatever it was my mother had left me; and yet on the other hand, I could never think it proper to discover the circumstances I was in, as well relating to the having a husband with me, as to my being brought over as a criminal; on both which accounts it was absolutely necessary to me to remove from the place where I was, and come again to him, as from another place and in another figure.

Upon those considerations, I went on with telling my husband the absolute necessity there was of our not settling in Potomac river, that we should presently be made public there; whereas if we went to any other place in the world, we could come in with as much reputation as any family that came to plant. That as it was always agreeable to the inhabitants to have families come among them to plant, who brought substance with them, so we should be sure of agreeable reception, and without any possibility of a discovery of our circumstances.

I told him too, that as I had several relations in the place where we was, and that I durst not now let myself be known to them, because they would soon come to know the occasion of my coming over, which would be to expose myself to the last degree; so I had reason to believe that my mother, who died here, had left me something, and perhaps considerable, which it might be very well worth my while to inquire after; but that this too could not be done without exposing us publicly, unless we went from hence; and then, wherever we settled, I might come as it were to visit and to see my brother and nephews, make myself known, inquire after what was my due, be received with respect, and at the same time have justice done me; whereas, if I did it now, I could expect nothing but with trouble, such as exacting it by force, receiving it with curses and reluctance, and with all kinds of affronts, which he would not perhaps bear to see. That in case of being obliged to legal proofs of being really her daughter, I might be at a loss, be obliged to have recourse to England, and it may be, to fail at last, and so lose it. With these arguments, and having thus acquainted my husband with the whole secret, so far as was needful to him, we resolved to go and seek a settlement in some other colony, and at first Carolina was the place pitched upon.

In order to this we began to make inquiry for vessels going to Carolina, and in a very little while got information, that on the other side the bay, as they call it, namely, in Maryland, there was a ship which came from Carolina, loaden with rice, and other goods, and was going back again thither. On this news we hired a sloop to take in our goods, and taking as it were a final farewell of Potomac river, we went with all our cargo over to Maryland.

This was a long and unpleasant voyage, and my spouse said it was worse to him than all the voyage from England, because the weather was bad, the water rough, and the vessel small and inconvenient; in the next place, we were full a hundred miles up Potomac river, in a part they call Westmorland county; and as that river is by far the greatest in Virginia, and I have heard say it is the greatest river in the world that falls into another river, and not directly into the sea, so we had base weather in it, and were frequently in great danger; for though they call it but a river, 'tis frequently so broad, that when we were in the middle we could not see land on either side for many leagues together. Then we had the great bay of Chesapeak to cross, which is, where the river Potomac falls into it, near thirty miles broad, so that our voyage was full two hundred mile, in a poor sorry sloop, with all our treasure, and if any accident had happened to us we might at last have been very miserable; supposing we had lost our goods and saved our lives only, and had then been left naked and destitute, and in a wild

strange place, not having one friend or acquaintance in all
that part of the world. The very thoughts of it gives me
some horror, even since the danger is past.

Well, we came to the place in five days' sailing, I think
they call it Philip's Point, and behold when we came
thither, the ship bound to Carolina was loaded and gone
away but three days before. This was a disappointment,
but however, I that was to be discouraged with nothing,
told my husband that since we could not get passage to
Carolina, and that the country we was in was very fertile
and good, we would see if we could find out anything for
our turn where we was, and that if he liked things we would
settle here.

We immediately went on shore, but found no conveniences
just at that place, either for our being on shore, or preserving
our goods on shore, but was directed by a very honest quaker,
who we found there, to go to a place about sixty miles east;
that is to say, nearer the mouth of the bay, where he said
he lived, and where we should be accommodated, either
to plant, or to wait for any other place to plant in that
might be more convenient; and he invited us with so much
kindness that we agreed to go, and the quaker himself went
with us.

Here we bought us two servants, viz., an English woman-
servant, just come on shore from a ship of Liverpool, and a
negro man-servant, things absolutely necessary for all people
that pretended to settle in that country. This honest quaker
was very helpful to us, and when we came to the place that
he proposed, found us out a convenient storehouse for our
goods, and lodging for ourselves and servants; and about
two months, or thereabout, afterwards, by his direction, we
took up a large piece of land from the government of that
country, in order to form our plantation, and so we laid the
thoughts of going to Carolina wholly aside, having been
very well received here, and accommodated with a convenient
lodging till we could prepare things, and have land enough
cured, and materials provided for building us a house, all
which we managed by the direction of the quaker; so that
in one year's time we had near fifty acres of land cleared, part
of it enclosed, and some of it planted with tobacco, though
not much; besides, we had garden-ground, and corn sufficient
to supply our servants with roots, and herbs, and bread.

And now I persuaded my husband to let me go over the bay again, and inquire after my friends; he was the willinger to consent to it now, because he had business upon his hands sufficient to employ him, besides his gun to divert him, which they call hunting there, and which he greatly delighted in; and indeed we used to look at one another, sometimes with a great deal of pleasure, reflecting how much better that was, not than Newgate only, but than the most prosperous of our circumstances in the wicked trade we had been both carrying on.

Our affair was now in a very good posture; we purchased of the proprietors of the colony as much land for 35*l.*, paid in ready money, as would make a sufficient plantation to us as long as we could either of us live; and as for children, I was past anything of that kind.

But our good fortune did not end here; I went, as I have said, over the bay, to the place where my brother, once a husband, lived; but I did not go to the same village where I was before, but went up another great river, on the east side of the river Potomac, called Rappahannoc river, and by this means came on the back of his plantation, which was large, and by the help of a navigable creek, that run into the Rappahannòc, I came very near it.

I was now fully resolved to go up point blank to my brother (husband) and to tell him who I was; but not knowing what temper I might find him in, or how much out of temper rather, I might make him by such a rash visit, I resolved to write a letter to him first, to let him know who I was, and that I was come not to give him any trouble upon the old relation, which I hoped was entirely forgot, but that I applied to him as a sister to a brother, desiring his assistance in the case of that provision which our mother, at her decease, had left for my support, and which I did not doubt but he would do me justice in, especially considering that I was come thus far to look after it.

I said some very tender kind things in the letter about his son, which I told him he knew to be my own child, and that as I was guilty of nothing in marrying him, any more than he was in marrying me, neither of us having then known our being at all related to one another, so I hoped he would allow me the most passionate desire of once seeing my own and only child, and of showing something of the infirmities of a

mother in preserving a violent affection for him, who had
never been able to retain any thought of me one way or
other.

I did believe that having received this letter he would
immediately give it to his son to read; his eyes being, I
knew, so dim, that he could not see to read it; but it fell
out better than so, for as his sight was dim, so he had
allowed his son to open all letters that came to his hand for
him, and the old gentleman being from home, or out of the
way when my messenger came, my letter came directly to
my son's hand, and he opened and read it.

He called the messenger in, after some little stay, and
asked him where the person was who gave him that letter?
The messenger told him the place, which was about seven
miles off, so he bid him stay, and ordering a horse to be got
ready, and two servants, away he came to me with the
messenger. Let any one judge the consternation I was in,
when my messenger came back and told me the old gentleman was not at home, but his son was come along with him,
and was just coming up to me. I was perfectly confounded,
for I knew not whether it was peace or war, nor could I tell
how to behave; however, I had but a very few moments to
think, for my son was at the heels of the messenger, and
coming up into my lodgings, asked the fellow at the door
something, I suppose it was, for I did not hear it, which was
the gentlewoman that sent him? for the messenger said,
There she is, sir; at which he comes directly up to me,
kisses me, took me in his arms, embraced me with so much
passion that he could not speak, but I could feel his breast
heave and throb like a child, that cries, but sobs, and cannot
cry it out.

I can neither express or describe the joy that touched my
very soul, when I found, for it was easy to discover that part,
that he came not as a stranger, but as a son to a mother, and
indeed a son who had never before known what a mother of
his own was; in short we cried over one another a considerable while, when at last he broke out first, My dear mother,
says he, are you still alive! I never expected to have seen
your face. As for me, I could say nothing a great while.

After we had both recovered ourselves a little, and were
able to talk, he told me how things stood. He told me he
had not showed my letter to his father, or told him anything

about it; that what his grandmother left me, was in his hands, and that he would do me justice to my full satisfaction; that as to his father, he was old and infirm both in body and mind; that he was very fretful and passionate, almost blind, and capable of nothing; and he questioned whether he would know how to act in an affair which was of so nice a nature as this; and that therefore he had come himself, as well to satisfy himself in seeing me, which he could not restrain himself from, as also to put it into my power to make a judgment; after I had seen how things were, whether I would discover myself to his father or no.

This was really so prudently and wisely managed, that I found my son was a man of sense, and needed no direction from me; I told him I did not wonder that his father was as he had described him, for that his head was a little touched before I went away; and principally his disturbance was, because I could not be persuaded to live with him as my husband, after I knew that he was my brother: that as he knew better than I, what his father's present condition was, I should readily join with him in such measures as he would direct: that I was indifferent as to seeing his father, since I had seen him first, and he could not have told me better news than to tell me that what his grandmother had left me, was intrusted in his hands, who I doubted not, now he knew who I was, would as he said, do me justice: I inquired then how long my mother had been dead, and where she died, and told so many particulars of the family, that I left him no room to doubt the truth of my being really and truly his mother.

My son then inquired where I was, and how I had disposed myself; I told him I was on the Maryland side of the bay, at the plantation of a particular friend, who came from England in the same ship with me; that as for that side of the bay where he was, I had no habitation. He told me I should go home with him, and live with him, if I pleased, as long as I lived: that as to his father, he knew nobody, and would never so much as guess at me; I considered of that a little, and told him, that though it was really no little concern to me to live at a distance from him, yet I could not say it would be the most comfortable thing in the world to me to live in the house with him; and to have that unhappy object always before me, which had been such a blow to my peace before; that though I should be glad to have his company

T 2

(my son), or to be as near him as possible, yet I could not
think of being in the house where I should be also under
constant restraint for fear of betraying myself in my discourse, nor should I be able to refrain some expressions in my
conversing with him as my son, that might discover the
whole affair, which would by no means be convenient.

He acknowledged that I was right in all this; But then,
dear mother, says he, you shall be as near me as you can.
So he took me with him on horseback to a plantation, next to
his own, and where I was as well entertained, as I could
have been in his own. Having left me there, he went away
home, telling me he would talk of the main business the next
day; and having first called me his aunt, and given a charge
to the people, who it seems were his tenants, to treat me with
all possible respect, about two hours after he was gone, he
sent me a maid-servant and a negro boy to wait on me, and
provisions ready dressed for my supper; and thus I was as if
I had been in a new world, and began almost to wish that I
had not brought my Lancashire husband from England at all.

However that wish was not hearty neither, for I loved my
Lancashire husband entirely, as I had ever done from the beginning; and he merited it as much as it was possible for a
man to do: but that by the way.

The next morning my son came to visit me again, almost
as soon as I was up. After a little discourse, he first of all
pulled out a deer-skin bag, and gave it me, with five-and-fifty
Spanish pistoles in it, and told me that was to supply my expenses from England, for though it was not his business to
inquire, yet he ought to think I did not bring a great deal of
money out with me, it not being usual to bring much money
into that country. Then he pulled out his grandmother's will,
and read it over to me, whereby it appeared that she left a
plantation on York River to me, with the stock of servants,
and cattle upon it, and had given it in trust to this son of
mine for my use, whenever he should hear of me, and to my
heirs, if I had any children, and in default of heirs, to whom-
soever I should by will dispose of it; but gave the income of
it, till I should be heard of, to my said son; and if I should
not be living, then it was to him, and his heirs..

This plantation, though remote from him, he said he did not
let out, but managed it by a head clerk, as he did another
that was his father's, that lay hard by it, and went over him-

self three or four times a year to look after it. I asked him what he thought the plantation might be worth : he said, if I would let it out, he would give me about 60*l.* a year for it; but if I would live on it, then it would be worth much more, and he believed would bring me in about 150*l.* a year. But seeing I was likely either to settle on the other side the bay, or might perhaps have a mind to go back to England, if I would let him be my steward he would manage it for me, as he had done for himself, and that he believed he should be able to send me as much tobacco from it, as would yield me about a 100*l.* a year, sometimes more.

This was all strange news to me, and things I had not been used to; and really my heart began to look up more seriously than I think it ever did before, and to look with great thankfulness to the hand of providence, which had done such wonders for me, who had been myself the greatest wonder of wickedness perhaps that had been suffered to live in the world; and I must again observe, that not on this occasion only, but even on all other occasions of thankfulness, my past wickedness and abominable life never looked so monstrous to me, and I never so completely abhorred it, and reproached myself with it, as when I had a sense upon me of providence doing good to me, while I had been making those vile returns on my part.

But I leave the reader to improve these thoughts, as no doubt they will see cause, and I go on to the fact. My son's tender carriage and kind offers fetched tears from me, almost all the while he talked with me. Indeed I could scarce discourse with him, but in the intervals of my passion; however, at length I began, and expressing myself with wonder at my being so happy to have the trust of what I had left, put into the hands of my own child, I told him, that as to the inheritance of it, I had no child but him in the world, and was now past having any if I should marry, and therefore would desire him to get a writing drawn, which I was ready to execute, by which I would, after me, give it wholly to him, and to his heirs. And in the mean time smiling, I asked him what made him continue a bachelor so long. His answer was kind, and ready, that Virginia did not yield any great plenty of wives, and that since I talked of going back to England, I should send him a wife from London.

This was the substance of our first day's conversation, the

pleasantest day that ever passed over my head in my life, and which gave me the truest satisfaction. He came every day after this, and spent great part of his time with me, and carried me about to several of his friend's houses, where I was entertained with great respect. Also I dined several times at his own house, when he took care always to see his half-dead father so out of the way, that I never saw him, or he me. I made him one present, and it was all I had of value, and that was one of the gold watches, of which, I said, I had two in my chest, and this I happened to have with me, and gave it him at his third visit. I told him I had nothing of any value to bestow but that, and I desired he would now and then kiss it for my sake. I did not indeed tell him that I stole it from a gentlewoman's side, at a meeting-house in London: that's by the way.

He stood a little while hesitating, as if doubtful whether to take it or no: but I pressed it on him, and made him accept it, and it was not much less worth than his leather pouch full of Spanish gold; no, though it were to be reckoned as if at London, whereas it was worth twice as much there. At length he took it, kissed it, told me the watch should be a debt upon him, that he would be paying as long as I lived.

A few days after, he brought the writings of gift, and the scrivener with him, and I signed them very freely, and delivered them to him with a hundred kisses : for sure nothing ever passed between a mother, and a tender dutiful child, with more affection. The next day he brings me an obligation under his hand and seal, whereby he engaged himself to manage the plantation for my account, and to remit the produce to my order wherever I should be; and withal, obliged himself to make up the produce a 100*l.* a year to me. When he had done so, he told me, that as I came to demand before the crop was off, I had a right to the produce of the current year, and so he paid a 100*l.* in Spanish pieces of eight, and desired me to give him a receipt for it as in full for that year, ending at Christmas following; this being about the latter end of August.

I stayed here above five weeks, and indeed had much ado to get away then. Nay, he would have come over the bay with me, but I would by no means allow it; however he would send me over in a sloop of his own, which was built like a yacht, and served him as well for pleasure as business.

This I accepted of, and so after the utmost expressions both of duty and affection, he let me come away, and I arrived safe in two days at my friend's the quaker's.

I brought over with me for the use of our plantation, three horses, with harness and saddles; some hogs, two cows, and a thousand other things, the gift of the kindest and tenderest child that ever woman had. I related to my husband all the particulars of this voyage, except that I called my son, my cousin; and first I told him, that I had lost my watch, which he seemed to take as a misfortune; but then I told him how kind my cousin had been, that my mother had left me such a plantation, and that he had preserved it for me, in hopes some time or other he should hear from me; then I told him that I had left it to his management, that he would render me a faithful account of its produce; and then I pulled him out the 100l. in silver, as the first year's produce; and then pulling out the deer-skin purse with the pistoles, And here my dear, says I, is the gold watch. Says my husband, So is heaven's goodness sure to work the same effects, in all sensible minds, where mercies touch the heart! lifted up both his hands, and with an ecstacy of joy, What is God a doing, says he, for such an ungrateful dog as I am! Then I let him know, what I had brought over in the sloop, besides all this; I mean the horses, hogs, and cows, and other stores for our plantation; all which added to his surprise, and filled his heart with thankfulness; and from this time forward I believe he was as sincere a penitent, and as thoroughly a reformed man, as ever God's goodness brought back from a profligate, a highwayman, and a robber. I could fill a larger history than this, with the evidences of this truth, and but that I doubt that part of the story will not be equally diverting as the wicked part.

But this is to be my own story, not my husband's: I return therefore to my own part. We went on with our own plantation, and managed it with the help and direction of such friends as we got there, and especially the honest quaker, who proved a faithful, generous, and steady friend to us; and we had very good success; for having a flourishing stock to begin with, as I have said, and this being now increased by the addition of 150l. sterling in money, we enlarged our number of servants, built us a very good house, and cured every year a great deal of land. The second

year I wrote to my old governess, giving her part with us of
the joy of our success, and ordered her how to lay out the
money I had left with her, which was 250l. as above, and
to send it to us in goods, which she performed with her usual
kindness and fidelity, and all this arrived safe to us.

Here we had a supply of all sorts of clothes, as well for
my husband as for myself; and I took especial care to buy
for him all those things that I knew he delighted to have; as
two good long wigs, two silver-hilted swords, three or four
fine fowling pieces, a fine saddle with holsters and pistols very
handsome, with a scarlet cloak; and in a word, everything
I could think of to oblige him, and to make him appear, as
he really was, a very fine gentleman: I ordered a good quantity
of such household-stuff as we wanted, with linen for us both;
as for myself, I wanted very little of clothes, or linen, being
very well furnished before.   The rest of my cargo consisted
in iron-work of all sorts, harness for horses, tools, clothes
for servants, and woollen-cloth, stuffs, serges, stockings,
shoes, hats, and the like, such as servants wear; and whole
pieces also, to make up for servants, all by direction of the
quaker; and all this cargo arrived safe, and in good condition,
with three women-servants, lusty wenches, which my old
governess had picked up for me, suitable enough to the place,
and to the work we had for them to do, one of which
happened to come double, having been got with child by one
of the seamen in the ship, as she owned afterwards, before
the ship got so far as Gravesend; so she brought us out a
stout boy, about seven months after our landing.

My husband, you may suppose, was a little surprised at the
arriving of this cargo from England; and talking with me
one day after he saw the particulars, My dear, says he, what
is the meaning of all this?   I fear you will run us too deep in
debt: when shall we be able to make returns for it all?   I
smiled, and told him that it was all paid for; and then I told
him, that not knowing what might befall us in the voyage,
and considering what our circumstances might expose us
to, I had not taken my whole stock with me, that I had
reserved so much in my friend's hands, which now we were
come over safe, and settled in a way to live, I had sent for
as he might see.

He was amazed, and stood awhile telling upon his fingers,
but said nothing: at last he began thus; Hold, let's see, say

he, telling upon his fingers still; and first on his thumb, there's 246l. in money at first, then two gold watches, diamond rings; and plate, says he, upon the forefinger: then upon the next finger, Here's a plantation on York·River, a 100l. a year, then 150l. in money, then a sloop load of horses, cows, hogs, and stores; and so on to the thumb again; And now, · says he, a cargo cost 250l. in England, and worth here twice the money. Well, says I, what do you make of all that? Make of it, says he, why who says I was deceived when I married a wife in Lancashire? I think I have married a fortune, and a very good fortune too, says he.

In a word, we were now in very considerable circumstances, and every year increasing; for our new plantation grew upon our hands insensibly, and in eight years which we lived upon it, we brought it to such a pitch that the produce was at least 300l. sterling a year: I mean, worth so much in England.

After I had been a year at home again, I went over the bay to see my son, and to receive another year's income of my plantation; and I was surprised to hear, just at my landing there, that my old husband was dead, and had not been . buried, above a fortnight. This, I confess, was not disagreeable news, because, now I could appear as I was, in a married condition: so I told my son before I came from him, that I believed I should marry a gentleman who had a plantation near mine; and though I was legally free to marry, as to any obligation that was on me before, yet that I was shy of it lest the plot should some time or other be revived, and it might make a husband uneasy. My son, the same kind, dutiful, and obliging creature as ever, treated me now at his own house, paid me my hundred pounds, and sent me home again loaded with presents.

Some time after this, I let my son know I was married, and invited him over to see us, and my husband wrote a very obliging letter to him also, inviting him to come and see him; and he came accordingly some months after, and happened to be there just when my cargo from England came in, which I let him believe belonged all to my husband's estate, and not to me.

It must be observed that when the old wretch, my brother (husband) was dead, I then freely gave my husband an account of all that affair, and of this cousin, as I called him before, being my own son by that mistaken match.   He was perfectly easy in the account, and told me he should have been easy if the old man, as we called him, had been alive. For, said he, it was no fault of yours, nor of his; it was a mistake impossible to be prevented.   He only reproached him with desiring me to conceal it, and to live with him as a wife, after I knew that he was my brother; that, he said, was a vile part.   Thus all these little difficulties were made easy, and we lived together with the greatest kindness and comfort imaginable; we are now grown old, I am come back to England, being almost seventy years of age, my husband sixty-eight, having performed much more than the limited terms of my transportation; and now, notwithstanding all the fatigues, and all the miseries we have both gone through, we are both in good heart and health.   My husband remained there some time after me to settle our affairs, and at first I had intended to go back to him, but at his desire I altered that resolution, and he is come over to England also, where we resolve to spend the remainder of our years in sincere penitence for the wicked lives we have lived.

WRITTEN IN THE YEAR 1683.

THE END.

THE
HISTORY
OF THE
DEVIL,
AS WELL
ANCIENT AS MODERN:
IN TWO PARTS.

PART I.

Containing a State of the Devil's Circumstances, and the various Turns of his Affairs, from his Expulsion out of Heaven, to the Creation of Man; with Remarks on the several Mistakes concerning the Reason and Manner of his Fall.

Also his Proceedings with Mankind ever since Adam, to the first planting of the Christian Religion in the world.

PART II.

Containing his more private Conduct, down to the present times: His Government, his Appearances, his Manner of Working, and the Tools he works with.

Bad as he is, the Devil may be abus'd,
Be falsely charg'd, and causelessly accus'd,
When Men unwilling to be blam'd alone,
Shift off those Crimes on Him which are their Own.

LONDON:

Printed for T. WARNER, at the *Black Boy*, in
Pater-noster Row, 1726.

DEDICATION.

IT is not the easiest thing in the case before me to determine who has the most right to a dedication of this work.

Ancient usage would have directed a solemn author to address these sheets to the great Majesty of Heaven, in congratulation of his glorious victory over the Devil and his angels; but I decline that method as profane.

The same reason forbids me addressing to Him who conquered him on earth, and who when the Devil was so insolent as to assault him, made him fly like a vanquished rebel, with but the word, *Get thee behind me.*

I had then some thoughts of inscribing it to Satan himself, but I did not really know how to relish holding a parley with the Devil, and talking to him in the first person; nay, and as it were, making all my readers do so too; and besides, as I knew there was so very little in the whole work that Satan would be pleased with, I was loath to compliment him, while I was exposing him; which would be to imitate the very hypocrisy by which he is distinguished, and you might say, I played the devil with the Devil.

These difficulties presenting, I think the giving my reasons for the making no dedication, is dedication enough.

SUGGESTIVE LINES ON THE DEVIL

(Alfred J. Hough, in Baltimore Sun.)

Men don't believe in a devil now, as their
fathers used to do;
They've forced the door of the broadest creed
to let his majesty through.
There isn't a print of his cloven foot, or a
fiery dart from his bow
To be found in earth or air today, for the
world has voted so.

But who is it mixing the fatal draught that
palsies heart and brain,
And loads the bier of each passing year with
ten hundred thousand slain?
Who blights the bloom of the land today with
the fiery breath of hell,
If the devil isn't and never was? Won't
somebody rise and tell?

Who dogs the steps of the toiling saint and
digs the pit for his feet?
Who sows the tares in the field of time
wherever God sows his wheat?
The devil is voted not to be, and, of course,
the thing is true;
But who is doing the kind of work the devil
alone should do?

We are told he does not go around like a
roaring lion now;
But whom shall we hold responsible for the
everlasting row
To be heard in home, in church and state, to
the earth's remotest bound,
If the devil by a unanimous vote is nowhere
to be found,

Won't somebody step to the front forthwith
and make his bow and show
How the frauds and the crimes of a single
day spring up? We want to know.
The devil was fairly voted out, and, of
course, the devil's gone;
But simple people would like to know who
carries his business on?

THE POLITICAL

HISTORY OF THE DEVIL.

CHAPTER I.

BEING AN INTRODUCTION TO THE WHOLE WORK.

1 DOUBT not but the title of this book will amuse some of my reading friends a little at first; they will make a pause, perhaps, as they do at a witch's prayer, and be some time a resolving whether they had best look into it or no, lest they should really raise the Devil by reading his story.

Children and old women have told themselves so many frightful things of the Devil, and have formed ideas of him in their minds, in so many horrible and monstrous shapes, that really it were enough to fright the Devil himself to meet himself in the dark, dressed up in the several figures which imagination has formed for him in the minds of men; and, as for themselves, I cannot think by any means that the Devil would terrify them half so much if they were to converse face to face with him.

It must certainly therefore be a most useful undertaking to give the true history of this tyrant of the air, this god of the world, this terror and aversion of mankind, which we call Devil; to show what he is, and what he is not; where he is, and where he is not; when he is in us, and when he is not; for I cannot doubt but that the Devil is really and *bona fide* in a great many of our honest weak-headed friends, when they themselves know nothing of the matter.

Nor is the work so difficult as some may imagine. The

Devil's history is not so hard to come at as it seems to be; his original and the first rise of his family is upon record; and as for his conduct, he has acted indeed in the dark, as to method, in many things, but in general, as cunning as he is, he has been fool enough to expose himself in some of the most considerable transactions of his life, and has not shown himself a politician at all.   Our old friend, Machiavel, outdid him in many things, and I may in the process of this work give an account of several of the sons of Adam, and some societies of them too, who have outwitted the Devil; nay, who have out-sinned the Devil, and that I think may be called out-shooting him in his own bow.

It may perhaps be expected of me in this history, that since I seem inclined to speak favourably of Satan, to do him justice, and to write his story impartially, I should take some pains to tell you what religion he is of; and even this part may not be so much a jest, as at first sight you may take it to be; for Satan has something of religion in him, I assure you; nor is he such an unprofitable Devil that way, as some may suppose him to be; for though, in reverence to my brethren, I will not reckon him among the clergy; yet I cannot deny but that he often preaches, and if it be not profitably to his hearers, it is as much their fault, as it is out of his design.

It has indeed been suggested that he has taken orders, and that a certain pope, famous for being an extraordinary favourite of his, gave him both institution and induction; but as this is not upon record, and therefore we have no authentic document for the probation, I shall not affirm it for a truth, for I would not slander the Devil.

It is said also, and I am apt to believe it, that he was very familiar with that holy father, Pope Silvester II., and some charge him with personating Pope Hildebrand the infamous, on an extraordinary occasion, and himself sitting in the chair apostolic, in a full congregation; and you may hear more of this hereafter: but as I do not meet with Pope Diabolus among the list, in all father Platina's Lives of the Popes, so I am willing to leave it as I find it.

But to speak to the point, and a nice point it is I acknowledge; namely, what religion the Devil is of; my answer will indeed be general, yet not at all ambiguous, for I love to speak positively and with undoubted evidence

1. **He is a believer.** And if, in saying so, it should follow that even the Devil has more religion than some of our men of fame can at this time be charged with, I hope my lord —— and his grace the —— of —— and some of the upper class in the redhot club, will not wear the coat, however well it may set to their shapes, or challenge the satire, as if it were pointed at them, because it is due to them, in a word, whatever their lordships are, I can assure them that the Devil is no infidel.

2. **He fears God.** We have such abundant evidence of this in sacred history, that if I were not at present, in common with a few others, talking to an infidel sort of gentleman, with whom those remote things called Scriptures, are not allowed in evidence, I might say it were sufficiently proved; but I doubt not in the process of this undertaking to show, that the Devil really fears God, and that after another manner than ever he feared St. Francis or St. Dunstan; and if that be proved, as I take upon me to advance, I shall leave it to judgment, who is the better Christian, the Devil who believes and trembles, or our modern gentry of —— who believe neither God nor Devil.

Having thus brought the Devil within the pale, I shall leave him among you for the present; not but that I may examine in its order who has the best claim to his brotherhood, the papists or the protestants, and among the latter the Lutherans or the Calvinists, and so descending to all the several denominations of churches, see who has less of the Devil in them, and who more; and whether less, or more, the Devil has not a seat in every synagogue, a pew in every church, a place in every pulpit, and a vote in every synod; even from the sanhedrim of the Jews, to our friends at the Bull and Mouth, &c., from the greatest to the least.

It will, I confess, come very much within the compass of this part of my discourse, to give an account, or at least make an essay towards it, of the share the Devil has had in the spreading religion in the world, and especially of dividing and subdividing opinions in religion ; perhaps, to eke it out and make it reach the farther: and also to show how far he is or has made himself a missionary of the famous clan *de propaganda fide*; it is true, we find him heartily employed in almost every corner of the world *ad propagandum errorem:* but that may require a history by itself.

As to his propagating religion, it is a little hard indeed, at

first sight, to charge the Devil with propagating religion, that
is to say, if we take it literally, and in the gross; but if you
take it as the Scots insisted to take the oath of fidelity, viz.,
with an explanation, it is plain Satan has very often had a
share in the method, if not in the design, of propagating
Christian faith : for example :

I think I do no injury at all to the Devil, to say that he
had a great hand in the holy war, as it was ignorantly and
enthusiastically called ; and in stirring up the Christian princes
and powers of Europe to run a madding after the Turks and
Saracens, and make war with those innocent people above
a thousand miles off, only because they entered into God's
heritage when he had forsaken it, grazed upon his ground when
he had fairly turned it into a common and laid it open for the
next comer; spending the nation's treasure, and embarking
their kings and people, I say, in a war above a thousand miles
off, filling their heads with that religious madness, called, in
those days, 'holy zeal' to recover the *terra sancta*, the se-
pulchres of Christ and the saints, and as they called it falsely,
the 'holy city,' though true religion says it was the accursed
city, and not worth spending one drop of blood for.

This religious bubble was certainly of Satan, who, as he
craftily drew them in, so like a true Devil he left them in the
lurch when they came there, faced about to the Saracens,
animated the immortal Saladin against them, and managed so
dexterously that he left the bones of about thirteen or fourteen
hundred thousand Christians there as a trophy of his infernal
politics ; and after the Christian world had run *à la santa terra*,
or in English, a sauntering about a hundred years, he dropped
it to play another game less foolish, but ten times wickeder
than that which went before it, namely, turning the crusadoes
of the Christians one against another; and, as Hudibras said
in another case,

> Made them fight like mad or drunk,
> For dame Religion as for punk.

Of this you have a complete account in the history of the
popes' decrees against the Count de Toulouse, and the Wal-
denses and Albigenses, with the crusadoes and massacres
which followed upon them, wherein, to do the Devil's politics
some justice, he met with all the success he could desire, and
the zealots of that day executed his infernal orders most

punctually, and planted religion in those countries in a glorious and triumphant manner, upon the destruction of an infinite number of innocent people, whose blood has fattened the soil for the growth of the Catholic faith, in a manner very particular, and to Satan's full satisfaction.

I might, to complete this part of his history, give you the detail of his progress in these first steps of his alliances with Rome, and add a long list of massacres, wars, and expeditions in behalf of religion, which he has had the honour to have a visible hand in; such as the Parisian massacre, the Flemish war under the Duke d'Alva, the Smithfield fires in the Marian days in England, and the massacres in Ireland; all which would most effectually convince us that the Devil has not been idle in his business; but I may meet with these again in my way, it is enough, while I am upon the generals only, to mention them thus in a summary way; I say, it is enough to prove that the Devil has really been as much concerned as anybody, in the methods taken by some people for propagating the Christian religion in the world.

Some have rashly, and I had almost said maliciously, charged the Devil with the great triumphs of his friends the Spaniards in America, and would place the conquest of Mexico and Peru to the credit of his account.

But I cannot join with them in this at all, I must say, I believe the Devil was innocent of that matter; my reason is, because Satan was never such a fool as to spend his time or his politics, or embark his allies to conquer nations who were already his own; that would be Satan against Beelzebub, a making war upon himself, and at least doing nothing to the purpose.

If they should charge him, indeed, with deluding Phillip II. of Spain into that preposterous attempt called the Armada (Anglicè, the Spanish Invasion), I should indeed more readily join with them; but whether he did it weakly, in hope, which was indeed not likely, that it should succeed; or wickedly, to destroy the great fleet of the Spaniards and draw them in within the reach of his own diminions, the elements; this being a question which authors differ exceedingly about, I shall leave it to decide itself.

But the greatest piece of management which we find the Devil has concerned himself in of late in the matter of religion, seems to be that of the mission into China; and here indeed Satan has acted his masterpiece. It was, no doubt, much for his service, that the Chinese should have no insight into matters of religion, I mean that we call Christian; and therefore, though popery and the Devil are not at so much variance as some may imagine, yet he did not think it safe to let the general system of Christianity be heard of among them in China. Hence, when the name of the Christian religion had but been received with some seeming approbation in the country of Japan, Satan immediately, as if alarmed at the thing, and dreading what the consequence of it might be, armed the Japanese against it with such fury, that they expelled it at once.

It was much safer to his designs, when, if the story be not a fiction, he put that Dutch witticism into the mouths of the States' commanders, when they came to Japan; who, having more wit than to own themselves Christians in such a place as that, when the question was put to them, answered negatively, that they were not, but that they were of another religion, called Hollanders.

However, it seems the diligent Jesuits outwitted the Devil in China, and, as I said above, overshot him in his own bow; for the mission being in danger, by the Devil and the Chinese emperor's joining together, of being wholly expelled there too, as they had been in Japan, they cunningly fell in with the ecclesiastics of the country, and joining the priestcraft of both religions together, they brought Jesus Christ and Confucius to be so reconcilable, that the Chinese and the Roman idolatry appeared capable of a confederacy, of going on hand in hand together, and consequently of being very good friends.

This was a masterpiece indeed, and, as they say, almost frightened Satan out of his wits; but he being a ready manager, and particularly famous for serving himself of the rogueries of the priests, faced about immediately to the mission, and making a virtue of necessity, clapped in, with all possible alacrity, with the proposal;* so the Jesuits and he formed a hotchpotch of religion, made up of popery and paganism, and calculated to leave the latter rather worse than they found it, blending the faith of Christ and the philosophy or morals of Confucius together, and formally christening them by the name of religion; by which means the politic interest of the

* N.B. He never refused setting his hand to any opinion which he thought it for his interest to acknowledge.

mission was preserved, and yet Satan lost not one inch of ground with the Chinese, no, not by the planting the gospel itself, such as it was, among them.

Nor has it been much advantage to him that this plan or scheme of a new-modelled religion would not go down at Rome, and that the Inquisition damned it with bell, book, and candle; distance of place served his new allies, the missionaries, in the stead of a protection from the Inquisition; and now and then a rich present well placed found them friends in the congregation itself; and where any nuncio with his impudent zeal pretended to take such a long voyage to oppose them, Satan took care to get him sent back *re infecta*, or inspired the mission to move him off the premises, by methods of their own, that is to say, being interpreted, to murder him.

Thus the mission has, in itself, been truly devilish, and the Devil has interested himself in the planting the Christian religion in China.

The influence the Devil has in the politics of mankind, is another especial part of his history, and would require, if it were possible, a very exact description; but here we shall necessarily be obliged to inquire so nicely into the arcana of circumstances, and unlock the cabinets of state in so many courts, canvass the councils of ministers and the conduct of princes so fully, and expose them so much, that it may, perhaps, make a combustion among the great politicians abroad; and in doing that we may come so near home too, that though personal safety and prudentials forbid our meddling with our own country, we may be taken in a double entendre, and fall unpitied for being only suspected of touching truths that are so tender, whether we are guilty or no; on these accounts I must meddle the less with that part, at least for the present.

Be it that the Devil has had a share in some of the late councils of Europe, influencing them this way or that way, to his own advantage, what is it to us? For example, what if he has had any concern in the late affair of Thorn? what need we put it upon him, seeing his confederates the Jesuits with the Assessorial tribunal of Poland take it upon themselves? I shall leave that part to the issue of time. I wish it were as easy to persuade the world that he had no hand in bringing the injured protestants to commit the arbitration of that affair to the very party, and leave the justice due to the cries of protestant blood to the arbitrement of a popish power, who dare say that the Devil must be in it, if justice should be obtained that way : I should rather say, the Devil is in it, or else it would never be expected.

It occurs next to inquire from the premises, whether the Devil has more influence or less in the affairs of the world now, than he had in former ages ; and this will depend upon comparing, as we go along, his methods and way of working in past times, and the modern politics by which he acts in our days ; with the differing reception which he has met with among the men of such distant ages.

But there is so much to inquire of about the Devil, before we can bring his story down to our modern times, that we must for the present let that drop, and look a little back to the remoter part of his history, and draw his picture that people may know him when they meet him, and see who and what he is, and what he has been doing ever since he got leave to act in the high station he now appears in.

In the mean time, if I might obtain leave to present an humble petition to Satan, it should be, that he would, according to modern usage, oblige us all with writing the history of his own times ; it would, as well as one that is gone before it, be a devilish good one ; for, as to the sincerity of the performance, the authority of the particulars, the justice of the characters, &c., if they were no better vouched, no more consistent with themselves, with charity, with truth, and with the honour of an historian, than the last of that kind which came abroad amongst us, it must be a reproach to the Devil himself to be author of it.

Were Satan to be brought under the least obligation to write truth, and that the matters of fact, which he should write, might be depended upon, he is certainly qualified by his knowledge of things to be a complete historian ; nor could the bishop himself, who, by the way, has given us already the devil of a history, come up to him. Milton's Pandemonium, though an excellent dramatic performance, would appear a mere trifling sing-song business, beneath the dignity of Chevy Chase ; the Devil could give us a true account of all the civil wars in heaven ; how and by whom, and in what manner he lost the day there, and was obliged to quit the field. The fiction of his refusing to acknowledge and submit to the Messiah, upon his being declared generalissimo of the heavenly forces, which Satan expected himself, as the eldest officer; and his not being able to brook another to be put in over his head; I say, that fine-spun thought of Mr. Milton would appear to be strained too far, and only serve to convince us that he (Milton) knew nothing of the matter. Satan knows very well, that the Messiah was not declared to be the Son of God with power till by and after the resurrection from the dead, and that all power was then given him in heaven and earth, and not before; so that Satan's rebellion must derive from other causes, and upon other occasions, as he himself can doubtless give us an account, if he thinks fit, and of which we shall speak farther in his history.

What a fine history might this old gentleman write of the antediluvian world, and of all the weighty affairs, as well of state as of religion, which happened during the fifteen hundred years of the patriarchal administration!

Then, who, like him, could give a full and complete account of the deluge, whether it was a mere vindictive, a blast from heaven, wrought by a supernatural power in the way of miracle? or whether, according to Mr. Burnet's theory, it was a consequence following antecedent causes by the mere necessities of nature, seen in constitution, natural position, and unavoidable working of things, as by the theory published by that learned enthusiast it seems to be?

Satan could easily account for all the difficulties of the theory, and tell us whether, as there was a natural necessity of the deluge, there is not the like necessity and natural tendency to a conflagration at last.

Would the Devil exert himself as an historian, for our improvement and diversion, how glorious an account could he give us of Noah's voyage round the world, in the famous ark! he could resolve all the difficulties about the building it, the furnishing it, and the laying up provisions in it for all the collection of kinds that he had made; he could tell us whether all the creatures came volunteer to him to go into the ark, or whether he went a-hunting for several years before, in order to bring them together.

He could give us a true relation how he wheedled the people of the next world into the absurd, ridiculous undertaking of building a Babel; how far that stupendous staircase, which was in imagination to reach up to heaven, was carried, before it was interrupted, and the builders confounded; how their speech was altered, how many tongues it was divided into, or whether they were divided at all; and how many subdivisions or dialects have been made since that, by which means very few of God's creatures, except the brutes, understand one another, or care one farthing whether they do or no.

In all these things Satan, who, no doubt, would make a very good chronologist, could settle every epoch, correct every calendar, and bring all our accounts of time to a general agreement, as well the Grecian Olympiads, the Turkish Hegira, the Chinese fictitious accounts of the world's duration, as our blind Julian and Gregorian accounts, which put the world, to this day, in such confusion, that we neither agree in our holy days or working days, fasts or feasts, nor keep the same sabbath in any part of the same globe.

This great antiquary could bring us to a certainty in all the difficulties of ancient story, and tell us whether the tale of the Siege of Troy, and the Rape of Helen, was a fable of Homer, or a history; whether the fictions of the poets are formed from their own brain, or founded in facts, and whether letters were invented by Cadmus the Phœnician, or dictated immediately from heaven at Mount Sinai.

Nay, he could tell us how and in what manner he wheedled Eve, deluded Adam, put Cain into a passion, till he made him murder his own brother; and made Noah, who was above five hundred years a preacher of righteousness, turn sot in his old age, dishonour all his ministry, debauch himself with wine, and by getting drunk and exposing himself, became the jest and laughing-stock of his children, and of all his posterity to this day.

And would Satan, according to the modern practice of the late right reverend historian, enter into the characters of the great men of his age, how should we be diverted with the just history of Adam, in Paradise and out of it, his character, and how he behaved at and after his expulsion; how Cain wandered in the land of Nod, what the mark was which God set upon him, whose daughter his wife was, and how big the city was he built there, according to a certain poet of noble extraction,

> How Cain in the land of Nod
> When the rascal was all alone
> Like an owl in an ivy tod
> Built a city as big as Roan.—Rʉ oʉ.

He could certainly have drawn Eve's picture, told us every feature in her face, and every inch in her shape, whether she was a perfect beauty or no, and whether with the fall she did grow crooked, ugly, ill-natured, and a scold; as the learned Valdemar suggests to be the effect of the curse.

Descending to the characters of the patriarchs in that age, he might, no doubt, give us in particular the characters of Belus, worshipped under the name of Baal, Saturn, and Jupiter, his successors, who they were here, and how they behaved; with all the Pharaohs of Egypt, the Abimilechs of Canaan, and the monarchs of Assyria and Babylon.

Hence also he is able to write the lives of all the heroes of the world, from Alexander of Macedon to Lewis XIV., and from Augustus to the great king George; nor could the bishop himself go beyond him for flattery, any more than the Devil himself could go beyond the bishop for falsehood.

I could enlarge with a particular satisfaction upon the many fine things which Satan, rummaging that inexhaustible storehouse of slander, could set down to blacken the characters of good men, and load the best princes of the world with infamy and reproach.

But we shall never prevail with him, I doubt, to do mankind so much service as resolving all those difficulties would be; for he has an indelible grudge against us; as he believes, and perhaps is assured, that men were at first created by his sovereign, to the intent that, after a certain state of probation in life, such of them as shall be approved, are appointed to fill up those vacancies in the heavenly host, which were made by the abdication and expulsion of him, the Devil and his angels; so that man is appointed to come in Satan's stead, to make good the breach, and enjoy all those ineffable joys and beatitudes which Satan enjoyed before his fall. No wonder, then, that the Devil swells with envy and rage at mankind in general, and at the best of them in particular; nay, the granting this point is giving an unanswerable reason why the Devil practises with such unwearied and indefatigable application upon the best men, if possible, to disappoint God Almighty's decree, that he should not find enough among the whole race to be proper subjects of his clemency, and qualified to succeed the Devil and his host, or fill up the places vacant by the fall! It is true, indeed, the Devil, who we have reason to say is no fool, ought to know better than to suppose that if he could seduce the whole race of mankind and make them as bad as himself, he could, by the success of his wickedness, thwart or disappoint the determined purposes of heaven; but that those which are appointed to inherit the thrones, which he and his followers abdicated and were deposed from, shall certainly be preserved in spite of all his devices for that inheritance, and shall have the possession secured to them, notwithstanding all that the Devil and all the host of Hell can do to prevent it.

But, however, he knows the certainty of this, and that when he endeavours the seducing the chosen servants of the Most High, he fights against God himself, struggles with irresistible grace, and makes war with infinite power, undermining the Church of God and that faith in him which are fortified with eternal promises of Jesus Christ, that the gates of Hell, that is to say, the Devil and all his power shall not prevail against them; I say, however, he knows how impossible it is that he should obtain his ends, yet so blind is his rage, so infatuate is his wisdom, that he cannot refrain breaking himself to pieces against this mountain, and splitting against this rock, *qui Jupiter vult perdere hos dementat.*

But to leave this serious part, which is a little too solemn, for the account of this rebel; seeing we are not to expect he will write his own history for our information and diversion, I shall see if I cannot write it for him: in order to this, I shall extract the substance of his whole story, from the beginning to our own times, which I shall collect out of what is come to hand, whether by revelation or inspiration, that is nothing to him, I shall take care so to improve my intelligence, as may make my account of him authentic, and, in a word, such as the Devil himself shall not be able to contradict.

In writing this uncouth story I shall be freed from the censures of the critics, in a more than ordinary manner, upon one account especially; that my story shall be so just and so well grounded, and, after all the good things I shall say of Satan, will be so little to his satisfaction, that the Devil himself will not be able to say, I dealt with the Devil in writing it; I might, perhaps, give you some account where I had my intelligence, and how all the arcana of his management have come to my hands; but pardon me, gentlemen, this would be to betray conversation, and to discover my agents, and you know statesmen are very careful to preserve the correspondence they keep in the enemy's country, lest they expose their friends to the resentment of the powers whose councils they betray.

Besides, the learned tell us, that ministers of state make an excellent plea of their not betraying their intelligence, against all party inquiries into the great sums of money pretended to be paid for secret service ; and whether the secret service was to bribe people to betray things abroad or at home; whether the money was paid to somebody or to nobody; employed to establish correspondences abroad, or to establish families and amass treasure at home; in a word, whether it was to serve their country or serve themselves, it has been the same thing, and the same plea has been their protection: likewise, in the important affair which I am upon, it is hoped you will not desire me to betray my correspondents ; for you know, Satan is naturally cruel and malicious, and who knows what he might do to show his resentment? at least it might endanger a stop of our intelligence for the future.

And yet, before I have done, I shall make it very plain, that, however my information may be secret and difficult, that yet I came very honestly by it, and shall make a very good use of it ; for it is a great mistake in those who think that an acquaintance with the affairs of the Devil may not be made very useful to us all : they that know no evil can know no good; and, as the learned tell us, that a stone taken out of the head of a toad is a good antidote against poison, so a competent knowledge of the Devil and all his ways, may be the best help to make us defy the Devil and all his works.

CHAPTER II.

OF THE WORD 'DEVIL,' AS IT IS A PROPER NAME TO THE DEVIL, AND ANY OR ALL HIS HOST, ANGELS, ETC.

IT is a question, not yet determined by the learned, whether the word Devil be a singular, that is to say, the name of a person standing by himself, or a noun of multitude; if it be a singular, and so must be used personally only as a proper name, it consequently implies one imperial devil, monarch, or god of the whole clan of Hell; justly distinguished by the term, The Devil, or as the Scots call him, The muckle-horned Dee'l, or as others in a wilder dialect, The Devil of Hell.

that is to say, The Devil of a devil; or (better still) as the
Scripture expresses it, by way of emphasis, the great red
dragon, the Devil, and Satan.

But if we take this word to be, as above, a noun of multitude, and so to be used ambidexter, as occasion presents, singular or plural, then the Devil signifies Satan by himself, or
Satan with all his legions at his heels, as you please, more or
less ; and this way of understanding the word, as it may be very
convenient for my purpose, in the account I am now to give of
the infernal powers, so it is not altogether improper in the nature
of the thing. It is thus expressed in Scripture, where the person
possessed (Matt. iv. 24.) is first said to be possessed of the
Devil, singular; and our Saviour asks him, as speaking to a
single person, *What is thy name ?* and is answered in the plural
and singular together, *My name is Legion, for we are many.*

Nor will it be any wrong to the Devil, supposing him a
single person ; seeing entitling him to the conduct of all his
inferior agents, is what he will take rather for an addition to
his infernal glory, than a diminution or lessening of him in
the extent of his fame.

Having thus articled with the Devil for liberty of speech,
I shall talk of him sometimes in the singular, as a person, and
sometimes in the plural, as a host of devils, or of infernal
spirits ; just as occasion requires, and as the history of his
affairs makes necessary.

But before I enter upon any part of his history, the nature
of the thing calls me back, and my Lord B— of —— in his
late famous orations in defence of liberty, summons me to
prove that there is such a thing or such a person as the Devil;
and, in short, unless I can give some evidence of his existence
as my lord —— said very well, I am talking of nobody.

D—mn me, sir, says a graceless comrade of his to a great
man, your grace will go to the Devil.

D—mn ye, sir, says the d——, then I shall go nowhere ; I
wonder where you intend to go ?

Nay, to the D——l too, I doubt, says Graceless, for I am
almost as wicked as my lord duke.

D. Thou art a silly empty dog, says the d——, and if there
is such a place as a hell, though I believe nothing of it, it is
a place for fools, such as thou art.

Gr. I wonder, then, what heaven the great wits go to,
such as my lord duke ? I don't care to go there, let it be where

it will; they are a plaguy tiresome kind of people, there's nc bearing them, they'll make a hell wherever they come.

D. Prithee, hold thy fool's tongue; I tell thee, if there is any such place as we call nowhere, that's all the heaven or hell that I know of, or believe anything about.

GR. Very good, my lord —; so that heaven is nowhere, and hell is nowhere, and the Devil is nobody, according to my lord duke!

D. Yes, sir, and what then?

GR. And you are to go nowhere when you die, are you?

D. Yes, you dog; don't you know what that incomparable noble genius, my Lord Rochester, sings upon the subject; I believe it unfeignedly;

(sings,)   After death nothing is,
                  And nothing death.

GR. You believe it, my lord! you mean, you would fain believe it if you could; but since you put that great genius, my Lord Rochester, upon me, let me play him back upon your grace; I am sure you have read his fine poem upon Nothing, in one of the stanzas of which is this beautiful thought,

             And to be part of thee *
             The wicked wisely pray.

D. You are a foolish dog.

GR. And my lord duke is a wise infidel.

D. Why! is it not wiser to believe no Devil, than to be always terrified at him?

GR. But shall I toss another poet upon you, my lord?

       If it should so fall out, as who can tell,
       But there may be a God, a heaven, and hell
       Mankind had best consider well, for fear
       't should be too late when their mistakes appear.

D. D—mn your foolish poet, that's not my Lord Rochester?

GR. But how must I be damn'd, if there's no Devil? Is not your grace a little inconsistent there? My Lord Rochester would not have said that, an't please your grace.

D. No, you dog, I am not inconsistent at all, and if I had the ordering of you, I'd make you sensible of it; I'd make you think yourself damn'd for want of a Devil.

GR. That's like one of your grace's paradoxes; such as when you swore by God, that you did not believe there was

           * Meant of nothing.

any such thing as a God or Devil; so you swear by nothing, and damn me to nowhere.

D. You are a critical dog; who taught you to believe these solemn trifles? who taught you to say there is a God.

GR. Nay, I had a better schoolmaster than my lord duke.

D. Why, who was your schoolmaster pray?

GR. The Devil, an't please your grace.

D. The Devil! the devil he did! What, you're going ·to quote Scripture, are you? Prithee don't tell me of Scripture, I know what you mean, *the devils believe and tremble;* why then I have the whip-hand of the Devil, for I hate trembling, and I am delivered from it effectually, for I never believed anything of it, and therefore I don't tremble.

GR. And there, indeed, I ám a wickeder creature than the Devil, or even than my lord duke, for I believe, and yet don't tremble neither.

D. Nay, if you are come to your penitentials, I have done with you.

GR. And I think I must have done with my lord duke, for he same reason.

D. Ay, ay, pray do, I'll go and enjoy myself; I won't throw away the pleasure of my life; I know the consequence of it.

GR. And I'll go and reform myself, else I know the consequence too.

This short dialogue happened between two men of quality, and both men of wit too; and the effect was, that the Lord brought the reality of the Devil into the question, and the debate brought the profligate to be a penitent; so, in short, the Devil was made a preacher of repentance.

The truth is, God and the Devil, however opposite in their nature, and remote from one another in their place of abiding, seem to stand pretty much upon a level in our faith; for as to our believing the reality of their existence, he that denies one, generally denies both; and he that believes one, necessarily believes both.

Very few, if any, of those who believe there is a God, and acknowledge the debt of homage which mankind owes to the supreme Governor of the world, doubt the existence of the Devil, except here and there one, whom we call practical atheists; and it is the character of an atheist, if there is such a creature on earth, that, like my lord duke, he believes neither God nor Devil.

As the belief of both these stands upon a level, and that God and the Devil seem to have an equal share in our faith, so the evidence of their existence seems to stand upon a level too, in many things; and as they are known by their works in the same particular cases, so they are discovered after the same manner of demonstration.

Nay, in some respects, it is equally criminal to deny the reality of them both, only with this difference, that to believe the existence of a God is a debt to nature, and to believe the existence of the Devil is a like debt to reason; one is a demonstration from the reality of visible causes, and the other a deduction from the like reality of their effects.

One demonstration of the existence of God, is from the universal well-guided consent of all nations to worship and adore a supreme power; one demonstration of the existence of the Devil, is from the avowed ill-guided consent of some nations, who, knowing no other god, make a god of the Devil for want of a better.

It may be true, that those nations have no other ideas of the Devil than as of a superior power; if they thought him a supreme power it would have other effects on them, and they would submit to and worship him with a different kind of fear.

But it is plain they have right notions of him as a devil, or evil spirit, because the best reason, and in some places the only reason, they give for worshipping him is, that he may do them no hurt; having no notions at all of his having any power, much less any inclination, to do them any good; so that, indeed, they make a mere devil of him, at the same time that they bow to him as to a god.

All the ages of paganism in the world have had this notion of the Devil; indeed, in some parts of the world, they had also some deities which they honoured above him, as being supposed to be beneficent, kind, and inclined, as well as capable, to give them good things; for this reason, the more polite heathens, such as the Grecians and the Romans, had their Lares, or household gods, who they paid a particular respect to, as being their protectors from hobgoblins, ghosts of the dead, evil spirits, frighful appearances, evil geniuses, and other noxious creatures from the invisible world; or, to

put it into the language of the day we live in, from the Devil,
in whatever shape or appearance he might come to them,
and from whatever might hurt them. And what was all
this but setting up devils against devils, supplicating one
devil, under the notion of a good spirit, to drive out and
protect them from another, whom they called a bad spirit;
the white devil against the black devil?

This proceeds from the natural notions mankind necessarily
entertain of things to come; superior or inferior, God and
the Devil, fill up all futurity in our thoughts; and it is
impossible for us to form any images in our minds of an
immortality and an invisible world, but under the notions of
perfect felicity, or extreme misery.

Now, as these two respect the eternal state of man after
life, they are respectively the object of our reverence and
affection, or of our horror and aversion; but notwithstanding
they are placed thus in a diametrical opposition in our
affections and passions, they are on an evident level as
to the certainty of their existence, and, as I said above, bear
an equal share in our faith.

It being then as certain that there is a Devil, as that there
is a God, I must from this time forward admit no more doubt
of his existence, nor take any more pains to convince you of
it; but speaking of him as a reality in being, proceed to
inquire who he is, and from whence, in order to enter directly
into the detail of his history.

Now, not to enter into all the metaphysical trumpery of
the schools, nor wholly to confine myself to the language of
the pulpit, where we are told, that to think of God and of
the Devil, we must endeavour first, to form ideas of those
things which illustrate the description of rewards and punishment; in the one the eternal presence of the highest good,
and, as a necessary attendant, the most perfect, consummate,
durable bliss and felicity, springing from the presence of that
being in whom all possible beatitude is inexpressibly present, and that in the highest perfection; and on the contrary,
to conceive of a sublime fallen archangel, attended with an innumerable host of degenerate, rebel seraphs or angels, cast out
of heaven together, all guilty of inexpressible rebellion, and
all suffering from that time, and to suffer for ever, the eternal
vengeance of the Almighty, in an inconceivable manner;
that his presence, though blessed in itself, is to them the most

complete article of terror; that they are in themselves perfectly miserable; and to be with whom for ever, adds an inexpressible misery to any state as well as place, and fills the minds of those who are to be, or expect to be, banished to them, with inconceivable horror and amazement.

But when you have gone over all this, and a great deal more of the like, though less intelligible language, which the passions of men collect to amuse one another with, you have said nothing if you omit the main article, namely, the personality of the Devil; and till you add to all the rest some description of the company with whom all this is to be suffered, viz., the Devil and his angels.

Now, who this Devil and his angels are, what share they have either actively or passively in the eternal miseries of a future state, how far they are agents in or partners with the sufferings of the place, is a difficulty yet not fully discovered by the most learned; nor do I believe it is made less a difficulty by their meddling with it.

But to come to the person and original of the Devil, or, as I said before, of devils; I allow him to come of an ancient family, for he is from heaven, and more truly than the Romans could say of their idolized Numa, he is of the race of the Gods.

That Satan is a fallen angel, a rebel seraph, cast out for his rebellion, it is the general opinion, and it is not my business to dispute things universally received; as he was tried, condemned, and the sentence of expulsion executed on him in heaven, he is in this world like a transported felon, never to return; his crime, whatever particular aggravations it might have, it is certain amounted to high treason against his lord and governor, who was also his maker, and against whom he rose in rebellion, took up arms, and, in a word, raised a horrid and unnatural war in his dominions; but being overcome in battle and made prisoner, he and all his host, whose numbers were infinite, all glorious angels like himself, lost at once their beauty and glory with their innocence, and commenced devils, being transformed by crime into monsters and frightful objects; such as, to describe, human fancy is obliged to draw pictures and descriptions in such forms as are most hateful and frightful to the imagination.

These notions, I doubt not, gave birth to all the beauteous images and sublime expressions in Milton's majestic poem;

where, though he has played the poet in a most luxuriant manner, he has sinned against Satan most egregiously, and done the Devil a manifest injury in a great many particulars, as I shall show in its place. And as I shall be obliged to do Satan justice when I come to that part of his history, Mr. Milton's admirers must pardon me if I let them see, that though I admire Mr. Milton as a poet, yet that he was greatly out in matters of history, and especially the history of the Devil; in short, that he has charged Satan falsely in several particulars; and so he has Adam and Eve too: but that I shall leave till I come to the history of the royal family of Eden; which I resolve to present you with when the Devil and I have done with one another.

But not to run down Mr. Milton neither, whose poetry, nor his judgment, cannot be reproached without injury to our own; all those bright ideas of his, which make his poem so justly valued, whether they are capable of proof as to the fact, are, notwithstanding, confirmations of my hypothesis; and are taken from a supposition of the personality of the Devil, placing him at the head of the infernal host as a sovereign, elevated spirit, and monarch of Hell; and as such it is that I undertake to write his history.

By the word Hell, I do not suppose, or at least not determine, that his residence, or that of the whole army of devils, is yet in the same local hell to which the divines tell us he shall be at last chained down; or, at least, that he is yet confined to it; for we shall find he is at present a prisoner at large; of both which circumstances of Satan I shall take occasion to speak in its course.

But when I call the Devil the monarch of Hell, I am to be understood as suits to the present purpose; that he is the sovereign of all the race of hell, that is to say, of all the devils or spirits of the infernal clan; let their numbers, quality, and powers, be what they will.

Upon this supposed personality and superiority of Satan, or, as I call it, the sovereignty and government of one Devil above all the rest; I say, upon this notion are formed all the systems of the dark side of futurity, that we can form in our minds; and so general is the opinion of it, that it will hardly bear to be opposed by any other argument, at least that will bear to be reasoned upon : all the notions of a parity of devils, or making a commonwealth among the black divan, seem to be enthusiastic and visionary, but with no consistency or certainty, and is so generally exploded that we must not venture so much as to debate the point.

Taking it, then, as the generality of mankind do, that there is a grand Devil, a superior of the whole black race ; that they all fell, together with their general Satan at the head of them ; that though he, Satan, could not maintain his high station in heaven, yet that he did continue his dignity among the rest who are called his servants, in Scripture, his angels ; that he has a kind of dominion or authority over the rest, and that they were all, how many millions soever in number, at his command ; employed by him in all his hellish designs, and in all his wicked contrivances for the destruction of man, and for the setting up his own kingdom in the world.

Supposing then, that there is such a superior master-Devil over the rest, it remains that we inquire into his character, and something of his history; in which, though we cannot perhaps produce such authentic documents as in the story of other great monarchs, tyrants, and furies of the world ; yet I shall endeavour to speak some things which the experience of mankind may be apt to confirm, and which the Devil himself will hardly be able to contradict.

It being then granted that there is such a thing or person, call him which we will, as a master-Devil ; that he is thus superior to all the rest in power and in authority, and that all the other evil spirits are his angels, or ministers, or officers, to execute his commands, and are employed in his business ; it remains to inquire, whence he came ? how he came hither into this world ? what that business is which he is employed about ? what his present state is, and where and to what part of the creation of God he is limited and restrained ? what the liberties are he takes, or is allowed to take ? in what manner he works, and how his instruments are likewise allowed to work ? what he has done ever since he commenced Devil, and what he is now doing, and what he may yet do before his last and closer confinement ? as also what he cannot.do, and how far we may or may not be said to be exposed to him, or have or have not reason to be afraid of him ?   These and whatever else occurs in the history and conduct of this arch-devil and his agents, that may be useful for information, caution, or diversion, you may expect in the process of this work.

I know it has been questioned by some, with more face than fear, how it consists with a complete victory of the Devil, which they say was at first obtained by the heavenly powers over Satan and his apostate army in heaven, that when he was cast out of the holy place, and dashed down into the abyss of eternal darkness, as into a place of punishment, a condemned hole, or place of confinement, to be reserved there to the judgment of the great day; I say, how it consists with that entire victory, to let him loose again and give him liberty, like a thief that has broke prison, to range about God's creation, and there to continue his rebellion, commit new ravages and acts of hostility against God, make new efforts at dethroning the Almighty Creator, and, in particular, to fall upon the weakest of his creatures, man ; how Satan being so entirely vanquished, he should be permitted to recover any of his wicked powers, and find room to do mischief to mankind.

Nay, they go farther, and suggest bold things against the wisdom of heaven in exposing mankind, weak in comparison of the immense extent of the Devil's power, to so manifest an overthrow, to so unequal a fight, in which he is sure, if alone in the conflict, to be worsted, to leave him such a dreadful enemy to engage with, and so ill furnished with weapons to resist him.

These objections I shall give as good an answer to as the case will admit in their course, but must adjourn them for the present.

That the Devil is not yet a close prisoner, we have evidence enough to confirm; I will not suggest, that, like our Newgate thieves (to bring little devils and great devils together), he is let out by connivance, and has some little latitudes and advantages for mischief, by that means ; returning at certain seasons to his confinement again.   This might hold, were it not, that the comparison must suggest, that the power which has cast him down could be deluded, and the under-keepers or jailers, under whose charge he was in custody, could wink at his excursions, and the lord of the place know nothing of the matter.   But this wants farther explanation.

CHAPTER III.

OF THE ORIGINAL OF THE DEVIL, WHO HE IS, AND WHAT HE WAS BEFORE HIS EXPULSION OUT OF HEAVEN, AND IN WHAT STATE HE WAS FROM THAT TIME TO THE CREATION OF MAN.

To come to a regular inquiry into Satan's affairs, it is needful we should go back to his original, as far as history and the opinion of the learned world give us leave.

It is agreed by all writers, as well sacred as profane, that this creature we now call a Devil, was originally an angel of light, a glorious seraph; perhaps the choicest of all the glorious seraphs. See how Milton describes his original glory:

> Satan, so call him now, his former name
> Is heard no more in Heaven; he of the first,
> If not the first archangel, great in power,
> In favour and preeminence.—Par. Lost, lib. v.

And again, the same author, and upon the same subject:

> Brighter ones amidst the host
> Of angels, than that star the stars among.—Ib. lib. vii.

The glorious figure which Satan is supposed to make among the thrones and dominions in heaven is such, as we might suppose the highest angel in that exalted train could make; and some think, as above, that he was the chief of the archangels.

Hence that notion, and not ill founded, namely, that the first cause of his disgrace, and on which ensued his rebellion, was occasioned upon God's proclaiming his Son generalissimo, and with himself supreme ruler in heaven, giving the dominion of all his works of creation, as well already finished as not then begun, to him; which post of honour, say they, Satan expected to be conferred on himself, as next in honour, majesty, and power, to God the supreme.

This opinion is followed by Mr. Milton, too, as appears in the following lines, where he makes all the angels attending at a general summons, and God the Father making the following declaration to them:

> Hear all ye angels, progeny of light,
> Thrones, dominations, princedoms, virtues, powers !
> Hear my decree, which unrevok'd shall stand.
> This day I have begot whom I declare

My only Son, and on this holy hill
Him have anointed, whom you now behold
At my right hand; your Head I him appoint;
And by myself have sworn to him shall bow
All knees in heaven, and shall confess him lord;
Under his great vice-gerent reign abide
United, as one individual soul,
For ever happy: him who disobeys,
Me disobeys, breaks union, and, that day
Cast out from God and blessed vision, falls
Into utter darkness, deep ingulf'd, his place
Ordained without redemption, without end.

Satan, affronted at the appearance of a new essence or
being in heaven, called the Son of God; for God, says Mr.
Milton (though erroneously), declared himself at that time,
saying, This day have I begotten him, and that he should be
set up above all the former powers of heaven, of whom Satan
(as above) was the chief, and expecting, if any higher post
could be granted, it might be his due; I say, affronted at this,
he resolved

With all his legions to dislodge, and leave
Unworship'd, unobey'd, the throne supreme
Contemptuous.—Par. Lost, lib. v.

But Mr. Milton is grossly erroneous in ascribing those
words, This day have I begotten thee, to that declaration of
the Father before Satan fell, and consequently to a time
before the creation; whereas, it is by interpreters agreed to
be understood of the incarnation of the Son of God, or at least
of the resurrection: see Pool, upon Acts xiii. 33.[*]

In a word, Satan withdrew, with all his followers, mal-
content and chagrined, resolved to disobey this new command,
and not yield obedience to the Son.

But Mr. Milton agrees in that opinion, that the number of
angels which rebelled with Satan was infinite; and suggests

---

[*] Mr. Pool's words are these: Some refer the words, 'this day have I
begotten thee,' to the incarnation of the Son of God, others to the
resurrection: our translators lay the stress on the preposition, of which the
verb is compounded, and by adding 'again,' (viz.) 'raised up Jesus again,'
Acts xiii. 33, intend it to be understood of the resurrection; and there is
ground for it, in the context, for the resurrection of Christ is that which
St. Paul had propounded in v. 30. of the same chapter, as his theme or
argument to preach upon.
Not that Christ at his resurrection began to be the Son of God, but that
he was manifested then to be so.

in one place, that they were the greatest half of all the angelic body or seraphic host.

> But Satan with his powers,
> ——————————————————————————an host
> Innumerable as the stars of night,
> Or stars of morning, dew drops, which the sun
> Impearls on every leaf and every flow'r.—*Ib.* lib. v.

Be their number as it is, numberless millions and legions of millions, that is no part of my present inquiry; Satan, the leader, guide, and superior, as he was author of the celestial rebellion, is still the great head and master-devil as before; and under his authority they still act, not obeying, but carrying on the same insurrection against God, which they begun in heaven; making war still against heaven, in the person of his image and creature man; and though vanquished by the thunder of the Son of God, and cast down headlong from heaven, they have yet resumed, or rather not lost, either the will or the power of doing mischief.

This fall of the angels, with the war in heaven which preceded it, is finely described by Ovid, in his war of the Titans against Jupiter, casting mountain upon mountain, and hill upon hill (Pelion upon Ossa), in order to scale the adamantine walls, and break open the gates of heaven, till Jupiter struck them with his thunderbolts and overwhelmed them in the abyss. Vide Ovid. Metam. new translation :—

> Nor were the Gods themselves secure on high,
> For now the Giants strove to storm the sky,
> The lawless brood with bold attempt invade
> The Gods, and mountains upon mountains laid.
>   But now the bolt, enraged the Father took,
> Olympus from her deep foundation shook,
> Their structure nodded at the mighty stroke,
> And Ossa's shattered top o'er Pelion broke,
> They're in their own ungodly ruins slain.—Lib. i. p. ix.

Then, again, speaking of Jupiter, resolving in council to destroy mankind by a deluge, and giving the reasons of it to the heavenly host, says thus, speaking of the demigods, alluding to the good men below :

> Think that they in safety can remain,
> When I, myself, who o'er immortals reign,
> Who send the lightning, and heaven's empire sway,
> The stern Lycaön* practised to betray ?—*Ib.*

* Satan.

Since, then, so much poetic liberty is taken with the Devil, relating to his most early state, and the time before his fall, give me leave to make an excursion of the like kind, relating to his history immediately after the fall, and till the creation of man; an interval which I think much of the Devil's story is to be seen in, and which Mr. Milton has taken little notice of, at least it does not seem completely filled up; after which I shall return to honest prose again, and pursue the duty of an historian.

Satan, with hideous ruin thus supprest,
Expell'd the seat of blessedness and rest,
Look'd back and saw the high eternal mound,
Where all his rebel host their outlet found
Restor'd impregnable: the breach made up,
And garrisons of angels ranged a top;
In front, a hundred thousand thunders roll,
And lightnings temper'd to transfix a soul,
Terror of Devils. Satan and his host,
Now to themselves as well as station lost,
Unable to support the hated sight,
Expand seraphic wings, and swift as light
Seek for new safety in eternal night.
  In the remotest gulf of dark they land,
Here vengeance gives them leave to make their stand;
Not that to steps and measures they pretend,
Councils and schemes their station to defend,
But broken, disconcerted, and dismay'd,
By guilt and fright to guilt and fright betray'd;
Rage and confusion every spirit possess'd,
And shame and horror swell'd in every breast;
Transforming envy to their essentials burns,
And beauteous angels frightful devils turns.
  Thus Hell began; the fire of conscious rage
No years can quench, no length of time assuage.
Material fire, with its intensest flame,
Compared with this can scarce deserve a name;
How should it up to immaterials rise?
When we're all flame, we shall all fire despise.
  This fire outrageous and its heat intense
Turns all the pain of loss to pain of sense.
The folding flames concave and inward roll,
Act upon spirit and penetrate the soul:
Not force of devils can its new powers repel,
Where'er it burns it finds or makes a hell;
For Satan flaming with unquench'd desire
Forms his own hell and kindles his own fire;
Vanquish'd, not humbl'd, not in will brought low,
But as his powers decline his passions grow;

The malice, viper like, takes vent within,
Gnaws its own bowels, and bursts in its own sin :
Impatient of the change he scorns to bow,
And never impotent in power till now ;
Ardent with hate, and with revenge distract,
A will to new attempts, but none to act ;
Yet all seraphic, and in just degree,
Suited to spirits' high sense of misery,
Derived from loss which nothing can repair,
And room for nothing left but mere despair.
Here's finish'd Hell! what fiercer fire can burn ?
Enough ten thousand worlds to overturn.
    Hell's but the frenzy of defeated pride,
Seraphic treason's strong impetuous tide,
Where vile ambition, disappointed first,
To its own rage and boundless hatred curst ;
The hate's fann'd up to fury, that to flame,
For fire and fury are in kind the same ;
These burn unquenchable in every face,
And the word 'endless' constitutes the place.
    O state of being! where being's the only grief,
And the chief torture's to be damn'd to life ;
O life ! the only thing they have to hate ;
The finish'd torment of a future state,
Complete in all the parts of endless misery,
And worse ten thousand times than not to be !
Could but the damn'd th' immortal law repeal,
And devils die, there'd be an end of hell ;
Could they that thing called 'being' annihilate,
There'd be no sorrows in a future state ;
The wretch, whose crimes had shut him out on high,
Could be revenged on God himself, and die ;
Job's wife was in the right, and always we   ⎫
Might end by death all human misery,   ⎬
Might have it in our choice, to be, or not to be. ⎭

CHAPTER IV.

OF THE NAME OF THE DEVIL, HIS ORIGINAL, AND THE NATURE
OF HIS CIRCUMSTANCES SINCE HE HAS BEEN CALLED BY THAT
NAME.

THE Scripture is the first writing on earth where we find
the Devil called by his own proper distinguishing denomination, Devil, or the Destroyer* ; nor indeed is there any other

* The meaning of the word Devil, is *destroyer*. See Pool, upon Acts
xiii. 10.

author of antiquity, or of sufficient authority, which says anything of that kind about him.

Here he makes his first appearance in the world, and on that occasion he is called the serpent; but the serpent, however, since made to signify the Devil, when spoken of in general terms, was but the Devil's representative, or the Devil *in quovis vehiculo*, for that time, clothed in a bodily shape, acting under cover and in disguise; or, if you will, the Devil in masquerade: nay, if we believe Mr. Milton, the angel Gabriel's spear had such a secret powerful influence, as to make him strip of a sudden, and with a touch to unmask, and stand upright in his naked original shape, mere Devil, without any disguises whatsoever.

Now as we go to the Scripture for much of his history, so we must go there also for some of his names; and he has a great variety of names indeed, as his several mischievous doings guide us to conceive of him. The truth is, all the ancient names given him, of which the Scripture is full, seem to be originals derived from and adapted to the several steps he has taken, and the several shapes he has appeared in to do mischief in the world.

Here he is called the serpent, Gen. iii. 1.

The old serpent, Rev. xii. 9.
The great red dragon, Rev. xii. 3.
The accuser of the brethren, Rev. xii. 10.
The enemy, Matt. xxiii. 29.
Satan, Job i.; Zech. iii. 1, 2.
Belial, 2 Cor. vi. 15.
Beelzebub, Matt. xii. 24.
Mammon, Matt. vi. 24.
The angel of light, 2 Cor. xi. 14.
The angel of the bottomless pit, Rev. ix. 11.
The prince of the power of the air, Eph. ii. 2.
Lucifer, Isa. xiv. 12.
Abbaddon, or Apollion, Rev. ix. 11.
Legion, Mark v. 9.
The god of this world, 2 Cor. iv. 4.
The foul spirit, Mark ix. 5.
The unclean spirit, Mark i. 27.
The lying spirit, 2 Chron. xxx.
The tempter, Matt. iv. 3.
The son of the morning, Isa. xiv. 12

But to sum them all up in one, he is called in the New Testament plain Devil; all his other names are varied according to the custom of speech, and the dialects of the several nations where he is spoken of; but in a word, Devil is the common name of the Devil in all the known languages of the earth. Nay, all the mischief he is empowered to do, is in Scripture placed to his account, under the particular title of the Devil, not of devils in the plural number, though they are sometimes mentioned too; but in the singular it is the identical individual Devil, in and under whom all the little devils, and all the great devils, if such there be, are supposed to act; nay, they are supposed to be governed and directed by him. Thus we are told in Scripture of the works of the devil, 1 John iii. 8; of casting out the devil, Mark i. 34; of resisting the devil, James iv. 5; of our Saviour being tempted of the devil, Matt. iv. 1; of Simon Magus, a child of the devil, Acts xiii. 10; the devil came down in a great wrath, Rev. xii. 12, and the like. And according to this usage in speech we go on to this day, and all the infernal things we converse with in the world, are fathered upon the Devil, as one undivided simple essence, by how many agents soever working: everything evil, frightful in appearance, wicked in its actings, horrible in its manner, monstrous in its effects, is called the Devil; in a word, Devil is the common name for all devils, that is to say, for all evil spirits, all evil powers, all evil works, and even all evil things; yet it is remarkable the Devil is no Old Testament word, and we never find it used in all the Old Testament but four times, and then not once in the singular number, and not once to signify Satan, as it is now understood.

It is true, the learned give a great many differing interpretations of the word Devil; the English commentators tell us, it means a destroyer, others that it signifies a deceiver, and the Greeks derive it from a calumniator, or false witness; for we find that Calumny was a goddess, to whom the Athenians built altars and offered sacrifices upon some solemn occasions, and they call her Διαβολὴ, from whence came the masculine Διάβολος, which we translate Devil.

Thus we take the name of Devil to signify not persons only, but actions and habits; making imaginary devils, and transforming that substantial creature called Devil, into everything noxious and offensive: thus St. Francis being tempted by the Devil in the shape of a bag of money lying in the highway, the saint having discovered the fraud, whether seeing his cloven foot hang out of the purse, or whether he distinguished him by his smell of sulphur, or how otherwise, authors are not agreed; but, I say, the saint, having discovered the cheat, and outwitted the Devil, took occasion to preach that eminent sermon to his disciples, where his text was, Money is the Devil.

Nor, upon the whole, is any wrong done to the Devil by this kind of treatment; it only gives him the sovereignty of the whole army of Hell, and making all the numberless legions of the bottomless pit servants, or, as the Scripture calls them, angels to Satan the grand devil; and all their actions, performances, and achievements, are justly attributed to him, not as the prince of devils only, but the emperor of devils, the prince of all the princes of devils.

Under this denomination then of Devil, all the powers of Hell, all the princes of the air, all the black armies of Satan are comprehended, and in this manner they are to be understood in this whole work, *mutatis mutandis*, according to the several circumstances in which we are to speak of them.

This being premised, and my authority being so good, Satan must not take it ill if I treat him after the manner of men, and give him those titles which he is best known by among us; for indeed, having so many, it is not very easy to call him out of his name.

However, as I am obliged by the duty of an historian to decency, as well as impartiality, so I thought it necessary, before I used too much freedom with Satan, to produce authentic documents, and bring antiquity upon the stage, to justify the manner of my writing, and let you see I shall describe him in no colours, nor call him by any name, but what he has been known by for many ages before me.

And now, though being writing to the common understanding of my reader, I am obliged to treat Satan very coarsely, and to speak of him in the common acceptation, calling him plain Devil; a word which in this mannerly age is not so sonorous as others might be, and which by the error of the times is apt to prejudice us against his person; yet it must be acknowledged he has a great many other names and surnames which he might be known by, of a less obnoxious import than that of Devil, or Destroyer, &c.

Mr. Milton, indeed, wanting titles of honour to give to the leaders of Satan's host, is obliged to borrow several of his Scripture names, and bestow them upon his infernal heroes, whom he makes the generals and leaders of the armies of Hell; and so he makes Beelzebub, Lucifer, Belial, Mammon, and some others, to be the names of particular devils, members of Satan's upper house, or Pandemonium; whereas, indeed, these are all names proper and peculiar to Satan himself.

The Scripture also has some names of a coarser kind, by which the Devil is understood; as particularly, as is noted already in the Apocalypse, he is called the Great Red Dragon, the Beast, the Old Serpent, and the like: but take it in the Scripture, or where you will in history, sacred or profane, you will find that in general the Devil is, as I have said above, his ordinary name in all languages and in all nations, the name by which he and his works are principally distinguished: also the Scripture, besides that it often gives him this name, speaks of the works of the devil, of the subtilty of the devil, of casting out devils, of being tempted of the devil, of being possessed with a devil; and so many other expressions of that kind, as I have said already, are made use of for us to understand the evil spirit by, that in a word, Devil is the common name of all wicked spirits: for Satan is no more the devil, as if he alone was so, and all the rest were a diminutive species who did not go by that name; but, I say, even in Scripture, every spirit, whether under his dominion or out of his dominion, is called the Devil, and is as much a real devil, that is to say, a condemned spirit, and employed in the same wicked work, as Satan himself.

His name, then, being thus ascertained, and his existence acknowledged, it should be a little inquired what he is; we believe there is such a thing, such a creature as the Devil; and that he has been, and may still with propriety of speech, and without injustice to his character, be called by his ancient name, Devil.

But who is he? what is his original? whence came he? and what is his present station and condition? for these things and these inquiries are very necessary to his history, nor, indeed, can any part of his history be complete without them.

That he is of an ancient and noble original must be acknowledged, for he is heaven-born and of angelic race, as has been touched already; if Scripture evidence may be of any weight in the question, there is no room to doubt the genealogy of the Devil; he is not only spoken of as an angel, but as a fallen angel, one that had been in heaven, had beheld the face of God in his full effulgence of glory, and had surrounded the throne of the Most High; from whence, commencing rebel, and being expelled, he was cast down, down, down, God and the Devil himself only know where; for indeed we cannot say that any man on earth knows it; and wherever it is, he has, ever since man's creation, been a plague to him, been a tempter, a deluder, a calumniator, an enemy, and the object of man's horror and aversion.

As his original is heaven-born, and his race angelic, so the angelic nature is evidently placed in a class superior to the human, and this the Scripture is express in also; when speaking of man, it says, *he made him a little lower than the angels.*

Thus the Devil, as mean thoughts as you may have of him, is of a better family than any of you, nay, than the best gentleman of you all; what he may be fallen to, is one thing, but what he is fallen from, is another; and therefore I must tell my learned and reverend friend J. W., LL.D., when he spoke so rudely of the Devil lately, in my opinion he abused his betters.

Nor is the Scripture more a help to us in the search after the Devil's original, than it is in our search after his nature; it is true, authors are not agreed about his age, what time he was created, how many years he enjoyed his state of blessedness before he fell, or how many years he continued with his whole army in a state of darkness before the creation of man. It is supposed it might be a considerable space, and that it was a part of his punishment too, being all the while inactive, unemployed, having no business, nothing to do but gnawing his own bowels, and rolling in the agony of his own self-reproaches, being a hell to himself in reflecting on the glorious state from whence he was fallen.

How long he remained thus, it is true we have no light into from history, and but little from tradition; Rabbi Judah says, the Jews were of the opinion that he remained twenty thousand years in that condition, and that the world shall continue twenty thousand more, in which he shall find work enough to satisfy his mischievous desires; but he shows no authority for his opinion.

Indeed, let the Devil have been as idle as they think he was before, it must be acknowledged that now he is the most busy, vigilant, and diligent, of all God's creatures, and very full of employment too, such as it is.

Scripture, indeed, gives us light into the enmity there is between the two natures, the diabolical and the human; the reason of it, and how and by what means the power of the Devil is restrained by the Messiah; and to those who are willing to trust to gospel light, and believe what the Scripture says of the Devil, there may much of his history be discovered; and therefore those that list may go there for a fuller account of the matter.

But to reserve all Scripture evidence of these things, as a magazine in store for the use of those with whom Scripture testimony is of force, I must for the present turn to other inquiries, being now directing my story to an age, wherein to be driven to Revelation and Scripture assertions is esteemed giving up the dispute; people now-a-days must have demonstration; and, in a word, nothing will satisfy the age, but such evidence as perhaps the nature of the question will not admit.

It is hard, indeed, to bring demonstrations in such a case as this: *No man has seen God at any time,* says the Scripture, 1 John iv. 12. So the Devil, being a spirit incorporeal, an angel of light, and consequently not visible in his own substance, nature, and form, it may in some sense be said, No man has seen the Devil at any time; all those pretences of frenziful and fanciful people, who tell us they have seen the Devil, I shall examine, and perhaps expose by themselves.

It might take up a great deal of our time here, to inquire whether the Devil has any particular shape or personality of substance, which can be visible to us, felt, heard, or understood, and which he cannot alter; and then, what shapes or appearances the Devil has at any time taken upon him; and whether he can really appear in a body which might be handled and seen; and yet so as to know it to have been the Devil at the time of his appearing; but this also I defer, as not of weight in the present inquiry.

We have divers accounts of witches conversing with the Devil; the Devil in a real body, with all the appearance of a body of a man or woman appearing to them; also of having a familiar, as they call it, an incubus, or little devil, which sucks their bodies, runs away with them into the air, and the like; much of this is said, but much more than it is easy to prove, and we ought to give but a just proportion of credit to those things.

As to his borrowed shapes and his subtle transformings, that we have such open testimony of, that there is no room for any question about it; and when I come to that part, I shall be obliged rather to give a history of the fact, than enter into any dissertation upon the nature and reason of it.

I do not find in any author, whom we can call creditable, that even in those countries where the dominion of Satan is more particularly established, and where they may be said to worship him in a more particular manner as a devil; which some tell us the Indians in America did, who worshipped the Devil that he might not hurt them; yet, I say, I do not find that even there the Devil appeared to them in any particular constant shape or personality peculiar to himself.

Scripture and history, therefore, giving us no light into that part of the question, I conclude and lay it down, not as my opinion only, but as what all ages seem to concur in, that the Devil has no particular body; that he is a spirit, and that though he may, Proteus-like, assume the appearance of either man or beast, yet it must be some borrowed shape, some assumed figure, *pro hac vice*, and that he has no visible body of his own.

I thought it needful to discuss this as a preliminary, and that the next discourse might go upon a certainty in this grand point, namely, that the Devil, however he may for his particular occasions put himself into a great many shapes, and clothe himself, perhaps, with what appearances he pleases, yet that he is himself still a mere spirit, that he retains the seraphic nature, is not visible by our eyes, which are human and organic, neither can he act with the ordinary powers, or in the ordinary manner as bodies do; and, therefore, when he has thought fit to descend to the meannesses of disturbing and frightening children and old women by noises and knockings, dislocating the chairs and stools, breaking windows, and such-like little ambulatory things, which would seem to be below the dignity of his character, and which, in particular, is ordinarily performed by organic powers, yet even then he has thought fit not to be seen, and rather to make the poor people believe he had a real shape and body, with hands to act, mouth to speak, and the like, than to give proof of it in common to the whole world, by showing himself, and acting visibly and openly, as a body usually and ordinarily does.

Nor is it any disadvantage to the Devil, that his seraphic nature is not confined or imprisoned in a body or shape, suppose that shape to be what monstrous thing we would; for this would, indeed, confine his actings within the narrow sphere of the organ or body to which he was limited; and though you were to suppose the body to have wings for a velocity of motion equal to spirit, yet if it had not a power of invisibility too, and a capacity of conveying itself, undiscovered, into all the secret recesses of mankind, and the same secret art or capacity of insinuation, suggestion, accusation, &c., by which his wicked designs are now propagated, and all his other devices assisted, by which he deludes and betrays mankind; I say, he would be no more a devil, that is, a destroyer, no more a deceiver, and no more a Satan, that is, a dangerous arch-enemy to the souls of men; nor would it be any difficulty to mankind to shun and avoid him, as I shall make plain in the other part of his history.

Had the Devil from the beginning been embodied, as he could not have been invisible to us, whose souls, equally seraphic, are only prescribed by being embodied and incased in flesh and blood as we are; so he would have been no more a devil to anybody but himself: the imprisonment in a body, had the powers of that body been all that we can conceive to make him formidable to us, would yet have been a hell to him. Consider him as a conquered exasperated rebel, retaining all that fury and swelling ambition, that hatred of God, and envy at his creatures which dwells now in his enraged spirits as a Devil; yet suppose him to have been condemned to organic powers, confined to corporeal motion, and restrained as a body must be supposed to restrain a spirit; it must, at the same time, suppose him to be effectually disabled from all the methods he is now allowed to make use of, for exerting his rage and enmity against God, any farther than as he might suppose it to affect his Maker at second hand, by wounding his glory through the sides of his weakest creature, man.

He must, certainly, be thus confined, because body can only act upon body, not upon spirit; no species being empowered to act out of the compass of its own sphere: he

might have been empowerd, indeed, to have acted terrible
and even destructive things upon mankind, especially if this
body had any powers given it which mankind had not,
by which man would be overmatched and not be in a
condition of self-defence; for example, suppose him to have
had wings to have flown in the air; or to be invulnerable,
and that no human invention, art, or engine could hurt,
ensnare, captivate, or restrain him.

But this is to suppose the righteous and wise Creator to
have made a creature and not be able to defend and preserve
him, or have left him defenceless to the mercy of another of
his own creatures, whom he had given power to destroy
him; this indeed, might have occasioned a general idolatry,
and made mankind, as the Americans do to this day, worship
the Devil, that he might not hurt them; but it could not have
prevented the destruction of mankind, supposing the Devil to
have had malice equal to his power; and he must put on a
new nature, be compassionate, generous, beneficent, and
steadily good in sparing the rival enemy he was able to
destroy, or he must have ruined mankind.   In short, he must
have ceased to have been a devil, and must have resumed his
original, angelic, heavenly nature, filled with the principles
of love, to delight in the works of his creator, and bent to
propagate his glory and interest; or he must have put an end
to the race of man, whom it would be in his power to destroy,
and oblige his Maker to create a new species, or fortify the
old with some kind of defence which must be invulnerable,
and which his fiery darts could not penetrate.

On this occasion suffer me to make an excursion from the
usual style of this work, and with some solemnity to express
my thoughts thus:

How glorious is the wisdom and goodness of the great
Creator of the world! in thus restraining these seraphic out-
casts from the power of assuming human or organic bodies,
which, could they do, invigorating them with the supernatural powers, which, as seraphs and angels, they now possess
and might exert, they would be able even to fright mankind
from the face of the earth, destroy and confound God's creation; nay, even as they are, were not their power limited,
they might destroy the creation itself, reverse and overturn
nature, and put the world into a general conflagration; but
were those immortal spirits embodied, though they were not

permitted to confound nature, they would be able :o harass poor, weak, and defenceless man out of his wits, and render him perfectly useless, either to his Maker or himself.

But the dragon is chained, the Devil's power is limited; he has indeed a vastly extended empire, being prince of the air; having, at least, the whole atmosphere to range in, and how far that atmosphere is extended, is not yet ascertained by the nicest observations; I say, at least, because we do not yet know how far he may be allowed to make excursions beyond the atmosphere of this globe into the planetary worlds, and what power he may exercise in all the habitable parts of the solar system; nay, of all the other solar systems, which, for aught we know, may exist in the mighty extent of created space, and of which you may hear farther in its order.

But let his power be what it will there, we are sure it is limited here, and that in two particulars; first, he is limited, as above, from assuming body or bodily shapes and substance; and secondly, from exerting seraphic powers, and acting with that supernatural force, which, as an angel, he was certainly vested with before the fall, and which we are not certain is yet taken from him; or at most, we do not know how much it may or may not be diminished by his degeneracy, and by the blow given him at his expulsion: this we are certain, that be his power greater or less, he is restrained from the exercise of it in this world; and he, who was once equal to the angel who killed a hundred and eighty thousand men in one night, is not able now, without a new commission, to take away the life of one Job, nor to touch anything he had.

But let us consider him then limited and restrained as he is, yet he remains a mighty, a terrible, an immortal being: infinitely superior to man, as well in the dignity of his nature, as in the dreadful powers he retains still about him; and though the brainsick heads of our enthusiastics paint him blacker than he is, and, as I have said, represent him clothed with terrors that do not really belong to him; as if the power of good and evil was wholly vested in him, and that he was placed in the throne of his Maker, to distribute both punishments and rewards; terrifying and deluding fanciful people about him till they turn their heads, and fright them into a belief that the Devil will let them alone if they do such and such good things, or carry them away with him, they know not whither, if they do not; as if the Devil, whose proper

business is mischief, seducing and deluding mankind, and
drawing him in to be a rebel like himself, should threaten to
seize upon them, carry them away, and, in a word, fall upon
them to hurt them, if they did evil, and on the contrary, be
favourable and civil to them, if they did well.

Thus a poor deluded country fellow in our town, that had
lived a wicked, abominable, debauched life, was frightened
with an apparition, as he called it, of the Devil; he fancied
that he spoke to him, and telling his tale to a good honest
Christian gentleman his neighbour, that had a little more
sense than himself, the gentleman asked him if he was sure
he really saw the Devil? Yes, yes, sir, says he, I saw him
very plain; and so they began the following discourse.

GENT. See him! see the Devil! art thou sure of it, Thomas?

THO. Yes, yes, I am sure enough of it, master; to be sure
it was the Devil.

GENT. And how do you know 'twas the Devil, Thomas?
had you ever seen the Devil before?

THO. No, no, I had never seen him before, to be sure, but
for all that I know it was the Devil.

GENT. Well, if you are sure, Thomas, there's no contradicting you; pray what clothes had he on?

THO. Nay, sir, don't jest with me, he had no clothes on,
he was clothed with fire and brimstone.

GENT. Was it dark or daylight when you saw him?

THO. O! it was very dark, for it was midnight.

GENT. How could you see him then? did you see by the
light of the fire you speak of?

THO. No, no, he gave me no light himself, but I saw him
for all that.

GENT. But was it within doors, or out in the street?

THO. It was within, it was in my own chamber, when I
was just going into bed, that I saw him.

GENT. Well, then, you had a candle, hadn't you?

THO. Yes, I had a candle, but it burnt as blue! and as
dim!

GENT. Well, but if the Devil was clothed with fire and
brimstone, he must give you some light; there can't be such
a fire as you speak of but it must give a light with it.

THO. No, no, he gave no light, but I smelt his fire and
brimstone; he left a smell of it behind him, when he was
gone.

GENT. Well, so you say he had fire, but gave no light: it was a devilish fire, indeed; did it feel warm? was the room hot while he was in it?

THO. No, no, but I was hot enough without it, for it put me into a great sweet with the fright.

GENT. Very well, he was all in fire, you say, but without light or heat, only it seems he stunk of brimstone; pray what shape was he in? what was he like? for you say you saw him.

THO. O! sir, I saw two great staring saucer eyes, enough to frighten anybody out of their wits.

GENT. And was that all you saw?

THO. No, I saw his cloven-foot very plain; t'was as big as one of our bullocks that goes to plough.

GENT. So you saw none of his body but his eyes and his feet? a fine vision, indeed!

THO. No, that was enough to send me going.

GENT. Going! what did you run away from him?

THO. No, but I fled into bed at one jump, and sunk down, and pull'd the bedclothes quite over me.

GENT. And what did you do that for?

THO. To hide myself from such a frightful creature.

GENT. Why, if it had really been the Devil, do you think the bedclothes would have secured you from him?

THO. Nay, I don't know, but in a fright it was all I could do.

GENT. Nay, 'twas as wise as all the rest; but come, Thomas, to be a little serious, pray did he speak to you?

THO. Yes, yes, I heard a voice, but who it was the Lord knows.

GENT. What kind of voice was it? was it like a man's voice?

THO. No; it was a hoarse ugly noise, like the croaking of a frog, and it called me by my name twice, Thomas Dawson, Thomas Dawson!

GENT. Well, did you answer?

THO. No, not I, I could not have spoken a word for my life; why, I was frightened to death!

GENT. Did it say anything else?

THO. Yes, when it saw that I did not speak, it said Thomas Dawson, Thomas Dawson, you are a wicked wretch; you lay with Jenny S——— last night; if you don't repent, I will take you away alive and carry you to hell, and you shall be damn'd, you wretch.

GENT. And was it true, Thomas? did you lie with Jenny S——— the night before?

THO. Indeed, master, it was true; but I was very sorry afterwards.

GENT. But how should the Devil know it, Thomas?

THO. Nay, he knows it to be sure; why, they say he knows everything.

GENT. Well, but why should he be angry at that? he would rather bid you lie with her again, and encourage you to lie with forty whores, than hinder you: this can't be the Devil, Thomas.

THO. Yes, yes, sir, 'twas the Devil to be sure.

GENT. But he bid you repent too, you say?

THO. Yes, he threatened me if I did not.

GENT. Why, Thomas, do you think the Devil would have you repent?

THO. Why no, that's true too; I don't know what to say to that; but what could it be? 'twas the Devil to be sure, it could be nobody else.

GENT. No, no, 'twas neither the Devil, Thomas, nor anybody else, but your own frightened imagination, Thomas; you had lain with that wench, and being a young sinner of that kind, your conscience terrified you, told you the Devil would fetch you away, and you would be damn'd; and you were so persuaded it would be so, that you at last imagined he was come for you indeed; that you saw him and heard him; whereas, you may depend upon it, if Jenny S——— will let you lie with her every night, the Devil will hold the candle, or do anything to forward it, but will never disturb you; he's too much a friend to your wickedness; it could never be the Devil, Thomas; 'twas only your own guilt frightened you, and that was devil enough, too, if you knew the worst of it; you need no other enemy.

THO. Why that's true, master, one would think the Devil should not bid me repent, that's true; but certainly 'twas the Devil for all that.

Now Thomas was not the only man that, having committed a flagitious crime, had been deluded by his own imagination, and the power of fancy, to think the Devil was come for him; whereas, the Devil, to give him his due, is too honest to pretend to such things; it is his business to persuade men to offend, not to repent, as he professes no other. He may press men to this or that action, by telling them it 's no sin, no offence, no breach of God's law, and the like, when really it is both; but to press them to repent, when they have offended, that is quite out of his way; it is none of his business, nor does he pretend to it; therefore, let no man charge the Devil with what he is not concerned in.

But to return to his person; he is, as I have said, notwithstanding his lost glory, a mighty, a terrible, and an immortal spirit; he is himself called a Prince, the Prince of the Power of the air, the Prince of Darkness, the Prince of Devils, and the like, and his attending spirits are called his angels; so that however Satan has lost the glory and rectitude of his nature, by his apostate state, yet he retains a greatness and magnificence, which places him above our rank, and indeed above our conception; for we know not what he is, any more than we know what the blessed angels are; of whom we can say no more than that they are ministering spirits, &c., as the Scripture has described them.

Two things, however, may give us some insight into the nature of the Devil, in the present state he is in; and these we have a clear discovery of in the whole series of his conduct from the beginning.

1. That he is the vanquished but implacable enemy of God his creator, who has conquered him, and expelled him from the habitations of bliss; on which account he is filled with envy, rage, malice, and all uncharitableness; would dethrone God, and overturn the thrones of heaven if it was in his power.

2. That he is man's irreconcilable enemy; not as he is a man, nor on his own account simply, nor for any advantage he (the Devil) can make by the ruin and destruction of man, but in mere envy at the felicity he is supposed to enjoy as Satan's rival; and as he is appointed to succeed Satan and his angels in the possession of those glories from which they are fallen.

And here I must take upon me to say, Mr. Milton makes a wrong judgment of the reason of Satan's resolution to disturb the felicity of man; he tells us it was merely to affront God his maker, rob him of the glory designed in his new work of creation, and to disappoint him in his main design, namely, the creating a new species of creatures, in a perfect rectitude of soul, and after his own image, from whom he might expect a new fund of glory should be raised, and who was to appear as the triumph of the Messiah's victory over the Devil. In all which Satan could not be fool enough not to know that he should be disappointed by the same power which had so eminently counteracted his rage before.

But, I believe, the Devil went upon a much more probable design; and though he may be said to act upon a meaner principle than that of pointing his rage at the personal glory of his Creator, yet I own, that in my opinion, it was by much the more rational undertaking, and more likely to succeed; and that was, that whereas he perceived this new species of creatures had a sublime as well as human part, and were made capable of possessing the mansions of eternal beatitude from whence he (Satan) and his angels were expelled and irretrievably banished; envy at such a rival moved him by all possible artifice (for he saw himself deprived of capacity to do it by force), to render him unworthy, like himself; and that bringing him to fall into rebellion and disobedience, he might see his rival damned with him; and those who were intended to fill up the empty spaces in heaven, made so by the absence of so many millions of fallen angels, be cast out into the same darkness with them.

How he came to know that this new species of creatures were liable to such imperfection, is best explained by the Devil's prying, vigilant disposition, judging or leading him to judge by himself (for he was as near being infallible as any of God's creatures had been), and then inclining him to try whether it was so or no.

Modern naturalists, especially some who have not so large a charity for the fair sex as I have, tell us, that as soon as ever Satan saw the woman, and looked in her face, he saw it evidently that she was the best-formed creature to make a fool of, and the best to make a hypocrite of, that could be made, and therefore the most fitted for his purpose.

1. He saw by some thwart lines in her face (legible, perhaps, to himself only) that there was a throne ready prepared for the sin of pride to sit in state upon, especially if it took an early possession. Eve, you may suppose, was a perfect beauty, if ever such a thing may be supposed in the human frame; her figure being so extraordinary was the

groundwork of his project; there needed no more than to bring her to be vain of it, and to conceit that it either was so, or was infinitely more sublime and beautiful than it really was; and having thus tickled her vanity, to introduce pride gradually, till at last he might persuade her that she was really angelic, or of heavenly race, and wanted nothing but to eat the forbidden fruit, and that would make her something more excellent still.

2. Looking farther into her frame, and with a nearer view to her imperfections, he saw room to conclude that she was of a constitution easy to be seduced, and especially by flattering her, raising a commotion in her soul, and a disturbance among her passions; and accordingly he set himself to work, to disturb her repose, and put dreams of great things into her head; together with something of a nameless nature, which (however some have been ill-natured enough to suggest) I shall not injure the Devil so much as to mention without better evidence.

3. But, besides this, he found, upon the very first survey of her outside, something so very charming in her mien and behaviour, so engaging as well as agreeable in the whole texture of her person, and withal such a sprightly wit, such a vivacity of parts, such a fluency of tongue, and, above all, such a winning prevailing whine in her smiles, or at least in her tears, that he made no doubt if he could but once delude her, she would easily be brought to delude Adam, whom he found set not only a great value upon her person, but was perfectly captivated by her charms; in a word, he saw plainly, that if he could but ruin her, he should easily make a devil of her, to ruin her husband, and draw him into any gulf of mischief, were it ever so black and dreadful, that she should first fall into herself. How far some may be wicked enough, from hence, to suggest of the fair sex, that they have been devils to their husbands ever since, I cannot say; I hope they will not be so unmerciful to discover truths of such fatal consequence, though they should come to their knowledge.

Thus subtle and penetrating has Satan been from the beginning; and who can wonder that, upon these discoveries made into the woman's inside, he went immediately to work with her, rather than with Adam? not but that one would think, if Adam was fool enough to be deluded by his wife, the Devil might have seen so much of it in his countenance, as to have encouraged him to make his attack directly upon him, and not go round about, beating the bush, and ploughing with the heifer; setting upon the woman first, and then setting her upon her husband, who might as easily have been imposed upon as she.

Other commentators upon this critical text suggest to us, that Eve was not so pleased with the hopes of being made a goddess; that the pride of a seraphic knowledge did not so much work upon her imagination to bring her to consent, as a certain secret notion, infused into her head by the same wicked instrument, that she should be wiser than Adam, and should by the superiority of her understanding, necessarily have the government over him; which, at present, she was sensible she had not, he being master of a particular air of gravity and majesty, as well as of strength, infinitely superior to her.

This is an ill-natured suggestion; but it must be confessed, the impatient desire of government which (since that) appears in the general behaviour of the sex, and particularly of governing husbands, leaves too much room to legitimate the supposition.

The philosophers and expositors who are of this opinion, add to it, that this being her original crime, or the particular temptation to that crime, Heaven thought fit to show his justice, in making her more entire subjection to her husband be a part of the curse, that she might read her sin in the punishment, viz., *He shall rule over thee.*

I only give the general hint of these things as they appear recorded in the annals of Satan's first tyranny, and at the beginning of his government in the world; those that would be more particularly informed, may inquire of him and know farther.

I cannot, however, but observe here, with some regret, how it appears by the consequence, that the Devil was not mistaken when he made an early judgment of Mrs. Eve; and how Satan really went the right way to work, to judge of her; it is certain the Devil had nothing to do but to look in her face, and upon a near steady view he might easily see there an instrument for his turn; nor has he failed to make her a tool ever since, by the very methods which he at first proposed; to which, perhaps, he has made some additions in the corrupting her composition, as well as her understanding; qualifying her to be a complete snare to the poor weaker vessel man; to wheedle him with her syren's voice, abuse him with her smiles, delude him with her crocodile tears, and sometimes cock her crown at him, and terrify him with the thunder of her treble; making the effeminated male apple-eater tremble at the noise of that very tongue which at first commanded him to sin.   For it is yet a debate, which the learned have not decided, whether she persuaded and entreated him, or, like a true she-tyrant, exercised her authority and obliged him to eat the forbidden fruit.

And therefore a certain author, whose name, for fear of the sex's resentment, I conceal, brings her in, calling to Adam at a great distance, in an imperious haughty manner, beckoning to him with her hand, thus; Here, says she, you cowardly faint-hearted wretch, take this branch of heavenly fruit, eat and be a stupid fool no longer; eat and be wise; eat and be a god; and know, to your eternal shame, that your wife has been made an enlightened goddess before you.

He tells you, Adam hung back a little at first, and trembled, afraid to trespass: What ails the sot? says the new termagant; what are you afraid of? did God forbid you! yes; and why? that we might not be knowing and wise like himself! what reason can there be that we, who have capacious souls, able to receive knowledge, should have it withheld? take it, you fool, and eat; don't you see how I am exalted in soul by it, and am quite another creature? take it, I say, or, if you don't, I will go and cut down the tree, and you shall never eat any of it at all, and you shall be still a fool, and be governed by your wife for ever.

Thus, if this interpretation of the thing is just, she scolded him into it, rated him, and brought him to it by the terror of her voice; a thing that has retained a dreadful influence over him ever since; nor have the greatest of Adam's successors, how light soever some husbands make of it in this age, been ever able, since that, to conceal their terror at the very sound; nay, if we may believe history, it prevailed even among the gods; not all the noise of Vulcan's hammers could silence the clamours of that outrageous whore, his goddess; nay, even Jupiter himself led such a life with a termagant wife, that once, they say, Juno outscolded the noise of all his thunders, and was within an ace of brawling him out of heaven. But to return to the Devil.

With these views he resolved, it seems, to attack the woman; and if we consider him as a devil, and what he aimed it, and consider the fair prospect he had of success, I must confess I do not see who can blame him, or at least, how anything less could be expected from him; but we shall meet with it again by and by.

CHAPTER V.

OF THE STATION SATAN HAD IN HEAVEN BEFORE HE FELL; THE
NATURE AND ORIGINAL OF HIS CRIME, AND SOME OF MR. MILTON'S
MISTAKES ABOUT IT.

THUS far I have gone upon general observation in this great affair of Satan and his empire in this world; I now come to my title, and shall enter upon the historical part, as the main work before me.

Besides what has been said poetically, relating to the fall and wandering condition of the Devil and his host, which poetical part I offer only as an excursion, and desire it should be taken so; I shall give you what I think is deduced from good originals on the part of Satan's story in a few words.

He was one of the created angels, formed by the same omnipotent hand and glorious power who created the heavens and the earth, and all that is therein: this innumerable heavenly host, as we have reason to believe, contained angels of higher and lower stations, of greater and of lesser degree, expressed in the Scripture by thrones, dominions, and principalities: this, I think, we have as much reason to believe, as we have that there are stars in the firmament (or starry heavens) of greater and of lesser magnitude.

What particular station among the immortal choir of angels this arch-seraph, this prince of devils, called Satan, was placed in before his expulsion, that, indeed, we cannot come at the knowledge of, at least, not with such an authority as may be depended upon; but as from Scripture authority, he is placed at the head of all the apostate armies, after he was fallen, we cannot think it in the least assuming to say, that he might be supposed to be one of the principal agents in the rebellion which happened in heaven, and, consequently, that he might be one of the highest in dignity there, before that rebellion.

The higher his station, the lower, and with the greater precipitation, was his overthrow ; and therefore, those words, though taken in another sense, may very well be applied to him : *How art thou fallen, O Lucifer! Son of the Morning.*

Having granted the dignity of his person, and the high station in which he was placed among the heavenly host, it would come then necessarily to inquire into the nature of his fall, and, above all, a little into the reason of it ; certain it is, he did fall, was guilty of rebellion and disobedience, the just effect of pride ; sins which, in that holy place, might well be called wonderful.

But what to me is more wonderful, and which, I think, will be very ill accounted for, is, How came seeds of crime to rise in the angelic nature ? created in a state of perfect, unspotted holiness ? how was it first found in a place where no unclean thing can enter ? how came ambition, pride, or envy, to generate there ? could there be offence where there was no crime ? could untainted purity breed corruption ? could the nature contaminate and infect, which was always partaking nourishment from, and taking in principles of, perfection ?

Happy it is to me, that writing the history, not solving the difficulties of Satan's affairs, is my province in this work; that I am to relate the fact, not give reasons for it, or assign causes; if it was otherwise, I should break off at this difficulty, for I acknowledge I do not see through it; neither do I think that the great Milton, after all his fine images and lofty excursions upon the subject, has left it one jot clearer than he found it. Some are of opinion, and among them the great Dr. B——s, that crime broke in upon them at some interval when they omitted, but one moment, fixing their eyes and thoughts on the glories of the divine face, to admire and adore, which is the full employment of angels ; but even this, though it goes as high as imagination can carry us, does not reach it, nor, to me, make it one jot more comprehensible than it was before ; all I can say to it here, is, that so it was, the fact was upon record, and the rejected troop are in being (whose circumstances confess the guilt), and still groan under the punishment.

If you will bear with a poetic excursion upon the subject, not to solve, but to illustrate, the difficulty, take it in a few lines, thus:

> Thou sin of witchcraft! first-born child of crime!
>   Produc'd before the bloom of time;
> Ambition's maiden sin, in heaven conceiv'd,
>   And who could have believed
> Defilement could in purity begin,
> And bright eternal day be soil'd with sin?
> Tell us, sly penetrating crime,
> How cam'st thou there, thou fault sublime?
> How didst thou pass the adamantine gate,
>   And into spirit thyself insinuate?
>   From what dark state? from what deep place?
>   From what strange uncreated race?
> Where was thy ancient habitation found,
> Before void chaos heard the forming sound?
>   Wast thou a substance, or an airy ghost,
>   A vapour flying in the fluid waste
>   Of unconcocted air?
>   And how at first didst thou come there?
> Sure there was once a time when thou wert not;
> By whom wast thou created? and for what?
> Art thou a stream from some contagious damp exhal'd?
>   How should contagion be entail'd,
>   On bright seraphic spirits, and in a place
> Where all's supreme, and glory fills the space?
>   No noxious vapour there could rise,
> For there no noxious matter lies;
>   Nothing that's evil could appear,
> Sin never could seraphic glory bear;
> The brightness of the eternal face,
> Which fills as well as constitutes the place,
> Would be a fire too hot for crime to bear,
> 'Twould calcine sin, or melt it into air.
> How then did first defilement enter in?
> Ambition, thou first vital seed of sin!
> Thou life of death! how cam'st thou there?
>   In what bright form didst thou appear?
>   In what seraphic orb didst thou arise?
> Surely that place admits of no disguise;
>   Eternal sight must know thee there,
>   And being known, thou soon must disappear.
> But since the fatal truth we know,
>   Without the matter whence or manner how:
> Thou high superlative of sin,
>   Tell us thy nature, where thou didst begin?
>   The first degree of thy increase,
> Debauch'd the regions of eternal peace,

And fill'd the breasts of loyal angels there
With the first treason and infernal war.
   Thou art the high extreme of pride,
   And dost o'er lesser crimes preside;
   Not for the mean attempt of vice design'd,
   But to embroil the world and damn mankind.
   Transforming mischief, how hast thou procur'd
      That loss that's ne'er to be restor'd,
   And made the bright seraphic morning star
      In horrid monstrous shapes appear?
      Satan, that while he dwelt in glorious light,
   Was always then as pure as he was bright,
   That in effulgent rays of glory shone,
   Excell'd by the eternal light, by Him alone;
   Distorted now, and stript of innocence,
   And banish'd with thee from the high pre-eminence:
   How as the splendid seraph chang'd his face,
   Transform'd by thee, and like thy monstrous race?
   Ugly as is the crime, for which he fell,   ⎫
   Fitted by thee to make a local hell,   ⎬
   For such must be the place where either of you dwell. ⎭

Thus, as I told you, I only moralise upon the subject, but as
to the difficulty, I must leave it as I find it, unless, as I hinted
at first, I could prevail with Satan to set pen to paper, and
write this part of his own history; no question but he could
let us into the secret. But to be plain, I doubt I shall tell
so many plain truths of the Devil, in this history, and discover so many of his secrets, which it is not for his interest
to have discovered, that, before I have done, the Devil and I
may not be so good friends as you may suppose we are; at
least, not friends enough to obtain such a favour of him,
though it be for public good; so we must be content till we
come 'tother side the Blue-blanket, and then we shall know
the whole story.

But now, though, as I said, I will not attempt to solve
the difficulty, I may, I hope, venture to tell you, that there
is not so much difficulty in it as at first sight appears, and
especially not so much as some people would make us believe;
let us see how others are mistaken in it, perhaps that may
help us a little in the inquiry; for to know what it is not, is
one help towards knowing what it is.

Mr. Milton has indeed told us a great many merry things
of the Devil, in a most formal, solemn manner; till, in short,
he has made a good play of Heaven and Hell; and no doubt,
if he had lived in our times, he might have had it acted with

our Pluto and Proserpine. He has made fine speeches both for God and the Devil, and a little addition might have turned it, *a la modern*, into a *Harlequin Dieu et Diable*.

I confess, I do not well know how far the dominion of poetry extends itself; it seems the butts and bounds of Parnassus are not yet ascertained; so that, for aught I know, by virtue of their ancient privileges, called *licentia poetarum*, there can be no blasphemy in verse, as some of our divines say there can be no treason in the pulpit. But they that will venture to write that way, ought to be better satisfied about that point than I am.

Upon this foot, Mr. Milton, to grace his poem, and give room for his towering fancy, has gone a length beyond all that ever went before him, since Ovid in his Metamorphoses. He has, indeed, complimented God Almighty with a flux of lofty words, and great sounds, and has made a very fine story of the Devil, but he has made a mere *je ne scai quoi* of Jesus Christ. In one line he has him riding on a cherub, and in another sitting on a throne, both in the very same moment of action. In another place he has brought him in making a speech to his saints, when it is evident he had none there, for we all know man was not created till a long while after; and nobody can be so dull as to say the angels may be called saints, without the greatest absurdity in nature. Besides, he makes Christ himself distinguish them, as in two several bands, and of differing persons and species, as to be sure they are.

> Stand still in bright array, ye saints ——
> —————————— Here stand,
> Ye angels.
>
> ✦   Par. Lost, lib. **vi.**

So that Christ here is brought in drawing up his army before the last battle, and making a speech to them, to tell them they shall only stand by in warlike order, but that they shall have no occasion to fight, for he alone will engage the rebels. Then, in embattling his legions, he places the saints here, and the angels there, as if one were the main battle of infantry, and the other the wings of cavalry. But who are those saints? they are indeed all of his own making, for it is certain there were no saints at all in heaven or earth at that time; God and his angels filled up the place; and till some of the angels fell, and men were created, had lived, and were dead, there could have been no saints there. Saint Abel was certainly the proto-saint of all that ever were seen in heaven, as well as the proto-martyr of all that have been upon earth.

Just such another mistake, not to call it a blunder, he makes about hell; which he not only makes local, but gives it a being before the fall of the angels, and brings it in opening its mouth to receive them. This is so contrary to the nature of the thing, and so great an absurdity, that no poetic license can account for it; for though poesy may form stories as idea and fancy may furnish materials, yet poesy must not break in upon chronology, and make things, which in time were to exist, act before they existed.

Thus a painter may make a fine piece of work, the fancy may be good, the strokes masterly, and the beauty of the workmanship inimitably curious and fine, and yet have some unpardonable improprieties which mar the whole work. So the famous painter of Toledo painted the story of the three wise men of the East coming to worship and bring their presents to our Lord upon his birth at Bethlehem, where he represents them as three Arabian or Indian kings; two of them are white, and one black; but unhappily, when he drew the latter part of them kneeling, which to be sure was done after their faces, their legs being necessarily a little intermixed, he made three black feet for the Negro king, and but three white feet for the two white kings, and yet never discovered the mistake till the piece was presented to the king, and hung up in the great church. As this is an unpardonable error in sculpture or limning, it must be much more so in poetry, where the images must have no improprieties, much less inconsistencies.

In a word, Mr. Milton has indeed made a fine poem, but it is the devil of a history. I can easily allow Mr. Milton to make hills and dales, flowery meadows and plains, and the like, in heaven; and places of retreat and contemplation in hell; though, I must add, it can be allowed to no poet on earth but Mr. Milton. Nay, I will allow Mr. Milton, if you please, to set the angels a dancing in heaven, lib. v., and the devils a singing in hell, lib. i., though they are, in short, especially the last, most horrid absurdities. But I cannot allow him to make their music in hell to be harmonious and charming as he does; such images being incongruous, and indeed shocking to nature. Neither can I think we should allow things to be placed out of time in poetry, any more than in history; it is a confusion of images which is allowed to be disallowed by all the critics of what tribe or species soever in the world, and is indeed unpardonable. But we shall find so many more of these things in Mr. Milton, that really taking notice of them all would carry me quite out of my way, I being at this time not writing the history of Mr. Milton, but of the Devil; besides, Mr. Milton is such a celebrated man, that who but he that can write the history of the Devil dare meddle with him.

But to come back to the business. As I had cautioned you against running to Scripture for shelter in cases of difficulty, Scripture weighing very little among the people I am directing my speech to, so indeed, Scripture gives but very little light into anything of the Devil's story before his fall, and but to very little of it for some time after.

Nor has Mr. Milton said one word to solve the main difficulty, viz., how the Devil came to fall, and how sin came into heaven, and how the spotless seraphic nature could receive infection, whence the contagion proceeded, what noxious matter could emit corruption, how and whence any vapour to poison the angelic frame could rise up, or how it increased and grew up to crime. But all this he passes over, and hurrying up that part in two or three words, only tells us,

> ———his pride
> Had cast him out from heaven, with all his host
> Of rebel angels, by whose aid aspiring
> To set himself in glory above his peers,
> He trusted to have equall'd the Most High.—Lib. i.

"His pride!" but how came Satan, while an archangel, to be proud? How did it consist, that pride and perfect holiness should meet in the same person? Here we must bid Mr. Milton good night; for, in plain terms, he is in the dark about it, and so we are all; and the most that can be said, is, that we know the fact is so, but nothing of the nature or reason of it.

But to come to the history: the angels fell, they sinned, (wonderful!) in heaven, and God cast them out; what their sin was is not explicit, but in general it is called a rebellion against God; all sin must be so.

Mr. Milton here takes upon him to give the history of it,

as particularly as if he had been born there, and came down hither on purpose to give us an account of it (I hope he is better informed by this time); but this he does in such a manner, as jostles with religion, and shocks our faith in so many points necessary to be believed, that we must forbear to give up to Milton, or must set aside part of the sacred text, in such a manner, as will assist some people to set it aside all.

I mean by this, his invented scheme of the Son's being declared in heaven to be begotten then, and then to be declared generalissimo of all the armies of heaven; and of the Father's summoning all the angels of the heavenly host to submit to him, and pay him homage. The words are quoted already, page 309.

I must own the invention, indeed, is very fine, the images exceeding magnificent, the thought rich and bright, and, in some respect, truly sublime: but the authorities fail most wretchedly, and the mistiming of it is unsufferably gross, as is noted in the introduction to this work; for Christ is not declared the Son of God but on earth; it is true, it is spoken from heaven, but then it is spoken as perfected on earth; it it was at all to be assigned to heaven, it was from eternity, and there, indeed, his eternal generation is allowed; but to take upon us to say, that, On a day; a certain day! for so our poet assumes, lib. v. :

————————When on a day,
————————On such day
As heaven's great year brings forth, th' empyreal host
Of angels, by imperial summons called,
Forthwith from all the ends of heaven appear'd.

This is, indeed, too gross; at this meeting he makes God declare the Son to be *that day begotten* as before; had he made him not begotten that day, but declared general that day, it would be reconcilable with Scripture and with sense; for either the begetting is meant of ordaining to an office, or else the eternal generation falls to the ground; and if it was to the office (mediator), then Mr. Milton is out in ascribing another fixed day to the work; see lib. x. But then the declaring him *that day*, is wrong chronology too, for Christ is declared *the Son of God with power*, only by the resurrection of the dead, and this is both a declaration in heaven and in earth; Rom. i. 4. And Milton can have no

z 2

authority to tell us there was any declaration of it in heaven before this, except it be that dull authority, called poetic license, which will not pass in so solemn an affair as that.

But the thing was necessary to Milton, who wanted to assign some cause or original of the Devil's rebellion; and so, as I said above, the design is well laid, it only wants two trifles called truth and history; so I leave it to struggle for itself.

This groundplot being laid, he has a fair field for the Devil to play the rebel in, for he immediately brings him in not satisfied with the exaltation of the Son of God. The case must be thus: Satan, being an eminent archangel, and perhaps the highest of all the angelic train, hearing this sovereign declaration, that the Son of God was declared to be head or generalissimo of all the heavenly host, took it ill to see another put into the high station over his head, as the soldiers call it; he, perhaps, being the senior officer, and disdaining to submit to any but to his former immediate sovereign; in short, he threw up his commission, and, in order not to be compelled to obey, revolted, and broke out in open rebellion.

All this part is a decoration noble and great, nor is there any objection to be made against the invention, because a deduction of probable events; but the plot is wrong laid, as is observed above, because contradicted by the Scripture account, according to which Christ was declared in heaven, not then, but from eternity, and not declared with power but on earth, viz., in his victory over sin and death, by the resurrection from the dead; so that Mr. Milton is not orthodox in this part, but lays an avowed foundation for the corrupt doctrine of Arius, which says, there was a time when Christ was not the Son of God.

But to leave Mr. Milton to his flights, I agree with him in this part, viz., that the wicked or sinning angels with the great archangel at the head of them, revolted from their obedience, even in heaven itself; that Satan began the wicked defection, and being a chief among the heavenly host, consequently carried over a great party with him, who altogether rebelled against God; that upon this rebellion they were sentenced, by the righteous judgment of God, to be expelled the holy habitation; this, besides the authority of Scripture, we have visible testimonies of from the devils themselves; their influences and operations among us every day, of which mankind are witnesses; in all the merry things they do in his name, and under his protection, in almost every scene of life they pass through, whether we talk of things done openly or in masquerade, things done in —— or out of it, things done in earnest or in jest.

But then, what comes of the long and bloody war that Mr. Milton gives such a full and particular account of, and the terrible battles in heaven between Michael with the royal army of angels on one hand, and Satan with his rebel host on the other; in which he supposes the numbers and strength to be pretty near equal? but at length brings in the Devil's army, upon doubling their rage, and bringing new engines of war into the field, putting Michael and all the faithful army to the worst; and, in a word, defeats them? For though they were not put to a plain flight, in which case he must, at least, have given an account of two or three thousand millions of angels cut in pieces and wounded, yet he allows them to give over the fight, and make a kind of retreat; so making way for the complete victory of the Son of God: now this is all invention, or at least, a borrowed thought from the old poets, and the fight of the giants against Jupiter, so nobly designed by Ovid, almost two thousand years ago; and there it was well enough; but whether poetic fancy should be allowed to fable upon heaven, or no, and upon the king of heaven too, that I leave to the sages.

By this expulsion of the devils, it is allowed by most authors, they are, *ipso facto*, stripped of the rectitude and holiness of their nature, which was their beauty and perfection; and being ingulphed in the abyss of irrevocable ruin, it is no matter where, from that very time they lost their angelic beautiful form, and commenced ugly frightful monsters and devils, and became evil doers, as well as evil spirits; filled with a horrid malignity and enmity against their Maker, and armed with a hellish resolution to show and exert it on all occasions; retaining however their exalted spirituous nature, and having a vast extensive power of action, all which they can exert in nothing else but doing evil, for they are entirely divested of either power or will to do good; and even in doing evil, they are under restraints and limitations of a superior power, which it is their torment, and, perhaps, a great part of their hell, that they cannot break through.

CHAPTER VI.

WHAT BECAME OF THE DEVIL AND HIS HOST OF FALLEN SPIRITS
AFTER THEIR BEING EXPELLED FROM HEAVEN, AND HIS WAN-
DERING CONDITION TILL THE CREATION; WITH SOME MORE OF
MR. MILTON'S ABSURDITIES ON THAT SUBJECT.

HAVING thus brought the Devil and his innumerable legions
to the edge of the bottomless pit, it remains, before I bring
them to action, that some inquiry should be made into the
posture of their affairs immediately after their precipitate fall,
and into the place of their immediate residence; for this
will appear to be very necessary to Satan's history, and
indeed, so as that, without it, all the farther account we have
to give of him will be inconsistent and imperfect.

And first, I take upon me to lay down some fundamentals,
which I believe I shall be able to make out historically, though,
perhaps, not so geographically as some have pretended to do.

1. That Satan was not immediately, nor is yet locked down
   into the abyss of a local hell, such as is supposed by some,
   and such as he shall be at last; or that,

2. If he was, he has certain liberties allowed him for
   excursions into the regions of this air, and certain
   spheres of action, in which he can and does move, to do
   like a very devil as he is, all the mischief he can, and of
   which we see so many examples both about us and in
   us: in the inquiry after which, I shall take occasion to
   examine whether the Devil is not in most of us sometimes, if not in all of us one time or other.

3. That Satan has no particular residence in this globe or
   earth where we live; that he rambles about among us,
   and marches over and over our whole country, he and
   his devils, in camps *volant*; but that he pitches his
   grand army or chief encampment in our adjacencies, or
   frontiers, which the philosophers call atmosphere, and
   whence he is called the prince of the power of that element or part of the world we call air; from whence he
   sends out his spies, his agents, and emissaries, to get
   intelligence, and to carry his commissions to his trusty
   and well-beloved cousins and councillors on earth, by
   which his business is done, and his affairs carried on in
   the world.

Here again. I meet Mr. Milton full in my face, who will have it, that the Devil, immediately at his expulsion, rolled down directly into a hell proper and local; nay, he measures the very distance, at least gives the length of the journey by the time they were passing or falling, which, he says, was nine days; a good poetical flight, but neither founded on Scripture or philosophy, for he might every jot as well have brought hell up to the walls of heaven, advanced to receive them, or he ought to have considered the space which is to be allowed to any locality, let him take what part of infinite distance between heaven and a created hell he pleases.

But let that be as Mr. Milton's extraordinary genius pleases to place it; the passage, it seems, is just nine days betwixt heaven and hell; well might Dives then see father Abraham, and talk to him too; but then the great gulph which Abraham tells him was fixed between them, does not seem to be so large as, according to Sir Isaac Newton, Dr. Halley, Mr. Whiston, and the rest of our men of science, we take it to be.

But suppose the passage to be nine days, according to Mr. Milton, what followed? why hell gaped wide, opened its frightful mouth and received them all at once; millions and thousands of millions as they were, it received them all at a gulp, as we call it; they had no difficulty to go in, no, none at all.

> Facilis descensus Averni sed revocare gradum
> Hoc opus hic labor est.——   Virg.

All this, as poetical, we may receive, but not at all as historical; for then come troubles insuperable in our way, some of which may be as follow: (1.) hell is here supposed to be a place; nay, a place created for the punishment of angels and men, and likewise created long before those had fallen, or these had being; this makes me say, Mr. Milton was a good poet, but a bad historian; Tophet was prepared of old, indeed, but it was for the king, that is to say, it was prepared for those whose lot it should be to come there; but this does not at all suppose it was prepared before it was resolved whether there should be subjects for it, or no; else we must suppose both men and angels were made by the glorious and upright Maker of all things on purpose for destruction, which would be incongruous and absurd.

But there is worse yet to come; for in the next place he adds, that hell having received them, closed upon them; that is to say, took them in, closed or shut its mouth; and, in a word, they were locked in, as it was said in another place; they were locked in, and the key is carried up to heaven and kept there, for we know the angel came down from heaven, having the key of the bottomless pit; but first, see Mr. Milton.

> Nine days they fell; confounded Chaos roar'd
> And felt tenfold confusion in their fall:
> ——Hell, at last,
> Yawning, receiv'd them whole, and on them clos'd;
> Down from the verge of heaven, eternal wrath
> Burnt after them——
> Unquenchable.

This scheme is certainly deficient, if not absurd, and I think is more so than any other he has laid; it is evident, neither Satan or his host of devils are, no, not any of them, yet, even now, confined in the eternal prison, where the Scripture says, *he shall be reserved in chains of darkness.* They must have mean thoughts of hell, as a prison, a local confinement, that can suppose the Devil able to break jail, knock off his fetters, and come abroad, if he had been once locked in there, as Mr. Milton says he was: now we know that he is abroad again; he presented himself before God, among his neighbours, when Job's case came to be discoursed of; and more than that, it is plain he was a prisoner at large, by his answer to God's question, which was, *Whence comest thou?* to which he answered, *From going to and fro through the earth, &c.;* this, I say, is plain, and if it be as certain that hell closed upon them, I demand then, how got he out? and why was there not a proclamation for apprehending him, as there usually is after such rogues as break out of prison?

In short, the true account of the Devil's circumstances, since his fall from heaven, is much more likely to be thus: that he is more of a vagrant than a prisoner; that he is a wanderer in the wild unbounded waste, where he and his legions, like the hordes of Tartary, who, in the wild countries of Karakathay, the deserts of Barkan, Cassan, and Astracan, live up and down where they find proper; so Satan and his innumerable legions rove about, *hic et ubique,* pitching their camps (being beasts of prey) where they find the most spoil;

watching over this world (and all the other worlds, for aught we know, and if there are any such); I say, watching and seeking who they may devour, that is, who they may deceive and delude, and so destroy, for devour they cannot.

Satan being thus confined to a vagabond, wandering, un-settled condition, is without any certain abode; for though he has, in consequence of his angelic nature, a kind of empire in the liquid waste or air, yet this is certainly part of his punishment, that he is continually hovering over this inha-bited globe of earth, swelling with the rage of envy at the felicity of his rival, man, and studying all the means possible to injure and ruin him; but extremely limited in power, to his unspeakable mortification; this is his present state, without any fixed abode, place, or space allowed him to rest the sole of his foot upon.

From his expulsion, I take his first view of horror to be that of looking back towards the heaven which he had lost, and there to see the chasm or opening made up, out at which, as at a breach in the wall of the holy place, he was thrust headlong by the power which expelled him; I say, to see the breach repaired, the mounds built up, the walls garrisoned with millions of angels, and armed with thunders; and, above all, made terrible by that glory from whose presence they were expelled, as is poetically hinted at before.

Upon this sight, it is no wonder (if there was such a place) that they fled till the darkness might cover them, and that they might be out of the view of so hated a sight.

Wherever they found it, you may be sure they pitched their first camp, and began, after many a sour reflection upon what was passed, to consider and think a little upon what was to come.

If I had as much personal acquaintance with the Devil as would admit it, and could depend upon the truth of what answer he would give me, the first question I would ask him, should be, what measures they resolved on at their first assembly; and the next should be, how they were employed in all that space of time, between their so flying the face of their almighty Conqueror, and the creation of man. As for the length of the time, which, according to the learned, was twenty thousand years, and according to the more learned, not a quarter so much, I would not concern my curiosity much about it; it is most certain, there was a considerable time between, but of that immediately; first let me inquire what they were doing all that time.

The Devil and his host being thus, I say, cast out of heaven, and not yet confined strictly to hell, it is plain they must be somewhere: Satan and all his legions did not lose their existence, no, nor the existence of devils neither. God was so far from annihilating him, that he still preserved his being: and this, not Mr. Milton only, but God himself has made known to us, having left his history so far upon record; several expressions in Scripture also make it evident, as particularly the story of Job, mentioned before; the like in our Saviour's time, and several others.

If hell did not immediately ingulf them, as Milton suggests, it is certain, I say, that they fled somewhere from the anger of heaven, from the face of the Avenger; and his absence, and their own guilt, wonder not at it, would make hell enough for them wherever they went.

Nor need we fly to the dreams of our astronomers, who take a great deal of pains to fill up the vast spaces of the starry heavens with innumerable habitable worlds, allowing as many solar systems as there are fixed stars, and that not only in the known constellations, but even in galaxy itself; who, to every such system, allow a certain number of planets, and to every one of those planets so many satellites or moons, and all these planets and moons to be worlds; solid, dark, opaque bodies, habitable, and (as they would have us believe) inhabited by the like animals and rational creatures as on this earth; so that they may, at this rate, find room enough for the Devil and all his angels, without making a hell on purpose; nay they may, for aught I know, find a world for every devil in all the Devil's host, and so every one may be a monarch, or master-devil, separately in his own sphere or world, and play the devil there by himself.

And even if this were so, it cannot be denied but that one devil in a place would be enough for a whole systemary world, and be able, if not restrained, to do mischief enough there too, and even to ruin and overthrow the whole body of people contained in it.

But, I say, we need not fly to these shifts, or consult the astronomers in the decision of this point; for, wherever Satan and his defeated host went at their expulsion from heaven, we think we are certain none of all these beautiful worlds or be they worlds or no, I mean the fixed stars, planets, &c., had then any existence; for *the beginning*, as the Scripture calls it, was not yet begun.

But to speak a little by the rules of philosophy, that is to say, so as to be understood by others, even when we speak of things we cannot fully understand ourselves: though in the beginning of time all this glorious creation was formed, the earth, the starry heavens, and all the furniture thereof, and there was a time when they were not; yet we cannot say so of the void, or that nameless nowhere, as I called it before, which now appears to be a somewhere, in which these glorious bodies are placed. That immense space which those take up, and which they move in at this time, must be supposed, before they had being, to be placed there: as God himself was, and existed before all being, time, or place, so the heaven of heavens, or the place where the thrones and dominions of his kingdom then existed, inconceivable and ineffable, had an existence before the glorious seraphs, the innumerable company of angels, which attended about the throne of God, existed; these all had a being long before, as the eternal Creator of them all had before them.

Into this void or abyss of nothing, however unmeasurable, infinite, and, even to those spirits themselves, inconceivable, they certainly launched from the bright precipice which they fell from, and shifted as well as they could.

Here, expanding those wings which fear and horror at their defeat furnished them, as I hinted before, they hurried away to the utmost distance possible from the face of God their conqueror, and then most dreaded enemy, formerly their joy and glory.

Be this utmost removed distance where it will, here, certainly, Satan and all his gang of devils, his numberless, though routed armies, retired. Here Milton might, with some good ground, have formed his Pandemonium, and have brought them in, consulting what was next to be done, and whether there was any room left to renew the war, or to carry on the rebellion; but had they been cast immediately into hell, closed up there, the bottomless pit locked upon them, and the key carried up to heaven to be kept there, as Mr. Milton himself in part confesses, and the Scripture affirms; I say, had this been so, the Devil himself could not have been so ignorant as to think of any future steps to be taken, to retreive his affairs, and therefore a Pandemonium or divan in hell, to consult of it, was ridiculous.

All Mr. Milton's schemes of Satan's future conduct, and all the Scripture expressions about the Devil and his numerous attendants, and of his actings since that time, make it not reasonable to suggest that the devils were confined to their eternal prison, at their expulsion out of heaven ; but that they were in a state of liberty to act, though limited in acting ; of which I shall also speak in its place.

CHAPTER VII.

OF THE NUMBER OF SATAN'S HOST; HOW THEY CAME FIRST TO KNOW OF THE NEW CREATED WORLDS, NOW IN BEING, AND THEIR MEASURES WITH MANKIND UPON THE DISCOVERY.

SEVERAL things have been suggested to set us a calculating the number of this frightful throng of devils, who, with Satan, the master-devil, was thus cast out of heaven ; I cannot say I am so much master of political arithmetic as to cast up the number of the beast, no, nor the number of the beasts or devils who make up this throng. St. Francis, they tell us, or some other saint, they do not say who, asked the Devil once, how strong he was; for St. Francis, you must know, was very familiar with him ; the Devil, it seems, did not tell him, but presently raised a great cloud of dust, by the help, I suppose, of a gust of wind, and bid that saint count it ; he was, I suppose, a calculator that would be called grave, who, dividing Satan's troops into three lines, cast up the number of the devils of all sorts in each battalia, at ten hundred times a hundred thousand millions of the first line, fifty millions of times as many in the second line, and three hundred thousand times as many as both in the third line.

The impertinence of this account would hardly have given it a place here, only to hint that it has always been the opinion, that Satan's name may well be called a noun of multitude, and that the Devil and his angels are certainly no inconsiderable number. It was a smart repartee that a Venetian nobleman made to a priest, who rallied him upon his refusing to give something to the church, which the priest demanded for the delivering him from purgatory ; when the priest asking him if he knew what an innumerable number of devils they were to take him, he answered, yes, he knew how many devils there were in all. How many? says the priest; his curiosity, I suppose, being raised by the novelty of the answer: Why ten millions, five hundred and eleven thousand, six hundred and seventy-five devils and a half, says the nobleman. A half! says the priest; pray what kind of a devil is that? Yourself, says the nobleman, for you are half a devil already, and will be a whole one when you come there, for you are for deluding all you deal with, and bringing us soul and body into your hands, that you may be paid for letting us go again. So much for their number.

Here also it would come in very aptly, to consider the state of that long interval between the time of their expulsion from heaven, and the creation of the world; and what the posture of the Devil's affairs might be, during that time. The horror of their condition can only be conceived of at a distance, and especially by us, who being embodied creatures, cannot fully judge of what is or is not a punishment to seraphs and spirits; but it is just to suppose they suffered all that spirits of a seraphic nature were capable to sustain, consistent with their existence; notwithstanding which they retained still the hellishness of their rebellious principle, namely, their hatred and rage against God, and their envy at the felicity of his creatures.

As to how long their time might be, I shall leave the search, no lights being given me that are either propable or rational, and we have so little room to make a judgment of it, that we may as well believe father M——, who supposes it to be a hundred thousand years, as those who judge it one thousand years; it is enough that we are sure it was before the creation; how long before is not material to the Devil's history, unless we had some records of what happened to him, or was done by him in the interval.

During the wandering condition the Devil was in at that time, we may suppose he and his whole clan to be employed in exerting their hatred and rage at the Almighty, and at the happiness of the remaining faithful angels, by all the ways they had power to show it.

From this determined stated enmity of Satan and his host against God, and at everything that brought glory to his name, Mr. Milton brings in Satan, when first he saw Adam in Paradise, and the felicity of his station there, swelling with age and envy, and taking up a dreadful resolution to ruin Adam and all his posterity, merely to disappoint his Maker of the glory of his creation ; I shall come to speak of that in its place.

How Satan, in his remote situation, got intelligence of the place where to find Adam out, or that any such thing as a man was created, is matter of just speculation, and there might be many rational schemes laid for it : Mr. Milton does not undertake to tell us the particulars, nor indeed could he find room for it; perhaps the Devil, having, as I have said, a liberty to range over the whole void or abyss, which we want as well a name for, as indeed powers to conceive of, might have discovered that the almighty Creator had formed a new and glorious work, with infinite beauty and variety, filling up the immense waste of space, in which he, the Devil and his angels, had roved for so long a time, without finding anything to work on, or to exert their apostate rage in against their Maker.

That at length they found the infinite untrodden space, on a sudden spread full with glorious bodies, shining in self-existing beauty, with a new, and to them unknown lustre, called light; they found these luminous bodies, though immense in bulk, and infinite in number, yet fixed in their wondrous stations, regular and exact in their motions, confined in their proper orbits, tending to their particular centres, and enjoying every one their peculiar systems, within which was contained innumerable planets with their satellites or moons, in which again a reciprocal influence, motion, and revolution, conspired to form the most admirable uniformity of the whole.

Surprised, to be sure, with this sudden and yet glorious work of the Almighty (for the creation was enough, with its lustre, even to surprise the devils), they might reasonably be supposed to start out of their dark retreat, and with a curiosity not below the seraphic dignity (for these are some of the things which the angels desire to look into), to take a flight through all the amazing systems of the fixed suns or stars, which we see now but at a distance, and only make astronomical guesses at.

Here the Devil found not subject of wonder only, but matter to swell his revolted spirit with more rage, and to revive the malignity of his mind against his Maker, and especially against this new increase of glory, which, to his infinite regret, was extended over the whole waste, and which he looked upon, as we say in human affairs, as a *pays conquis*, or, if you will have it in the language of devils, as an invasion upon their kingdom.

Here it naturally occurred to them, in their state of envy and rebellion, that though they could not assault the impregnable walls of Heaven, and could no more pretend to raise war in the place of blessedness and peace, yet that perhaps they might find room in this new, and, however glorious, yet inferior kingdom or creation, to work some despite to their great Creator, or to affront his majesty in the person of some of his new creatures; and upon this they may be justly supposed to double their vigilance, in the survey they resolved to take of these new worlds, however great, numberless, and wonderful.

What discoveries they may have made in the other and greater worlds than this earth, we have not yet had an account; possibly they are conversant with other parts of God's creation besides this little, little globe, which is but as a point in comparison of the rest; and with other of God's creatures besides man, who may, according to the opinion of our philosophers, inhabit those worlds; but as nobody knows that part but the Devil, we shall not trouble ourselves with the inquiry.

But it is very reasonable, and indeed probable, that the devils were more than ordinarily surprised at the nature and reason of all this glorious creation, after they had, with the utmost curiosity, viewed all the parts of it; the glories of the several systems; the immense spaces in which the glorious bodies that were created and made part of it, were allowed respectively to move; the innumerable fixed stars, as so many suns in the centre of so many distant solar systems; the (likewise innumerable) dark opaque bodies receiving light and depending upon those suns respectively for such light, and then reflecting that light again upon and for the use of one another; to see the beauty and splendour of their forms, the regularity of their position, the order and exactness, and yet inconceivable velocity of their motions, the certainty of their revolutions, and the variety and virtue of their influences; and then, which was even to the devils themselves most astonishing, that after all the rest of their observations they should find this whole immense work was adapted for, and made subservient to, the use, delight, and blessing only of one poor species, in itself small, and in appearance contemptible; the meanest of all the kinds supposed to inhabit so many glorious worlds, as appeared now to be formed; I mean, that moon called the Earth, and the creature called Man; that all was made for him, upheld by the wise Creator, on his account only, and would necessarily end and cease whenever that species should end and be determined.

That this creature was to be found nowhere but (as above) in one little individual moon; a spot less than almost any of the moons, which were in such great numbers to be found attendant upon, and prescribed with, in every system of the whole created heavens; this was astonishing, even to the Devil himself, nay, the whole clan of devils could scarce entertain any just ideas of the thing; till, at last, Satan, indefatigable in his search or inquiry into the nature and reason of this new work, and particularly searching into the species of man, whom he found God had thus placed in the little globe, called earth; he soon came to an *eclaircissement*, or a clear under standing of the whole.   For example,

1. He found this creature, called man, was, however mean and small in his appearance, a kind of a seraphic species; that he was made in the very image of God, endowed with reasonable faculties to know good and evil, and possessed of a certain thing till then unknown and unheard of even in hell itself; that is, in the habitation of devils, let that be where it would, (viz.),

2. That God had made him indeed of the lowest and coarsest materials, but that he had breathed into him the breath of life, and that he became a living thing called soul, being a kind of an extraordinary heavenly and divine emanation; and consequently that man, however mean and terrestrial his body might be, was yet heaven-born; in his spirituous part completely seraphic; and, after a space of life here (determined to be a state of probation), he should be translated through the regions of death into a life purely and truly seraphic, and which should remain so for ever: being capable of knowing and enjoying God his Maker, and standing in his presence as the glorified angels do.

3. That he had the most sublime faculties infused into him

was capable not only of knowing and contemplating God, and which was still more, of enjoying him, as above, but (which the Devil now was not) capable of honouring and glorifying his Maker, who also had condescended to accept of honour from him.

4. And, which was still more, that being of an angelic nature, though mixed with, and confined for the present in, a case of mortal flesh; he was intended to be removed from this earth after a certain time of life here to inhabit that heaven, and enjoy that very glory and felicity, from which Satan and his angels had been expelled.

When he found all this, it presently occurred to him, that God had done it all as an act of triumph over him (Satan); and that these creatures were only created to people heaven, depopulated, or stripped of its inhabitants, by their expulsion; and that these were all to be made angels in the Devil's stead.

If this thought increased his fury and envy as far as rage of devils can be capable of being made greater; it doubtless set him on work to give a vent to that rage and envy, by searching into the nature and constitution of this creature called man; and to find out whether he was invulnerable, and could by no means be hurt by the power of hell, or deluded, by his subtilty; or whether he might be beguiled and deluded, and so, instead of being preserved in holiness and purity, wherein he was certainly created, be brought to fall and rebel as he (Satan) had done before him; by which, instead of being transplanted into a glorious state, after this life in heaven, as his Maker had designed him to be, to fill up the angelic choir, and supply the place from whence he (Satan) had fallen, he might be made to fall also like him, and, in a word, be made a devil like himself.

This convinces us that the Devil has not lost his natural powers by his fall, and our learned commentator, Mr. Pool, is of the same opinion; though he grants that the Devil has lost his moral power, or his power of doing good, which he can never recover. Vide Mr. Pool, upon Acts xix. 17; where we may particularly observe, when the man possessed with an evil spirit flew upon the seven sons of Scæva the Jew (who would have exorcised them in the name of Jesus, without the authority of Jesus, or without faith in him), he flew on them and mastered them, so that they fled out of the house from the Devil, conquered, naked, and wounded ; but of this power of the Devil I shall speak by itself.

In a word, and to sum up all the Devil's story from his first expulsion, it stands thus: for so many years as were between his fall and the creation of man, though we have no memoirs of his particular affairs, we have reason to believe he was without any manner of employment, but a certain tormenting endeavour to be always expressing his rage and enmity against heaven. I call it tormenting, because ever disappointed; every thought about it proving empty; every attempt towards it abortive; leaving them only light enough to see still more and more reason to despair of success; and that this made his condition still more and more a hell than it was before.

After a space of duration in this misery, which we have no light given us to measure or judge of, he at length discovered the new creation of man, as above, upon which he soon found matter to set himself to work upon, and has been busily employed ever since.

And now, indeed, there may be room to suggest a local hell, and the confinement of souls (made corrupt and degenerate by him) to it, as a place; though he himself, as is still apparent by his actings, is not yet confined to it; of this hell, its locality, extent, dimensions, continuance, and nature, as it does not belong to Satan's history, I have a good excuse for saying nothing, and so put off my meddling with that, which if I would meddle with, I could say nothing to the purpose.

CHAPTER VIII.

OF THE POWER OF THE DEVIL AT THE TIME OF THE CREATION OF THIS WORLD ; AND WHETHER IT HAS NOT BEEN FARTHER STRAITENED AND LIMITED SINCE THAT TIME, AND WHAT SHIFTS AND STRATAGEMS HE IS OBLIGED TO MAKE USE OF TO COMPASS HIS DESIGNS UPON MANKIND.

CUNNING men have fabled, and though it be without either religion, authority, or physical foundation, it may be we may like it never the worse for that, that when God made the stars and all the heavenly luminaries, the Devil, to mimic his Maker, and insult his new creation, made comets, in imitation of the fixed stars; but that the composition of them being combustible, when they came to wander in the abyss, rolling by an irregular ill-grounded motion, they took fire, in their approach to some of those great bodies of flame, the fixed stars ; and being thus kindled, like a firework unskilfully let off, they then took wild and eccentric, as also different motions of their own, out of Satan's direction, and beyond his power to regulate ever after.

Let this thought stand by itself, it matters not to our purpose whether we believe anything of it or no ; it is enough to our case, that if Satan had any such power then, he has no such power now, and that leads me to inquire into his more recent limitations.

I am to suppose, he and all his accomplices being confounded at the discovery of the new creation, and racking their wits to find out the meaning of it, had at last, no matter how, discovered the whole system, and concluded, as I have said, that the creature called man was to be their successor in the heavenly mansions; upon which, I suggest that the first motion of hell was to destroy this new work, and, if possible, to overwhelm it ; but when they came to make the attempt, they found their chains were not long enough, and that they could not reach to the extremes of the system; they had no power either to break the order, or stop the motion, dislocate the parts, or confound the situation of things. They traversed, no doubt, the whole work, visited every star, landed upon every solid, and sailed upon every fluid in the whole scheme, to see what mischief they could do ; but, upon a long and full survey, came to this point in their inquiry, that, in short, they could do nothing by force ; that they could not displace any part, annihilate any atom, or destroy any life in the whole creation ; but that as omnipotence had created it, so the same omnipotence had armed it at all points against the utmost power of hell, had made the smallest creature in it invulnerable, as to Satan ; so that without the permission of the same power which had made heaven, and conquered the Devil, he could do nothing at all, as to destroying anything that God had made, no, not the little diminutive thing called man, who Satan saw so much reason to hate, as being created to succeed him in happiness in heaven ; Satan found him placed out of his power to hurt, or out of his reach to touch ; and here, by the way, appears the second conquest of heaven over the Devil ; that having placed his rival, as it were, just before his face, and showed the hateful sight to him, he saw written upon his image, *Touch him, if you dare.*

It cannot be doubted, but, had it not been thus, man is so far from being a match for the Devil, .that one of Satan's least imps or angels could destroy all the race of them in the world, ay, world and all, in a moment; as he is prince of the power of the air, taking the air there for the elementary world, how easily could he, at one blast, sweep all the surface of the earth into the sea, or drive the weighty immense surges of the ocean over the whole plane of the earth, and deluge the globe at once with a storm; or how easily could he, who, by the situation of his empire, must be supposed able to manage the clouds, draw them up in such position as should naturally produce thunders and lightnings, cause those lightnings to blast the earth, dash in pieces all the fine buildings, burn all the populous towns and cities, and lay waste the world; at the same time command suited quantities of sublimated air to burst out of the bowels of the earth, and overwhelm and swallow up in the opening chasms, all the inhabitants of the globe. In a word, Satan, left to himself as a Devil, and to the power, which by virtue of his seraphic original he must be vested with, was able to have made devilish work in the world, if by a superior power he was not restrained.

But there is no doubt, at least to me, but that with his fall from heaven, as he lost the rectitude and glory of his angelic nature, I mean his innocence, so he lost the power too that he had before; and that when he first commenced devil, he received the chains of restraint too, as the badge of his apostacy, viz., a general prohibition to do anything to the prejudice of this creation, or to act anything by force or violence without special permission.

This prohibition was not sent him by a messenger, or by an order in writing, or proclaimed from heaven by a law; but Satan, by a strange, invisible, and unaccountable impression felt the restraint within him; and at the same time that his moral capacity was not taken away, yet his power of exerting that capacity felt the restraint, and left him unable to do, even what he was able to do, at the same time.

I make no question but the Devil is sensible of this restraint, that is to say, not as it is a restraint only, or as an effect of his expulsion from heaven; but as it prevents his capital

design against man, who, for the reason I have given already,
he entertains a mortal hatred of, and would destroy with all
his heart, if he might; and, therefore, like a chained mastiff,
we find him oftentimes making a horrid hellish clamour and
noise, barking and howling, and frightening the people, letting
them know that if he was loose he would tear them to pieces;
but at the same time his very fury shakes his chain, which lets
them know to their satisfaction, he can only bark, but cannot
bite.

Some are of opinion that the Devil is not restrained so
much by the superior power of his sovereign and Maker; but
that all his milder measures with man are the effect of a
political scheme, and done upon mature deliberation; that it
was resolved to act thus in the great council or p——t of
devils, called upon this very occasion, when they first were
informed of the creation of man; and especially when they
considered what kind of creature he was, and what might
probably be the reason of making him, viz., to fill up the
vacancies in heaven; I say, that then the devils resolved,
that it was not for their interest to fall upon him with fury
and rage, and so destroy the species, for that this would be
no benefit at all to them, and would only cause another
original man to be created; for that they knew God could,
by the same omnipotence, form as many new species of
creatures as he pleased; and, if he thought fit, create them
in heaven too, out of the reach of devils or evil spirits, and
that therefore to destroy man would no way answer their end.

On the other hand, examining strictly the mould of this
new creature, and of what materials he was formed; how
mixed up of a nature convertible and pervertible, capable
indeed of infinite excellence, and consequently of eternal
felicity; but subject likewise to corruption and degeneracy,
and consequently to eternal misery; that instead of being
fit to supply the places of Satan and his rejected tribe (the
expelled angels) in heaven, and filling up the thrones or
stalls in the celestial choir, they might, if they could but be
brought into crime, become a race of rebels and traitors like
the rest, and so come at last to keep them company, as well
in the place of eternal misery, as in the merit of it; and, in
a word, become devils instead of angels.

Upon this discovery, I say, they found it infinitely more
for the interest of Satan's infernal kingdom, to go another

way to work with mankind, and see if it were possible, by the strength of all their infernal wit and councils, to lay some snare for him, and by some stratagem to bring him to eternal ruin and misery.

This being then approved as their only method (and the Devil showed he was no fool in the choice), he next resolved that there was no time to be lost; that it was to be set about immediately, before the race was multiplied, and before, by that means, the work be not made greater only, but perhaps the more difficult too; accordingly, the diligent Devil went instantly about it, agreeable to all the story of Eve and the serpent, as before; the belief of which, whether historically or allegorically, is not at all obstructed by this hypothesis.

I do not affirm that this was the case at first, because being not present in that black divan, at least not that I know of, for who knows where he was or was not in his pre-existent state? I cannot be positive in the resolve that passed there; but except for some very little contradiction, which we find in the sacred writings, I should, I confess, incline to believe it historically; and I shall speak of those things which I call contradictions to it, more largely hereafter.

In the mean time, be it one way or other, that is to say, either that Satan had no power to have proceeded with man by violence, and to have destroyed him as soon as he was made; or that he had the power, but chose rather to proceed by other methods to deceive and debauch him; I say, be it which you please, I am still of the opinion that it really was not the Devil's business to destroy the species; that it would have been nothing to the purpose, and no advantage at all to him, if he had done it; for that, as above, God could immediately have created another species to the same end, whom he either could have made invulnerable, and not subject to the Devil's power, or removed him out of Satan's reach, placed him out of the Devil's ken, in heaven, or some other place, where the Devil could not come to hurt him; and that, therefore, it is infinitely more his advantage, and more suited to his real design of defeating the end of man's creation, to debauch him and make a devil of him, that he may be rejected like himself, and increase the infernal kingdom and company in the lake of misery *in æternum.*

It may be true, for aught I know, that Satan has not the power of destruction put into his hand, and that he cannot take away the life of a man; and it seems probable to be so, from the story of Satan and Job, when Satan appeared among the sons of God, as the text says, Job i. 6. Now when God gave such a character of Job to him, and asked him if he had considered his servant Job, v. 8, why did not the Devil go immediately and exert his malice against the good man at once, to let his Maker see what would become of his servant Job in his distress? On the contrary, we see he only answers by showing the reason of Job's good behaviour; that it was but common gratitude for the blessing and protection he enjoyed, v. 10; and pleading that if his estate was taken away, and he was exposed as he (Satan) was, to be a beggar and a vagabond, going to and fro in the earth, and walking up and down therein, he would be a very devil too, like himself, and curse God to his face.

Upon this, the text says, that God answered, v. 11, *Behold, all that he hath is in thy power;* now it is plain here, that God gave up Job's wealth and estate, nay, his family, and the lives of his children and servants into the Devil's power; and, accordingly, like a true merciless devil, as he is, he destroyed them all; he moved the Sabeans to fall upon the oxen and the asses, and carry them off; he moved the Chaldeans to fall upon the camels and the servants, to carry off the first, and murder the last; he made lightning flash upon the poor sheep, and kill them all; and he blowed the house down upon his poor children, and buried them all in the ruins.

Now here is (1.) a specimen of Satan's good will to mankind, and what a havoc the Devil would make in the world, if he might; and here is a testimony too, that he could not do this without leave; so that I cannot but be of the opinion he has some limitations, some bounds set to his natural fury; a certain number of links in his chain, which he cannot exceed, or, in a word, that he cannot go a foot beyond his tether.

The same kind of evidence we have in the Gospel, Matt. viii. 31, where Satan could not so much as possess the filthiest and meanest of all creatures, the swine, till he had asked leave; and that still to show his good will, as soon as he had gotten leave, he hurried them all into the sea and choked them; these, I say, are some of the reasons why I am not willing to say the Devil is not restrained in power; but, on the other side, we are told of so many mischievous things the Devil has done in the world, by virtue of his dominion over the elements, and by other testimonies of his power, that I do not know what to think of it, though, upon the whole, the first is the safest opinion; for if we believe the last, we may, for aught I know, be brought, like the American Indians, to worship him that he may do us no harm.

And now I have named those people in America, I confess it would go a great way in favour of Satan's generosity, as well as in testimony of his power, if we might believe all the accounts, which indeed authors are pretty well agreed in the truth of, namely, of the mischiefs the Devil does in those countries where his dominion seems to be established; how he uses them when they deny him that homage he claims of them as his due; what havoc and combustion he makes among them; and how beneficent he is, or at least negative in his mischiefs when they appease him by their hellish sacrifices.

Likewise we see a test of his wicked subtilty in his management of those dark nations, when he was more immediately worshipped by them; namely, the making them believe that all their good weather, rains, dews, and kind influences upon the earth, to make it fruitful, was from him; whereas they really were the common blessings of a higher hand, and came not from him, the Devil, but from him that made the Devil, and made him a devil or fallen angel by his curse.

But to go back to the method the Devil took with the first of mankind; it is plain the policy of hell was right, though the execution of the resolves they took did not fully answer their end neither; for Satan fastening upon poor, proud, ridiculous mother Eve, as I have said before, made presently a true judgment of her capacities, and of her temper; took her by the right handle, and soothing her vanity, which is to this day the softest place in the head of all the sex, wheedled her out of her senses, by praising her beauty, and promising to make her a goddess.

The foolish woman yielded presently, and that we are told is the reason why the same method so strangely takes with all her posterity, viz , that you are sure to prevail with them, if you can but once persuade them that you believe they are witty and handsome; for the Devil, you may observe, never quits any hold he gets, and having once found a way into the heart, always takes care to keep the door open, that any of his agents may enter after him without any more difficulty; hence the same argument, especially the last, has so bewitching an influence on the sex, that they never deny you anything, after they are but weak enough and vain enough to accept of the praises you offer them on that head; on the other hand, you are sure they never forgive you the unpardonable crime of saying they are ugly or disagreeable. It is suggested that the first method the Devil took to insinuate all those fine things into Eve's giddy head, was by creeping close to her one night, when she was asleep, and laying his mouth to her ear, whispering all the fine things to her, which he knew would set her fancy a tiptoe, and so made her receive them involuntarily into her mind, knowing well enough that when she had formed such ideas in her soul, however they came there, she would never be quiet till she had worked them up to some extraordinary thing or other.

It was evident what the Devil aimed at, namely, that she should break in upon the command of God, and so having corrupted herself, bring the curse upon herself and all her race, as God had threatened; but why the pride of Eve should be so easily tickled by the notion of her exquisite beauty, when there then was no prospect of the use or want of those charms; that indeed makes a kind of difficulty here, which the learned have not determined: for,

1. If she had been as ugly as the Devil, she had nobody to rival her, so that she need not fear Adam should leave her and get another mistress.

2. If she had been bright and beautiful as an angel, she had no other admirer but poor Adam, and he could have no room to be jealous of her, or afraid she should cuckold him; so that in short, Eve had no such occasion for her beauty, nor could she make any use of it, either to a bad purpose or to a good; and therefore I believe the Devil, who is too cunning to do anything that signifies nothing, rather tempted her by the hope of increasing her wit, than her beauty.

But to come back to the method of Satan's tempting her, viz., by whispering to her in her sleep; it was a cunning trick, that's the truth of it, and by that means he certainly set her head a madding after deism, and to be made a goddess, and then backed it by the subtle talk he had with her afterwards.

I am the more particular upon this part, because, however the devil may have been the first that ever practised it, yet I can assure him the experiment has been tried upon many a woman since, to the wheedling her out of her modesty, as well as her simplicity; and the cunning men tell us still, that if you can come at a woman when she is in a deep sleep, and whisper to her close to her ear, she will certainly dream of the thing you say to her, and so will a man too.

Well, be this so to her race or not, it was it seems so to her; for she waked with her head filled with pleasing ideas, and, as some will have it, unlawful desires; such as, to be sure, she never had entertained before, fatally infused in her dream, and suggested to her waking soul, when the organ ear which conveyed them was dosed and insensible. Strange fate of sleeping in Paradise! that we seem to have notice but of two sleeps there, and that in one, a woman should go out of him, and in the other, the Devil should come into her.

Certainly, when Satan first made the attempt upon Eve, he did not think he should have so easily conquered her, or have brought his business about so soon; the Devil himself could not have imagined she should have been so soon brought to forget the command given, or at least who gave it, and have ventured to transgress against him; and made her forget that God had told her it should be death to her to touch it; and, above all, that she should aspire to be as wise as him, who was so ignorant before, as to believe it was for fear of her being like himself, that he had forbid it her.

Well might she be said to be the weaker vessel, though Adam himself had little enough to say for his being the stronger of the two, when he was over-persuaded (if it were done by persuasion) by his wife to do the same thing.

And mark how wise they were after they had eaten, and what fools they both acted like, even to one another; nay, even all the knowledge they attained to by it was, for aught I see, only to know that they were fools to be sensible of sin and shame; and see how simply they acted, I say, upon their having committed.the crime, and being detected in it.

> View them to-day conversing with their God,
> His image both enjoy'd and understood,
> To-morrow skulking with a sordid flight,
> Among the bushes from the infinite,
> As if that power was blind which gave them sight;
> With senseless labour tagging fig-leaf vests,
> To hide their bodies from the sight of beasts.
> Hark! how the fool pleads faint, for forfeit life,
> First he reproaches heaven, and then his wife:
> The woman which thou gav'st, as if the gift
> Could rob him of the little reason left,
> A weak pretence to shift his early crime,
> As if accusing her would excuse him;
> But thus encroaching crime dethrones the sense,
> And intercepts the heavenly influence;
> Debauches reason, makes the man a fool,
> And turns his active light to ridicule.

It must be confessed, that it was unaccountable degeneracy, even of their common reasoning, which Adam and Eve both fell into upon the first committing the offence of taking the forbidden fruit: if that was their being made as gods, it made but a poor appearance in its first coming, to hide their nakedness when there was nobody to see them, and cover themselves among the bushes from their Maker; but thus it was, and this the Devil had brought them to, and well might he and all the clan of hell, as Mr. Milton brings them in, laugh and triumph over the man after the blow was given, as having so egregiously abused and deluded them both.

But here, to be sure, began the Devil's new kingdom; as he had now seduced the two first creatures, he was pretty sure of success upon all the race, and therefore prepared to attack them also, as soon as they came on; nor was their increasing multitude any discouragement to his attempt, but just the contrary; for he had agents enough to employ, if every man and woman that should be born was to want a devil to wait upon them, separately and singly to seduce them; whereas some whole nations have been such willing subjects to him, that one of his seraphic imps may, for aught we know, have been enough to guide a whole country; the people being entirely subjected to his government for many ages; as in America, for example, where some will have it, that he conveyed the first inhabitants, at least, if he did not, we don't well know who did, or how they got thither.

And how came all the communication to be so entirely cut off between the nations of Europe and Africa, from whence America must certainly have been peopled, or else the Devil must have done it indeed? I say, how came the communication to be so entirely cut off between them, that except the time, whenever it was, that people did at first reach from one to the other, none ever came back to give their friends any account of their success, or invite them to follow? Nor did they hear of one another afterwards, as we have reason to think: did Satan politically keep them thus asunder, lest news from heaven should reach them, and so they should be recovered out of his government? We cannot tell how to give any other rational account of it, that a nation, nay, a quarter of the world, or as some will have it be, half the globe, should be peopled from Europe or Africa, or both, and nobody ever go after them, or come back from them in above three thousand years after.

Nay, that those countries should be peopled when there was no navigation in use in these parts of the world, no ships made that could carry provisions enough to support the people that sailed in them, but that they must have been starved to death before they could reach the shore of America; the ferry from Europe or Africa, in any part (which we have known navigation to be practised in) being at least a thousand miles, and in most places much more.

But as to the Americans, let the Devil and they alone to account for their coming thither, this we are certain of, that we knew nothing of them for many hundred years; and when we did, when the discovery was made, they that went from hence, found Satan in a full and quiet possession of them, ruling them with an arbitrary government, particular to himself. He had led them into a blind subjection to himself, nay, I might call it devotion (for it was all of religion that was to be found among them), worshipping horrible idols in his name, to whom he directed human sacrifices continually to be made, till he deluged the country with blood, and ripened them up for the destruction that followed from the invasion of the Spaniards, who he knew would hurry them all out of the world as fast as he (the Devil) himself could desire of them.

But to go back a little to the original of things, it is evident that Satan has made a much better market of mankind,
by thus subtilly attacking them, and bringing them to break
with their Maker, as he had done before them, than he could
have done by fulminating upon them at first, and sending
them all out of the world at once: for now he has peopled
his own dominions with them, and though a remnant are
snatched, as it were, out of his clutches, by the agency of
invincible grace, of which I am not to discourse in this place;
yet this may be said of the Devil, without offence, that he
has in some sense carried his point, and, as it were, forced
his maker to be satisfied with a part of mankind, and the
least part too, instead of the great glory he would have brought
to himself by keeping them all in his service.

Mr. Milton, as I have noted above, brings in the Devil and
all hell with him, making a *feu de joie* for the victory Satan
obtained over one silly woman; indeed, it was a piece of
success, greater in its consequence than in the immediate
appearance; nor was the conquest so complete as Satan himself imagined to make, since the promise of a redemption out
of his hands, which was immediately made to the man, in
behalf of himself and his believing posterity, was a great
disappointment to Satan; and, as it were, snatched the best
part of his victory out of his hands.

It is certain the devils knew what the meaning of that
promise was, and who was to be the *seed of the woman*, namely,
the incarnate Son of God, and that it was a second blow to
the whole infernal body; but, as if they had resolved to let
that alone, Satan went on with his business; and as he had
introduced crime into the common parent of mankind, and
thereby secured the contamination of blood, and the descent
or propagation of the corrupt seed, he had nothing to do but
to assist nature in time to come, to carry on its own rebellion,
and act itself in the breasts of Eve's tainted posterity; and
that indeed has been the Devil's business ever since his first
victory upon the kind, to this day.

His success in this part has been such, that we see upon
innumerable occasions a general defection has followed; a
kind of a taint upon nature, call it what you will, a blast upon
the race of mankind; and were it not for one thing, he had
ruined the whole family; I say, were it not for one thing,
namely, a selected company or number, who his Maker has

resolved he shall not be able to corrupt, or if he does, the sending the promised seed shall recover back again from him, by the power of irresistible grace; which number thus selected, or elected, call it which we will, are still to supply the vacancies in heaven, which Satan's defection left open; and what was before filled up with created seraphs, is now to be restored by recovered saints, by whom infinite glory is to accrue to the kingdom of the Redeemer.

This glorious establishment has robbed Satan of all the joy of his victory, and left him just where he was, defeated and disappointed; nor does the possession of all the myriads of the sons of perdition, who yet some are of the opinion will be snatched from him too at last; I say, the possession of all these makes no amends to him, for he is such a devil in his nature, that the envy at those he cannot seduce, eats out all the satisfaction of the mischief he has done in seducing all the rest; but I must not preach, so I return to things as much needful to know, though less solemn.

CHAPTER IX.

OF THE PROGRESS OF SATAN IN CARRYING ON HIS CONQUEST OVER MANKIND, FROM THE FALL OF EVE TO THE DELUGE.

I DOUBT if the Devil was asked the question plainly, he would confess, that after he had conquered Eve by his own wicked contrivance, and then by her assistance had brought Adam too, like a fool as he was, into the same gulf of misery, he thought he had done his work, compassed the whole race, that they were now his own, and that he had put an end to the grand design of their creation; namely, of peopling heaven with a new angelic race of souls, who when glorified, should make up the defection of the host of hell, that had been expunged by their crime; and that, in a word, he had gotten a better conquest than if he had destroyed them all.

But that in the midst of his conquest, he found a check put to the advantages he expected to reap from his victory, by the immediate promise of grace to a part of the posterity of Adam, who, notwithstanding the fall, were to be purchased by the Messiah, and snatched out of his (Satan's) hands, and over whom he could make no final conquest; so that his power met with a new limitation, and that such, as indeed fully disappointed him in the main thing he aimed at, viz., preventing the beatitudes of mankind, which were thus secured; (and what if the numbers of mankind were, upon this account, increased in such a manner, that the selected number should, by length of time, amount to just as many as the whole race, had they not fallen, would have amounted to in all?) and thus, indeed, the world may be said to be upheld and continued for the sake of those few, since till their number can be completed, the creation cannot fall, any more than that without them, or but for them, it would not have stood.

But leaving this speculation, and not having inquired of Satan what he has to say on that subject, let us go back to the antediluvian world; the Devil, to be sure, gained his point upon Eve, and in her upon all her race; he drew her into sin; got her turned out of Paradise, and the man with her: the next thing was to go to work with her posterity, and particularly with her two sons, Cain and Abel.

Adam having, notwithstanding his fall, repented very sincerely of his sin, received the promise of redemption and pardon, with an humble but believing heart; charity bids us suppose that he led a very religious and sober life ever after, and especially in the first part of his time; that he brought up his children very soberly, and gave them all the necessary advantages of a religious education, and a good introduction into the world, that he was capable of, and that Eve assisted to both in her place and degree.

Their two eldest sons, Cain and Abel, the one heir apparent to the patriarchal empire, and the other heir presumptive, I suppose also, lived very sober and religious lives; and as the principles of natural religion dictated a homage and subjection due to the Almighty Maker, as an acknowledgment of his mercies, and a recognition of their obedience; so the received usage of religion dictating at that time that this homage was to be paid by a sacrifice, they either of them brought a free-will offering to be dedicated to God, respectively for themselves and families.

How it was, and for what reason, that God had respect to the offering of Abel, which, the learned say, was a lamb of the firstlings of the flock, and did not give any testimony of the like respect to Cain and his offering, which was of the first-fruits of the earth, the offerings being equally suited to the respective employment of the men, that is not my present business; but this we find made heart-burnings, and raised envy and jealousy in the mind of Cain, and at that door the Devil immediately entered; for he, from the beginning was very diligent in his way, never slipped any opportunity, or missed any advantages, that the circumstances of mankind offered him, to do mischief.

What shape or appearance the Devil took up to enter into a conversation with Cain upon the subject, that authors do not take upon them to determine; but it is generally supposed he personated some of Cain's sons or grandsons to begin the discourse, who attacked their father, or perhaps grandfather, upon this occasion, in the following manner, or to that purpose.

D. Sir, I perceive your majesty (for the first race were certainly all monarchs, as great as kings, to their immediate posterity) to be greatly disturbed of late, your countenance is changed, your noble cheerfulness (the glories of your face) are strangely sunk and gone, and you are not the man you used to be; please your majesty to communicate your griefs to us, your children; you may be sure that, if it be possible, we would procure you relief, and restore your delights, the loss of which, if thus you go on to subject yourself to too much melancholy, will be very hurtful to you, and in the end destroy you.

CAIN. It is very kind, my dear children, to show your respect thus to your true progenitor, and to offer your assistance. I confess, as you say, my mind is oppressed and displeased; but though it is very heavy, yet I know not which way to look for relief, for the distemper is above our reach, no cure can be found for it on earth.

D. Do not say so, sir; there can be no disease sure on earth but may be cured on earth; if it be a mental evil, we have heard that your great ancestor, the first father of us all, who lives still on the great western plains towards the sea, is the oracle to which all his children fly for direction in such cases as are out of the reach of the ordinary understanding of mankind; please you to give leave, we will take a journey to him, and, representing your case to him, we will hear his advice, and bring it to you with all speed, for the ease of your mind.

CAIN. I know not whether he can reach my case or no.

D. Doubtless he may, and if not, the labour of our journey is nothing when placed in competition with the ease of your mind; it is but a few days' travel lost, and you will not be the worse if we fail of the desired success.

CAIN. The offer is filial, and I accept your affectionate concern for me, with a just sense of an obliged parent; go, then, and my blessing be upon you; but, alas! why do I bless? can he bless whom God has not blessed?

D. O! sir, do not say so; has not God blessed you? are you not the second sovereign of the earth? and does he not converse with you face to face? are not you the oracle to all your growing posterity, and next after his sovereign imperial majesty Lord Adam, patriarch of the world?

CAIN. But has not God rejected me, and refused to converse any more with me, while he daily favours and countenances my younger brother Abel, as if he resolved to set him up to rule over me?

D. No, sir, that cannot be, you cannot be disturbed at such a thing; is not the right of sovereignty yours by primogeniture? can God himself take that away when it is once given? are not you Lord Adam's eldest son? are you not the first-born glory of the creation? and does not the government descend to you by right of birth and blood?

CAIN. But what does all that signify to me, while God appears to favour and caress my younger brother, and to shine upon him, while a black dejection and token of displeasure surrounds me every day, and he does not appear to me as he used to do?

D. And what need your majesty be concerned at that, if it be so? if he does not appear pleased, you have the whole world to enjoy yourself in, and all your numerous and rising posterity adore and honour you; what need those remote things be any disturbance to you?

CAIN. How! my children; not the favour of God be valued! yes, yes, in his favour is life; what can all the world avail without the smiles and countenance of him that made it?

D. Doubtless, sir, he that made the world and placed you at the head of it all, to govern and direct it, has made it agreeable, and it is able to give you a full satisfaction and enjoyment, if you please to consider it well, though you were never to converse with him all the while you live in it.

CAIN. You are quite wrong there, my children, quite wrong.

D. But do you not, great sir, see all your children as well as us rejoicing in the plenty of all things, and are they not completely happy, and yet they know little of this great God, he seldom converses among us; we hear of him indeed by your sage advices, and we bring our offerings to you for him, as you direct, and when that is done, we enjoy whatever our hearts desire; and so doubtless may you in an abundant manner if you please.

CAIN. But your felicity is wrong placed then, or you suppose that God is pleased and satisfied in that your offerings are brought to me; but what would you say, if you knew that God is displeased? that he does not accept your offerings? that, when I sacrificed to him in behalf of you all, he rejected my offerings, though I brought a princely gift, being of the finest of the wheat, the choicest and earliest fruits, and sweetest of the oil, an offering suited to the giver of them all?

D. But if you offered them, sir, how are you sure they were not accepted?

CAIN. Yes, yes, I am sure; did not my brother Abel offer at the same time a lamb of his flock (for he, you know, delights in cattle, and covers the mountains with his herds), over him, all the while he was sacrificing, a bright emanation shone, cheering and enlivening, a pledge of favour; and light ambient flames played hovering in the lower air, as if attending his sacrifice; and, when ready prepared, immediately descended and burnt up the flesh, a sweet odoriferous savour ascending to him, who thus testified his acceptance; whereas, over my head a black cloud, misty, and distilling vapour, hung dripping upon the humble altar I had raised, and, wetting the finest and choicest things I had prepared, spoiled and defaced them; the wood unapt to burn by the moisture which fell, scarce received the fire I brought to kindle it, and even then, rather smothered and choked, than kindled into a flame; in a word, it went quite out, without consuming what was brought to be offered up.

D. Let not our truly reverenced lord and father be disquieted at all this: if he accepts not what you bring, you are discharged of the debt, and need bring no more, nor have the trouble of such laboured collections of rarities any more, when he thinks fit to require it again you will have notice,

L

no question, and then it being called for, will be accepted, or else why should it be required ?

CAIN. That may indeed be the case, nor do I think of attempting any more to bring an offering, for I rather take it, that I am forbidden for the present; but then, what is it that my younger brother triumphs in ? and how am I insulted, in that he and his house are all joy and triumph, as if they had some great advantage over me, in that their offering was accepted when mine was not ?

D. Does he triumph over your majesty, our lord and sovereign ? give us but your order, and we will go and pull him and all his generation in pieces; for to triumph over you who are his elder brother, is a horrid rebellion and treason, and he ought to be expelled the society of mankind.

CAIN. I think so too, indeed; however, my dear children and faithful subjects, though I accept your offer of duty and service, yet I will consider very well, before I take up arms against my brother; besides, our sovereign father and lord, patriarchal Adam, being yet alive, it is not in my right to act offensively without his command.

D. We are ready therefore to carry your petition to him, and doubt not to obtain his license and commission too, to empower you to do yourself justice upon your younger brother; who, being your vassal, or at least inferior, as he is junior in birth, insults you upon the fancied opinion of having a larger share in the divine favour, and receiving a blessing on his sacrifices, on pretence of the same favour being denied you.

CAIN. I am content; go then, and give a just account of the state of our affairs.

D. We shall soon return with the agreeable answer; let not our lord and father continue sad and dejected, but depend upon a speedy relief, by the assistance of thy numerous issue, all devoted to thy interest and felicity.

CAIN. My blessing be with you in your way, and give you a favourable reception at the venerable tent of our universal lord and father.

Note. Here the cursed race being fully given up to the direction of the evil spirit, which so early possessed them, and swelling with rage at the innocent Abel and his whole family, they resolved upon forming a most wicked and detestable lie, to bring about the advice which they had already

given their father Cain a touch of; and to pretend that
Adam being justly provoked at the undutiful behaviour of
Abel, had given Cain a commission to chastise him, and by
force to cut him off and all his family, as guilty of rebellion
and pride.

Filled with this mischievous and bloody resolution, they
came back to their father Cain, after staying a few days, such
as were sufficient to make Cain believe they had been at the
plains of Shinnar, where Adam dwelt; the same which are
now called the blessed valleys, or the plains of Mecca in
Arabia Felix, near the banks of the Red Sea.

Note here also, that Cain having received a wicked hint
from these men, his children and subjects, as before intimating
that Abel had broken the laws of primogeniture in his
behaviour towards him (Cain), and that he might be
justly punished for it; Satan, that cunning manager of all
our wayward passions, fanned the fire of envy and jealousy
with his utmost skill all the while his other agents were
absent; and by the time they came back had blown it up
into such a heat of fury and rage, that it wanted nothing but
air to make it burn out, as it soon afterwards did, in a furious
flame of wrath and revenge, even to blood and destruction.

Just in the very critical moment, while things stood thus
with Cain, Satan brings in his wicked instruments, as if just
arrived with the return of his message from Adam, at whose
court they had been for orders; and thus they, that is the
Devil, assuming to speak by them, approach their father
with an air of solemn but cheerful satisfaction at the success
of their embassy.

D. Hail, sovereign, reverend, patriarchal lord! we come
with joy to render thee an account of the success of our
message.

CAIN. Have you then seen the venerable tents, where
dwell the heaven-born, the angelic pair, to whom all human
reverence highly due, is and ought always to be humbly
paid?

D. We have.

CAIN. Did you, together with my grand request, a just, a
humble homage for me pay to the great sire and mother of
mankind?

D. We did.

CAIN. Did you in humble language represent the griefs and anguish which oppress my soul?

D. We did, and back their blessing to thee bring.

CAIN. I hope with humblest signs of filial duty you took it for me on your bending knees?

D. We did, and had our share; the patriarch, lifting his hands to heaven, expressed his joy to see his spreading race, and blessed us all.

CAIN. Did you my solemn message too deliver, my injuries impartially lay down, and due assistance and direction crave?

D. We did.

CAIN. What spoke the oracle? he's God to me; what just command d'ye bring? what's to be done? am I to bear the insulting junior's rage, and meekly suffer what unjustly he, affronting primogeniture and laws of God and man, imposes by his pride unsufferable? am I to be crushed, and be no more the first-born son on earth, but bow and kneel to him?

D. Forbid it heaven! as Adam too forbids; who, with a justice godlike, and peculiar to injured parents, Abel's pride resents, and gives his high command to thee to punish.

CAIN. To punish, say you! Did he use the word, the very word? am I commissioned then to punish Abel?

D. Not Abel only, but his rebel race; as they, alike in crime, alike are joined in punishment.

CAIN. The race indeed have shared the merit with him; how did they all insult, and with a shout of triumph mock my sorrow, when they saw me from my sacrifice dejected come; as if my disappointment was their joy.

D. This, too, the venerable prince resents; and to preserve the race in bounds of laws subordinate and limited to duty, commands that this first breach be not passed by, lest the precedent upon record stand to future times to encourage like rebellion.

CAIN. And is it then my sovereign parent's will?

D. It is his will, that thou, his eldest son, his image, his beloved, should be maintained in all the rights of sovereignty derived to thee from him; and not be left exposed to injury and power usurped, but should do thyself justice on the rebel race.

CAIN. And so I will. Abel shall quickly know what it is to trample on his elder brother; shall know that he is thus sentenced by his father, and I am commissioned but to execute his high command, his sentence, which is God's; and that he falls by the hand of heavenly justice.

So now Satan had done his work; he had deluded the mother to a breach against the first and only command; he had drawn Adam to the same snare; and now he brings in Cain, prompted by his own rage, and deluded by his (Satan's) craft, to commit murder, nay, a fratricide, an aggravated murder.

Upon this he sends out Cain, while the bloody rage was in its ferment, and wickedly at the same time bringing Abel, innocent and fearing no ill, just in his way, he suggests to his thoughts such words as these.

Look you, Cain, see how divine justice concurs with your father's righteous sentence; see there is thy brother Abel directed by heaven to fall into thy hands unarmed, unguarded, that thou mayest do thyself justice upon him without fear; see, thou mayest kill him, and if thou hast a mind to conceal it, no eyes can see, or will the world ever know it, so that no resentment or revenge upon thee or thy posterity can be apprehended, but it may be said some wild beast had rent him; nor will any one suggest that thou, his brother and superior, could be possibly the person.

Cain, prepared for the fact by his former avowed rage and resolution of revenge, was so much the less prepared to avoid the snare thus artfully contrived by the master of all subtilty, the Devil; so he immediately runs upon his brother Abel, and, after a little unarmed resistance, the innocent poor man, expecting no such mischief, was conquered and murdered; after which, as is to be supposed, the exasperated crew of Cain's outrageous race, overrun all his family and household, killing man, woman, and child.

It is objected here that we have no authority in Scripture to prove this part of the story; but I answer, it is not likely but that Abel, as well as Cain, being at man's estate long before this, had several children by their own sisters, for they were the only men in the world who were allowed the marrying their own sisters, there being no other women then in the world; and as we never read of any of Abel's posterity, it is likewise as probable they were all murdered, as that they should kill Abel only, whose sons might immediately fall upon Cain for the blood of their father, and so the world have been involved in a civil war as soon as there were two families in it.

But be it so or not, it is not doubted the Devil wrought with Cain in the horrid murder, or he had never done it; whether it was directly or by agents is not material, nor is the latter unlikely; and if the latter, then there is no improbability in the story, for why might not he that made use of the serpent to tempt Eve, be as well supposed to make a tool of some of Cain's sons or grandsons to prompt him in the wicked attempt of murdering his brother? and why must we be obliged to bring in a miracle or an apparition into the story, to make it probable that the Devil had any hand in it, when it was so natural to a degenerate race to act in such a manner?

However it was, and by whatever tool the Devil wrought, it is certain, that this was the consequence, poor Abel was butchered; and thus the Devil made a second conquest in God's creation; for Adam was now, as may be said, really childless, for his two sons were thus far lost, Abel was killed, and Cain was cursed and driven out from the presence of the Lord, and his race blasted with him.

It would be a useful inquiry here, and worthy our giving an account of, could we come to a certainty in it, namely, what was the mark that God set upon Cain by which he was kept from being fallen upon by Abel's friends or relations? but as this does not belong to the Devil's history, and it was God's mark, not the Devil's, I have nothing to do with it here.

The Devil had now gained his point, the kingdom of grace, so newly erected, had been, as it were, extinct, without a new creation, had not Adam and Eve been alive, and had not Eve, though now one hundred and thirty years of age, been a breeding young lady, for we must suppose the women in that state of longevity bare children till they were seven or eight hundred years old: this teeming of Eve peopled not the world so much as it restored the blessed race; for though Abel was killed, Cain had a numerous offspring presently, which, had Seth, Adam's third son, never been born, would soon have replenished the world with people, such as they were; the seed of a murderer, cursed of God, branded with a mark of infamy, and who afterwards fell altogether in the universal ruin of the race by the Deluge

But after the murder of Abel, Adam had another son born, namely, Seth, the father of Enos, and indeed the father of the holy race ; for during his time and his son Enos, the text says, that men began to call on the name of the Lord ; that is to say, they began to look back upon Cain and his wicked race, and being convinced of the wickedness they had committed, and led their whole posterity into, they began to sue to heaven for pardon of what was past, and to lead a new sort of life.

But the Devil had met with too much success in his first attempts, not to go on with his general resolution of debauching the minds of men, and bringing them off from God ; and, therefore, as he kept his hold upon Cain's cursed race, embroiled already in blood and murder, so he proceeded with his degenerate offspring, till, in a word, he brought both the holy seed and the degenerate race to join in one universal consent of crime, and to go on in it with such aggravating circumstances, as that it repented the Lord that he had made man, and he resolved to overwhelm them again with a general destruction, and clear the world of them.

The succession of blood in the royal original line of Adam, is preserved in the sacred histories, and brought down as low as Noah and his three sons, for a continued series of 1540 years, say some ; 1640, say others ; in which time sin spread itself so generally through the whole race, and the sons of God, so the Scripture calls the men of the righteous seed, the progeny of Seth came in unto the daughters of men, that is, joined themselves to the cursed race of Cain, and married promiscuously with them, according to their fancies, the women it seems being beautiful and tempting ; and though the Devil could not make the women handsome or ugly on one or other families, yet he might work up the gust of wicked inclination on either side, so as to make both the men and women tempting and agreeable to one another where they ought not to have been so ; and perhaps, as it is often seen to this day, the more tempting for being under legal restraint.

It is objected here, that we do not find in the Scripture that the men of either race were at that time forbid intermarrying with one another ; and it is true that, literally, it is not forbid ; but if we did not search rather to make doubts than to explain them, we might suppose it was forbidden by

some particular command at that time; seeing we may reasonably allow everything to be forbidden, which they are taxed
with a crime in committing; and as the sons of God taking
them wives as they thought fit to choose, though from among
the daughters of the cursed race, is there charged upon them
as a general depravation, and a great crime, and for which,
it is said, God even repented that he had made them, we
need go no farther to satisfy ourselves that it was certainly
forbidden.

Satan, no doubt, too, had a hand in this wickedness; for as
it was his business to prompt men to do everything which God
had prohibited, so the reason given why the men of those days
did this thing was, they saw the daughters of men, that is of the
wicked race or forbidden sort, were fair, he tempted them by
the lust of the eye; in a word, the ladies were beautiful and
agreeable, and the Devil knew how to make use of the allurement; the men liked and took them by the mere direction of
their fancy and appetite, without regarding the supreme prohibition; *They took them wives of all which they chose*, or such
as they liked to choose.

But the text adds, that this promiscuous generation went
farther than the mere outward crime of it, for it showed that
the wickedness of the heart of man was great before God,
and that he resented it; in short, God perceived a degeneracy
or defect of virtue had seized upon the whole race, that there
was a general corruption of manners and a depravity of
nature upon them, that even the holy seed was tainted with
it, that the Devil had broken in upon them, and prevailed to
a great degree; that not only the practice of the age was
corrupt, for that God could easily have restrained, but that
the very heart of man was debauched, his desires wholly
vitiated, and his senses engaged in it; so that, in a word, it
became necessary to show the divine displeasure, not in the
ordinary manner, by judgment and reproofs of such kind as
usually reclaim men, but by a general destruction to sweep
them away, clear the earth of them, and put an end to the
wickedness at once, removing the offence and the offenders
all together; this is signified at large, Gen. vi. 5, *God saw
that the wickedness of man was great in the earth, and that every
imagination of the thoughts of his heart was only evil continually*
And again, v. 11, 12, *The earth also was corrupt before God;
and the earth was filled with violence. And God looked upon the*

earth, and behold it was corrupt; for all flesh had corrupted his way upon the earth.

It must be confessed, it was a strange conquest the Devil had made in the antediluvian world; that he had, as I may say, brought the whole race of mankind into a general revolt from God; Noah was indeed a preacher of righteousness, and he had preached about five hundred years, to as little purpose as most of the good ministers ever did; for we do not read there was one man converted by him, or at least not one of them left, for that at the Deluge there was either none of them alive, or none spared but Noah and his three sons and their wives; and even they are, it is evident, recorded, not so much to be saved for their own goodness, but because they were his sons; nay, without breach of charity, we may conclude that at least one went to the Devil, even of those three, namely Canaan, for triumphing in a brutal manner over his father's drunkenness; for we find the special curse reached to him and his posterity for many ages; and whether it went no farther than the present state of life with them, we cannot tell.

We will suppose now, that through this whole fifteen hundred years, the Devil, having so effectually debauched mankind, had advanced his infernal kingdom to a prodigious height; for the text says, *the whole earth was filled with violence;* in a word, blood, murder, rape, robbery, oppression and injustice, prevailed everywhere; and man, like the wild bear in the forest, lived by prey, biting and devouring one another.

At this time, Noah begins to preach a new doctrine to them, for as he had before been a preacher of righteousness, now he becomes a preacher of vengeance; first, he tells them they shall be all overwhelmed with a Deluge; that for their sins God repented they were made, and that he would destroy them all; adding, that to prevent the ruin of himself and family, he resolved to build him a ship to have recourse to when the water should come over the rest of the world.

What jesting, what scorn, what contempt did this work expose the good old man to for above a hundred years; for so long the work was building, as ancient authors say. Let us represent to ourselves, in the most lively manner, how the witty world at that time behaved to poor old Noah; how they took their evening walks to see what he was doing, and passed their judgment upon it, and upon the progress of it; I

say, to represent this to ourselves, we need go no farther than
to our own witticisms upon religion, and upon the most
solemn mysteries of divine worship; how we damn the serious
for enthusiasts, think the grave mad, and the sober melancholy;
call religion itself *flatus* and *hyppo* ; make the devout ignorant,
the divine mercenary, and the whole scheme of divinity a
frame of priestcraft; and thus no doubt the building an ark
or boat, or whatever they called it, to float over the mountains
and dance over the plains, what could it be but a religous
frenzy, and the man that so busied himself, a lunatic ; and all
this in an age when divine things came by immediate revelation into the minds of men! The Devil must therefore have
made a strange conquest upon mankind, to obliterate all the
reverence, which, but a little before, was so strangely impressed
upon them concerning their Maker.

This was certainly the height of the Devil's kingdom, and
we shall never find him arrive to such a pitch again; he was
then truly and literally the universal monarch, nay, the god of
this world; and as all tyrants do, he governs them with an
arbitrary absolute sway; and had not God thought fit to give
him a writ of ejectment, and afterwards drown him out of
possession, I know not what would have been the case; he
might have kept his hold, for aught I know, till the seed of
the woman came to bruise his head, that is to say, cripple
his government, dethrone him, and depose his power, as has
been fulfilled in the Messiah.

But as he was, I say, drowned out of the world, his king·
dom for the present was at an end; at least, if he had a do
minion he had no subjects, and as the creation was in a man
ner renewed, so the Devil had all his work to do over again
Unhappy man! how has he, by his weak resistance, made
the Devil, recovering his hold too easy to him, and given him
all the advantages, except as before excepted, which he had
before? Now whither he retired in the mean time, and how
he got footing again after Noah and his family were landed
upon the new surface. that we come next to inquire.

CHAPTER X.

OF THE DEVIL'S SECOND KINGDOM, AND HOW HE GOT FOOTING IN
THE RENEWED WORLD, BY HIS VICTORY OVER NOAH AND HIS
RACE.

THE story of Noah, his building the ark, his embarking himself and all nature's stock for a new world on board it; the long voyage they took, and the bad weather they met with, though it would embellish this work very well, and come in very much to the purpose in this place, yet as it does not belong to the Devil's story (for I cannot prove what some suggest, viz., that he was in the ark among the rest), I say, for that reason I must omit it.

And now, having mentioned Satan's being in the ark, as I say I cannot prove it, so there are, I think some good reasons to believe he was not there: first, I know no business he had there; secondly, we read of no mischief done there, and these joined together make me conclude he was absent; the last I chiefly insist upon, that we read of no mischief done there, which if he had been in the ark would certainly have happened; and therefore I suppose rather, that when he saw his kingdom dissolved, his subjects all ingulfed in an inevitable ruin and desolation (a sight suitable enough to him, except as it might un-king him for a time), I say, when he saw this, he took care to speed himself away as well as he could, and make his retreat to a place of safety, where that was, is no more difficult to us, than it was to him.

It is suggested, that as he is prince of the power of the air, he retired only into that region. It is most rational to suppose he went no farther on many accounts, of which I shall speak by and by : here he stayed hovering in the earth's atmosphere, as he has often done since, and perhaps now does; or if the atmosphere of this globe was affected by the indraft of the absorption, as some think, then he kept himself upon the watch to see what the event of the new phenomenon would be; and this watch, wherever it was, I doubt not, was as near the earth as he could place himself, perhaps in the atmosphere of the moon, or, in a word, the next place of retreat he could find.

From hence I take upon me to insist, that Satan has not a more certain knowledge of events than we: I say, he has not a more certain knowledge; that he may be able to make stronger conjectures and more rational conclusions from what he sees, I will not deny; and that which he most outdoes us in is, that he sees more to conclude from than we can, but I am satisfied he knows nothing of futurity more than he can see by observation and inference: nor, for example, did he know whether God would repeople the world any more or no.

I must therefore allow that he only waited to see what would be the event of this strange eruption of water, and what God purposed to do with the ark, and all that was in it.

Some philosophers tell us, besides what I hinted above, that the Devil could have no retreat in the earth's atmosphere, for that the air being wholly condensed into water, and having continually poured down its streams to deluge the earth, that body was become so small, and had suffered such convulsions, that there was but just enough air left to surround the water, or as might serve by its pressure to preserve the natural position of things, and supply the creatures in the ark with a part to breathe in.

The atmosphere, indeed, might suffer some strange and unnatural motions at that time, but not, I believe, to that degree; however, I will not affirm that there could be room in it, or is now, for the Devil, much less for all the numberless legions of Satan's host; but there was, and now certainly is, sufficient space to receive him, and a sufficient body of his troops for the business he had for them at that time, and that is enough to the purpose; or, if the earth's atmosphere did suffer any particular convulsion on that occasion, he might make his retreat to the atmosphere of the moon, or of Mars, or of Venus, or of any of the other planets; or to any other place; for he that is prince of the air could not want retreats in such a case, from whence he might watch for the issue of things; certainly he did not go far, because his business lay here, and he never goes out of his way of doing mischief.

In particular, his more than ordinary concern was to see what would become of the ark; he was wise enough doubtless to see that God, who had directed its making, nay, even the very structure of it, would certainly take care of it, preserve it upon the water, and bring it to some place of safety or

other; though where it should be, the Devil with all his
cunning could not resolve, whether on the same surface, the
waters drawing off, or in any other created or to be created
place; and this state of uncertainty being evidently his case,
and which proves his ignorance of futurity, it was his business, I say, to watch with the utmost vigilance for the event.

If the ark was, as Mr. Burnet thinks, guided by two angels,
they not only held it from foundering or being swallowed up
in the water, but certainly kept the waters calm about it,
especially when the Lord brought a strong wind to blow over
the whole globe, which by the way was the first, and, I suppose, the only universal storm that ever blew, for to be
sure it blew over the whole surface at once; I say, if it was
thus guided, to be sure the Devil saw it, and that with envy
and regret that he could do it no injury; for, doubtless, had
it been in the Devil's power, as God had drowned the whole
race of man, except what was in the ark, he would have
taken care to have dispatched them too, and so made an end
of the creation at once; but either he was not empowered to
go to the ark, or it was so well guarded by angels, that when
he came near it he could do it no harm: so it rested at length,
the waters abating, on the mountains of Arrarat, in Armenia,
or somewhere else that way, and where they say a .piece of
the keel is remaining to this day, of which, however, with
Dr. ——, I say, I believe not a word.

The ark being safe landed, it is reasonable to believe Noah
prepared to go on shore, as the seamen call it, as soon as the
dry land began to appear; and here you must allow me to
suppose Satan; though himself clothed with a cloud, so as
not to be seen, came immediately, and perching on the roof,
saw all the heaven-kept household safely landed, and all the
host of living creatures dispersing themselves down the sides
of the mountain, as the search of their food or other proper
occasions directed them.

This sight was enough; Satan was at no loss to conclude
from hence that the design of God was to repeople the world,
by the way of ordinary generation, from the posterity of these
eight persons, without creating any new species.

Very well, says the Devil, then my advantage over them,
by the snare I laid for poor Eve, is good still; and I am
now just where I was after Adam's expulsion from the garden, and when I had Cain and his race to go to work with,

for here is the old expunged corrupted race still; as Cain was the object then, so Noah is my man now, and if I do not master him one way or another, I am mistaken in my mark. Pardon me for making a speech for the Devil.

Noah, big with a sense of his late condition, and while the wonders of the Deluge were fresh in his mind, spent his first days in the ecstacies of his soul, giving thanks, and praising the power that had been his protection in and through the floods of water, and which had in so miraculous a manner safely landed him on the surface of the newly-discovered land; and the text tells us, as one of the first things he was employed in, *He built an altar unto the Lord, and offered burnt-offerings upon the altar.* Gen. viii. 20.

While Noah was thus employed he was safe, the Devil himself could nowhere break in upon him; and we may suppose very reasonably, as he found the old father invulnerable, he left him for some years, watching, notwithstanding, all possible advantages against his sons and their children; for now the family began to increase, and Noah's sons had several children; whether himself had any more children after the Flood or not, that we are not arrived to any certainty about.

Among his sons, the Devil found Japhet and Shem, good, pious, religious, and very devout persons; serving God daily, after the example of their good old father Noah, and he could make nothing of them, or of any of their posterity; but Ham the second, or, according to some, the younger son of Noah, had a son who was named Canaan, a loose, young, profligate fellow; his education was probably but cursory and superficial, his father Ham being not near so religious and serious a man as his brothers Shem and Japhet were; and as Canaan's education was defective, so he proved, as untaught youth generally do, a wild, and, in short, a very wicked fellow, and consequently a fit tool for the Devil to go to work with.

Noah, a diligent industrious man, being, with all his family, thus planted in the rich fruitful plains of Armenia, or whereever you please, let it be near the mountains of Caucasûs or Arrarat; went immediately to work, cultivating and improving the soil, increasing his cattle and pastures, sowing corn, and, among other things, planting trees for food; and among the fruit-trees he planted vines, of the grapes whereof he made, no doubt, as they still in the same country do make, most excellent wine, rich, luscious, strong, and pleasant.

I cannot come into the notion of our critics, who to excuse Noah from the guilt of what followed, or at least from the censure, tell us he knew not the strength or the nature of wine, but that gathering the heavy clusters of the grapes, and their own weight crushing out their balmy juices into his hand, he tasted the tempting liquor, and that, the Devil assisting, he was charmed with the delicious fragrance, and tasted again and again; pressing it out into a bowl or dish; that he might take a larger quantity, till at length the heady froth ascended, and seizing his brain he became intoxicate and drunk, not in the least imagining there was any such strength in the juice of that excellent fruit.

But to make out this story, which is, indeed, very favourable for Noah, but in itself extremely ridiculous, you must necessarily fall into some absurdities, and beg the question most egregiously in some particular cases, which way of arguing will by no means support what is suggested; at first you must suppose there was no such thing as wine made before the Deluge, and that nobody had been ever made drunk with the juice of the grape before Noah, which, I say, is begging the question in the grossest manner.

If the contrary is true, as I see no reason to question, if, I say, it was true that there was wine drank, and that men were or had been drunk with it before, they cannot then but suppose that Noah, who was a wise, a great, and a good man, and a preacher of righteousness, both knew of it, and without doubt had, in his preaching against their crimes, preached against this among the rest; upbraided them with it, reproved them for it, and exhorted them against it.

Again; it is highly probable they had grapes growing, and consequently wines made from them, in the antediluvian world; how else did Noah come by the vines which he planted? For we are to suppose, he could plant no trees or shrubs, but such as he found the roots of in the earth, and which no doubt had been there before in their highest perfection, and had consequently grown up and brought forth the same luscious fruit before.

Besides, as he found the roots of the vines, so he understood what they were, and what fruit they bore, or else it may be supposed also he would not have planted them; for he planted them for their fruit, as he did it in the provision he was making for his subsistence, and the subsistence of his family; and if he did not know what they were, he would not have set them, for he was not planting for diversion, but for profit.

Upon the whole, it seems plain to me he knew what he did, as well when he planted the vines as when he pressed out the grapes; and also, when he drank the juice, that he knew it was wine, was strong, and would make him drunk if he took enough of it: he knew that other men had been drunk with such liquor before the Flood, and that he had reprehended them for it; and therefore it was not his ignorance, but the Devil took him at some advantage, when his appetite was eager, or he thirsty, and the liquor cooling and pleasant; and, in short, as Eve said, *The serpent beguiled her, and she did eat,* so the Devil beguiled Noah, and *he did drink;* the temptation was too strong for Noah, not the wine; he knew well enough what he did, but as the drunkards say to this day, it was so good he could not forbear it, and so he got drunk before he was aware; or, as our ordinary speech expresses it, he was overtaken with drink; and Mr. Pool and other expositors are partly of the same mind.

No sooner was the poor old man conquered, and the wine had lightened his head, but it may be supposed he falls off from the chair or bench where he sat, and tumbling backwards, his clothes, which in those hot countries were only loose open robes, like the vests which the Armenians wear to this day, flying abroad, or the Devil so assisting on purpose to expose him, he lay there in a naked indecent posture, not fit to be seen.

In this juncture, who should come by but young Canaan, say some; or as others think, this young fellow first attacked him by way of kindness and pretended affection; prompted his grandfather to drink, on pretence of the wine being good for him, and proper for the support of his old age, and subtilly set upon him, drinking also with him, and so (his head being too strong for the old man's) drank him down, and then, Devil like, triumphed over him; boasted of his conquest, insulted the body as it were dead, uncovered him on purpose to expose him; and, leaving him in that indecent posture, went and made sport with it to his father Ham, who in that part, wicked like himself, did the same to his brethren Japhet and Shem; but they, like modest and good men, far from carrying on the wicked insult on their parent, went and covered him, as the Scripture expresses it, and, as may be supposed, informed him how he had been abused, and by who.

Why else should Noah, when he came to himself, shew his resentment so much against Canaan his grandson, rather than against Ham his father, and who it is supposed in the story, the guilt chiefly lay upon? we see the curse is, as it were, laid wholly upon Canaan the grandson, and not a word of the father is mentioned, Gen. ix. 25, 26, 27, *Cursed be Canaan, a servant of servants shall he be, &c.*

That Ham was guilty, that is certain from the history of fact, but I cannot but suppose his grandson was the occasion of it; and in this case the Devil seems to have made Canaan the instrument or tool to delude Noah, and draw him into drunkenness, as he made the serpent the tool to beguile Eve, and draw her into disobedience.

Possibly Canaan might do it without design at first, but might be brought in to ridicule and make a jest of the old patriarch afterwards, as is too frequent since in the practice of our days; but I rather believe he did it really with a wicked design, and on purpose to expose and insult his reverend old parent; and this seems more likely too, because of the great bitterness with which Noah resented it, after he came to be informed of it.

But be that as it will, the Devil certainly made a great conquest here, and as to outward appearance, no less than that which he gained before over Adam; nor did the Devil's victory consist barely in his having drawn in the only righteous man of the whole antediluvian world, and so beginning or initiating the new young progeny with a crime; but here was the great oracle silenced at once; the preacher of righteousness, for such no doubt he would have been to the new world, as he was to the old, I say, the preacher was turned out of office, or his mouth stopped, which was worse; nay, it was a stopping of his mouth in the worst kind, far worse than stopping his breath, for had he died, the office had descended to his sons, Shem and Japhet, but he was dead to the office of an instructor, though alive as to his being; for of what force could his preachings be, who had thus fallen himself into the most shameful and beastly excess?

Besides, some are of the opinion, though I hope without ground, that Noah was not only overtaken once in his drink, but that being fallen into that sin it became habitual, and he continued in it a great while, and that it was this which is the meaning of his being uncovered in his tent, and that his son saw his nakedness; that is, he continually exposed himself for a long time, a hundred years, say they, and that his son Ham, and his grandson Canaan, having drawn him into it, kept him in it, encouraged and prompted it, and all the while Satan still prompting them, joined their scoffs and contempt of him, with their wicked endeavours to promote the wickedness; and both with as much success as the Devil himself could wish for.

Then, as for his two sons modestly and decently covering their father, they tell us that represents Shem and Japhet applying themselves in an humble and dutiful manner to their father, to entreat and beseech him to consider his ancient glory, his own pious exhortations to the late drowned world, and to consider the offence which he gave by his evil course to God, and the scandal to his whole family, and also that they are brought in effectually prevailing upon him; and that then Noah cursed the wickedness of Ham's degenerate race, in testimony of his sincere repentance after the fact.

The story is not so very unlikely, as it is certain that it is not to be proved, and therefore we had better take it as we find it, viz., for one single act; but suppose it was so, it is still certain that Noah's preaching was sadly interrupted, the energy of his words scattered, and the force of his persuasions enervated and abated, by this shameful fall; that he was effectually silenced for an instructor ever after, and this was as much as the Devil had occasion for; and therefore indeed we read little more of him, except that he lived three hundred and fifty years after the Flood; nay, we do not so much as read that he had any more children, but the contrary, nor indeed could Noah have any more children, except by his old and perhaps superannuated wife, who it was very likely he had had four or five hundred years, unless you will suppose he was allowed to marry some of his own progeny, daughters or granddaughters, which we do not suppose was allowed, no, not to Adam himself.

This was certainly a masterpiece of the Devil's policy, and a fatal instance of his unhappy diligence; viz., that the door of the ark was no sooner open, and the face of the world hardly dry from the universal destruction of mankind, but he was at work among them; and that not only to form a general defection among the race, upon the foot of the original taint of nature, but like a bold devil, he strikes at the very root, and flies at the next general representative of mankind, attacks the head of the family, that in his miscarriage the rise and progress of a reformation of the new world should receive an early check, and should be at once prevented; I say, like a bold devil, he strikes at the root, and, alas! poor unhappy Noah, he proved too weak for him, Satan prevailed in his very first attempt, and got the victory over him at once.

Noah, thus overcome, and Satan's conquest carried on to the utmost of his own wishes, the Devil had little more to do in the world for some ages, than to carry on an universal degeneracy among mankind, and to finish it by a like diligent application, in deluding the generality of the race, and them as they came on gradually into life; this he found the less difficult, because of the first defection, which spread like a contagion upon the earth immediately after.

The first evidence we have of his success in this mischievous design, was in the building that great stupendous staircase, for such it seems it was intended, called Babel, which, if the whole world had not been drunk, or otherwise infatuated, they would never have undertaken; even Satan himself could never have prevailed with them to undertake such a preposterous piece of work, for it had neither end or means, possibility or probability in it.

I must confess I am sometimes apt to vindicate our old ancestors in my thoughts, from the charge itself, as we generally understand it, namely, that they really designed to build a tower which should reach up to heaven, or that it should secure them in case of another flood; and Father Casaubon is of my opinion, whether I am of his or no, is a question by itself; his opinion is, that the confusion was nothing but a breach among the undertakers and directors of the work, and that the building was designed chiefly for a storehouse for provisions, in case of a second Deluge; as to their notion of its reaching up to heaven, he takes the expression to be allegorical rather than literal, and only to mean that it should be exceeding high; perhaps they might not be astronomers enough to measure the distance of space between the earth and heaven, as we pretend to do now : but as Noah was then alive, and as we believe all his three sons were so too, they were able to have informed them how absurd it was to suppose either the one or the other, viz. 1. that they could build up to heaven; or, 2. that they could build firm enough to resist, or high enough to overtop the waters, supposing such another flood should happen. I would rather think it was only that they intended to build a most glorious and magnificent city, where they might all inhabit together; and that this tower was to be built for ornament and also for strength, or, as above, and for a storehouse to lay up vast magazines of provisions, in case of extraordinary floods or other events, the city being built in a great plain, namely, the plains of Shinnar, near the river Euphrates.

But the story, as it is recorded, suits better with Satan's measures at that time; and as he was from the beginning prompting them to everything that was contrary to the happiness of man, so the more preposterous it was, and the more inconsistent with common sense, the more to his purpose, and it showed the more what a complete conquest he had gained over the reason as well as the religion of mankind at that time.

Again; it is evident in this case, they were not only acting contrary to the nature of things, but contrary to the design and to the command of heaven ; for God's command was that they should replenish the earth, that is, that they should spread their habitations over it, and people the whole globe; whereas they were pitching in one place, as if they were not to multiply sufficient to take up any more.

But what cared the Devil for that; or, to put it a little handsomer, that was what Satan aimed at; for it was enough to him to bring mankind to act just contrary to what heaven had directed or commanded them in anything, and if possible in everything.

But God himself put a stop to this foolish piece of work, and it was time indeed to do so, for a madder thing the Devil himself never proposed to them ; I say, God himself put a stop to this new undertaking, and disappointed the Devil ; and how was it done? not in judgment and anger, as perhaps the Devil expected and hoped for, but, as pitying the simpliciy of that dreaming creature man, he confused their speech, or as some say, divided and confused their councils, so that they could not agree with one another, which would be the same thing as not to understand one another: or he put a new Shibboleth upon their tongues, thereby separating them into tribes or families, for, by this, every family found themselves under a necessity of keeping together, and this naturally increased that differing jargons of language, for at first it might be no more.

What a confusion this was to them we all know, by their being obliged to leave off their building, and immediately separating one from another; but what a surprise it was to the old serpent, that remains to be considered of, for indeed it belongs to his history.

Satan had never met with any disappointment in all his wicked attempts till now; for first, he succeeded even to triumph upon Eve, he did the like upon Cain, and, in short, upon the whole world, one man (Noah) excepted, when he blended the sons of God and the daughters of hell, for so the word is understood, together, in promiscuous voluptuous living as well as generation.

As to the Deluge, authors are not agreed whether it was a disappointment to the Devil or no, it might be indeed a surprise to him, for though Noah had preached of it for a hundred years together, yet as he (Satan) daily prompted the people not to heed or believe what that old fellow Noah said to them, and to ridicule his whimsical building a monstrous tub to swim or float in, when the said Deluge should come, so I am of the opinion he did not believe it himself, and am positive he could not foresee it, by any insight into futurity that he was master of.

It is true, the astronomers tell us, there was a very terrible comet seen in the air, that it appeared for one hundred and eighty days before the Flood, continually, and that as it approached nearer and nearer every day all the while, so that at last it burst and fell down in a continual spout or stream of water, being of a watery substance, and the quantity so great that it was forty days a falling; so that this comet not only foretold the Deluge or drowning of the earth, but actually performed it, and drowned it from itself.

But, to leave this tale to them that told it, let us consider the Devil, surprised, and a little amazed, at the absorption or inundation, or whatever we are to call it, of the earth in the Deluge; not, I say, that he was much concerned at it, perhaps just the contrary; and if God would drown it again, and as often as he thought fit, I do not see, by anything I meet with in Satan's history, or in the nature of him, that he would be at all disturbed at it; all that I can see in it, that could give Satan any concern, would be that all his favourites were gone, and he had his work to do over again, to lay a foundation for a new conquest in the generation that was to come; but in this his prospect was fair enough, for why should he be discouraged, when he had now eight people to work upon, who met with such success when he had but two? and why should he question breaking in now where nature was already vitiated and corrupted, when he had before conquered the same nature when in its primitive rectitude · and purity, just come out of the hands of its Maker, and fortified with the awe of his high and solemn command just given them, and the threatening of death also annexed to it if broken?

But I go back to the affair of Babel: this confusion of language or of councils, take it which way you will, was the first disappointment that I find the Devil met with in all his attempts and practices upon mankind, or upon the new creation, which I mentioned above; for now he foresaw what would follow; namely, that the people would separat and spread themselves over the whole surface of the earth and a thousand new scenes of action would appear, in whic; he therefore prepares himself to behave as he should se occasion.

How·the Devil learned to speak all the languages that were now to be used, and how many languages they were, the several ancient writers of the Devil's story have not yet determined; some tell us they were divided only into fifteen, some into seventy-two, others into one hundred and eighty, and others again into several thousands.

It also remains a doubt with me, and, I suppose, will be so with others also, whether Satan has yet found out a method to converse with mankind without the help of language and words, or not; seeing man has no other medium of conversing, no not with himself: this I have not time to enter upon here; however, this seems plain to me, viz., that the Devil soon learned to make mankind understand him, whatever language he spoke, and no doubt but he found ways and · means to understand them, whatever language they spoke.

After the confusion of languages, the people necessarily sorted themselves into families and tribes, every family understanding their own particular speech, and that only; and these families multiplying grew into nations, and those nations wanting room, and seeking out habitations, wandered some this way, some that, till they found out countries respectively proper for their settling; and they became a kingdom, spreading and possessing still more and more land as their people increased, till at last the whole earth was scarce big enough for them. This presented Satan with an opportunity to break in upon their morals at another door, viz., their pride; for men being naturally proud and envious, nations and tribes began to jostle with one another for room; either one nation enjoyed better accommodations, or had a better soil or a more favourable climate than another; and these being numerous and strong thrust the other out, and encroached upon their land; the other liking their situation, prepare for their defence, and so began oppression, invasion, war, battle, and blood; Satan all the while beating the drums, and his attendants clapping their hands, as men do when they set dogs on upon one another.

The bringing mankind thus to war and confusion, as it was the first game the Devil played after the confounding of languages and divisions at Babel, so it was a conquest upon mankind, purely devilish, born from hell, and so exactly tinctured with Satan's original sin, ambition, that it really transformed men into mere devils; for when is man transformed into the very image of Satan himself, when is he turned into a mere devil, if it is not when he is fighting with his fellow creatures, and dipping his hands in the blood of his own kind? Let his picture be considered,—the fire of hell, flames or sparkles in his eyes, a voracious grin sits upon his countenance, rage and fury distort the muscles of his face, his passions agitate his whole body, and he is metamorphosed from a comely beauteous angelic creature into a fury, a satyr, a terrible and frightful monster, nay, into a devil; for Satan himself is described by the same word, which on his very account is changed into a substantive, and the devils are called Furies.

This sowing the seeds of strife in the world, and bringing nations to fight and make war upon one another, would take up a great part of the Devil's history, and abundance of extraordinary things would occur in relating the particulars; for there have been very great conflagrations kindled in the world, by the artifice of hell under this head, viz., of making war; in which it has been the Devil's masterpiece, and he has indeed shown himself a workman in it, that he has wheedled mankind into strange unnatural notions of things, in order to propagate and support the fighting principle in the world; such as laws of war, fair fighting, behaving like men of honour, fighting to the last drop, and the like, by which killing and murdering is understood to be justifiable. Virtue and a true greatness of spirit is rated now by rules which God never appointed, and the standard of honour is quite different from that of reason and of nature : bravery is denominated, not from a fearless undaunted spirit in the just defence of life and liberty, but from a daring defiance of God and man, fighting, killing, and treading under foot his fellow creatures, at the ordinary command of the officer, whether it be right or wrong, and whether it be in a just defence of life, and our country's life, that is liberty, or whether it be for the support of injury and oppression.

A prudent avoiding causeless quarrel is called cowardice, and to take an affront, baseness, and meanness of spirit; to refuse fighting, and put life at a cast on the point of a sword, a practise forbid by the laws of God and of all good government, is yet called cowardice; and a man is bound to die, duelling, or live and be laughed at.

This trumping up these imaginary things called bravery and gallantry, naming them virtue and honour, is all from the Devil's new management, and his subtle influencing the minds of men to fly in the face of God and nature, and to act against his senses; nor but for his artifice in the management, could it be possible that such inconsistencies could go down with mankind, or they could pass such absurd things among them for reasoning; for example, A. is found in bed with B.'s wife, B. is the person injured, and therefore offended and coming into the chamber with his sword in his hand, A. exclaims loudly, Why sir, you won't murder me, will you? as you are a man of honour let me rise and take my sword.

A very good story indeed! fit for nobody but the Devil to put into any man's head; but so it is, B. being put in mind, forsooth, that he is a man of honour, starts back and must act the honourable part; so he lets A. get up, put on

his clothes and take his sword; then they fight, and B.
is killed for his honour; whereas, had the laws of God, of
nature, and of reason, taken place, the adulterer and the
adulteress should have been taken prisoners and carried before
the judge; and being taken in the fact, should have been
immediately sentenced, he to the block, and she to the stake,
and the innocent abused husband had no reason to have run
any risk of his life for being made a cuckold.

But thus has Satan abused the reason of man, and if a
man does me the greatest injury in the world, I must do
myself justice upon him, by venturing my life upon an even
lay with him, and must fight him upon an equal hazard, in
which the injured person is as often killed as the person
offering the injury; suppose now it be in the same case as
above, a man abuses my wife, and then, to give me satisfaction, tells me, he will fight me, which the French call doing
me reason; No, sir, say I, let me lie with your wife too, and
then, if you desire it, I may fight you; then I am upon even
terms with you: but this indeed is the reasoning which the
Devil has brought mankind to at this day.   But to go back
to the subject, viz., the Devil bringing the nations to fall out,
and to quarrel for room in the world, and so to fight, in
order to dispossess one another of their settlements.   This
began at a time when certainly there were places enough in
the world for every one to choose in, and therefore the Devil,
not the want of elbowroom, must be the occasion of it; and
it is carried on ever since, as apparently from the same interest, and by the same original.

But we shall meet with this part again very often in the
Devil's story, and as we bring him farther on in the management of mankind; I therefore lay it by for the present, and
come to the next step the Devil took with mankind after the
confusion of languages, and this was in the affair of worship.
It does not appear yet that ever the Devil was so bold, as
either,

1. To set himself up to be worshipped as a god; or, which
ras still worse,

2. To persuade men to believe there was no God at all to
worship.

Both these are introduced since the Deluge, one indeed by
the Devil, who soon found means to set himself up for a god
in many parts of the world, and holds it to this day; but the

last is brought in by the invention of men, in which it must be confessed man has outsinned the Devil; for to do Satan justice, he never thought it could ever pass upon mankind, or that anything so gross would go down with them; so that, in short, these modern casuists, in the reach of our days, have, I say, outsinned the Devil.

As then both these are modern inventions, Satan went on gradually, and being to work upon human nature by stratagem, not by force, it would have been too gross to have set himself up as an object of worship at first, it was to be done step by step; for example:

1. It was sufficient to bring mankind to a neglect of God, to worship him by halves, and give little or no regard to his laws, and so grow loose and immoral, in direct contradiction to his commands; this would not go down with them at first, so the Devil went on gradually.

2. From a negligence in worshipping the true God, he by degrees introduced the worship of false gods; and to introduce this, he began with the sun, moon, and stars, called, in the holy text, the host of heaven; these had a greater majesty upon them, and seemed fitter to command the homage of mankind; so it was not the hardest thing in the world to bring men, when they had once forgotten the true God, to embrace the worship of such gods as those.

3. Having thus debauched their principles in worship, and led them from the true and only object of worship, to a false, it was the easier to carry them on; so, in a few gradations more, he brought them to downright idolatry, and even in that idolatry he proceeded gradually too: for he began with awful names, such as were venerable in the thoughts of men, as Baal or Bell, which, in Chaldaic and Hebrew, signifies lord or sovereign, or mighty and magnificent, and this was therefore a name ascribed at first to the true God, but afterwards they descended to make images and figures to represent him, and then they were called by the same name as Baal, Baalim, and afterwards Bell, from which, by a hellish degeneracy, Satan brought mankind to adore every block of their own hewing, and to worshipping stocks, stones, monsters, hobgoblins, and every sordid frightful thing, and at last, the Devil himself.

What notions some people may entertain of the forward-ness of the first ages of the world, to run into idolatry, I do not inquire here; I know they tell us strange things, of its being the product of mere nature, one remove from its primitive state; but I, who pretend to have so critically inquired into Satan's history, can assure you, and that from very good authority, that the Devil did not find it so easy a task, to obliterate the knowledge of the true God, in the minds and consciences of men, as those people suggest.

It is true, he carried things a great length under the patriarchal government of the first ages, but still he was sixteen hundred years bringing it to pass; and though we have reason to believe the old world, before the Flood, was arrived to a very great height of wickedness, and Ovid very nobly describes it by the war of the Titans against Jupiter, yet we do not read that ever Satan was come to such a length as to bring them to idolatry; indeed we do read of wars carried on among them, whether it was one nation against another, or only personal, we cannot tell: but the world seemed to be swallowed up in a life of wickedness, that is to say, of luxury and lewdness, rapine and violence, and there were giants among them, and men of renown, that is to say, men famed for their mighty valour, great actions in war we may suppose, and their strength, who personally oppressed others. We read of no considerable wars, indeed, but it is not to be doubted there were such wars, or else it is to be understood that they lived, in common, a life somewhat like the brutes, the strong devouring the weak; for the text says, *the whole earth was filled with violence*, hunting and tearing one another to pieces, either for dominion or for wealth, either for ambition or for avarice, we know not well which.

Thus far the old antediluvian world went, and very wicked they were, there is no doubt of that; but we have reason to believe there was no idolatry, the Devil had not brought them to that length yet; perhaps it would soon have followed, but the Deluge intervened.

After the Deluge, as I have said, he had all his work to do over again, and he went on by the same steps; first he brought them to violence and war, then to oppression and tyranny, then to neglect of true worship, then to false worship, and then idolatry by the mere natural consequence of the thing. Who were the first nation or people that fell from the worship of the true God, is something hard to determine; the Devil, who certainly of all God's creatures is best able to inform us, having left us nothing upon record upon that subject, but we have reason to believe it was thus introduced:

Nimrod was the grandson of Ham, Noah's second son, the same who was cursed by his father for exposing him in his drunkenness; this Nimrod was the first who it seems Satan picked out for a hero: here he inspired him with ambitious thoughts, dreams of empire, and having the government of all the rest, that is to say, universal monarchy; the very same bait with which he has played upon the frailty of princes, and ensnared the greatest of them ever since, even from his most august imperial majesty, King Nimrod the First, to his most Christian majesty, Louis XIV., and many a mighty monarch between.

When these mighty monarchs and men of fame went off the stage, the world had their memories in esteem many ages after; and as their great actions were no otherwise recorded than by oral tradition, and the tongues and memories of fallible men, time and the custom of magnifying the past actions of kings, men soon fabled up their histories, Satan assisting, into miracle and wonder; hence their names were had in veneration more and more; statues and bustoes representing their persons and great actions were set up in public places, till from heroes and champions they made gods of them, and thus, Satan prompting, the world was quickly filled with idols.

This Nimrod is he who, according to the received opinion, though I do not find Satan's history exactly concurring with it, was first called Belus, then Baal, and worshipped in most of the eastern countries under those names; sometimes with additions of surnames, according to the several countries, or people, or towns where he was particularly set up, as Baal Peor, Baal Zephon, Baal Phegor, and in other places plain Baal; as Jupiter, in after times, had the like additions, as Jupiter Ammon, Jupiter Capitolinus, Jupiter Pistor, Jupiter Feretrius, and about ten or twelve Jupiters more.

I must acknowledge, that I think it was a masterpiece of hell to bring the world to idolatry so soon after they had had such an eminent example of the infinite power of the true God, as was seen in the Deluge; and particularly in the escape of Noah in the ark, to bring them (even before Noah or his sons were dead) to forget whose hand it was, and give the homage of the world to a name, and that a name of a mortal man, dead and rotten, who was famous for nothing when he was alive but blood and war; I say, to bring the world to set up this nothing, this mere name, nay, the very image and picture of him, for a god, it was first a mark of most prodigious stupidity in the whole race of man, a monstrous degeneracy from nature, and even from common sense; and, in the next place, it was a token of an inexpressible craft and subtlety in the Devil, who had now gotten the people into so full and complete a management, that, in short, he could have brought them, by the same rule, to have worshipped anything; and in a little while more, did bring many of them to worship himself, plain devil as he was, and knowing him to be such.

As to the antiquity of this horrible defection of mankind, though we do not find the beginning of it particularly recorded, yet we are certain it was not long after the confusion of Babel; for Ninrod, as is said, was no more than Noah's great grandson, and Noah himself, I suppose, might be alive some years after Nimrod was born; and as Nimrod was not long dead before they forgot that he was a tyrant and a murderer, and made a Baal, that is a lord or idol, of him; I say, he was not long dead, for Nimrod was born in the year of the world 1847, and built Babylon, the year 1879 ; and we find Terah, the father of Abram, who lived from the year 1879, was an idolater, as was doubtless Bethuel, who was Terah's grandson; for we find Laban, who was Bethuel's son, was so, and all this was during the life of the first postdiluvian family, for Terah was born within one hundred and ninety-three years after the Flood, and one hundred and fifty-seven years before Noah was dead; and even Abram himself was eight-and-fifty years old before Noah died, and yet idolatry had been then, in all probability, above a hundred years practised in the world.

N.B. It is worth remark here, what a terrible advantage the Devil gained by the debauching poor Noah, and drawing him into the sin of Drunkenness ; for by this, as I said, he silenced and stopped the mouth of the great preacher of righteousness, that father and patriarch of the whole world, who not being able, for the shame of his own foul miscarriage, to pretend to instruct or reprove the world any more, the Devil took hold of them immediately, and for want of a prophet to warn and admonish, run that little of religion which there might be left in Shem and Japhet, quite out of the world, and deluged them all in idolatry.

How long the whole world may be said to be thus over-whelmed in ignorance and idolatry, we may make some toler-able guess at by the history of Abraham ; for it was not till God called him from his father's house, that any such thing as a church was established in the world ; nor even then, except in his own family and successors, for almost four hundred years after that call ; and till God brought the Israelites back out of Egypt, the whole world may be said to be involved in idolatry and Devil worship.

So absolute a conquest had the Devil made over mankind immediately after the Flood, and all taking its rise and beginning at the fatal defeat of Noah, who had he lived untainted and invulnerable, as he had done for six hundred years before, would have gone a great way to have stemmed the torrent of wickedness which broke in upon mankind ; and therefore the Devil, I say, was very cunning, and very much in the right of it, take him as he is a mere devil, to attack Noah personally, and give him a blow so soon.

It is true, the Devil did not immediately rase out the notion of religion, and of a God, from the minds of men, nor could he easily suppress the principle of worship and homage to be paid to a sovereign being, the author of nature and guide of the world ; the Devil saw this clearly in the first ages of the new world, and therefore, as I have said, he proceeded poli-tically and by degrees. That it was so, is evident from the story of Job and his three friends, who, if we may take it for a history, not a fable, and may judge of the time of it by the length of Job's life, and by the family of Eliphaz the Temanite, who, it is manifest, was at least grandson or great grandson to Esau, Isaac's eldest son, and by the language of Abimelech, King of Gerar, to Abraham, and of Laban to Jacob, both the latter being at the same time idolaters ; I say, if we may judge of it by all these, there were still very sound notions of religion in the minds of men ; nor could Satan with all his cunning and policy deface those ideas, and root them out of the minds of the people.

And this put him upon taking new measures to keep up his interest and preserve the hold he got upon mankind; and his method was, like himself, subtle and politic to the last degree, as his whole history makes appear; for seeing he found they could not but believe the being of a God, and that they would needs worship something, it is evident he had no game left him to play but this, namely, to set up wrong notions of worship, and bring them to a false worship instead of a true, supposing the object worshipped to be still the same.

To finish this stratagem, he first insinuates that the true God was a terrible, a dreadful, unapproachable being; that to see him was so frightful, that it would be present death; that to worship him immediately, was a presumption which would provoke his wrath; and that as he was a consuming fire in himself, so he would burn up those in his anger that dared to offer up any sacrifice to him, but by the interposition of some medium which might receive their adorations in his name.

Hence it occurred presently, that subordinate gods were to be found out and set up, to whom the people might pay the homage due to the supreme God, and who they might worship in his name; this I take from the most ancient account of idolatry in the world; nor indeed could the Devil himself find out any other reason why men should canonize, or rather deify, their princes and men of fame, and worship them after they were dead, as if they could save them from death and calamity, who were not able to save themselves when they were alive; much less could Satan bring men to swallow so gross, so absurd a thing, as the bowing the knee to a stock or a stone, a calf, an ox, a lion, nay, the image or figure of a calf, such as the Israelites made at Mount Sinai, and say, *These be thy gods, O Israel, who brought thee out oj the land of Egypt.*

Having thus, I say, brought them to satisfy themselves that they worshipped the true God and no other, under the figures and appearances which they made to represent him, it was easy after that to worship anything for the true God; and thus in a few ages they worshipped nothing but idols, even throughout the whole world; nor has the Devil lost this hold in some parts of the world, nay, not in most parts of the world to this day; he holds still all the eastern parts of Asia, and the southern parts of Africa, and the northern parts of Europe, and in them the vast countries of China and Tartary, Persia and India, Guinea, Ethiopia, Zanquebar, Congo, Angola, Monomotapa, &c., in all which, except Ethiopia, we find no vestiges of any other worship but that of idols, monsters, and even the Devil himself; till after the very coming of our Saviour, and even then, if it be true, that the Gospel was preached in the Indies and China by St. Thomas, and in other remote countries by other of the apostles; we see that whatever ground Satan lost, he seems to have recovered it again; and all Asia and Africa is at present overrun with Paganism or Mahometanism, which I think of the two is rather the worst; besides all America, a part of the world, as some say, equal in bigness to all the other, in which the Devil's kingdom was never interrupted from its first being inhabited, whenever it was, to the first discovery of it by the European nations in the sixteenth century.

In a word, the Devil got what we may call an entire victory over mankind, and drove the worship of the true God, in a manner, quite out of the world, forcing, as it were, his Maker in a new kind of creation, the old one proving thus ineffectual to recover a certain number by force and mere omnipotence to return to their duty, serve him, and worship him; but of that hereafter.

CHAPTER XL

OF GOD'S CALLING A CHURCH OUT OF THE MIDST OF A DEGENERATE WORLD, AND OF SATAN'S NEW MEASURES UPON THAT INCIDENT; HOW HE ATTACKED THEM IMMEDIATELY, AND HIS SUCCESS IN THOSE ATTACKS.

SATAN having, as I have said in the preceding chapter, made, as it were, a full conquest of mankind, debauching them all to idolatry, and brought them at least to worshipping the true God by the wretched medium of corrupt and idolatrous representations; God seemed to have no true servants or worshippers left in the world, but, if I may be allowed to speak so, was obliged, in order to restore the world to their senses again, to call a select number out from among the rest, who he himself undertook should own his godhead or supreme authority, and worship him as he required to be worshipped; this, I say, God was obliged to do, because it is evident it has not been done so much by the choice and council of men, for Satan would have overruled that part, as by the power and energy of some irresistible and invincible operation, and this our divines give high names to; but be it what they will, it is the second defeat or disappointment that the Devil has met with in his progress in the world; the first I have spoken of already.

It is true, Satan very well understood what was threatened to him in the original promise to the woman, immediately after the fall, namely, *Thou shalt bruise his head, &c.*, but he did not expect it so suddenly, but thought himself sure of mankind, till the fulness of time when the Messiah should come; and therefore it was a great surprise to him to see that Abraham, being called, was so immediately received and established, though he did not so immediately follow the voice that directed him; yet in him, in his loins, was all God's church at that time contained.

In the calling Abraham, it is easy to see that there was no other way for God to form a Church, that is to say, to single out a people to himself, as the world was then stated, but by immediate revolution and voice from heaven. All mankind were gone over to the enemy, overwhelmed in idolatry, in a word, were engaged to the Devil; God Almighty, or, as the Scripture distinguishes him, the Lord, the true God, was out of the question; mankind knew little or nothing of him, much less did they know anything of his worship, or that there was such a being in the world.

Well might it be said the Lord appeared to Abraham, Gen. xii. 7, for if God had not appeared himself, he must have sent a messenger from heaven, and perhaps it was so too, for he had not one true servant or worshipper that we know of, then on earth, to send on that errand; no prophet, no preacher of righteousness; Noah was dead, and had been so above seventeen years; and if he had not, his preaching, as I observed after his great miscarriage, had but little effect; we are indeed told, that Noah left behind him certain rules and orders for the true worship of God, which were called the precepts of Noah, and remained in the world for a long time; though, how written, when neither any letters, much less writing, were known in the world, is a difficulty which remains to be solved; and this makes me look upon those laws, called the Precepts of Noah, to be a modern invention, as I do also the *Alphabetum Noachi*, which Bochart pretends to give an account of.

But to leave that fiction, and come back to Abraham; God called him, whether at first by voice, without any vision; whether in a dream or night vision, which was very significant in those days; or whether by some awful appearance, we know not; the second time, it is indeed said expressly, God appeared to him; be it which way it will, God himself called him, showed him the land of Canaan, gave him the promise of it for his posterity, and, withal, gave him such a faith, that the Devil soon found there was no room for him to meddle with Abraham. This is certain, we do not read that the Devil ever so much as attempted Abraham at all: some will suggest that the command to Abraham, to go and offer up his son Isaac, was a temptation of the Devil, if possible, to defeat the glorious work of God's calling a holy seed into the world; for the first, if Abraham had disobeyed that call, the new favourite had been overcome and made a rebel of, or secondly, if he had obeyed, then the promised seed had been cut off, and Abraham defeated; but as the text is express that God himself proposed it to Abraham, I shall not start the suggestions of the critics in bar of the sacred oracle.

Be it one way or other, Abraham showed a hero-like faith and courage, and if the Devil had been the author of it, he had seen himself disappointed in both his views; 1. by Abraham's ready and bold compliance, as believing it to be God's command; and, 2. by the divine countermand of the execution, just as the fatal knife was lifted up.

But if the Devil left Abraham, and made no attack upon him, seeing him invulnerable, he made himself amends upon the other branch of his family, his poor nephew, Lot; who, notwithstanding he was so immediately under the particular care of heaven, as that the angel who was sent to destroy Sodom could do nothing till he was out of it; and who, though after he had left Zoar, and was retired into a cave to dwell, yet the subtle Devil found him out, deluded his two daughters, took an advantage of the fright they had been in about Sodom

and Gomorrah, made them believe the whole world was burnt
too, as well as those cities, and that, in short, they could
never have any husbands, &c., and so in their abundant concern to repeople the world, and that the race of mankind
might not be destroyed, they go and lie with their own father;
the Devil telling them doubtless how to do it, by intoxicating
his head with wine; in all which story, whether they were
not as drunk as their father, seems to be a question, or else
they could not have supposed all the men in the earth were
consumed, when they knew that the little city Zoar had been
preserved for their sakes.

This now was the third conquest Satan obtained by the
gust of human appetite; that is to say, once by eating and
twice by drinking, or drunkenness, and still the last was the
worst and most shameful; for Lot, however his daughters
managed him, could not pretend he did not understand what
the strength of wine was; and one would have thought after
so terrible a judgment as that of Sodom was, which was, as
we may say, executed before his face, his thoughts should
have been too solemnly engaged in praising God for sparing
his life, to be made drunk, and that two nights together.

But the Devil played his game sure, he set his two daughters to work, and as the Devil's instruments seldom fail, so
he secured his by that hellish stratagem of deluding the
daughters to think all the world was consumed but they
two and their father: to be sure the old man could not suspect that his daughters' design was so wicked as indeed it
was, or that they intended to debauch him with wine, and
made him drink till he knew not what he did.

Now the Devil, having carried his game here, gained a
great point; for as there were but two religious families in
the world before, from whence a twofold generation might be
supposed to rise, religious and righteous like their parents,
viz., that of Abraham and this of Lot; this crime ruined the
hopes of one of them; it could no more be said that just Lot
was in being, who vexed his righteous soul from day to day
with the wicked behaviour of the people of Sodom; righteous
Lot was degenerated into drunken incestuous Lot; Lot, fallen
from what he was, to be a wicked and unrighteous man; no
pattern of virtue, no reprover of the age, but a poor fallen
degenerate patriarch, who could now no more reprove or
exhort, but look down and be ashamed, and had nothing to

do but to repent; and see the poor mean excuses of all the three :

Eve says, *The serpent beguiled me, and I did eat.*

Noah says, *My grandson beguiled me, or the wine beguiled me, and I did drink.*

Lot says, *My daughters beguiled me, and I also did drink.*

It is observable, that, as I said above, Noah was silenced, and his preaching at an end, after that one action, so the like may be said of Lot; and, in short, you never hear one word more of either of them after it; as for mankind, both were useless to them, and as to themselves, we never read of any of their repentance, nor have we much reason to believe they did repent.

From this attack of the Devil upon Lot, we hear no more of the Devil being so busily employed as he had been before in the world; he had indeed but little to do, for all the rest of the world was his own, lulled asleep under the witchcraft of idolatry, and are so still.

But it could not be long that the Devil lay idle : as soon as God called himself a people, the Devil could not be at rest till he attacked them.

> Wherever God sets up a house of prayer,
> The Devil always builds a chapel there.

'Abraham indeed went off the stage free, and so did Isaac too, they were a kind of first-rate saints ; we do not so much as read of any failing they had, or of anything the Devil had ever the face to offer to them ; no, or with Jacob either, if you will excuse him for beguiling his brother Esau, of both his birthright and his blessing, but he was busy enough with all his children : for example,—

He sent Judah to his sheep-shearing, and placed a whore (Tamar) in his way, in the posture of temptation, so made him commit incest and whoredom both together.

He sent incestuous Reuben to lie with his father's concubine, Billah.

He sent Dinah to the ball, to dance with the Sichemite ladies, and play the whore with their master.

He enraged Simeon and Levi, at the supposed injury, and then prompted them to revenge, for which their father heartily cursed them.

He sent them altogether to fall upon poor Joseph, first to

murder him intentionally, and then actually sell him to the Midianites.

He made them show the party coloured coat and tell a lie to their father, to make the poor old man believe Joseph was killed by a lion, &c.

He sent Potiphar's wife to attack Joseph's chastity, and filled her with rage at the disappointment.

He taught Joseph to swear by the life of Pharaoh.

In a word, he debauched the whole race, except Benjamin, and never man had such a set of sons, so wicked and so notorious, after so good an introduction into the world as they all of them had, to be sure; for Jacob, no doubt, gave them as good instruction as the circumstances of his wandering condition would allow him to do.

We must now consider the Devil and his affairs in a quite differing situation : when the world first appeared, peopled by the creating power of God, he had only Adam and Eve to take care of, and I think he plied his time with them to purpose enough ; after the Deluge he had Noah only to pitch upon, and he quickly conquered him by the instigation of his grandson.

At the building of Babel, he guided them by their acting all in a body as one man, so that in short, he managed them with ease, taking them as a body politic, and we find they came into his snare as one man ; but now, the children of Israel multiplying in the land of their bondage, and God seeming to show a particular concern for them, the Devil was obliged to new measures, stand at a distance, and look on for some time.

The Egyptians were plagued even without his help, nor though the cunning artist, as I said, stood and looked on, yet he durst not meddle; nor could he make a few lice, the least and meanest of the armies of insects raised to afflict the Egyptians.

However, when he perceived that God resolved to bring the Israelites out, he prepared to attend them, to watch them, and be at hand upon all the wicked occasions that might offer, as if he had been fully satisfied such occasions would offer, and that he should not fail to have an opportunity to draw them into some snare or another, and that therefore it was his business not to be out of the way, but to be ready, as we say, to make his market of them in the best manner he could: how many ways he attempted them, nay, how many times he conquered them in their journey, we shall see presently.

First, he put them in a fright at Baal-Zephon, where he thought he had drawn them into a noose, and where he sent Pharaoh and his army to block them up between the mountains of Piahiroth and the Red Sea; but there indeed Satan was outwitted by Moses, so far as it appeared to be a human action, for he little thought of their going dry-footed through the sea, but depended upon having them all cut in pieces the next morning, by the Egyptians; an eminent proof, by the way, that the Devil has no knowledge of events, or any insight into futurity; nay, that he has not so much as a second sight, or knows to-day what his Maker intends to do to-morrow; for had Satan known that God intended to ford them over the sea, if he had not been able to have prevented the miracle, he would certainly have prevented the escape, by sending out Pharaoh and his army time enough to have taken the strand before them, and so have driven them to the necessity of travelling on foot round the north point of that sea, by the wilderness of Etan, where he would have pursued and harassed them with his cavalry, and in all probability have destroyed them: but the blind short-sighted Devil, perfectly in the dark, and unacquainted with futurity, knew nothing of the matter, was as much deceived as Pharaoh himself, stood still, flattering himself with the hopes of his booty, and the revenge he should take upon them the next morning; till he saw the frighted waves in an uproar, and to his utter astonishment and confusion, saw the passage laid open, and Moses leading his vast army in full march over the dry space; nay, even then it is very probable Satan did not know, that if the Egyptians followed them, the sea would return upon and overwhelm them; for I can hardly think so hard of the Devil himself, that if he had, he would have suffered, much less prompted, Pharaoh to follow the chase at such an expense; so that either he must be an ignorant, unforeseeing Devil, or a very ungrateful false Devil to his friends the Egyptians.

I am inclined also to the more charitable opinion of Satan too, because the escape of the Israelites was really a triumph over himself; for the war was certainly his, or at least he was auxiliary to Pharaoh: it was a victory over hell and

Egypt together, and he would never have suffered the disgrace
if he had known it beforehand; that is to say, though he
could not have prevented the escape of Israel, or the dividing
the water, yet he might have warned the Egyptians, and
cautioned them not to venture in after them.

But we shall see a great many weak steps taken by the
Devil in the affair of this very people, and their forty years'
wandering in the wilderness; and though he was in some
things successful, and wheedled them into many foolish and
miserable murmurings and wrangling against God, and
mutinies against poor Moses, yet the Devil was oftentimes
baulked and disappointed; and it is for this reason, that I
choose to finish the first part of his history with the particular
relation of his behaviour among the Jews, because also, we
do not find any extraordinary things happening anywhere
else in the world, for above one thousand five hundred years;
no variety, no revolutions, all the rest of mankind lay still
under his yoke, quietly submitted to his government, did just
as he bade them, worshipped every idol he set up, and, in a
word, he had no difficulty with anybody but the Jews, and
for this reason, I say, this part of his story will be the more
useful and instructing.

To return, therefore, to Moses, and his dividing the Red
Sea: that the people went over or through it, that we have
the sacred history for; but how the Devil behaved, that you
must come to me for, or I know not where you will find a
true account of it, at least not in print.

1. It was in the night they marched through; whether the
Devil saw it in the dark or no, that's not my business.

But when he had daylight for it, and viewed the next day's
work, I make no question but all Hell felt the surprise, the
prey being thus snatched out of their hands unexpectedly.
It is true, the Egyptian host was sent to him in their room,
but that was not what he aimed at; for he was sure enough
of them his own way, and if it was not just at that time, yet
he knew what and who they were; but as he had devoured
the whole Israelitish host in his imagination, to the tune of at
least a million and a half of souls; men, women, and children;
it was, no doubt, a great disappointment to the Devil to miss
of his prey, and to see them all triumphing on the other side
in safety.

. It is true, Satan's annals do not mention this defeat, for historians are generally backward to register their own misfortunes ; but as we have an account of the fact from other hands, so as we cannot. question the truth of it, the nature of the thing will tell us it was a disappointment to the Devil, and a very great one too.

I cannot but observe here, that I think this part of the Devil's story very entertaining, because of the great variety of incidents which appear in every part of it ; sometimes he is like a hunted fox, curveting and counter-running to avoid his being pursued and found out, while, at the same time, he is carrying on his secret designs to draw the people he pretends to manage, into some snare or other to their hurt ; at another time, though the comparison is a little too low for his dignity, like a monkey that has done mischief, and who, making his own escape, sits and chatters at a distance, as if he had triumphed in what he had done ; so Satan, when he had drawn them in to worship a calf, to offer strange fire, to set up a schism, and the like, and so to bring the divine vengeance upon themselves, leaving them in their distress, kept at a distance, as if he looked on with satisfaction to see them burned, swallowed up, swept away, and the like ; as the several stories relate.

His indefatigable vigilance is, on the other hand, a useful caveat, as well as an improving view to us ; no sooner is he routed and exposed, defeated and disappointed in one enterprise, but he begins another, and, like a cunning gladiator, warily defends himself and boldly attacks his enemy at the same time. Thus we see him, up and down, conquering and conquered, through this whole part of his story, till at last, he receives a total defeat, of which you shall hear in its place ; in the mean time, let us take up his story again at the Red Sea, where he received a great blow, instead of which he, expected a complete victory ; for, doubtless the Devil, and the King of Egypt too, thought of nothing but conquest at Piahiroth.

However, though the triumph of the Israelites over the Egyptians must needs be a great mortification to the Devil, and exasperated him very much. yet the consequence was only this, viz,, that Satan, like an enemy who is baulked and defeated, but not overcome, redoubles his rage, and re-enforces his army, and what the Egyptians could not do for him, he resolves to do for himself ; in order then to take his opportunity for what mischief might offer, being defeated, and provoked, I say, at the slur that was put upon him, he resolves to follow them into the wilderness, and many a vile prank he played them there; as first, he straitens them for water, and makes them murmur against God, and against Moses, within a very few days, nay, hours, of their great deliverance of all.

Nor was this all; but in less than one year more, we find them (at his instigation too), setting up a golden calf, and making all the people dance about it at mount Sinai; even when God himself had but just before appeared to them in the terrors of a burning fire upon the top of the mountain; and what was the pretence? Truly, nothing but that they had lost Moses, who used to be their guide, and he had hid himself in the mount, and had not been seen in forty days, so that they could not tell what was become of him. This put them all into confusion; a poor pretence, indeed, to turn them all back to idolatry! but the watchful Devil took the hint, pushed the advantage, and insinuated that they should never see Moses again, that he was certainly devoured by venturing too near the flashes of fire in the mount, and presuming upon the liberty he had taken before; in a word, that God had destroyed Moses, or he was starved to death for want of food, having been forty days and forty nights absent.

All these were, it is true, in themselves most foolish suggestions, considering Moses was admitted to the vision of God, and that God had been pleased to appear to him in the most intimate manner; that as they might depend God would not destroy his faithful servant, so they might have concluded he was able to support his being without food as long as he thought fit; but to a people so easy to believe anything, what could be too gross for the Devil to persuade them to?

A people who could dance round a calf, and call it their god, might do anything; that could say to one another, that this was the great Jehovah *that brought them out of the land of Egypt;* and that within so few days after God's miraculous appearance to them, and for them; I say, such a people were really fitted to be imposed upon, nothing could be too gross for them.

This was, indeed, his first considerable experiment upon them as a people, or as a body; and the truth is, his affairs required it, for Satan, who has been a successful devil in

most of his attempts upon mankind, could hardly doubt of
success in anything after he had carried his point at mount
Sinai: to bring them to idolatry in the very face of their de-
liverer, and just after their deliverance! It was more
astonishing, in the main, than even their passing the Red Sea.
In a word, the Devil's whole history does not furnish us with
a story equally surprising.

And how was poor Aaron bewildered in it too? He that
was Moses's partner in all the great things that Moses did in
Pharaoh's sight, and that was appointed to be his assistant
and oracle, or orator rather, upon all public occasions; that
he, above all the rest, should come into this absurd and
ridiculous proposal, he that was singled out for the sacred
priesthood; for him to defile his holy hands with a polluted
abominable sacrifice, and with making the idol for them too,
(for it is plain that he made it), how monstrous was it!

And see what an answer he gives to his brother Moses;
how weak! how simple! I did so and so, indeed, I bade them
bring the earrings, &c., and I cast the gold into the fire, and
it came out this calf. Ridiculous! as if the calf came out by
mere fortuitous adventure, without a mould to cast it in;
which could not be supposed; and if it had not come out so
without a mould, Moses would certainly have known of it.
Had Aaron been innocent, he would have answered after quite
another manner, and told Moses honestly that the whole body
of the people came to him in a fright, that they forced him to
make them an idol; which he did, by making first a proper
mould to cast it in, and then taking the proper metal to cast it
from; that indeed he had sinned in so doing, but that he was
mobbed into it, and the people terrified him, perhaps they
threatened to kill him; and if he had added, that the Devil,
prompting his fear, beguiled him, he had said nothing but
what was certainly true; for if it was in Satan's power to
make the people insolent and outrageous enough to threaten
and bully the old venerable prophet (for he was not yet a
priest) who was the brother of their oracle, Moses, and had
been partner with him in so many of his commissions; I say,
if he could bring up the passions of the people to a height to
be rude and unmannerly to him (Aaron), and perhaps to
threaten and insult him, he may be easily supposed to be able
to intimidate Aaron, and terrify him into a compliance.

See this cunning agent, when he has man's destruction in

his view, how securely he acts! he never wants a handle; the best of men have one weak place or other, and he always finds it out, takes the advantage of it, and conquers them by one artifice or another; only, take it with you as you go, it is always by stratagem, never by force; a proof that he is not empowered to use violence. He may tempt, and he does prevail; but it is all legerdemain, it is all craft and artifice, he is still Διαβολή, the calumniator and deceiver, that is, the misrepresenter; he misrepresents man to God, and misrepresents God to man; also he misrepresents things; he puts false colours, and then manages the eye to see them with an imperfect view, raising clouds and fogs to intercept our sight; in short, he deceives all our senses, and imposes upon us in things which otherwise would be the easiest to discern and judge of.

This, indeed, is in part the benefit of the Devil's history, to let us see that he has used the same method all along; and that ever since he has had anything to do with mankind, he has practised upon them with stratagem and cunning; also it is observable that he has carried his point better that way than he would have done by fury and violence, if he had been allowed to make use of it; for, by his power indeed he might have laid the world desolate, and made a heap of rubbish of it long ago. But, as I have observed before, that would not have answered his ends half so well, for by destroying men he would have made martyrs, and sent abundance of good men to heaven, who would much rather have died than yielded to serve him, and, as he aimed to have it, to fall down and worship him; I say, he would have made martyrs, and that not a few; but this was none of Satan's business; his design lies quite another way; his business is to make men sin, not to make them suffer; to make devils of them, not saints; to delude them, and draw them away from their Maker, not send them away to him; and there fore he works by stratagem, not by force.

We are now come to his story, as it relates to the Jewish church in the wilderness, and to the children of Israel in their travelling circumstances; and this was the first scene of public management that the Devil had upon his hands in the world; for, as I have said, till now, he dealt with mankind either in their separate condition, one by one, or else carried all before him, engrossing whole nations in his systems

of idolatry, and overwhelming them in an ignorant destruction.

But having now a whole people, as it were, snatched away
from him, taken out of his government, and, which was still
worse, having a view of a kingdom being set up independent
of him, and superior to his authority, it is not to be wondered
at if he endeavoured to overthrow them in the infancy of
their constitution, and tried all possible arts to bring them
back into his own hands again.

He found them not only carried away from the country
where they were even in his clutches, surrounded with idols,
and where we have reason to believe the greatest part of them
were polluted with the idolatry of the Egyptians; for we do
not read of any stated worship which they had of their own,
or if they did worship the true God, we scarce know in what
manner they did it; they had no law given them, nothing
but the covenant of circumcision, and even Moses himself
had not strictly observed that, till he was frightened into it;
we read of no sacrifices among them, no feasts were ordained,
no solemn worship appointed, and how, or in what manner
they performed their homage, we know not; the Passover
was not ordained till just at their coming away; so that there
was not much religion among them, at least that we have
any account of; and we may suppose the Devil was pretty
easy with them all the while they were in the house of their
bondage.

But now, to have a million of people fetched out of his
hands, as it were all at once, and to have the immediate
power of heaven engaged in it, and that Satan saw evidently
God had singled' them out in a miraculous manner to favour
them, and call them his own; this alarmed him at once, and
therefore he resolves to follow them, lay close siege to them,
and take all the measures possible to bring them to rebel
against, and disobey God, that he might be provoked to
destroy them; and how near he went to bring it to pass, we
shall see presently.

This making a calf, and paying an idolatrous worship to
it (for they acted the heathens and idolaters, not in the setting
up the calf only, but in the manner of their worshipping, viz.,
dancing and music, things they had not been acquainted with
in the worship of the true God) I mention here, to observe
how the Devil not only imposed upon their principles, but

upon their senses too; as if the awful majesty of heaven, whose glory they had seen in mount Sinai, where they stood, and whose pillar of cloud and fire was their guide and protection, would be worshipped by dancing round a calf! and that not a living creature, or a real calf, but the mere image of a calf cast in gold, or, as some think, in brass gilded over.

But this was the Devil's way with mankind, namely, to impose upon their senses, and bring them into the grossest follies and absurdities; and then having first made them fools, it was much the easier to make them offenders.

In this very manner he acted with them through all the course of their wilderness travels; for, as they were led by the hand like children, defended by omnipotence, fed by miracles, instructed immediately from heaven, and in all things had Moses for their guide, they had no room to miscarry, but by acting the greatest absurdities, and committing the greatest follies in nature; and even these the Devil brought them to be guilty of in a surprising manner: 1. As God himself relieved them in every exigence, and supplied them in every want, one would think it was impossible they should be ever brought to question either his willingness or his ability, and yet they really objected against both; which was indeed very provoking, and I doubt not, that when the Devil had brought them to act in such a preposterous manner, he really hoped and believed God would be provoked effectually. The testimonies of his care of them, and ability to supply them were miraculous and undeniable; he gave them water from the rock, bread from the air, sent the fowls to feed them with flesh, and supported them all the way by miracles; their health was preserved, none were sick among them, their clothes did not wear out, nor the shoes grow old upon their feet; could anything be more absurd, than to doubt whether he could provide for them, who had never let them want for so many years.

But the Devil managed them in spite of miracle; nor did he ever give them over till he had brought six hundred thousand of them to provoke God so highly that he would not suffer above two of them to go into the land of promise; so that, in short, Satan gained his point as to that generation, for all their carcases fell in the wilderness. Let us take but a short view to what a height he brought them, and in what a rude, absurd manner they acted; how he set them upon murmuring upon every occasion, now for water, then for bread : nay, they murmured at their bread when they had it ; *Our soul loathes this light bread.*

He sowed the seeds of church rebellion in the sons of Aaron, and made Nadab and Abihu offer strange fire till they were strangely consumed by fire for the doing it.

He set them complaining at Taberah ; and a lusting for flesh at the first three days' journey from mount Sinai.

He planted envy in the hearts of Miriam and Aaron against the authority of Moses, to pretend God had spoken by them as well as by him, till he humbled the father, and made a leper of the daughter.

He debauched ten of the spies, frightened them with sham appearances of things, when they went out to search the land, and made them frighten the whole people out of their understanding, as well as duty, for which six hundred thousand of their carcases fell in the wilderness

He raised the rebellion of Korah and the two hundred and fifty princes, till he brought them to be swallowed up alive.

He put Moses into a passion at Meribah, and ruffled the temper of the meekest man upon earth, by which he made both him and Aaron forfeit their share of the promise, and be shut out from the Holy Land.

He raised a mutiny among them when they travelled from mount Hor, till they brought fiery serpents among them to destroy them.

He tried to make Balaam the prophet curse them ; but there the Devil was disappointed ; however, he brought the Midianites to debauch them with women, as in the case of Zimri and Cosbi.

He tempted Achan with the wedge of gold and the Babylonish garment, that he might take of the accursed thing and be destroyed.

He tempted the whole people not effectually to drive out the cursed inhabitants of the land of promise, that they might remain and be goads in their sides, till at last they often oppressed them for their idolatry, and, which was worse, debauched them to idolatry.

He prompted the Benjamites to refuse satisfaction to the people in the case of the wickedness of the men of Gibeah, to the destruction of the whole tribe, four hundred men ex cepted, in the rock Rimmon.   •

At last he tempted them to reject the theocracy of their Maker, and call upon Samuel to make them a king; and most of those kings he made plagues and sorrows to them in their time, as you shall hear in their order.

Thus he plagued the whole body of the people continually, making them sin against God, and bring judgments upon themselves, to the consuming some millions of them, first and last, by the vengeance of their Maker.

As he did with the whole congregation, so he did with their rulers and several of the judges who were made instruments to deliver the people, yet were drawn into snares by this subtle serpent to ruin themselves or the people they had delivered.

He tempted Gideon to make an ephod, contrary to the law of the tabernacle, and made the children of Israel go a whoring (that is, a worshipping) after it.

He tempted Samson to debauch himself with a harlot, and betray his own happy secret to a whore, at the expense of both his eyes, and at last of his life.

He tempted Eli's sons to lie with the women in the very doors of the tabernacle, when they came to bring their offerings to the priest; and he tempted poor Eli to connive at them, or not sufficiently reprove them.

He tempted the people to carry the ark of God into the camp, that it might fall into the hands of the Philistines. And

He tempted Uzzi to reach out his hand to hold it up; as if he that had preserved in the house of Dagon, the idol of the Philistines, could not keep it from falling out of a cart.

When the people had gotten a king, he immediately set to work in divers ways to bring that king to load them with plagues and calamities, not a few.

He tempted Saul to spare the king of Amalek, contrary to God's express command.

He not tempted Saul only, but possessed him with an evil spirit, by which he was left to wayward dispositions, and was forced to have it fiddled out of him with a minstrel.

He tempted Saul with a spirit of discontent, and with a spirit of envy at poor David, to hunt him like a partridge upon the mountains.

He tempted Saul with a spirit of divination, and sent him to a witch to inquire of Samuel for him; as if God would help him when he was dead, that had forsaken him when he was alive.

After that, he tempted him to kill himself, on a pretence that he might not fall into the hands of the uncircumcised; as if self-murder was not half so bad, either for sin against God, or disgrace among men, as being taken prisoner by a Philistine! A piece of madness none but the Devil could have brought mankind to submit to, though, some ages' after that he made it a fashion among the Romans.

After Saul was dead, and David come to the throne, by how much he was a man chosen and particularly favoured by heaven, the Devil fell upon him with the more vigour, attacked him so many ways, and conquered him so very often, that, as no man was so good a king, so hardly any good king was ever a worse man; in many cases one would have almost thought the Devil had made sport with David, to show how easily he could overthrow the best man God could choose of the whole congregation.

He made him distrust his benefactor so much as to feign himself mad before the king of Gath, when he had fled to him for shelter.

He made him march with his four hundred cut-throats, to cut off poor Nabal, and all his household, only because he would not send him the good cheer he had provided for his honest sheep-shearers.

He made him, for his word's sake, give Ziba half his master's estate for his treachery, after he knew he had been the traitor, and betrayed poor Mephibosheth for the sake of it; in which,

> The good old king, it seems, was very loath
> To break his word, and therefore broke his oath.

Then he tempted him to the ridiculous project of numbering the people, though against God's express command; a thing Joab himself was not wicked enough to do, till David and the Devil forced him to it.

And, to make him completely wicked, he carried him to the top of his house, and showed him a naked lady bathing herself in her garden, in which it appeared that the Devil knew David too well, and what was the particular sin of his inclination; and so took him by the right handle, drawing him at once into the sins of murder and adultery.

Then, that he might not quite give him over (though David's repentance for the last sin kept the Devil off for a while), when he could attack him no farther personally, he fell upon him in his family, and made him as miserable as he could desire him to be, in his children, three of whom he brought to destruction before his face, and another after his death.

First, he tempted Amnon to ravish his sister Tamar; so there was an end of her (poor girl!) as to this world, for we never hear any more of her.

Then he tempted Absalom to murder his brother Amnon, in revenge for Tamar's maidenhead.

Then he made Joab run Absalom through the body, contrary to David's command.

And, after David's death, he brought Adonijah (weak man!) to the block, for usurping King Solomon's throne.

As to Absalom, he tempted him to rebellion, and raising war against his father, to the turning him shamefully out of Jerusalem, and almost out of the kingdom.

He tempted him, for David's farther mortification, to lie with his father's wives, in the face of the whole city; and had Ahithophel's honest counsel been followed, he had certainly sent him to sleep with his fathers long before his time. But there Satan and Ahithophel were both outwitted together.

Through all the reigns of the several successors of David, the Devil took care to carry on his own game, to the continual insulting the measures which God himself had taken for the establishing his people in the world, and especially as a church; till, at last, he so effectually debauched them to idolatry, that crime, which, of all others, was most provoking to God, as it was carrying the people away from their allegiance, and transposing the homage they owed God their Maker, to a contemptible block of wood, or an image of a brute beast; and this, how sordid and brutish soever it was in itself, yet so did his artifice prevail among them, that, first or last, he brought them all into it, the ten tribes as well as the two tribes; till, at last, God himself was provoked to unchurch them, give them up to their enemies; and the few that were left of them, after incredible slaughters and desolation, were hurried away, some into Tartary, and others into Babylon; from whence very few, of that few that were carried away, ever found their way home again; and some, when they might have come, would not accept of it, but con-

tinued there to the very coming of the Messiah.   See epistles
of St. James and of St. Peter, at the beginning.

But to look a little back upon this part (for it cannot be
omitted, it makes so considerable a part of the Devil's history), I mean his drawing God's people, kings, and all, into
all the sins and mischiefs which gradually contributed to their
destruction.

First (for he began immediately with the very best and
wisest of the race), he drew in King Solomon, in the midst
of all his zeal for the building God's house, and for the
making the most glorious and magnificent appearance for
God's worship that ever the world saw; I say, in the middle of
all this, he drew him into such immoderate and insatiable an
appetite for women, as to set up the first, and, perhaps, the
greatest seraglio of whores that ever any prince in the world
had, or pretended to before : nay, and to bring whoring so
much into reputation, that, as the text says, seven hundred
of them were princesses, that is to say, ladies of quality;
not as the grand seigniors, and great moguls (other princes of
the eastern world), have since practised, namely, to pick up
their most beautiful slaves; but these, it seems, were women
of rank, kings' daughters, as Pharaoh's daughters, and the
daughters of the princes and prime men among the Moabites,
Ammonites, Zidonians, Hittites, &c.—1 Kings xi. 1.

Nor was this all; but as he drew him into the love of
these forbidden women (for such they were, as to their nation
as well as number), so he ensnared him by those women to a
familiarity with their worship; and, by degrees, brought
that famous prince (famous for his wisdom) to be the greatest,
and most-imposed-upon old fool in the world; bowing down
to those idols, by the enticings of his whores, whom he had
abhorred and detested in his youth, as dishonouring that God
for whom, and for whose worship, he had finished and dedicated the most magnificent building and temple in the
world.   Nothing but the invincible subtlety of this archdevil
could ever have brought such a man as Solomon to such a
degeneracy of manners, and to such meannesses: no, not the
Devil himself, without the assistance of his whores, nor the
whores themselves, without the Devil to help them.

As to Solomon, Satan had made conquest enough there,
we need hear no more of him; the next advance he made
was in the person of his son Rehoboam; had not the Devil

E E 2

prompted his pride and tyrannical humour, he would never have given the people such an answer as he did; and when he saw a fellow at the head of them too, whom he knew wanted and waited for an occasion to raise a rebellion, and had ripened up the people's humour to the occasion. Well might the text call it 'listening to the counsel of the young heads:' that it was, indeed, with a vengeance! but those young heads too, were acted by an old Devil, who, for his craft, is called, as I have observed, the *old serpent.*

Having thus paved the way, Jeroboam revolts. So far God had directed him; for the text says expressly, speaking in the first person of God himself, *This thing is of me.*

But though God might appoint Jeroboam to be king (that is to say, of ten tribes), yet God did not appoint him to set up the two calves in the two extreme parts of the land, viz., in Dan and in Bethel; that was Jeroboam's own doing, and done on purpose to keep the people from falling back to Rehoboam, by being obliged to go to Jerusalem to the public worship; and the text adds, *Jeroboam made Israel to sin.* This was, indeed, a masterpiece of the Devil's policy, and it was effectual to answer the end; nothing could have been more to the purpose : what reason he had to expect the people would so universally come into it, and be so well satisfied with a couple of calves, instead of the true worship of God at Jerusalem, or what arts and management he (Satan) made use of afterwards, to bring the people in, to join with such a delusion, that we find but little of in all the annals of Satan, nor is it much to the case. It is certain the Devil found a strange kind of propensity to worshipping idols rooted in the temper of that whole people, even from their first breaking away from the Egyptian bondage; so that he had nothing to do but to work upon the old stock, and propagate the crime that he found was so natural to them. And this is Satan's general way of working, not with them only, but with us also, and with all the world, even then, and ever since.

When he had thus secured Jeroboam's revolt, we need not trace him among his successors; for the same reason of state that held for the setting up the calves at Bethel and Dan, held good for the keeping them up to all Jeroboam's posterity; nor had they one good king ever after; even Jehu, who called his friends to come and see his zeal for the Lord, and who fulfilled the threatenings of God upon Ahab

and his family, and upon Queen Jezebel and her offspring,
and knew all the while that he was executing the judgment
of the true God upon an idolatrous race; yet he would not
part with his calves, but would have thought it to have been
parting with his kingdom, and that as the people would have
gone up to Jerusalem to worship, so they would at the same
time have transferred their civil obedience to the King of
Judah, whose right it really was, as far as they could claim
by birth and right line; so that, by the way, Satan any more
than other politicians, is not for the *jus divinum* of lineal succession, or what we call hereditary right, any farther than
serves for his purpose.

Thus Satan ridded his hands of ten of the twelve tribes;
let us now see how he went on with the rest, for his work
was now brought into a narrower compass: the church of
God was now reduced to two tribes, except a few religious
people, who separated from the schism of Jeroboam, and
came and planted themselves among the tribes of Judah and
Benjamin; the first thing the Devil did after this, was to
foment a war between the two kings, while Judah was
governed by a boy or youth, Abijah by name, and he none of
the best neither; but God's time was not come, and the Devil
received a great disappointment, when Jeroboam was so
entirely overthrown, that if the records of those ages do not
mistake, no less than five hundred thousand men of Israel
were killed; such a slaughter, that one would think the army
of Judah, had they known how to improve as well as gain a
victory, might have brought all the rest back again, and have
entirely reduced the house of Jeroboam, and the ten tribes
that followed him, to their obedience; nay, they did take a
great deal of the country from him, and amongst the rest,
Bethel itself; and yet so cunningly did Satan manage, that
the king of Judah, who was himself a wicked king, and perhaps
an idolater in his heart, did not take down the golden calf
that Jeroboam had there, no, nor destroy the idolatry itself,
so that, in short, his victory signified nothing.

From hence to the captivity, we find the Devil busy with
the kings of Judah, especially the best of them; as for such
as Manasseh and those who transgressed by the general tenor
of their lives, those he had no great trouble with.

But such as Asa, Jehoshaphat, Hezekiah, and Josiah, he

hung about them and their courts, till he brought every one
of them into some mischief or another.

As first, good king Asa, of whom the scripture says, *his
heart was perfect all his days*, yet the subtle spirit, that could
break in upon him nowhere else, tempted him when the king
of Israel came out against him, to send to hire Benhadad
the king of Syria to help him; as if God, who had before
enabled him to conquer the Ethiopians, with an army of ten
hundred thousand men, could not have saved him from the
king of the ten tribes.

In the same manner he tempted Jehoshaphat to join with
that wicked king Ahab against the king of Syria, and also to
marry his son to Ahab's daughter, which was fatal to
Jehoshaphat, and to his posterity.

Again, he tempted Hezekiah to show all his riches to the
king of Babylon's messengers; and who can doubt, but that
he (Satan) is to be understood by the wicked spirit which
stood before the Lord, 2 Chron. xviii. 20, and offered his
service to entice Ahab the king of Israel to come out to battle
to his ruin, by being a lying spirit in the mouths of all his
prophets; and who for that time had a special commission,
as he had another time in the case of Job? and indeed it was
a commission fit for nobody but the Devil; *Thou shalt entice
him, and thou shalt also prevail; go out and do even so*, ver. 21.

Even good Josiah himself, of whom it is recorded, that
*like him there was no king before him, neither after him arose there
any like him*, 2 Kings xxiii. 25, yet the Devil never left him
with his machinations, till finding he could not tempt him to
anything wicked in his government, he tempted or moved
him to a needless war with the king of Egypt, in which he
lost his life.

From the death of this good king, the Devil prevailed so
with the whole nation of the Jews, and brought them to such
an incorrigible pitch of wickedness that God gave them up,
forsook his habitation of glory, the temple, which he suffered
to be spoiled first, then burnt and demolished; destroying the
whole nation of the Jews, except a small number that were
left, and those the enemy carried away into captivity.

Nor was he satisfied with this general destruction of the
whole people of Israel (for the ten tribes were gone before),
but he followed them even into their captivity; those that

fled away to Egypt, which they tell us were seventy thousand, he first corrupted, and then they were destroyed there upon the overthrow of Egypt, by the same king of Babylon.

Also he went very near to have them rooted out, young and old, man, woman, and child, who were in captivity in Babylon, by the ministry of that true agent of hell, Haman the Agagite; but there Satan met with a disappointment too, as in the story of Esther, which was but the fourth that he had met with in all his management since the creation; I say, there he was disappointed, and his prime minister Haman was exalted, as he deserved.

Having thus far traced the government and dominion of the Devil, from the creation of man to the captivity, I think I may call upon him to set up his standard of universal empire, at that period: it seemed just then as if God had really forsaken the earth, and given the entire dominion of mankind up to his outrageous enemy the Devil; for excepting the few Israelites which were left in the territories of the king of Babylon, and they were but a few; I say, except among them, there was not one corner of the world left where the true God was called upon, or his dominion so much as acknowledged; all the world was buried in idolatry, and that of so many horrid kinds, that one would think the light of reason should have convinced mankind, that he who exacted such bloody sacrifices as that of Moloch, and such a bloody cutting themselves with knives, as the priests of Baal did, could not be a god, a good and benificent being, but must be a cruel, voracious, and devouring devil, whose end was not the good, but the destruction of his creatures: but to such a height was the blind demented world arrived to at that time, that in these sordid and corrupt ways, they went on worshipping dumb idols, and offering human sacrifices to them, and in a word, committing all the most horrid and absurd abominations that they were capable of, or that the Devil could prompt them to, till Heaven was again put as it were to the necessity of bringing about a revolution, in favour of his own forsaken people, by miracle and surprise, as he had done before.

We come therefore to the restoration or return from the captivity: had Satan been able to have acted anything by force, as I have observed before, all the princes and powers of the world, having been, as they really were, at his devotion, he might easily have made use of them, armed all the world against the Jews, and prevented the rebuilding the temple, and even the return of the captivity.

But now the Devil's power manifestly received a check, and the hand of God appeared in it, and that he was resolved to re-establish his people the Jews, and to have a second temple built: the Devil who knew the extent of his own power too well, and what limitations were laid upon him, stood still, as it were looking on, and not daring to oppose the return of the captivity, which he very well knew had been prophesied, and would come to pass.

He did indeed make some little opposition to the building, and to the fortifying the city, but as it was to no purpose, so he was soon obliged to give it over; and thus the captivity being returned, and the temple rebuilt, the people of the Jews increased and multiplied to an infinite number and strength; and from this time, we may say the power of the Devil rather declined and decreased, than went on with success, as it had done before; it is true the Jews fell into sects and errors, and divisions of many kinds, after the return from the captivity, and no doubt the Devil had a great hand in those divisions; but he could never bring them back to idolatry, and his not being able to do that, made him turn his hand so many ways to plague and oppress them; as particularly by Antiochus the Great, who brought the abomination of desolation into the holy place; and there the Devil triumphed over them for some time; but they were delivered many ways, till at last they came peaceably under the protection, rather than the dominion, of the Roman empire; when Herod the Great governed them as a king, and re-edified, nay, almost rebuilt their temple, with so great an expense and magnificence, that he made it, as some say, greater and more glorious than that of Solomon's, though that I take to be a great—fable, to say no worse of it.

In this condition the Jewish church stood, when the fulness of time, as it is called in Scripture, was come; and the Devil was kept at bay, though he had made some encroachments upon them as above; for there was a glorious remnant of saints among them, such as old Zacharias, the father of John the Baptist, and old Simeon, who waited for the salvation of Israel; I say, in this condition the Jewish church stood when the Messiah came into the world, which was such another mortal stab to the thrones and principalities infernal, as that of which I have spoken already in chap. iii. at the creation of man; and therefore with this I break off the antiquities of the Devil's history, or the ancient part of his kingdom; for from hence downward we shall find his empire has declined gradually; and though by his wonderful address, his prodigious application, and the vigilance and fidelity of his instruments, as well human as infernal and diabolical, and of the human, as well the ecclesiastic as the secular, he has many times retrieved what he has lost, and sometimes bid fair for recovering the universal empire he once possessed over mankind, yet he has still been defeated again, repulsed and beaten back, and his kingdom has greatly declined in many parts of the world; and especially in the northern parts, except Great Britian; and how he has politically maintained his interest, and increased his dominion among the wise and righteous generation that we cohabit with and among, will be the subject of the modern part of Satan's history, and of which we are next to give an account.

THE MODERN

HISTORY OF THE DEVIL.

PART II.

CHAPTER I.

I HAVE examined the antiquites of Satan's history in the former part of this work, and brought his affairs down from the creation, as far as to our blessed Christian times; especially to the coming of the Messiah, when one would think the Devil could have nothing to do among us. I have indeed but touched at some things which might have admitted of a farther description of Satan's affairs, and the particulars of which we may all come to a farther knowledge of hereafter; yet I think I have spoken to the material part of his conduct, as it relates to his empire in this world; what has happened to his more sublimated government, and his angelic capacities, I shall have an occasion to touch at in several solid particulars as we go along.

The Messiah was now born, *the fulness of time was come*, that the old serpent was to have his head broken; that is to say, his empire or dominion over man, which he gained by the fall of our first father and mother in Paradise, received a downfall or overthrow.

It is worth observing, in order to confirm what I have already mentioned of the limitation of Satan's power, that not only his angelic. strength seems to have received a farther blow upon the coming of the Son of God into the world, but he seems to have had a blow upon his intellects; his serpentine craft and devil-like subtilty seems to have been circumscribed and cut short; and instead of his being so cunning a fellow as before, when, as I said, it is evident he outwitted all mankind, not only Eve, Cain, Noah, Lot, and all the patriarchs, but even nations of men, and that in their public capacity, and thereby led them into absurd and ridiculous things, such as the building of Babel, and deifying and worshipping their kings, when dead and rotten; idolizing beasts, stocks, stones, anything, and even nothing; and, in a word, when he managed mankind just as he pleased.

Now, and from this time forward, he appeared a weak, foolish, ignorant devil, compared to what he was before; he was upon almost every occasion resisted, disappointed, balked and defeated, especially in all his attempts to thwart or cross the mission and ministry of the Messiah, while he was upon earth, and sometimes upon other and very mean occasions too.

And first, how foolish a project was it, and how below Satan's celebrated artifice in like cases, to put Herod upon sending to kill the poor innocent children in Bethlehem, in hopes to destroy the infant? for I take it for granted, it was the Devil put into Herod's thoughts that execution, how simple and foolish soever; now we must allow him to be very ignorant of the nativity himself, or else he might easily have guided his friend Herod to the place where the infant was.

This shows that either the Devil is in general ignorant as we are, of what is to come in the world, before it is really come to pass, and consequently can foretel nothing, no, not so much as our famous old Merlin or Mother Shipton did, or else that great event was hid from him by an immediate power superior to his, which I cannot think neither, considering how much he was concerned in it, and how certainly he knew that it was once to come to pass.

But be that as it will, it is certain the Devil knew nothing where Christ was born, or when; nor was he able to direct Herod to find him out, and therefore put him upon that foolish, as well as cruel order, to kill all the children, that he might be sure to destroy the Messiah among the rest.

The next simple step that the Devil took, and, indeed, the most foolish one that he could ever be charged with, unworthy the very dignity of a devil, and below the understanding that he always was allowed to act with, was that of coming to tempt the Messiah in the wilderness; it is certain, and he owned it himself afterwards upon many occasions, that the

Devil knew our Saviour to be the Son of God; and it is as certain that he knew, that as such he could have no power or advantage over him; how foolish then was it in him to attack him in that manner, *If thou beest the Son 'of God!* why he knew him to be the Son of God well enough; he said so afterwards, *I know thee, who thou art, the holy one of God;* how then could he be so weak a devil as to say, If thou art, then do so and so?

The case is plain, the Devil, though he knew him to be the Son of God, did not fully know the mystery of the incarnation; nor did he know how far the inanition of Christ extended, and whether as man, he was not subject to fall, as Adam was, though his reserved Godhead might be still immaculate and pure; and upon this foot, as he would leave no method untried, he attempts him three times, one immediately after another; but then, finding himself disappointed, he fled.

This evidently proves that the Devil was ignorant of *the great mystery of godliness,* as the text calls it, *God manifest in the flesh;* and therefore made that foolish attempt upon Christ, thinking to have conquered his human nature, as capable of sin, which it was not; and at this repulse hell groaned, the whole army of regimented devils received a wound, and felt the shock of it; it was a second overthrow to them, they had had a long chain of success, carried a devilish conquest over the greatest part of the creation of God; but now they were cut short, *the seed of the woman* was now come *to break the serpent's head,* that is, to cut short his power, to contract the limits of his kingdom, and, in a word, to dethrone him in the world: no doubt the Devil received a shock, for you find him always afterwards crying out in a horrible manner, whenever Christ met with him, or else very humble and submissive, as when he begged leave to go into the herd of swine, a thing he has often done since.

Defeated here, the first stratagem I find him concerned in after it, was his entering into Judas, and putting him upon betraying Christ to the chief priest; but here again he was entirely mistaken, for he did not see, as much a devil as he was, what the event would be; but when he came to know, that if Christ was put to death he would become a propitiatory, and be the great sacrifice of mankind, so to rescue the fallen race from that death they had incurred the penalty of by the fall, that this was the fulfilling of all Scripture prophecy, and that thus it was that Christ was to be *the end of the law;* I say, as soon as he perceived this, he strove all he could to prevent it, and disturbed Pilate's wife in her sleep, in order to set her upon her husband to hinder his delivering him up to the Jews; for then, and not till then, he knew how Christ was to vanquish hell by the power of his cross.

Thus the Devil was disappointed and exposed in every step he took; and as he now plainly saw his kingdom declining, and even the temporal kingdom of Christ rising up upon the ruins of his (Satan's) power, he seemed to retreat into his own region, the air, and to consult there with his fellow devils, what measures he should take next to preserve his dominion among men; here it was that he resolved upon that truly hellish thing called Persecution, by which, though he proved a foolish devil in that too, he flattered himself he should be able to destroy God's church, and root out its professors from the earth, even almost as soon as it was established; whereas, on the contrary, Heaven counteracted him there too, and though he armed the whole Roman empire against the Christians, that is to say, the whole world, and they were fallen upon everywhere, with all the fury and rage of some of the most flaming tyrants that the world ever saw, of whom Nero was the first; yet, in spite of hell, God made all the blood which the Devil caused to be spilt, to be *semen ecclesiæ,* and the Devil had the mortification to see that the number of Christians increased, even under the very means he made use of to root them out and destroy them; this was the case through the reign of all the Roman emperors for the first three hundred years after Christ.

Having thus tried all the methods that best suited his inclination, I mean those of blood and death, complicated with tortures and all kinds of cruelty, and that for so long a stage of time as above; the Devil, all on a sudden, as if glutted with blood, and satiated with destruction, sits still and becomes a peaceable spectator for a good while; as if he either found himself unable, or had no disposition to hinder the progress of Christianity in the first ages of its settlement in the world; in this interval the Christian church was established under Constantine, religion flourished in peace, and under the most perfect tranquillity; the Devil seemed to be at a loss what he should do next, and things began to look as if Satan's kingdom was at an end; but he soon let them see that he was the same indefatigable devil that ever he was, and the prosperity of the church gave him a large field of action; for knowing the disposition of mankind to quarrel and dispute, the universal passion rooted in nature, especially among the churchmen, for precedency and dominion, he fell to work with them immediately; so that turning the tables, and reassuming the subtlety and craft, which, I say, he seemed to have lost in the former four hundred years, he gained more ground in the next ages of the church, and went farther towards restoring his power and empire in the world, and towards overthrowing that very church which was so lately established, than all he had done by fire and blood before.

His policy now seemed to be edged with resentment for the mistakes he had made; as if the Devil, looking back with anger at himself, to see what a fool he had been to expect to crush religion by persecution, rejoiced for having discovered that liberty and dominion was the only way to ruin the church, not fire and faggot; and that he had nothing to do but to give the zealous people their utmost liberty in religion, only sowing error and variety of opinion among them, and they would bring fire and faggot in fast enough among themselves.

It must be confessed these were devilish politics; and so sure was the aim, and so certain was the Devil to hit his mark by them, that we find he not only did not fail then, but the same hellish methods have prevailed still, and will do so to the end of the world. Nor had the Devil ever a better game to play than this, for the ruin of religion, as we shall have room to show in many examples, besides that of the dissenters in England, who are evidently weakened by the late toleration: whether the Devil had any hand in baiting his hook with an a— of parliament or no, history is silent, but it is too evident he has catched the fish by it; and if the honest Church of England does not, in pity and Christian charity to the dissenters, straighten her hand a little, I cannot but fear the Devil will gain his point, and the dissenters will be undone by it.

Upon this new foot of politics the Devil began with the emperors themselves. Arius, the father of the heretics of that age, having broached his opinions, and Athanasius the orthodox bishop of the East opposing him, the Devil no sooner saw the door open to strife and imposition, but he thrust himself in, and raising the quarrel up to a suited degree of rage and spleen, he involved the good emperor himself in it first, and Athanasius was banished and recalled, and banished and recalled again, several times, as error ran high, and as the Devil either got or lost ground: after Constantine, the next emperor was a child of his own (Arian), and then the court came all into the quarrel, as courts often do, and then the Arians and the orthodox persecuted one another as furiously as the pagans persecuted them all before. To such a height the Devil brought his conquest in the very infancy of the question, and so much did he prevail over the true Christianity of the primitive church, even before they had enjoyed the liberty of the pure worship twenty years.

Flushed with this success, the Devil made one push for the restoring paganism, and bringing on the old worship of the heathen idols and temples; but, like our king James II., he drove too hard, and Julian had so provoked the whole Roman empire, which was generally at that time become Christian, that, had the apostate lived, he would not have been able to have held the throne; and as he was cut off in his beginning, paganism expired with him, and the Devil himself might have cried out, as Julian did, and with much more propriety, *Vicisti Galilean.*

Jovian, the next emperor, being a glorious Christian and a very good and great man, the Devil abdicated for a while, and left the Christian armies to re-establish the orthodox faith; nor could he bring the Christians to a breach again among themselves a great while after.

However, time and a dilligent devil did the work at last, and when the emperors' concerning themselves one way or other, did not appear sufficient to answer his end, he changed hands again, and went to work with the clergy; to set the doctors effectually together by the ears, he threw in the new notion of primacy among them, for a bone of contention; the bait took, the priests swallowed it eagerly down, and the Devil, a cunninger fisherman than ever St. Peter was, struck them (as the anglers call it) with a quick hand, and hung them fast upon the hook.

Having them thus in his clutches, and they being now, as we may say, his own, they took their measures afterwards

from him, and most obe liently followed his directions ; nay,
I will not say but he may have had pretty much the management of the whole society ever since, of what profession or
party soever they may have been, with exception only to the
reverend and right reverend among ourselves.

The sacred, as above, being thus hooked in, and the Devil
being at the head of their affairs, matters went on most glo-
riously his own way ; first, the bishops fell to bandying and
party-making for the superiority, as heartily as ever temporal
tyrants did for dominion, and took as black and devilish
methods to carry it on, as the worst of those tyrants ever
had done before them.

At last Satan declared for the Roman pontiff, and that upon
excellent conditions, in the reign of the emperor Mauritius ;
for Boniface, who had long contended for the title of supreme,
fell into a treaty with Phocas, captain of the emperor's guards :
whether the bargain was from hell or not, let any one judge,
the conditions absolutely entitle the Devil to the honour
of making the contract, viz., that Phocas first murdering his
master (the emperor) and his sons, Boniface should countenance the treason, and declare him emperor ; and in return
Phocas should acknowledge the primacy of the Church of
Rome, and declare Boniface universal bishop. A blessed
compact ! which at once set the Devil at the head of affairs
in the Christian world, as well spiritual as temporal, ecclesiastic and civil. Since the conquest over Eve in Paradise,
by which Death and the Devil, hand in hand, established
their first empire upon earth, the Devil never gained a more
important point than he gained at this time.

He had indeed prospered in his affairs tolerably well for
some time before this, and his interest among the clergy had
got ground for some ages; but that was indeed a secret
management, was carried on privately, and with difficulty ;
as in sowing discord and faction among the people, perplexing the councils of their princes, and secretly wheedling in
with the dignified clergy.

Also he had raised abundance of little church rebellions,
by setting up heretics of several kinds, and raising them
favourers among the clergy, such as Ebion, Cerinthius, Pelagius, and others.

He had drawn in the bishops of Rome to set up the ridiculous pageantry of the key; and while he, the Devil, set

open the gates of hell to them all, set them upon locking up
the gates of heaven, and giving the bishop the key; a cheat
which, as gross as it was, the Devil so gilded over, or so
blinded the age to receive it, that, like Gideon's ephod, all
the catholic world went a whoring after the idol; and the
bishop of Rome sent more fools to the Devil by it than ever
he pretended to let into heaven, though he opened the door
as wide as his key was able to do.

The story of this key being given to the bishop of Rome
by St. Peter (who, by the way, never had it himself), and of
its being lost by somebody or other (the Devil it seems did
not tell them who), and its being found again by a Lombard
soldier in the army of king Antharis, who attempting to cut
it with his knife, was miraculously forced to direct the wound
to himself, and cut his own throat; that king Antharis and
his nobles happened to see the fellow do it, and were converted to Christianity by it, and that the king sent the key,
with another made like it, to pope Pelagius, then bishop of
Rome, who thereupon assumed the power of opening and
shutting heaven's gates; and he afterwards setting a price or
toll upon the entrance, as we do here at passing a turnpike;
these fine things, I say, were successfully managed for some
years before this I am now speaking of, and the Devil got a
great deal of ground by it too; but now he triumphed openly,
and having set up a murderer upon the temporal throne, and
a church emperor upon the ecclesiastic throne, and both of
his own choosing, the Devil may be said to begin his new
kingdom from this epocha, and call it the restoration.

Since this time indeed the Devil's affairs went very merrily
on, and the clergy brought so many gewgaws into their worship, and such devilish principles were mixed with that which
we call the Christian faith, that, in a word, from this time
the bishop of Rome commenced whore of Babylon, in all the
most express terms that could be imagined : tyranny of the
worst sort crept into the pontificate, errors of all sorts into
the profession, and they proceeded from one thing to another,
till the very popes (for so the bishop of Rome was now called,
by way of distinction), I say, the popes themselves, their
spiritual guides, professed openly to confederate with the
Devil, and to carry on a personal and private correspondence
with him at the same time, taking upon them the title of

Christ's vicar, and the infallible guide of the consciences cf Christians.

This we have sundry instances of in some merry popes, who, if fame lies not, were sorcerers, magicians, had familiar spirits, and immediate conversation with the Devil, as well visibly as invisibly, and by this means became what we call devils incarnate : upon this account it.is that I have left the conversation that passes between devils and men to this place, as well because I believe it differs much now in his modern state, from what it was in his ancient state, and therefore that which most concerns us belongs rather to this part of his history; as also because, as I am now writing to the present age, I choose to bring the most significant parts of his history, especially as they relate to ourselves, into that part of time that we are most concerned in.

The Devil had once, as I observed before, the universal monarchy or government of mankind in himself, and I doubt not but in that flourishing state of his affairs, he governed them like what he is, viz., an absolute tyrant; during this theocracy of his (for Satan is called the god of this world), he did not familiarize himself to mankind so much as he finds occasion to do now, there was not then so much need of it; he governed then with an absolute sway ; he had his oracles, where he gave audience to his votaries like a deity, and he had his sub-gods, who, under his several dispositions, received the homage of mankind in their names; such were all the rabble of the heathen deities, from Jupiter the supreme, to the Lares or household gods of every family ; these, I say, like residents, received the prostrations, but the homage was all Satan's; the Devil had the substance of it all, which was the idolatry.

During this administration of hell, there was less witchcraft, less true literal magic, than there has been since ; there was indeed no need of it, the Devil did not stoop to the mechanism of his more modern operations, but ruled as a deity, and received the vows and the bows of his subjects in more state, and with more solemnity; whereas, since that, he is content to employ more agents and take more pains himself too ; now he runs up and down hackney in the world, more like a drudge than a prince, and much more than he did then.

Hence all those things we call apparitions and visions of ghosts, familiar spirits, and dealings with the Devil, of which there is so great a variety in the world at this time, were not so much known among the people in those first ages of the Devil's kingdom; in a word, the Devil seems to be put to his shifts, and to fly to art and stratagem for the carrying on his affairs, much more now than he did then.

One reason for this may be, that he has been more discovered and exposed in these ages, than he was before; then he could appear in the world in his own proper shapes, and yet not be known; when the sons of God appeared at the divine summons, Satan came along with them : but now he has played so many scurvy tricks upon men, and they know him so well that he is obliged to play quite out of sight, and act in disguise; mankind will allow nothing of his doing, and hear nothing of his saying, in his own name; and if you propose anything to be done, and it be but said the Devil is to help in the doing it, or if you say of any man, ' he deals with the Devil,' or ' the Devil has a hand in it,' everybody flies him and shuns him, as the most frightful thing in the world.

Nay, if anything strange and improbable be done, or related to be done, we presently say the Devil was at the doing it.   Thus the great ditch at Newmarket Heath is called the Devil's ditch; so the Devil built Crowland abbey, and the whispering-place in Gloucester cathedral; nay, the cave at Castleton, only because there is no getting to the farther end of it, is called the Devil's a——, and the like.   The poor people of Wiltshire, when you ask them how the great stones at Stonehenge were brought thither, they will all tell you the Devil brought them.   If any mischief extraordinary befalls us, we presently say ' the Devil was in it,' and ' the Devil would have it so :' in a word, the Devil has got an ill name among us, and so he is fain to act more *in tenebris*, more *incog.*, than he used to do, play out of sight himself, and work by the sap, as the engineers call it, and not openly and avowedly in his own name and person, as formerly, though, perhaps, not with less success than he did before ; and this leads me to inquire more narrowly into the manner of the Devil's management of his affairs since the Christian religion began to spread in the world, which manifestly differs from his conduct in more ancient times; in which if we discover some of the most consummate fool's policy, the most profound simple craft,

and the most subtle shallow management of things that can
by our weak understandings be conceived, we must only resolve it into this—that, in short, it is the Devil.

CHAPTER II.

OF HELL, AS IT IS REPRESENTED TO US, AND HOW THE DEVIL IS
TO BE UNDERSTOOD AS BEING PERSONALLY IN HELL, WHEN, AT
THE SAME TIME, WE FIND HIM AT LIBERTY, RANGING OVER THE
WORLD.

IT is true, as that learned and pleasant author, the inimitable
Dr. Brown, says, 'The Devil is his own hell;' one of the
most constituting parts of his infelicity is, that he cannot act
upon mankind *brevi manu*, by his own inherent power, as well
as rage; that he cannot unhinge this creation, which, as I have
observed in its place, he had the utmost aversion to from its
beginning, as it was a stated design in the Creator to supply his
place in heaven with a new species of being called man, and fill
the vacancies occasioned by his degeneracy and rebellion.

This filled him with rage inexpressible, and horrible resolutions of revenge, and the impossibility of executing those
resolutions torments him with despair; this, added to what
he was before, makes him a complete devil, with a hell in his
own breast, and a fire unquenchable burning about his heart.

I might enlarge here, and very much to the purpose, in
describing spherically and mathematically, that exquisite
quality called a devilish spirit, in which it would naturally
occur to give you a whole chapter upon the glorious articles
of malice and envy, and especially upon that luscious, delightful, triumphant passion, called revenge: how natural to man,
nay, even to both sexes: how pleasant in the very contemplation,
though there be not, just at that time, a power of execution:
how palatable it is in itself, and how well it relishes when
dished up with its proper sauces, such as plot, contrivance,
scheme, and confederacy, all leading on to execution: how
it possesses the human soul in all the most sensible parts: how
it empowers mankind to sin in imagination, as effectually, to
all future intents and purposes (damnation), as if he had sinned actually; how safe a practice it is too, as to punishment
in this life, namely, that it empowers us to cut throats clear
of the gallows, to slander virtue, reproach innocence, wound

honour, and stab reputation ; and, in a word, to do all the wicked things in the world, out of the reach of the law.

It would also require some few words to describe the secret operations of those nice qualities when they reach the human soul; how effectually they form a hell within us, and how imperceptibly they assimilate and transform us into devils, mere human devils, as really devils as Satan himself, or any of his angels; and that, therefore, it is not so much out of the way as some imagine, to say, such a man is an incarnate devil; for, as crime made Satan a devil, who was before a bright immortal seraph, or angel of light, how much more easily may the same crime make the same devil, though every way meaner and more contemptible, of a man or woman either! But this is too grave a subject for me at this time.

The Devil being thus, I say, fired with rage and'envy, in consequence of his jealousy upon the creation of man, his torment is increased to the highest by the limitation of his power, and his being forbid to act against mankind by force of arms; this is, I say, part of his hell, which, as above, is within him, and which he carries with him wherever he goes; nor is it so difficult to conceive of hell, or of the Devil either, under this just description, as it is by all the usual notions that we are taught to entertain of them, by (the old woman) our instructers ; for every man may, by taking but a common view of himself, and making a just scrutiny into his own passions, or some of their particular excursions, see a hell within himself, and himself a mere devil as long as the inflammation lasts ; and that as really, and to all intents and purposes, as if he had the angel (Satan) before his face, in his locality and personality ; that is to say, all devil and monster in his person, and an immaterial, but intense fire flaming about and from within him, at all the pores of his body.

The notions we receive of the Devil, as a person being in hell as a place, are infinitely absurd and ridiculous. The first, we are certain is not true in fact, because he has a certain liberty (however limited, that is not to the purpose), is daily visible, and to be traced in his several attacks upon mankind, and has been so ever since his first appearance in Paradise : as to his corporal visibility, that is not the present question neither ; it is enough that we can hunt him by the foot, that we can follow him as hounds do a fox upon a hot scent : we can see him as plainly by the effect, by the mischief he does, and more by the mischief he puts us upon doing, I say, as plainly, as if we saw him by the eye.

It is not to be doubted but the Devil can see us when and where we cannot see him ; and as he has a personality, though it be spiritous, he and his angels too may be reasonably supposed to inhabit the world of spirits, and to have free access from thence to the regions of life, and to pass and repass in the air, as really, though not perceptible to us, as the spirits of men do, after their release from the body, pass to the place (wherever that is) which is appointed for them.

If the Devil was confined to a place (Hell) as a prison, he could then have no business here; and if we pretend to describe hell, as not a prison, but that the Devil has liberty to be there or not be there, as he pleased, then he would certainly never be there, or hell is not such a place as we are taught to understand it to be.

Indeed, according to some, hell should be a place of fire and torment to the souls that are cast into it, but not to the devils themselves; who we make little more or less than keepers and turnkeys to hell, as a jail; that they are sent about to bring souls thither, lock them in when they come, and then away upon the scent to fetch more. That one sort of devils are made to live in the world among men, and to be busy continually debauching and deluding mankind, bringing them, as it were, to the gates of hell ; and then another sort are porters and carriers to fetch them in.

This is, in short, little more or less than the old story of Pluto, of Cerberus, and of Charon ; only that our tale is not half so well told, nor the parts of the fable so well laid together.

In all these notions of hell and devil, the torments of the first, and the agency of the last, tormenting, we meet with not one word of the main, and perhaps only, accent of horror which belongs to us to judge of about hell, I mean the absence of heaven; expulsion and exclusion from the presence and face of the chief ultimate, the only eternal and sufficient Good; and this loss sustained by a sordid neglect of our concern in that excellent part, in exchange for the most contemptible and justly condemned trifles, and all this eternal and irrecoverable ; these people tell us nothing of the eternal reproaches of conscience, the horror of desperation, and the anguish of a mind hopeless of ever seeing the glory which alone constitutes heaven, and which makes all other places dreadful, and even darkness itself.

And this brings me directly to the point in hand, viz., the state of that hell which we ought to have in view when we speak of the Devil as in hell; this is the very hell which is the torment of the Devil; in short, the Devil is in hell, and hell is in the Devil; he is filled with this unquenchable fire, he is expelled the place of glory, banished from the regions of light; absence from the life of all beatitude is his curse, despair is the reigning passion in his mind; and all the little constituting parts of his torment, such as rage, envy, malice, and jealousy, are consolidated in this, to make his misery complete, viz., the duration of it all, the eternity of his condition; that he is without hope, without redemption, without recovery.

If anything can inflame this hell, and make it hotter, it is this only, and this does add an inexpressible horror to the Devil himself; namely, the seeing man (the only creature he hates) placed in a state of recovery, a glorious establishment of redemption formed for him in heaven, and the scheme of it perfected on earth; by which this man, though even the Devil by his art may have deluded him, and drawn him into crime, is yet in a state of recovery, which the Devil is not; and that it is not in his (Satan's) power to prevent it. Now take the Devil as he is in his own nature, angelic, a bright immortal seraph, heaven-born, and having tasted the eternal beatitude, which these are appointed to enjoy; the loss of that state to himself, the possession of it granted to his rival, though wicked like and as himself; I say, take the Devil as he is, having a quick sense of his own perdition, and a stinging sight of his rival's felicity, it is hell enough, and more than enough, even for an angel to support; nothing we can conceive of can be worse.

As to any other fire than this, such and so immaterially intense as to torment a spirit, which is itself fire also, I will not say it cannot be, because to Infinite everything is possible, but, I must say, I cannot conceive rightly of it.

I will not enter here into the wisdom or reasonableness of representing the torments of hell to be fire, and that fire to be a commixture of flame and sulphur; it has pleased God to let the horror of those eternal agonies about a lost heaven be laid before us by those similitudes or allegories which are most moving to our senses and to our understandings ; nor will I dispute the possibility, much less will I doubt but that there is to be a consummation of misery to all the objects of misery, when the Devil's kingdom in this world, ending with the world itself, that liberty he has now may be farther abridged ; when he may be returned to the same state he was in between the time of his fall and the creation of the world, with perhaps some additional vengeance on him, such as at present we cannot describe, for all that treason and those high crimes and misdemeanors which he has been guilty of here in his conversation with mankind.

As his infelicity will be then consummated and completed, so the infelicity of that part of mankind who are condemned with him may receive a considerable addition from those words in their sentence, *to be tormented with the Devil and his angels;* for, as the absence of the supreme Good is a complete hell, so the hated company of the Deceiver, who was the great cause of their ruin, must be a subject of additional horror ; and they will be always saying as a Scotch gentleman who died of his excesses said to the famous Dr. P—— who came to see him on his death-bed, but had been too much his companion in his life,

O tu fundamenta gessisti ————.

I would not treat the very subject itself with any indecency, nor do I think my opinion of that hell which, I say, consists in the absence of him in whom is heaven, one jot less solemn than theirs who believe it all fire and brimstone ; but I must own, that to me, nothing can be more ridiculous than the notions that we entertain and fill our heads with about hell, and about the devils being there tormenting of souls, broiling them upon gridirons, hanging them up upon hooks, carrying them upon their backs, and the like ; with the several pictures of hell, represented by a great mouth with horrible teeth, gaping like a cave on the side of a mountain ; suppose that appropriated to Satan in the Peak, which indeed is not much unlike it, with a stream of fire coming out of it, as there is of water, and smaller devils going and coming continually in and out, to fetch and carry souls the Lord knows whither, and for the Lord knows what.

These things, however, intended for terror, are indeed so ridiculous, that the Devil himself, to be sure, mocks at them, and a man of sense can hardly refrain doing the like, only I avoid it, because I would not give offence to weaker heads.

However, I must not compliment the brains of other men at the expense of my own, or talk nonsense because they can understand no other; I think all these notions and representations of hell and of the Devil to be as profane as they are ridiculous, and I ought no more to talk profanely than merrily of them.

Let us learn to talk of these things, then, as we should do; and as we really cannot describe them to our reason and understanding, why should we describe them to our senses? we had, I think, much better not describe them at all, that is to say, not attempt it: the blessed apostle St. Paul was, as he said himself, carried up, or caught up, into the third heaven, yet when he came down again he could neither tell what he heard, or describe what he saw; all he could say of it was, that what he heard was unutterable, and what he saw was inconceivable.

It is the same thing as to the state of the Devil in those regions which he now possesses, and where he now more particularly inhabits; my present business, then, is not to enter into those grave things so as to make them ridiculous, as I think most people do that talk of them; but as the Devil, let his residence be where it will, has evidently free leave to come and go, not into this world only (I mean, the region of our atmosphere), but, for aught we know, to all the other inhabited worlds which God has made, wherever they are, and by whatsoever names they are, or may be, known or distinguished; for, if he is not confined in one place, we have no reason to believe he is excluded from any place, heaven only excepted, from whence he was expelled for his treason and rebellion.

His liberty, then, being thus ascertained, three things seem to be material for us to give an account of, in order to form this part of his history.

1. What his business is on this globe of earth, which we vulgarly call the world; how he acts among us; what affairs mankind and he have together; and how far his conduct here relates to us, and ours is, or may be, influenced by him.

2. Where his principal residence is, and whether he has not a particular empire of his own, to which he retreats upon proper occasions, where he entertains his friends when they come under his particular administration,

and where, when he gets any victory over his enemies, he carries his prisoners of war.

3. What may probably be the great business this black emperor has at present upon his hands, either in this world or out of it, and by what agents he works.

As these things may perhaps run promiscuously through the course of this whole work, and frequently be touched at under other branches of the Devil's history, so I do not propose them as heads of chapters or particular sections, for the order of discourse to be handled apart; for, by the way, as Satan's actings have not been the most regular things in the world, so, in our discourse about him, it must not be expected that we can always tie ourselves down to order and regularity, either as to time, or place, or persons; for Satan being *hic et ubique*, a loose, ungoverned fellow, we must be content to trace him where we can find him.

It is true, in the foregoing chapter I showed you the Devil entered into the herd ecclesiastic, and gave you some account of the first successful step he took with mankind since the Christian epoch; how, having secretly managed both temporal and spiritual power apart, and by themselves, he now united them, in point of management, and brought the church usurpation and the army's usurpation together: the pope to bless the general, in desposing and murdering his master, the emperor; and the general to recognise the pope in dethroning his master, Christ Jesus.

From this time forward you are to allow the Devil a mystical empire in this world; not an action of moment done without him, not a treason but he has a hand in it, not a tyrant but he prompts him, not a government but he has a —— in it; not a fool but he tickles him, not a knave but he guides him; he has a finger in every fraud, a key to every cabinet, from the divan at Constantinople to the Mississippi in France, and to the South-Sea cheats at ——; from the first attack upon the Christian world in the person of the Romish antichrist, down to the bull *Unigenitus;* and from the mixture of St. Peter and Confucius in China, to the holy office in Spain; and down to the Emlins and Dodwells of the current age.

How he has managed, and does manage, and how in all probability he will manage till his kingdom shall come to a period, and how at last he will probably be managed himself, inquire within, and you shall know farther.

CHAPTER III.

OF THE MANNER OF SATAN'S ACTING AND CARRYING ON HIS AFFAIRS IN THIS WORLD, AND PARTICULARLY OF HIS ORDINARY WORKINGS IN THE DARK, BY POSSESSION AND AGITATION.

THE Devil being thus reduced to act upon mankind by stratagem only, it remains to inquire how he performs, and which way he directs his attacks; the faculties of man are a kind of a garrison in a strong castle, which as they defend it on the one hand under the command of the reasoning power of man's soul, so they are prescribed on the other hand, and can not sally out without leave; for the governor of a fort does not permit his soldiers to hold any correspondence with the enemy, without special order and direction.   Now the great inquiry before us is, How comes the Devil to a parley with us? how does he converse with our senses, and with the understanding? how does he reach us? which way does he come at the affections? and which way does he move the passions?   It is a little difficult to discover this treasonable correspondence, and that difficulty is indeed the Devil's advantage, and, for aught I see, the chief advantage he has over mankind.

It is also a great inquiry here, whether the Devil knows our thoughts or no: if I may give my opinion, I am with a negative; I deny that he knows anything of our thoughts, except of those thoughts which he puts us upon thinking, for I will not doubt but he has the art to inject thoughts, and to revive dormant thoughts in us: it is not so wild a scheme as some take it to be, that Mr. Milton lays down, to represent the Devil injecting corrupt desires and wandering thoughts into the head of Eve, by dreams, and that he brought her to dream whatever he put into her thoughts, by whispering to her vocally when she was asleep; and to this end, he imagines the Devil laying himself close to her ear, in the shape of a toad, when she was fast asleep; I say, this is not so wild a scheme, seeing even now, if you can whisper anything close to the ear of a person in a deep sleep, so as to speak distinctly to the person, and yet not awaken him, as has been frequently tried, the person sleeping shall dream distinctly of what you say to him; nay, shall dream the very words you say.

We have, then, no more to ask, but how the Devil can convey himself to the ear of a sleeping person; and it is granted then that he may have power to make us dream what he pleases: but this is not all, for if he can so forcibly, by his invisible application, cause us to dream what he pleases, why can he not with the same facility prompt our thoughts, whether sleeping or waking? To dream is nothing else but to think sleeping; and we have abundance of deep-headed gentlemen among us, who give us ample testimony that they dream waking.

But if the Devil can prompt us to dream, that is to say, to think, yet if he does not know our thoughts, how then can he tell whether the whisper had its effect? The answer is plain; the Devil, like the angler, baits the hook, if the fish bite he lies ready to take the advantage; he whispers to the imagination, and then waits to see how it works; as Naomi said to Ruth, chap. iii. 5, 18, *Sit still, my daughter, until thou know how the matter will fall, for the man will not be at rest until he have finished the thing.* Thus when the Devil had whispered to Eve in her sleep, according to Milton, and suggested mischief to her imagination, he only sat still to see how the matter would work, for he knew if it took with her, he should hear more of it; and then by finding her alone the next day, without her ordinary guard, her husband, he presently concluded she had swallowed the bait, and so attacked her afresh.

A small deal of craft, and less by far than we have reason to believe the Devil is master of, will serve to discover whether such and such thoughts, as he knows he has suggested, have taken place or no; the action of the person presently discovers it, at least to him that lies always upon the watch, and has every word, every gesture, every step we take subsequent to his operation, open to him; it may, therefore, for aught we know, be a great mistake, and what most of us are guilty of, to tell our dreams to one another in the morning, after we have been disturbed with them in the night; for, if the Devil converses with us so insensibly as some are of the opinion he does, that is to say, if he can hear us far as we can see, we may be telling our story to him indeed, when we think we are only talking to one another.

This brings me most naturally to the important inquiry, whether the Devil can walk about the world invisibly or no. The truth is, this is no question to me; for as I have taken away his visibility already, and have denied him all prescience of futurity too, and have proved he cannot know our thoughts, nor put any force upon persons or actions, if we should take away his invisibility too, we should undevil him quite, to all intents and purposes, as to any mischief he could do; nay, it would banish him the world, and he might e'en go and seek his fortune somewhere else ; for if he could neither be visible or invisible, neither act in public or in private, he could neither have business or being in this sphere, nor could we be any way concerned with him.

The Devil, therefore, most certainly has a power and liberty of moving about in this world, after some manner or another; this is verified, as well by way of allegory as by way of history, in the Scripture itself; and as the first strongly suggests and supposes it to be so, the last positively asserts it ; and, not to crowd this work with quotations from a book which we have not much to do with in the Devil's story, at least not much to his satisfaction, I only hint his personal appearance to our Saviour in the wilderness, where it is said, *the Devil taketh him up to an exceeding high mountain;* and, in another place, *the Devil departed from him.* What shape or figure he appeared in we do not find mentioned, but I cannot doubt his appearing to him there, any more than I can his talking to our Saviour in the mouths and with the voices of the several persons who were under the terrible affliction of an actual possession.

These things leave us no room to doubt of what is advanced above, namely, that he (the Devil) has a certain residence, or liberty of residing in, and moving about upon, the surface of this earth, as well as in the compass of the atmosphere vulgarly called the air, in some manner or other : that is the general.

It remains to inquire into the manner, which I resolve into two kinds:

1. Ordinary, which I suppose to be his invisible motions as a spirit; under which consideration I suppose him to have an unconfined, unlimited, unrestrained liberty, as to the manner of acting; and this either in persons, by possession ; or in things, by agitation.

2. Extraordinary, which I understand to be his appearances in borrowed shapes and bodies, or shadows rather of bodies; assuming speech, figure, posture, and several powers, of which we can give little or no account; in which extraordinary manner of appearances, he is either limited by a superior power, or limits himself politically, as being not the way most for his interest or purpose to act in his business, which is more effectually done in his state of obscurity.

Hence we must suppose the Devil has it very much in his own choice, whether to act in one capacity, or in the other, or in both; that is to say, of appearing and not appearing, as he finds for his purpose: in this state of invisibility, and under the operation of these powers and liberties, he performs all his functions and offices, as Devil, as prince of darkness, as god of this world, as tempter, accuser, deceiver, and all whatsoever other names of office or titles of honour he is known by.

Now taking him in this large unlimited, or little limited state of action, he is well called the god of this world, for he has very much of the attribute of omnipresence, and may be said, either by himself or his agents, to be everywhere, and see everything; that is to say, everything that is visible; for I cannot allow him any share of omniscience at all.

That he ranges about everywhere, is with us, and sometimes in us, sees when he is not seen, hears when he is not heard, comes in without leave, and goes out without noise, is neither to be shut in or shut out; that when he runs from us we cannot catch him, and when he runs after us we cannot escape him, is seen when he is not known, and is known when he is not seen; all these things, and more, we have knowledge enough about to convince us of the truth of them; so that, as I have said above, he is certainly walking to and fro through the earth, &c., after some manner or other, and in some figure or other, visible or invisible, as he finds occasion. Now in order to make our history of him complete, the next question before us is, how, and in what manner, he acts with mankind: how his kingdom is carried on, and by what methods he does his business, for he certainly has a great deal of business to do; he is not an idle spectator, nor is he walking about *incognito*, and clothed in mist and darkness, purely in kindness to us, that we should

not be frightened at him; but it is in policy, that he may act
undiscovered, that he may see and not be seen, may play his
game in the dark, and not be detected in his roguery; that
he may prompt mischief, raise tempests, blow up coals,
kindle strife, embroil nations, use instruments, and not be
known to have his hand in anything, when at the same time
he really has a hand in everything.

Some are of opinion, and I among the rest, that if the
Devil was personally and visibly present among us, and we
conversed with him face to face, we should be so familiar
with him in a little time, that his ugly figure would not
affect us at all, that his terrors would not frighten us, or that
we should any more trouble ourselves about him than we
did with the last great comet in 1678, which appeared so
long and so constantly without any particular known event,
that at last we took no more notice of it than of the other
ordinary stars, which had appeared before we or our ancestors were born.

Nor, indeed, should we have much reason to be frightened
at him, or at least none of those silly things could be said of
him which we now amuse ourselves about, and by which we
set him up like a scarecrow to frighten children and old
women, to fill up old stories, make songs and ballads, and,
in a word, carry on the low-prized buffoonery of the common people; we should either see him in his angelic form,
as he was from the original, or if he has any deformities
entailed upon him by the supreme sentence, and in justice to
the deformity of his crime, they would be of a superior
nature, and fitted more for our contempt, as well as horror,
than those weak-fancied trifles contrived by our ancient
devil-raisers and devil-makers, to feed the wayward fancies
of old witches and sorcerers, who cheated the ignorant world
with a devil of their own making, set forth, *in terrorem*,
with bat's wings, horns, cloven foot, long tail, forked tongue,
and the like.

In the next place, be his frightful figure what it would,
and his legions as numerous as the host of heaven, we
should see him still, as the prince of devils, though monstrous as a dragon, flaming as a comet, tall as a mountain,
yet dragging his chain after him equal to the utmost of his
supposed strength; always in custody of his jailers the
angels, his power overpowered, his rage cowed and abated,

or at least awed and under correction, limited and restrained; in a word, we should see him a vanquished slave, his spirit broken, his malice, though not abated, yet handcuffed and overpowered, and he not able to work anything against us by force; so that he would be to us but like the lions in the Tower, encaged and locked up, unable to do the hurt he wishes to do, and that we fear, or indeed any hurt at all.

From hence it is evident, that it is not his business to be public, or to walk up and down in the world visibly, and in his own shape; his affairs require a quite different management, as might be made apparent from the nature of things, and the manner of our actings, as men, either with ourselves or to one another.

Nor could he be serviceable in his generation, as a public person, as now he is; or answer the end of his party who employ him, and who, if he was to do their business in public as he does in private, would not be able to employ him at all.

As in our modern meetings for the propagation of impudence and other virtues, there would be no entertainment, and no improvement for the good of the age, if the people did not all appear in mask, and concealed from the common observation; so neither could Satan (from whose management those more happy assemblies are taken as copies of a glorious original) perform the usual and necessary business of his profession, if he did not appear wholly in covert and under needful disguises. How, but for the convenience of his habit, could he cast himself into so many shapes, act on so many different scenes, and turn so many wheels of state in the world, as he has done? as a mere professed devil he could do nothing.

Had he been obliged always to act the mere devil in his own clothes, and with his own shape appearing uppermost in all cases and places, he could never have preached in so many pulpits, presided in so many councils, voted in so many committees, sat in so many courts, and influenced so many parties and factions in church and state, as we have reason to believe he has done in our nation, and in our memories too, as well as in other nations and in more ancient times. The share Satan has had in all the weighty confusions of the times, ever since the first ages of Christianity in the world, has been carried on with so much secrecy, and so much with an air of cabal and intrigue, that nothing can have been managed more subtly and closely; and in the same manner has he acted in our times, in order to conceal his interest, and conceal the influence he has had in the councils of the world.

Had it been possible for him to have raised the flames ot rebellion and war so often in this nation, as he certainly has done? could he have agitated the parties on both sides, and inflamed the spirits of three nations, if he had appeared in his own dress, a mere naked devil? It is not the Devil as a devil, that does the mischief, but the Devil in masquerade, Satan in full disguise, and acting at the head of civil confusion and distraction.

If history may be credited, the French court at the time of our old confusions was made the scene of Satan's politics, and prompted both parties in England and in Scotland also to quarrel; and how was it done? will any man offer to scandalize the Devil so much as to say, or so much as to suggest, that Satan had no hand in it all? did not the Devil, by the agency of Cardinal Richelieu, send four hundred thousand crowns at one time, and six hundred thousand at another, to the Scots, to raise an army and march boldly into England? and did not the same Devil, at the same time, by other agents, remit eight hundred thousand crowns to the other party, in order to raise an army to fall upon the Scots? nay, did not the Devil with the same subtlety send down the archbishop's order to impose the service-book upon the people in Scotland, and at the same time raise a mob against it, in the great church (at St. Giles's)? nay, did not he actually, in the person of an old woman (his favourite instrument), throw the three-legged stool at the service-book, and animate the zealous people to take up arms for religion, and turn rebels for God's sake?

All these happy and successful undertakings, though it is no more to be doubted they were done by the agency of Satan, and in a very surprising manner too, yet were all done in secret, by what I call possession and injection, and by the agency and contrivance of such instruments, or by the Devil in the disguise of such servants, as he found out fitted to be employed in his work, and who he took a more effectual care in concealing of.

But we shall have occasion to touch all this part over again, when we come to discourse of the particular habits and disguises which the Devil has made use of all along in the world, the better to cover his actions, and to conceal his being concerned in them.

In the mean time, the cunn'r.g or artifice the Devil makes use of in all these things, is, in itself, very considerable; it is an old practice of his using, and he has gone on in divers measures, for the better concealing himself in it; which measures, though he varies sometimes, as his extraordinary affairs require, yet they are in all ages much the same, and have the same tendency; namely, that he may get all his business carried on by the instrumentality of fools; that he may make mankind agents in their own destruction, and that he may have all his work done in such a manner as that he may seem to have no hand in it; nay, he contrives so well, that the very name, Devil, is put upon his opposite party, and the scandal of the black agent lies all upon them.

In order, then, to look a little into his conduct, let us inquire into the common mistakes about him, see what use is made of them to his advantage, and how far mankind is imposed upon in those particulars, and to what purpose.

CHATPER IV.

OF SATAN'S AGENTS OR MISSIONARIES, AND THEIR ACTINGS UPON AND IN THE MINDS OF MEN IN HIS NAME.

INFINITE advantages attend the Devil in his retired government, as they respect the management of his interests, and the carrying on his absolute monarchy in the world; particularly as it gives him room to act by the agency of his inferior ministers and messengers, called on many occasions his angels, of whom he has an innumerable multitude at his command, enough, for aught we know, to spare one to attend every man and woman now alive in the world; and of whom, if we may believe our second-sight Christians, the air is always as full as a beam of the evening sun is of insects, where they are ever ready for business, and to go and come as their great governor issues out orders for their directions.

These, as they are all of the same spiritous quality with himself, and consequently invisible like him, except as above, are ready upon all occasions to be sent to and into any such person, and for such purposes, superior limitations only excepted, as the grand director of devils (the Devil, properly so called) guides them; and be the subject or the object what it will, that is to say, be the person they are sent to, or into, as above, who it will, and the business the messenger is to do, what it will, they are sufficiently qualified; for this is a particular to Satan's messengers or agents, that they are not like us human devils here in the world, some bred up one way, some another; some of one trade, some of another; and consequently some fit for some business, some for another; some good for something, and some good for nothing; but his people are every one fit for everything, can find their way everywhere, and are a match for everybody they are sent to; in a word, they are no foolish devils, they are all fully qualified for their employment, fit for anything he sets them about, and very seldom mistake their errand, or fail in the business they are sent to do.

Nor is it strange at all, that the Devil should have such a numberless train of deputy devils to act under him; for it must be acknowledged he has a great deal of business upon his hands, a vast deal of work to do, abundance of public affairs under his direction, and an infinite variety of particular cases always before him; for example:

How many governments in the world are wholly in his administration? how many divans and great councils under his direction? nay, I believe, it would be hard to prove that there is or has been one council of state in the world for many hundred years past, down to the year 1713 (we do not pretend to come nearer home), where the Devil, by himself or his agents, in one shape or another, has not sat as a member, if not taken the chair.

And though some learned authors may dispute this point with me, by giving some examples where the councils of princes have been acted by a better hand, and where things have been carried against Satan's interest, and even to his great mortification, it amounts to no more than this; namely, that in such cases the Devil has been outvoted; but it does not argue but he might have been present there, and have pushed his interest as far as he could, only that he had not the success he expected; for I do not pretend to say that he has never been disappointed: but those examples are so rare, and of so small signification, that when I come to the particulars, as I shall do in the sequel of this history, you will find them hardly worth naming; and that, take it one time with another, the Devil has met with such a series of success in all his affairs, and has so seldom been balked; and where he has met with a little check in his politics, has, notwithstanding, so soon and so easily recovered himself, regained his lost ground, or replaced himself in another country when he has been supplanted in one, that his empire is far from being lessened in the world, for the last thousand years of the Christian establishment.

Suppose we take an observation from the beginning of Luther, or from the year 1420, and call the Reformation a blow to the Devil's kingdom, which, before that, was come to such a height in Christendom, that it is a question not yet thoroughly decided, whether that medley of superstition and horrible heresies, that mass of enthusiasm and idols, called the catholic hierarchy, was a church of God, or a church of the Devil; whether it was an assembly of saints, or a synagogue of Satan: I say, take that time to be the epoch of Satan's declension, and of Lucifer's falling from heaven, that is, from the top of his terrestrial glory, yet whether he did not gain in the defection of the Greek church, about that time and since, as much as he lost in the reformation of the Roman, is what authors are not yet agreed about, not reckoning what he has regained since of the ground which he had lost even by the Reformation, viz., the countries of the Duke of Savoy's dominion, where the Reformation is almost eaten out by persecution; the whole Valtoline, and some adjacent countries; the whole kingdom of Poland, and almost all Hungary; for, since the last war, the Reformation, as it were, lies gasping for breath, and expiring in that country; also several large provinces in Germany, as Austria, Carinthia, and the whole kingdom of Bohemia, where the Reformation, once powerfully planted, received its death's wound at the battle of Prague, ann. 1627, and languished but a very little while, died, and was buried, and good king popery reigned in its stead.

To these countries, thus regained to Satan's infernal empire, let us add his modern conquests, and the encroachments he has made upon the Reformation in the present age, which are, however light we make of them, very considerable; viz., the electorate of the Rhine and the Palatinate, the one fallen to the house of Bavaria, and the other to that of Neuburg, both popish ; the duchy of Deux Ponts, fallen just now to a popish branch ; the whole electorate of Saxony, fallen under the power of popish government, by the apostacy of their princes, and more likely to follow the fate of Bohemia, whenever the dilligent Devil can bring his new project in Poland to bear, as it is more than probable he will do some time or other, by the growing zeal as well as power of (that house of bigots) the house of A——.

But to sum up the dull story; we must add in the roll of the Devil's conquests, the whole kingdom of France, where we have in one year seen, to the immortal glory of the Devil's politics, that his measures have prevailed to the total extirpation of the protestant churches, without a war; and that interest, which for two hundred years had supported itself in spite of persecutions, massacres, five civil wars, and innumerable battles and slaughters, at last received its mortal wound from its own champion Henry IV., and sunk into utter oblivion, by Satan's most exquisite management, under the agency of his two prime ministers Cardinal Richelieu and Lewis XIV., whom he entirely possessed.

Thus far we have a melancholy view of the Devil's new conquests, and the ground he has regained upon the Reformation, in which his secret management has been so exquisite, and his politics so good, that could he bring but one thing to pass, which, by his own former mistake (for the devil is not infallible), he has rendered impossible, he would bring the protestant interest so near its ruin, that heaven would be, as it were, put to the necessity of working by miracle to prevent it ; the case is thus :

Ancient historians tell us, and from good authority, that the Devil, finding it for his interest to bring his favourite Mahomet upon the stage, and spread the victorious half-moon upon the ruin of the cross, having with great success raised first the Saracen empire, and then the Turkish, to such a height, as that the name of Christian seemed to be extirpated in those two quarters of the world, which were then not the greatest only, but by far the most powerful, I mean Asia and Africa; having totally laid waste all those ancient and flourishing churches of Africa, the labours of St. Cyprian, Tertullian, St. Augustine, and six hundred and seventy Christian bishops and fathers, who governed there at once, also all the churches of Smyrna, Philadelphia, Ephesus, Sardis, Antioch, Laodicea, and innumerable others in Pontus, Bithynia, and the provinces of the Lesser Asia.

The Devil having, I say, finished these conquests so much to his satisfaction, began to turn his eyes northward, and though he had a considerable interest in the whore of Babylon, and had brought his power, by the subjection of the Roman hierarchy, to a great height, yet finding the interest of Mahomet most suitable to his devilish purposes, as most adapted to the destruction of mankind, and laying waste the world, he resolved to espouse the growing power of the Turk, and bring him in upon Europe like a deluge.

In order to this, and to make way for an easy conquest, like a true devil, he worked under ground, and sapped the foundation of the Christian power by sowing discord among the reigning princes of Europe; that so, envying one another, they might be content to stand still and look on while the Turk devoured them one by one, and at last might swallow them all up.

This devilish policy took, to his heart's content; the Christian princes stood still, stupid, dosing, and unconcerned till the Turk conquered Thrace, overrun Servia, Macedonia, Bulgaria, and all the remains of the Grecian empire, and at last the imperial city of Constantinople itself.

Finding this politic method so well answer his ends, the Devil, who always improves upon the success of his own experiments, resolved from that time to lay a foundation for the making those divisions and jealousies of the Christian princes immortal; whereas they were at first only personal, and founded in private quarrels between the princes respectively; such as emulation of one another's glory, envy at the extraordinary valour or other merit of this or that leader, or revenge of some little affront; for which, notwithstanding, so great was the piety of Christian princes in those days, that they made no scruple to sacrifice whole armies, yea, nations, to their piques and private quarrels, a certain sign whose management they were under.

These being the causes by which the Devil first sowed the seeds of mischief among them, and the success so well answering his design, he could not but wish to have the same advantage always ready at his hand; and therefore he resolved to order it so, that these divisions, which, however useful to him, were only personal, and consequently temporary, like an annual in the garden, which must be raised anew every season, might for the future be national, and consequently durable and immortal.

To this end it was necessary to lay the foundation of eternal feud, not in the humours and passions of men only, but in the interests of nations: the way to do this was to form and state the dominion of those princes, by such a plan drawn in hell, and laid out from a scheme truly political, of which the Devil was chief engineer, that the divisions should always remain; being made a natural consequence of the situation of the country, the temper of their people, the nature of their commerce, the climate, the manner of living, or something which should for ever render it impossible for them to unite.

This, I say, was a scheme truly infernal, in which the Devil was as certainly the principal operator (to illustrate great things by small), as ever John of Leyden was of the high Dutch rebellion, or Sir John B——t of the late project, called the South-sea stock. Nor did this contrivance of the Devil at all dishonour its author, or the success appear unworthy of the undertaker; for we see it not only answer the end, and made the Turk victorious at the same time, and formidable to Europe ever after, but it works to this day, the foundation of the divisions remains in all the several nations, and that to such a degree that it is impossible they should unite.

This is what I hinted before, in which the Devil was mistaken, and is another instance that he knows nothing of what is to come; for this very foundation of immortal jealousy and discord between the several nations of Spain, France, Germany, and others, which the Devil himself with so much policy contrived, and which served his interests so long, is now the only obstruction to his designs, and prevents the entire ruin of the Reformation; for though the reformed countries are very powerful, and some of them, as Great Britain and Prussia in particular, more powerful than ever, yet it cannot be said that the protestant interests in general are stronger than formerly, or so strong as they were in 1632, under the victorious arms of the Swede; on the other hand, were it possible that the popish powers, to wit, of France,

Spain, Germany, Italy, and Poland, which are entirely popish, could heartily unite their interests, and should join their powers to attack the protestants, the latter would find it very difficult, if not impossible, to defend themselves.

But as fatal as such an union of the popish powers would be, and as useful as it would be to the Devil's cause at this time, not the Devil with all his angels are able to bring it to pass; no, not with all his craft and cunning; he divided them, but he cannot unite them; so that, even just as it is with men, so it is with devils, they may do in an hour what they cannot undo in an age.

This may comfort those faint-hearted Christians among us, who cry out of the danger of a religious war in Europe, and what terrible things will happen, when France, and Spain, and Germany, and Italy, and Poland, shall all unite; let this answer satisfy them, the Devil himself can never make France and Spain, or France and the emperor unite; jarring humours may be reconciled, but jarring interests never can: they may unite so as to make a peace, though that can hardly be long, but never so as to make conquests together; they are too much afraid of one another, for one to bear that any addition of strength should come to the other. But this is a digression. We shall find the Devil mistaken and disappointed too on several other occasions, as we go along.

I return to Satan's interest in the several governments and nations, by virtue of his invisibility, and which he carries on by possession; it is by this invisibility that he presides in all the councils of foreign powers (for we never mean our own, that we always premise); and what though it is alleged by the critics, that he does not preside, because there is always a president? I say, if he is not in the president's chair, yet if he be in the president himself, the difference is not much; and if he does not vote as a councillor, if he votes in the councillor, it is much the same; and here, as it was in the story of Ahab, the king of Israel, as he was a lying spirit in the mouths of all his prophets, so we find him a spirit of some particular evil quality or other, in all the transactions and transactors on that stage of life we call the state.

Thus he was a dissembling spirit in Charles IX., a turbulent spirit in Charles V., emperors; a bigoted spirit of fire and faggot in our Queen Mary; an apostate spirit in Henry IV.;

a cruel spirit in Peter of Castile; a revengeful spirit in Fer-
dinand II.; a Phaeton in Lewis XIV.; a Sardanapalus in
C ...... II.

In the great men of the world, take them a degree lower
than the class of crowned heads, he has the same secret
influence; and hence it comes to pass, that the greatest
heroes, and men of the highest character for achievements of
glory, either by their virtue or valour, however they have
been crowned with victories, and elevated by human tongues,
whatever the most consummate virtues or good qualities they
have been known by, yet they have always had some devil
or other in them, to preserve Satan's claim to them uninterrupted, and prevent their escape out of his hands; thus we
have seen a bloody devil in a D'Alva; a profligate devil in
a Buckingham; a lying, artful, or politic devil in a Richelieu;
a treacherous devil in a Mazarin; a cruel, merciless devil in
a Cortez; a debauched devil in an Eugene; a conjuring
devil in a Luxemburg; and a covetous devil in a M........ h:
in a word, tell me the man, I tell you the spirit that reigned
in him.

Nor does he thus carry on this secret management, by
possession, in men of the first magnitude only, but have we
not had evidences of it among ourselves? how has he been a
lying spirit in the mouths of our prophets, a factious spirit
in the heads of our politicians; a profuse devil in a B ..... s;
a corrupt devil in M ......; a proud spirit in my Lord
Plausible; a bullying spirit in my Lord Bugbear; a talkative
spirit in his grace the D ... of Rattle-hall; a scribbling
spirit in my Lord H ....; a runaway spirit in my Lord
Frightful; and so through a long roll of heroes, whose
exceeding, and particular qualifications, proclaim loudly what
handle the Devil took them by, and how fast he held them
for these were all men of ancient fame, I hope you know that.

From men of figure, we descend to the mob, and it is there
the same thing; possession, like the plague, is *morbus plebæi*;
not a family, but he is a spirit of strife and contention among
them; not a man, but he has a part in him; he is a drunken
devil in one, a whoring devil in another, a thieving devil in
a third, a lying devil in the fourth, and so on to a thousand,
and a hundred thousand, *ad infinitum*.

Nay, even the ladies have their share in the possession;
and if they have not the Devil in their heads or in their tails,

in their faces or their tongues, it must be some poor despicable she-devil, that Satan did not think it worth his while to meddle with; and the number of those that are below his operation, I doubt is very small. But that part I have much more to say to in its place.

From degrees of persons to professions and employments, it is the same; we find the Devil is a true posture-master, he assumes any dress, appears in any shape, counterfeits every voice, acts upon every stage; here he wears a gown, there a long robe; here he wears the jack-boots, there the small sword; is here an enthusiast, there a buffoon; on this side he acts the mountebank, on that side the merry-andrew; nothing comes amiss to him, from the Great Mogul, to the scaramouch; the Devil is in them, more or less, and plays his game so well, that he makes sure work with them all: he knows where the common foible lies, which is universal passion, what handle to take hold of every man by, and how to cultivate his interest, so as not to fail of his end, or mistake the means.

How, then, can it be denied, but that his acting thus *in tenebris*, and keeping out of the sight of the world, is abundantly his interest, and that he could do nothing, comparatively speaking, by any other method?

What would his public appearance have signified? who would have entertained him in his own proper shape and person? even B.... B..... himself, though all the world knows him to have a foolish devil in him, would not have been fool enough to have taken him into his service, if he had known him; and my Lord Simpleton, also, who Satan has set up for a cunning fool, seems to have it sit much better upon him, now he passes for a fool of art, than it would have done if the naked devil had come and challenged him for a fool in nature.

Infinite variety illustrate the Devil's reign among the sons of men, all which he manages with admirable dexterity, and a sleight particular to himself, by the mere advantage of his present concealed situation, and which, had he been obliged to have appeared in public, had been all lost, and he capable of just nothing at all, or, at least, of nothing more than the other ordinary politicians of wickedness could have done without him.

Now, authors are much divided as to the manner how the Devil manages his proper instruments for mischief: for Satan has a great many agents in the dark, who neither have the

Devil in them, nor are they much acquainted with him, and yet he serves himself of them; whether of their folly, or of that other frailty called wit, it is all one, he makes them do his work when they think they are doing their own; nay, so cunning is he in his guiding the weak part of the world, that even when they think they are serving God, they are doing nothing less or more than serving the Devil; nay, it is some of the nicest part of his operation to make them believe they are serving God when they do his work.   Thus, those who the Scripture foretold should persecute Christ's church in the latter days, were to think they did God good service; thus the Inquisition, for example, it may be, at this time, in all the acts of Christian cruelty which they are so famous for, if any of them are ignorant enough not to know that they are devils incarnate, they may, for aught we know, go on for God's sake; torture, murder, starve to death, mangle, and macerate, and all for God, and God's catholic church; and it is certainly the Devil's master-piece to bring mankind to such a perfection of devilism as that of the Inquisition is, for, if the Devil had not been in them, could they christen such a hell-fire judicature as the Inquisition is by the name of the Holy Office?   And so in paganism; how could so many nations among the poor Indians offer human sacrifices to their idols, and murder thousands of men, women, and children, to appease this god of the air when he is angry, if the Devil did not act in them under the visor of devotion?

But we need not go to America, or to the Inquisition, nor to paganism, or to popery either, to look for people that are sacrificing to the Devil, or that give their peace-offerings to him while they are offered upon God's altar; are not our churches (aye, and meeting-houses, too, as much as they pretend to be more sanctified than their neighbours) full of Devil-worshippers?   where do his devotees gratulate one another, and congratulate him, more than at church?   where, while they hold up their hands, and turn up their eyes towards heaven, they make all their vows to Satan, or, at least, to the fair devils, his representatives, which I shall speak of in their place.

Do not the sons of God, make assignations with the daughters of men, in the very house of worship?   do they not talk to them in the language of the eyes?   and what is at the bottom of it, while one eye is upon the prayer-book, and the other adjusting their dress? are they not sacrificing to Venus and Mercury, nay, and to the very Devil they dress at.

Let any man impartially survey the church gestures, the air, the postures, and the behaviour; let him keep an exact roll, and if I do not show him two Devil-worshippers for one true saint, then the word *saint* must have another signification than I ever yet understood it by.

The church as a place, is the receptacle of the dead, as well as the assembly of the living; what relates to those below, I doubt Satan, if he would be so kind, could give a better account of than I can; but as to the superficies, I pretend to so much penetration as to tell you, that there are more spectres, more apparitions always there, than you, that know nothing of the matter, may be aware of.

I happened to be at an eminent place of God's most devout worship the other day, with a gentleman of my acquaintance, who, I observed, minded very little the business he ought to come about; first I saw him always busy staring about him, and bowing this way and that way; nay, he made two or three bows and scrapes when he was repeating the responses to the Ten Commandments, and, I assure you, he made it correspond strangely, so that the harmony was not so broken in upon as you would expect it should; thus: *Lord*—and a bow to a fine lady, just come up to her seat—*have mercy upon us;*—three bows to a throng of ladies that came into the next pew altogether—*and incline*—then stopped to make a great scrape to my lord ——,— *our hearts*—just then the hearts of all the church were gone off from the subject, for the response was over, so he huddled up the rest in whisper, for God a'mighty could hear him well enough, he said, nay, as well as if he had spoken as loud as his neighbours did.

After we were come home, I asked him what he meant by all this, and what he thought of it.

How could I help it? said he; I must not be rude.

What? says I; rude to who?

Why, says he, there came in so many she-devils, I could not help it.

What, said I, could you not help bowing when you were saying your prayers?

O, sir, says he, the ladies would have thought I had slighted them; I could not avoid it.

Ladies! said I, I thought you called them devils just now.

Ay, ay, devils, said he, little charming devils; but I must not be rude to them, however.

Very well, said I, then you would be rude to God a'mighty, because you could not be rude to the Devil?

Why, that is true, said he; but what can we do? there is no going to church, as the case stands now, if we must not worship the Devil a little between whiles.

This is the case, indeed, and Satan carries his point on every hand; for if the fair-speaking, world, and the fair-looking world, are generally devils, that is to say, are in his management, we are sure the foul-speaking and the foul-doing world are all on his side; and you have then only the fair-doing part of the world that are out of his class, and when we speak of them, O, how few!

But I return to the Devil's managing our wicked part, for this he does with most exquisite subtlety; and this is one part of it, viz., he thrusts our vices into our virtues, by which he mixes the clean and the unclean, and thus by the corruption of the one, poisons and debauches the other; so that the slave he governs cannot account for his own common actions, and is fain to be obliged to his Maker to accept of the heart without the hands and feet; to take, as we vulgarly express it, the will for the deed, and if heaven was not so good to come into that half-in-half service, I do not see but the Devil would carry away all his servants. Here, indeed, I should enter into a long detail of involuntary wickedness, which, in short, is neither more or less than the Devil in everybody, ay, in every one of you, our governors excepted, take it as you please.

What is our language when we look back with reflection and reproach on past follies? I think I was bewitched, I was possessed; certainly; the Devil was in me, or else I had never been such a sot. Devil in you sir! ay, who doubts it? you may be sure the Devil was in you, and there he is still, and next time he can catch you in the same snare, you will be just the same sot that you say you were before.

In short, the Devil is too cunning for us, and manages us his own way; he governs the vices of men by his own methods: though every crime will not make a man a devil, yet it must be owned that every crime puts the criminal in some measure into the Devil's power, gives him a title to the man, and he treats him magisterially ever after.

Some tell us every single man, every individual, has a

devil attending him, to execute the orders of the (grand seignior) devil of the whole clan; that this attending evil angel, for so he is called, sees every step you take, is with you in every action, prompts you to every mischief, and leaves you to do everything that is pernicious to yourself; they also allege that there is a good spirit which attends him too, which latter is always accessary to everything that we do that is good, and reluctant to evil; if this is true, how comes it to pass that those two opposite spirits do not quarrel about it when they are pressing us to contrary actions, one good and the other evil? and why does the evil tempting spirit so often prevail? Instead of answering this difficult question, I shall only tell you, as to this story of good and evil angels attending every particular person, it is a good allegory, indeed, to represent the struggle in the mind of man between good and evil inclinations; but as to the rest, the best thing I can say of it is, that I think it is a fib.

But to take things as they are, and only talk by way of natural consequence (for to argue from nature is certainly the best way to find out the Devil's story), if there are good and evil spirits attending us, that is to say, a good angel and a devil, then it is no unjust reproach upon anybody to say, when they follow the dictates of the latter, the Devil is in them; or they are devils; nay, I must carry it farther still, namely, that as the generality and greatest number of people do follow and obey the evil spirit and not the good, and that the predominate power is allowed to be the nominating power, you must then allow that, in short, the greater part of mankind has the Devil in them, and so I come to my text:

To this purpose give me leave to borrow a few lines of a friend on this very part of the Devil's management.

> To places and persons he suits his disguises,
>   And dresses up all his banditti,
> Who, as pickpockets flock to a country assizes,
>   Crowd up to the court and the city.
>
> They're at every elbow and every ear,
>   And ready at every call, Sir;
> The vigilant scout plants his agents about,
>   And has something to do with us all, Sir.
>
> In some he has part, and in some he's the whole,
>   And of some (like the vicar of Baddow),
> It can neither be said they have body or soul,
>   But only are devils in shadow.

The pretty and witty are devils in mask,
  The beauties are mere apparitions ;
The homely alone by their faces are known,
  And the good by their ugly conditions.

The beaus walk about like the shadows of men,
  And wherever he leads 'em they follow,
But take 'em and shake 'em, there's not one in ten
  But's as light as a feather, and hollow.

Thus all his affairs he drives on in disguise,
  And he tickles mankind with a feather :
Creeps in at our ears, and looks out at our eyes,
  And jumbles our senses together.

He raises the vapours, and prompts the desires,
  And to ev'ry dark deed holds the candle ;
The passions inflames and the appetite fires ;
  And takes ev'rything by the right handle.

Thus he walks up and down in complete masquerade,
  And with every company mixes,
Sells in every shop, works at every trade,
  And ev'rything doubtful perplexes.

How Satan comes by this governing influence in the minds
and upon the actions of men, is a question I am not yet come
to, nor indeed does it so particularly belong to the Devil's
history; it seems rather a polemic, so it may pass at school
among the metaphysics, and puzzle the heads of our masters ;
wherefore I think to write to the learned Dr. B. . . about
it, imploring his most sublime haughtiness, that when his
other more momentous avocations of pedantry and pedagogism
will give him an interval from wrath and contention, he will
set apart a moment to consider human nature devilized, and
give us a mathematical, anatomical description of it; with
a map of Satan's kingdom in the microcosm of mankind,
and such other illuminations as to him and his contemporaries
—— and —— &c., in their great wisdom shall seem meet.

CHAPTER V.

OF THE DEVIL'S MANAGEMENT IN THE PAGAN HIERARCHY BY
OMENS, ENTRAILS, AUGURS, ORACLES, AND SUCH-LIKE PAGEANTRY
OF HELL ; AND HOW THEY WENT OFF THE STAGE AT LAST, BY
THE INTRODUCTION OF TRUE RELIGION.

I HAVE adjourned, not finished my account of the Devil's
secret management by possession, and shall re-assume it, in

its place; but I must take leave to mention some other parts
of his retired scheme, by which he has hitherto managed
mankind, and the first of these is by that fraud of all frauds,
called oracle.

Here his trumpet yielded an uncertain sound for some
ages, and like what he was, and according to what he
practised from the beginning, he delivered out falsehood and
delusion by retail: the priests of Apollo acted this farce for
him to a great nicety at Delphos; there were divers others
at the same time, and some, which to give the Devil his
due, he had very little hand in, as we shall see presently.

There were also some smaller, some greater, some more,
some less famous places where those oracles were seated, and
audience given to the inquirers, in all which the Devil, or
somebody for him, *permissu superiorum*, for either vindictive
or other hidden ends and purposes, was allowed to make at
least a pretension to the knowledge of things to come; but,
as public cheats generally do, they acted in masquerade, and
gave such uncertain and inconsistent responses, that they
were obliged to use the utmost art to reconcile events to the
prediction, even after things were come to pass.

Here the Devil was a lying spirit, in a particular and
extraordinary manner, in the mouths of all the prophets;
and yet he had the cunning to express himself so, that whatever happened, the oracle was supposed to have meant as it
fell out; and so all their auguries, omens, and voices, by
which the Devil amused the world, not at that time only,
but since, have been likewise interpreted.

Julian the Apostate dealt mightily in these amusements;
but the Devil, who neither wished his fall or presaged it to
him, evidenced that he knew nothing of Julian's fate; for
that, as he sent almost to all the oracles of the East, and
summoned all the priests together, to inform him of the success of his Persian expedition, they all, like Ahab's prophets,
having a lying spirit in them, encouraged him and promised
him success.

Nay, all the ill omens which disturbed him, they presaged
good from; for example, he was at a prodigious expense
when he was at Antioch, to buy up white beasts and white
fowls for sacrifices, and for predicting from the entrails; from
whence the Antiochians, in contempt, called him Victimarius;
but whenever the entrails foreboded evil, the cunning Devil

made the priests put a different construction upon them, and promise him good : when he entered into the temple of the Genii, to offer sacrifice, one of the priests dropped down dead ; this, had it any signification more than a man falling dead of an apoplectic, would have signified something fatal to Julian, who made himself a brother sacrist or priest; whereas the priests turned it presently to signify the death of his colleague, the consul Sallust, which happened just at the same time, though eight hundred miles off. So in another case, Julian thought it ominous, that he, who was Augustus, should be named with two other names of persons, both already dead : the case was thus; the style of the emperor was Julianus Felix Augustus, and two of his principal officers were Julianus, and Felix; now both Julianus and Felix died within a few days of one another, which disturbed him much, who was the third of the three names; but his flattering devil told him it all imported good to him, viz., that though Julianus and Felix should die, Augustus should be immortal.

Thus whatever happened, and whatever was foretold, and how much soever they differed from one another, the lying spirit was sure to reconcile the prediction and the event, and make them at least seem to correspond in favour of the person inquiring.

Now, we are told, oracles are ceased, and the Devil is farther limited for the good of mankind, not being allowed to vent his delusions by the mouths of the priests and augurs, as formerly. I will not take upon me to say how far they are really ceased, more than they were before; I think it is much more reasonable to believe there was never any reality in them at all, or that any oracle ever gave out any answers but what were the invention of the priests, and the delusions of the Devil. I have a great many ancient authors on my side in this opinion, as Eusebius, Tertullian, Aristotle, and others, who, as they lived so near the pagan times, and when even some of those rites were yet in use, they had much more reason to know, and could probably pass a better judgment upon them ; nay, Cicero himself ridicules them in the openest manner. Again, other authors descend to particulars, and show how the cheat was managed by the heathen sacrists and priests, and in what enthusiastic manner they spoke ; namely, by going into the hollow images, such as the brazen bull, and the image of Apollo ; and how subtly they gave out dubious and ambigious answers; that when the people did not find their expectations answered by the event, they might be imposed upon by the priests, and confidently told they did not rightly understand the oracle's meaning : however, I cannot say but that indeed there are some authors of good credit too, who will have it that there was a real prophetic spirit in the voice or answers given by the oracles, and that oftentimes they were miraculously exact in those answers; and they give that of the Delphic oracle answering the question which was given about Crœsus for an example, viz., what Crœsus was doing at that time : to wit, that he was boiling a lamb and the flesh of a tortoise together, in a brass vessel, or boiler, with a cover of the same metal; that is to say, in a kettle with a brass cover.

To affirm therefore, that they were all cheats, a man must encounter with antiquity, and set his private judgment up against an established opinion : but it is no matter for that; if I do not see anything in that received opinion capable of evidence, much less of demonstration, I must be allowed still to think as I do; others may believe as they list; I see nothing hard or difficult in the thing; the priests, who were always historically informed of the circumstance of the inquirer, or at least something about them, might easily find some ambiguous speech to make, and put some *double entendre* upon them, which, upon the event, solved the credit of the oracle, were it one way or other; and this they certainly did, or we have room to think the Devil knows less of things now than he did in former days.

It is true that by these delusions the priests got infinite sums of money, and this makes it still probable that they would labour hard, and use the utmost of their skill to uphold the credit of their oracles; and it is a full discovery, as well of the subtlety of the sacrists, as of the ignorance and stupidity of the people, in those early days of Satan's witchcraft, to see what merry work the Devil made with the world, and what gross things he put upon mankind. Such was the story of the Dordonian oracle in Epirus, viz., that two pigeons flew out of Thebes (N.B. it was the Egyptian Thebes), from the temple of Belus, erected there by the ancient sacrists, and that one of these fled eastward into Libya, and the deserts of Africa, and the other into Greece, namely, to Dordona, and these communicated the divine mysteries to one another, and afterwards gave mystical solutions to the devout inquirers; first the Dordonian pigeon perching upon an oak, spoke audibly to the people there, that the gods commanded them to build an oracle, or temple, to Jupiter in that place, which was accordingly done: the other pigeon did the like on the hill in Africa, where it commanded them to build another to Jupiter Ammon, or Hammon.

Wise Cicero contemned all this, and, as authors tell us, ridiculed the answer which, as I have hinted above, the oracle gave to Crœsus, proving that the oracle itself was a lie; that it could not come from Apollo, for that Apollo never spoke Latin. In a word, Cicero rejected them all; and Demosthenes also mentions the cheats of the oracles, when, speaking of the oracle of Apollo, he said, Pythia Philippized; that is, that when the priests were bribed with money, they always gave their answers in favour of Philip of Macedon.

But that which is most strange to me is, that in this dispute about the reality of oracles, the heathen who made use of them are the people who expose them, and who insist, most positively, upon their being cheats and impostors, as in particular those mentioned above; while the Christians who reject them, yet believe they did really foretell things, answer questions, &c.; only with this difference, that the heathen authors who oppose them, insist that it is all delusion and cheat, and charge it upon the priests; and the Christian opposers insist that it was real, but that the Devil, not the gods, gave the answers; and that he was permitted to do it by a superior power, to magnify that power in the total silencing them at last.

But, as I said before, I am with the heathen here, against the Christian writers, for I take it all to be a cheat and delusion. I must give my reason for it, or I do nothing: my reason is this; I insist Satan is as blind in matters of futurity as we are, and can tell nothing of what is to come. These oracles, often pretending to predict, could be nothing else, therefore, but a cheat, formed by the money-getting priests to amuse the world, and bring grist to their mill. If I meet with anything in my way to open my eyes to a better opinion of them, I shall tell you as I go on.

On the other hand, whether the Devil really spake in those oracles, or set the cunning priests to speak for him; whether they predicted, or only made the people believe they predicted;

whether they gave answers which came to pass, or prevailed upon the people to believe that what was said did come to pass, it was much at one, and fully answered the Devil's end ; namely, to amuse and delude the world; and as to do, or to cause to be done, is the same part of speech, so, whoever did it, the Devil's interest was carried on by it, his government preserved, and all the mischief he could desire was effectually brought to pass; so that every way they were the Devil's oracles, that is out of the question.

Indeed, I have wondered sometimes why, since by this sorcery the Devil performed such wonders, that is, played so many tricks in the world, and had such universal success, he should set up no more of them; but there might be a great many reasons given for that, too long to tire you with at present. It is true, there were not many of them; and yet, considering what a great deal of business they despatched, it was enough, for six or eight oracles were more than sufficient to amuse all the world: the chief oracles we meet with in history, are among the Greeks and the Romans, viz.,

> That of Jupiter Hammon, in Libya, as above.
> The Dordonian, in Epirus.
> Apollo Delphicus, in the country of Phocis in Greece.
> Apollo Clavius, in Asia Minor.
> Serapis, in Alexandria, in Egypt.
> Trophomis, in Bœotia.
> Sybilla Cumæa, in Italy.
> Diana, at Ephesus.
> Apollo Daphneus, at Antioch.

Besides many of lesser note, in several other places, as I have hinted before.

I have nothing to do here with the story mentioned by Plutarch, of a voice being heard at sea, from some of the islands called the Echinades, and calling upon one Thamuz, an Egyptian, who was on board a ship, bidding him, when he came to the Palodes, other islands in the Ionian seas, tell them there, that the great god Pan was dead; and when Thamuz performed it, great groanings, and howlings, and lamentations, were heard from the shore.

This tale tells but indifferently, though indeed it looks more like a Christian fable than a pagan, because it seems as if made to honour the Christian worship, and blast all the pagan idolatry; and for that reason I reject it, the Christian profession needing no such fabulous stuff to confirm it.

Nor is it true, in fact, that the oracles did cease immediately upon the death of Christ; but, as I noted before, the sum of the matter is this; the Christian religion spreading itself universally, as well as miraculously, and that too by the foolishness of preaching, into all parts of the world, the oracles ceased; that is to say, their trade ceased, their rogueries were daily detected; the deluded people being better taught, came no more after them, and being ashamed, as well as discouraged, they sneaked out of the world as well as they could; in short, the customers fell off, and the priests, who were the shopkeepers, having no business to do, shut up their shops, broke, and went away; the trade and the tradesmen were hissed off the stage together; so that the Devil, who, it must be confessed, got infinitely by the cheat, became bankrupt, and was obliged to set other engines at work, as other cheats and deceivers do, who, when one trick grows stale, and will serve no longer, are forced to try another.

Nor was the Devil to seek of new measures; for though he could not give out his delusive trash as he did before, in pomp and state, with the solemnity of a temple and a set of enthusiasts called priests, who played a thousand tricks to amuse the world, he then had recourse to his old Egyptian method, which indeed was more ancient than that of oracles; and that was by magic, sorcery, familiars, witchcraft, and the like.

Of this we find the people of the south, that is, of Arabia and Chaldea, were the first, from whence we are told the wise men, that is to say, magicians, were called Chaldeans and Southsayers. Hence also we find Ahaziah, the king of Israel, sent to Baal-zebub, the god of Ekron, to inquire whether he should live or die. This, some think, was a kind of an oracle, though others think it was only some overgrown magician, who counterfeited himself to be a devil, and obtained upon that idol-hunting age to make a cunning man of him; and for that purpose he got himself made the priest of Baal-zebub, the god of Ekron, and gave out answers in his name. Thus those merry fellows in Egypt, Jannes and Jambres, are said to mimic Moses and Aaron when they worked the miraculous plagues upon the Egyptians; and we have some instances in Scripture that support this, such as the witch of Endor, the king Manasses, who dealt with the Devil openly, and had a familiar; the woman mentioned Acts xvi., who had a spirit of divination, and who got money by playing the oracle, that is, answering doubtful questions, &c., which spirit, or devil, the apostle cast out.

Now, though it is true that the old women in the world have filled us with tales, some improbable, others impossible, some weak, some ridiculous; and that this puts a general discredit upon all the graver matrons, who entertain us with stories better put together; yet it is certain, and I must be allowed to affirm, that the Devil does not disdain to take into his service many troops of good old women, and old women-men too, who he finds it is for his service to keep in constant pay; to these he is found frequently to communicate his mind, and oftentimes we find them such proficients, that they know much more than the Devil can teach them.

How far our ancient friend Merlin, or the grave matron his (Satan's) most trusty and well-beloved cousin and counsellor, mother Shipton, were commissioned by him to give out their prophetic oracles, and what degree of possession he may have arrived to in them upon their midnight excursions, I will not undertake to prove; but that he might be acquainted with them both, as well as with several of our modern gentlemen, I will not deny neither.

I confess it is not very incongruous with the Devil's temper, or with the nature of his business, to shift hands: possibly he found that he had tired the world with oracular cheats; that men began to be surfeited with them, and grew sick of the frauds which were so frequently detected; that it was time to take new measures, and contrive some new trick to bite the world, that he might not be exposed to contempt; or perhaps he saw the approach of new light, which the Christian doctrine bringing with it began to spread in the minds of men; that it would outshine the dim-burning *ignis fatui*, with which he had so long cheated mankind, and was afraid to stand it, lest he should be mobbed off the stage by his own people, when their eyes should begin to open; that upon this foot he might, in policy, withdraw from those old retreats the oracles, and restrain those responses before they lost all their credit; for we find the people seemed to be at a mighty loss for some time, for want of them, so that

It made them run up and down to conjurers, and man-gossips, to brazen heads, speaking calves, and innumerable simple things, so gross that they are scarce fit to be named, to satisfy the itch of having their fortunes told them, as we call it.

. Now as the Devil is very seldom blind to his own interest, and therefore thought fit to quit his old way of imposing upon the world by his oracles, only because he found the world began to be too wise to be imposed upon that way; so, on the other hand, finding there was still a possibility to delude the world, though by other instruments, he no sooner laid down his oracles, and the solemn pageantry, magnificent appearances, and other frauds of his priests and votaries, in their temples and shrines, but he set up a new trade, and having, as I have said, agents and instruments sufficient for any business that he could have to employ them in, he begins in corners, as the learned and merry Dr. Brown says, and exercises his minor trumperies by ways of his own contriving, listing a great number of new-found operators, such as witches, magicians, diviners, figure-casters, astrologers, and such inferior seducers.

Now it is true, as that doctor says, this was running into corners, as if he had been expelled his more triumphant way of giving audience in form, which for so many ages had been allowed him; yet I must add, that as it seemed to be the Devil's own doing, from a right judgment of his affairs, which had taken a new turn in the world, upon the shining of new lights from the Christian doctrine, so it must be acknowledged the Devil made himself amends upon mankind, by the various methods he took, and the multitude of instruments he employed, and perhaps deluded mankind in a more fatal and sensible manner than he did before, though not so universally.

He had, indeed, before more pomp and figure put upon it, and he cheated mankind then in a way of magnificence and splendour; but this was not in above eight or ten principal places, and not fifty places in all, public or private; whereas now, fifty thousand of his angels and instruments, visible and invisible, hardly may be said to suffice for one town or city; but in short, as his invisible agents fill the air, and are at hand for mischief on every emergence, so his visible fools swarm in every village, and you have scarce a hamlet or a town but his emissaries are at hand for business; and, which is still worse, in all places he finds business; nay, even where religion is planted, and seems to flourish, yet he keeps his ground and pushes his interest according to what has been said elsewhere upon the same subject, that wherever religion plants, the Devil plants close by it.

· Nor, as I say, does he fail of success; delusion spreads like a plague, and the Devil is sure of votaries; like a true mountebank, he can always bring a crowd about his stage, and that sometimes faster than other people.

What I observe upon this subject is this, that the world is at a strange loss for want of the Devil; if it was not so, what is the reason, that upon the silencing the oracles, and religion telling them that miracles are ceased, and that God has done speaking by prophets, they never inquire whether heaven has established any other or new way of revelation, but away they ran with their doubts and difficulties to these dreamers of dreams, tellers of fortunes, and personal oracles to be resolved; as if, when they acknowledge the Devil is dumb, these could speak; and as if the wicked spirit could do more than the good, the diabolical more than the divine, or that heaven having taken away the Devil's voice, had furnished him with an equivalant, by allowing scolds, termagants, and old, weak, and superannuated wretches, to speak for him; for these are the people we go to now in our doubts and emergencies.

While this blindness continues among us, it is nonsense to say that oracles are silenced, or the Devil is dumb, for the Devil gives audience still by his deputies; only as Jeroboam made priests of the meanest of the people, so he is grown a little humble, and makes use of meaner instruments than he did before; for whereas the priests of Apollo, and of Jupiter, were splendid in their appearance, of grave and venerable aspect, and sometimes of no mean quality, now he makes use of scoundrels and rabble, beggars and vagabonds, old hags, superanuated miserable hermits, gipseys and strollers, the pictures of envy and ill luck.

Either the Devil is grown an ill master, and gives but mean wages, that he can get no better servants; or else common sense is grown very low-prized and contemptible, that such as these are fit tools to continue the succession of fraud, and carry on the Devil's interest in the world; for were not the passions and temper of mankind deeply pre-engaged in favour of this dark prince, we could never suffer ourselves to accept of his favours by the hands of such contemptible agents as these! how do we receive his oracles from an old witch of particular eminence, and who we believe to be more than ordinarily inspired from hell! I say, we receive the oracle with reverence, that is to say, with a kind of horror, with regard to the black prince it comes from, and at the same time turn our faces away from the wretch that mumbles out the answers, lest she should cast an evil eye, as we call it, upon us, and put a devil into us when she plays the devil before us! how do we listen to the cant of those worst of vagabonds, the gipseys, when, at the same time, we watch our hedges and henroosts for fear of their thieving!

Either the Devil uses us more like fools than he did our ancestors, or we really are worse fools than those ages produced, for they were never deluded by such low-prized devils as we are, by such despicable Bridewell devils, that are fitter for a whipping-post than an altar, and instead of being received as the voice of an oracle, should be sent to the house of correction for pickpockets.

Nor is this accidental, and here and there one of these wretches to be seen, but, in short, if it has been in other nations as it is with us, I do not see that the Devil was able to get any better people into his pay, or at least very rarely: where have we seen anything above a tinker turn wizard? and where have we had a witch of quality among us, mother Je——gs excepted? and if she had not been more of something else than a witch, it was thought she had never got so much money by her profession.

Magicians, southsayers, devil-raisers, and such people, we have heard much of, but seldom above the degree of the meanest of the mean people, the lowest of the lowest rank: indeed the word, *wisemen* which the Devil would fain have had his agents honoured with, was used awhile in Egypt, and in Persia, among the Chaldeans, but it continued but a little while, and never reached so far northward as our country; nor, however the Devil has managed it, have many of our great men, who have been most acquainted with him, ever been able to acquire the title of wise men.

I have heard that in older times, I suppose in good Queen Bess's days, or beyond (for little is to be said here for anything on this side of her time), there were some councillors and statesmen who merited the character of wise, in the best sense; that is say, good, and wise, as they stand in conjunction; but as to what has happened since that, or, as we may call it, from that queen's funeral to the late revolution, I have little to say; but I will tell you what honest Andrew Marvel said of those times, and by that you may, if you please, make your calculation or let it alone, it is all one:

> To see a white staff-maker, a beggar, a lord,
> And scarce a wise man at a long council-board.

But I may be told this relates to wise men in another construction, or wise men as they are opposed to fools; whereas we are talking of them now under another class, namely, as wisemen or magicians, southsayers, &c., such as were in former times called by that name.

But to this I answer, that take them in which sense you please, it may be the same; for if I were to ask the Devil the character of the best statesman he had employed among us for many years past, I am apt to think that though oracles are ceased, he would honestly, according to the old ambiguous way, when I asked if they were Christians, answer they were (his) privy-councillors.

It is but a little while ago, that I happened, in conversation, to meet with a long list of the magistrates of that age, in a neighbouring country, that is to say, the men of fame among them; and it was a very diverting thing to see the judgment which was passed upon them among a great deal of good company; it is not for me to tell you how many white staves, golden keys, marshal's batons, cordons blue, gordon rouge and gordon blanc, there were among them, or by what titles, as dukes, counts, marquis, abbot, bishop, or judge, they were to be distinguished; but the marginal notes I found upon most of them were (being marked with an asterisk) as follows:—

Such a duke, such eminent offices added to his titles (* in the margin) —— 'no saint.'

Such an arch—— with the title of noble added, —— 'no archangel.'

Such an eminent statesman and prime minister, —— 'no witch.'

Such a ribbon with a set of great letters added, —— 'no conjurer.'

It presently occurred to me that though oracles were ceased, and we had now no more *double entendre* in such a degree as before, yet that ambiguous answers were not at an end; and that whether those negatives were meant so by the writers, or not, it was certain custom led the readers to conclude them to be satires, that they were to be rung backward, like the bells when the town is on fire; though, in short, I durst not read them backward anywhere, but as speaking of foreign people, for fear of raising the devil I am talking of.

But to return to the subject : to such mean things is the Devil now reduced in his ordinary way of carrying on his business in the world, that his oracles are delivered now by the bellmen and the chimney-sweepers, by the meanest of those that speak in the dark, and if he operates by them, you may expect it accordingly; his agents seem to me as if the Devil had singled them out by their deformity, or that there was something particular required in their aspect to qualify them for their employment; whence it is become proverbial, when our looks are very dismal and frightful, to say ' I look like a witch ; ' or in other cases to say, ' as ugly as a witch ; ' in another case, ' to look as envious as a witch.' Now whether there is anything particularly required in the looks of the Devil's modern agents, which is assisting in the discharge of their offices, and which makes their answers appear more solemn, this the Devil has not yet revealed, at least not to me; and, therefore, why it is that he singles out such creatures as are fit only to frighten the people that come to them with their inquiries, I do not take upon me to determine.

Perhaps it is necessary they should be thus extraordinary in their aspect, that they might strike an awe into the minds of their votaries, as if they were Satan's true and real representatives, and that the said votaries may think when they speak to the witches they are really talking to the Devil ; or perhaps it is necessary to the witches themselves, that they should be so exquisitely ugly, that they might not be surprised at whatever figure the Devil makes when he first appears to them, being certain they can see nothing uglier than themselves.

Some are of the opinion that the communication with the Devil, or between the Devil and those creatures his agents, has something assimilating in it, and that if they were tolerable before, they are, *ipso facto*, turned into devils by talking with him ; I will not say but that a tremor in the limbs, a horror in the aspect, and a surprising stare in the eyes, may seize upon some of them when they really see the Devil, and that the frequent repetition may make those distortions, which we so constantly see in their faces, become natural to them ; by which, if it does not continue always upon the countenance, they can at least, like the posturemasters, cast themselves into such figures and frightful dislocations of the lines and features in their faces, and so assume a devil's face suitable to the occasion, or as may serve the turn for which they take it up, and as often as they have any use for it.

But be it which of these the inquirer pleases, it is all one to the case in hand ; this is certain, that such deformed, devil-like creatures, most of those we call hags and witches are in their shapes and aspects, and that they give out their sentences and frightful messages with an air of revenge for some injury received, for witches are famed chiefly for doing mischief.

It seems the Devil has always picked out the most ugly and frightful old women to do his business ; mother Shipton, our famous English witch or prophetess, is very much wronged in her picture, if she was not of the most terrible aspect imaginable ; and if it be true that Merlin, the famous Welsh fortuneteller, was a frightful figure, it will seem the more rational to believe, if we credit another story, viz., that he was begotten by the Devil himself, of which I shall speak by itself ; but to go back to the Devil's instruments being so ugly, it may be observed, I say, that the Devil has always dealt in such sort of cattle ; the sibyls, of whom so many strange prophetic things are recorded, whether true or no is not to the question, are (if the Italian painters may have any credit given them) all represented as very old women ; and, as if ugliness were a beauty to old age, they seem to paint them out as ugly and frightful as, not they, the painters, but even as the Devil himself could make them ; not that I believe there are any original pictures of them really extant ; but it is not unlikely that the Italians might have some traditional knowledge of them, or some remaining notions of them, or particularly that ancient sibyl named Anus, who sold the fatal book to Tarquin ; it is said of her that Tarquin supposed she doated with age.

I had thoughts, indeed, here to have entered into a learned

disquisition of the excellency of old women in all diabolical operations, and particularly of the necessity of having recourse to them for Satan's more exquisite administration, which also may serve to solve the great difficulty in the natural philosophy of hell; namely, why it comes to pass that the Devil is obliged, for want of old women, properly so called, to turn so many ancient fathers, grave counsellors both of law and state, and especially civilians, or doctors of the law, into old women, and how the extra-ordinary operation is performed; but this, as a thing of great consequence in Satan's management of human affairs, and particularly as it may lead us into the necessary history as well as characters of some of the most eminent of these sects among us, I have purposely reserved for a work by itself, to be published, if Satan hinders not, in fifteen volumes in folio, wherein I shall, in the first place, define in the most exact manner possible, what is to be understood by a male old woman, of what heterogeneous kind they are produced; give you the monstrous anatomy of the parts, and especially those of the head, which being filled with innumerable globules of a sublime nature, and which being of a fine contexture without, but particularly hollow in the cavity, defines most philosophically that ancient paradoxical saying, viz., being full of emptiness, and makes it very consistent with nature and common sense.

I shall likewise spend some time, and it must be labour too, I assure you, when it is done, in determining whether this new species of wonderfuls are not derived from that famous old woman Merlin, which I prove to be very reasonable for us to suppose, because of the many several judicious authors, who affirm the said Merlin, as I hinted before, to have been begotten by the Devil.

As to the deriving his gift of prophecy from the Devil, by that pretended generation, I shall omit that part, because, as I have all along insisted upon it, that Satan himself has no prophetic or predicting powers of his own, it is not very clear to me that he could convey it to his posterity, *nil dat quod non habet.*

However, in deriving this so much magnified prophet in a right line from the Devil, much may be said in favour of his ugly face, in which it was said he was very remarkable, for it is no new thing for a child to be like the father; but all

these weighty things I adjourn for the present, and proceed
to the affair in hand, namely, the several branches of the
Devil's management since his quitting his temples and oracles.

CHAPTER VI.

OF THE EXTRAORDINARY APPEARANCE OF THE DEVIL, AND PARTICULARLY OF THE CLOVEN FOOT.

SOME people would fain have us treat this tale of the Devil's
appearing with a cloven-foot with more solemnity than I
believe the Devil himself does; for Satan, who knows how
much of a cheat it is, must certainly ridicule it, in his
own thoughts, to the last degree; but as he is glad of any
way to hoodwink the understandings, and bubble the weak
part of the world; so if he sees men willing to take every
scarecrow for a devil, it is not his business to undeceive
them; on the other hand, he finds it his interest to foster the
cheat, and serve himself of the consequence: nor could I
doubt but the Devil, if any mirth be allowed him, often laughs
at the many frightful shapes and figures we dress him up in,
and especially to see how willing we are first to paint him as
black, and make him as ugly as we can, and then stare and
start at the spectrum of our own making.

The truth is, that among all the horribles that we dress up
Satan in, I cannot but think we show the least of invention
in this of a goat, or a thing with a goat's foot, of all the rest;
for though a goat is a creature made use of by our Saviour in
the allegory of the day of judgment, and is said there to
represent the wicked rejected party, yet it seems to be only
on account of their similitude to the sheep, and so to represent
the just fate of hypocrisy and hypocrites, and, in particular,
to form the necessary antithesis in the story; for else, our
whimsical fancies excepted, a sheep or a lamb has a cloven
foot as well as a goat; nay, if the Scripture be of any value
in the case, it is to the Devil's advantage, for the dividing
the hoof was the distinguishing character or mark of a
clean beast, and how the Devil can be brought into that
number is pretty hard to say.

One would have thought if we had intended to have given
a just figure of the Devil, it would have been more apposite

to have ranked him among the cat-kind, and given him a foot (if he is to be known by his foot) like a lion, or like a red dragon, being the same creatures which he is represented by in the text, and so his claws would have had some terror in them, as well as his teeth.

But neither is the goat a true representative of the Devil at all, for we do not rank the goats among the subtle or cunning part of the brutes; he is counted a fierce creature indeed of his kind, though nothing like these other above mentioned; and he is emblematically used to represent a lustful temper, but even that part does not fully serve to describe the Devil, whose operation lies principally another way.

Besides, it is not the goat himself that is made use of, it is the cloven hoof only, and that so particularly, that the cloven foot of a ram or a swine, or any other creature, may serve as well as that of a goat, only that history gives us some cause to call it the goat's foot.

In the next place, it is understood by us not as a bare token to know Satan by, but as if it were a brand upon him, and that, like the mark God put upon Cain, it was given him for a punishment, so that he cannot get leave to appear without it, nay, cannot conceal it, whatever other dress or disguise he may put on; and, as if it was to make him as ridiculous as possible, they will have it be, that whenever Satan has occasion to dress himself in any human shape, be it of what degree soever, from the king to the beggar, be it of a fine lady, or of an old woman (the latter it seems he most often assumes), yet still he not only must have this cloven foot about him, but he is obliged to show it too; nay, they will not allow him any dress, whether it be a prince's robes, a lord cha——r's gown, or a lady's hoops and long petticoats, but the cloven foot must be showed from under them; they will not so much as allow him an artificial shoe, or a jack-boot, as we often see contrived to conceal a club-foot, or a wooden-leg; but that the Devil may be known wherever he goes, he is bound to show his foot; they might as well oblige him to set a bill upon his cap, as folks do upon a house to be let, and have it written in capital letters, I am the Devil.

It must be confessed, this is very particular, and would be very hard upon the Devil, if it had not another article in it, which is some advantage to him, and that is, that the fact is not true; but the belief of this is so universal, that all the world runs away with it; by which mistake the good people miss the Devil many times where they look for him, and meet him as often where they did not expect him, and when, for want of this cloven foot, they do not know him.

Upon this very account I have sometimes thought, not that this has been put upon him by mere fancy, and the cheat of a heavy imagination, propagated by fable and chimney-corner divinity, but that it has been a contrivance of his own; and that, in short, the Devil raised this scandal upon himself, that he might keep his disguise the better, and might go a visiting among his friends without being known; for were it really so, that he could go nowhere without this particular brand of infamy, he could not come into company, could not dine with my lord mayor, nor drink tea with the ladies, could not go to the drawing-r—— at ——, could not have gone to Fontainbleau to the King of France's wedding, or to the Diet of Poland to prevent the grandees there coming to an agreement; nay, which would be still worse than all, he could not go to the masquerade, nor to any of our balls; the reason is plain, he would be always discovered, exposed and forced to leave the good company, or, which would be as bad, the company would all cry out, the Devil, and run out of the room as if they were frightened; nor could all the help of invention do him any service, no dress he could put on would cover him; not all our friends at Tavistock Corner could furnish him with a habit that would disguise or conceal him, this unhappy foot would spoil it all. Now this would be so great a loss to him, that I question whether he could carry on any of his most important affairs in the world without it; for though he has access to mankind in his complete disguise, I mean that of his invisibility, yet the learned very much agree in this, that his corporal presence in the world is absolutely necessary upon many occasions, to support his interest, and keep up his correspondences, and particularly to encourage his friends, when numbers are requisite to carry on his affairs; but this part I shall have occasion to speak of again, when I come to consider him as a gentleman of business in his locality, and under the head of visible apparition; but I return to the foot.

As I have thus suggested that the Devil himself has politically spread about this notion concerning his appearing with a cloven foot, so I doubt not that he has thought it for his purpose to paint this cloven foot so lively in the imaginations of many of our people, and especially of those clear-sighted folks who see the Devil when he is not to be seen, that they would make no scruple to say, nay, and to make affidavit too, even before Satan himself, whenever he sat upon the bench, that they had seen his worship's foot at such and such a time; this I advance the rather because it is very much for his interest to do this, for if we had not many witnesses, *viva voce*, to testify it, we should have had some obstinate fellows always among us, who would have denied the fact, or at least have spoken doubtfully of it, and so have raised disputes and objections against it as impossible, or at least as improbable; buzzing one ridiculous notion or other into our ears, as if the Devil was not so black as he was painted, that he had no more a cloven foot than a pope, whose apostolical toes have so often been reverentially kissed by kings and emperors.   But now, alas! this part is out of the question, not the man in the moon, not the groaning-board, not the speaking of friar Bacon's brazen-head, not the inspiration of mother Shipton, or the miracles of Dr. Faustus, things as certain as death and taxes, can be more firmly believed : the Devil not have a cloven foot! I doubt not but I could, in a short time, bring you a thousand old women together, that would as soon believe there was no Devil at all, nay, they will tell you, he could not be a devil without it, any more than he could come into the room and the candles not burn blue, or go out and not leave a smell of brimstone behind him.

Since then the certainty of the thing is so well established, and there are so many good and substantial witnesses ready to testify that he has a cloven foot, and that they have seen it too; nay, and that we have antiquity on our side, for we have this truth confirmed by the testimony of many ages; why should we doubt it any longer? We can prove that many of our ancestors have been of this opinion, and divers learned authors have left it upon record, as particularly that learned familiarist, mother Hazel, whose writings are to be found in MS. in the famous library at Pie-Corner; also the admired Joan of Amesbury, the History of the Lancashire Witches, and the reverend exorcist of the Devils of Loudon, whose history is extant among us to this day; all these and many more may be

quoted, and their writings referred to for the confirmation
of the antiquity of this truth; but there seems to be no
occasion for farther evidence, it is enough; Satan himself,
if he did not raise the report, yet tacitly owns the fact, at
least he appears willing to have it believed, and be received
as a general truth for the reasons above.

But besides all this, and as much a jest as some unbeliev-
ing people would have this story pass for, who knows but
that if Satan is empowered to assume any shape or body,
and to appear to us visibly, as if really so shaped; I say, who
knows but he may, by the same authority, be allowed to
assume the addition of the cloven foot, or two or four cloven
feet, if he pleased? and why not a cloven foot as well as any
other foot, if he thinks fit? for if the Devil can assume a
shape, and can appear to mankind in a visible form, it may, I
doubt not, with as good authority be advanced that he is left
at liberty to assume what shape he pleases, and to choose
what case of flesh and blood he will please to wear, whether
real or imaginary; and, if this liberty be allowed him, it is
an admirable disguise for him to come generally with his
cloven foot, that when he finds it for his purpose on special
occasions to come without it, as I said above, he may not be
suspected; but take this with you as you go, that all this is
upon a supposition that the Devil can assume a visible shape,
and can make a real appearance, which, however, I do not
think fit to grant or deny.

Certain it is, the first people who bestowed a cloven foot
upon the Devil, were not so despicable as you may imagine,
but were real favourites of heaven; for did not Aaron set up
the devil of a calf in the congregation, and set the people a
dancing about it for a god? Upon which occasion, expositors
tell us, that particular command was given, Lev. xvii. 7.
*They shall no more offer their sacrifices unto devils, after whom
they have gone a whoring;* likewise King Jeroboam set up the
two calves, one at Dan, and the other at Bethel, and we find
them charged afterwards with setting up the worship of
devils, instead of the worship of God.

After this, we find some nations actually sacrificed to the
Devil, in the form of a ram, and others of a goat, from which,
and that above of the calves at Horeb, I doubt not the story
of the cloven foot first derived; and it is plain, that the worship of that calf at Horeb, is meant in the Scripture quoted

above, Lev. xvii. 7. *Thou shalt no more offer sacrifices unto devils :* the original is *Seghnirim ;* that is, rough and hairy goats or calves ; and some think also in this shape the Devil most ordinarily appeared to the Egyptians and Arabians, from whence it was derived.

Also in the old writings of the Egyptians, I mean their hieroglyphic writing, before the use of letters was known, we are told this was the mark that he was known by; and the figure of a goat was the hieroglyphic of the Devil ; some will affirm, that the Devil was particularly pleased to be so re-presented ; how they came by their information, and whether they had it from his own mouth or not, authors have not yet determined.

But be this as it will, I do not see that Satan could have been at a loss for some extraordinary figure to have bantered mankind with, though this had not been thought of; but thinking of the cloven foot first, and the matter being indif-ferent, this took place, and easily rooted itself in the bewildered fancy of the people, and now it is riveted too fast for the Devil himself to remove it, if he was disposed to try ; but as I said above, it is none of his business to solve doubts, or remove difficulties out of our heads, but to perplex us with more, as much as he can.

Some people carry this matter a great deal higher still, and will have the cloven foot to be like the great stone which the Brazilian conjurers used to solve all difficult questions upon, after having used a great many monstrous and bar-barous gestures and distortions of their bodies, and cut certain marks or magical figures upon the stone; so, I say, they will have this cloven foot be a kind of a conjuring-stone, and tell us that in former times, when Satan drove a greater trade with mankind in public than he has done of late, he gave this cloven foot as a token to his particular favourites to work wonders with, and to conjure by ; and that witches, fairies, hobgoblins, and such things, of which the ancients had several kinds, at least in their imagination, had all a goat's leg, with a cloven foot, to put on upon extraordinary occasions ; it seems this method is of late grown out of prac-tice, and so, like the melting of marble, and the painting of glass, it is laid aside among the various useful arts which history tells us are lost to the world ; what may be practised

I I 2

in the fairy world, if such a place there be, we can give no particular account at present.

But neither is this all, for other would-be-wise people take upon them to make farther and more considerable improvements upon this doctrine of the cloven foot, and treat it as a most significant instrument of Satan's private operation, and that as Joseph is said to divine, that is to say, to conjure, by his golden cup which was put into Benjamin's sack, so the Devil has managed several of his secret operations, and possessions, and other hellish mechanisms, upon the spirits as well as bodies of men, by the medium or instrumentality of the cloven foot; accordingly, it had a kind of a hellish inspiration in it, and a separate and magical power, by which he wrought his infernal miracles; that the cloven foot had a superior signification, and was not only emblematic and significative of the conduct of men, but really guided their conduct in the most important affairs of life; and that the agents the Devil employed to influence mankind and to delude them, and draw them into all the snares and traps that he lays continually for their destruction, were equipped with this foot in aid of their other powers for mischief.

Here they read us learned lectures upon the sovereign operations which the Devil is at present master of, in the government of human affairs; and how the cloven foot is an emblem of the true *double entendre* or divided aspect, which the great men of the world generally act with, and by which all their affairs are directed; from whence it comes to pass that there is no such thing as a single-hearted intergity, or an upright meaning, to be found in the world; that mankind, worse than the ravenous brutes, preys upon his own kind, and devours them by all the laudable methods of flattery, whine, cheat, and treachery; crocodile-like, weeping over those it will devour, destroying those it smiles upon, and, in a word, devours its own kind, which the very beasts refuse, and that by all the ways of fraud and allurement that hell can invent; holding out a cloven divided hoof, or hand, pretending to save, when the very pretence is made use of to ensnare and destroy.

Thus the divided hoof is the representative of a divided double tongue and heart, an emblem of the most exquisite hypocrisy, the most fawning and fatally deceiving flattery;

and here they give us very diverting histories, though tragical
in themselves, of the manner which some of the Devil's inspired agents have managed themselves under the especial
influence of the cloven foot; how they have made war under
the pretence of peace, murdered garrisons under the most
sacred capitulations, massacred innocent multitudes after sur-
renders to mercy.

Again, they tell us the cloven foot has been made use of
in all treasons, plots, assassinations, and secret as well as
open murders and rebellions. Thus Joab under the treason
of an embrace, showed how dexterously he could manage
the cloven foot, and struck Abner under the fifth rib; thus
David played the cloven foot upon poor Uriah, when he had
a mind to lie with his wife; thus Brutus played it upon
Cæsar; and, to come nearer home, we have had a great
many retrograde motions in this country, by this magical im-
plement the foot; such as that of the Earl of Essex's fate,
beheading the Queen of Scots, and divers others in Queen
Elizabeth's time; that of the Earl of Shrewsbury and Sir
Thomas Overbury, Gondamor and Sir Walter Raleigh, and
many others in King James the First's time; in all which,
if the cloven foot had not been dexterously managed, those
murders had not been so dexterously managed, or the murderers have so well been screened from justice; for which,
and the imprecated justice of heaven unappeased, some have
thought the innocent branches of the royal house of Stuart
did not fare the better in the ages which followed.

It must be confessed, the cloven foot was in its full exercise
in the next reign, and the generation that rose up immediately after them arrived to the most exquisite skill for
management of it; here they fasted and prayed, there they
plundered and murdered; here they raised war for the king,
and there they fought against him; cutting throats for God's
sake, and deposing both king and kingly government according to law.

Nor was the cloven foot unemployed on all sides; for it is
the main excellency of this instrument of hell, that it acts
on every side, it is its denominating quality, and is for that
reason called a cloven, or divided, hoof.

This mutilated apparition has been so public in other
countries, too, that it seems to convince us the Devil is not
confined to England only, but that as his empire extended

to all the sublunarv world, so he gives them all room to **see** he is qualified to manage them his own way.

What abundant use did that prince of dissemblers, Charles V., make of this foot. It was by the help of this apparition of the foot that he baited his hook with the city of Milan, and tickled Francis I. of France so well with it, that when he passed through France, and was in that king's power, he let him go, and never got the bait off of the hook neither; it seems the foot was not on king Francis's side at that time.

How cruelly did Phillip II. of Spain manage this foot in the murder of the nobility of the Spanish Netherlands, the assassination of the Prince of Orange, and, at last, in that of his own son, Don Carlos, infant of Spain; and yet such was the Devil's craft, and so nicely did he bestir this cloven hoof, that this monarch died consoled, though impenitent, in the arms of the church, and with the benediction of the clergy, too, those second best managers of the said hoof in the world.

I must acknowledge, I agree with this opinion thus far; namely, that the Devil, acting by this cloven foot, as a machine, has done great things in the world for the propagating his dark empire among us; and history is full of examples, besides the little, low-prized things done among us; for we are come to such a kind of degeneracy in folly, that we have even dishonoured the Devil, and put this glorious engine, the cloven foot, to such mean uses, that the Devil himself seems to be ashamed of us.

But, to return a little to foreign history, besides what has been mentioned above, we find flaming examples of most glorious mischief done by this weapon, when put into the hands of kings and men of fame in the world: how many games have the kings of France played with this cloven foot, and that within a few years of one another! First, Charles IX. played the cloven foot upon Gaspar Coligni, admiral of France, when he caressed him, complimented him, invited him to Paris, to the wedding of the King of Navarre, called him father, kissed him, and, when he was wounded, sent his own surgeons to take care of him, and yet, three days after, ordered him to be assassinated and murdered, used with a thousand indignities, and, at last, thrown out of the window into the street, to be insulted by the rabble.

Did not Henry III., in the same country, play the cloven

foot upon the Duke of Guise, when he called him to his council, and caused him to be murdered as he went in at the door. The Guises, again, played the same game back upon the king, when they sent out a Jacobin friar to assassinate him in his tent, as he lay at the siege of Paris.

In a word, this opera of the cloven foot has been acted all over the Christian world, ever since Judas betrayed the Son of God with a kiss; nay, our Saviour says expressly of him, *One of you is a devil;* and the sacred text says, in another place, *The Devil entered into Judas.*

' It would take up a great deal of time, and paper, too, to give you a full acconnt of the travels of this cloven foot, its progress into all the courts of Europe, and with what most accurate hypocrisy Satan has made use of it upon many occasions, and with what success; but as, in the elaborate work of which I just now gave you a specimen, I design one whole volume upon this subject, and which I shall call The Complete History of the Cloven Foot, I say, for that reason, and divers others, I shall say but very little more of it in this place.

It remains to tell you, that this merry story of the cloven foot is very essential to the history which I am now writing, as it has been all along the great emblem of the Devil's government in the world, and by which all his most considerable engagements have been answered and executed; for, as he is said not to be able to conceal this foot, but that he carries it always with him, it imports most plainly, that the Devil would be no devil, if he was not a dissembler, a deceiver, and carried a *double entendre* in all he does or says; that he cannot but say one thing, and mean another; promise one thing and do another; engage, and not perform; declare, and not intend; and act, like a true devil, as he is, with a countenance that is no index of his heart.

I might, indeed, go back to originals, and derive this cloven foot from Satan's primitive state, as a cherubim, or a celestial being, which cherubims, as Moses is said to have seen them about the throne of God in Mount Sinai, and as the same Moses, from the original, represented them afterwards covering the ark, had the head and face of a man, wings of an eagle, body of a lion, and legs and feet of a calf; but this is not so much to our present purpose, for, as we are to allow that whatever Satan had of heavenly beauty before the fall,

he lost it all when he commenced devil; so to fetch his
original so far up, would be only to say that he retained
nothing but the cloven foot, and that all the rest of him was
altered and deformed, become frightful and horrible as the
devil; but his cloven foot, as we now understand it, is rather
mystical and emblematic, and describes him only as the
fountain of mischief and treason, and the prince of hypocrites,
and as such we are now to speak of him.

It is from this original all the hypocritic world copy; he
wears the foot on their account, and from this model they
act; this made our blessed Lord tell them, *The works of your
father ye will do*, meaning the Devil, as he had expressed it
just before.

Nor does he deny the use of the foot to the meaner class
of his disciples in the world, but decently equips them all,
upon every occasion, with a needful proportion of hypocrisy
and deceit, that they may hand on the power of promiscuous
fraud through all his temporal dominions, and wear the foot
always about them, as a badge of their professed share in
whatever is done by that means.

Thus every dissembler, every false friend, every secret
cheat, every bearskin-jobber has a cloven foot, and so far
hands on the Devil's interest by the same powerful agency of
art, as the Devil himself uses to act when he appears in
person, or would act if he was just now upon the spot; for
this foot is a machine which is to be wound up and wound
down, as the cause it appears for requires; and there are
agents and engineers to act in it by directions of Satan (the
grand engineer), who lies still in his retirement, only issuing
out his orders as he sees convenient.

Again, every class, every trade, every shopkeeper, every
pedlar, nay, that meanest of tradesmen, that church pedlar,
the pope, has a cloven foot, with which he *paw wa's* upon
the world, wishes them all well, and at the same time cheats
them; wishes them all fed, and at the same time starves
them; wishes them all in heaven, and at the same time
marches before them directly to the Devil, *a la mode de cloven
foot.*

Nay, the very bench, the everliving foundation of justice
in the world; how often has it been made the tool of violence,
the refuge of oppression, the seat of bribery and corruption,
by this monster in masquerade, and that everywhere (our

own country always excepted!) they had much better wipe
out the picture of Justice blinded, and having the sword and
scales in her hand, which in foreign countries is generally
painted over the seat of those who sit to do justice, and place
instead thereof a naked unarmed cloven hoof, a proper
emblem of that spirit that influences the world, and of the
justice we often see administered among them; human imagination cannot form an idea more suitable, nor the Devil
propose an engine more or better qualified for an operation
of justice, by the influence of bribery and corruption; it is
this magnipotent instrument in the hands of the Devil, which,
under the closest disguise, agitates every passion, bribes
every affection, blackens every virtue, gives a double face to
words and actions, and to all persons who have any concern
in them, and, in a word, makes us all devils to one another.

Indeed the Devil has taken but a dark emblem to be distinguished by, for this of a goat was said to be a creature
hated by mankind from the beginning, and that there is a
natural antipathy in mankind against them : hence the scape-
goat was to bear the sins of the people, and to go into the
wilderness with all that burthen upon him.

But we have a saying among us, in defence of which we
must inquire into the proper sphere of action which may be
assigned to this cloven foot, as hitherto described : the
proverb is this; Every devil has not a cloven foot. This
proverb, instead of giving us some more favourable thoughts
of the Devil, confirms what I have said already, that the
Devil raised this scandal upon himself; I mean, the report
that he cannot conceal or disguise his Devil's foot, or hoof,
but that it must appear under whatever habit he shows himself; and the reason I give holds good still, namely, that he
may be more effectually concealed when he goes abroad
without it : for if the people were fully persuaded that the
Devil could not appear without this badge of his honour, or
mark of his infamy, take it as you will; and that he was
bound also to show it upon all occasions, it would be natural
to conclude, that whatever frightful appearances might be
seen in the world, if the cloven foot did not also appear, we
had no occasion to look for the Devil, or so much as to think
of him, much less to apprehend he was near us ; and as this
might be a mistake, and that the Devil might be there while
we thought ourselves so secure it might on many occasions

be a mistake of very ill consequence, and in particular, as it would give the Devil room to act in the dark, and not be discovered, where it might be most needful to know him.

From this short hint, thus repeated, I draw a new thesis, namely, that devil is most dangerous that has no cloven foot; or, if you will have it in words more to the common understanding, the Devil seems to be most dangerous when he goes without his cloven foot.

And here a learned speculation offers itself to our debate, and which indeed I ought to call a council of casuists, and men learned in the Devil's politics, to determine :—

Whether is most hurtful to the world, the Devil walking about without his cloven foot, or the cloven foot walking about without the Devil?

It is, indeed, a nice and difficult question, and merits to be well inquired into; for which reason, and divers others, I have referred it to be treated with some decency, and as a dispute of dignity sufficient to take up a chapter by itself.

CHAPTER VII.

WHETHER IS MOST HURTFUL TO THE WORLD, THE DEVIL WALKING ABOUT WITH HIS CLOVEN FOOT, OR THE CLOVEN FOOT WALKING ABOUT WITHOUT THE DEVIL?

In discussing this most critical distinction of Satan's private motions, I must, as the pulpit gentlemen direct us, explain the text, and let you know what I mean by several dark expressions in it, that I may not be understood to talk (as the Devil walks) in the dark.

1. As to the Devil's walking about.
2. His walking without his cloven foot.
3. The cloven foot walking about without the Devil.

Now as I study brevity, and yet would be understood too, you may please to understand me as I understand myself, thus :—

1. That I must be allowed to suppose the Devil really has a full intercourse in, and through, and about this globe, with egress and regress, for the carrying on his special affairs, when, how, and where, to his majesty, in his great wisdom, it shall seem meet; that sometimes he appears and becomes visible, and that, like a mastiff

without his clog, he does not always carry his cloven foot with him. This will necessarily bring me to some debate upon the most important question of apparitions, hauntings, walkings, &c., whether of Satan in human shape, or of human creatures in the Devil's shape, or in any other manner whatsoever.

2. I must also be allowed to tell you that Satan has a great deal of wrong done him by the general embracing vulgar errors, and that there is a cloven foot oftentimes without a devil; or, in short, that Satan is not guilty of all the simple things, no, or of all the wicked things, we charge him with.

These two heads, well settled, will fully explain the title of this chapter, answer the query mentioned in it, and, at the same time, correspond very well with, and give us a farther prospect into, the main and original design of this work, namely, The History of the Devil. We are so fond of, and pleased with, the general notion of seeing the Devil, that I am loath to disoblige my readers so much as calling in question his visibility would do. Nor is it my business, any more than it is his, to undeceive them, where the belief is so agreeable to them; especially since upon the whole it is not one farthing matter, either on one side or on the other, whether it be so or no, or whether the truth of fact be ever discovered or not.

Certain it is, whether we see him or no, here he is, and I make no doubt but he is looking on while I am writing this part of his story, whether behind me, or at my elbow, or over my shoulder, is not material to me, nor have I once turned my head about to see whether he is there or no; for if he be not in the inside, I have so mean an opinion of all his extravasated powers, that it seems of very little consequence to me what shape he takes up, or in what posture he appears; nor indeed can I find in all my inquiry that ever the Devil appeared (*qua Devil*) in any of the most dangerous or important of his designs in the world; the most of his projects, especially of the significant part of them, having been carried on another way.

However, as I am satisfied nobody will be pleased if I should dispute the reality of his appearance, and the world runs away with it as a received point, and that admits no dispute, I shall most readily grant the general, and give you some account of the particulars.

History is fruitful of particulars, whether invention has supplied them or not, I will not say, where the Devil is brought upon the stage in plain and undeniable apparition: the story of Samuel being raised by the witch of Endor, I shall leave quite out of my list, because there are so many scruples and objections against that story; and as I shall not dispute with the Scripture, so, on the other hand, I have so much deference for the dignity of the Devil, as not to determine rashly how far it may be in the power of every old (witch) woman, to call him up whenever she pleases, and that he must come, whatever the pretence is, or whatever business of consequence he may be engaged in, as often as it is needful for her to *paw wa* for half a crown, or perhaps less than half the money.

Nor will I undertake to tell you, till I have talked farther with him about it, how far the Devil is concerned to discover frauds, detect murders, reveal secrets, and especially to tell where any money is hid, and show folks where to find it; it is an odd thing that Satan should think it of consequence to come and tell us where such a miser hid a strong box, or where such an old woman buried her chamberpot full of money, the value of all which is perhaps but a trifle, when, at the same time, he lets so many veins of gold, so many unexhausted mines, nay, mountains of silver (as we may depend upon it are hid in the bowels of the earth, and which it would be so much to the good of whole nations to discover), lie still there, and never say one word of them to anybody. Besides, how does the Devil's doing things so foreign to himself, and so out of his way, agree with the rest of his character; namely, showing a kind of a friendly disposition to mankind, or doing beneficent things? this is so beneath Satan's quality, and looks so little, that I scarce know what to say to it; but that which is still more pungent in the case is, these things are so out of his road, and so foreign to his calling, that it shocks our faith in them, and seems to clash with all the just notions we have of him, and of his business in the world. The like is to be said of those little merry turns we bring him in acting with us, and upon us, upon trifling and simple occasions, such as tumbling chairs and stools about house, setting pots and vessels bottom upward, tossing the glass and crockery-ware about without breaking; and such-like mean foolish things, beneath the dignity of the Devil, who, in my opinion, is rather employed in setting the world with the bottom upward, tumbling kings and crowns about, and dashing the nations one against another; raising tempests and storms, whether at sea, or on shore; and, in a word, doing capital mischiefs, suitable to his nature, and, agreeable to his name, Devil; and suited to that circumstance of his condition, which I have fully represented in the primitive part of his exiled state.

But to bring in the Devil playing at push-pin with the world, or, like Domitian, catching flies, that is to say, doing nothing to the purpose, this is not only deluding ourselves, but putting a slur upon the Devil himself; and, I say, I shall not dishonour Satan so much as to suppose anything in it; however, as I must have a care too how I take away the proper materials of winter-evening frippery, and leave the good wives nothing of the Devil to frighten the children with, I shall carry the weighty point no farther. No doubt the Devil and Dr. Faustus were very intimate; I should rob you of a very significant proverb,* if I should so much as doubt it? no doubt the Devil showed himself in the glass to that fair lady who looked in it to see where to place her patches; but then it should follow too that the Devil is an enemy to the ladies wearing patches, and that has some difficulties in it which we cannot so easily reconcile; but we must tell the story, and leave out the consequences.

But to come to more remarkable things, and in which the Devil has thought fit to act in a figure more suitable to his dignity, and on occasions consistent with himself; take the story of the appearance of Julius Cæsar, or the Devil assuming that murdered emperor, to the great Marcus Brutus, who, notwithstanding all the good things said to justify it, was no less than a king-killer and an assassinator, which we in our language call by a very good name, and peculiar to the English tongue, a ruffian.

The spectre had certainly the appearance of Cæsar, with his wounds bleeding fresh, as if he had just received the fatal blow: he had reproached him with his ingratitude, with a *Tu Brute! tu quoque, mi fili:* What thou, Brutus! thou, my

* As great as the Devil and Doctor Faustus. Vulg. Dr. Foster.

adopted son! Now history seems to agree universally, not only in the story itself, but in the circumstances of it; we have only to observe that the Devil had certainly power to assume, not a human shape only, but the shape of Julius Cæsar in particular.

Had Brutus been a timorous, conscience-harried, weak-headed wretch, had he been under the horror of the guilt, and terrified with the dangers that were before him at that time, we might suggest that he was overrun with the vapours, that the terrors which were upon his mind disordered him, that his head was delirious and prepossessed, and that his fancy only placed Cæsar so continually in his eye, that it realized him to his imagination, and he believed he saw him: with many other suggested difficulties to invalidate the story, and render the reality of it doubtful.

But the contrary, to an extreme, was the case of Brutus: his known character placed him above the power of all hypochondriacs, or fanciful delusions; Brutus was of a true Roman spirit, a bold hero, of an intrepid courage; one that scorned to fear even the Devil, as the story allows; besides, he gloried in the action, there could be no terror of mind upon him, he valued himself upon it, as done in the service of liberty, and the cause of his country; and was so far from being frightened at the Devil, in the worst shape, that he spoke first to him, and asked him what art thou? and when he was cited to see him again at Philippi, answered, with a gallantry that knew no fear, Well, I will see thee there. Whatever the Devil's business was with Brutus, this is certain, according to all the historians who give us the account of it, that Brutus discovered no fear; he did not, like Saul at Endor, fall to the ground in a swoon, 1 Sam. xxviii. 20. *Then Saul fell all along upon the earth, and there was no strength in him, and was sore afraid.* In a word, I see no room to charge Brutus with being overrun with the hyppo, or with vapours, or with fright and terror of mind; but he saw the Devil, that is certain, and with eyes open, his courage not at all daunted, his mind resolute, and, with the utmost composure, spoke to him, replied to his answer, and defied his summons to death, which, indeed, he feared not, as appeared afterwards.

I come next to an instance as eminent in history as the other; this was in Charles VI. of France, surnamed the

Beloved, who, riding over the forest near Mans, a ghastly, frightful fellow (that is to say, the Devil, so clothed in human vizor), came up to his horse, and, taking hold of his bridle, stopped him, with the addition of these words, Stop, king, whither go you? you are betrayed! and immediately disappeared. It is true, the king had been distempered in his head before, and so he might have been deceived, and we might have charged it to the account of a whimsical brain, or the power of his imagination; but this was in the face of his attendants, several of his great officers, courtiers, and princes of the blood being with him, who all saw the man, heard the words, and immediately, to their astonishment, lost sight of the spectre, who vanished from them all.

Two witnesses will convict a murderer; why not a traitor? This must be the Old Gentleman, emblematically so called; or who must it be? nay, who else could it be? His ugliness is not the case, though *ugly as the Devil* is a proverb in his favour; but vanishing out of sight is an essential to a spirit, and to an evil spirit, in our times especially.

These are some of the Devil's extraordinaries, and, it must be confessed, they are not the most agreeable to mankind, for sometimes he takes upon him to disorder his friends very much on these occasions, as in the above case of Charles VI. of France; the king, they say, was really demented ever after, that is, as we vulgarly, but not always improperly, express it, he was really frightened out of his wits. Whether the malicious Devil intended it so or not, is not certain; though it was not so foreign to his particular disposition if he did.

But where he is more intimate, we are told, he appears in a manner less disagreeable; and there he is more properly a familiar spirit, that is, in short, a devil of their acquaintance; it is true, the ancients understood the word, *a familiar spirit*, to be one of the kinds of possession; but if it serves our turn as well under the denomination of an intimate devil, or a devil visitant, it must be acknowledged to be as near, in the literal sense and acceptation of the word, as the other; nay, it must be allowed, it is a very great piece of familiarity in the Devil to make visits, and show none of his disagreeables, not appear formidable, or in the shape of what he is, respectfully withholding his dismal part, in compassion to the infirmities of his friends.

It is true, Satan may be obliged to make different appearances, as the several circumstances of things call for it; in
some cases he makes his public entry, and then he must show
himself in his habit of ceremony; in other cases he comes
upon private business, and then he appears in disguise; in
some public cases he may think fit to be incog., and then he
appears dressed *à la masque;* so, they say, he appeared at the
famous Bartholomew wedding at Paris, where he came
in dressed up like a trumpeter, danced in his habit, sounded
a levet, and then went out and rung the alarm-bell (which
was the signal to begin the massacre) half an hour before
the time appointed, lest the king's mind should alter, and
his heart fail him.

If the story be not made upon him (for we should not
slander the Devil), it should seem he was not thoroughly
satisfied in King Charles IX.'s steadiness in his cause; for
the king, it seems, had relaxed a little once before, and Satan
might be afraid he would fall off again, and so prevent the
execution; others say, the king did relent immediately after
the ringing the alarm-bell, but that then it was too late, the
work was begun, and the rage of blood having been let loose
among the people, there was no recalling the order. If the
Devil was thus brought to the necessity of a secret management, it must be owned he did it dexterously; but I have
not authority enough for the story to charge him with the
particulars, so I leave it *au croc.*

I have much better vouchers for the story following, which
I had so solemnly confirmed by one that lived in the family,
that I never doubted the truth of it. There lived in the
parish of St. Bennet Fynk, near the Royal Exchange, an
honest, poor, widow woman, who, her husband being lately
dead, took lodgers into her house; that is, she let out some
of her rooms, in order to lessen her own charge of rent;
among the rest, she let her garrets to a working watchwheel
maker, or one some way concerned in making the movements
of watches, and who worked to those shopkeepers who sell
watches, as is usual.

It happened that a man and woman went up to speak with
this movement-maker upon some business which related to
his trade, and when they were near the top of the stairs, the
garret-door where he usually worked being wide open, they
saw the poor man (the watchmaker, or wheelmaker) had

hanged himself upon a beam which was left open in the room, a little lower than the plaster, or ceiling; surprised at the sight, the woman stopped, and cried out to the man who was behind her on the stairs, that he should run up and cut the poor creature down.

At that very moment comes a man hastily from another part of the room which they upon the stairs could not see, bringing a joint-stool in his hand, as if in great haste, and sets it down just by the wretch that was hanged, and getting up as hastily upon it, pulls a knife out of his pocket, and taking hold of the rope with one of his hands, beckoned to the woman and the man behind her with his head, as if to stop and not come up, showing them the knife in his other hand, as if he was just going to cut the poor man down.

Upon this, the woman stopped awhile, but the man who stood on the joint-stool continued with his hand and knife as if fumbling at the knot, but did not yet cut the man down; at which the woman cried out again, and the man behind her called to her, Go up, says he, and help the man upon the stool! supposing something hindered. But the man upon the stool made signs to them again to be quiet, and not come on, as if saying, I shall do it immediately; then he made two strokes with his knife, as if cutting the rope, and then stopped again; and still the poor man was hanging, and consequently dying: upon this, the woman on the stairs cried out to him, What ails you? why don't you cut the poor man down? And the man behind her, having no more patience, thrusts her by, and said to her, Let me come, I'll warrant you I'll do it; and with that runs up and forward into the room to the man; but when he came there, behold, the poor man was there hanging: but no man with a knife, or joint-stool, or any such thing to be seen, all that was spectre and delusion, in order, no doubt, to let the poor creature that had hanged himself perish and expire.

The man was so frightened and surprised, that, with all the courage he had before, he dropped on the floor as one dead, and the woman at last was fain to cut the poor man down with a pair of scissors, and had much to do to effect it.

As I have no room to doubt the truth of this story, which I had from persons on whose honesty I could depend, so I think it needs very little trouble to convince us who the man upon the stool must be, and that it was the Devil who placed himself there in order to finish the murder of the man whom he had, devil-like, tempted before, and prevailed with to be his own executioner. Besides, it corresponds so well with the Devil's nature, and with his business, viz., that of a murderer, that I never questioned it; nor can I think we wrong the Devil at all to charge him with it.

> N.B. I cannot be positive in the remaining part of this story, viz., whether the man was cut down soon enough to be recovered, or whether the Devil carried his point, and kept off the man and woman till it was too late; but be it which it will, it is plain he did his devilish endeavour, and stayed till he was forced to abscond again.

We have many solid tales well attested, as well in history as in the reports of honest people, who could not be deceived, intimating the Devil's personal appearance, some in one place, some in another; as also sometimes in one habit or dress, and sometimes in another; and it is to be observed, that in none of those which are most like to be real, and in which there is least of fancy and vapour, you have any mention of the cloven foot, which rather seems to be a mere invention of men, and perhaps chiefly of those who had a cloven understanding; I mean a shallow kind of craft, the effect of an empty and simple head, thinking by such a well-meant, though weak fraud, to represent the Devil to the old women and children of the age, with some addition suitable to the weakness of their intellects, and suited to making them afraid of him.

I have another account of a person who travelled upwards of four years with the Devil in his company, and conversed most intimately with him all the while; nay, if I may believe the story, he knew most part of the time that he was the Devil, and yet conversed with him, and that very profitably, for he performed many very useful services for him, and constantly preserved him from the danger of wolves and wild beasts, which the country he travelled through was intolerably full of: where, by the way, you are to understand that the wolves and bears in those countries knew the Devil, whatever disguise he went in; or that the Devil has some way to fright bears, and such creatures, more than we know of: nor could this devil ever be prevailed upon to hurt him or any of his company. This account has an innumerable number of diverting incidents attending it; but they are equal to all the rest in bulk, and, therefore, too long for this book.

I find, too, upon some more ordinary occasions, the Devil has appeared to several people at their call. This, indeed, shows abundance of good humour in him, considering him as a devil, and that he was mighty complaisant: nay, some, they tell us, have a power to raise the Devil whenever they think fit; this I cannot bring the Devil to a level with, unless I should allow him to be *servus servorum*, as another devil in disguise calls himself, subjected to every old wizard's call; or that he is under a necessity of appearing on such or such particular occasions, whoever it is that calls him; which would bring the Devil's circumstances to a pitch of slavery which I see no reason to believe of them.

Here, also, I must take notice again, that though I say the Devil, when I speak of all these apparitions, whether of a greater or lesser kind, yet I am not obliged to suppose Satan himself, in person, is concerned to show himself, but that some of his agents, deputies, and servants, are sent to that purpose, and directed what disguise of flesh and blood to put on, as may be suitable to the occasion.

This seems to be the only way to reconcile all those simple and ridiculous appearances which, not Satan, but his emissaries (which we old women call imps), sometimes make, and the mean and sorry employment they are put to. Thus fame tells us of a certain witch of quality, who called the Devil once to carry her over a brook where the water was swelled with a hasty rain, and lashed him soundly with her whip for letting her ladyship fall into the water before she was quite over. Thus also, as fame tells us, she set the Devil to work, and made him build Croiland Abbey, where there was no foundation to be found, only for disturbing the workmen a little who were first set about it. So, it seems, another laborious devil was obliged to dig the great ditch across the country from the fen country to the edge of Suffolk and Essex; which, however, he has preserved the reputation of, and, where it crosses Newmarket heath, it is called Devil's Ditch to this day.

Another piece of punishment, no doubt it was, when the Devil was obliged to bring the stones out of Wales into Wiltshire to build Stonehenge. How this was ordered in those days, when it seems they kept Satan to hard labour, I know not; I believe it must be registered among the ancient pieces of art which are lost in the world, such as melting of stones, painting of glass, &c. Certainly they had the Devil under correction in those days, that is to say, those lesser sort of devils; but I cannot think that the 'muckle thief Devil,' as they call him in the North, the grand seignior Devil of all, was ever reduced to discipline. What devil it was that Dunstan took by the nose with his red hot tongs, I have not yet examined antiquity enough to be certain of, any more than I can what devil it was that St. Francis played so many warm tricks with, and made him run away from him so often. However, this I take upon me to say in the Devil's behalf, that it could not be our Satan, the arch-devil of all devils, of whom I have been talking so long.

Nor is it unworthy the occasion, to take notice that we really wrong the Devil, and speak of him very much to his disadvantage, when we say of such a great lord, or of such a lady of quality, I think the Devil is in your grace. No, no, Satan has other business; he very rarely possesses f—ls: besides, some are so far from having the Devil in them, that they are really transmigrated into the very essence of the Devil themselves; and others again, not transmigrated, or assimilated, but in deed and in truth show us that they are, or have, mere native devils in every part or parcel of them, and that the rest is only mask and disguise. Thus, if rage, envy, pride, and revenge, can constitute the parts of a devil, why should not a lady of such quality, in whom all those extraordinaries abound, have a right to the title of being a devil really and substantially, and to all intents and purposes, in the most perfect and absolute sense, according to the most exquisite descriptions of devils already given by me or anybody else; and even just as Joan of Arc, or Joan, Queen of Naples, were, who were both sent home to their native country, as soon as it was discovered that they were real devils, and that Satan acknowledged them in that quality.

Nor does my lady d——ss's, wearing sometimes a case of humanity about her, called flesh and blood, at all alter the case: for so it is evident, according to our present hypothesis, Satan has been always allowed to do, upon urgent occasions; ay, and to make his personal appearance as such, among even the sons and daughters of God too, as well as among the children of men; and, therefore, her grace may have

appeared in the shape of a fine lady, as long she has been
supposed to do, without any impeachment of her just claim
to the title of Devil; which, being her true and natural
original, she ought not, nor indeed shall not, by me, be denied
her shapes of honour, whenever she pleases to declare for a
re-assumption.

And farther, to give every truth its due illustration, this
need not be thought so strange; and is far from being
unjust; her grace (as she, it may be, is now styled) has not
acted, at least that I ever heard of, so unworthy her great
and illustrious original, that we should think she has lost
anything by walking about the world so many years in apparition; but to give her the due homage of her quality, she
has acted as consonant to the essence and nature of devil,
which she has such a claim to, as was consistent with the need
ful reserve of her present disguise.

Nor shall we lead the reader into any mistake concerning
this part of our work, as if this was, or is meant to be, a
particular satire upon the d——ss of ————, and upon her
only, as if we had no devils among us in the phenomena of
fair ladies but this one; if Satan would be so honest to us
as he might be (and it would be very ingenuous in him, that
must be acknowledged, to give us a little of his illumination
in this case), we should soon be able to unmask a great
many notable figures among us, to our real surprise.

Indeed it is a point worth our farther inquiry, and would
be a discovery many ways to our advantage, were we
blessed with it, to see how many real devils we have walking
up and down the world in mask, and how many hoop-petti-
coats complete the entire mask that disguises the Devil in
the shape of that thing called woman.

As for the men, nature has satisfied herself in letting them
be their own disguise, and in suffering them to act the old
woman, as old women are vulgarly understood, in matters of
council and politics; but if at any time they have occasion
for the Devil in person, they are obliged to call him to their
aid in such shape as he pleases to make use of, *pro hac vice;*
and of all those shapes, the most agreeable to him seems to
be that of a female of quality, in which he has infinite
opportunity to act to perfection what part soever he is called
in for.

How happy are those people who they say have the par

ticular quality, or acquired habit, called the second sight; one sort of whom they tell us are able to distinguish the Devil, in whatever case or outside of flesh and blood he is pleased to put on, and consequently could know the Devil wherever they met him! Were I blessed with this excellent and useful accomplishment, how pleasant would it be, and how would it particularly gratify my spleen, and all that which I, in common with my fellow creatures carry about me, called ill-nature, to stand in the Mall, or at the entrance to any of our assemblies of beauties, and point them out as they pass by, with this particular mark, That's a devil; that fine young toast is a devil; there's a devil dressed in a new habit for the ball; there's a devil in a coach and six, *cum aliis*. In short, it would make a merry world among us if we could but enter upon some proper method of such discriminations: but, Lawr'd, what a hurricane would it raise, if, like ———, who they say scourged the Devil so often that he durst not come near him in any shape whatever, we could find some new method out to make the Devil unmask; like the angel Uriel, who, Mr. Milton says, had an enchanted spear, with which if he did but touch the Devil, in whatever disguise he had put on, it obliged him immediately to start up, and show himself in his true original shape, mere devil as he was.

This would do nicely, and as I who am originally a projector, have spent some time upon this study, and doubt not in a little time to finish my engine, which I am contriving, to screw the Devil out of everybody, or anybody; I question not, when I have brought it to perfection, but I shall make most excellent discoveries by it; and besides the many extraordinary advantages of it to human society, I doubt not but it will make good sport in the world too; wherefore, when I publish my proposals, and divide it into shares, as other less useful projects have been done, I question not, for all the severe act lately passed against bubbles, but I shall get subscribers enough, &c.

In a word, a secret power of discovering what devils we have among us, and where and what business they are doing, would be a vast advantage to us all; that we might know among the crowd of devils that walk about streets, who are apparitions, and who are not.

Now I, you must know, at certain intervals, when the old

gentleman's illuminations are upon me, and when I have something of an eclaircissement with him, have some degrees of this discriminating second sight, and therefore it is no strange thing for me to tell a great many of my acquaintance that they are really devils, when they themselves know nothing of the matter: sometimes, indeed, I find it pretty hard to convince them of it, or at least they are very unwilling to own it, but it is not the less so for that.

I had a long discourse upon this subject one day, with a young beautiful lady of my acquaintance, whom the world very much admired ; and as the world judges no farther than they can see (and how should they? you would say), they took her to be, as she really was, a most charming creature.

To me, indeed, she discovered herself many ways, besides the advantage I had of my extraordinary penetration by the magic powers which I am vested with : to me, I say, she appeared a fury, a satyr, a fiery little fiend, as could possibly be dressed up in flesh; in short, she appeared to me what really she was, a very devil. It is natural to human creatures to desire to discover any extraordinary powers they are possessed of superior to others, and this itch prevailing in me, among the rest, I was impatient to let this lady know that I understood her composition perfectly well, nay, as well as she did herself.

In order to this, happening to be in the family once for some days, and having the honour to be very intimate with her and her husband too, I took an opportunity on an extraordinary occasion, when she was in the height of good humour, to talk with her. You must note that, as I said, the lady was in an extraordinary good humour, and there had been a great deal of mirth in the family for some days ; but one evening, Sir Ed——, her husband, upon some very sharp turn she gave to another gentleman, which made all the company pleasant, ran to her, and with a passion of good humour, takes her in his arms, and turning to me, says he, Jack, this wife of mine is full of wit and good humour, but when she has a mind to be smart, she is the keenest little devil in the world : this was alluding to the quick turn she had given the other gentleman.

Is that the best language you can give your wife? says my lady. O madam, says I, such devils as you, are all angels. Ay, ay, says my lady, I know that, he has only let a truth fly out that he does not understand. Look ye there, now, says Sir Edward, could anything but such a dear devil as this have said a thing so pointed? Well, well, adds he, devil to a lady in a man's arms, is a word of divers interpretations. Thus they rallied for a good while, he holding her fast all the while in his arms, and frequently kissing her; and at last it went off, all in sunshine and mirth.

But the next day (for I had the honour to lodge in the lady's father's house, where it all happened), I say, the next day my lady begins with me upon the subject, and that very smartly, so that at first I did not know whether she was in jest or earnest. Ay, ay, says she, you men make nothing of your wives after you have them; alluding to the discourse with Sir Edward, the night before.

Why madam, says I, we men, as you are pleased to term it, if we meet with good wives, worship them, and make idols of them; what would you have more of us?

No, no, says she, before you have them, they are angels; but when you have been in heaven, adds she, and smiled, then they are devils.

Why madam, says I, devils are angels, you know, and were the highest sort of angels once.

Yes, says she, very smartly, all devils are angels, but all angels are not devils.

But madam, says I, you should never take it ill to be called devil, you know.

I know! says she, hastily, what d'ye mean by that?

Why madam, says I (and looked very gravely and serious), I thought you had known that I knew it, or else I would not have said so, for I would not offend you; but you may depend I shall never discover it, unless you order me to do so for your particular service.

Upon this she looked hard and wild, and bid me explain myself.

I told her I was ready to explain myself, if she would give me her word she would not resent it, and would take nothing ill.

She gave me her word solemnly she would not, though, like a true devil, she broke her promise with me all at once.

Well, however, being unconcerned whether she kept her word or no, I began by telling her that I had long since obtained the second sight, and had some years studied magic, by which I could penetrate into many things which to ordinary perception were invisible, and had some glasses by the help of which I could see into all visionary or imaginary appearances in a different manner than other people did.

Very well, says she, suppose you can, what's that to me?

I told her it was nothing to her any farther than that as she knew herself to be originally not the same creature she seemed to be, but was of a sublime angelic original; so, by the help of my recited art, I knew it too, and so far it might relate to her.

Very fine, says she: so you would make a devil of me, indeed.

I took that occasion to tell her I would make nothing of her but what she was; that I supposed she knew well enough God Almighty never thought fit to make any human creature so perfect and completely beautiful as she was, but that such were only reserved for figures to be assumed by angels of one kind or another.

She rallied me upon that, and told me that would not bring me off, for I had not determined her for anything angelic, but a mere devil; and how could I flatter her with being handsome and a devil both at the same time?

I told her, as Satan, whom we abusively called Devil, was an immortal seraph, and of an original angelic nature, so, abstracted from anything wicked, he was a most glorious being; that when he thought fit to incase himself with flesh, and walk about in disguise, it was in his power, equally with the other angels, to make the form he took upon himself be, as he thought fit, beautiful or deformed.

Here she disputed the possibility of that, and after charging me faintly with flattering her face, told me the Devil could not be represented by anything handsome, alleging our constant picturing the Devil in all the frightful appearances imaginable.

I told her we wronged him very much in that, and quoted St. Francis, to whom the Devil frequently appeared in the form of the most incomparably beautiful naked woman, to allure him, and what means he used to turn the appearance into a devil again, and how he effected it.

She put by the discourse, and returned to that of angels,

and insisted that angels did not always assume beautiful appearances; that sometimes they appeared in terrible shapes, but that when they did not, it was at best only amiable faces, not exquisite; and that therefore it would not hold, that to be handsome should always render them suspected.

I told her the Devil had more occasion to form beauties than other angels had, his business being principally to deceive and ensnare mankind. And then I gave her some examples upon the whole.

I found, by her discourse, she was willing enough to pass for an angel, but it was the hardest thing in the world to convince her that she was a devil, and she would not come into that by any means; she argued that I knew her father, and that her mother was a very good woman, and was delivered of her in the ordinary way, and that there were such and such ladies who were present in the room when she was born, and that had often told her so.

I told her that was nothing in such a case as hers; that when the old gentleman had occasion to transform himself into a fine lady, he could easily dispose of a child, and place himself in the cradle instead of it, when the nurse or mother were asleep; nay, or when they were broad awake either, it was the same thing to him; and I quoted Luther to her upon that occasion, who affirms that it had been so. However, I said, to convince her that I knew it (for I would have it that she knew it already), if she pleased I would go to my chamber and fetch her my magic looking-glass, where she should see her own picture, not only as it was an angelic picture for the world to admire, but a devil also frightful enough to anybody but herself and me that understood it.

No, no, said she, I will look in none of your conjuring glasses; I know myself well enough, and I desire to look no otherwise than I am.

No, madam, says I, I know that very well; nor do you need any better shape than that you appear in, it is most exquisitely fine; all the world knows you are a complete beauty, and that is a clear evidence what you would be, if your present appearing form was reduced to its proper personality.

Appearing form! says she, why, what! would you make an apparition of me?

An apparition, madam! said I; yes, to be sure: why you

know you are nothing else but an apparition; and what else would you be, when it is so infinitely to your advantage?

With that, she turned pale and angry, and then rose up hastily, and looked into the glass (a large pier-glass being in the room), where she stood surveying herself from head to foot, with vanity not a little.

I took that time to slip away, and running up into my apartment, I fetched my magic glass, as I called it, in which I had a hollow case, so framed, behind a looking-glass, that in the first she would see her own face only; in the second, she would see the Devil's face, ugly and frightful enough, but dressed up with a lady's head-clothes in a circle, the Devil's face in the centre, and, as it were, at a little distance behind.

I came down again so soon that she did not think the time long, especially having spent it in surveying her fair self; when I returned, I said, Come, madam, do not trouble yourself to look there, that is not a glass capable of showing you anything; come, take this glass.

It will show me as much of myself, says she, a little scornfully, as I desire to see; so she continued looking in the pier-glass; after some time more (for seeing her a little out of humour, I waited to see what observation she would make), I asked her if she had viewed herself to her satisfaction? She said she had, and she had seen nothing of devil about her. Come, madam, said I, look here; and with that I opened the looking-glass, and she looked in it, but saw nothing but her own face. Well, says she, the glasses agree well enough, I see no difference; what can you make of it? With that I took it a little away. Don't you? says I, then I should be mistaken very much; so I looked in it myself, and giving it a turn imperceptible to her, I showed it her again, where she saw the Devil indeed, dressed up like a fine lady, but ugly and devil-like as could be desired for a devil to be.

She started, and cried out most horribly, and told me she thought I was more of a devil than she, for that she knew nothing of all those tricks, and I did it to frighten her, she believed I had raised the Devil.

I told her it was nothing but her own natural picture, and that she knew well enough, and that I did not show it her to inform her of it, but to let her know that I knew it too; that so she might make no pretences of being offended when I talked familiarly to her of a thing of this nature.

Very well; so, says she, I am a real frightful devil, am I?

O, madam, says I, don't say, Am I? why you know what you are, don't you? A devil! ay, certainly; as sure as the rest of the world believes you a lady.

I had a great deal of farther discourse with her upon that subject, though she would fain have beat me off of it, and two or three times she put the talk off, and brought something else on; but I always found means to revive it, and to attack her upon the reality of her being a devil, till at last I made her downright angry, and then she showed it.

First she cried, told me I came to affront her, that I would not talk so if Sir Ed—— was by, and that she ought not to be used so. I endeavoured to pacify her, and told her I had not treated her with any indecency, nor I would not; because while she thought fit to walk abroad incog., it was none of my business to discover her; that if she thought fit to tell Sir Ed—— anything of the discourse, she was very welcome, or to conceal it (which I thought the wisest course), she should do just as she pleased; but I made no question I should convince Sir Ed——, her husband, that what I said was just, and that it was really so; whether it was for her service or no for him to know it, was for her to consider.

This calmed her a little, and she looked hard at me a minute, without speaking a word, when, on a sudden, she broke out thus: And you will undertake, says she, to convince Sir Ed—— that he has married a devil, will ye? a fine story indeed! and what follows? why then it must follow, that the child I go with (for she was big with child) will be a devil too, will it? a fine story for Sir Ed——, indeed! isn't it?

I don't know that, madam, said I, that's as you order it; by the father's side, said I, I know it will not, but what it may by the mother's side, that's a doubt I can't resolve till the Devil and I talk farther about it.

You and the Devil talk together! says she, and looks ruefully at me; why, do you talk with the Devil, then?

Ay, madam, says I, as sure as ever you did yourself; besides, said I, can you question that? pray who am I talking to now?

I think you are mad, says she; why you will make devils

of all the family, it may be, and particularly I must be with child of a devil, that's certain.

No, madam, said I, 'tis not certain; as I said before, I question it.

Why, you say I am the Devil; the child, you know, has always most of the mother in it, then that must be a devil too, I think; what else can it be? says she.

I can't tell that, madam, said I; that's as you agree among yourselves: this kind does not go by generation; that's a dispute foreign to the present purpose.

Then I entered into a discourse with her of the ends and purposes for which the Devil takes up such beautiful forms as hers, and why it always gave me a suspicion when I saw a lady handsomer than ordinary, and set me upon the search, to be satisfied whether she was really a woman, or an apparition: a lady or a devil; allowing all along that her being a devil was quite out of the question.

Upon that very foot she took me up again roundly; And so, says she, you are very civil to me through all your discourse, for I see it ends all in that, and you take it as a thing confessed, that I am a devil! a very pretty piece of good usage indeed, says she; I thank you for it.

Nay, madam, says I, do not take it ill of me, for I only discover to you that I knew it; I do not tell it you as a secret, for you are satisfied of that another way.

Satisfied of what? says she; that I am a devil? I think the Devil's in you; and so began to be hot.

A devil! yes, madam, says I, without doubt a mere devil; take it as you please, I can't help that; and so I began to take it ill that she should be disgusted at opening such a well-known truth to her.

With that she discovered it all at once, for she turned fury, in the very letter of it; flew out in a passion, railed at me, cursed me most heartily, and immediately disappeared; which, you know, is the particular mark of a spirit or apparition.

We had a great deal of discourse besides this, relating to several other young ladies of her acquaintance, some of which I said, were mere apparitions like herself; and told her which were so, and which not; and the reason why they were so, and for what uses and purposes, some to delude the world one way, and some another; and she was pretty well pleased to hear that, but she could not bear to hear her own true character, which, however, as cunning as she was, made her act the devil at last, as you have heard; and then vanished out of my sight.

I have seen her in miniature several times since, but she proves herself still to be the devil of a lady, for she bears malice, and will never forgive me that I would not let her be an angel; but like a very devil as she is, she endeavours to kill me at a distance; and indeed the poison of her eyes (basilisk-like) is very strong, and she has a strange influence upon me; but I, that know her to be a devil, strive very hard with myself to drive the memory of her out of my thoughts.

I have had two or three engagements since this, with other apparitions of the same sex, and I find they are all alike, they are willing enough to be thought angels, but the word devil does not go down at all with them; but it is all one, whenever we see an apparition, it is so natural to say we have seen the Devil, that there is no prevailing with mankind to talk any other language. A gentleman of my acquaintance, the other day, that had courted a lady a long time, had the misfortune to come a little suddenly upon her, when she did not expect him, and found her in such a rage at some of her servants, that it quite disordered her, especially a footman; the fellow had done something that was indeed provoking, but not sufficient to put her into such a passion, and so out of herself; nor was she able to restrain herself when she saw her lover come in, but damned the fellow, and raged like a fury at him.

My friend did his best to compose her, and begged the fellow's pardon of her, but it would not do; nay, the poor fellow made all the submissions that could be expected, but it was the same thing; and so the gentleman, not caring to engage himself farther than became him, withdrew, and came no more at her for three days, in all which time she was hardly cool.

The next day my friend came to me, and talking of it in confidence to me, I am afraid, says he, I am going to marry a she-devil; and so told me the story: I took no notice to him, but finding out his mistress, and taking proper measures with some of my particular skill, I soon found out that it was really so, that she was a mere apparition; and had it not been for that accidental disorder of her passions, which discovered her inside, she might indeed have cheated any man, for she was a lovely devil as ever was seen; she talked like an angel, sung like a syren, did everything, and said everything, that was taking and charming; but what then? it was all apparition, for she was a mere devil. It is true, my friend married her, and though she was a devil without doubt, yet either she behaved so well, or he was so good, I never could hear him find fault with her.

These are particular instances; but, alas! I could run you a length beyond all those examples, and give you such a list of devils among the gay things of the town, that would frighten you to think of; and you would presently conclude with me, that all the perfect beauties are devils, mere apparitions; but time and paper fails, so we must only leave the men the caution, let them venture at their peril. I return to the subject.

We have a great many charming apparitions of like kind go daily about the world in complete masquerade, and, though we must not say so, they are in themselves mere devils, wicked, dangerous, murdering devils, that kill various ways; some, basilisk-like, with their eyes; some, syren-like, with their tongues; all murderers, even from the beginning. It is true, it is pity these pretty apparitions should be devils, and be so mischievous as they are; but, since it is so, I can do no less than to advertise you of it, that you may shun the Devil in whatever shape you meet with him.

Again, there are some half devils, they say, like the Sagittarii, half man, half horse; or rather, like the Satyr, who, they say, is half devil, half man; or, like my lord bishop, who, they say, was half-headed: whether they mean half-witted or no, I do not find authors agreed about it; but if they had voted him such, it had been as kind a thing as any they could say of him, because it would have cleared him from the scandal of being a devil or half a devil, for we don't find the Devil makes any alliance with f—ls.

Then as to merry devils, there is my master G——, he may indeed have the Devil in him, but it must be said, to the credit of possession in general, that Satan would have scorned to have entered into a soul so narrow that there was not room to hold him, or to take up with so discording a creature, so abject, so scoundrel, as never made a figure among mankind greater than that of a thief, a marauder moulded up into quality, and a rapparee dressed up, a-la-masque, with a robe and a coronet.

Some little dog-kennel devil may, indeed, take up his quarters in or near him, and so run into and out of him as his drum beats a call: but to him that was born a devil, Satan, that never acts to no purpose, could not think him worth being possessed by anything better than a devil of a dirty quality; that is to say, a spirit too mean to wear the name of devil, without some badge or addition of infamy and meanness to distinguish it by.

Thus what devil of quality would be confined to a P———n, who, inheriting all the pride and insolence of his ancestors, without one of their good qualities; the bully, the Billingsgate, and all the hereditary ill language of his family, without an ounce of their courage; that has been rescued five or six times from the scandal of a coward, by the bravery, and at the hazard, of friends, and never failed to be ungrateful; that if ever he committed a murder, did it in cold blood, because nobody could prove he ever had any hot; who, possessed with a poltroon devil, was always wickeder in the dark than he durst be by daylight; and who, after innumerable passive sufferings, has been turned out of human society, because he could not be kicked or cuffed either into good manners or good humour.

To say this was a devil, an apparition, or even a half devil, would be unkind to Satan himself, since though he (the Devil) has so many millions of inferior devils under his command, not one could be found base enough to match him, nor one devil found but what would think himself dishonoured to be employed about him.

Some merry, good for nothing devils we have, indeed, which we might, if we had room, speak of at large, and divert you, too, with the relation; such as my Lady Hatt's devil in Essex, who, upon laying a joiner's mallet in the window of a certain chamber, would come very orderly and knock with it all night upon the window, or against the wainscot, and disturb the neighbourhood, and then go away in the morning, as well satisfied as may be; whereas, if the mallet was not left, he would think himself affronted, and be as unsufferable and terrifying as possible, breaking the windows, splitting the wainscot, committing all the disorders, and doing all the damage that he was able to the house, and to the goods in it. And, again, such as the drumming devil in the well at Oundle, in Northamptonshire, and such-like.

A great many antic devils have been seen also who seemed to have little or nothing to do, but only to assure us that they can appear if they please, and that there is a reality in the thing called apparition.

As to shadows of devils, and imaginary appearances, such as appear and yet are invisible at the same time, I had thought to have bestowed a chapter upon them by themselves, but it may be as much to the purpose to let them alone as to meddle with them; it is said our old friend Luther used to be exceedingly troubled with such invisible apparitions, and he tells us much of them in what they call his Table-talk; but, with Master Luther's leave, though the Devil passes for a very great liar, I could swallow many things of his own proper making, as soon as some of those I find in a book that goes by his name; particularly the story of the Devil in a basket, the child flying out of the cradle, and the like.

In a word, the walking devils that we have generally among us are of the female sex; whether it be that the Devil finds less difficulty to manage them, or that he lives quieter with them, or that they are fitter for his business than the men, I shall not now enter into a dispute about that; perhaps he goes better disguised in the fair sex than otherwise. Antiquity gives us many histories of she-devils, such as we can very seldom match for wickedness among the men ; such, now, as in the text, Lot's daughters, Joseph's mistress, Samson's Delilah, Herod's Herodias, these were certainly devils, or played the devil sufficiently in their turn; one male apparition, indeed, the Scripture furnishes you with, and that is Judas; for his master says expressly of him, *One of you is a devil*, not 'has' the Devil, or is 'possessed' of the Devil; but really 'is' a devil, or is a real devil.

How happy is it, that this great secret comes thus to be discovered to mankind! certainly the world has gone on in ignorance a long time, and at a strange rate, that we should have so many devils continually walking about among us in human shape, and we know it not.

Philosophers tell us that there is a world of spirits, and many learned pieces of guess-work they make at it, representing the world to be so near us, that the air, as they describe it, must be full of dragons and devils, enough to frighten our imaginations with the very thoughts of them; and, if they say true, it is our great felicity that we cannot see any farther into it than we do, which, if we could, would appear as frightful as hell itself; but none of those sages ever told us, till now, that half the people we converse with are apparitions, especially of the women; and, among them, especially this valuable part, the women of figure, the fair, the beautiful, or the patched and painted.

This unusual phenomenon has been seen but a little while, and but a little way, and the general part of mankind cannot come into the same notions about it; nay, perhaps they will all think it strange; but be it as strange as it will, the nature of the thing confirms it, this lower sphere is full of devils; and some of both sexes have given strange testimonies of the reality of their pre-existent devilism for many ages past, though I think it never came to that height as it has now.

It is true, in former times Satan dealt much in old women, and those, as I have observed already, very ugly; 'ugly as a witch,' 'black as a witch,' 'I look like a witch,' all proverbial speeches, and which testified what tools it was Satan generally worked with; and these old spectres, they tell us, used to ride through the air in the night, and upon broomsticks, too; all mighty homely doings. Some say they used to go to visit their grand seignior, the Devil, in those nocturnal perambulations; but be that as it will, it is certain the Devil has changed hands, and that now he walks about the world clothed in beauty, covered with the charms of the lovely; and he fails not to disguise himself effectually by it, for who would think a beautiful lady could be a mask to the devil? and that a fine face, a divine shape, a heavenly aspect, should bring the Devil in her company, nay, should be herself an apparition, a mere devil?

The inquiry is, indeed, worth our while, and therefore I hope all the enamoured beaus and boys, all the beauty-hunters and fortune-hunters, will take heed, for I suppose, if they get the Devil, they will not complain for want of a fortune; and there is danger enough, I assure you, for the world is full of apparitions, *non rosa sine spinis*, not a beauty without a devil; the old women spectres, and the young women apparitions, the ugly ones witches, and the handsome ones devils; Lord ha' mercy! and a + may be set on the man's door that goes a-courting.

CHAPTER VIII.

OF THE CLOVEN FOOT WALKING ABOUT THE WORLD WITHOUT THE DEVIL; VIZ., OF WITCHES MAKING BARGAINS FOR THE DEVIL, AND PARTICULARLY OF SELLING THE SOUL TO THE DEVIL.

I HAVE dwelt long upon the Devil in mask, as he goes about the world incog., and especially without his cloven foot, and have touched upon some of his disguises in the management of his interest in the world; I must say some of his disguises only, for who can give a full account of all his tricks and arts in so narrow a compass as I am prescribed to?

But as I said that every devil has not a cloven foot, so I must add now, for the present purpose, that every cloven foot is not the Devil.

Not but that, wherever I should meet the cloven hoof, I should expect that the Devil was not far off, and should be apt to raise the posse against him, to apprehend him; yet it may happen otherwise, that's certain: every coin has its counterfeit, every art its pretender, every whore her admirer, every error its patron, and every day has its devil.

I have had some thought of making a full and complete discovery here of that great doubt which has so long puzzled the world, namely, whether there is any such thing as secret making bargains with the Devil; and the first positive assurance I can give you in the case, is, that if there is not, it is not his fault, it is not for want of his endeavour; it is plain, if you will pardon me for taking so mean a step as that of quoting Scripture, I say, it is evident he would fain have made a contract with our Saviour; and he bid boldly, give him his due, namely, all the kingdoms of the world for one bend of his knee. Impudent seraph! to think thy Lord should pay thee homage! How many would agree with him here for a less price! They say Oliver Cromwell struck a bargain with him, and that he gave Oliver the protectorship, but would not let him call himself king, which stuck so close to that furioso, that the mortification spread into his soul, and it is said he died of a gangrene in the spleen. But take notice,

L L 2

and do Oliver justice; I do not vouch the story, neither does
the bishop say one word of it.

Fame used to say, that the old famous Duke of Luxemburg
made a magic compact of this kind; nay, I have heard many
an (old woman) officer of the troops, who never cared to see
his face, declare that he carried the Devil at his back. I
remember a certain author of a newspaper in London was
once taken up, and they say it cost him 50*l.* for printing in
his news, that Luxemburg was humpbacked. Now if I have
solved the difficulty, namely, that he was not humped, only
carried the Devil at his back, I think the poor man should
have his 50*l.* again, or I should have it for the discovery.

I confess, I do not well understand this compacting with
such a fellow as can neither write nor read; nor do I know
who is the scrivener between them, or how the indenture
can be executed; but that which is worse than all the rest is,
that in the first place, the Devil never keeps articles; he will
contract perhaps, and they say he is mighty forward to make
conditions; but who shall bind him to the performance, and
where is the penalty if he fails? if we agree with him, he
will be apt enough to claim his bargain and demand payment;
nay, perhaps before it is due; but who shall make him stand
to his word?

Besides, he is a knave in his dealing, for he really promises
what he cannot perform; witness his impudent proposal to
our Lord, mentioned above, *All these kingdoms will I give thee!*
Lying spirit! why they were none of thine to give, no, not
one of them; for *the earth is the Lord's, and the kingdoms
thereof,* nor were they in his power any more than in his
right. So I have heard that some poor dismal creatures have
sold themselves to the Devil for a sum of money, for so much
cash; and yet even in that case, when the day of payment
came, I never heard that he brought his money or paid the
purchase, so that he is a scoundrel in his treaties, for you
shall trust for your bargain, but not be able to get your money;
and yet for your part, he comes for you to an hour: of which
by itself.

In a word, let me caution you all, when you trade with the
Devil, either get the price or quit the bargain; the Devil is
a cunning shaver, he will wriggle himself out of the performance on his side if possible, and yet expect you should
be punctual on your side. They tell you of a poor fellow in

Herefordshire, that offered to sell his soul to him for a cow, and though the Devil promised, and as they say, signed the writings, yet the poor countryman could never get the cow of him, but still as he brought a cow to him, somebody or other came and challenged it, proving that it was lost or stolen from them; so that the man got nothing but the name of a cow-stealer, and was at last carried to Hereford jail, and condemned to be hanged for stealing two cows, one after the other: the wicked fellow was then in the greatest distress imaginable, he summoned his devil to help him out, but he failed him, as the Devil always will; he really had not stolen the cows, but they were found in his possession, and he could give no account how he came by them. At last, he was driven to confess the truth, told the horrid bargain he had made, and how the Devil often promised him a cow, but never gave him one, except that several times in the morning early he found a cow put into his yard, but it always proved to belong to some of his neighbours: whether the man was hanged or no, the story does not relate; but this part is to my purpose, that they that make bargains with the Devil, ought to make him give security for the performance of covenants, and who the Devil would get to be bound for him, I cannot tell, they must look to that who make the bargain: besides, if he had not had a mind to cheat or baffle the poor man, what need he have taken a cow so near home? If he had such and such powers as we talk of, and as fancy and fable furnish for him, could not he have carried a cow in the air upon a broomstick, as well as an old woman? could he not have stole a cow for him in Lincolnshire, and set it down in Herefordshire, and so have performed his bargain, saved his credit, and kept the poor man out of trouble? so that if the story is true, as I really believe it is, either it is not the Devil that makes those bargains, or the Devil has not such power as we bestow on him, except on special occasions he gets a permit, and is bid go, as in the case of Job, the Gadarene hogs, and the like.

We have another example of a man's selling himself to the Devil, that is very remarkable, and that is in the Bible too; and even in that, I do not find what the Devil did for him, in payment of the purchase price. The person selling was .Ahab, of whom the text says expressly, *there was none like him, who did sell himself to work wickedness in the sight of the*

Lord, 1 Kings xxi. 20, and the 25th. I think it might have been rendered, if not translated, 'in spite of the Lord,' or, 'in defiance of God;' for certainly that is the meaning of it; and now allowing me to preach a little upon this text, my sermon shall be very short. Ahab sold himself; who did he sell himself to? I answer that question by a question; who would buy him? who, as we say, would give anything for him? and the answer to that is plain also, you may judge of the purchaser by the work he was to do; he that buys a slave in the market, buys him to work for him, and to do such business as he has for him to do: Ahab was bought to work wickedness, and who would buy him for that but the Devil?

I think there is no room to doubt but Ahab sold himself to the Devil; the text is plain that he sold himself, and the work he was sold to do points out the master that bought him: what price he agreed with the Devil for, that indeed the text is silent in, so we may let it alone, nor is it much to our purpose, unless it be to inquire whether the Devil stood to his bargain or not, and whether he paid the money according to agreement, or cheated him as he did the farmer at Hereford.

This buying and selling between the Devil and us, is, I must confess, an odd kind of stock-jobbing, and, indeed, the Devil may be said to sell the bear-skin, whatever he buys; but the strangest part is, when he comes to demand the transfer; for, as I hinted before, whether he performs or no, he expects his bargain to a tittle; there is, indeed, some difficulty in resolving how and in what manner payment is made. The stories we meet with in our chimney-corner histories, and which are so many ways made use of to make the Devil frightful to us and our heirs for ever, are generally so foolish and ridiculous, as, if true or not true, they have nothing material in them, are of no signification, or else so impossible in their nature, that they make no impression upon anybody above twelve years old and under seventy; or else are so tragical that antiquity has fabled them down to our taste, that we might be able to hear them and repeat them with less horror than is due to them.

This variety has taken off our relish of the thing in general, and made the trade of soul-selling, like our late more eminent bubbles, be taken to be a cheat, and to have little in it.

However, to speak a little more gravely to it, I cannot say

but that since, by the two eminent instances of it above in Ahab, and in Christ himself, the fact is evidently ascertained, and that the Devil has attempted to make such a bargain on one, and actually did make it with the other, the possibility of it is not to be disputed; but then I must explain the manner of it a little, and bring it down nearer to our understanding, that it may be more intelligible than it is; for, as for this selling the soul, and making a bargain to give the Devil possession by livery and seisin on the day appointed, that I cannot come into by any means; no, nor into the other part, namely, of the Devil coming to claim his bargain, and to demand the soul according to agreement, and upon default of a fair delivery, taking it away by violence, case and all, of which we have many historical relations pretty current among us; some of which, for aught I know, we might have hoped had been true, if we had not been sure they were false, and others we had reason to fear were false, because it was impossible they should be true.

The bargains of this kind, according to the best accounts we have of them, used to consist of two main articles, according to the ordinary stipulations in all covenants ; namely,

1. Something to be performed on the Devil's part, buying.

2. Something to be performed on the man's part, selling.

1. The Devil's part: this was generally some poor trifle, for the Devil generally bought good pennyworths, and oftentimes, like a complete sharper, agreed to give what he was not able to procure; that is to say, would bargain for a price he could not pay, as in the case of the Hereford man and the cow; for example, 1. Long life: this, though the deluded chapman has often had folly enough to contract for, the Devil never had power to make good; and we have a famous story, how true I know not, of a wretch that sold himself to the Devil on condition he, Satan, should assure him (1.) That he should never want victuals; (2.) That he should never be a-cold; (3.) That he should always come to him when he called him; and (4.) That he should let him live one-and-twenty years, and then Satan was at liberty to have him; that is, I suppose, to take him wherever he could find him.

It seems, the fellow's desire to be assured of twenty-one years' life, was chiefly, that during that time, he might be as wicked as he would, and should yet be sure not to be hanged, nay, to be free from all punishment; upon this foot it is said he commenced rogue, and committed a great many robberies and other villanous things. Now it seems the Devil was pretty true to his bargain in several of those things; particularly, that two or three times when the fellow was taken up for petty crimes, and called for his old friend, he came and frightened the constables so, that they let the offender get away from them; but at length, having done some capital crime, a set of constables, or such-like officers, seized upon him, who were not to be frightened with the Devil, in what shape soever he appeared; so that they carried him off, and he was committed to Newgate, or some other prison as effectual.

Nor could Satan, with all his skill, unlock his fetters, much less the prison doors; but he was tried, convicted, and executed. The fellow in his extremity, they say, expostulated with the Devil for his bargain, the term of twenty-one years it seems not being expired. But the Devil, it is said, shuffled with him, told him a good while he would get him out, bid him have patience and stay a little, and thus led him on, till he came as it were within sight of the gallows, that is to say, within a day or two of his execution, when the Devil cavilled upon his bargain, told him he agreed to let him live twenty-one years, and he had not hindered him, but that he did not covenant to cause him to live that time; that there was a great deal of difference between doing and suffering; that he was to suffer him to live, and that he did; but he could not make him live when he had brought himself to the gallows.

Whether this story were true or not (for you must not expect we historians should answer for the discourse between the Devil and his chaps, because we were not privy to the bargain), I say, whether it was true or not, the inference is to our purpose several ways.

1. It confirms what I have said of the knavery of the Devil in his dealings, and that when he has stock-jobbed with us on the best conditions he can get, he very seldom performs his bargain.

2. It confirms what I have likewise said, that the Devil's power is limited; with this addition, that he not only cannot destroy the life of man, but that he cannot preserve it; in short, he can neither prevent or bring on our destruction.

I may be allowed, I hope, for the sake of the present discourse, to suppose that the Devil would have been so just to
this wicked, though foolish creature, as to have saved him
from the gallows if he could ; but it seems, he at last acknowledged that it was not in his power; nay, he could not keep
him from being taken and carried to prison, after he was
gotten into the hands of a bold fellow or two, that were not
to be scared with his bluster, as some foolish creatures had
been before.

And how simple, how weak, how unlike anything of an
angelic nature, was it to attempt to save the poor wretch
only by little noises and sham appearances, putting out the
candles, rushing and jostling in the dark, and the like. If
the Devil was that mighty seraph which we have heard of,
if he is a god of this world, a prince of the air, a spirit able
to destroy cities and make havoc in the world; if he can
raise tempests and storms, throw fire about the world, and
do wonderful things, as an unchained devil no doubt could
do, what need all this frippery ? and what need he try so
many ridiculous ways, by the emptiness, nay, the silly non-
sensical manner, of which, he shows that he is able to do no
better, and that his power is extinguished ? In a word, he
would certainly act otherwise, if he could. *Sed caret pedibus*,
he wants power.

How weak a thing is it then, for any man to expect performance from the Devil, if he has not power to do mischief,
which is his element, his very nature, and on many accounts,
is the very sum of his desires !   How should he have power
to do good ? how power to deliver from danger or from
death ? which deliverance would be in itself a good, and we
know it is not in his nature to do good to or for any man.

In a word, the Devil is strangely impudent, to think that
any man should depend upon him for the performance of an
agreement of any kind whatever, when he knows himself
that he is not able, if he was honest enough, to be as good
as his word.

Come we next to his expecting our performance to him;
though he is not so just to us, yet, it seems, he never fails to
come and demand payment of us at the very day appointed.
He was but a weak trader in things of this nature, who
having sold his soul to the Devil (so our old women's tales
call the thing), and when the Devil came to demand his bar-

gain, put it off as a thing of no force, for that it was done so long ago, he thought he (the Devil) had forgot it. It was a better answer, which they tell us a Lutheran divine gave the Devil in the name of a poor wretch who had sold himself to the Devil, and who was in a terrible fright about his coming for his bargain, as he might well be indeed, if the Devil has such a power as really to come and take it by force. The story, if you can bear a serious one, is this:

The man was in great horror of mind, and the family feared he would destroy himself; at length they sent for a Lutheran minister to talk with him, and who, after some labour with him, got out the truth, viz., that he had sold himself to the Devil, and that the time was almost expired when he expected the Devil would come and fetch him away, and he was sure he would not fail coming to the time to a minute. The minister first endeavoured to convince him of the horrid crime, and to bring him to a true penitence for that part; and having, as he thought, made him a sincere penitent, he then began to encourage him, and particularly, desired of him, that when the time was come that the Devil should fetch him away, he, the minister, should be in the house with him; accordingly, to make the story short, the time came, the Devil came, and the minister was present when the Devil came; what shape he was in, the story does not say; the man said he saw him, and cried out; the minister could not see him, but the man affirming he was in the room, the minister said aloud, In the name of the living God, Satan, what comest thou here for? The Devil answered, I come for my own; the minister answered, He is not thy own, for Jesus Christ has redeemed him, and in his name I charge thee to avoid and touch him not; at which, says the story, the Devil gave a furious stamp (with his cloven foot I suppose) and went away, and was never known to molest him afterwards.

Another story, though it be in itself a long one, I shall abridge (for your reading with the less uneasiness) as follows:

A young gentleman of ——berg, in the elector of Brandenburgh's (now the King of Prussia's) dominions, being deeply in love with a beautiful lady, but something above his fortune, and whom he could by no means bring to love him again, applied himself to an old thing, called a witch, for her assistance, and promised her great things if she could bring the lady to love him, or any how compass her so as he might have his will of her; nay, at last he told her he would give up his soul to her, if she would answer his desire.

The old hag, it seems, having had some of his money, had very honestly tried what she could do, but all to no purpose, the lady would not comply; but when he offered such a great price, she told him she would consider farther against such a time, and so appointed him the next evening.

At the time appointed, he comes, and the witch made a long speech to him upon the nicety of the affair; I suppose to prepare him not to be surprised at what was to come, for she supposed he was not so very desperately bent as he appeared to be; she told him it was a thing of very great difficulty, but as he had made such a great offer, of selling his soul for it, she had an acquaintance in the house, who was better skilled than she was in such particular things, and would treat with him farther, and she doubted not but that both together might answer his end. The fellow, it seems, was still of the same mind, and told her he cared not what he pawned or sold, if he could but obtain the lady; Well, says the old hag, sit still awhile; and with that she withdraws.

By and by she comes in again with a question in her mouth; Pray, says she, do you seek this lady for a wife, or for a mistress? would you marry her, or would you only lie with her? The young man told her, no, no, he did not expect she would lie with him, therefore he would be satisfied to marry her, but asks her the reason of the question; Why truly, says the old hag, my reason is very weighty; for if you would have her for your wife, I doubt we can do you no service; but if you have a mind to lie with her, the person I speak of will undertake it.

The man was surprised at that, only he objected that this was a transient or short felicity, and that he should perhaps have her no more; the old hag bid him not fear, but that if she once yielded to be his whore, he might have her as often as he pleased; upon this he consents, for he was stark mad for the lady: he having consented, she told him then, he should follow her, but told him, whoever he saw, he must speak to nobody but her, till she gave him leave, and that he should not be surprised, whatever happened, for no hurt should befall him; all which he agreed to, and the old woman going out he followed her.

Being, upon this, led into another room, where there was but very little light, yet enough to let him see that there was nobody in it but himself and the woman, he was desired to sit down in a chair next to a table, and the old woman clapping the door to after her, he asked her why she shut the door, and where was the person she told him of. At which she answered, There he is, pointing to a chair at a little distance: the young gentleman turned his head, saw a grave kind of a man sitting in an elbow-chair, though he said, he could have sworn there was nobody in the chair when the old woman shut the door; however, having promised not to speak to anybody but the old woman, he said not a word.

By and by the woman making abundance of strange gestures and motions, and mumbling over several things which he could not understand, on a sudden a large wicker chair, which stood by the chimney, removes to the other end of the table which he sat by, but there was nobody in the chair; in about two minutes after that the chair removed, there appeared a person sitting in that too, who, the room being, as is said, almost dark, could not be so distinguished by the eye as to see his countenance.

After some while, the first man, and the chair he sat in, moved, as if they had been one body, to the table also; and the old woman and the two men seemed to talk together, but the young man could not understand anything they said; after some time the old witch turned to the young gentleman, told him his request was granted, but not for marriage, but the lady should love and receive him.

The witch then gave him a stick dipped in tar at both ends, and bid him hold it to a candle, which he did, and instead of burning like a stick, it burnt out like a torch; then she bid him break it off in the middle, and light the other end; he did that too, and all the room seemed to be in a light flame; then, she said, Deliver one piece here, pointing to one only of the persons; so he gave the first fire-stick to the first man or apparition; Now, says she, deliver the other here; so he gave the other piece to the other apparition, at which they both rose up and spoke to him words, which he said he understood not, and could not repeat, and immediately vanished with the fire-sticks and all, leaving the room full of smoke. I do not remember that the story says anything of brimstone, or the smell of it, but it says the door continued fast locked, and nobody was left in the room but the young gentleman and the witch.

Now the ceremony being over, he asked the witch if the business was done. She said, Yes. Well, but says he, have I sold my soul to the Devil? Yes, says she, you have, and you gave him possession when you delivered the two fire-sticks to him. To him! says he; why, was that the Devil? Yes, says the old hag. At which the young man was in a terrible fright for a while, but it went off again.

And what's next? says he; when shall I see the lady for whose sake I have done all this? You shall know that presently, said she; and opening the door, in the next room she presents him with a most beautiful lady, but had charged him not to speak a word to her: she was exactly dressed like, and he presently knew her to be the lady he desired; upon which he flew to her, and clasped her in his arms, but that moment he had her fast, as he thought, in his arms, she vanished out of his sight.

Finding himself thus disappointed, he upbraids the old woman with betraying him, and flew out with ill language at her, in a great rage. The Devil often deluded him thus, after this, with shows and appearances, but still no per-formance; after a while he gets an opportunity to speak with the lady herself in reality, but she was as positive in her denial as ever, and even took away all hopes of his ever obtaining her, which put him into despair, for now he thought he had given himself up to the Devil for nothing; and this brought him to himself, so that he made a penitent confession of his crime to some friends, who took great care of him, and encouraged him, and at last furnished him with such an answer as put the Devil into a fright, when he came for the bargain.

For Satan, it seems, as the story says, had the imprudence to demand his agreement, notwithstanding he had failed in the performance on his part; what the answer was, I do not pretend to have seen, but it seems it was something like what is mentioned above, viz., that he was in better hands, and that he durst not touch him.

I have heard of another person that had actually signed a contract with the Devil; and upon a fast kept by some protestant or Christian divines, while they were praying for the poor man, the Devil was obliged to come and throw the contract in at the window.

But I vouch none of these stories; there may be much in them, and much use made of them, even whether exactly such in fact, as they are related, or no; the best use I can make of them is this; if any wicked desperate wretches have made bargain and sale with Satan, their only way is to repent, if they know how, and that before he comes to claim them; then batter him with his own guns; play religion against devilism, and perhaps they may drive the Devil out of their reach; at least he will not come at them, which is as well.

On the other hand, how many stories have we handed about of the Devil's really coming with a terrible appearance at the time appointed, and powerfully, or by violence, carrying away those that have given themselves thus up to him; nay, and sometimes a piece of the house along with them, as in the famous instance of Sudbury, anno 1662. It seems he comes with rage and fury upon such occasions, pretending he only comes to take his own, or as if he had leave given him to come and take his goods, as we say, where he could find them, and would strike a terror into all that should oppose him.

The greatest part of the terror we are usually in upon this occasion, is from a supposition, that when this hell-fire contract is once made, God allows the Devil to come and take the wicked creature, how and in what manner he thinks fit, as being given up to him by his own act and deed; but in my opinion there's no divinity at all in that; for as, in our law, we punish a *felo de se* or self-murderer, because, as the law suggests, he had no right to dismiss his own life; that he being a subject of the commonwealth, the government claims the ward or custody of him, and so it was not murder only, but robbery, and is a felony against the state, robbing the king of his liegeman, as it is justly called; so neither has any man a right to dispose of his soul, which belongs to his Maker in property, and in right of creation: the man, then, having no right to sell, Satan has no right to buy, or at best he has made a purchase without a title, and consequently has no just claim to the possession.

It is therefore a mistake to say, that when any of us have been so mad to make such a pretended contract with the Devil, that God gives him leave to take it as his due; it is

no such thing; the Devil has bought what you had no right
to sell, and therefore, as an unlawful oath is to be repented
of, and then broken, so your business is to repent of the
crime, and then tell the Devil you have better considered of
it, and that you won't stand to your bargain, for you had no
power to sell; and if he pretends to violence after that, I am
mistaken; I believe the Devil knows better.

It is true, our old mothers and nurses have told us
other things, but they only told us what their mothers and
nurses told them, and so the tale has been handed down
from one generation of old women to another; but we have
no vouchers for the fact, other than oral tradition, the credit
of which, I confess, goes but a very little way with me; nor
do I believe it one jot the more for all the frightful addenda
which they generally join to the tale, for it never wants a
great variety of that kind.

Thus they tell us the Devil carried away Dr. Faustus, and
took a piece of the wall of his garden along with them: thus
at Salisbury, the Devil, as it is said, and publicly printed,
carried away two fellows that had given themselves up to
him, and carried away the roof of the house with them,
and the like, all which I believe my share of. Besides,
if these stories were really true, they are all against the
Devil's true interest, Satan must be a fool, which is
indeed what I never took him to be in the main; this would
be the way not to increase the number of desperadoes, who
should thus put themselves into his hand, but to make himself a terror to them; and this is one of the most powerful
objections I have against the thing, for the Devil, I say, is
no fool, that must be acknowledged; he knows his own game,
and generally plays it sure.

I might, before I quit this point, seriously reflect here
upon our *beau monde*, viz., the gay part of mankind, especially
those of the times we live in, who walk about in a composure
and tranquillity inexpressible, and yet, as we all know, must
certainly have all sold themselves to the Devil, for the power
of acting the foolishest things with the greater applause; it
is true, to be a fool is the most pleasant life in the world, if
the fool has but the particular felicity, which few fools want,
viz., to think themselves wise: the learned say, it is the dignity and perfection of fools, that they never fail trusting
themselves; they believe themselves sufficient and able for

everything; and hence their want or waste of brains is no grievance to them, but they hug themselves in the satiety of their own wit; but to bring other people to have the same notion of them, which they have of themselves, and to have their apish and ridiculous conduct make the same impression on the minds of others, as it does on their own; this requires a general infatuation, and must either be a judgment from heaven, or a mist of hell; nothing but the Devil can make all the men of brains applaud a fool; and can any man believe that the Devil will do this for nothing? no, no, he will be well paid for it, and I know no other way they have to compound with him, but this of bargain and sale.

It is the same thing with rakes and bullies, as it is with fools and beaus; and this brings me to the subject of buying and selling itself, and to examine what is understood by it in the world, what people mean by such and such a man selling himself to the Devil: I know the common acceptation of it is, that they make some capitulation for some indulgence in wickedness, on conditions of safety and impunity, which the Devil promises them; though, as I said above, he is a bite in that too, for he cannot perform the conditions; however, I say, he promises boldly, and they believe him, and for this privilege in wickedness, they consent that he shall come and fetch them for his own, at such or such a time.

This is the state of the case in the general acceptation of it; I do not say it is really so, nay, it is even an inconsistency in itself, for one would think they need not capitulate with the Devil to be so and so superlatively wicked, and give him such a price for it, seeing, unless we have a wrong notion of him, he is naturally inclined, as well as avowedly willing, to have all men be as superlatively wicked as possibly they can, and must necessarily be always ready to issue out his licenses gratis, as far as his authority will go in the case; and therefore I do not see why the wretches that deal with him, should article with him for a price; but suppose, for argument sake, that it is so, then the next thing is, some capital crime follows the contract, and then the wretch is forsaken, for the Devil cannot protect him, as he promised, so he is trussed up, and, like Coleman at the gallows, he exclaims that there is no truth in devils.

It may be true, however, that under the powerful guard and protection of the Devil, men do sometimes go a great way in crime, and that, perhaps, farther in these our days of boasted morals, than was known among our fathers; the only difference that I meet with between the sons of Belial in former days and those of our ages, seems to be in the Devil's management, not in theirs; the sum of which amounts to this, that Satan seems to act with more cunning, and they with less; for, in the former ages of Satan's dominion, he had much business upon his hands; all his art and engines, and engineers also, were kept fully employed, to wheedle, allure, betray, and circumvent people, and draw them into crimes, and they found him, as we may say, a full employment. I doubt not, he was called the Tempter on that very account; but the case seems quite altered now, the tables are turned; then the Devil tempted men to sin, but now, in short, they tempt the Devil; men push into crimes before he pushes them; they outshoot him in his own bow, outrun him on his own ground, and, as we say of some hotspurs who ride post, they whip the postboy; in a word, the Devil seems to have no business now but to sit still and look on.

This I must confess, seems to intimate some secret compact between the Devil and them; but then it looks, not as if they had contracted with the Devil for leave to sin, but that the Devil had contracted with them that they should sin so and so, up to such a degree, and that without giving him the trouble of daily solicitation, private management, and artful screwing up their passions, their affections, and their most retired faculties, as he was before obliged to do.

This also appears more agreeable to the nature of the thing; and as it is a most exquisite part of Satan's cunning, so it is an undoubted testimony of his success; if it was not so, he could never bring his kingdom to such a height of absolute power as he has done: this also solves several difficulties in the affair of the world's present way of sinning, which otherwise it would be very hard to understand; as particularly how some eminent men of quality among us, whose upper rooms are not extraordinary well furnished in other cases, yet are so very witty in their wickedness, that they gather admirers by hundreds and thousands; who, however heavy, lumpish, slow, and backward, even by nature and in force of constitution, in better things, yet, in their race devilwards, th foot, and outrun all their neighbours; fellows that are as empty of sense as beggars are of honesty, and as far from brains as a whore is of modesty; on a sudden you shall find them dip into polemics, study Michael Servetus, Socinus, and the most learned of their disciples; they shall reason against all religion, as strongly as a philosopher, blaspheme with such a keenness of wit, and satirize God and eternity with such a brightness of fancy, as if the soul of a Rochester or a Hobbes was transmigrated into them; in a little length of time more they banter heaven, burlesque the Trinity, and jest with every sacred thing, and all so sharp, so ready, and so terribly witty, as if they were born buffoons, and were singled out by nature to be champions for the Devil.

Whence can all this come? how is the change wrought? who but the Devil can inject wit in spite of natural dulness, create brains, fill empty heads, and supply the vacuities in the understanding? And will Satan do all this for nothing? No, no, he is too wise for that; I can never doubt a secret compact, if there is such a thing in nature; when I see a head where there was no head, sense in *posse* where there is no sense in *esse*, wit without brains, and sight without eyes, it is all devil-work: could G—— write satires, that could neither read Latin or spell English; like old Sir William Read, who wrote a book of optics, which when it was printed, he did not know which was the right side uppermost and which the wrong? Could this eminent uninformed beau turn atheist, and make wise speeches against that Being which made him a fool, if the Devil had not sold him some wit in exchange for that trifle of his, called soul? Had he not bartered his inside with that son of the morning, to have his tongue tipped with blasphemy, he that knew nothing of a God, but only to swear by him, could never have set up for a wit to burlesque his providence and ridicule his government of the world.

But the Devil, as he is god of the world, has one particular advantage, and that is, that when he has work to do he very seldom wants instruments; with this circumstance also, that the degeneracy of human nature supplies him. As the late King of France said of himself, when they told him what a calamity was like to befall his kingdom by the famine: Well, says the king, then I shall not want soldiers; and it was so; want of bread supplied his army with recruits, so want of grace supplies the Devil with reprobates for his work.

Another reason why I think the Devil has made more bargains of that kind we speak of, in this age, is, because he seems to have laid by his cloven foot; all his old emissaries, the tools of his trade, the engineers which he employed in his mines, such as witches, warlocks, magicians, conjurors, astrologers, and all the hellish train or rabble of human devils, who did his drudgery in former days, seem to be out of work: I shall give you a fuller enumeration of them in the next chapter.

These, I say, seem to be laid aside; not that his work is abated, or that his business with mankind, for their delusion and destruction, is not the same, or perhaps more than ever; but the Devil seems to have changed hands; the temper and genius if mankind is altered, and they are not to be taken by fright and horror, as they were then: the figures of those creatures were always dismal and horrible, and that is it which I mean by the cloven foot; but now wit, beauty, and gay things, are the sum of his craft; he manages by the soft and the smooth, the fair and the artful, the kind and the cunning, not by the frightful and terrible, the ugly and the odious.

When the Devil, for weighty despatches,
    Wanted messengers cunning and bold,
He pass'd by the beautiful faces,
    And pick'd out the ugly and old.

Of these he made warlocks and witches,
    To run of his errands by night;
Till the over-wrought hag-ridden wretches,
    Were as fit as the Devil to fright.

But whoever has been his adviser,
    As his kingdom increases in growth;
He now takes his measures much wiser,
    And traffics with beauty and youth.

Disguis'd in the wanton and witty,
    He haunts both the church and the court;
And sometimes he visits the city,
    Where all the best Christians resort.

Thus dress'd up in full masquerade,
    He the bolder can range up and down;
For he better can drive on his trade,
    In any one's name than his own.

CHAPTER IX.

OF THE TOOLS THE DEVIL WORKS WITH; VIZ., WITCHES, WIZARDS OR WARLOCKS, CONJURERS, MAGICIANS, DIVINES, ASTROLOGERS, INTERPRETERS OF DREAMS, TELLERS OF FORTUNES; AND, ABOVE ALL THE REST, HIS PARTICULAR MODERN PRIVY-COUNCILLORS CALLED WITS AND FOOLS.

THOUGH, as I have advanced in the foregoing chapter, the Devil has very much changed hands in his modern management of the world, and that, instead of the rabble and long train of implements reckoned up above, he now walks about in beaus, beauties, wits, and fools; yet I must not omit to tell you that he has not dismissed his former regiments, but, like officers in time of peace, he keeps them all in half-pay; or, like extraordinary men at the custom-house, they are kept at a call, to be ready to fill up vacancies, or to employ when he is more than ordinarily full of business; and therefore it may not be amiss to give some brief account of them from Satan's own memoirs, their performance being no inconsiderable part of his history.

Nor will it be an unprofitable digression to go back a little to the primitive institution of all these orders, for they are very ancient, and I assure you it requires great knowledge of antiquity to give a particular of their original; I shall be very brief in it.

In order then to this inquiry, you must know that it was not for want of servants that Satan took this sort of people into his pay; he had, as I have observed in its place, millions of diligent devils at his call, whatever business, and however difficult, he had for them to do; but, as I have said above, that our modern people are forwarder than even the Devil himself can desire them to be, and that they come before they are called, run before they are sent, and crowd themselves into his service; so it seems it was in those early days, when the world was one universal monarchy under his dominion, as I have at large described it in its place.

In those days, the wickedness of the world keeping a just pace with their ignorance, this inferior sort of low-prized instruments did the Devil's work mighty well; they drudged on in his black art so laboriously, and with such good success, that he found it was better to employ them as tools to delude about, and oblige them to take such shapes and dresses as were necessary, upon every trifling occasion; which, perhaps, was more cost than worship, more pains than pay.

Having then a set of these volunteers in his service, the true Devil had nothing to do but to keep an exact correspondence with them, and communicate some needful powers to them, to make them be and do something extraordinary, and give them a reputation in their business; and these, in a word, did a great part of, nay, almost all the Devil's business in the world.

To this purpose gave he them power (if we may believe old Glanville, Baxter, Hicks, and other learned consulters of oracles), to walk invisible, to fly in the air, ride upon broomsticks, and other wooden gear, to interpret dreams, answer questions, betray secrets, to talk (gibberish) the universal language, to raise storms, sell winds, bring up spirits, disturb the dead, and torment the living, with a thousand other needful tricks to amuse the world, keep themselves in veneration, and carry on the Devil's empire in the world.

The first nations among whom these infernal practices were found, were the Chaldeans; and, that I may do justice in earnest, as well as in jest, it must be allowed that the Chaldeans, or those of them so called, were not conjurers or magicians, only philosophers and studiers of nature, wise, sober, and studious men at first; and we have an extraordinary account of them; and if we may believe some of our best writers of fame, Abraham was himself famous among them for such magic, as Sir Walter Raleigh expresses it, *Qui contemplatione creaturarum cognovit Creatorem.*

Now granting this, it is all to my purpose, namely, that the Devil drew these wise men in, to search after more knowledge than nature could instruct them in; and the knowledge of the true God being at that time sunk very low, he debauched them all with dreams, apparitions, conjurers, &c., till he ruined the just notions they had, and made devils of them all, like himself.

The learned Senensis, speaking of this Chaldean kind of learning, gives us an account of five sorts of them; you will pardon me for being so grave as to go this length back.

1. Chascedin or Chaldeans, properly so called, being astronomers.
2. Asaphim or magicians, such was Zoroastres, and Balaam the son of Beor.

3. Chatumim or interpreters of dreams and hard speeches, enchanters, &c.

4. Mecasphim or witches, called at first prophets, afterwards *malefici* or *venefici*, poisoners.

5. Gazarim or auruspices, and diviners, such as divined by the entrails of beasts, the liver in particular; mentioned in Ezek.; or, as others, called augurs.

Now as to all these, I suppose I may do them no wrong, if I say, however justifiable they were in the beginning, the Devil got them all into his service at last; and that brings me to my text again, from which the rest was a digression.

1. The Chascedin, or Chaldean astronomers, turned astrologers, fortune-tellers, calculators of nativities, and vile deluders of the people, as if the wisdom of the holy God was in them, as Nebuchadnezzar said of Daniel on that very account.

2. The Asaphim, or magi, or magicians; Sixtus Senensis says, they were such as wrought by covenants with devils, but turned to it from their wisdom, which was to study the practical part of natural philosophy, working admirable effects by the mutual application of natural causes.

3. The Chatumim, from being reasoners or disputers upon difficult points in philosophy, became enchanters and conjurers. So,

4. The Mecasphim, or prophets, they turned to be sorcerers, raisers of spirits, such as wounded by an evil eye, and by bitter curses, and were afterwards famed for having familiar converse with the Devil, and were called witches.

5. The Gazarim, from the bare observing of the good and bad omens, by the entrails of beasts, flying of birds, &c., were turned to sacrists, or priests of the heathen idols and sacrificers.

Thus, I say, first or last, the Devil engrossed all the wise men of the East (for so they are called), made them all his own, and by them he worked wonders; that is, he filled the world with lying wonders, as if wrought by these men, when, indeed, it was all his own from beginning to the end, and set on foot merely to propagate delusion, and impose upon blinded and ignorant men: the god of this world blinded their minds, and they were led away by the subtlety of the Devil, to say no worse of it, till they became devils themselves, as to mankind; for they carried on the Devil's work upon all occasions, and the race of them still continue in other ations, and some of them among ourselves, as we shall see presently.

The Arabians followed the Chaldeans in this study, while it was kept within its due bounds, and after them the Egyptians; and, among the latter, we find that Jannes and Jambres were famous for their leading Pharaoh, by their pretended magic performances, to reject the real miracles of Moses; and history tells us of strange pranks the wise men, the magicians, and the southsayers, played to delude the people in the most early ages of the world.

But, as I say, now the Devil has improved himself, so he did then; for the Grecian and Roman heathen rites coming on, they outdid all the magicians and southsayers, by establishing the Devil's lying oracles, which, as a masterpiece of hell, did the Devil more honour, and brought more homage to him, than ever he had before, or could arrive to since.

Again, as by the setting up the oracles, all the magicians and southsayers grew out of credit, so at the ceasing of those oracles, the Devil was fain to go back to the old game again, and take up with the agency of witches, divinations, enchantments, and conjurings, as I hinted before, answerable to the four sorts mentioned in the story of Nebuchadnezzar, viz., magicians, astrologers, the Chaldeans, and the southsayers. How these began to be out of request, I have mentioned already; but, as the Devil has not quite given them over, only laid them aside a little for the present, we may venture to ask what they were, and what use he made of them when he did employ them.

The truth is, I think, as it was a very mean employment for anything that wears a human countenance to take up, so I must acknowledge, I think it was a mean low-prized business for Satan to take up with; below the very Devil; below his dignity as an angelic, though condemned creature; below him even as a Devil, to go to talk to a parcel of ugly, deformed, spiteful, malicious old women; to give them power to do mischief, who never had a will, after they entered into the state of old-womanhood, to do anything else. Why the Devil always chose the ugliest old women he could find, whether wizardism made them ugly that were not so before, and whether the ugliness, as it was a beauty in witchcraft, did not increase according to the meritorious performance in the black trade; these are all questions of moment, to be decided (if human learning can arrive to so much perfection) in ages to come.

Some say the evil eye, and the wicked look were parts of the enchantment, and that the witches, when they were in the height of their business, had a powerful influence with both; that by looking upon any person they could bewitch them, and make the Devil, as the Scotch express it, ride through them booted and spurred; and that hence came that very significant saying, ' to look like a witch.'

The strange work which the Devil has made in the world by this sort of his agents called witches, is such, and so extravagantly wild, that except our hope that most of those tales happen not to be true, I know not how any one could be easy to live near a widow after she was five-and-fifty.

All the other sorts of emissaries which Satan employs, come short of these ghosts; and apparitions sometimes come and show themselves on particular accounts, and some of those particulars respect doing justice, repairing wrongs, preventing mischief; sometimes in matters very considerable, and on things so necessary to public benefit, that we are tempted to believe they proceed from some vigilant spirit who wishes us well; but, on the other hand, these witches are never concerned in anything but mischief; nay, if what they do portends good to one, it issues in hurt to many; the whole tenor of their life, their design in general, is to do mischief, and they are only employed in mischief, and nothing else. How far they are furnished with ability suitable to the horrid will they are vested with, remains to be described.

. These witches, it is said, are furnished with power suitable to the occasion that is before them, and particularly that which deserves to be considered as prediction, and foretelling events, which, I insist, the author of withcraft is not accomplished with himself, nor can he communicate it to any other. How then witches come to be able to foretell things to come, which it is said, the Devil himself cannot know, and which, as I have shown, it is evident he does not know himself, is yet to be determined; that witches do foretel, is certain, from the witch of Endor, who foretold things to Saul. which he knew not before, namely, that he should be slain in battle the next day, which accordingly came to pass.

There are, however, and notwithstanding this particular case, many instances wherein the Devil has not been able to foretel approaching events, and that in things of the utmost consequence, and he has given certain foolish or false answers in such cases; the Devil's priests, which were summoned in by the prophet Elijah, to decide the dispute between God and Baal, had the Devil been able to have informed them of it, would certainly have received notice from him, of what was intended against them by Elijah; that is to say, that they would be all cut in pieces; for Satan was not such a fool as not to know that Baal was a nonentity, a nothing, at best a dead man, perished and rotting in his grave; for Baal was Bel or Belus, an ancient king of the Assyrian monarchy, and he could no more answer by fire to consume the sacrifice than he could raise himself from the dead.

But the priests of Baal were left of their master to their just fate; namely, to be a sacrifice to the fury of a deluded people; hence I infer his inability, for it would have been very unkind and ungrateful in him not to have answered them, if he had been able.   There is another argument raised here most justly against the Devil, with relation to his being under restraint, and that of greater eminence than we imagine, and it is drawn from this very passage, thus : it is not to be doubted but that Satan, who has much of the element put into his hands, as prince of the air, had a power, or was able, potentially speaking, to have answered Baal's priests by fire, fire being, in virtue of his airy principality, a part of his dominion; but he was certainly withheld by the superior hand which gave him that dominion, I mean withheld for the occasion only. So, in another case, it was plain that Balaam, who was one of those sorts of Chaldeans mentioned above who dealt in divinations and enchantments, was withheld from cursing Israel.

Some are of opinion that Balaam was not a witch, or a dealer with the Devil, because it is said of him, or rather he says it of himself, that he saw the visions of God, Numb. xxiv. 16; *He hath said,* who *heard the words of God, and knew the knowledge of the Most High, which saw the visions of the Almighty, falling into a trance, but having his eyes open.* Hence they allege he was one of those magi which St. Augustine speaks of, *de Divinatione,* who, by the study of nature, and by the contemplation of created beings, came to the knowledge of the creature ; and that Balaam's fault was, that being tempted by the rewards and honours that the king promised him, he intended to have cursed Israel; but when his eyes were opened, and that he saw they were God's own people, he durst not do it. They will have it, therefore, that except, as above, Balaam was a good man, or, at least, that he had the knowledge of the true God, and the fear of that God upon him, and that he honestly declares this, Numb. xxii. 18, *If Balak would give me his house full of silver and gold, I cannot go beyond the word of the Lord my God;* where, though he is called a false prophet by some, he evidently owns God, and assumes a property in him, as other prophets did; 'my God,' and 'I cannot go beyond his orders.' But that which gives me a better opinion of Balaam than all this, is his plain prophecy of Christ, chap. xxiv. 17, where he calls him the star of Jacob, and declares, *I shall see him, but not now; I shall behold him, but not nigh; there shall come a star out of Jacob, and a sceptre shall rise out of Israel, and shall smite the corners of Moab, and destroy all the children of Seth;* all which express not a knowledge only, but a faith in Christ: but I have done preaching, this is all by-the-by; I return to my business, which is the history.

There is another piece of dark practice here which lies between Satan and his particular agents, and which they may give us an answer to when they can, which, I think, will not be in haste; and that is about the obsequious Devil submitting to be called up into visibility whenever an old woman has her hand crossed with a white sixpence, as they call it. One would think that instead of these vile things called witches being sold to the Devil, the Devil was really sold for a slave to them ; for how far soever Satan's residence is off of this state of life, they have power, it seems, to fetch him from home, and oblige him to come at their call.

I can give little account of this, only that indeed so it is. Nor is the thing so strange in itself, as the methods to do it are mean, foolish, and ridiculous; as making a circle and dancing in it, pronouncing such and such words, saying the Lord's prayer backward, and the like. Now is this agreeable to the dignity of the prince of the air or atmosphere, that he should be commanded forth with no more pomp or ceremony than that of muttering a few words, such as the old witches and he agree about? or is there something else in it, which none of us or themselves understand?

Perhaps, indeed, he is always with those people called witches and conjurers, or, at least, some of his *camp volant* are always present, and so, upon the least call of the wizard, it is but putting off the misty cloak and showing themselves.

Then we have a piece of mock pageantry in bringing those things called witches or conjurers to justice ; that is, first, to know if a woman be a witch, throw her into a pond, and if she be a witch she will swim, and it is not in her own power to prevent it ; if she does all she can to sink herself it will not do, she will swim like a cork ; then, that a rope will not hang a witch, but you must get a withe, a green osier ; that if you nail a horseshoe on the sill of the door she cannot come into the house, or go out of it if she be in ; these and a thousand more, too simple to be believed, are yet so vouched, so taken for granted, and so universally received for truth, that there is no resisting them without being thought atheistical.

What methods to take to know who are witches, I really know not ; but, on the other side, I think there are a variety of methods to be used to know who are not : W—— G——; Esq., is a man of fame, his parts are great, because his estate is so ; he has threescore and eight lines of Virgil by rote, and they take up many of the intervals of his merry discourses ; he has just as many witty stories to please society, when they are well told once over he begins again ; and so he lives in a round of wit and learning : he is a man of great simplicity and sincerity ; you must be careful not to mistake my meaning as to the word simplicity ; some take it to mean honesty, and so do I, only that it has a negative attending it in his particular case. In a word, W—— G—— is an honest man, and no conjurer ; a good character, I think, and, without impeachment to his understanding, he may be a man of worth for all that. Take the other sex : there is the Lady H——, is another discovery ; bless us, what charms in that face ! how bright those eyes ! how flowing white her breasts ! how sweet her voice ! add to all, how heavenly, divinely good, her temper ! how inimitable her behaviour ! how spotless her virtue ! how perfect her innocence ! and, to sum up her character, we may add, the Lady H—— is no witch. Sure, none of our beau critics will be so unkind now, as to censure me in those honest descriptions, as if I meant that my good friend W—— G—— Esq., or my adored angel, the bright, the charming Lady H——, were fools ; but what will not those savages called critics do, whose barbarous nature inclines them to trample on the brightest characters, and to cavil at the clearest expressions ?

It might be expected of me, however, in justice to my

friends, and to the bright characters of abundance of gentlemen of this age, who, by the depth of their politics, and the
height of their elevations, might be suspected, and might
give us room to charge them with subterranean intelligence ;
I say, it might be expected that I should clear up their fame,
and assure the world concerning them, even by name,
that they are no conjurers, that they do not deal with the
Devil, at least, not by way of witchcraft and divination, such
as Sir T——k, E—— B——, Esq., my Lord Homily, Col.
Swagger, Geoffry Wellwith, Esq., Capt. Harry Godeeper,
Mr. Wellcome Woollen, citizen and merchant-tailor of London, Henry Cadaver, Esq., the D—— of Caerfilly, the
Marquis of Sillyhoo, Sir Edward Thro'-and-Thro', Bart.,
and a world of fine gentlemen more, whose great heads and
weighty understandings have given the world such occasion
to challenge them with being at least descended from the
magi, and perhaps engaged with old Satan in his politics and
experiments ; but I, that have such good intelligence among
Satan's ministers of state as is necessary to the present undertaking, am thereby well able to clear up their characters ;
and I doubt not but they will value themselves upon it, and
acknowledge their obligation to me, for letting the world
know the Devil does not pretend to have had any business
with them, or to have enrolled them in the list of his operators ; in a word, that none of them are conjurors.   Upon
which testimony of mine, I expect they be no longer charged
with, or so much as suspected of, having an unlawful quantity of wit, or having any sorts of it about them that are
contraband or prohibited, but that for the future they pass
unmolested, and be taken for nothing but what they are,
viz., very honest worthy gentlemen.

CHAPTER X.

OF THE VARIOUS METHODS THE DEVIL TAKES TO CONVERSE WITH MANKIND.

HAVING spoken something of persons, and particularly of
such as the Devil thinks fit to employ in his affairs in the
world, it comes next of course to say something of the manner how he communicates his mind to them, and by them to
the rest of his acquaintance in the world.

I take the Devil to be under great difficulties in his affairs on his part, especially occasioned by the bounds which are set him, or which policy obliges him to set to himself, in his access to the conversing with mankind; it is evident he is not permitted to fall upon them with force and arms, that is to say, to muster up his infernal troops, and attack them with fire and sword; if he was let loose to act in this manner, as he was able, by his own seraphic power, to have destroyed the whole race, and even the earth they dwelt upon, so he would certainly and long ago have effectually done it; his particular interests and inclinations are well enough known.

But, in the next place, as he is thus restrained from violence, so prudentials restrain him in all his other actings with mankind; and being confined to stratagem, and soft still methods, such as persuasion, allurement, feeding the appetite, prompting, and then gratifying corrupt desires, and the like, he finds it for his purpose not to appear in person, except very rarely, and then in disguise; but to act all the rest in the dark, under the visor of art and craft, making use of persons and methods concealed, or at least not fully understood or discovered.

As to the persons whom he employs, I have taken some pains you see to discover some of them; but the methods he uses with them, either to inform and instruct, and give orders to them, or to converse with other people by them, these are very particular, and deserve some place in our memoirs, particularly as they may serve to remove some of our mistakes, and to take off some of the frightful ideas we are apt to entertain in prejudice of this great manager; as if he was no more to be matched in his politics, than he would be to be matched in his power, if it was let loose; which is so much a mistake, that, on the contrary, we read of several people that have abused and cheated the Devil, a thing, which I cannot say is very honest nor just, notwithstanding the old Latin proverb, *Fallere fallentem non est fraus*, which men construe, or rather render, by way of banter upon Satan, It is no sin to cheat the Devil, which for all that, upon the whole, I deny, and allege that let the Devil act how he will by us, we ought to deal fairly by him.

But to come to the business, without circumlocutions; I am to inquire how Satan issues out his orders, gives his instructions, and fully delivers his mind to his emissaries, of w

order to this, you must form an idea of the Devil sitting in
great state, in open campagain, with all his legions about him,
in the height of the atmosphere ; or, if you will, at a certain
distance from the atmosphere, and above it, that the plan of
his encampment might not be hurried round its own axis,
with the earth's diurnal motion, which might be some disturbance to him.

By this fixed situation, the earth performing its rotation,
he has every part and parcel of it brought to a direct opposition to him, and consequently to his view, once in twenty-
four hours.   The last time I was there, if I remember right,
he had this quarter of the world, which we call Christendom,
just under his eye ; and as the motion is not so swift, but
that his piercing optics can take a strict view of it *en passant*;
for the circumference of it being but twenty-one thousand
miles, and its circular motion being full twenty-four hours
performing, he has something more than an hour to view
every thousand miles, which, to his supernatural penetration,
is not worth naming.

As he takes thus a daily view of all the circle, and an
hourly view of the parts, he is fully master of all transactions,
at least, such as are done above board by all mankind; and
then he despatches his emissaries, or *aid du camps*, to every
part with his orders and instructions.   Now these emissaries,
you are to understand, are not the witches and diviners, who
I spoke of above, for I call them also emissaries ; but they are
all devils or (as you know they are called) devil's angels ;
and these may, perhaps, come and converse personally with
the sub-emissaries I mentioned, to be ready for their support
and assistance on all occasions of business : these are those
devils which the witches are said to raise ; for we can hardly
suppose the master devil comes himself at the summons of
every ugly old woman.

These run about into every nook and corner, wherever
Satan's business calls them, and are never wanting to him:
but are the most diligent devils imaginable ; like the Turkish
chaiux, they no sooner receive their errand, but they execute it with the utmost alacrity ; and as to their speed, it
may be truly written as a motto, upon the head of every
individual devil,

Non indiget calcaribus.

These are those, who they tell us, our witches, sorcerers,
wizards, and such sorts of folks, converse freely with, and

are therefore called their familiars; and, as they tell us, come to them in human shapes, talk to them with articulate plain voices, as if men, and that yet the said witches, &c., know them to be devils.

History has not yet enlightened us in this part of useful knowledge, or at least not sufficiently for a description of the persons or habits of these sorts of appearances; as what shapes they take up, what language they speak, and what particular works they perform, so we must refer it to farther inquiry; but if we may credit history, we are told many famous stories of these appearances; for example, the famous Mother Lakland, who was burnt for a witch at Ipswich, anno 1645, confessed, at the time of her execution, or a little before it, that she had frequent conversations with the Devil himself; that she being very poor, and withal of a devilish, passionate, cruel and revengeful disposition before, used to wish she had it in her power to do such and such mischievous things to some that she hated, and that the Devil himself, who, it seems, knew her temper, came to her one night as she lay in her bed, and was between sleeping and waking, and speaking in a deep hollow voice, told her, if she would serve him in some things he would employ her to do, she should have her will of all her enemies, and should want for nothing: that she was much afraid at first, but that he soliciting her very often, bade her not be afraid of him, and still urged her to yield, and, as she says, struck his claw into her hand, and though it did not hurt her, made it bleed, and with the blood wrote the covenants, that is to say, the bargain between them. Being asked what was in them, and whether he required her to curse or deny God or Christ, she said, No.

N.B. I do not find she told them whether the Devil wrote it with a pen, or whether on paper or parchment, nor whether she signed it or no, but it seems he carried it away with him. I suppose, if Satan's register were examined, it might be found among the archives of hell, the rolls of his *acta publica*; and when his historiographer royal publishes them, we may look for it among them.

Then he furnished her with three devils, to wait upon her (I suppose) for she confessed they were to be employed in her service; they attended in the shapes of two little dogs and a mole. The first she bewitched was her own husband, ly which he lay awhile in great misery and died; then she sent to one Captain Beal, and burnt a new ship of his just built, which had never been at sea; these, and many other horrid things she did and confessed, and having been twenty years a witch, at last the Devil left her, and she was burnt as she deserved.

That some extraordinary occasions may bring these agents of the Devil, nay, sometimes the Devil himself, to assume human shapes, and appear to other people, we cannot doubt; he did thus in the case of our Saviour as a tempter, and some think he did so to Manasses as a familiar, who the Scripture charges with sorcery, and having a familiar or devil. Fame tells us that St. Dunstan frequently conversed with him, and finally, took him by the nose; and so of others.

But in these modern ages of the world, he finds it much more to his purpose to work under ground, as I have observed, and to keep upon the reserve; so that we have no authentic account of his personal appearance, but what are very ancient or very remote from our faith, as well as our inquiry.

It seems to be a question that would bear some debating whether all apparitions are not devils, or from the Devil; but there being so many of those apparitions which we call spirits, which really assume shapes and make appearances in the world, upon such accounts as we know Satan himself scorns to be employed in, that I must dismiss the question in favour of the Devil; assuring them, that as he never willingly did any good in his life, so he would be far from giving himself the trouble of setting one foot into the world on such an errand; and for that reason we may be assured those certain apparitions, which we are told came to detect a murder in Gloucestershire, and others who appeared to prevent the ruining an orphan for want of finding a deed, that was not lost, was certainly some other power equally concerned, and not the Devil.

On the other hand, neither will it follow that Satan never appears in human shape; for though every apparition may not be the Devil, yet it does not follow that the Devil never makes an apparition: all I shall say to it is, as I have mentioned before, that, generally speaking, the Devil finds it more for his purpose to have his interest in the world propagated another way: namely, in private, and his personal consequence, and, as I may say, of evident necessity, where his honour is concerned, and where his interest could be carried on no other way; not forgetting to take notice that this is very seldom.

. It remains to inquire, what then those things are which we make so much stir about, and which are called apparitions, or spirits assuming human shapes, and showing themselves to people on particular occasions? whether they are evil spirits or good? and though, indeed, this is out of my way at this time, and does not relate at all to the Devil's history, yet I thought it not amiss to mention it. 1st, Because, as I have said, I do not wholly exclude Satan from all concerning such things; and 2ndly, because I shall dismiss the question with so very short an answer, namely, that we may determine which are and which are not the Devil's, by the errand they come upon; every one to his own business. If it comes of a good errand, you may certainly acquit the Devil of it, conclude him innocent, and that he has no hand in it; if it comes of a wicked and devilish errand, you may e'en take him up upon suspicion, 'tis ten to one but you find him at the bottom of it.

Next to apparitions, we find mankind disturbed by abundance of little odd reserved ways which the Devil is shrewdly suspected of having a hand in, such as dreams, noises, voices, &c., smells of brimstone, candles burning blue, and the like.

As to dreams, I have nothing to say in Satan's prejudice at all there; I make no question but he deals very much in that kind of intelligence, and why should he not? We know Heaven itself formerly conversed very often with the greatest of men by the same method, and the Devil is known to mimic the methods, as well as the actions, of his Maker; whether Heaven has not quite left off that way of working we are not certain; but we pretty well know the Devil has not left it, and I believe some instances may be given where his worship has been really seen and talked to in sleep, as much as if the person had been awake with his eyes open.

These are to be distinguished too, pretty much by the goodness or badness of the subject; how often have men committed murder, robbery, and adultery in a dream, and at the same time except an extraordinary agitation of the soul, and expressed by extraordinary noises in the sleep, by violent sweating, and other such ways, the head has never been removed from the pillow, or the body so much as turned in the bed.

Whether in such cases, the soul, with all the passions and affections, being agitated, and giving their full assent to the facts, of whatever kind soever, the man is not as guilty as if the sins so dreamed of his committing, had been actually committed; though it be no doubt to me, but that it is so, yet as it is foreign to the present affair, and not at all relating to the Devil's history, I leave it to the reverend doctors of the church, as properly belonging to them to decide.

I knew a person who the Devil so haunted with naked women, fine beautiful ladies in bed with him, and ladies of his acquaintance too, offering their favours to him, and all in his sleep, so that he seldom slept without some such entertainment; the particulars are too gross for my story, but he gave me several long accounts of his nights' amours, and being a man of a virtuous life and good morals, it was the greatest surprise to him imaginable; for you cannot doubt but that the cunning Devil made everything he acted to the life with him, and in a manner the most wicked; he owned with grief to me, that the very first attack the Devil made upon him, was with a very beautiful lady of his acquaintance, who he had been really something freer than ordinary with in their common conversation. This lady he brought to him in a posture for wickedness, and wrought up his inclination so high in his sleep, that he, as he thought, actually went about to debauch her, she not at all resisting; but that he waked in the very moment, to his particular satisfaction.

He was greatly concerned at this part, namely, that he really gave the consent of his will to the fact, and wanted to know if he was not as guilty of adultery as if he had lain with her; indeed he decided the question against himself so forcibly, that I, who was of the same opinion before, had nothing to say against it; however, I confirmed him in it, by asking him these questions:

1. Whether he did not think the Devil had the chief hand in such a dream? He answered, it could certainly be nobody else, it must be the Devil.

2. I then asked him what reason the Devil could have for it, if his consent to the fact in sleep had not been criminal? That's true indeed, says he, I am answered. But then he asked another question, which, I confess, is not

so easy to answer, namely, how he should prevent being served so again?

Nor could all my divinity or his own keep the Devil from attacking him again: on the other hand, as I have said, he worried him to that degree, that he injured his health, bringing naked women to him, sometimes one, sometimes another, sometimes in one posture of lewdness, sometimes in another, sometimes into his very arms, sometimes with such additions as I am not merry enough, and sometimes such as I am not wicked enough to put into your heads; the man, indeed, could not help it, and so the Devil was more faulty than he; but as I hinted to him, he might bring his mind to such a stated habit of virtue, as to prevent its assenting to any wicked motion, even in sleep, and that would be the way to put an end to the attempt; and this advice he relished very well, and practised, I believe, with success.

By this same method, the same devil injects powerful incentives to other crimes, provokes avarice by laying a great quantity of gold in your view, and nobody present, giving you an opportunity to steal it, or some of it, at the same time, perhaps, knowing your circumstances to be such as that you are at that time in a great want of the money.

I knew another, who, being a tradesman, and in great distress for money in his business, dreamed that he was walking all alone in a great wood, and that he met a little child with a bag of gold in its hand, and a fine necklace of diamonds on its neck; upon the sight, his wants presently dictated to him to rob the child; the little innocent creature (just so he dreamed), not being able to resist, or to tell who it was; accordingly, he consented to take the money from the child, and then to take the diamond necklace from it too, and did so.

But the Devil (a full testimony, as I told him, that it was the Devil), not contented with that, hinted to him, that perhaps the child might some time or other know him, and single him out, by crying or pointing, or some such thing, especially if he was suspected and showed to it, and therefore it would be better for him to kill the child, prompting him to kill it for his own safety, and that he need do no more but twist the neck of it a little, or crush it with his knee: he told me he stood debating with himself whether he should do so or not: but that in that instant his heart struck him with the word murder, and he entertained a horror of it, refused to do it, and immediately waked.

He told me that when he waked, he found himself in so violent a sweat as he had never known the like; that his pulse beat with that heat and rage, that it was like a palpitation of the heart to him, and that the agitation of his spirits was such, that he was not fully composed in some hours; though the satisfaction and joy that attended him when he found it was but a dream, assisted much to return his spirits to their due temperament.

It is neither my business or inclination to turn divine here, nor is the age I write to sufficiently grave to relish a sermon, if I was disposed to preach, though they must allow the subject would very well bear it; but I shall only ask them if they think this is not the Devil, what they think it is? if they believe it is the Devil, they will act accordingly I hope, or let it alone, as Satan and they can agree about it.

I should not oblige the Devil over much, whatever I might do to those that read it, if I should enter here upon a debate of interests, viz., to inquire whether the Devil has not a vast advantage upon mankind this way, and whether it is not much his interest to preserve it; and if I prove the affirmative, I leave it to you to inquire whose interest it is to disappoint and supplant him.

In short, I take dreams to be the second best of the advantages the Devil has over mankind; the first, I suppose, you all know, viz., the treachery of the garrison within; by dreams he may be said to get into the inside of us without opposition; here he opens and locks without a key, and like an enemy laying siege to a fortified city, reason and nature, the governor of the city, keep him out by day, and keep the garrison true to their duty; but in the dark he gets in and parleys with the garrison (the affections and passions), debauches their loyalty, stirring up them to disloyalty and rebellion, so they betray their trust, revolt, mutiny, and go over to the besieger.

Thus he manages his interest, I say, and insinuates himself into the inside of us, without our consent, nay, without our knowledge; for whatever speculation may do, it is evident demonstration does not assist us to discover which way he gets access to the soul, while the organ tied up, and dozed with sleep, has locked it up from action; that it is so

is clear, but how he does it is a secret which I do not find
the ancients or moderns have yet made a discovery of.

That devil of a creature, Mother Lakland, whose story I
mentioned above, acknowledged that the first time the Devil
attempted to draw her in to be a witch, was in a dream, and
even when she consented, she said, she was between sleeping
and waking; that is, she did not know whether she was
awake or asleep, and the cunning devil it seems was satisfied
with her assent given so, when she was asleep, or neither
asleep or awake, so taking advantage of her incapacity to act
rationally.

The stories of her bewitching several people, and the manner
in which they died, are so formidable and extravagant, that I
care not to put any one's faith to the stretch about them, though
published by authority, and testified by abundance of witnesses; but this is recorded in particular, and to my purpose,
whether from her own mouth or not, I do not say, namely,
the description of a witch, and the difference between witches
and those other of Satan's acquaintance who act in his name.

1. They have consulted and covenanted with a spirit or
   devil.
2. They have a deputy devil, sometimes several, to ser—
   and assist them.
3. These they employ as they please, call them by name,
   and command their appearance in whatever shape they
   think fit.
4. They send them abroad, to or into the persons who
   they design to bewitch, who they always torment, and
   often murder them, as Mother Lakland did several.

As to the difference between the several devils that appear,
it relates to the office of the persons who employ them; as
conjurers, who seem to command the particular devil that waits
upon them with more authority, and raise them and lay
them at pleasure, drawing circles, casting figures, and the
like; but the witch, in a more familiar manner, whispers with
the Devil, keeps the Devil in a bag or a sack, sometimes in her
pocket, and the like, and, like Mr. Faux, shows tricks with him.

But all these kinds deal much in dreams, talk with the
Devil in their sleep, and make other people talk with him in
their sleep too; and it is on this occasion I mention it here
in short, the Devil may well take this opportunity with mankind, for not half the world that came into his measures
would comply if they were awake; but of that hereafter.

And yet his thus insinuating himself by dream, does not seem sufficient, in my opinion, to answer the Devil's end, and to carry on his business; and therefore we must be forced to allow him a kind of actual possession, in particular cases, and that in the souls of some people by different methods from others. Luther is of the opinion that the Devil gets a familiarity with some souls just at, or rather before, their being embodied; as to the manner and method how he gets in, that is another question, and may be spoken of by itself; besides, why may not He, that at Satan's request to enter into the herd of swine, said *Go*, give the same commission to possess a sort of creatures so many degrees below the dignity of the Gadarenian swine, and open the door too? But as for that, when our Lord said *Go*, the Devil never inquired which way he should get in.

When I see nations, or indeed herds of nations, set on fire of hell, and as I may say, inflamed by the Devil; when I see towns, parties, factions and rabbles of people visibly possessed; it is enough to me that the great Master of the Devils has said to him, *Go;* there is no need to inquire which way he finds open, or at what postern gate he gets in; as to his appearing, it is plain he often gets in without appearing, and therefore the question about his appearing still remains a doubt; and is not very easy to be resolved.

In the Scripture we have some light into it, and that is all the help I find from antiquity, and it goes a great way to solve the phenomena of Satan's appearing; what I mean by the Scripture giving some light to it, is this; it is said in several places, and of several persons, God came to them in a dream; Gen. xx. 3, *God came to Abimelech in a dream by night.* Gen. xxxi. 24, *And God came to Laban the Syrian in a dream.* Matt. ii. 13, *The angel of the Lord appeared to Joseph in a dream;* short comments are sufficient to plain texts, applying this to my friend when he wanted to be satisfied about the how, relating to his dream, viz., how he should come to dream such wicked things? I told him, in short, the case was plain, the Devil came to him in a dream by night. How and in what manner he formed the wicked representations, and spread debauched appearances before his fancy, by real whispers and voice, according to Milton, or by what other methods, the learned are not arrived to any certainty about it.

This leads me necessarily to inquire whether the Devil or

some of nis agents are not always in our company, whether they make any visible appearances or no? For my part I make no question of it, how else could he come at the knowledge of what we do; for as I can allow him no prescience at all (as for many reasons I have observed already), he must be able to see and know us, and what we are about when we know nothing of him, or else he could know nothing of us and our affairs; which yet we find otherwise; and this gives him infinite advantage to influence our actions, to judge of our inclinations, and to bring our passions to clash with our reason, as they often do, and get the better of it too.

All this he obtains by his being able to walk about invisible, and see when he is not seen, of which I have spoken already; hence that most wise and solid suggestion, that when the candles burn blue the Devil is in the room, which great secret in nature, that you may more fully be convinced of its imaginary reality, I must tell you the following story, which I saw in a letter directed to a particular friend, take it word for word as in the letter; because I do not make myself accountable for the facts, but take them *ad referendum*: —

SIR,

WE had one day, very early in the morning, and for the most part of the day, a great deal of rain, with a high wind, and the clouds very thick and dark all day.

In the evening, the cloudy thick weather continued, though not the rain, when, being at a friend's house in ——lane, London, and several ladies and some gentlemen in the room, besides two or three servants (for we had been eating), the following interlude happened for our entertainment: when the cloth was taken away, two large candles were brought upon the table and placed there, with some bottles and glasses for the gentlemen, who, it seems, were intending to drink and be very merry; two large wax candles were also set on another table, the ladies being going to cards; also there were two large candles in sconces over or near the chimney, and one more in a looking-glass sconce on a pier by the window.

With all this apparatus, the company, separating, sat down, the gentlemen at their table, and the ladies at theirs, to play as above; when, after some time, the gentleman of the house said hastily to a servant, What a p—— ails the candles; and, turning to the servant, raps out an oath or two, and bids him snuff the candles, for they burned as if the Devil was in the room.

The fellow going to snuff one of the candles, snuffs it out, at which, his master being in a passion, the fellow lights it again immediately at the other candle, and then, being in a little hurry, going to snuff the other candle, snuffed that out too.

The first candle that was relighted (as is usual in such cases) burned dim and dull for a good while, and the other being out, the room was much darker than before, and a wench that stood by the ladies' table, bawls out to her mistress, Law, madam! the candles burn blue! An old lady that sat by says, Ay, Betty! so they do: upon this one of the ladies starts up, Mercy upon us, says she, what is the matter? In this unlucky moment another servant, without orders, went to the great pier sconce, and because, as he thought, he would be sure to snuff the candle well, he offers to take it down, but, very unhappily, I say, the hook came out, down falls the sconce, candle and all, and the looking-glass broke all to pieces, with a horrible noise; however, the candle falling out of the sconce did not go out, but lay on the floor burning dully, and, as it is usual on such cases, all on one side. Betty cries out again, Law, madam, that candle burns blue too. The very moment she said this, the footman, that had thrown down the sconce, says to his fellow-servant that came to his assistance, I think the Devil is in the candles to-night, and away he run out of the room for fear of his master.

The old lady, who, upon the maid Betty's notion of the candles burning blue, had her head just full of that old chimney-corner story, 'the candles burn blue when spirits are in the room,' heard the footman say the word devil, but heard nothing else of what he said; upon this she rises up in a terrible fright, and cries out that the footman said the Devil was in the room; as she was, indeed, frightened out of her wits, she frightened the ladies most terribly, and they all starting up together, down goes the card table, and put the wax candles out.

Mrs. Betty, that had frightened them all, runs to the sconce next the chimney, but that having a long snuff, she cried out it burnt blue too, and she durst not touch it; in short, though there were three candles left still burning in the room, yet the ladies were all so frightened, that they and the maids too run out of the parlour screaming like mad folks. The master in a rage kicked his first man out of the room, and the second man was run out to avoid, as I said before, the like, so that no servant was to be had, but all was in confusion.

The two other gentlemen, who were sitting at the first table, kept their seats, composed and easy enough, only concerned to see all the house in such a fright; it was true, they said, the candles burnt dim, and very oddly, but they could not perceive they burnt blue, except one of those over the chimney, and that on the table, which was relighted after the fellow had snuffed it out.

However, the maid, the old lady, and the footman that pulled down the sconce, all insist that the candles burnt blue, and all pretend that the Devil was certainly in the room, and was the occasion of it; and they now came to me with the story, to desire my opinion of it.

This put me upon inquiry into the notion of candles burning blue when spirits are in a room, which, upon all the search into things, that I am able to make, amounts to no more than this; that upon any extraordinary emission of sulphurous or of nitrous particles, either in a close room, or in any not very open place, if the quantity be great, a candle or lamp, or any such little blaze of fire, will seem to be, or to burn blue; and if then they can prove that any such effluvia attends, or is emitted from a spirit, then, when Satan is at hand, it may be so.

But then, it is begging the question grossly, because no man can assure us that the Devil has any such sulphurous particles about him.

It is true, the candles burn thus in mines and vaults, and damp places; and it is as true that they will do so upon occasion of very damp, stormy, and moist air, when an extraordinary quantity of vapours are supposed to be dispersed abroad, as was the case when this happened; and if there was anything of that in it on that Monday night, the candles might, perhaps, burn blue upon that occasion; but that the Devil was abroad upon any extraordinary business that night, that I cannot grant, unless I have some better testimony than the old lady that heard the footman's outcry but by halves, or than Mrs. Betty, who first fancied the candles burnt blue; so I must suspend my judgment till I hear farther.

This story, however, may solve a great many of those things which pass for apparitions in the world, and which are laid to the Devil's charge, though he really may know nothing of the matter; and this would bring me to defend Satan in many things wherein he may truly be said to suffer wrongfully; and, if I thought it would oblige him, I might say something to his advantage this way; however, I will venture a word or two for an injured devil, take it as you will.

First, it is certain, that as this invisibility of the Devil is very much to our prejudice, so the doctrine of his visibility is a great prejudice to him, as we make use of it.

By his invisibility he is certainly vested with infinite advantages against us; while he can be present with us, and we know nothing of the matter, he informs himself of all our measures, and arms himself in the best and most suitable manner to injure and assault us, as he can counteract all our secret concerted designs, disappoint all our schemes, and, except when heaven apparently concerns itself to overrule him, can defeat all our enterprises, break all our measures, and do us mischief in almost every part of our life; and all this because we are not privy to all his motions, as he is to ours.

But now for his visibility, and his real appearance in the world, and particularly among his disciples and emissaries, such as witches and wizards, demoniasts, and the like; here I think Satan has a great deal of loss, suffers manifest injury, and has great injustice done him; and that therefore I ought to clear this matter up a little, if it be possible to do justice to Satan, and set matters right in the world about him, according to that useful old maxim of setting the saddle upon the right horse, or giving the Devil his due.

First, as I have said, we are not to believe every idle head, who pretends even to converse face to face with the Devil, and who tell us they have thus seen him and been acquainted with him every day; many of these pretenders are manifest cheats, and however they would have the honour of a private interest in him, and boast how they have him at their beck, can call him this way and send him that, as they please, raise him and lay him, when, and how, and as often as they find for their purpose; I say, whatever boasts they make of this kind, they really have nothing of truth in them.

Now the injuries and injustice done to the Devil in these cases are manifest; namely, that they entitle the Devil to all the mischief they are pleased to do in the world; and if they commit a murder or a robbery, fire a house, or do any act of violence in the world, they presently are said to do it by the agency of the Devil, and the Devil helps them; so Satan bears the reproach, and they have all the guilt. This is, 1, a grand cheat upon the world, and 2, a notorious slander upon the Devil; and it would be a public benefit to mankind to have such would-be devils as these turned inside out, that we might know when the Devil was really at work among us, and when not; what mischiefs were of his doing, and which were not; and that these fellows might not slip their necks out of the halter by continually laying the blame of their wickedness upon the Devil.

Not that the Devil is not very willing to have his hand in any mischief, or in all the mischief that is done in the world; but there are some low-prized rogueries that are too little for him, beneath the dignity of his operation, and which it is really a scandal to the Devil to charge upon him. I remember the Devil had such a cheat put upon him in East Smithfield once, where a person pretended to converse with the Devil face to face, and that in open day, too, and to cause him to tell fortunes, foretell good and evil, &c., discover stolen goods, tell where they were who stole them, and how to find them again, nay, and even to find out the thieves; but Satan was really slandered in the case, the fellow had no more to do with the Devil than other people, and perhaps not so much neither: this was one of those they called 'cunning men,' or, at least, he endeavoured to pass for such a one; but it was all a cheat.

Besides, what had the Devil to do to detect thieves and restore stolen goods? Thieving and robbing, trick and cheat, are part of the craft of his agency, and of the employments which it is his business to encourage: they greatly mistake him, who think he will assist anybody in suppressing and detecting such laudable arts and such diligent servants.

I will not say, but the Devil, to draw these people we call cunning men into a snare, and to push on his farther designs, may encourage them privately, and in a manner that they themselves know nothing of, to make use of his name, and abuse the world about him; till at last they may really believe that they do deal with the Devil, when, indeed, it is only he deals with them, and they know nothing of the matter.

In other cases he may encourage them in these little frauds and cheats, and give them leave, as above, to make use of his name, to bring them afterwards, and by degrees, to have a real acquaintance with him; so bringing the jest of their trade into earnest, till, at length, prompting them to commit some great villany, he secures them to be his own by their very fear of his leaving them to be exposed to the world; thus he puts a Jonathan Wild upon them, and makes them be the very wretches they only pretended to be before; so old Parsons of Clithroe, as fame tells, was twenty-five years a cunning man, and twenty-two years a witch; that is to say, for five-and-twenty years he was only pretending to deal with the Devil, when Satan and he had no manner of acquaintance, and he only put his legerdemain upon the people in the Devil's name, without his leave; but, at length, the Devil's patience being tired quite out, he told the old counterfeit that, in short, he had been his stalking-horse long enough, and that now, if he thought fit to enter himself and take a commission, well and good, and he should have a lease to carry on his trade for so many years more, to his heart's content; but if not, he would expose his knavery to the world, for that he should take away his people's trade no longer, but that he (Satan) would set up another in his room that should make a mere fool of him, and carry away all his customers.

Upon this the old man considered of it, took the Devil's counsel, and listed in his pay; so he, that had played his pranks twenty-five years as a conjuror when he was no conjuror, was then forced really to deal with the Devil for fear the people should know he did not: till now he had *ambo dexter*, cheated the Devil on one hand, and the people on the other; but the Devil gained his point at last, and so he was a real wizard ever after.

But this is not the only way the Devil is injured neither, for we have often found people pretend upon him in other cases, and of nearer concern to him a great deal, and in articles more weighty; as, in particular, in the great business of possession. It is true, this point is not thoroughly understood among men, neither has the Devil thought fit to give us those illuminations about it, as, I believe, he might do; particularly that great and important article is not, for aught

I can see, rightly explained, namely, whether there are not two several kinds of possession; viz., some wherein the Devil possesses us, and some in which we really possess the Devil; the nicety of which, I doubt, this age, with all its penetration, is not qualified to explain; and a dissertation upon it being too long for this work, especially so near its conclusion, I am obliged to omit, as I am also all the practical discourses upon the usefulness and advantages of real possession, whether considered one way or other to mankind, all which I must leave to hereafter.

But to come back to the point in hand, and to consider the injustice done to the Devil, in the various turns and tricks which men put upon him very often in this one article, viz., pretending to possession, and to have the Devil in them, when really it is not so; certainly the Devil must take it very ill, to have all their demented lunatic tricks charged upon him, some of which, nay, most of which are so gross, so simple, so empty, and so little to the purpose, that the Devil must be ashamed to see such things pass in his name, or that the world should think he was concerned in them.

It is true, that possession, being one of the principal pieces of the Devil's artifice in his managing mankind, and in which, with the most exquisite skill, he plays the Devil among us, he has the more reason to be affronted when he finds himself invaded in this part, and angry that anybody should pretend to possess, or be possessed, without his leave; and this may be the reason, for aught we know, why so many blunders have been made, when people have pretended to it without him, and he has thought fit not to own them in it : of which we have many examples in history, as in Simon Magus, the Devil of London, the Fair Maid of Kent, and several others, whose history it is not worth while to enlarge upon.

In short, possessions, as I have said, are nice things, and it is not so easy to mimic the Devil in that part, as it may be in some other : designing men have attempted it often, but their manner has been easily distinguished, even without the Devil's assistance.

Thus the people of Salem, in New England, pretended to be bewitched, and that a black man tormented them by the instigation of such and such, whom they resolved to bring to the gallows : this black man they would have be the Devil, employed by the person who they accused for a witch : thus

making the Devil a page or a footman to the wizard, to go
and torment whoever the said wizard commanded, till the
Devil himself was so weary of the foolish part, that he left
them to go on their own way, and at last they overacted the
murdering part so far, that when they confessed themselves
to be witches, and possessed, and that they had correspondence with the Devil, Satan not appearing to vouch for them,
no jury would condemn them upon their own evidence, and
they could not get themselves hanged, whatever pains they
took to bring it to pass.

Thus you see the Devil may be wronged, and falsely
accused in many particulars, and often has been so; there
are likewise some other sorts of counterfeit devils in the
world, such as gipseys, fortune-tellers, foretellers of good
and bad luck, sellers of winds, raisers of storms, and many
more, some practised among us, some in foreign parts, too
many almost to reckon up; nay, I almost doubt whether the
Devil himself knows all the sorts of them; for it is evident
he has little or nothing to do with them, I mean not in the
way of their craft.

These I take to be interlopers, or, with the Guinea merchants leave, separate traders, and who act under the screen
and protection of Satan's power, but without his license or
authority; no doubt these carry away a great deal of his
trade, that is to say, the trade which otherwise the Devil
might have carried on by agents of his own; I cannot but
say, that while these people would fain be thought devils,
though they really are not, it is but just they should be really
made as much devils as they pretended to be, or that Satan
should do himself justice upon them, as he threatened to do
upon old Parsons of Clithroe, above mentioned, and let the
world know them.

CHAPTER XI.

OF DIVINATION, SORZERY, THE BLACK ART, PAWAWING, AND SUCH
LIKE PRETENDERS TO DEVILISM, AND HOW FAR THE DEVIL IS OR
IS NOT CONCERNED IN THEM.

THOUGH I am writing the history of the Devil, I have not
undertaken to do the like of all the kinds of people, male or
female, who set up for devils in the world: this would be a
task for the Devil indeed, and fit only for him to undertake,

for their number is and has been prodigious great, and may, with his other legions, be ranked among the innumerable.

What a world do we inhabit! where there is not only with us a great roaring lion-devil daily seeking whom of us he may devour, and innumerable millions of lesser devils hovering in the whole atmosphere ever us, nay, and for aught we know, other millions always invisibly moving about us, and perhaps in us, or at least in many of us; but that have, besides all these, a vast many counterfeit hocus-pocus devils; human devils, who are visible among us, of our own species and fraternity, conversing with us upon all occasions; who, like mountebanks, set up their stages in every town, chat with us at every tea-table, converse with us in every coffee-house, and impudently tell us to our faces that they are devils, boast of it, and use a thousand tricks and arts to make us believe it too, and that too often with success.

It must be confessed, there is a strong propensity in man's nature, especially the more ignorant part of mankind, to resolve every strange thing, or whether really strange or no, if it be but strange to us, into devilism, and to say everything is the Devil, that they can give no account of.

Thus the famous doctors of the faculty at Paris, when John Faustus brought the first printed books that had then been seen in the world, or at least seen there, into the city, and sold them for manuscripts: they were surprised at the performance, and questioned Faustus about it; but he affirming they were manuscripts, and that he kept a great many clerks employed to write them, they were satisfied for awhile.

But looking farther into the work, they observed the exact agreement of every book, one with another, that every line stood in the same place, every page a like number of lines, every line a like number of words; if a word was mis-spelt in one, it was mis-spelt also in all, nay, that if there was a blot in one, it was alike in all; they began again to muse, how this should be: in a word, the learned divines not being able to comprehend the thing (and that was always sufficient), concluded it must be the Devil, that it was done by magic and witchcraft, and that in short, poor Faustus (who was indeed nothing but a mere printer), dealt with the Devil.

N. B. John Faustus was servant, or journeyman, or compositor, or what you please to call it, to Koster of Harlem, the frst inventor of printing, and having printed the Psalter, sold them at Paris as manuscripts; because as such they yielded a better price.

But the learned doctors not being able to understand how the work was performed, concluded as above it was all the Devil, and that the man was a witch; accordingly they took him up for a magician and a conjurer, and one that worked by the black art, that is to say, by the help of the Devil; and, in a word, they threatened to hang him for a witch, and, in order to it, commenced a process against him in their criminal courts, which made such a noise in the world as raised the fame of poor John Faustus to a frightful height, till at last he was obliged, for fear of the gallows, to discover the whole secret to them.

N. B. This is the true original of the famous Dr. Faustus, or Foster, of whom we have believed such strange things, as that it is become a proverb, 'as great as the Devil and Dr. Foster :' whereas poor Faustus was no doctor, and knew no more of the Devil than another body.

Thus the magistrates of Bern in Switzerland, finding a gang of French actors of puppet-show opened their stage in the town, upon hearing the surprising accounts which the people gave of their wonderful puppets, how they made them speak, answer questions, and discourse, appear and disappear in a moment, pop up here, as if they rise out of the earth, and down there, as if they vanished, and abundance more feats of art, censured them as demons; and if they had not packed up their trinkets, and disappeared almost as dexterously as their puppets, they had certainly condemned the poor puppets to the flames for devils, and censured, if not otherwise punished their masters. See the Count de Rochfort's Memoirs, p. 179.

Wonderful operations astonish the mind, especially where the head is not over-burthened with brains; and custom has made it so natural to give the Devil either the honour or scandal of everything that we cannot otherwise account for, that it is not possible to put the people out of the road of it.

The magicians were, in the Chaldean monarchy, called the wisemen; and though they are joined with the sorcerers and astrologers in the same place, Daniel ii. 4, yet they were generally so understood among those people; but in our language we understand them to be people that have an art to reveal secrets, interpret dreams, foretel events, &c., and that use enchantments and sorceries, by all which we understand the same thing; which now, in a more vulgar way, we express by one general coarse expression, 'dealing with the Devil.'

The Scripture speaks of a spirit of divination, Acts xvi. 16, and a wench that was possessed by this spirit *brought her master much gain by southsaying*, that is to say, according to the learned, by oracling or answering questions; whence you will see in the margin, that this southsaying devil is there called Python, that is, Apollo, who is often called Python, and who, at the oracle of Delphos gave out such answers and *double entendres*, as this wench possibly did; and hence all those spirits which were called spirits of divination, were in another sense called Pythons.

Now when the apostle St. Paul came to see this creature, this spirit takes upon it to declare that *those men*, meaning St. Paul and Timotheus, *were the servants of the most high God, which shewed unto them the way of salvation;* this was a good turn of the Devil, to preserve his authority in the possessed girl; she brought them gain by southsaying, that is to say, resolving difficult questions, answering doubts, interpreting dreams, &c. Among these doubts, he makes her give testimony to Paul and Timotheus, to wheedle in with the new Christians, and perhaps (though very ignorantly) even with Paul and Timotheus themselves, so to give a kind of credit and respect to her for speaking.

But the Devil, who never speaks truth, but with some sinister end, was discovered here, and detected; his flattering recognition not accepted, and he himself unkennelled as he deserved; there the Devil was over-shot in his own bow again.

Here now was a real possession, and the evil spirits who possessed her, did stoop to sundry little acts of servitude, that we could give little or no reason for, only that the girl's master might get money by her; but perhaps this was a particular case, and prepared to honour the authority and power the apostles had over evil spirits.

But we find these things carried a great way farther in many cases, that is to say, where the parties are thus really possessed; namely, the Devil makes agents of the possessed parties to do many things for the propagating his interest and kingdom, and particularly for the carrying on his dominion in the world: but I am for the present not so much upon the real possession as the pretended, and particularly we have had many that have believed themselves possessed, when the Devil never believed it of them, and perhaps knew them better; some of these are really poor devils to be pitied, and are what I call *diables imaginaire*; these have, notwithstanding, done the Devil good service, and brought their masters good gain by southsaying.

We find possessions acknowledged in Scripture to be really and personally the Devil, or, according to the text, legions of devils, in the plural. The devil, or devils, rather, which possessed the man among the tombs, is positively affirmed to be the Devil in the Scripture; all the evangelists agree in calling him so, and his very works show it; namely, the mischief he did, as well to the poor creature among the tombs, who was made so fierce that he was the terror of all the country, as to the herd of swine and to the country in the loss of them.

I might preach you a lecture here of the Devil's terror upon the approach of our Saviour, the dread of. his government, and how he acknowledged that there was a time for his torment, which was not yet come. *Art thou come to torment us before our time?* It is evident the Devil apprehended that Christ would chain them up before the day of judgment; and therefore some think the Devil here, being, as it were, caught out of his due bounds, possessing the poor man in such a furious manner, was afraid, and petitioned Christ not to chain him up for it, and as the text says, *They besought him to suffer them to go away, &c.*; that is to say, when they say, Art thou come to torment us before the time? the meaning is, they begged he would not cast them into torment before the time, which was already fixed; but that if he would cast them out of the man, he would let them go away, &c.

The Evangelist St. Luke says, *The Devil besought him that he would not command them to go out into the deep:* our learned annotators think that part is not rightly rendered; adding, that they do not believe the Devil fears drowning; but with submission, I believe the meaning is, that they would not be confined to the vast ocean, where, no inhabitants being to be seen, they would be effectually imprisoned and tied down from doing mischief, which would be a hell to them. As to their going into the swine, that might afford us some allegory;

but I am not disposed to jest with the Scripture, no, nor the Devil neither, farther than needs must.

It is evident the Devil makes use of very mean instruments sometimes, such as the damsel possessed with a spirit of divination, and several others.

I remember a story, how true I know not, of a weak creature next door to an idiot, who was established in the country for an oracle, and would tell people strange things that should be, long before they came to pass; when people were sick, would tell them whether they should live or die; if people where married, tell how many children they should have; and a hundred such things, as filled the people with admiration, and they were the easier brought to believe that the girl was possessed; but then they were divided about her too, and that was the finest-spun thread the Devil could work, for he carried a great point in it; some said she had a good spirit, and some a bad, some said she was a prophetess, and some that she was the Devil.

Now had I been there to decide the question, I should certainly have given it for the latter; if it were only upon this account, namely, that the Devil has often found fools very necessary agents for the propagating his interest and kingdom, but we never knew the good spirits do so; on the other hand, it does not seem likely that Heaven should deprive a poor creature of its senses, and as it were take her soul from her, and then make her an instrument of instruction to others, and an oracle to declare his decrees by; this does not seem to be rational.

But as far as this kind of divination is in use in our days, yet I do not find room to charge the Devil with making any great use of fools, unless it be such as he has particularly qualified for his work, for as to idiots and naturals, they are perfectly useless to him; but a sort of fools called the magi, indeed, we have some reason to think he often works with.

We are not arrived to a certainty yet, in the settling this great point, namely, what magic is? whether a diabolical art or a branch of the mathematics? Our most learned Lexicon Technicum is of the latter opinion, and gives the magic square and the magic lantern, two terms of art.

The magic square is when numbers in arithmetical proportion are disposed into such parallels or equal ranks, as that the sums of each row, as well diagonally as laterally shall be all equal; for example, 2, 3, 4, 5, 6, 7, 8, 9, 10. Place these nine in a square of three, they will directly and diagonally make eighteen. Thus,

5	10	3
4	6	8
9	2	7

This he calls the magic square, but gives no reason for the term, nor any account of what infernal operations are wrought by this concurrence of the numbers; neither do I see that there can be any such use made of it.

The magic lantern is an optic machine, by the means of which are represented, on a wall in the dark, many phantasms and terrible appearances, but no devil in all this, only that they are taken for the effects of magic, by those that are not acquainted with the secret.

All this is done by the help of several little painted pieces of glass, only so and so situated, placed in certain oppositions to one another, and painted with different figures, the most formidable being placed foremost, and such as are most capable of terrifying the spectators; and by this all the figures may be represented upon the opposite wall, in the largest size.

I cannot but take notice, that this very piece of optic delusion seems too much akin to the mock possessions and infernal accomplishments, which most of the possessionists of this age pretend to, so that they are most of them mere phantasms and appearances, and no more; nor is the spirit of divination, the magic, the necromancing, and other arts which were called diabolical, found to be of any use in modern practice, at least, in these parts of the world; but the Devil seems to do most of his work himself, and by shorter methods; for he has so complete an influence among those that he now lists in his service, that he brings all the common affairs of mankind into a narrower compass in his management, with a dexterity particular to himself, and by which he carries on his interest silently and surely, much more to the detriment of virtue and good government, and consequently much more to his satisfaction, than ever he did before.

There is a kind of magic or sorcery, or what else you may please to call it, which, though unknown to us, is yet, it seems, still very much encouraged by the Devil; but this is a great way off, and in countries where the politer instruments, which he finds here, are not to be had; namely, among the Indians of North America: this is called pawawing, and they have their divines, which they call pawaws, or witches, who use strange gestures, distortions, horrid smokes, burnings, and scents, and several such things which the sorcerors and witches in ancient times are said to use in casting nativities, in philtres, and in determining, or as they pretended, directing, the fate of persons, by burning such and such herbs and roots, such as hellebore, wormwood, storax, devilwort, mandrake, nightshade, and abundance more such, which are called noxious plants, or the product of noxious plants; also melting such and such minerals, gums, and poisonous things, and by several hellish mutterings and markings over them, the like do these pawaws; and the Devil is pleased, it seems (or is permitted), to fall in with these things, and as some people think, appears often to them for their assistance upon those occasions.

But be that as it will, he is eased of all that trouble here; he can pawaw here himself, without their aid, and having laid them all aside, he negotiates much of his business without ambassadors; he is his own plenipotentiary, for he finds man so easy to come at, and so easy when he is come at, that he stands in no need of secret emissaries, or at least not so much as he used to do.

Upon the whole, as the world, within the compass of a few past years, is advanced in all kinds of knowledge and arts, and every useful branch of what they knew before improved, and innumerable useful parts of knowledge, which were concealed before, are discovered, why should we think the Devil alone should stand at a stay, has taken no steps to his farther accomplishment, and made no useful discoveries in his way? that he alone should stand at a stay, and be just the same unimproved devil that he was before? No, no, as the world is improved every day, and every age is grown wiser and wiser than their fathers; so, no doubt, he has bestirred himself too, in order to an increase of knowledge and discovery, and that he finds every day a nearer way to go to work with mankind than he had before.

Besides, as men in general seem to have altered their manner, and that they move in a higher and more exalted sphere, especially as to vice and virtue, so the Devil may have been obliged to change his measures, and alter his way of working; particularly those things which would take in former times, and which a stupid age would come easily into, won't ~ down with us now; as the taste of vice and virtue

alters, the Devil is forced to bait his hook with new com-
positions; the very thing called temptation is altered in its
nature, and that which served to delude our ancestors, whose
gross conceptions of things caused them to be manageable
with less art, will not do now; the case is quite altered; in
some things, perhaps, as I hinted above, we come into crime
with ease, and may be led by a finger; but when we come
to a more refined way of sinning, which our ancestors never
understood, other and more refined politics must be made use
of, and the Devil has been put upon many useful projects and
inventions, to make many new discoveries and experiments
to carry on his affairs; and to speak impartially, he is strangely
improved either in knowledge or experiment, within these few
years; he has found out a great many new inventions to
shorten his own labour, and carry on his business in the
world currently, which he never was master of before, or at
least we never knew he was.

No wonder then that he has changed hands too, and that
he has left off pawawing in these parts of the world; that we
don't find our houses disturbed as they used to be, and the stools
and chairs walking about out of one room into another, as
formerly; that children don't vomit crooked pins and rusty
stub nails, as of old, the air is not full of noises, nor the church-
yard full of hobgoblins; ghosts don't walk about in winding-
sheets, and the good old scolding wives visit and plague their
husbands after they are dead, as they did when they were
alive.

The age is grown too wise to be agitated by these dull
scarecrow things which their forefathers were tickled with;
Satan has been obliged to lay by his puppet-shows and his
tumblers, those things are grown stale; his morrice-dancing
devils, his mountebanking and quacking won't do now; those
things, as they may be supposed to be very troublesome to
him (and but that he has servants enough, would be charge-
able too), are now of no great use in the new management of
his affairs.

In a word, men are too much devils themselves, in the sense
that I have called them so, to be frighted with such little low-
prized appearances as these; they are better acquainted with
the old archangel than so, and they seem to tell him they
must be treated after another manner, and that then, as
they are good-natured and tractable, he may deal with them
upon better terms.

Hence the Devil goes to work with mankind a much shorter way; for instead of the art of wheedling and whining, together with the laborious part of tricking and sharping, hurrying and driving, frightening and terrifying, all which the Devil was put to the trouble of before; in short, he acts the 'grand manner,' as the architects call it: I don't know whether our freemasons may understand the word, and therefore I may hereafter explain it, as it is to be diabolically as well as mathematically understood.

At present my meaning is, he acts with them immediately and personally by a magnificent transformation, making them mere devils to themselves, upon all needful occasions, and devils to one another too, whenever he (Satan) has need of their services.

This way of embarking mankind in the Devil's particular engagement, is really very modern; and though the Devil himself may have been long acquainted with the method, and, as I have heard, began to practise it towards the close of the Roman empire, when men began to act upon very polite principles, and were capable of the most refined wickedness, and afterwards with some popes, who likewise were a kind of church devils, such as Satan himself could hardly expect to find in the world; yet I do not find that he was ever able to bring it into practice, at least not so universally as he does now. But now the case is altered, and men being generally more expert in wickedness than they were formerly, they suffer the smaller alteration of the species, in being transmigrated; in a word, they turn into devils with no trouble at all hardly, either to the Devil or themselves.

This particular would want much the less explanation, could I obtain a license from Sir Hellebore Wormwood, bart., or from my Lord Thwartover, baron of Scoundrel Hall, in the kingdom of Ireland, to write the true history of their own conduct; and how early, and above all how easily, they commenced devils, without the least impeachment of their characters as wise men, and without any diminution of that part of their denomination which established them for fools.

How many mad fellows appear among us every day in the critical juncture of their transmigration, just when they have so much of the man left as to be known by their names, and enough of the Devil taken up to settle their characters! This easiness of the Devil's access to these people, and the great convenience it is to him in his general business, is a proof to me that he has no more occasion of diviners, magicians, sorcerers, and whatever else we please to call those people who were formerly so great with him; for what occasion has he to employ devils and wizards to confound mankind, when he is arrived to such a perfection of art as to bring men, at least in these parts of the world, to do it all themselves. Upon this account, we do not find any of the old sorcerers and diviners, magicians or witches, appear among us; not that the Devil might not be as well able to employ such people as formerly, and qualify them for the employment too, but that really there is no need of them hereabout, the Devil having a shorter way, and mankind being much more easily possessed; not the old herd of swine were sooner agitated, though there was full two thousand of them together; nature has opened the door, and the Devil has egress and regress at pleasure, so that witches and diviners are quite out of the question.

Nor let any man be alarmed at this alteration in the case, as it stands between mankind and the Devil, and think the Devil having gained so much ground, may in time, by encroachment, come to a general possession of the whole race, and so we should all come to be devils incarnate. I say, let us not be alarmed, for Satan does not get these advantages by encroachment, and by his infernal power or art; no, not at all; but it is the man himself does it by his indolence and negligence on one hand, and his complaisance to the Devil on the other; and both ways he, as it were, opens the door to him, beckons him with his very hand to come in, and the Devil has nothing to do but enter and take possession. Now if it be so, and man is so frank to him, you know the Devil is no fool not to take the advantage when it is offered him, and therefore it is no wonder if the consequences which I have been just now naming follow.

But let no man be discouraged by this, from reassuming his natural and religious powers, and venturing to shut the Devil out; for the case is plain he may be shut out; the soul is a strong castle, and has a good garrison placed within to defend it; if the garrison behave well, and do their duty, it is impregnable, and the cowardly Devil must raise his siege and be gone; nay, he must fly, or, as we call it, make his escape, lest he be laid by the heels, that is, lest his weakness be exposed, and all his lurking, lying in wait, ambuscade-tricks. This part would bear a great enlargement, but I have not oom to be witty upon him, so you must take it in the gross; the Devil lies at Blye Bush, as our country people call it, to watch you coming out of your hold; and if you happen to go abroad unarmed, he seizes upon and masters you with ease

Unarmed; you'll say, what arms should I take? what fence against a flail? what weapons can a man take to fight the Devil? I could tell you what to fight him with, and what you might fright him with, for the Devil is to be frightened with several things besides holy water; but it is too serious for you, and you will tell me I am a preaching and a canting, and the like, so I must let the Devil manage you rather than displease you with talking Scripture and religion.

Well, but may not the Devil be fought with some of his own weapons? Is there no dealing with him in a way of human nature? This would require a long answer, and some philosophy might be acted, or at least imitated, and some magic, perhaps; for they tell us there are spells to draw away even the Devil himself; as, in some places, they nail horseshoes upon the threshold of the door to keep him out; in other places, old pieces of flint, with so many holes, and so many corners, and the like. But I must answer in the negative; I don't know what Satan might be scared at in those days, but he is either grown cunninger since or bolder, for he values none of those things now; I question much whether he would value St. Dunstan and his redhot tongs if he was to meet him now, or St. Francis, or any of the saints, no, not the host itself, in full procession; and, therefore, though you don't care I should preach, yet, in short, if you are afraid he should charge upon you and attack you, if you won't make use of those Scripture weapons I should have mentioned, and which you may hear of, if you inquire at Eph. vi. 19, you must look for better where you can find them.

But to go on with my work; the Devil, 1 say, is not to be scared with maukins; nor does he employ his old instruments, but does much of his work himself, without instruments.

And yet I must enter a caveat here too, against being misunderstood in my saying the Devil stands in need of no agents; for, when I speak so, I am to be taken in a limited sense. I don't say he needs them nowhere, but only that he does not need them in those polite parts of the world which I have been speaking of, and perhaps not much here; but in

many remote countries it is otherwise still; the Indians of
America are particularly said to have witches among them,
as well in those countries where the Spaniards, and the
English, and other nations, have planted themselves, as
amongst those where the European nations seldom come:
for example, the people of Canada, that is, of the countries
under the French government of Quebec, the Esquimeaux,
and other northern climates, have magicians, wizards, and
witches, who they call Pilloatas, or Pillotoas ; these pretend
they speak intimately and familiarly with the Devil, and
receive from him the knowledge of things to come; all
which, by the way, I take to be little more than this, that
these fellows being a little more cunning than the rest, think
that by pretending to something more than human, they
shall make the stronger impressions on the ignorant people ;
as Mahomet amused the world with his pigeon, using it to
pick peas out of his ear, and persuaded the people it brought
him superior revelations and inspirations from Paradise.

Thus these Pillotoas, gaining an opinion among the people,
behave like so many mountebanks of hell, pretending to
understand dark things, cure diseases, practise surgery,
physic, and necromancy altogether. I will not say but
Satan may pick out such tools to work with, and I believe
does in those parts, but I think he has found a nearer way to
the wood with us, and that is sufficient to my present
purpose.

Some would persuade me the Devil had a great hand in
the late religious breaches in France, among the clergy, viz.,
about the pope's constitution Unigenitus, and that he made
a fair attempt to set the pope and the Gallican church
together by the ears, for they were all just upon the point of
breaking out into a church war, that, for aught we knew,
might have gone farther than the Devil himself cared it
should. Now I am of the quite contrary opinion ; I believe
the Devil really did not make the breach, but rather healed
it, for fear it should have gone so far among them as to have
set them all in a flame, and have opened the door to the
return of the Huguenots again, which it was in a fair way
to have done.

But be it one way or t'other, the historical part seems to
be a little against me; for it is certain the Devil both
wanted and made use of legions of agents, as well human as
infernal, visible and invisible, in that great and important

affair, and we cannot doubt but he has innumerable instruments still at work about it.

Like as in Poland, I make no question but the Devil has thousands of his banditti at work at this time, and in another country not far from it, perhaps, preparing matters for the next general Diet, taking care to prevent giving any relaxation to the protestants, and to justify the moderate executions at Thorn; to excite a nation to quarrel with everybody, who are able to fight with nobody; to erect the apostate race of S——y upon a throne which they have no title to, and turn an elective throne into an hereditary, in favour of popery.

I might anticipate all your objections, by granting the busy Devil at this time employing all his agents and instruments (for I never told you they were idle and useless), in striving to inflame the Christian world, and bring a new war to overspread Europe : I might, perhaps, point out to you some of the measures he takes, the provocatives which his state physicians administer to the courts and counsellors of princes, to foment and ferment the spirits and members of nations, kingdoms, empires, and states, in the world, in order to bring these glorious ends of blood and war to pass; for you cannot think but he that knows so much of the Devil's affairs as to write his history, must know something of all these matters more than those that do not know so much as he.

But all this is remote to the present case, for this is no impeachment of Satan's new methods with mankind in this part of the world, and in his private and separate capacity; all this only signifies that, in his more general and national affairs, the Devil acts still by his old methods; and when he is to seduce or embroil nations, he, like other conquerors, subdues them by armies, employs mighty squadrons of devils, and sends out strong detachments, with generals and generalissimos to lead them, some to one part of the world, some to another, some to influence one nation, some to manage and direct another, according as business presents, and his occasions require, that his affairs may be carried on currently and to his satisfaction.

If it were not thus, but that the Devil, by his new and exquisite management, of which I have said so much, had brought mankind in general to be the agents of their own mischiefs, and that the world were so at his beck that he need but command them to go and fight, declare war, raise armies, destroy cities, kingdoms, countries, and people, the world would be a field of blood indeed, and all things would run into confusion presently.

But this is not the case at all; Heaven has not let go the government of the creation to his subdued enemy, the Devil; that would overturn the whole system of God, and give Satan more power than ever he was or will be vested with. When, therefore, I speak of a few forward wretches in our day, who are so warm in their wickedness, that they anticipate the Devil, save him the trouble to tempt, turn devils to themselves, and gallop hellward faster than he drives, I speak of them as single persons, and acting in their own personal and private capacity; but when I speak of nations and kingdoms, there the Devil is obliged to go on in the old road, and act by stratagem, by his proper machinery, and to make use of all his arts and all his agents, just as he has done in all ages, from the beginning of his politic government to this day.

And if it was not thus, too, what would become of all his numberless legions, of which all ages have heard so much, and all parts of the world have had so much fatal experience?

They would seem to be quite out of employment, and be rendered useless in the world of spirits, where it is to be supposed they reside; not the Devil himself could find any business for them, which by the way, to busy and mischievous spirits as they are, would be a hell to them, even before their time; they would be, as it were, doomed to a state of inactivity, which, we may suppose, was one part of their expulsion from blessedness and the creation of man; or as they were for the surprising interval between the destruction of mankind by the deluge and Noah's coming out of the ark, when, indeed, they might be said to have had nothing at all to do.

But this is not Satan's case; and therefore let me tell you, too (that you may not think I treat the case with more levity than I really do, and than, I am sure, I intend to do), though it is too true that our modern and modish sinners have arrived to more exquisite ways of being wicked than their fathers, and really seem, as I have said, to need no Devil to tempt them; nay, that they do Satan's work for him as to others also, and make themselves devils to their neighbours, tempting others to crime even faster than the Devil desires them, running before they are sent, and going of the Devil's errands gratis; by which means Satan's work is, as to them, done to his hand, and they may be said to save him a great deal of trouble; yet, after all, the Devil has still a great deal of business upon his hands, and, as well himself as all his legions, find themselves a full employment in disturbing the world, and opposing the glory and kingdom of their great superior; whose kingdom it is their whole business, however vain in its end, to overthrow and destroy, if they were able, or, at least, to endeavour it.

This being the case, it follows, of course, that the general mischiefs of mankind, as well national and public as family mischiefs, and even personal (except as before excepted), lie all still at the Devil's door as much as ever, let his advocates bring him off of it if they can. And this brings us back again to the manner of the Devil's management, and the way of his working by human agents, or if you will, the way of human devils working in affairs of low life, such as we call divination, sorcery, black art, necromancy, and the like; all which I take to consist of two material parts, and both very necessary for us to be rightly informed of.

1. The part which Satan by himself, or his inferior devils, empowers such people to do as he is in confederacy with here on earth; to whom he may be said, like the master of an opera or comedy, to give their parts to act, and to qualify them to act it; whether he obliges them to a rehearsal in his presence, to try their talents, and see that they are capable of performing, that indeed I have not inquired into.

2. That part which these empowered people do volunteer for beyond their commission, to show their diligence in the service of their new master, and either, 1. to bring grist to their own mill, and make their market of their employment in the best manner they can; or, 2. to gain applause, be admired, wondered at, and applauded, as if they were ten times more devils than really they are.

In a word, the matter consists of what the Devil does by the help of these people, and what they do in his name without him. The Devil is sometimes cheated in his own business; there are pretenders to witchcraft and black art who Satan never made any bargain with, but who he connives at, because, at least, they do his cause no harm; though their business is rather to get money than to render him any service, of which I gave you a remarkable instance before.

But to go back to his real agents, of which I reckon two.

1. Those who act by direction and confederacy, as I have said already many do.

2. Those whom he acts in, and by, and they (perhaps) know it not, of which sort history gives us plenty of examples, from Machiavel's first disciple ——— to the famous Cardinal Alberoni, and even to some more modern than his eminence, of whom I can say no more till farther occasion offers.

1. Those who act by immediate direction of the Devil, and in confederacy with him; these are such as I mentioned in the beginning of this chapter, whose arts are truly black, because really infernal. It will be very hard to decide the dispute between those who really act thus in confederacy with the Devil, and those who only pretend to it; so I shall leave that dispute where I find it; but that there are, or at least have been, a set of people in the world, who really are of his acquaintance, and very intimate with him; and though, as I have said, he has much altered his schemes, and changed hands of late; yet that there are such people, perhaps of all sorts, and that the Devil keeps up his correspondence with them, I must not venture to deny that part, lest I bring upon me the whole posse of the conjuring and betwitching crew, male and female, and they should mob me for pretending to deny them the honour of dealing with the Devil, which they are so exceeding willing to have the fame of.

Not that I am hereby obliged to believe all the strange things the witches and wizards, who have been allowed to be such, nay, who have been hanged for it, have said of themselves; nay, that they have confessed of themselves, even at the gallows; and if I come to have an occasion to speak freely of the matter, I may perhaps convince you that the Devil's possessing power is much lessened of late, and that he either is limited, and his fetter shortened more than it has been, or that he does not find the whole way, as I said before, so fit for his purpose as he did formerly, and therefore takes other measures; but I must adjourn that to a time and place by itself. But we are told that there are another sort of people, and, perhaps, a great many of them too, in whom and by whom the Devil really acts, and they know it not.

It would take up a great deal of time and room, too much for this place, so near the close of this work, to describe and mark out the involuntary devils which there are in the world; of whom it may be truly said, that really the Devil is in them, and they know it not. Now though the Devil is cunning and managing, and can be very silent where he finds it for his interest not to be known; yet it is very hard for him to conceal himself, and to give so little disturbance in the house, as that the family should not know who lodged in it; yet I say, the Devil is so subtle and so mischievous an agent, that he uses all manner of methods and craft to reside in such people as he finds for his purpose, whether they will or no, and, which is more, whether they know it or no.

And let none of my readers be angry, or think themselves ill used, when I tell them the Devil may be in them, and may act in them, and by them, and they not know it; for I must add, it may, perhaps, be one of the greatest pieces of human wisdom in the world, for a man to know when the Devil is in him, and when not; when he is a tool and agent of hell, and when he is not; in a word, when he is doing the Devil's work, and under his direction, and when not.

It is true, this is a very weighty point, and might deserve to be handled in a more serious way than I seem to be talking in all this book; but give me leave to talk of things my own way, and withal, to tell you that there is no part of this work so seemingly ludicrous, but a grave and well weighed mind may make a serious and solid application of it, if they please: nor is there any part of this work, in which a clear sight and a good sense may not see that the author's design is, that they should do so; and as I am now so near the end of my book, I thought it was meet to tell you so, and lead you to it as far. as I can.

I say, it is a great part of human wisdom to know when the Devil is acting in us and by us, and when not; the next, and still greater part, would be to prevent him, put a stop to his progress, bid him go about his business, and let him know he should carry on his designs no farther in that manner; that we will be his tools no longer; in short, to turn him out of doors, and bring a stronger power to take possession; but this, indeed, is too solid a subject, and too great to begin with here.

But now, as to the bare knowing when he is at work with us; I say, this, though it is considerable, may be done, nor is it so very difficult; for example, you have no more to do but look a little into the microcosm of the soul, and see there how the passions, which are the blood, and the affections, which are the spirit, move in their particular vessels; how they circulate, and in what temper the pulse beats there, and you may easily see who turns the wheel. If a perfect calm possesses the soul; if peace and temper prevail, and the mind feels no tempests rising; if the affections are regular, and exalted to virtuous and sublime objects; the spirits cool, and the mind sedate, the man is in a general rectitude of mind; he may be truly said to be his own man; heaven shines upon his soul with its benign influences, and he is out of the reach of the evil spirit; for the divine spirit is an influence of peace, all calm and bright, happy and sweet like itself, and tending to everything that is good, both present and future.

But on the other hand, if at any time the mind is ruffled, if vapours rise, clouds gather, if passions swell the breast, if anger, envy, revenge, hatred, wrath, strife; if these, or any of these, hover over you; much more, if you feel them within you; if the affections are possessed, and the soul hurried down the stream to embrace low and base objects; if those spirits, which are the life and enlivening powers of the soul, are drawn off to parties, and to be engaged in a vicious and corrupt manner, shooting out wild and wicked desires, and running the man headlong into crime, the case is easily resolved, the man is possessed, the Devil is in him; and having taken the fort, or at least the counterscarp and outworks, is making his lodgment to cover and secure himself in his hold, that he may not be dispossessed.

Nor can he be easily dispossessed when he has got such hold as this; and it is no wonder that, being lodged thus upon the outworks of the soul, he continues to sap the foundation of the rest, and by his incessant and furious assaults, reduces the man at last to a surrender.

If the allegory be not as just and apposite as you would have it be, you may, however, see by it, in a full view, the state of the man, and how the Devil carries on his designs; nothing is more common, and I believe there are few thinking minds but may reflect upon it in their own compass, than for our passions and affections to flow out of the ordinary channel; the spirits and blood of the soul to be extravasated, the passions grow violent and outrageous, the affections impetuous, corrupt, and violently vicious. Whence does all this proceed? from heaven we cannot pretend it comes; if we must not say it is the Devil, whose door must it lie at? Pride swells the passions; avarice moves the affections; and what is pride, and what is avarice, but the Devil in the inside of the man? ay, as personally and really as ever he was in the herd of swine.

Let not any man then, who is a slave to his passions, or who is chained down to his covetousness, pretend to take it ill, when I say he has the Devil in him, or that he is a devil: what else can it be, and how comes it to pass that passion and revenge so often dispossess the man of himself, as to lead him to commit murder, to lay plots and snares for the life of his enemies, and so to thirst for blood, how comes this but by the Devil's putting those spirits of the soul into so violent a ferment, into a fever? that the circulation is precipitated to that degree, and that the man too is precipitated into mischief, and at last into ruin? it is all the Devil, though the man does not know it.

In like manner, avarice leads him to rob, plunder, and destroy for money, and to commit sometimes the worst of violences to obtain the wicked reward. How many have had their throats cut for their money, have been murdered on the highway, or in their beds, for the desire of what they had? It is the same thing in other articles, every vice is the Devil in a man; lust of rule is the devil of great men, and that ambition is their devil, as much as whoring is father . . . . .'s devil; one has a devil of one class acting him, one another, and every man's reigning vice is a devil to him.

Thus the Devil has his involuntary instruments, as well as those who act in confederacy with him; he has a very great share in many of us, and acts us, and in us, unknown to ourselves, though we know nothing of it, and indeed though we may not suspect it of ourselves; like Hazael the Assyrian, who, when the prophet told him how he would act the devil upon the poor Israelites, answered with detestation, *Is thy servant a dog, that he should do this thing?* and yet he was that dog, and did all those cruel things for all that; the Devil acting him, or acting in him, to make him wickeder than ever he thought it was possible for him to be.

THE CONCLUSION.

OF THE DEVIL'S LAST SCENE OF LIBERTY, AND WHAT MAY BE SUPPOSED TO BE HIS END, WITH WHAT WE ARE TO UNDERSTAND OF HIS BEING TORMENTED FOR EVER AND EVER.

As the Devil is a prince of the power of the air, his kingdom is mortal, and must have an end; and as he is called the god of this world, that is, the great usurper of the homage and reverence which mankind ought of right to pay to their Maker, so his usurpation also, like the world itself, must have an end: Satan is called the God of the world, as men too much prostrate and prostitute themselves to him, yet he is not the governor of this world; and therefore the homage and worship he has from the world, is an usurpation ; and this will have an end because the world itself will have an end ; and all mankind, as they had a beginning in time, so must expire and be removed before the end of time.

Since, then, the Devil's empire is to expire and come to an end, and that the Devil himself and all his host of devils are immortal seraphs, spirits that are not embodied, and cannot die, but are to remain in being; the question before us next will be, what is to become of him ? what is his state to be ? whither is he to wander, and in what condition is he to remain to that eternity to which he is still to exist ?

I hope no man will mistake me so much in what I have said as to spirits, which are all flame, not being affected with fire, as if I supposed there was no place of punishment for the Devil, nor any kind of punishment that could affect them ; and so of our spirits also, when transformed into flame.

I must be allowed to speak there of that material fire, by which, as by an allegory, all the terrors of an eternal state are represented to us in Scripture, and in the writings of the learned commentators, and by which the pain of sense is described ; this, perhaps, I do not understand as they seem to do, and therefore have said,

When we are all flame (that is, all spirit) we shall all fire (that is, all such fire as this) despise. And thus I claim to be understood.

It does not follow from hence, neither do I suggest or so much as think that infinite power cannot form a something (though inconceivable to us here) which shall be as tormenting and as insupportable to a devil, an apostate seraph, and to a spirit, though exalted, unembodied and rarefied into flame, as fire would be to other bodies; in which I think I am orthodox, and do not give the least occasion to an enemy to charge me with profane speaking in those words, or to plead for thinking profanely himself.

It must be atheistical to the last degree to suggest, that whereas the Devil has been heaping up and amassing guilt ever since the creation of man, increasing in hatred of God and rebellion against him, and in all possible endeavour to dethrone and depose the Majesty of heaven, that yet Heaven had not prepared, or could not prepare, a just penalty for him; and that it should not all end in God's entire victory over hell, and in Satan's open condemnation. Heaven could not be just to its own glory, if he should not avenge himself upon this rebel, for all his superlative wickedness in his modern as well as ancient station; for the blood of so many millions of his faithful subjects and saints whom he has destroyed; and if nothing else offered itself to prove this part, it would appear undoubted to me; but this, I confess, does not belong to Satan's history, and therefore I have reserved it to this place, and shall also be the shorter in it.

That his condition is to be a state of punishment, and that by torment, the Devil himself has owned; and his calling out to our blessed Lord when he cast him out of the furious man among the tombs, is a proof of it; *What have we to do with thee,* and *art thou come to torment us before the time?* Luke viii. 28; where the Devil acknowledges four things, and three of them are directly to my present purpose, and if you won't believe the Word of God, I hope you will believe the Devil, especially when it is an open confession against himself.

1. He confessed Christ to be the Son of God (that by the way) and no thanks to him, for that does not want the Devil's evidence.

2. He acknowledges he may be tormented.

3. He acknowledges Christ was able to torment him.

4. He acknowledges that there is a time appointed when he shall be tormented.

As to how, in what manner, and by what means, this tormenting the Devil is to be performed or executed, that I take to be as needless to us as it is impossible to know, and being not at present inclined to fill your heads and thoughts with weak and imperfect guesses, I leave it where I find it.

It is enough to us, that this torment of the Devil is represented to us by fire, it being impossible for our confined thoughts to conceive of torment by anything in the world more exquisite; whence I conclude, that devils shall at last receive a punishment suitable to their spiritous nature, and as exquisitely tormenting as a burning fire would be to our bodies.

Having thus settled my own belief of this matter, and stated it so as I think will let you see it is rightly founded, the matter stands thus:

Satan having been let loose to play his game in this world, has improved his time to the utmost; he has not failed on all occasions to exert his hatred, rage, and malice, at his conqueror and enemy, namely, his Maker; he has not failed, from principles of mere envy and pride, to pursue mankind with all possible rancour, in order to deprive him of the honour and felicity which he was created for, namely, to succeed the Devil and his angels in the state of glory from which they fell.

This hatred of God, and envy at man, having broken out in so many several ways in the whole series of time from the creation, must necessarily have greatly increased his guilt; and as Heaven is righteous to judge him, must terminate in an increase of punishment, adequate to his crime, and sufficient to his nature.

Some have suggested, that there is yet a time to come, when the Devil shall exert more rage, and do more mischief than ever yet he has been permitted to do; whether he shall break his chain, or be unchained for a time, they cannot tell, nor I neither; and it is happy for my work, that even this part too does not belong to his history; if ever it shall be given an account of by mankind, it must be after it is come to pass, for my part is not prophecy, or foretelling what the Devil shall do, but history of what he has done.

Thus, good people, I have brought the history of the Devil down to your own times; I have, as it were, raised him for you, and set him in your view, that you may know him, and have a care of him.

If any cunninger men among you think they are able now to lay him again, and so dispose of him out of your sight, that you shall be troubled no more with him, either here or hereafter, let them go to work with him in their own way; you know things future do not belong to an historian, so I leave him among you, wishing you may be able to give no worse an account of him for the time to come, than I have done for the time past.

THE END OF THE HISTORY OF THE DEVIL.

CATALOGUE OF

BOHN'S LIBRARIES.

N.B.—It is requested that all orders be accompanied by payment. Books are sent carriage free on the receipt of the published price in stamps or otherwise.

The Works to which the letters 'N. S.' (denoting New Style) are appended are kept in neat cloth bindings of various colours, as well as in the regular Library style. All Orders are executed in the New binding, unless the contrary is expressly stated.

Complete Sets or Separate Volumes can be had at short notice, half-bound in calf or morocco.

New Volumes of Standard Works in the various branches of Literature are constantly being added to this Series, which is already unsurpassed in respect to the number, variety, and cheapness of the Works contained in it. The Publishers have to announce the following Volumes as recently issued or now in preparation :—

Boswell's Life of Johnson. New Edition. 6 vols.
[*Ready, see p.* 1.

Vasari's Lives of the Painters. Additional Notes by J. P. Richter. *Ready, see p.* 8.

Roger Ascham's Scholemaster. Edited by Prof. Mayor.

Grimm's German Tales. 2 vols. With the Notes of the Original. [*Ready, see p.* 5.

Coleridge's Table-Talk, &c. [*Ready, see p.* 4.

Coleridge's Miscellaneous Works. [*In the press.*

Manual of Philosophy. By E. Belfort Bax. 1 vol.

Goldsmith's Works. Vols. I. and II. [*Ready, see p.* 5.

Fairholt's History of Costume. [*In the press.*

Hoffmann's Stories. Translated by Major Ewing.
[*In the press.*

LONDON : G. BELL & SONS, 4 YORK STREET, COVENT GARDEN.

BOHN'S LIBRARIES.

STANDARD LIBRARY.

294 Vols. at 3s. 6d. each, excepting those marked otherwise. (51*l*. 10*s*. 6*d*. *per set*.)

ADDISON'S Works. Notes of Bishop Hurd. Short Memoir, Portrait, and 8 Plates of Medals. 6 vols. *N. S.*
This is the most complete edition of Addison's Works issued.

ALFIERI'S Tragedies. In English Verse. With Notes, Arguments, and Introduction, by E. A. Bowring, C.B. 2 vols. *N. S.*

AMERICAN POETRY. — *See Poetry of America.*

ASCHAM'S Scholemaster. Edit. by by Prof. J. E. B. Mayor. [*In the press.*

BACON'S Moral and Historical Works, including Essays, Apophthegms, Wisdom of the Ancients, New Atlantis, Henry VII., Henry VIII., Elizabeth, Henry Prince of Wales, History of Great Britain, Julius Cæsar, and Augustus Cæsar. With Critical and Biographical Introduction and Notes by J. Devey, M.A. Portrait. *N. S.*

—— *See also Philosophical Library.*

BALLADS AND SONGS of the Peasantry of England, from Oral Recitation, private MSS., Broadsides, &c. Edit. by R. Bell. *N. S.*

BEAUMONT AND FLETCHER. Selections. With Notes and Introduction by Leigh Hunt.

BECKMANN (J.) History of Inventions, Discoveries, and Origins. With Portraits of Beckmann and James Watt. 2 vols. *N. S.*

BELL (Robert). — *See Ballads, Chaucer, Green.*

BOSWELL'S Life of Johnson, with the TOUR in the HEBRIDES and JOHNSONIANA. New Edition, with Notes and Appendices, by the Rev. A. Napier, M.A., Trinity College, Cambridge, Vicar of Holkham, Editor of the 'Cambridge Edition of the 'Theological Works' of Barrow.' With Frontispiece to each vol. 6 vols. *N.S.*

BREMER'S (Frederika) Works. Trans. by M. Howitt. Portrait. 4 vols. *N.S.*

BRINK (B. T.) Early English Literature (to Wiclif). By Bernhard Ten Brink. Trans. by Prof. H. M. Kennedy. *N. S.*

BRITISH POETS, from Milton to Kirke White. Cabinet Edition. With Frontispiece. 4 vols. *N. S.*

BROWNE'S (Sir Thomas) Works. Edit. by S. Wilkin, with Dr. Johnson's Life of Browne. Portrait. 3 vols.

BURKE'S Works. 6 vols. *N. S.*

—— **Speeches on the Impeachment** of Warren Hastings ; and Letters. 2 vols. *N. S.*

—— **Life.** By J. Prior. Portrait. *N. S.*

BURNS (Robert). Life of. By J. G. Lockhart, D.C.L. A new and enlarged edition. With Notes and Appendices by W. S. Douglas. Portrait. *N. S.*

BUTLER'S (Bp.) Analogy of Religion; Natural and Revealed, to the Constitution and Course of Nature ; with Two Dissertations on Identity and Virtue, and Fifteen Sermons. With Introductions, Notes, and Memoir. Portrait. *N. S.*

CAMOEN'S Lusiad, or the Discovery of India. An Epic Poem. Trans. from the Portuguese, with Dissertation, Historical Sketch, and Life, by W. J. Mickle. 5th edition. *N. S.*

CARAFAS (The) of Maddaloni. Naples under Spanish Dominion. Trans. by Alfred de Reumont. Portrait of Massaniello.

CARREL. The Counter-Revolution in England for the Re-establishment of Popery under Charles II. and James II., by Armand Carrel ; with Fox's History of James II. and Lord Lonsdale's Memoir of James II. Portrait of Carrel.

CARRUTHERS. — *See Pope, in Illustrated Library.*

CARY'S Dante. The Vision of Hell, Purgatory, and Paradise. Trans. by Rev. H. F. Cary, M.A. With Life, Chronological View of his Age, Notes, and Index of Proper Names. Portrait. *N. S.*
This is the authentic edition, containing Mr. Cary's last corrections, with additional notes.

CELLINI (Benvenuto). Memoirs of, by himself. With Notes of G. P. Carpani. Trans. by T. Roscoe. Portrait. *N. S.*

CERVANTES' Galatea. A Pastoral Romance. Trans. by G. W. J. Gyll. *N. S.*

—— **Exemplary Novels.** Trans. by W. K. Kelly. *N. S.*

—— **Don Quixote de la Mancha.** Motteux's Translation revised. With Lockhart's Life and Notes. 2 vols. *N. S.*

CHAUCER'S Poetical Works. With Poems formerly attributed to him. With a Memoir, Introduction, Notes, and a Glossary, by R. Bell. Improved edition, with Preliminary Essay by Rev. W. W. Skeat, M.A. Portrait. 4 vols. *N. S.*

CLASSIC TALES, containing Rasselas, Vicar of Wakefield, Gulliver's Travels, and The Sentimental Journey. *N. S.*

COLERIDGE'S (S. T.) Friend. A Series of Essays on Morals, Politics, and Religion. Portrait. *N. S.*

—— **Confessions of an Inquiring Spirit;** and Essays on Faith and the Common Prayer-book. New Edition, revised. *N. S.*

—— **Aids to Reflection.** *N.S.*

—— **Table-Talk and Omniana.** By T. Ashe, B.A. *N.S.*

—— **Lectures on Shakspere and** other Poets. Edit. by T. Ashe, B.A. *N.S.* Containing the lectures taken down in 1811-12 by J. P. Collier, and those delivered at Bristol in 1813.

—— **Biographia Literaria; or, Bio-** graphical Sketches of my Literary Life and Opinions; with Two Lay Sermons. *N. S.*

COMMINES.—*See Philip.*

CONDÉ'S History of the Dominion of the Arabs in Spain. Trans. by Mrs. Foster. Portrait of Abderahmen ben Moavia. 3 vols.

COWPER'S Complete Works, Poems, Correspondence, and Translations. Edit. with Memoir by R. Southey. 45 Engravings. 8 vols.

COXE'S Memoirs of the Duke of Marlborough. With his original Correspondence, from family records at Blenheim. Revised edition. Portraits. 3 vols.
⁎⁎ An Atlas of the plans of Marlborough's campaigns, 4to. 10*s*. 6*d*.

COXE'S History of the House of Austria. From the Foundation of the Monarchy by Rhodolph of Hapsburgh to the Death of Leopold II., 1218-1792. By Archdn. Coxe. With Continuation from the Accession of Francis I. to the Revolution of 1848. 4 Portraits. 4 vols.

CUNNINGHAM'S Lives of the most Eminent British Painters. With Notes and 16 fresh Lives by Mrs. Heaton. 3 vols. *N. S.*

DEFOE'S Novels and Miscellaneous Works. With Prefaces and Notes, including those attributed to Sir W. Scott. Portrait. 7 vols. *N. S.*

DE LOLME'S Constitution of Eng- land, in which it is compared both with the Republican form of Government and the other Monarchies of Europe. Edit., with Life and Notes, by J. Macgregor, M.P.

EMERSON'S Works. 3 vols. Most complete edition published. *N. S.*
Vol. I.—Essays, Lectures, and Poems.
Vol. II.—English Traits, Nature, and Conduct of Life.
Vol. III.—Society and Solitude—Letters and Social Aims—Miscellaneous Papers (hitherto uncollected)—May-Day, &c.

FOSTER'S (John) Life and Corre- spondence. Edit. by J. E. Ryland. Portrait. 2 vols. *N. S.*

—— **Lectures at Broadmead Chapel.** Edit. by J. E. Ryland. 2 vols. *N. S.*

—— **Critical Essays contributed to** the 'Eclectic Review.' Edit. by J. E. Ryland. 2 vols. *N. S.*

—— **Essays: On Decision of Charac-** ter; on a Man's writing Memoirs of Himself; on the epithet Romantic; on the aversion of Men of Taste to Evangelical Religion. *N. S.*

—— **Essays on the Evils of Popular** Ignorance, and a Discourse on the Propagation of Christianity in India. *N. S.*

—— **Fosteriana:** selected from periodical papers, edit. by H. G. Bohn. 5*s*. *N. S.*

FOX (Rt. Hon. C. J.)—*See Carrel.*

GIBBON'S Decline and Fall of the Roman Empire. Complete and unabridged, with variorum Notes; including those of Guizot, Wenck, Niebuhr, Hugo, Neander, and others. 7 vols. 2 Maps and Portrait. *N. S.*

GOETHE'S Works. Trans. into English by E. A. Bowring, C.B., Anna Swanwick, Sir Walter Scott, &c. &c. 12 vols. *N. S.*
Vols. I. and II.—Autobiography and Annals. Portrait.
Vol. III.—Faust. Complete.

GOETHE'S Works.—*Continued.*

Vol. IV.—Novels and Tales: containing Elective Affinities, Sorrows of Werther, The German Emigrants, The Good Women, and a Nouvelette.

Vol. V.—Wilhelm Meister's Apprenticeship.

Vol. VI.—Conversations with Eckerman and Soret.

Vol. VII.—Poems and Ballads in the original Metres, including Hermann and Dorothea.

Vol. VIII.—Götz von Berlichingen, Torquato Tasso, Egmont, Iphigenia, Clavigo, Wayward Lover, and Fellow Culprits.

Vol. IX. — Wilhelm Meister's Travels. Complete Edition.

Vol. X. — Tour in Italy. Two Parts. And Second Residence in Rome.

Vol. XI.—Miscellaneous Travels, Letters from Switzerland, Campaign in France, Siege of Mainz, and Rhine Tour.

Vol. XII.—Early and Miscellaneous Letters, including Letters to his Mother, with Biography and Notes. Edited by Edw. Bell, M.A.

—— Correspondence with Schiller. 2 vols.—*See Schiller.*

GOLDSMITH'S Works. 5 vols. *N.S.*

Vol. I.—Life, Vicar of Wakefield, Essays, and Letters.

Vol. II.—Poems, Plays, Bee, Cock Lane Ghost.

[Vols. III. and IV. *in the press.*

GREENE, MARLOW, and BEN JONSON (Poems of). With Notes and Memoirs by R. Bell. *N. S.*

GREGORY'S (Dr.) The Evidences, Doctrines, and Duties of the Christian Religion.

GRIMM'S Household Tales. With the Original Notes. Trans. by Mrs. A. Hunt. Introduction by Andrew Lang, M.A. 2 vols. *N. S.*

GUIZOT'S History of Representative Government in Europe. Trans. by A. R. Scoble.

—— **English Revolution of 1640.** From the Accession of Charles I. to his Death. Trans. by W. Hazlitt. Portrait.

—— **History of Civilisation.** From the Roman Empire to the French Revolution. Trans. by W. Hazlitt. Portraits. 3 vols.

HALL'S (Rev. Robert) Works and Remains. Memoir by Dr. Gregory and Essay by J. Foster. Portrait.

HAWTHORNE'S Tales. 3 vols. *N. S.*

Vol. I.—Twice-told Tales, and the Snow Image.

Vol. II.—Scarlet Letter, and the House with Seven Gables.

Vol. III. — Transformation, and Blithedale Romance.

HAZLITT'S (W.) Works. 6 vols. *N.S.*

—— **Table-Talk.**

—— **The Literature of the Age of** Elizabeth and Characters of Shakespeare's Plays. *N. S.*

—— **English Poets and English Comic** Writers. *N. S.*

HAZLITT'S (W.) Works.—*Continued.*

—— **The Plain Speaker.** Opinions on Books, Men, and Things. *N. S.*

—— **Round Table.** Conversations of James Northcote, R.A.; Characteristics. *N. S.*

—— **Sketches and Essays,** and Winterslow. *N. S.*

HEINE'S Poems. Translated in the original Metres, with Life by E. A. Bowring, C.B. 5*s. N. S.*

HUNGARY: its History and Revo- lution, with Memoir of Kossuth. Portrait.

HUTCHINSON (Colonel). Memoirs of. By his Widow, with her Autobiography, and the Siege of Lathom House. Portrait. *N. S.*

IRVING'S (Washington) Complete Works. 15 vols. *N. S.*

—— **Life and Letters.** By his Nephew, Pierre E. Irving. With Index and a Portrait. 2 vols. *N. S.*

JAMES'S (G. P. R.) Life of Richard Cœur de Lion. Portraits of Richard and Philip Augustus. 2 vols.

—— **Louis XIV.** Portraits. 2 vols.

JAMESON (Mrs.) Shakespeare's Heroines. Characteristics of Women. By Mrs. Jameson. *N. S.*

JEAN PAUL.—*See Richter.*

JONSON (Ben). Poems of.—*See Greene.*

JUNIUS'S Letters. With Woodfall's Notes. An Essay on the Authorship. Facsimiles of Handwriting. 2 vols. *N. S.*

LA FONTAINE'S Fables. In English Verse, with Essay on the Fabulists. By Elizur Wright. *N. S.*

LAMARTINE'S The Girondists, or Personal Memoirs of the Patriots of the French Revolution. Trans. by H. T. Ryde. Portraits of Robespierre, Madame Roland, and Charlotte Corday. 3 vols.

—— **The Restoration of Monarchy** in France (a Sequel to The Girondists). 5 Portraits. 4 vols.

—— **The French Revolution of 1848.** 6 Portraits.

LAMB'S (Charles) Elia and Eliana. Complete Edition. Portrait. *N. S.*

—— **Specimens of English Dramatic** Poets of the time of Elizabeth. Notes, with the Extracts from the Garrick Plays. *N. S.*

LAPPENBERG'S England under the Anglo-Saxon Kings. Trans. by B. Thorpe, F.S.A. 2 vols. *N. S.*

LANZI'S History of Painting in Italy, from the Period of the Revival of the Fine Arts to the End of the 18th Century. With Memoir of the Author. Portraits of Raffaelle, Titian, and Correggio, after the Artists themselves. Trans. by T. Roscoe. 3 vols.

LESSING'S Dramatic Works. Complete. By E. Bell, M.A. With Memoir by H. Zimmern. Portrait. 2 vols. *N. S.*

—— **Laokoon, Dramatic Notes, and** Representation of Death by the Ancients. Frontispiece. *N. S.*

LOCKE'S Philosophical Works, containing Human Understanding, with Bishop of Worcester, Malebranche's Opinions, Natural Philosophy, Reading and Study. With Preliminary Discourse, Analysis, and Notes, by J. A. St. John. Portrait. 2 vols. *N. S.*

—— **Life and Letters,** with Extracts from his Common-place Books. By Lord King.

LOCKHART (J. G.)—*See Burns.*

LONSDALE (Lord).—*See Carrel.*

LUTHER'S Table-Talk. Trans. by W. Hazlitt. With Life by A. Chalmers, and LUTHER'S CATECHISM. Portrait after Cranach. *N, S.*

—— **Autobiography.**—*See Michelet.*

MACHIAVELLI'S History of Florence, THE PRINCE, Savonarola, Historical Tracts, and Memoir. Portrait. *N. S.*

MARLOWE. Poems of.—*See Greene.*

MARTINEAU'S (Harriet) History of England (including History of the Peace) from 1800-1846. 5 vols. *N. S.*

MENZEL'S History of Germany, from the Earliest Period to the Crimean War. 3 Portraits. 3 vols.

MICHELET'S Autobiography of Luther. Trans. by W. Hazlitt. With Notes. *N. S.*

—— **The French Revolution** to the Flight of the King in 1791. *N. S.*

MIGNET'S The French Revolution, from 1789 to 1814. Portrait of Napoleon. *N. S.*

MILTON'S Prose Works. With Preface, Preliminary Remarks by J. A. St. John, and Index. 5 vols.

MITFORD'S (Miss) Our Village. Sketches of Rural Character and Scenery. 2 Engravings. 2 vols. *N. S.*

MOLIÈRE'S Dramatic Works. In English Prose, by C. H. Wall. With a Life and a Portrait. 3 vols. *N. S.*
'It is not too much to say that we have here probably as good a translation of Molière as can be given.'—*Academy.*

MONTESQUIEU'S Spirit of Laws. Revised Edition, with D'Alembert's Analysis, Notes, and Memoir. 2 vols. *N. S.*

NEANDER (Dr. A.) History of the Christian Religion and Church. Trans. by J. Torrey. With Short Memoir. 10 vols.*

—— **Life of Jesus Christ, in its His**torical Connexion and Development. *N. S.*

—— **The Planting and Training of** the Christian Church by the Apostles. With the Antignosticus, or Spirit of Tertullian. Trans. by J. E. Ryland. 2 vols.

—— **Lectures on the History of** Christian Dogmas. Trans. by J. E. Ryland. 2 vols.

—— **Memorials of Christian Life in** the Early and Middle Ages; including Light in Dark Places. Trans. by J. E. Ryland.

OCKLEY (S.) History of the Saracens and their Conquests in Syria, Persia, and Egypt. Comprising the Lives of Mohammed and his Successors to the Death of Abdalmelik, the Eleventh Caliph. By Simon Ockley, B.D., Prof. of Arabic in Univ. of Cambridge. Portrait of Mohammed.

PERCY'S Reliques of Ancient English Poetry, consisting of Ballads, Songs, and other Pieces of our earlier Poets, with some few of later date. With Essay on Ancient Minstrels, and Glossary. 2 vols. *N. S.*

PHILIP DE COMMINES. Memoirs of. Containing the Histories of Louis XI. and Charles VIII., and Charles the Bold, Duke of Burgundy. With the History of Louis XI., by J. de Troyes. With a Life and Notes by A. R. Scoble. Portraits. 2 vols.

PLUTARCH'S LIVES. Newly Translated, with Notes and Life, by A. Stewart, M.A., late Fellow of Trinity College, Cambridge, and G. Long, M.A. 4 vols. *N. S.*

POETRY OF AMERICA. Selections from One Hundred Poets, from 1776 to 1876. With Introductory Review, and Specimens of Negro Melody, by W. J. Linton. Portrait of W. Whitman. *N. S.*

RANKE (L.) History of the Popes, their Church and State, and their Conflicts with Protestantism in the 16th and 17th Centuries. Trans. by E. Foster. Portraits of Julius II. (after Raphael), Innocent X. (after Velasquez), and Clement VII. (after Titian). 3 vols. *N. S.*

—— **History of Servia.** Trans. by Mrs. Kerr. To which is added, The Slave Provinces of Turkey, by Cyprien Robert. *N. S.*

REUMONT (Alfred de).—*See Carafas.*

REYNOLDS' (Sir J.) Literary Works. With Memoir and Remarks by H. W. Beechy. 2 vols. *N. S.*

RICHTER (Jean Paul). Levana, a Treatise on Education; together with the Autobiography, and a short Memoir. *N. S.*

—— **Flower, Fruit, and Thorn Pieces,** or the Wedded Life, Death, and Marriage of Siebenkaes. Translated by Alex. Ewing. *N. S.* The only complete English translation.

ROSCOE'S (W.) Life of Leo X., with Notes, Historical Documents, and Dissertation on Lucretia Borgia. 3 Portraits. 2 vols.

—— **Lorenzo de' Medici,** called 'The Magnificent,' with Copyright Notes, Poems, Letters, &c. With Memoir of Roscoe and Portrait of Lorenzo.

RUSSIA, History of, from the earliest Period to the Crimean War. By W. K. Kelly. 3 Portraits. 2 vols.

SCHILLER'S Works. 6 vols. *N. S.*
Vol. I.—Thirty Years' War—Revolt in the Netherlands. Rev. A. J. W. Morrison, M.A. Portrait.
Vol. II.—Revolt in the Netherlands, *completed*—Wallenstein. By J. Churchill and S. T. Coleridge.—William Tell. Sir Theodore Martin. Engraving (after Vandyck).
Vol. III.—Don Carlos. R. D. Boylan —Mary Stuart. Mellish — Maid of Orleans. Anna Swanwick—Bride of Messina. A. Lodge, M.A. Together with the Use of the Chorus in Tragedy (a short Essay). Engravings.
These Dramas are all translated in metre.
Vol. IV.—Robbers—Fiesco—Love and Intrigue—Demetrius—Ghost Seer—Sport of Divinity.
The Dramas in this volume are in prose.
Vol. V.—Poems. E. A. Bowring, C.B.
Vol. VI.—Essays, Æsthetical and Philosophical, including the Dissertation on the Connexion between the Animal and Spiritual in Man.

SCHILLER and GOETHE. Correspondence between, from A.D. 1794-1805. With Short Notes by L. Dora Schmitz. 2 vols. *N. S.*

SCHLEGEL'S (F.) Lectures on the Philosophy of Life and the Philosophy of Language. By A. J. W. Morrison.

—— **The History of Literature,** Ancient and Modern.

—— **The Philosophy of History.** With Memoir and Portrait.

SCHLEGEL'S Works.—*Continued.*
—— **Modern History,** with the Lectures entitled Cæsar and Alexander, and The Beginning of our History. By L. Purcel. and R. H. Whitelock.

—— **Æsthetic and Miscellaneous** Works, containing Letters on Christian Art, Essay on Gothic Architecture, Remarks on the Romance Poetry of the Middle Ages, on Shakspeare, the Limits of the Beautiful, and on the Language and Wisdom of the Indians. By E. J. Millington.

SCHLEGEL (A. W.) Dramatic Art and Literature. By J. Black. With Memoir by A. J. W. Morrison. Portrait.

SHAKESPEARE'S Dramatic Art. The History and Character of Shakspeare's Plays. By Dr. H. Ulrici. Trans. by L. Dora Schmitz. 2 vols. *N. S.*

SHERIDAN'S Dramatic Works. With Memoir. Portrait (after Reynolds). *N. S.*

SKEAT (Rev. W. W.)—*See Chaucer.*

SISMONDI'S History of the Litera-ture of the South of Europe. With Notes and Memoir by T. Roscoe. Portraits of Sismondi and Dante. 2 vols.
The specimens of early French, Italian, Spanish, and Portugese Poetry, in English Verse, by Cary and others.

SMITH'S (Adam) Theory of Moral Sentiments; with Essay on the First Formation of Languages, and Critical Memoir by Dugald Stewart.

SMYTH'S (Professor) Lectures on Modern History; from the Irruption of the Northern Nations to the close of the American Revolution. 2 vols.

—— **Lectures on the French Revolu-**tion. With Index. 2 vols.

SOUTHEY.—*See Cowper, Wesley, and* (*Illustrated Library*) *Nelson.*

STURM'S Morning Communings with God, or Devotional Meditations for Every Day. Trans. by W. Johnstone, M.A.

SULLY. Memoirs of the Duke of, Prime Minister to Henry the Great. With Notes and Historical Introduction. 4 Portraits. 4 vols.

TAYLOR'S (Bishop Jeremy) Holy Living and Dying, with Prayers, containing the Whole Duty of a Christian and the parts of Devotion fitted to all Occasions. Portrait. *N. S.*

THIERRY'S Conquest of England by the Normans; its Causes, and its Consequences in England and the Continent. By W. Hazlitt. With short Memoir. 2 Portraits. 2 vols. *N. S.*

TROYE'S (Jean de).—*See Philip de Comines.*

ULRICI (Dr.)—*See Shakespeare.*

VASARI. Lives of the most Eminent Painters, Sculptors, and Architects. By Mrs. J. Foster, with selected Notes. Portrait. 6 vols., Vol. VI. being an additional Volume of Notes by J. P. Richter. *N. S.*

WESLEY, the Life of, and the Rise and Progress of Methodism. By Robert Southey. Portrait. 5s. *N. S.*

WHEATLEY. A Rational Illustra- tion of the Book of Common Prayer, being the Substance of everything Liturgical in all former Ritualist Commentators upon the subject. Frontispiece. *N. S.*

HISTORICAL LIBRARY.

21 Volumes at 5s. each.　(5l. 5s. per set.)

EVELYN'S Diary and Correspond- dence, with the Private Correspondence of Charles I and Sir Edward Nicholas, and between Sir Edward Hyde (Earl of Clarendon) and Sir Richard Browne. Edited from the Original MSS. by W. Bray, F.A.S. 4 vols. *N. S.* 45 Engravings (after Vandyke, Lely, Kneller, and Jamieson, &c.).

N.B.—This edition contains 130 letters from Evelyn and his wife, contained in no other edition.

PEPYS' Diary and Correspondence. With Life and Notes, by Lord Braybrooke. 4 vols. *N. S.* With Appendix containing additional Letters, an Index, and 31 Engravings (after Vandyke, Sir P. Lely, Holbein, Kneller, &c.).

JESSE'S Memoirs of the Court of England under the Stuarts, including the Protectorate. 3 vols. With Index and 42 Portraits (after Vandyke, Lely, &c.).

—— **Memoirs of the Pretenders and** their Adherents. 7 Portraits.

NUGENT'S (Lord) Memorials of Hampden, his Party and Times. With Memoir. 12 Portraits (after Vandyke and others). *N. S.*

STRICKLAND'S (Agnes) Lives of the Queens of England from the Norman Conquest. From authentic Documents, public and private. 6 Portraits. 6 vols. *N. S.*

—— **Life of Mary Queen of Scots.** 2 Portraits. 2 vols. *N. S.*

PHILOSOPHICAL LIBRARY.

15 Vols. at 5s. each, excepting those marked otherwise.　(3l. 9s. 0d. per set.)

BACON'S Novum Organum and Ad- vancement of Learning. With Notes by J. Devey, M.A.

COMTE'S Philosophy of the Sciences. An Exposition of the Principles of the *Cours de Philosophie Positive.* By G. H. Lewes, Author of 'The Life of Goethe.'

DRAPER (Dr. J. W.) A History of the Intellectual Development of Europe. 2 vols. *N. S.*

HEGEL'S Philosophy of History. By J. Sibree, M.A.

KANT'S Critique of Pure Reason. By J. M. D. Meiklejohn. *N. S.*

—— **Prolegomena and Metaphysical** Foundations of Natural Science, with Biography and Memoir by E. Belfort Bax. Portrait. *N. S.*

LOGIC, or the Science of Inference. A Popular Manual. By J. Devey.

MILLER (Professor). History Philo- sophically Illustrated, from the Fall of the Roman Empire to the French Revolution. With Memoir. 4 vols. 3s. 6d. each.

SPINOZA'S Chief Works. Trans. with Introduction by R. H. M. Elwes. 2 vols. *N.S.*

Vol. I.—Tractatus Theologico-Politicus —Political Treatise.

Vol. II.—Improvement of the Understanding—Ethics—Letters.

TENNEMANN'S Manual of the His- tory of Philosophy. Trans. by Rev. A. Johnson, M.A.

THEOLOGICAL LIBRARY.

15 *Vols. at 5s. each, excepting those marked otherwise.* (3l. 13s. 6d. per set.)

BLEEK. **Introduction to the Old Testament.** By Friedrich Bleek. Trans. under the supervision of Rev. E. Venables, Residentiary Canon of Lincoln. 2 vols. *N. S.*

CHILLINGWORTH'S Religion of Protestants. 3s. 6d.

EUSEBIUS. **Ecclesiastical History** of Eusebius Pamphilius, Bishop of Cæsarea. Trans. by Rev. C. F. Cruse, M.A. With Notes, Life, and Chronological Tables.

EVAGRIUS. **History of the Church.** —*See Theodoret.*

HARDWICK. History of the Articles of Religion; to which is added a Series of Documents from A.D. 1536 to A.D. 1615. Ed. by Rev. F. Proctor. *N. S.*

HENRY'S (Matthew) Exposition of the Book of Psalms. Numerous Woodcuts.

PEARSON (John, D.D.) Exposition of the Creed. Edit. by E. Walford, M.A. With Notes, Analysis, and Indexes. *N. S.*

PHILO-JUDÆUS, Works of. The Contemporary of Josephus. Trans. by C. D. Yonge. 4 vols.

PHILOSTORGIUS. **Ecclesiastical** History of.—*See Sozomen.*

SOCRATES' Ecclesiastical History. Comprising a History of the Church from Constantine, A.D. 305, to the 38th year of Theodosius II. With Short Account of the Author, and selected Notes.

SOZOMEN'S Ecclesiastical History. A.D. 324-440. With Notes, Prefatory Remarks by Valesius, and Short Memoir. Together with the ECCLESIASTICAL HISTORY OF PHILOSTORGIUS, as epitomised by Photius. Trans. by Rev. E. Walford, M.A. With Notes and brief Life.

THEODORET and EVAGRIUS. Histories of the Church from A.D. 332 to the Death of Theodore of Mopsuestia, A.D. 427; and from A.D. 431 to A.D. 544. With Memoirs.

WIESELER'S (Karl) Chronological Synopsis of the Four Gospels. Trans. by Rev. Canon Venables. *N. S.*

ANTIQUARIAN LIBRARY.

35 *Vols. at 5s. each.* (8l. 15s. per set.)

ANGLO-SAXON CHRONICLE. — See *Bede.*
ASSER'S Life of Alfred.—*See Six O. E. Chronicles.*
BEDE'S (Venerable) Ecclesiastical History of England. Together with the ANGLO-SAXON CHRONICLE. With Notes, Short Life, Analysis, and Map. Edit. by J. A. Giles, D.C.L.
BOETHIUS'S Consolation of Philo-sophy. King Alfred's Anglo-Saxon Version of. With an English Translation on opposite pages, Notes, Introduction, and Glossary, by Rev. S. Fox, M.A. To which is added the Anglo-Saxon Version of the METRES OF BOETHIUS, with a free Translation by Martin F. Tupper, D.C.L.
BRAND'S Popular Antiquities of England, Scotland, and Ireland. Illustrating the Origin of our Vulgar and Provincial Customs, Ceremonies, and Superstitions. By Sir Henry Ellis, K.H., F.R.S. Frontispiece. 3 vols.

CHRONICLES of the CRUSADES. Contemporary Narratives of Richard Cœur de Lion, by Richard of Devizes and Geoffrey de Vinsauf; and of the Crusade at Saint Louis, by Lord John de Joinville. With Short Notes. Illuminated Frontispiece from an old MS.

DYER'S (T. F. T.) British Popular Customs, Present and Past. An Account of the various Games and Customs associated with different Days of the Year in the British Isles, arranged according to the Calendar. By the Rev. T. F. Thiselton Dyer, M.A.

EARLY TRAVELS IN PALESTINE. Comprising the Narratives of Arculf, Willibald, Bernard, Sæwulf, Sigurd, Benjamin of Tudela, Sir John Maundeville, De la Brocquière, and Maundrell; all unabridged. With Introduction and Notes by Thomas Wright. Map of Jerusalem.

ELLIS (G.) Specimens of Early En-
glish Metrical Romances, relating to
Arthur, Merlin, Guy of Warwick, Richard
Cœur de Lion, Charlemagne, Roland, &c.
&c. With Historical Introduction by J. O.
Halliwell, F.R.S. Illuminated Frontispiece from an old MS.

ETHELWERD. Chronicle of.—*See
Six O. E. Chronicles.*

FLORENCE OF WORCESTER'S
Chronicle, with the Two Continuations :
comprising Annals of English History
from the Departure of the Romans to the
Reign of Edward I. Trans., with Notes,
by Thomas Forester, M.A.

GESTA ROMANORUM, or Enter-
taining Moral Stories invented by the
Monks. Trans. with Notes by the Rev.
Charles Swan. Edit. by W. Hooper, M.A.

GIRALDUS CAMBRENSIS' Histori-
cal Works. Containing Topography of
Ireland, and History of the Conquest of
Ireland, by Th. Forester, M A. Itinerary
through Wales, and Description of Wales,
by Sir R. Colt Hoare.

GEOFFREY OF MONMOUTH.
Chronicle of.—*See Six O. E. Chronicles.*

GILDAS. Chronicle of.—*See Six O. E.
Chronicles.*

HENRY OF HUNTINGDON'S His-
tory of the English, from the Roman Invasion to the Accession of Henry II. ;
with the Acts of King Stephen, and the
Letter to Walter. By T. Forester, M.A.
Frontispiece from au old MS.

INGULPH'S Chronicles of the Abbey
of Croyland, with the CONTINUATION by
Peter of Blois and others. Trans. with
Notes by H. T. Riley, B.A.

KEIGHTLEY'S (Thomas) Fairy My-
thology, illustrative of the Romance and
Superstition of Various Countries. Frontispiece by Cruikshank. *N. S.*

LEPSIUS'S Letters from Egypt,
Ethiopia, and the Peninsula of Sinai ; to
which are added, Extracts from his
Chronology of the Egyptians, with refer-
ence to the Exodus of the Israelites. By
L. and J. B. Horner. Maps and Coloured
View of Mount Barkal.

MALLET'S Northern Antiquities, or
an Historical Account of the Manners,
Customs, Religions, and Literature of the
Ancient Scandinavians. Trans. by Bishop
Percy. With Translation of the PROSE
EDDA, and Notes by J. A. Blackwell.
Also an Abstract of the ' Eyrbyggia Saga '
by Sir Walter Scott. With Glossary
and Coloured Frontispiece.

MARCO POLO'S Travels; with Notes
and Introduction. Edit. by T. Wright.

MATTHEW PARIS'S English His-
tory, from 1235 to 1273. By Rev. J. A.
Giles, D.C.L. With Frontispiece. 3 vols.—
See also Roger of Wendover.

MATTHEW OF WESTMINSTER'S
·Flowers of History, especially such as relate to the affairs of Britain, from the beginning of the World to A.D. 1307. By
C. D. Yonge. 2 vols.

NENNIUS. Chronicle of.—*See Six
O. E. Chronicles.*

ORDERICUS VITALIS' Ecclesiastical
History of England and Normandy. With
Notes, Introduction of Guizot, and the
Critical Notice of M. Delille, by T.
Forester, M.A. To which is added the
CHRONICLE OF St. EVROULT. With Gene-
ral and Chronological Indexes. 4 vols.

PAULI'S (Dr. R.) Life of Alfred the
Great. To which is appended Alfred's
ANGLO-SAXON VERSION OF OROSIUS. With
literal Translation interpaged, Notes, and
an ANGLO-SAXON GRAMMAR and Glossary,
by B. Thorpe, Esq. Frontispiece.

RICHARD OF CIRENCESTER.
Chronicle of.—*See Six O. E. Chronicles.*

ROGER DE HOVEDEN'S Annals of
English History, comprising the History
of England and of other Countries of Europe from A.D. 732 to A.D. 1201. With
Notes by H. T. Riley, B.A. 2 vols.

ROGER OF WENDOVER'S Flowers
of History, comprising the History of
England from the Descent of the Saxons to
A.D. 1235, formerly ascribed to Matthew
Paris. With Notes and Index by J. A.
Giles, D.C.L. 2 vols.

SIX OLD ENGLISH CHRONICLES :
viz., Asser's Life of Alfred and the Chronicles of Ethelwerd, Gildas, Nennius, Geoffrey of Monmouth, and Richard of Cirencester. Edit., with Notes, by J. A. Giles,
D.C.L. Portrait of Alfred.

WILLIAM OF MALMESBURY'S
Chronicle of the Kings of England, from
the Earliest Period to King Stephen. By
Rev. J. Sharpe. With Notes by J. A.
Giles, D.C.L. Frontispiece.

YULE-TIDE STORIES. A Collection
of Scandinavian and North-German Popular Tales and Traditions, from the Swedish,
Danish, and German. Edit. by B. Thorpe.

ILLUSTRATED LIBRARY.

85 Vols. at 5s. each, excepting those marked otherwise. (*23l. 2s. 6d. per set.*)

ALLEN'S (Joseph, R.N.) Battles of the British Navy. Revised edition, with Indexes of Names and Events, and 57 Portraits and Plans. 2 vols.

ANDERSEN'S Danish Fairy Tales. By Caroline Peachey. With Short Life and 120 Wood Engravings.

ARIOSTO'S Orlando Furioso. In English Verse by W. S. Rose. With Notes and Short Memoir. Portrait after Titian, and 24 Steel Engravings. 2 vols.

BECHSTEIN'S Cage and Chamber Birds: their Natural History, Habits, &c. Together with SWEET'S BRITISH WARBLERS. 43 Plates and Woodcuts. *N. S.*

—— or with the Plates Coloured, 7s. 6d.

BONOMI'S Nineveh and its Palaces. The Discoveries of Botta and Layard applied to the Elucidation of Holy Writ. 7 Plates and 294 Woodcuts. *N. S.*

BUTLER'S Hudibras, with Variorum Notes and Biography. Portrait and 28 Illustrations.

CATTERMOLE'S Evenings at Haddon Hall. Romantic Tales of the Olden Times. With 24 Steel Engravings after Cattermole.

CHINA, Pictorial, Descriptive, and Historical, with some account of Ava and the Burmese, Siam, and Anam. Map, and nearly 100 Illustrations.

CRAIK'S (G. L.) Pursuit of Knowledge under Difficulties. Illustrated by Anecdotes and Memoirs. Numerous Woodcut Portraits. *N. S.*

CRUIKSHANK'S Three Courses and a Dessert; comprising three Sets of Tales, West Country, Irish, and Legal; and a Mélange. With 50 Illustrations by Cruikshank. *N. S.*

—— **Punch and Judy.** The Dialogue of the Puppet Show; an Account of its Origin, &c. 24 Illustrations by Cruikshank. *N. S.*

—— With Coloured Plates. 7s. 6d.

DANTE, in English Verse, by I. C. Wright, M.A. With Introduction and Memoir. Portrait and 34 Steel Engravings after Flaxman. *N. S.*

DIDRON'S Christian Iconography; a History of Christian Art in the Middle Ages. Trans. by E. J. Millington. 150 Outline Engravings.

DYER (Dr. T. H.) Pompeii: its Buildings and Antiquities. An Account of the City, with full Description of the Remains and Recent Excavations, and an Itinerary for Visitors. By T. H. Dyer, LL.D. Nearly 300 Wood Engravings, Map, and Plan. 7s. 6d. *N. S.*

—— **Rome:** History of the City, with Introduction on recent Excavations. 8 Engravings, Frontispiece, and 2 Maps.

GIL BLAS. The Adventures of. From the French of Lesage by Smollett. 24 Engravings after Smirke, and 10 Etchings by Cruikshank. 612 pages. 6s.

GRIMM'S Gammer Grethel; or, German Fairy Tales and Popular Stories, containing 42 Fairy Tales. By Edgar Taylor. Numerous Woodcuts after Cruikshank and Ludwig Grimm. 3s. 6d.

HOLBEIN'S Dance of Death and Bible Cuts. Upwards of 150 Subjects, engraved in facsimile, with Introduction and Descriptions by the late Francis Douce and Dr. Dibdin. 7s. 6d.

HOWITT'S (Mary) Pictorial Calendar of the Seasons; embodying AIKIN'S CALENDAR OF NATURE. Upwards of 100 Woodcuts.

INDIA, Pictorial, Descriptive, and Historical, from the Earliest Times. 100 Engravings on Wood and Map.

JESSE'S Anecdotes of Dogs. With 40 Woodcuts after Harvey, Bewick, and others. *N. S.*

—— With 34 additional Steel Engravings after Cooper, Landseer, &c. 7s. 6d. *N. S.*

KING'S (C. W.) Natural History of Gems or Decorative Stones. Illustrations. 6s.

—— **Natural History of Precious** Stones and Metals. Illustrations. 6s.

—— **Handbook of Engraved Gems.** Numerous Illustrations. 6s.

KITTO'S Scripture Lands. Described in a series of Historical, Geographical, and Topographical Sketches. 42 Maps.

—— With the Maps coloured, 7s. 6d.

KRUMMACHER'S Parables. 40 Illustrations.

LINDSAY'S (Lord) Letters on Egypt, Edom, and the Holy Land. 36 Wood Engravings and 2 Maps.

LODGE'S Portraits of Illustrious Personages of Great Britain, with Biographical and Historical Memoirs. 240 Portraits engraved on Steel, with the respective Biographies unabridged. Complete in 8 vols.

LONGFELLOW'S Poetical Works, including his Translations and Notes. 24 full-page Woodcuts by Birket Foster and others, and a Portrait. *N. S.*

—— Without the Illustrations, 3*s. 6d. N. S.*

—— **Prose Works.** With 16 full-page Woodcuts by Birket Foster and others.

LOUDON'S (Mrs.) Entertaining Na- turalist. Popular Descriptions, Tales, and Anecdotes, of more than 500 Animals. Numerous Woodcuts. *N. S.*

MARRYAT'S (Capt., R.N.) Master- man Ready; or, the Wreck of the *Pacific.* (Written for Young People.) With 93 Woodcuts. 3*s. 6d. N. S.*

—— **Mission; or, Scenes in Africa.** (Written for Young People.) Illustrated by Gilbert and Dalziel. 3*s. 6d. N. S.*

—— **Pirate and Three Cutters.** (Written for Young People.) With a Memoir. 8 Steel Engravings after Clarkson Stanfield, R.A. 3*s. 6d. N. S.*

—— **Privateersman.** Adventures by Sea and Land One Hundred Years Ago. (Written for Young People.) 8 Steel Engravings. 3*s. 6d. N. S.*

—— **Settlers in Canada.** (Written for Young People.) 10 Engravings by Gilbert and Dalziel. 3*s. 6d. N. S.*

—— **Poor Jack.** (Written for Young People.) With 16 Illustrations after Clarkson Stanfield, R.A. 3*s. 6d. N. S.*

MAXWELL'S Victories of Welling- ton and the British Armies. Frontispiece and 4 Portraits.

MICHAEL ANGELO and RAPHAEL, Their Lives and Works. By Duppa and Quatremère de Quincy. Portraits and Engravings, including the Last Judgment, and Cartoons. *N. S.*

MILLER'S History of the Anglo- Saxons, from the Earliest Period to the Norman Conquest. Portrait of Alfred, Map of Saxon Britain, and 12 Steel Engravings.

MILTON'S Poetical Works, with a Memoir and Notes by J. Montgomery, an Index to Paradise Lost, Todd's Verbal Index to all the Poems, and Notes. 120 Wood Engravings. 2 vols. *N. S.*

MUDIE'S History of British Birds. Revised by W. C. L. Martin. 52 Figures of Birds and 7 Plates of Eggs. 2 vols. *N.S.*

—— With the Plates coloured, 7*s. 6d.* per vol.

NAVAL and MILITARY HEROES of Great Britain; a Record of British Valour on every Day in the year, from William the Conqueror to the Battle of Inkermann. By Major Johns, R.M., and Lieut. P. H. Nicolas, R.M. Indexes. 24 Portraits after Holbein, Reynolds, &c. 6*s.*

NICOLINI'S History of the Jesuits: their Origin, Progress, Doctrines, and Designs. 8 Portraits.

PETRARCH'S Sonnets, Triumphs, and other Poems, in English Verse. With Life by Thomas Campbell. Portrait and 15 Steel Engravings.

PICKERING'S History of the Races, of Man, and their Geographical Distribution; with AN ANALYTICAL SYNOPSIS OF THE NATURAL HISTORY OF MAN. By Dr. Hall. Map of the World and 12 Plates.

—— With the Plates coloured, 7*s. 6d.*

PICTORIAL HANDBOOK OF Modern Geography on a Popular Plan. Compiled from the best Authorities, English and Foreign, by H. G. Bohn. 150 Woodcuts and 51 Maps. 6*s.*

—— With the Maps coloured, 7*s. 6d.*

—— Without the Maps, 3*s. 6d.*

POPE'S Poetical Works, including Translations. Edit., with Notes, by R. Carruthers. 2 vols.

—— **Homer's Iliad,** with Introduction and Notes by Rev. J. S. Watson, M.A. With Flaxman's Designs. *N. S.*

—— **Homer's Odyssey,** with the BATTLE OF FROGS AND MICE, Hymns, &c., by other translators, including Chapman. Introduction and Notes by J. S. Watson, M.A. With Flaxman's Designs. *N. S.*

—— **Life,** including many of his Letters. By R. Carruthers. Numerous Illustrations.

POTTERY AND PORCELAIN, and other objects of Vertu. Comprising an Illustrated Catalogue of the Bernal Collection, with the prices and names of the Possessors. Also an Introductory Lecture on Pottery and Porcelain, and an Engraved List of all Marks and Monograms. By H. G. Bohn. Numerous Woodcuts.

—— With coloured Illustrations, 10*s. 6d.*

PROUT'S (Father) Reliques. Edited by Rev. F. Mahony. Copyright edition, with the Author's last corrections and additions. 21 Etchings by D. Maclise, R.A. Nearly 600 pages. 5*s. N. S.*

RECREATIONS IN SHOOTING. With some Account of the Game found in the British Isles, and Directions for the Management of Dog and Gun. By 'Craven.' 62 Woodcuts and 9 Steel Engravings after A. Cooper, R.A.

REDDING'S History and Descrip-
tions of Wines, Ancient and Modern. 20
Woodcuts.

RENNIE. Insect Architecture. Revised by Rev. J. G. Wood, M.A. 186
Woodcuts. *N. S.*

ROBINSON CRUSOE. With Memoir of
Defoe, 12 Steel Engravings and 74 Woodcuts after Stothard and Harvey.

—— Without the Engravings, 3s. 6d.

ROME IN THE NINETEENTH CEN-
tury. An Account in 1817 of the Ruins of
the Ancient City, and Monuments of Modern
Times. By C. A. Eaton. 34 Steel Engravings. 2 vols.

SHARPE (S.) The History of Egypt,
from the Earliest Times till the Conquest
by the Arabs, A.D. 640. 2 Maps and upwards of 400 Woodcuts. 2 vols. *N. S.*

SOUTHEY'S Life of Nelson. With
Additional Notes, Facsimiles of Nelson's
Writing, Portraits, Plans, and 50 Engrav-
ings, after Birket Foster, &c. *N. S.*

STARLING'S (Miss) Noble Deeds of
Women ; or, Examples of Female Courage,
Fortitude, and Virtue. With 14 Steel Por-
traits. *N. S.*

STUART and REVETT'S Antiquities
of Athens, and other Monuments of Greece ;
with Glossary of Terms used in Grecian
Architecture. 71 Steel Plates and numerous
Woodcuts.

SWEET'S British Warblers. 5s.—*See
Bechstein.*

TALES OF THE GENII ; or, the
Delightful Lessons of Horam, the Son of
Asmar. Trans. by Sir C. Morrell. Numer-
ous Woodcuts.

TASSO'S Jerusalem Delivered. In
English Spenserian Verse, with Life, by
J. H. Wiffen. With 8 Engravings and 24
Woodcuts. *N. S.*

WALKER'S Manly Exercises; containing Skating, Riding, Driving, Hunting,
Shooting, Sailing, Rowing, Swimming, &c.
44 Engravings and numerous Woodcuts.

WALTON'S Complete Angler, or the
Contemplative Man's Recreation, by Izaak
Walton and Charles Cotton. With Memoirs and Notes by E. Jesse. Also an
Account of Fishing Stations, Tackle, &c.,
by H. G. Bohn. Portrait and 203 Woodcuts. *N. S.*

—— With 26 additional Engravings on Steel,
7s. 6d.

—— Lives of Donne, Wotton, Hooker,
&c., with Notes. A New Edition, re-
revised by A. H. Bullen, with a Memoir
of Izaak Walton by William Dowling. 6
Portraits, 6 Autograph Signatures, &c.
N.S.

WELLINGTON, Life of. From the
Materials of Maxwell. 18 Steel Engravings.

—— Victories of.—*See Maxwell.*

WESTROPP (H. M.) A Handbook of
Archæology, Egyptian, Greek, Etruscan,
Roman. By H. M. Westropp. Numerous
Illustrations. 7s. 6d. *N. S.*

WHITE'S Natural History of Sel-
borne, with Observations on various Parts
of Nature, and the Naturalists' Calendar.
Sir W. Jardine. Edit., with Notes and
Memoir, by E. Jesse. 40 Portraits. *N. S.*

—— With the Plates coloured, 7s. 6d. *N. S.*

YOUNG LADY'S BOOK, The. A
Manual of Recreations, Arts, Sciences, and
Accomplishments. 1200 Woodcut Illustra-
tions. 7s. 6d.

—— cloth gilt, gilt edges, 9s.

CLASSICAL LIBRARY.

TRANSLATIONS FROM THE GREEK AND LATIN.

95 *Vols. at* 5s. *each, excepting those marked otherwise.* (23l. 7s. *per set.*)

ÆSCHYLUS, The Dramas of. In
English Verse by Anna Swanwick. 3rd
edition. *N. S.*

—— **The Tragedies of.** In Prose, with
Notes and Introduction, by T. A. Buckley,
B.A. Portrait. 3s. 6d.

AMMIANUS MARCELLINUS. His-
tory of Rome during the Reigns of Con-
stantius, Julian, Jovianus, Valentinian, and
Valens, by C. D. Yonge, B.A. Double
volume. 7s. 6d.

ANTONINUS (M. Aurelius), The
Thoughts of. Translated literally, with
Notes, Biographical Sketch, and Essay on
the Philosophy, by George Long, M.A.
3s. 6d. *N. S.*

APULEIUS, The Works of. Comprising the Golden Ass, God of Socrates,
Florida, and Discourse of Magic. With
a Metrical Version of Cupid and Psyche,
and Mrs. Tighe's Psyche. Frontispiece.

ARISTOPHANES' Comedies. Trans.,
with Notes and Extracts from Frere's and
other Metrical Versions, by W. J. Hickie.
Portrait. 2 vols.

ARISTOTLE'S Nicomachean Ethics.
Trans., with Notes, Analytical Introduc-
tion, and Questions for Students, by Ven.
Archdn. Browne.

—— **Politics and Economics.** Trans.,
with Notes, Analyses, and Index, by E.
Walford, M.A., and an Essay and Life by
Dr. Gillies.

—— **Metaphysics.** Trans., with Notes,
Analysis, and Examination Questions, by
Rev. John H. M'Mahon, M.A.

—— **History of Animals.** In Ten Books.
Trans., with Notes and Index, by R.
Cresswell, M.A.

—— **Organon;** or, Logical Treatises, and
the Introduction of Porphyry. With Notes,
Analysis, and Introduction, by Rev. O.
F. Owen, M.A. 2 vols. 3s. 6d. each.

—— **Rhetoric and Poetics.** Trans., with
Hobbes' Analysis, Exam. Questions, and
Notes, by T. Buckley, B.A. Portrait.

ATHENÆUS. The Deipnosophists;
or, the Banquet of the Learned. By C. D.
Yonge, B.A. With an Appendix of Poetical Fragments. 3 vols.

ATLAS of Classical Geography. 22
large Coloured Maps. With a complete
Index. Imp. 8vo. 7s. 6d.

BION.—*See Theocritus.*

CÆSAR. Commentaries on the
Gallic and Civil Wars, with the Supplementary Books attributed to Hirtius, including the complete Alexandrian, African,
and Spanish Wars. Trans. with Notes.
Portrait.

CATULLUS, Tibullus, and the Vigil
of Venus. Trans. with Notes and Biographical Introduction. To which are
added, Metrical Versions by Lamb,
Grainger, and others. Frontispiece.

CICERO'S Orations. Trans. by C. D.
Yonge, B.A. 4 vols.

—— **On Oratory and Orators.** With
Letters to Quintus and Brutus. Trans.,
with Notes, by Rev. J. S. Watson, M.A.

—— **On the Nature of the Gods,** Divination, Fate, Laws, a Republic, Consul-
ship. Trans., with Notes, by C. D. Yonge,
B.A.

—— **Academics,** De Finibus, and Tuscu-
lan Questions. By C. D. Yonge, B.A.
With Sketch of the Greek Philosophers
mentioned by Cicero.

CICERO'S Orations.—*Continued.*
—— **Offices;** or, Moral Duties. Cato
Major, an Essay on Old Age; Lælius, an
Essay on Friendship; Scipio's Dream;
Paradoxes; Letter to Quintus on Magis-
trates. Trans., with Notes, by C. R. Ed-
monds. Portrait. 3s. 6d.

DEMOSTHENES' Orations. Trans.,
with Notes, Arguments, a Chronological
Abstract, and Appendices, by C. Rann
Kennedy. 5 vols.

DICTIONARY of LATIN and GREEK
Quotations; including Proverbs, Maxims,
Mottoes, Law Terms and Phrases. With
the Quantities marked, and English Translations.

—— With Index Verborum (622 pages). 6s.

—— Index Verborum to the above, with the
Quantities and Accents marked (56 pages),
limp cloth. 1s.

DIOGENES LAERTIUS. Lives and
Opinions of the Ancient Philosophers.
Trans., with Notes, by C. D. Yonge, B.A.

EPICTETUS. The Discourses of.
With the Encheiridion and Fragments.
With Notes, Life, and View of his Philo-
sophy, by George Long, M.A. *N. S.*

EURIPIDES. Trans., with Notes and Introduction, by T. A. Buckley, B.A. Portrait. 2 vols.

GREEK ANTHOLOGY. In English
Prose by G. Burges, M.A. With Metrical
Versions by Bland, Merivale, Lord Den-
man, &c.

GREEK ROMANCES of Heliodorus,
Longus, and Achilles Tatius: viz., The
Adventures of Theagenes and Chariclea;
Amours of Daphnis and Chloe; and Loves
of Clitopho and Leucippe. Trans., with
Notes, by Rev. R. Smith, M.A.

HERODOTUS. Literally trans. by Rev.
Henry Cary, M.A. Portrait.

HESIOD, CALLIMACHUS, and
Theognis. In Prose, with Notes and
Biographical Notices by Rev. J. Banks,
M.A. Together with the Metrical Ver-
sions of Hesiod, by Elton; Callimachus,
by Tytler; and Theognis, by Frere.

HOMER'S Iliad. In English Prose, with
Notes by T. A. Buckley, B.A. Portrait.

—— **Odyssey,** Hymns, Epigrams, and
Battle of the Frogs and Mice. In English
Prose, with Notes and Memoir by T. A.
Buckley, B.A.

HORACE. In Prose by Smart, with Notes
selected by T. A. Buckley, B.A. Portrait. 3s. 6d.

JUSTIN, CORNELIUS NEPOS, and Eutropius. Trans., with Notes, by Rev. J. S. Watson, M.A.

JUVENAL, PERSIUS, SULPICIA, and Lucilius. In Prose, with Notes, Chronological Tables, Arguments, by L. Evans, M.A. To which is added the Metrical Version of Juvenal and Persius by Gifford. Frontispiece.

LIVY. The History of Rome. Trans. by Dr. Spillan and others. 4 vols. Portrait.

LUCAN'S Pharsalia. In Prose, with Notes by H. T. Riley.

LUCRETIUS. In Prose, with Notes and Biographical Introduction by Rev. J. S. Watson, M.A. To which is added the Metrical Version by J. M. Good.

MARTIAL'S Epigrams, complete. In Prose, with Verse Translations selected from English Poets, and other sources. Dble. vol. (670 pages). 7s. 6d.

MOSCHUS.—*See Theocritus.*

OVID'S Works, complete. In Prose, with Notes and Introduction. 3 vols.

PHALARIS. Bentley's Dissertations upon the Epistles of Phalaris, Themistocles, Socrates, Euripides, and the Fables of Æsop. With Introduction and Notes by Prof. W. Wagner, Ph.D.

PINDAR. In Prose, with Introduction and Notes by Dawson W. Turner. Together with the Metrical Version by Abraham Moore. Portrait.

PLATO'S Works. Trans., with Introduction and Notes. 6 vols.

—— **Dialogues.** A Summary and Analysis of. With Analytical Index to the Greek text of modern editions and to the above translations, by A. Day, LL.D.

PLAUTUS'S Comedies. In Prose, with Notes and Index by H. T. Riley, B.A. 2 vols.

PLINY'S Natural History. Trans., with Notes, by J. Bostock, M.D., F.R.S., and H. T. Riley, B.A. 6 vols.

PLINY. The Letters of Pliny the Younger. Melmoth's Translation, revised, with Notes and short Life, by Rev. F. C. T. Bosanquet, M.A.

PLUTARCH'S Morals. Theosophical Essays. Trans. by C. W. King, M.A. *N. S.*

—— **Lives.** *See page 6.*

PROPERTIUS, The Elegies of. With Notes, Literally translated by the Rev. P. J. F. Gantillon, M.A., with metrical versions of Select Elegies by Nott and Elton. 3s. 6d.

QUINTILIAN'S Institutes of Oratory. Trans., with Notes and Biographical Notice, by Rev. J. S. Watson, M.A. 2 vols.

SALLUST, FLORUS, and VELLEIUS Paterculus. Trans., with Notes and Biographical Notices, by J. S. Watson, M.A.

SENECA. [*Preparing.*

SOPHOCLES. The Tragedies of. In Prose, with Notes, Arguments, and Introduction. Portrait.

STRABO'S Geography. Trans., with Notes, by W. Falconer, M.A., and H. C. Hamilton. Copious Index, giving Ancient and Modern Names. 3 vols.

SUETONIUS' Lives of the Twelve Cæsars and Lives of the Grammarians. The Translation of Thomson, revised, with Notes, by T. Forester.

TACITUS. The Works of. Trans., with Notes. 2 vols.

TERENCE and PHÆDRUS. In English Prose, with Notes and Arguments, by H. T. Riley, B.A. To which is added Smart's Metrical Version of Phædrus. With Frontispiece.

THEOCRITUS, BION, MOSCHUS, and Tyrtæus. In Prose, with Notes and Arguments, by Rev. J. Banks, M.A. To which are appended the METRICAL VERSIONS of Chapman. Portrait of Theocritus.

THUCYDIDES. The Peloponnesian War. Trans., with Notes, by Rev. H. Dale. Portrait. 2 vols. 3s. 6d. each.

TYRTÆUS.—*See Theocritus.*

VIRGIL. The Works of. In Prose, with Notes by Davidson. Revised, with additional Notes and Biographical Notice, by T. A. Buckley, B.A. Portrait. 3s. 6d.

XENOPHON'S Works. Trans., with Notes, by J. S. Watson, M.A., and others. Portrait. In 3 vols.

COLLEGIATE SERIES.

10 *Vols. at* 5*s. each.*   (2*l.* 10*s. per set.*)

DANTE. The Inferno. Prose Trans., with the Text of the Original on the same page, and Explanatory Notes, by John A. Carlyle, M.D. Portrait. *N. S.*

—— **The Purgatorio.** Prose Trans., with the Original on the same page, and Explanatory Notes, by W. S. Dugdale. *N. S.*

NEW TESTAMENT (The) in Greek. Griesbach's Text, with the Readings of Mill and Scholz at the foot of the page, and Parallel References in the margin. Also a Critical Introduction and Chronological Tables. Two Fac-similes of Greek Manuscripts. 650 pages. 3*s.* 6*d.*

—— or bound up with a Greek and English Lexicon to the New Testament (250 pages additional, making in all 900). 5*s.*
The Lexicon may be had separately, price 2*s.*

DOBREE'S Adversaria. (Notes on the Greek and Latin Classics.) Edited by the late Prof. Wagner. 2 vols.

DONALDSON (Dr.) The Theatre of the Greeks. With Supplementary Treatise on the Language, Metres, and Prosody of the Greek Dramatists. Numerous Illustrations and 3 Plans. By J. W. Donaldson, D.D. *N. S.*

KEIGHTLEY'S (Thomas) Mythology of Ancient Greece and Italy. Revised by Leonhard Schmitz, Ph.D., LL.D. 12 Plates. *N. S.*

HERODOTUS, Notes on. Original and Selected from the best Commentators. By D. W. Turner, M.A. Coloured Map.

—— **Analysis and Summary of,** with a Synchronistical Table of Events—Tables of Weights, Measures, Money, and Distances — an Outline of the History and Geography—and the Dates completed from Gaisford, Baehr, &c. By J. T. Wheeler.

THUCYDIDES. An Analysis and Summary of. With Chronological Table of Events, &c., by J. T. Wheeler.

SCIENTIFIC LIBRARY.

57 *Vols. at* 5*s. each, excepting those marked otherwise.*   (15*l.* 2*s. per set.*)

AGASSIZ and GOULD. Outline of Comparative Physiology touching the Structure and Development of the Races of Animals living and extinct. For Schools and Colleges. Enlarged by Dr. Wright. With Index and 300 Illustrative Woodcuts.

BOLLEY'S Manual of Technical Analysis; a Guide for the Testing and Valuation of the various Natural and Artificial Substances employed in the Arts and Domestic Economy, founded on the work of Dr. Bolley. Edit. by Dr. Paul. 100 Woodcuts.

BRIDGEWATER TREATISES.

—— **Bell (Sir Charles) on the Hand;** its Mechanism and Vital Endowments, as evincing Design. Preceded by an Account of the Author's Discoveries in the Nervous System by A. Shaw. Numerous Woodcuts.

—— **Kirby on the History, Habits,** and Instincts of Animals. With Notes by T. Rymer Jones. 100 Woodcuts. 2 vols.

—— **Kidd on the Adaptation of Ex-** ternal Nature to the Physical Condition of Man, principally with reference to the Supply of his Wants and the Exercises of his Intellectual Faculties. 3*s.* 6*d.*

BRIDGEWATER TREATISES.—
Continued.

—— **Whewell's Astronomy and** General Physics, considered with reference to Natural Theology. Portrait of the Earl of Bridgewater. 3*s.* 6*d.*

—— **Chalmers on the Adaptation of** External Nature to the Moral and Intellectual Constitution of Man. With Memoir by Rev. Dr. Cumming. Portrait.

—— **Prout's Treatise on Chemistry,** Meteorology, and the Function of Digestion, with reference to Natural Theology. Edit. by Dr. J. W. Griffith. 2 Maps.

—— **Buckland's Geology and Miner-** alogy. With Additions by Prof. Owen, Prof. Phillips, and R. Brown. Memoir of Buckland. Portrait. 2 vols. 15*s.* Vol. I. Text. Vol. II. 90 large plates with letterpress.

—— **Roget's Animal and Vegetable** Physiology. 463 Woodcuts. 2 vols. 6*s.* each.

BROWNE. Manual of Geology. By A. J. Jukes Browne. With numerous Diagrams and Illustrations, 6*s.*

CARPENTER'S (Dr. W. B.) Zoology.
A Systematic View of the Structure, Habits, Instincts, and Uses of the principal Families of the Animal Kingdom, and of the chief Forms of Fossil Remains. Revised by W. S. Dallas, F.L.S. Numerous Woodcuts. 2 vols. 6s. each.

—— **Mechanical Philosophy, Astronomy, and Horology.** A Popular Exposition. 181 Woodcuts.

—— **Vegetable Physiology and Systematic Botany.** A complete Introduction to the Knowledge of Plants. Revised by E. Lankester, M.D., &c. Numerous Woodcuts. 6s.

—— **Animal Physiology.** Revised Edition. 300 Woodcuts. 6s.

CHEVREUL on Colour. Containing the Principles of Harmony and Contrast of Colours, and their Application to the Arts ; including Painting, Decoration, Tapestries, Carpets, Mosaics, Glazing, Staining, Calico Printing, Letterpress Printing, Map Colouring, Dress, Landscape and Flower Gardening, &c. Trans. by C. Martel. Several Plates.

—— With an additional series of 16 Plates in Colours, 7s. 6d.

ENNEMOSER'S History of Magic. Trans. by W. Howitt. With an Appendix of the most remarkable and best authenticated Stories of Apparitions, Dreams, Second Sight, Table-Turning, and Spirit-Rapping, &c. 2 vols.

HIND'S Introduction to Astronomy. With Vocabulary of the Terms in present use. Numerous Woodcuts. 3s. 6d. *N.S.*

HOGG'S (Jabez) Elements of Experimental and Natural Philosophy. Being an Easy Introduction to the Study of Mechanics, Pneumatics, Hydrostatics, Hydraulics, Acoustics, Optics, Caloric, Electricity, Voltaism, and Magnetism. 400 Woodcuts.

HUMBOLDT'S Cosmos ; or, Sketch of a Physical Description of the Universe. Trans. by E. C. Otté, B. H. Paul, and W. S. Dallas, F.L.S. Portrait. 5 vols. 3s. 6d. each, excepting vol. v., 5s.

—— **Personal Narrative of his Travels** in America during the years 1799-1804. Trans., with Notes, by T. Ross. 3 vols.

—— **Views of Nature ; or, Contemplations of the Sublime Phenomena of Creation, with Scientific Illustrations.** Trans. by E. C. Otté.

HUNT'S (Robert) Poetry of Science ; or, Studies of the Physical Phenomena of Nature. By Robert Hunt, Professor at the School of Mines.

JOYCE'S Scientific Dialogues. A Familiar Introduction to the Arts and Sciences. For Schools and Young People. Numerous Woodcuts.

—— **Introduction to the Arts and** Sciences, for Schools and Young People. Divided into Lessons with Examination Questions. Woodcuts. 3s. 6d.

JUKES-BROWNE'S Student's Handbook of Physical Geology. By A. J. Jukes-Browne, of the Geological Survey of England. With numerous Diagrams and Illustrations, 6s. *N.S.*

KNIGHT'S (Charles) Knowledge is Power. A Popular Manual of Political Economy.

LECTURES ON PAINTING by the Royal Academicians, Barry, Opie, Fuseli. With Introductory Essay and Notes by R. Wornum. Portrait of Fuseli.

LILLY. Introduction to Astrology. With a Grammar of Astrology and Tables for calculating Nativities, by Zadkiel.

MANTELL'S (Dr.) Geological Excursions through the Isle of Wight and along the Dorset Coast. Numerous Woodcuts and Geological Map.

—— **Medals of Creation ; or, First** Lessons in Geology : including Geological Excursions. Coloured Plates and several hundred Woodcuts. 2 vols. 7s. 6d. each.

—— **Petrifactions and their Teachings.** Handbook to the Organic Remains in the British Museum. Numerous Woodcuts. 6s.

—— **Wonders of Geology ; or, a** Familiar Exposition of Geological Phenomena. A coloured Geological Map of England, Plates, and 200 Woodcuts. 2 vols. 7s. 6d. each.

MORPHY'S Games of Chess, being the Matches and best Games played by the American Champion, with explanatory and analytical Notes by J. Löwenthal. With short Memoir and Portrait of Morphy.

SCHOUW'S Earth, Plants, and Man. Popular Pictures of Nature. And Kobell's Sketches from the Mineral Kingdom. Trans. by A. Henfrey, F.R.S. Coloured Map of the Geography of Plants.

SMITH'S (Pye) Geology and Scripture ; or, the Relation between the Scriptures and Geological Science. With Memoir.

STANLEY'S Classified Synopsis of the Principal Painters of the Dutch and Flemish Schools, including an Account of some of the early German Masters. By George Stanley.

STAUNTON'S Chess-Player's Handbook. A Popular and Scientific Introduction to the Game, with numerous Diagrams and Coloured Frontispiece. *N.S.*

STAUNTON.—*Continued.*

—— **Chess Praxis.** A Supplement to the Chess-player's Handbook. Containing the most important modern Improvements in the Openings; Code of Chess Laws; and a Selection of Morphy's Games. Annotated. 636 pages. Diagrams. 6*s.*

—— **Chess-Player's Companion.** Comprising a Treatise on Odds, Collection of Match Games, including the French Match with M. St. Amant, and a Selection of Original Problems. Diagrams and Coloured Frontispiece.

—— **Chess Tournament of 1851.** A Collection of Games played at this celebrated assemblage. With Introduction and Notes. Numerous Diagrams.

STOCKHARDT'S Experimental Chemistry. A Handbook for the Study of the Science by simple Experiments. Edit. by C. W. Heaton, F.C.S. Numerous Woodcuts. *N. S.*

URE'S (Dr. A.) Cotton Manufacture of Great Britain, systematically investigated; with an Introductory View of its Comparative State in Foreign Countries. Revised by P. L. Simmonds. 150 Illustrations. 2 vols.

—— **Philosophy of Manufactures,** or an Exposition of the Scientific, Moral, and Commercial Economy of the Factory System of Great Britain. Revised by P. L. Simmonds. Numerous Figures. 800 pages. 7*s.* 6*d.*

ECONOMICS AND FINANCE.

GILBART'S History, Principles, and Practice of Banking. Revised to 1881 by A. S. Michie, of the Royal Bank of Scotland. Portrait of Gilbart. 2 vols. 10*s. N. S.*

REFERENCE LIBRARY.

27 Volumes at Various Prices. (8*l.* 4*s. per set.*)

BOHN'S Dictionary of Poetical Quotations. Fourth Edition. 6*s.*

BUCHANAN'S Dictionary of Science and Technical Terms used in Philosophy, Literature, Professions, Commerce, Arts, and Trades. By W. H. Buchanan, with Supplement. Edited by Jas. A. Smith. 6*s.*

BLAIR'S Chronological Tables. Comprehending the Chronology and History of the World, from the Earliest Times to the Russian Treaty of Peace, April 1856. By J. W. Rosse. 800 pages. 10*s.*

—— **Index of Dates.** Comprehending the principal Facts in the Chronology and History of the World, from the Earliest to the Present, alphabetically arranged; being a complete Index to the foregoing. By J. W. Rosse. 2 vols. 5*s.* each.

BOHN'S Dictionary of Quotations from the English Poets. 4th and cheaper Edition. 6*s.*

BUCHANAN'S Dictionary of Science and Technical Terms. With Supplement. 820 pp. 6*s.*

CLARK'S (Hugh) Introduction to Heraldry. Revised by J. R. Planché. 5*s.* 950 Illustrations.

—— *With the Illustrations coloured,* 15*s. N. S.*

CHRONICLES OF THE TOMBS. A Select Collection of Epitaphs, with Essay on Epitaphs and Observations on Sepulchral Antiquities. By T. J. Pettigrew, F.R.S., F.S.A. 5*s.*

COINS, Manual of.—*See Humphreys.*

DATES, Index of.—*See Blair.*

DICTIONARY of Obsolete and Provincial English. Containing Words from English Writers previous to the 19th Century. By Thomas Wright, M.A., F.S.A., &c. 2 vols. 5*s.* each.

EPIGRAMMATISTS (The). A Selection from the Epigrammatic Literature of Ancient, Mediæval, and Modern Times. With Introduction, Notes, Observations, Illustrations, an Appendix on Works connected with Epigrammatic Literature, by Rev. H. Dodd, M.A. 6*s. N. S.*

GAMES, Handbook of. Comprising Treatises on above 40 Games of Chance, Skill, and Manual Dexterity, including Whist, Billiards, &c. Edit. by Henry G. Bohn. Numerous Diagrams. 5*s. N. S.*

HUMPHREYS' Coin Collectors' Manual. An Historical Account of the Progress of Coinage from the Earliest Time, by H. N. Humphreys. 140 Illustrations. 2 vols. 5*s.* each. *N. S.*

LOWNDES' Bibliographer's Manual of English Literature. Containing an Account of Rare and Curious Books published in or relating to Great Britain and Ireland, from the Invention of Printing, with Biographical Notices and Prices, by W. T. Lowndes. Parts I.-X. (A to Z), 3*s.* 6*d.* each. Part XI. (Appendix Vol.), 5*s.* Or the 11 parts in 4 vols., half morocco, 2*l.* 2*s.*

MEDICINE, Handbook of Domestic, Popularly Arranged. By Dr. H. Davies. 700 pages. 5*s.*

NOTED NAMES OF FICTION. Dictionary of. Including also Familiar Pseudonyms, Surnames bestowed on Eminent Men, &c. By W. A. Wheeler, M.A. 5*s.* *N. S.*

POLITICAL CYCLOPÆDIA. A Dictionary of Political, Constitutional, Statistical, and Forensic Knowledge; forming a Work of Reference on subjects of Civil Administration, Political Economy, Finance, Commerce, Laws, and Social Relations. 4 vols. 3*s.* 6*d.* each.

PROVERBS, Handbook of. Containing an entire Republication of Ray's Collection, with Additions from Foreign Languages and Sayings, Maxims, and Phrases, collected by H. G. Bohn. 5*s.*

—— **A Polyglot of Foreign.** Comprising French, Italian, German, Dutch, Spanish, Portuguese, and Danish. With English Translations. 5*s.*

SYNONYMS and ANTONYMS; or, Kindred Words and their Opposites, Collected and Contrasted by Ven. C. J. Smith, M.A. 5*s.* *N. S.*

WRIGHT (Th.)—*See Dictionary.*

NOVELISTS' LIBRARY.

10 *Volumes at* 3*s.* 6*d. each, excepting those marked otherwise.* (1*l.* 18*s. per set.*)

BURNEY'S Evelina; or, a Young Lady's Entrance into the World. By F. Burney (Mme. D'Arblay). With Introduction and Notes by A. R. Ellis, Author of 'Sylvestra,' &c. *N. S.*

—— **Cecilia.** With Introduction and Notes by A. R. Ellis. 2 vols. *N. S.*

FIELDING'S Joseph Andrews and his Friend Mr. Abraham Adams. With Roscoe's Biography. *Cruikshank's Illustrations. N. S.*

—— **History of Tom Jones, a Found-**ling. Roscoe's Edition. *Cruikshank's Illustrations.* 2 vols. *N. S.*

FIELDING.—*Continued.*

—— **Amelia.** Roscoe's Edition, revised. *Cruikshank's Illustrations.* 5*s. N. S.*

GROSSI'S Marco Visconti. Trans. by A. F. D. *N. S.*

MANZONI. The Betrothed: being a Translation of 'I Promessi Sposi.' Numerous Woodcuts. 1 vol. (732 pages), 5*s. N. S.*

STOWE (Mrs. H. B.) Uncle Tom's Cabin; or, Life among the Lowly. 8 full-page Illustrations. *N. S.*

ARTISTS' LIBRARY.

5 *Volumes at Various Prices.* (1*l.* 8*s.* 6*d. per set.*)

BELL (Sir Charles). The Anatomy and Philosophy of Expression, as Connected with the Fine Arts. 5*s. N. S.*

DEMMIN. History of Arms and Armour from the Earliest Period. By Auguste Demmin. Trans. by C. C. Black, M.A., Assistant Keeper, S. K. Museum. 1900 Illustrations. 7*s.* 6*d. N. S.*

FLAXMAN. Lectures on Sculpture. With Three Addresses to the R.A. by Sir

R. Westmacott, R.A., and Memoir of Flaxman. Portrait and 53 Plates. 6*s. N.S.*

LEONARDO DA VINCI'S Treatise on Painting. Trans. by J. F. Rigaud, R.A. With a Life and an Account of his Works by J. W. Brown. Numerous Plates. 5*s. N. S.*

PLANCHÉ'S History of British Costume, from the Earliest Time to the 19th Century. By J. R. Planché. 400 Illustrations. *s. N. S.*

BOHN'S CHEAP SERIES.

PRICE ONE SHILLING EACH.

A Series of Complete Stories or Essays, mostly reprinted from Vols. in Bohn's Libraries, and neatly bound in stiff paper cover, with cut edges, suitable for Railway Reading.

ASCHAM (ROGER).—
SCHOLEMASTER. By PROFESSOR MAYOR.

CARPENTER (DR. W. B.).—
PHYSIOLOGY OF TEMPERANCE AND TOTAL AB-
STINENCE.

EMERSON.—
ENGLAND AND ENGLISH CHARACTERISTICS. Lectures
on the Race, Ability, Manners, Truth, Character, Wealth, Religion, &c. &c.
NATURE : An Essay. To which are added Orations, Lectures,
and Addresses.
REPRESENTATIVE MEN : Seven Lectures on PLATO, SWE-
DENBORG, MONTAIGNE, SHAKESPEARE, NAPOLEON, and GOETHE.
TWENTY ESSAYS on Various Subjects.
THE CONDUCT OF LIFE.

FRANKLIN (BENJAMIN).—
AUTOBIOGRAPHY. Edited by J. SPARKS.

HAWTHORNE (NATHANIEL).—
TWICE-TOLD TALES. Two Vols. in One.
SNOW IMAGE, and other Tales.
SCARLET LETTER.
HOUSE WITH THE SEVEN GABLES.
TRANSFORMATION ; or the Marble Fawn. Two Parts.

HAZLITT (W.).—
TABLE-TALK : Essays on Men and Manners. Three Parts.
PLAIN SPEAKER : Opinions on Books, Men, and Things.
Three Parts.
LECTURES ON THE ENGLISH COMIC WRITERS.
LECTURES ON THE ENGLISH POETS.

HAZLITT (W.).—Continued.

LECTURES ON THE CHARACTERS OF SHAKE-SPEARE'S PLAYS.

LECTURES ON THE LITERATURE OF THE AGE OF ELIZABETH, chiefly Dramatic.

IRVING (WASHINGTON).—

LIFE OF MOHAMMED. With Portrait.

LIVES OF SUCCESSORS OF MOHAMMED.

LIFE OF GOLDSMITH.

SKETCH-BOOK.

TALES OF A TRAVELLER.

TOUR ON THE PRAIRIES.

CONQUESTS OF GRANADA AND SPAIN. Two Parts.

LIFE AND VOYAGES OF COLUMBUS. Two Parts.

COMPANIONS OF COLUMBUS: Their Voyages and Discoveries.

ADVENTURES OF CAPTAIN BONNEVILLE in the Rocky Mountains and the Far West.

KNICKERBOCKER'S HISTORY OF NEW YORK, from the Beginning of the World to the End of the Dutch Dynasty.

TALES OF THE ALHAMBRA.

CONQUEST OF FLORIDA UNDER HERNANDO DE SOTO.

ABBOTSFORD AND NEWSTEAD ABBEY.

SALMAGUNDI; or, The Whim-Whams and Opinions of LAUNCELOT LANGSTAFF, Esq.

BRACEBRIDGE HALL; or, The Humourists.

ASTORIA; or, Anecdotes of an Enterprise beyond the Rocky Mountains.

WOLFERT'S ROOST, and Other Tsles.

LAMB (CHARLES).—

ESSAYS OF ELIA. With a Portrait.

LAST ESSAYS OF ELIA.

ELIANA. With Biographical Sketch.

MARRYAT (CAPTAIN).

PIRATE AND THE THREE CUTTERS. With a Memoir of the Author.

*The only authorised Edition; no others published in England contain
the Derivations and Etymological Notes of Dr. Mahn, who
devoted several years to this portion of the Work.*

WEBSTER'S DICTIONARY

OF THE ENGLISH LANGUAGE.

Thoroughly revised and improved by CHAUNCEY A. GOODRICH, D.D., LL.D.,
and NOAH PORTER, D.D., of Yale College.

THE GUINEA DICTIONARY.

New Edition [1880], with a Supplement of upwards of 4600 New Words and
Meanings.

1628 Pages. 3000 Illustrations.

The features of this volume, which render it perhaps the most useful
Dictionary for general reference extant, as it is undoubtedly one of the cheapest
books ever published, are as follows :—

1. COMPLETENESS.—It contains 114,000 words—more by 10,000 than any
   other Dictionary ; and these are, for the most part, unusual or technical
   terms, for the explanation of which a Dictionary is most wanted.

2. ACCURACY OF DEFINITION.—In the present edition all the definitions have
   been carefully and methodically analysed by W. G. Webster, the Rev. C.
   Goodrich. Prof. Lyman, Prof. Whitney, and Prof. Gilman, under the
   superintendence of Prof. Goodrich.

3. SCIENTIFIC AND TECHNICAL TERMS.—In order to secure the utmost
   completeness and accuracy of definition, this department has been sub-
   divided among eminent scholars and experts, including Prof. Dana, Prof.
   Lyman, &c.

4. ETYMOLOGY.—The eminent philologist, Dr. C. F. Mahn, has devoted five
   years to completing this department.

5. THE ORTHOGRAPHY is based, as far as possible, on Fixed Principles. *In
   all cases of doubt an alternative spelling is given.*

6. PRONUNCIATION.—This has been entrusted to Mr. W. G. Webster and Mr.
   Wheeler, assisted by other scholars. The pronunciation of each word is
   indicated by typographical signs *printed at the bottom of each page.*

7. THE ILLUSTRATIVE CITATIONS.—No labour has been spared to embody
   such quotations from standard authors as may throw light on the definitions, or possess any special interest of thought or language.

8. THE SYNONYMS.—These are subjoined to the words to which they belong,
   and are very complete.

9. THE ILLUSTRATIONS, which exceed 3000, are inserted, not for the sake of
   ornament, but to elucidate the meaning of words.

Cloth, 21*s.* ; half-bound in calf, 30*s.* ; calf or half russia, 31*s.* 6*d.* ; russia, 2*l.*

To be obtained through all Booksellers.

WEBSTER'S DICTIONARY.

' SEVENTY years passed before Johnson was followed by Webster, an American writer, who faced the task of the English Dictionary with a full appreciation of its requirements, leading to better practical results.' . . .

' His laborious comparison of twenty languages, though never published, bore fruit in his own mind, and his training placed him both in knowledge and judgment far in advance of Johnson as a philologist. Webster's *American Dictionary of the English Language* was published in 1828, and of course appeared at once in England, where successive re-editing *has yet kept it in the highest place as a practical Dictionary.*'

' The acceptance of an American Dictionary in England has itself had immense effect in keeping up the community of speech, to break which would be a grievous harm, not to English-speaking nations alone, but to mankind. The result of this has been that the common Dictionary must suit both sides of the Atlantic.' . . .

' The good average business-like character of Webster's Dictionary, both in style and matter, made it as distinctly suited as Johnson's was distinctly unsuited to be expanded and re-edited by other hands. Professor Goodrich's edition of 1847 is not much more than enlarged and amended ; but other revisions since have so much novelty of plan as to be described as distinct works.' . . .

' The American revised Webster's Dictionary of 1864, published in America and England, is of an altogether higher order than these last [The London Imperial and Student's]. It bears on its title-page the names of Drs. Goodrich and Porter, but inasmuch as its especial improvement is in the etymological department, the care of which was committed to Dr. Mahn of Berlin, we prefer to describe it in short as the Webster-Mahn Dictionary. Many other literary men, among them Professors Whitney and Dana, aided in the task of compilation and revision. On consideration it seems that the editors and contributors have gone far toward improving Webster to the utmost that he will bear improvement. The *vocabulary has become almost complete as regards usual words, while the definitions keep throughout to Webster's simple careful style, and the derivations are assigned with the aid of good modern authorities.*'

' On the whole, the Webster-Mahn Dictionary as it stands is most respectable, and **certainly the best Practical English Dictionary extant.**'—From the *Quarterly Review*, Oct. 1873.

LONDON : G. BELL & SONS, YORK STREET, COVENT GARDEN.

Printed in the United States
139021LV00006B/74/A